The Prints of Michael Mazur

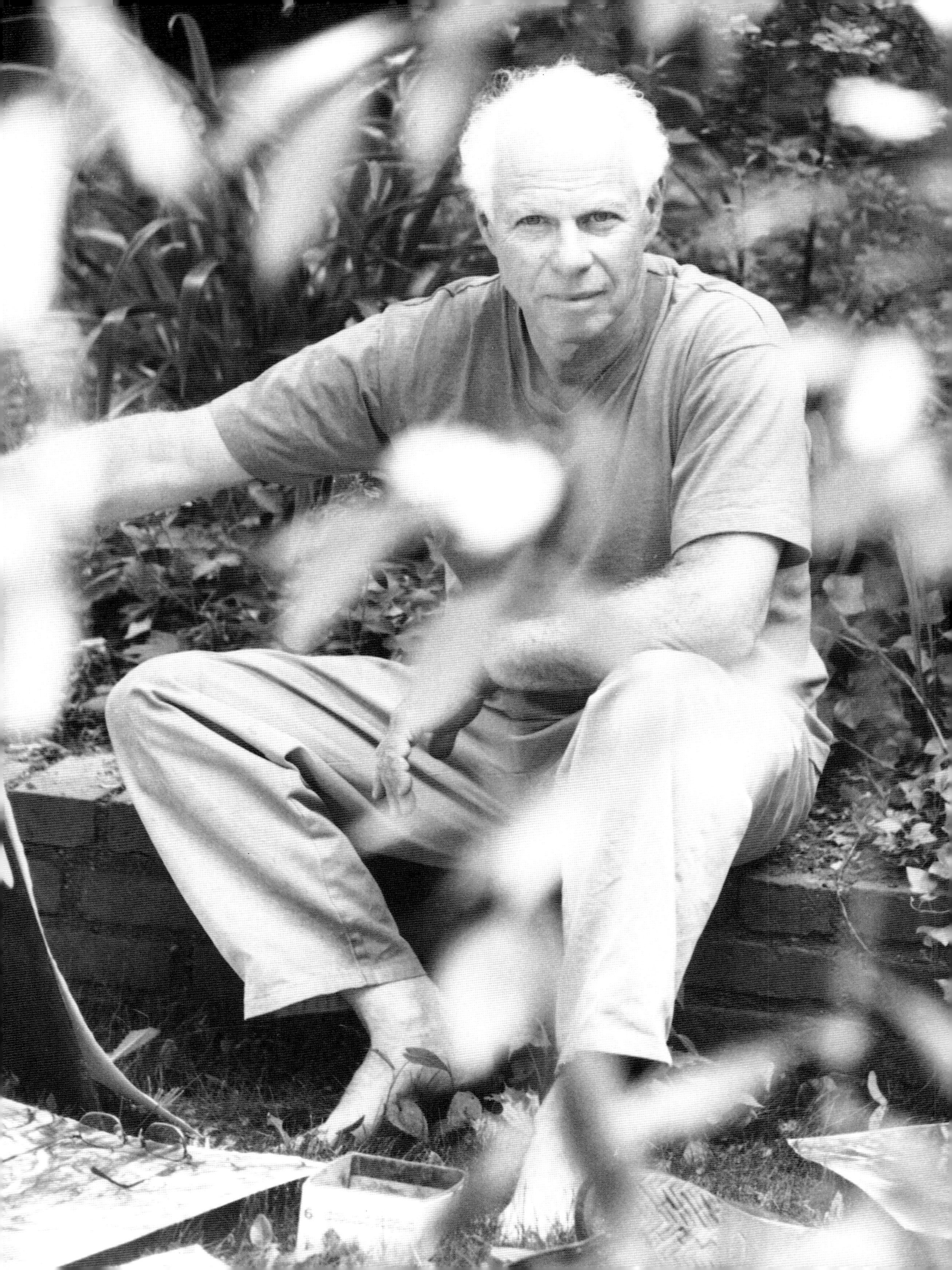

The Prints of
MICHAEL MAZUR

With a Catalogue Raisonné 1956–1999

TRUDY V. HANSEN

With Essays by Barry Walker, Clifford S. Ackley, and Lloyd Schwartz

HUDSON HILLS PRESS · NEW YORK

in Association with Jane Voorhees Zimmerli Art Museum

First Edition

Published in the United States by
Hudson Hills Press, Inc., 122 East 25th Street, 5th Floor, New York, NY 10010-2936.

The Prints of Michael Mazur is published in conjunction with the exhibition
Michael Mazur: A Print Retrospective. Exhibition dates:

February 16 – May 14, 2000
Museum of Fine Arts, Boston

July 11 – September 17, 2000
Iris and B. Gerald Cantor Center for Visual Arts, Stanford University, California

November 28, 2000 – February 16, 2001
Jane Voorhees Zimmerli Art Museum, Rutgers,
The State University of New Jersey, New Brunswick

March 15 – May 31, 2001
Minneapolis Institute of Arts

This publication has been made possible in part by generous support from
the National Endowment for the Arts, a Federal agency in Washington, D.C.

Distributed in the United States, its territories and possessions, and Canada
by National Book Network.
Distributed in the United Kingdom, Eire, and Europe by Art Books International Ltd.

Editor and Publisher: Paul Anbinder

Manuscript Editor: Virginia Wageman

Proofreader: Lydia Edwards

Indexer: Karla J. Knight

Designer: Howard I. Gralla

Composition: Angela Taormina

Manufactured in Japan by Toppan Printing Company

Library of Congress Cataloguing-in-Publication Data

Hansen, T. Victoria.
The prints of Michael Mazur with a catalogue raisonné 1956–1999 / Trudy V. Hansen ;
with essays by Barry Walker, Clifford S. Ackley, and Lloyd Schwartz. — 1st ed.
p. cm.
Published in conjunction with the exhibition "Michael Mazur: a print retrospective."
Exhibition dates, Museum of Fine Arts, Boston, Feb. 16 – May 14, 2000 and others.
Includes bibliographical references and index.
ISBN 1-55595-162-7 (paperback : alk. paper)
1. Mazur, Michael, 1935 — Exhibitions. 2. Mazur, Michael, 1935 — Catalogues raisonnés.
I. Walker, Barry, 1945– II. Ackley, Clifford S. III. Schwartz, Lloyd. IV. Museum of Fine
Arts, Boston. V. Title.
NE539.M33 A4 2000
769.92 — dc21

99-54001

Cover illustrations: *Wakeby Night* (1984) and detail (catalogue raisonne 246)
Frontispiece: Michael Mazur, Cambridge, Mass., 1997

Contents

Foreword

IN 1981 the Rutgers University Art Gallery — expanded and renamed in 1983 the Jane Voorhees Zimmerli Art Museum — acquired two hundred prints, monotypes, drawings, and paintings by Michael Mazur representing his, then, twenty-five-year career. That fall we exhibited a selection of seventy-six works from this incredible treasure trove of one artist's oeuvre. At that time I promised Michael that in the not too distant future we would publish a catalogue documenting his printmaking achievements. Thanks to Trudy Hansen and her colleagues, my long overdue commitment to Michael has been elegantly and expertly fulfilled with the present publication.

Nearly two decades have passed since I first met Michael and encountered the wide range and richness of his art. My goal in the early stage of developing the museum's collection of contemporary American prints was to acquire an in-depth group of works by an important contemporary artist in order to better demonstrate the creative process and the interrelationship of media. As a historian of nineteenth-century French graphic arts, I had often regretted the dearth of such documentation for many of my favorite fin-de-siècle painter/printmakers. My initial interest in acquiring Michael Mazur's art, therefore, was motivated by a didactic approach to collection development; ultimately, however, the acquisition of Michael's work was the result of great enthusiasm and admiration for his distinctive aesthetic accomplishments in all media.

Within the last twenty years the Zimmerli holdings of American prints have been tremendously enhanced, first by the establishment in 1982 of the Rutgers Archives for Printmaking Studios, and recently with the generous donation by David and Ruth Eisenberg of eighteen hundred prints covering more than one hundred years of American printmaking.

Michael Mazur is an artist steeped in the history of printmaking. It is that knowledge combined with his instincts that makes his work technically and aesthetically sound as well as enormously innovative. As this publication so convincingly reveals, the seductive but complex nature of Mazur's work — filled with allusions to the history of art and of literature — is a major artistic resource, in general, and as such is an essential component of the Zimmerli's graphic art collection.

Phillip Dennis Cate, *Director*
Jane Voorhees Zimmerli Art Museum

Acknowledgments

ORGANIZING a retrospective exhibition and accompanying publication of Michael Mazur's prints has proven a project filled with professional and personal rewards. Foremost among the rewards has been the opportunity to work closely with a dynamic and creative individual whose intelligence and talent are matched only by his generosity. I would like to extend my deepest gratitude to Michael Mazur for his enthusiasm, his insights, and his extraordinary patience as the exhibition was selected, his entire print history was documented, and the publication was prepared. Both Gail and Michael Mazur made important factual corrections and suggestions, and provided additional information as the essays and chronology were prepared, and their unflagging hospitality and willingness to answer innumerable questions were greatly appreciated.

We are grateful to the lenders to the exhibition, whose loans of artwork were critical to an accurate representation of Mazur's print oeuvre. Several institutions have lent key works, and I would especially like to thank George Goldner and Elliot Davis at the Metropolitan Museum of Art; Deborah Wye at the Museum of Modern Art; Marilyn Kushner at The Brooklyn Museum; Roberta Waddell at The New York Public Library; Clifford S. Ackley at the Museum of Fine Arts, Boston; and Joann Moser at the National Museum of American Art, Smithsonian Institution. My special thanks are also extended to each of the private lenders for their willingness to part with their art and for special insights and information regarding key works. The exhibition was also made possible by the interest of other institutions in sharing the exhibition on its national tour, and I would like to thank Malcolm Rogers and Katherine Getchell at the Museum of Fine Arts, Boston; Thomas Seligman, Hilarie Faberman, and Betsy Fryberger at the Iris and B. Gerald Cantor Center for Visual Arts, Stanford University; and Evan Maurer, Richard Campbell, and Patrick Noon at the Minneapolis Institute of Arts for their many efforts.

My deepest appreciation is extended to my collaborators on the project, fellow essayists Clifford S. Ackley, Barry Walker, and Lloyd Schwartz. It has been a pleasure working with each, and their support and advice as well as their written contributions have added depth and a broader perspective to the exhibition and publication.

Many colleagues, dealers, and other individuals were instrumental to the project, and I would particularly like to thank Mazur's current dealers, Mary Ryan and Barbara Krakow; Robert Brown, Cathy McLaurin, and Eva Crider of the Archives of American Art; Ellen Doon; photographers Greg Heins, Jack Abraham, and David and Louise Webber; Michael C. Henry; Katy Kline of the Hayden Gallery, Massachusetts Institute of Technology; and Peter Walch and Floramae Cates at the University of New Mexico Art Museum.

Many of the printers and publishers Michael Mazur has collaborated with over the years have been extremely helpful in lending works and answering countless technical questions, and I would especially like to thank Robert Townsend of R. E. Townsend Studio; Judith Solodkin of Solo Impression; Herb Fox of Fox Graphics – Merrimac Editions; Andrew Mockler of Jungle Press Editions; Marge Devon of The Tamarind Institute; and Ann McLaughlin and Will Foo of Experimental Workshop.

For their support, I wish to recognize and thank former colleagues at the Jane Voorhees Zimmerli Art Museum for their many efforts on behalf of the project, including Phillip Dennis Cate, Carma Fauntleroy, Edward Schwab, Ruth Berson, Anne Schneider, Donna DeBlasis, Roberto Delgado, Sharon Matt, and Gail Aaron. A very special thanks goes to Patricia A. Cudd for her involvement in every aspect of the project, especially the compilation of information for the catalogue raisonné, Barbara Trelstad for overseeing the myriad registrarial details, and Marguerite Santos for managing all of the contracts, requisitions, and other administrative aspects of the project.

In addition to those listed above, Michael Mazur would also like to extend his personal thanks to the following for their support of his printmaking career over the years: Sylan Cole, the late Agnes Mongan, Robert Miller, John Stoller, Jane Haslem, Barbara Mathes, Robert Brown, David Godine, Dick Solomon and Jan Turner, Jonathan Galassi, Andrew Hoyem, Judith Goldman, Kathy Halbreich, David Kiehl, Anne Anninger, Paula Z. Kirkeby and Kathryn Kain of Smith Andersen Editions, and assistants Michael Gitlin, David Small, Anne Clarke, Amanda Barrow, Tama Hochbaum, and Torey Fair. Mazur would also like to give a special note of acknowledgment and express his gratitude to Robert Townsend, who has collaborated with him as his printer for over twenty years.

We would both like to thank Paul Anbinder of Hudson Hills Press for enabling this publication, and for his enthusiasm and desire to support the preparation of the catalogue raisonné of Mazur's editioned prints. Additional support for this publication was provided by the National Endowment for the Arts, and their support for this project is greatly appreciated.

Trudy V. Hansen

Lenders to the Exhibition

The Brooklyn Museum of Art

Experimental Workshop, Emeryville, California

Barbara Krakow Gallery, Boston

Michael and Gail Mazur

Metropolitan Museum of Art, New York

Museum of Fine Arts, Boston

The Museum of Modern Art, New York

National Museum of American Art, Smithsonian Institution, Washington, D.C.

The New York Public Library

Mary Ryan Gallery, New York

Jane Voorhees Zimmerli Art Museum, Rutgers, The State University of New Jersey, New Brunswick

Private collections

The Prints of Michael Mazur

Michael Mazur: Entering the Stream: An Introduction

Trudy V. Hansen

. . . he was at once all the artists he had known and all the books he had read . . . and was still profoundly original.

— Charles Baudelaire, "La Fanfarlo"[1]

ONCE, when asked why he chose representational subject matter at a time when many young artists were rejecting it, Michael Mazur replied, quite automatically, that "it all depends on where one enters the stream."[2] He was referring, of course, to the historical times, the artistic climate, and the influences one encounters — the environment, the circumstances, and individual genetic codes of one's life.

Mazur's artistic genetic code is a complex one. While the artist has been best known for a remarkable body of printed works, his career has included regular exhibitions of paintings, drawings, pastels, and even sculpture and installations. Whether in his choice of subject matter, mood, or medium, Mazur's focus has been on the dualities that coexist in nature and in the human condition. Just as the world around him presents its daily contradictions and extremes, so has Mazur attempted to recognize the dualities of his own nature, balancing a romantic and expressive response to the horror/beauty of nature with an analytical and intellectual approach to the challenges of perception and representation inherent in even the simplest of objects. Technically, Mazur has spent over four decades reconciling the ease with which he creates printed images with the constant challenges of painting — balancing a career's worth of graphic innovation, achievement, and recognition with a determined effort to paint with the same satisfaction that printmaking has given him. It is only slightly ironic that, just as his forty-year commitment to printmaking is being examined and documented, breakthroughs made in his painting in the past decade have brought unprecedented critical appreciation.

Dualities have existed in other ways in the artist's career. Mazur refused, at a very early stage in his career, to be locked into an external and amorphous "art world" mandate to find a signature style or theme. Although a native New Yorker, the artist chose to work outside the contemporary art mecca of New York — in a place, in fact, that the art world regarded as a conservative backwater. Recognizing a primal need to be close to nature and to live somewhere that allowed both physical and psychological distance yet offered a lively intellectual and cultural life, Mazur chose to live in New England. His life, like that of many artists, has revolved around the day-to-day activities of living, working, and participating in the contemporary dialogue of the art world, balanced by the need to retreat and isolate himself in the studio. With wide-ranging friendships among three generations of artists, writers, and other creative spirits, Mazur has a broad frame of reference, and he has collaborated extensively with artists, writers, and master printers on a variety of projects. As a printmaker, his ability to create prints alone or in collaboration with others adds to the diversity of his body of work. Mazur has also resisted a strict linear progression and the temptation never to look back. Instead, his pattern of artistic development has been one of constant return and revision — to early subjects, to problems of perception and representation, and to continuing reevaluations made necessary by the passage of time.

Mazur is often called a humanist, for his choice of subjects and his approach to them stem from his life and the world around him. It is a life filled with reading, observation, and action, all centered on a strong social conscience and set of political convictions. Active on numerous fronts, Mazur has participated in wide-ranging liberal causes, lending his voice and donating both his art and time. Although he left the world of full-time teaching at age forty, Mazur teaches often, finding teaching to be a "generous" activity that balances the self-absorption of the studio. Mazur characterizes his teaching as more biographical than autobiographical, encouraging his students to "get a life" and then examine it rather than to search for a style, a market, or other external guideposts. At the same time, he has followed in the footsteps of his many mentors, enthusiastically sharing an encyclopedia of knowledge, tools, and techniques.

This publication celebrates the many achievements of Mazur as printmaker, from his extraordinary technical virtuosity to the leading role he played in the contemporary revival of the monotype, a hybrid "painterly print" that has figured prominently in the breakdown of barriers between art-making media in recent times. Just as Mazur recognizes no hierarchy among media, and has worked simultaneously on prints, paintings, pastels, and drawings throughout his career, neither does he recognize a hierarchy in subject matter. From confined residents in a psychiatric ward to caged monkeys and other animals at the Stoneham Zoo (colorplate 15; figs. 11 and 76) and the Boston Aquarium (figs. 1 and 2), from the light in his studio to the compositional challenges of representing an ashtray on a table, from studies that capture the simultaneous order and chaos of the natural world to narrative scenes of his imagination inspired, perhaps, by a world-shaking event or a masterpiece of literature, Mazur has gently insisted that an artist need not fit a mold. In a truly humanist spirit, Mazur recognizes man's need to comprehend the world from differing vantage points, from the analytical to the emotional. Viewers — whether critics, collectors, or museum and gallery goers — are drawn to his numerous works for a wide variety of reasons.

Mentors and Sources: The Early Years

There was never much question that Michael Mazur would become an artist. He was born in Manhattan in 1935, and his parents encouraged their only child's artistic activities from an early age.[3] As he was growing up on Manhattan's Upper East Side, the great museums of the city were favorite haunts, from the Metropolitan Museum of Art and the Museum of Modern Art to later visits to the Whitney Museum of American Art and the Solomon R. Guggenheim Museum. By the time Mazur reached his teens, the romantic notion of being an artist had already taken hold. At the progressive Horace Mann School, he was part of an ad hoc "art club" along with fellow members Henry Geldzahler and Ed Koren, who would later go on to distinguished careers as art critic / curator and artist / cartoonist respectively. All three worked together on the school's literary magazine, *Manuscript,* and they also advocated the addition of art classes to the school's curriculum. It was during this time that Mazur began exploring the bohemian life of Greenwich Village and learning about the artists who were radicalizing the contemporary art scene. In 1949 and 1950 Mazur worked on Saturdays as a studio assistant for the painter Alan Ullman in his Greenwich Village studio, where he learned "to drink coffee and talk about art."[4] He also took more formal art lessons with the painter Morris Davidson on West Fifty-seventh Street near the Art Students League.[5] While he had no firsthand interaction at that time with the artists who were causing such a commotion in the art world — including Jackson Pollock, Robert Motherwell, and Willem de Kooning — he was well aware of the Cedar Bar and the new art and theoretical arguments of the Abstract Expressionists. He was still, however, most impressed with the work of the late-nineteenth- and early-twentieth-century artists, particularly Edgar Degas and the young Pablo Picasso.

Upon finishing high school, Mazur wanted to study painting at Cooper Union in New York. His father, however, felt that a broader liberal arts education would prove to be a more valuable experience. Mazur decided to go to Amherst College after a recruiting officer from the school, at that time a men's college in western Massachusetts with a reputation for its strong academic curriculum, visited Horace Mann and described the new art facility and program for studio majors. It was at Amherst that Mazur's lifelong interest in poetry, art, and their unique interrelationship came into focus.

Mazur's undergraduate years at Amherst were significant for many reasons. As a fine arts major with a minor in English literature, Mazur took courses with the noted American literature scholar and critic Alfred Kazin and, by his sophomore year, began to study with the sculptor and printmaker Leonard Baskin (fig. 3) as part of a collaborative arrangement with Smith College. Baskin not only taught his students the fundamentals of printmaking, particularly relief printing, but also exposed them to his outstanding print collection and lessons in print connoisseurship. Mazur's classes with Baskin resulted in his first solid efforts in printmaking. He also honed his skills as a printer when Baskin hired him to help edition Baskin's Kafkaesque *Horned Beetles and Other Insects.*[6]

It was during Mazur's Amherst years that he met Smith College student Gail Beckwith, whom he would marry in 1958. Their union, one of artist and poet, strengthened the foundation of Mazur's dual preoccupation with the verbal and the visual. Their ongoing dialogue, and the tacit, if often unspoken, absorption and understanding of each other's careers, surfaces in the visual passages of Gail's poems and the poetic passages and references of Michael's images. Their family life has also formed the core of both of their lives, providing the sometimes chaotic normalcy of the everyday and the subjects of many of Mazur's prints.[7]

Just as Baskin was an important mentor early in his career, Mazur was also deeply affected by the books he read and studied. He recalls a few key works that had a major impact, including the well-illustrated *Modern Prints and Drawings* by Paul Sachs, *The Dehumanization of Art and Other Writings* by José Ortega y Gasset, and *Concerning the Spiritual in Art* by Wassily Kandinsky.[8] Many of Mazur's early prints show strong references to masterworks in Sachs's survey, from Francisco de Goya, Honoré Daumier, and Degas to Edvard Munch and the German Expressionists. Of course, he had already been reading contemporary material such as the avant-garde periodical *It Is,*[9] the reviews of Thomas Hess, Irving Sandler, and Fairfield Porter and other articles in *Art News* and numerous other contemporary periodicals.

Early travels also played a major role in Mazur's education and served to spark his imagination and broaden his frame of reference. In 1956 Mazur took a year off from his studies at Amherst to travel to Italy. In Florence he studied drawing at the Accademia di Belle Arti and also became familiar with the work of Italian neorealists such as Renzo Vespignani at the same time he was absorbing the art of the Renaissance masters. He visited the studio of American sculptor and printmaker Bernard Reder (fig. 4), whose expressionistic, and often surrealistic subjects drew upon diverse religious and mythological sources. Mazur also purchased his first artworks during this year, including prints by Reder, Käthe Kollwitz, Rodolphe Bresdin, and Georges Rouault, as well as illustrations from the German periodi-

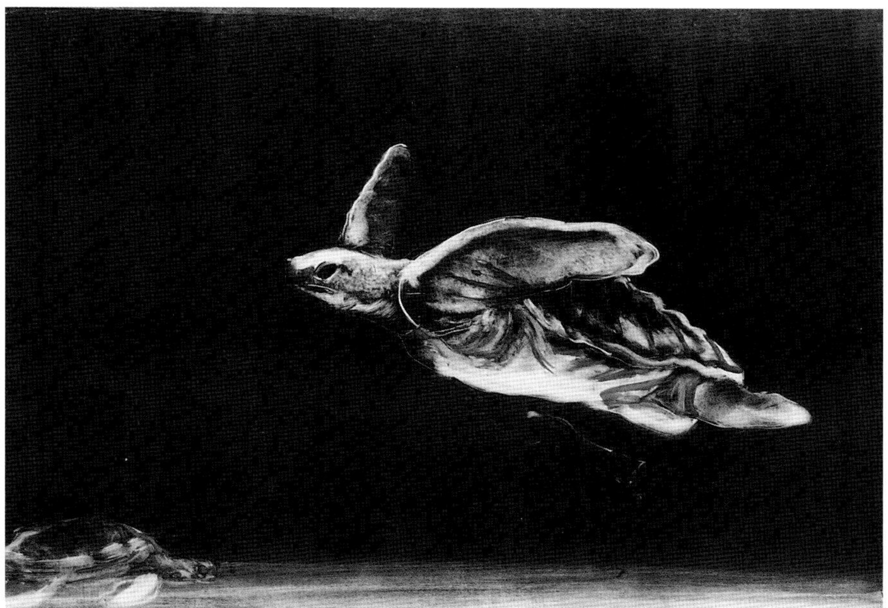

Fig. 1 *Sea Turtle II,* from the *Aquarium Series,* 1974, monotype (a/b), 23¾ × 31¾ in. (55.2 × 80.7 cm). Private Collection.

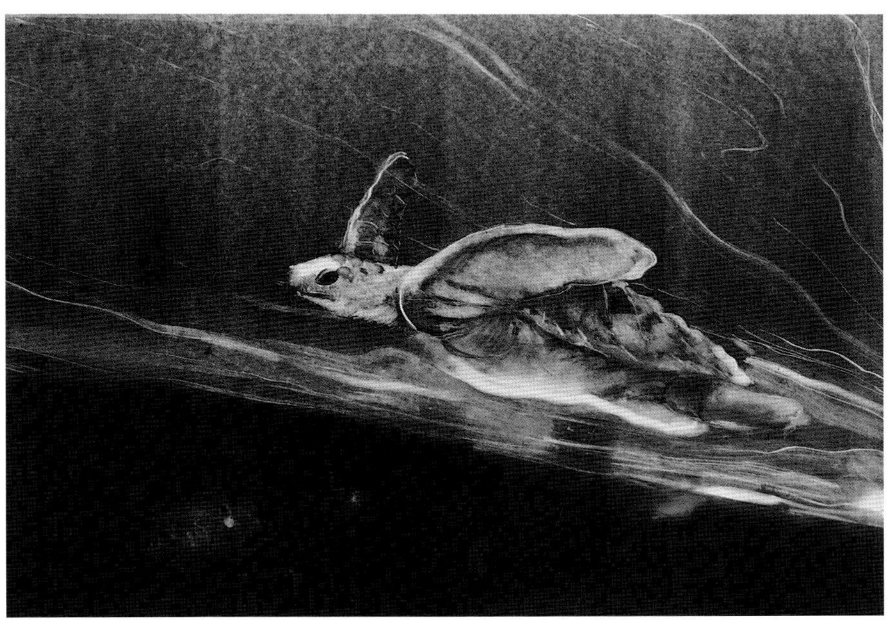

Fig. 2 *Sea Turtle II,* from the *Aquarium Series,* 1974, monotype (b/b), 23¾ × 31¾ in. (55.2 × 80.7 cm). Collection of Joel Janowitz.

cal *Die Stürm.* In Florence, the city of Dante, Mazur's fascination with *The Divine Comedy* began, an interest that would resurface throughout his career. Mazur learned to read Italian and, upon returning to the United States, read the opus in its original language for the first time. He also made frequent trips to Venice during the year, where he was most impressed by the paintings of Antonio Guardi and the Tiepolos and the prints of Giovanni Battista Piranesi.

While in Italy, Mazur began to make wood relief prints, simple images that he printed by hand. Subjects ranged from interiors and views from the room he rented to studies of *commedia dell'arte* figures (colorplate 1) that had captured his imagination in Venice. The expressive influence of both Reder and Baskin is evident. These first prints, single block images printed in black, clearly reveal the young artist's initial attempts to master the tools and explore the expressive possibilities of one printmaking technique. While relatively unsophisticated, several of the prints contain a balance of textural variety and dramatic contrasts that reveal Mazur's talent even at this early stage.

Mazur returned to Amherst for his final college year, spending most of his time working on *An Image of Salomé,*

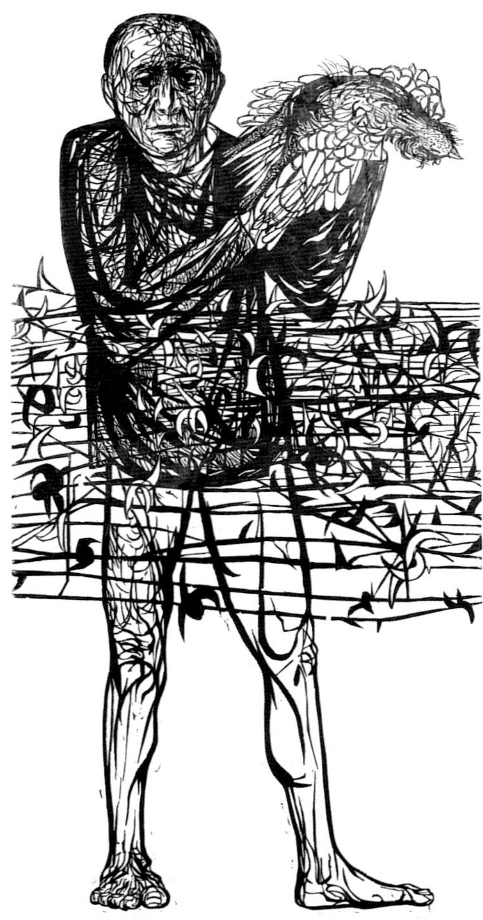

Fig. 3 Leonard Baskin (American, born 1922), *Man of Peace,* 1952, woodcut, 58⅞ × 30½ in. (149.5 × 77.5 cm). The Brooklyn Museum of Art, New York (53.38).

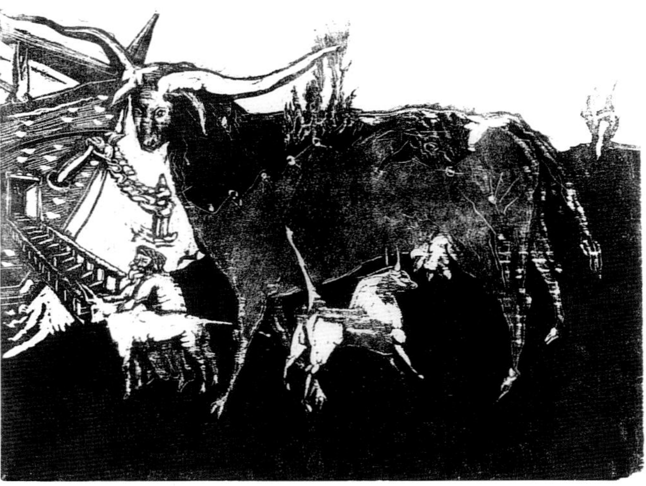

Fig. 4 Bernard Reder (American, 1897–1963), *Untitled (Noah's Ark),* 1957, wood relief, 11 × 14¼ in. (28.0 × 36.8 cm). Collection of Michael Mazur.

a visual narrative of symbolist texts (colorplate 2). The project took the form of an artist's book that included sixteen wood reliefs and wood engravings. In describing the project, Mazur stated: "My main objective in the prints was to carry the possibility of expression to the wood itself—exploiting its natural textures as well as those suggested by the very shapes of the cutting tools."[10] More accomplished than his earliest Italian prints, the Salomé images are layered and more intricate in their compositions and rhythms.

After receiving his baccalaureate with honors from Amherst in 1958, Mazur began graduate study in the fine arts program at Yale University, where he was introduced to another circle of mentors. Among his teachers at Yale, Gabor Peterdi (fig. 5) and Rico Lebrun (fig. 6) proved the strongest influences. However, other professors, including Bernard Chaet, Josef Albers, William Bailey, and visiting artist Fairfield Porter in the art department, the art historians Egbert Haverkamp-Begemann and Nelson Wu, and architectural historian and critic Vincent Scully, also provided important lessons in technique, philosophy, and connoisseurship. Peterdi was immensely important in Mazur's development, above all for introducing him to the myriad possibilities of intaglio printing. Peterdi was one of several postwar émigré artist-printmakers who played a major role in the promotion of printmaking during the 1940s and 1950s.[11] Peterdi was also receiving recognition, unprecedented for a printmaker, for his work during the late 1950s, and his artistic success seemed to suggest that a focus on printmaking and the graphic arts was viable for a contemporary artist.[12] An eager student, Mazur mastered engraving and etching techniques, experimenting widely with plate preparation, inking, and printing to find countless ways to add depth and variety to the primarily black-and-white prints he was creating.

During his last semester at Yale, Mazur met the Constructivist sculptor Naum Gabo and for three months assisted Gabo in printing two editions of etchings. Gabo showed the young artist the wood-engraved monoprints

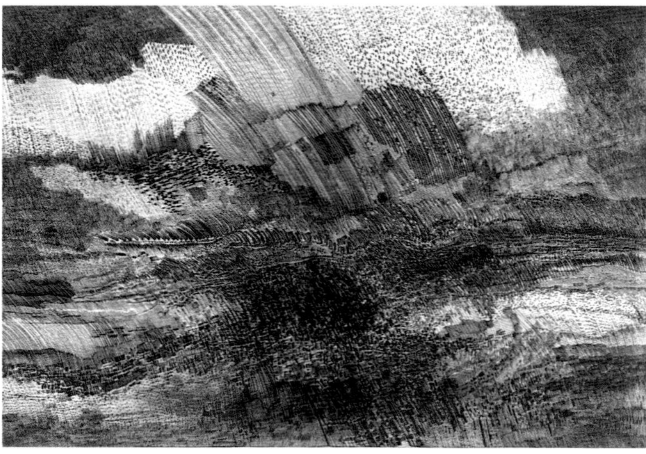

Fig. 5 Gabor Peterdi (American, born 1915), *Angry Skies,* 1959, etching, 23½ × 33 in. (59.7 × 83.9 cm). Collection of Michael Mazur.

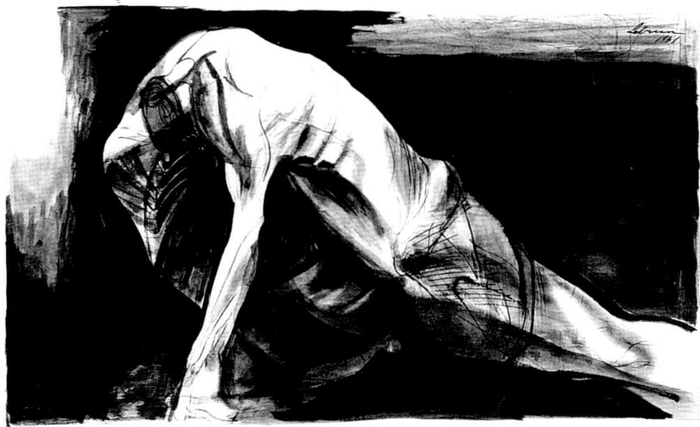

Fig. 6 Rico Lebrun (American, 1900–1964), *Reclining Figure,* from *Drawings for a Dante's Inferno by Rico Lebrun,* 1963, lithograph, 20 × 26 in. (50.8 × 66.1 cm). Collection of Michael Mazur.

that he had been printing by hand (fig. 36), providing Mazur with an early introduction to the concept of the one-of-a-kind print. Although these works were totally abstract, Mazur was drawn to the images for their lyrical and textural qualities and for the ways in which Gabo varied the images by printing the blocks, or sections of a block, with varying pressure. Gabo's subtle use of color, the incorporation of imperfections in the woodblock into the design, the carving, and the methods of printing demonstrated to Mazur yet another range of nuances he could add to his growing technical repertoire.

The Yale years were critical in cementing Mazur's commitment to figurative and nature-based subject matter. Indeed, after spending his teens absorbing contemporary arguments surrounding abstraction versus figuration, and after having a progression of artist-teachers who reiterated the arguments, Mazur felt that by 1960 the question of subject matter was to a large degree a moot point. At Yale, the battles were waged by Albers and Lebrun as they argued optical abstraction as opposed to figurative expressionism. At the same time, artists such as Bailey, Porter, and others were working with realistic subjects. Certainly, despite the overwhelming presence and impact of the New York–based Abstract Expressionist movement, many artists of the late 1950s and early 1960s were still actively and successfully committed to representational subject matter. Nor was the art establishment single-mindedly devoted to abstraction. Mazur recalls visiting the *New Images of Man* exhibition at the Museum of Modern Art in 1959, a major survey of the work of twenty-three painters and sculptors working primarily (at that time) with the figure.[13] Early works by the Pop artists were also becoming highly visible, and Mazur felt strongly that the art world had already become pluralistic. Based on his concern for social issues and a growing political awareness, Mazur chose to take his subjects from the world around him, believing that "the creative act is an act of imagination which applies to any choice of subject matter."[14] The diverse directions taken

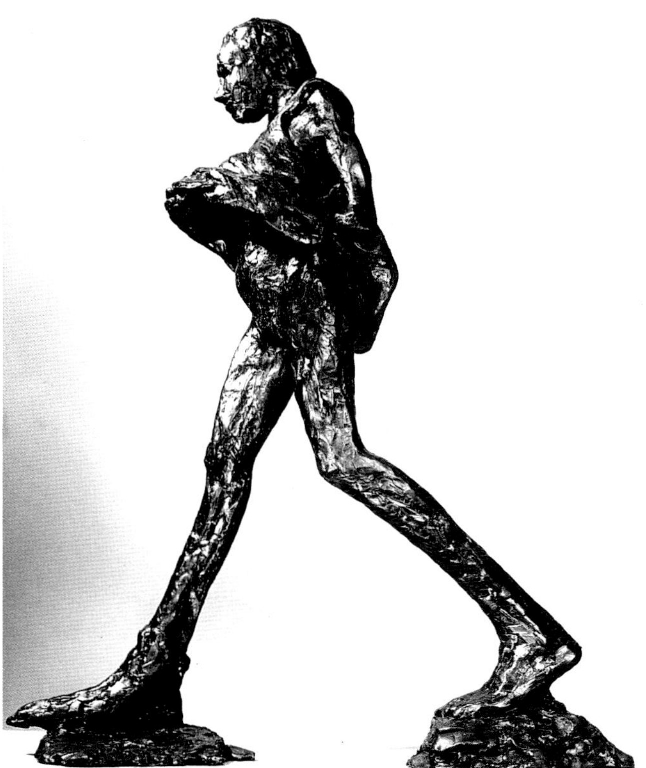

Fig. 7 *Walking Figure,* 1962–63, bronze, 24 in. (61.0 cm) high. Collection of the artist.

by Mazur's classmates at Yale, artists including Robert Mangold, Sylvia Plimack Mangold, Eva Hesse, Peter Milton, Richard Ziemann, and Robert Birmelin, clearly demonstrate a growing pluralism even in this small microcosm of the art world in the early 1960s.

Upon receiving his M.F.A. from Yale in 1961, Mazur was offered a position teaching anatomy, life drawing, and printmaking at the Rhode Island School of Design. Living in Providence, Rhode Island, with his young family, Mazur focused on drawing, etching, and engraving using his family and surrounding landscape as inspiration. In his earliest landscapes, such as the *Lily Growths* series (figs. 15, 16, and 17) or *Night Pine, Norfolk* (colorplate 3), Mazur captured dualities of nature through the wild and dramatic line quality of the etchings placed within a definite structure, a subtle gridwork recalling Peterdi's compositions and serving to contain the biomorphic chaos. During his three years in Providence, Mazur volunteered to conduct art therapy sessions with some of his students at the Howard State Institute of Mental Health, an experience that resulted in the *Closed Ward* (colorplate 4; figs. 8, 9, and 19–25) and *Locked Ward* (figs. 10, 26, and 47) print series. Upon returning home from these visits, Mazur would make drawings or sometimes create small sculptures to use as studies for the prints he made in the Rhode Island School of Design print shop (fig. 7).

The *Closed Ward* prints, dense and tortured, present haunting images of humans existing outside the civilized

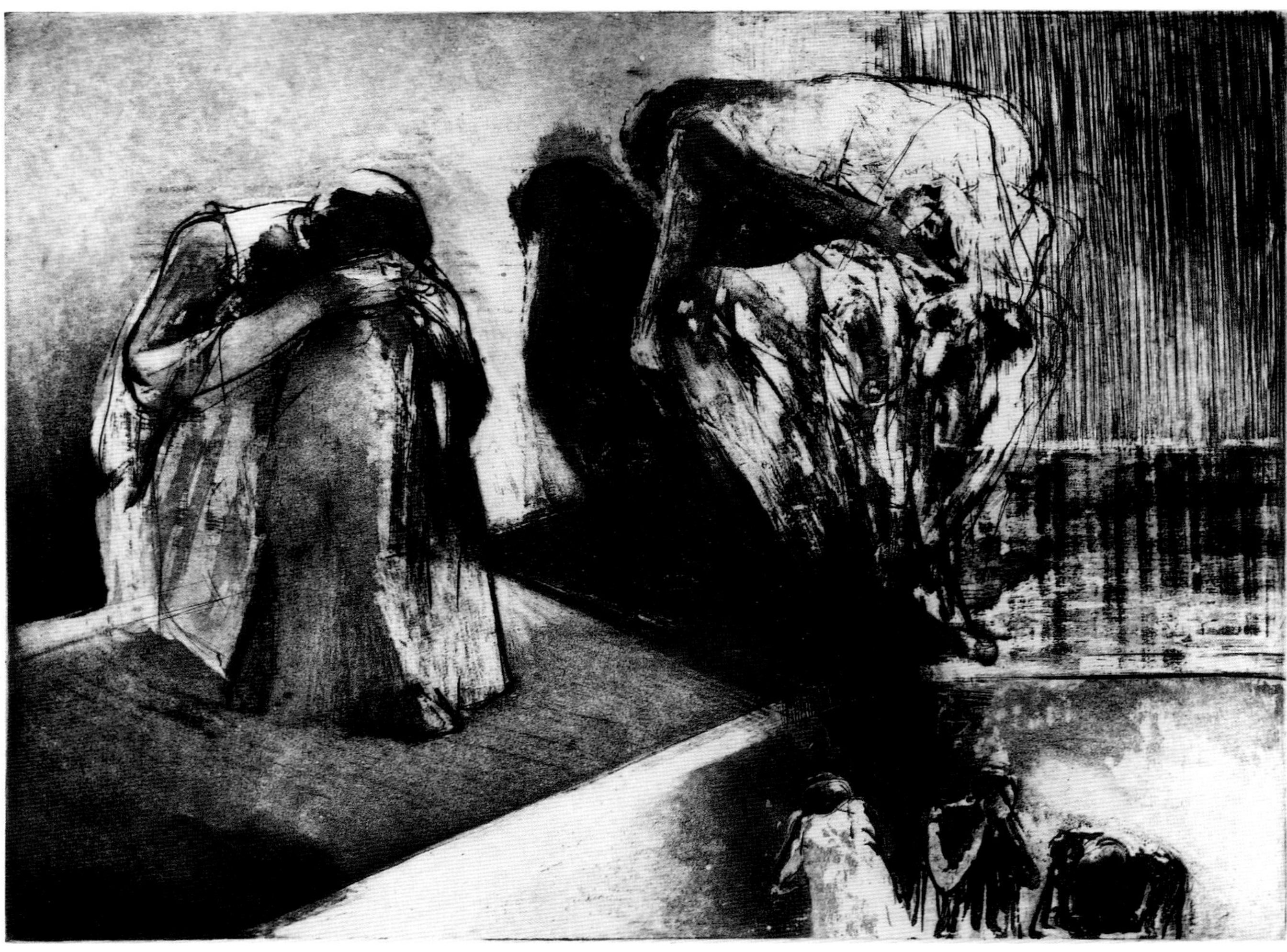

Fig. 8 *Closed Ward #6 (A Still and Rocking Figure — Below the Restless),* 1962, etching and aquatint, 20¾ × 26⅞ in. (52.7 × 68.3 cm). Jane Voorhees Zimmerli Art Museum (82.017.032). (Catalogue raisonné 105)

world, individuals who have lost their humanity and are left with only loneliness and desperation. The compositions, dark and confining, reveal Mazur's expressionistic side and are as much a representation of the artist's reaction to the condition of mental institutions as an objective rendering of real space and individuals. A comparison with Piranesi's *Carceri,* both in atmosphere and in the use of aggressive and dynamic line, is appropriate. In *Closed Ward* (figs. 8 and 9), the idea of containment resurfaces as the residents of the asylum are seen struggling with their constraints and boxed within dark, walled spaces. The subsequent *Locked Ward* series (fig. 10) took the form of a portfolio of fourteen lithographs and represented Mazur's first significant efforts in this medium. Deriving from the same series of asylum drawings, these images evoke similar feelings as the *Closed Ward,* although the technique resulted in a completely different surface and line quality. Mazur's sweeping crayon, sometimes used on its point and sometimes on its side, would break abruptly or change direction to create tension, as opposed to the *Closed Ward* etchings, which appear as long, unbroken webs of line reminiscent of automatic drawing. The two series received much critical attention and established Mazur as a strong talent at an extremely early age. For the next few years Mazur enjoyed extraordinary success as he won awards, received grants, and mounted his first solo exhibitions.[15] A 1964 Guggenheim fellowship allowed him to spend a year working primarily in sculpture (fig. 70), a hiatus that would prove fruitful for his printmaking activities in several ways.

Coming of Age: Themes and Formats

In 1965 Mazur accepted a position as assistant professor at Brandeis University in Waltham, Massachusetts, and he spent the next ten years teaching, exhibiting, and establishing the patterns of his professional life. This decade was one of great changes, and Mazur found himself involved alternately in the very public activities of campus political life, the peace movement, and artists' rights issues and the more private preoccupations of the studio and family life. Mazur had begun painting again after a hiatus of nearly a decade, and it was not unusual for him to be working in several media simultaneously, from painting, drawing,

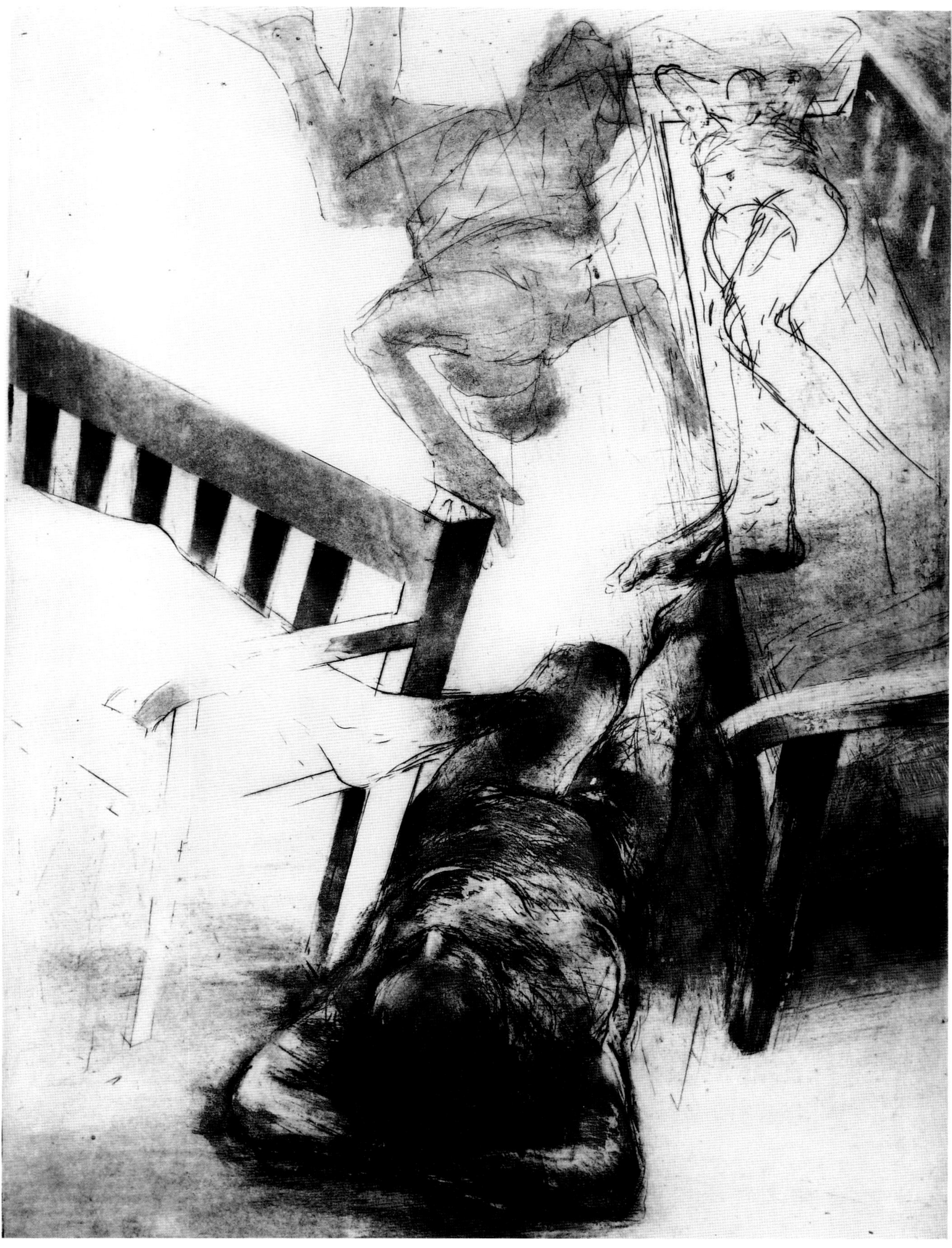

Fig. 9 *Closed Ward (Figure Fixed on Figure Falling)*, 1965, etching and aquatint, 35½ × 26¾ in. (90.2 × 68.0 cm). Collection of the artist. (Catalogue raisonné 124)

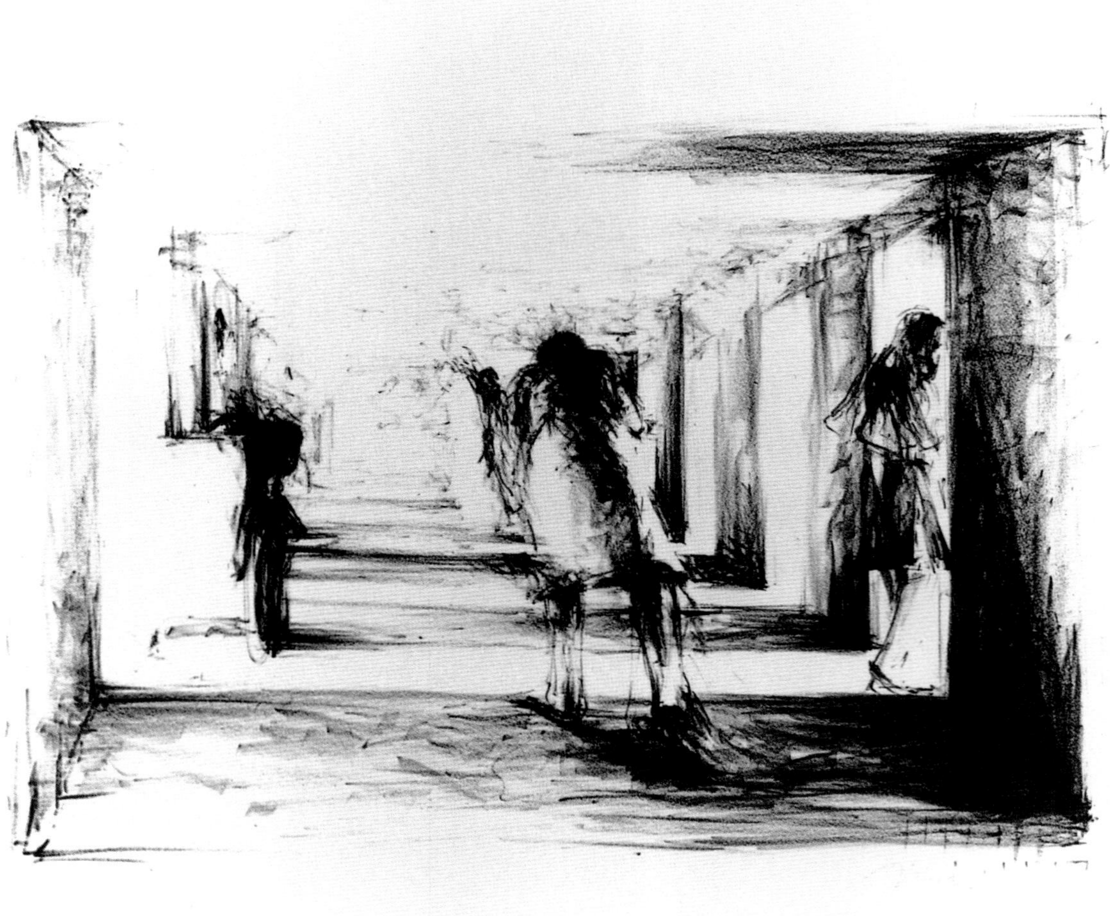

Fig. 10 *Images from a Locked Ward #2 (The Corridor),* 1965, lithograph, 20 × 26 in. (50.8 × 66.1 cm). Jane Voorhees Zimmerli Art Museum (82.017.044). (Catalogue raisonné 133)

pastel, and sculpture to printmaking. He also began keeping the detailed work journals that today provide fascinating insights into his work methods and creative process.[16] The earliest journals contain numerous preliminary sketches and notes for works, often with almost daily revisions as a subject and format developed.

The late 1960s signaled a change in Mazur's work, a shift toward a cooler and more analytical approach that may, in part, be understood as the artist's reaction to working in such an intensely expressive and emotional vein for several years combined with a more personal reaction to the tumultuous events of the times, particularly the year of 1968. Early in that year Mazur created a portfolio of images entitled *The Artist and the Model.*[17] This group of images stemmed from the sculptures Mazur produced working from the model during the year of his Guggenheim fellowship, followed by two years of making hundreds of drawings and small terra-cotta figures in which he explored, with directness and intimacy, not only the human form but the relationship of artist and model. After working with the tactile materials and techniques of the sculptor and draftsman, Mazur moved on to a new objectivity in the *Artist and the Model* print series (fig. 27) as he began to intellectualize, conceptualize, and abstract the figures to create "a complex study of the observer and the observed and the charged dynamic space between them."[18] The prints are radically different in spirit and style from earlier works, as Mazur began experimenting with cut and shaped plates as a two-dimensional extension of his sculptural studies. Figures and shadows, edges, and positive/negative spaces play games with the eye, just as the tension between the figures plays out its own ambiguous drama. The work also reflected the times, as several artists such as Alex Katz, Wayne Thiebaud, Yvonne Jacquette, Robert Cottingham, and Richard Estes reacted to the excesses of the Pop and Minimal movements with a cool and often stylized realism. Mazur continued the ideas developed in the *Artist and the Model* series when he went to Los Angeles to work at Tamarind Lithography Workshop on a fellowship in the early summer of 1968, creating thirty-four editions of lithographs working with several different printers. By then he was more than ready to leave the figure for a time and move on to new subjects.

For the next several years, including a sojourn in New York between 1970 and 1972, Mazur focused on the objects in his studio, views out his studio window (figs. 73 and 74), and other seemingly simple subjects devoid of subjectivity and emotion. Mazur became increasingly preoccupied with the nature of visual perception and an exploration of the eye-to-brain-to-hand relationships the artist experiences and the mental and physical processes of representation and illusion. As his activities in painting and drawing in pastel increased, Mazur also became interested in introducing more color into his printed work. A series of both black-and-white and color prints emerged that at first glance appear deceptively simple. Each work, however, presented its own set of formal and conceptual challenges and solutions. From time to time the work journals note that a subject "presented itself," reinforcing the fact that Mazur trusted his instinct and imagination and was open to an intriguing compositional challenge, a certain quality or movement of light, or a distraction that led his eye to a previously unnoticed object, thus starting a process that was far more important to the artist than the end result. New tools and techniques continued to be incorporated and explored, including a fascination with the airbrush that Mazur experimented with to create tonal effects for his printing plates after learning the basics from the artist Billy Al Bengston while they were both at Tamarind.

This activity, however, was overshadowed by Mazur's beginning exploration of the monotype process, a journey that has informed his work in all media and that was the pivotal event of his midcareer. Having been reminded of the possibility of the unique print, both monotypes and monoprints, by an extraordinary exhibition of the monotypes of Degas that Mazur visited at the Fogg Art Museum at Harvard University in 1968,[19] Mazur found a unique bridge to close the gap between painting and printmaking. Now, concurrent with his experimentation with printmaking tools such as the electric engraving needle and the airbrush to create aquatint textures, Mazur began to paint freely on unworked plates.

The variety of his prints during this period is remarkable; so are the formats. Expanding his conceptual concerns to include the passage of time, the monotype medium was suitable for creating series of works by printing a monotype and then continuing to work with the "ghost" impression on the plate, print again, rework, print again, in much the same manner as a film animator. Works such as *The Visit* (fig. 38), the *New York Memory* series (fig. 39), and *Window Sequence (Fire)* (fig. 40) now created their own implied or direct narratives. As importantly, they documented the artist's process, an intellectual and physical process that Mazur had previously achieved — and then lost — in his editioned prints through the many states he often created in developing the final image. Never leaving

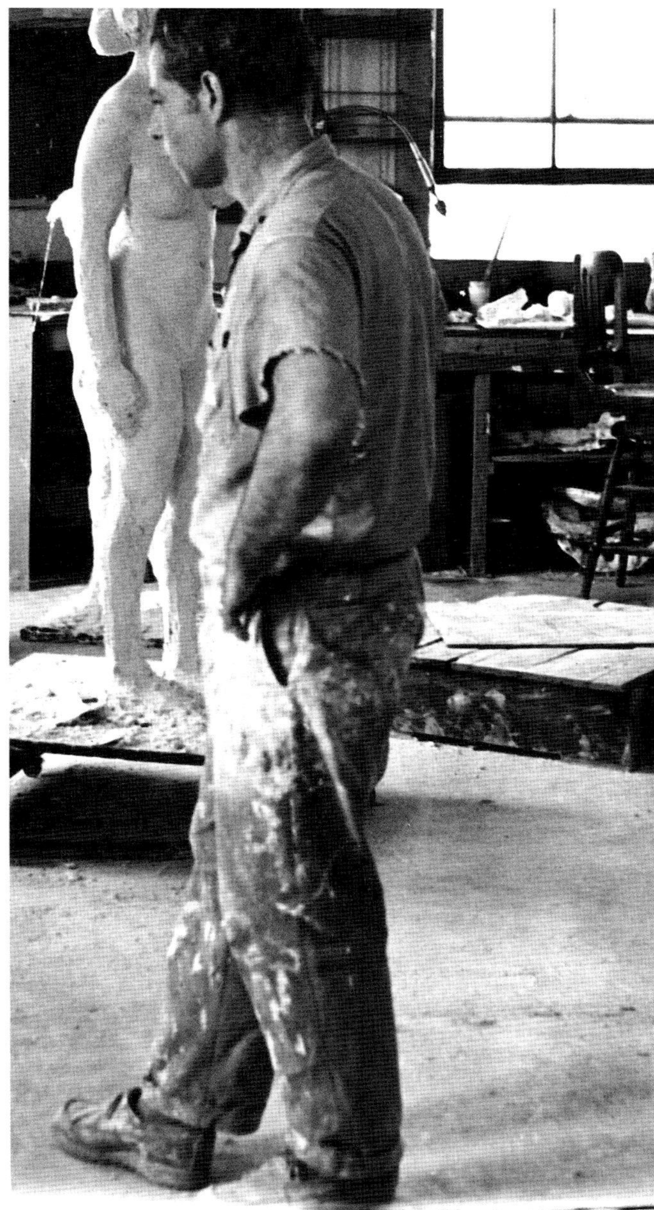

Mazur in studio with plaster sculpture of model, 1964

his expressive side completely behind, Mazur found the monotype an ideal medium for a series of work based on his observations of animals at the Stoneham Zoo (fig. 11). Mazur would spend hours there, observing and drawing monkeys, baboons, and other animals. On trips to New York he would often visit the Central Park Zoo in the company of his friend, artist Mary Frank. The drawings and monotypes, which Mazur would often supplement with pastel, are lush and remarkably keen in their observation and depiction of the animals and their behaviors (colorplate 15). They are strikingly similar in feel to the black-and-white images from the *Closed Ward* and *Locked Ward* series, with the obvious theme of containment and the difficult comparison of society's often inhumane fascination with, and need to collect and confine, nature.

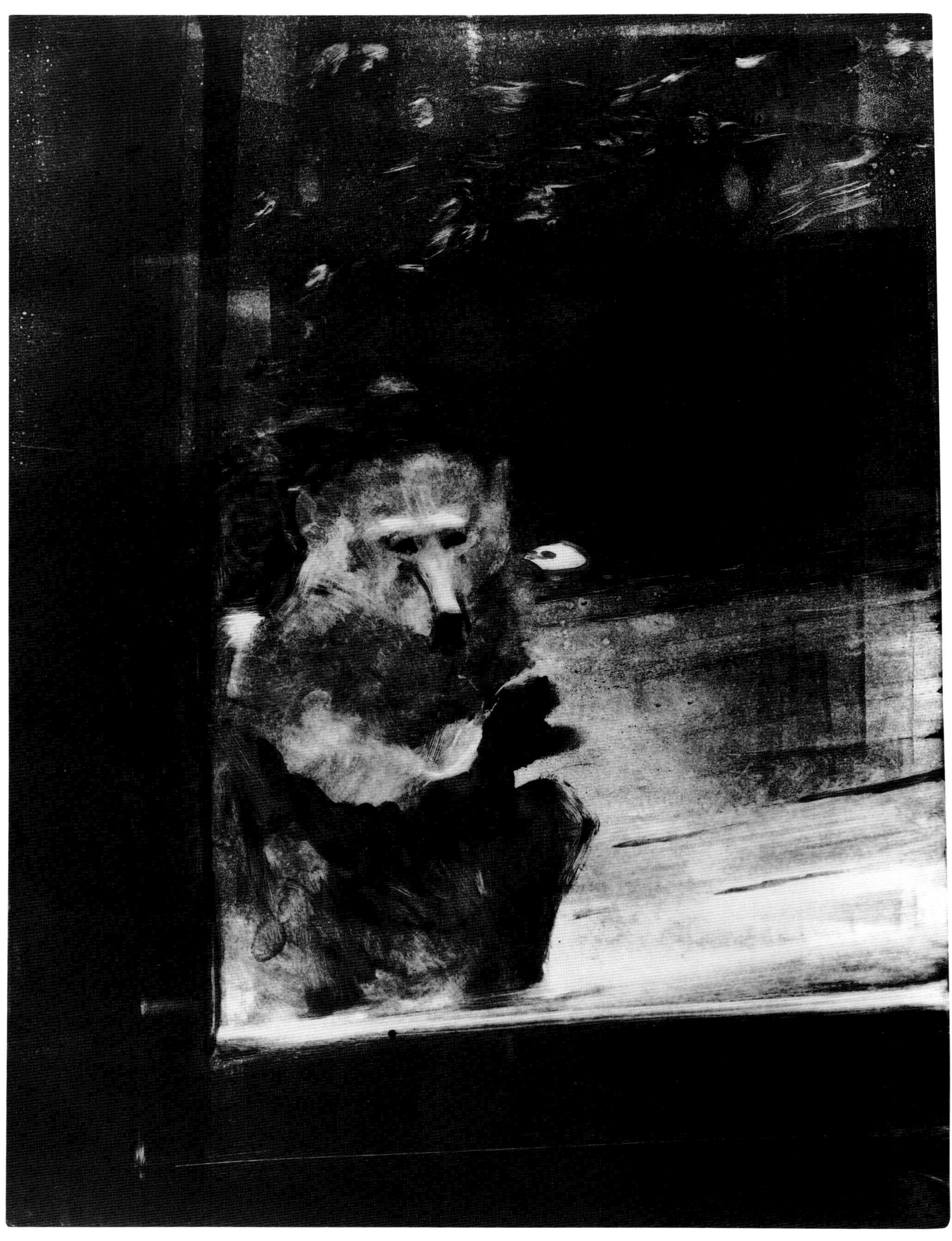

Fig. 11 *Monkey at Window,* 1974, monotype (cognates a/c and b/c), 26⅞ × 20⅝ in. (68.3 × 52.4 cm) each. Collection of the artist.

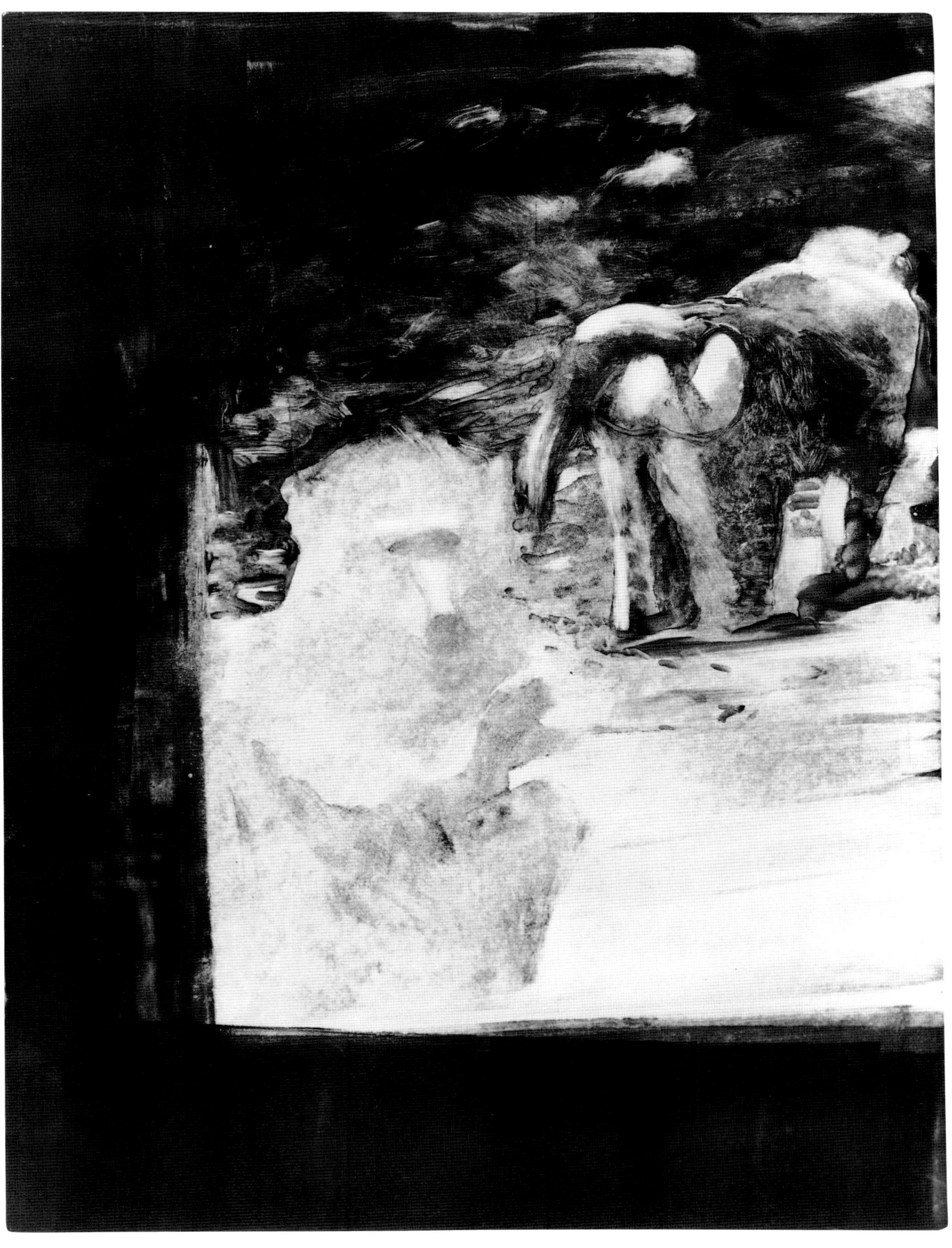

By the late 1970s Mazur's production of etchings, lithographs, and other editioned prints dropped off as his involvement with unique printmaking grew. And it was no wonder. Mazur, along with a handful of artists including Frank, Nathan Oliveira, Matt Phillips, and Joe Zirker became the vanguard for renewed interest in the unique print. Of course, many other contemporary artists had experimented with monotype and there had been a long history of one-of-a-kind prints, but it took the special qualities of artists of equal technical virtuosity and artistic vision to show a new generation the suitability and versatility of the medium.[20] Mazur became an advocate for the medium, generously sharing his techniques and writing and speaking about unique prints. Soon, many major painters, sculptors, and other artists began making monotypes and monoprints, just as many of them had added other basic types of printmaking to their everyday artistic activity years earlier. Mazur was also working with master printers at collaborative printmaking workshops during the 1980s, creating editioned prints as well as monoprints and monotypes.[21] In this way, he shared many of his techniques with printers who then proceeded to share their new skills with other artists. Today it is not unusual for artists to visit print workshops and create editioned prints and monotypes simultaneously, something that rarely happened in the 1970s when print shops were focused on producing large editions of identically printed impressions. Throughout the 1980s the notion of the variant edition of monoprints or a series of monotypes became a common option for artists arriving at print workshops to collaborate with master printers. In this way Mazur played a major role in helping to break down the barriers between visual media.

Mazur continued to innovate in the monotype medium, just as he had with intaglio and relief printmaking. An early flower study, the *Night Cyclamen* monotype of 1980 (colorplate 16), bears a strangely textured background that Mazur created by using an old, damaged ink roller his teacher Peterdi had given him. He would also paint an image with printing ink on one plate, pick up the image on a roller, and then offset it onto another plate or elsewhere on the original plate to create multilayered "ghosts within ghosts." He began using turpentine and other solvents to make the inks bleed and run before printing, creating veils of watercolorlike layers. His black-and-white monotypes were equally interesting. In 1982 Mazur was commissioned to create illustrations for Richard Howard's translation of Charles Baudelaire's *Les Fleurs du Mal*.[22] The resulting flower images display a stunning variance in texture and mood, as Mazur's marks range from spiky, threatening slashes of leaves to delicately layered and ghostly tones creating a curving and gently seductive stem of cyclamen (fig. 12). A full range of expression, accompanied by a full range of marks and deletions, was evident in the representation of a few simple flowers.

Another major change in Mazur's working life had occurred in 1975, when, at age forty, he made the decision to quit university teaching to devote himself full-time to his art making. He was now free to work even more intensely and to lecture and guest teach more selectively. His output during the late 1970s and 1980s was prolific. Mazur describes work sessions in which he would create eight to ten monotypes, often after having spent the earlier part of the day painting, drawing, writing, or doing paperwork. As the monotype movement caught on, Mazur's monotypes were included in virtually every major exhibition of the medium, and his name became synonymous with monotype. He continued to make editioned prints, of course, and the eighties and early nineties saw a series of color prints, many based on the notion of duality and the passage of time. *Two Ideas about a Garden* of 1990 (colorplate 24), for example, contrasts vastly different concepts of landscape and gardens by showing a "natural" western garden (the view from Mazur's studio) as a background within which an inset carries the notion of the formal Chinese garden. Mazur varied the printmaking processes as well, with the natural landscape printed using aquatint and etching, while the *chine collé* inset was printed using wood relief for textural contrast. Mazur had begun working out his ideas for the print by creating a series of monotypes; a study created during the previous winter (colorplate 25), while similar in composition, evokes a completely different mood.

Other experiments led Mazur to print monotypes on silk and to create large, multipaneled screens with silk monotype insets (colorplate 28). These experiments started in 1988 when Mazur visited the Experimental Workshop in San Francisco and, together with the master printer Will Foo, solved many technical problems presented in printing on silk. He also created works that pieced several monotypes together, in much the same way that other artists have experimented with shaped and pieced canvases to create monumental works. Several of Mazur's works in this vein, such as the 84½-by-45½-inch *Weeping Beech* of 1988 (colorplate 29), continued to demonstrate the versatility of printmaking as a fundamental form of visual expression.

These works of the late 1980s followed one of the most important projects of Mazur's career, the monumental *Wakeby Day/Wakeby Night* triptychs of 1983 (colorplates 18, 26, and 27). The project centered around a commission from the Committee on the Visual Arts at the Massachusetts Institute of Technology to create two six-by-twelve-foot murals for a new dormitory on campus.[23] Mazur's masterful use of the curving wall space, the charged contrasts of day and night in compositions that embody nature's full cycle of birth, life, death, and renewal, and the richness of countless layers of ink and marks make the *Wakeby* prints and the many monotype studies (colorplate 21) a compendium of possibilities for the medium. The range of technical nuances, from the offsetting of an image on one plate to another plate using the roller, the use of solvents to create painterly drips and layers, the marks made by fingers, palm, rags, wooden sticks, and the like, all make it difficult to believe the speed at which it was necessary to

Fig. 12 *Parisian Scenes,* from *Les Fleurs du Mal,* 1981, monotype, 37⅝ × 26 in. (95.6 × 66.1 cm). The New York Public Library, Gift of Michael Mazur and David R. Godine, in memory of Morton Godine.

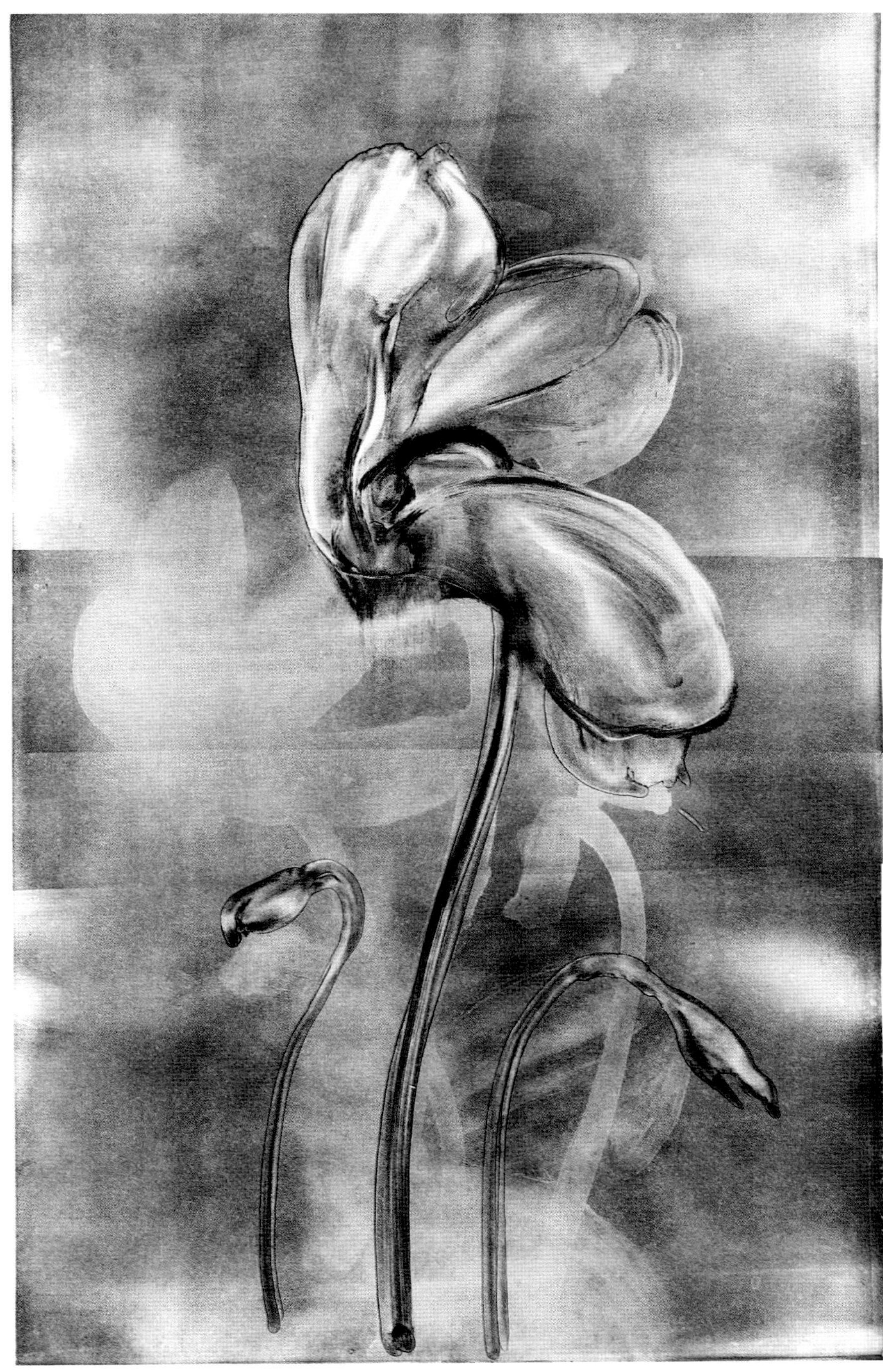

create and print the panels before the inks began to dry. Looking at the still photographs or the videotape made during the *Wakeby* sessions,[24] one realizes the poetry in motion of the artist, the choreography of Mazur and master printer Robert Townsend working in tandem to manipulate and print the gigantic plates. It also becomes clear that the project was, in many ways, a performance piece. Mazur created dozens of large and small studies, or rehearsals, as he worked out the structure, all leading up to the final full-scale production sessions where Mazur, having already worked through the details, focused entirely on the process.

Revision and Renewal: The Journey Continued

Despite the many successes and a steady stream of production in the late 1980s, Mazur arrived at midlife with a certain feeling of malaise and frustration. An abortive return to working with the figure in the early 1980s was seen in the *Dancer or the Dance* prints and paintings (fig. 78), and in a series of self-portraits begun in 1985 when the artist turned fifty, which can only be described as bordering on the bizarre (colorplates 8 and 9). Beginning with a fairly benign self-portrait, Mazur's flights of fancy led to a surreal series of images and a mixture of printing, sometimes with cut and pieced plates, with monotype and handwork. Mazur recalls feeling as though he was literally "pushing himself around on the plate" and saw the series as a soul-searching experience. Far more intriguing during this period was the artist's exploration of yet another technique, the trace monotype. This technique, which involves inking a plate and then covering it with a sheet of paper and drawing on it to transfer an image to the paper, could be more accurately described as a transfer drawing. In Mazur's hands, however, nuances appeared as the artist varied the tools and began to experiment with printing the inked plate after the first traced print had been pulled to create a second, very different print. Mazur's *Self-Portrait (Bronze)* of 1986 (colorplate 7) and the majestically anthropomorphic *Copper Beech* of 1987 (fig. 13), a tree in a neighbor's yard that Mazur had drawn many times, give some indication of the range of the process in Mazur's skilled hands. These images, and a continuing series of tree images, saw a return of expressiveness and mood reminiscent of Mazur's earliest figure and landscape subjects. Prints such as *Texas Tree* of 1988 (figs. 43 and 44), a foreboding tangle of branches pushing at the borders of an almost square format, also show Mazur's constant experimentation. In the *Texas Tree* series, monotype was combined with a wood relief image that had first been printed onto a metal plate and then offset printed to create additional textures.

At the same time Mazur was busy in the studio, he was also involved in a dizzying array of other activities. A growing fascination with Asian landscape traditions and garden design had led to a trip to China in 1987, along with other regular travel. In 1990 Mazur founded the New Provincetown Print Project at the Fine Arts Work Center in Provincetown, and for several years he not only collaborated with invited guest artists to explore monotype techniques in intensive work sessions with Robert Townsend, but also directed the program and led the fund-raising and print marketing efforts.[25] He was also teaching, both on a regular basis at Harvard and on numerous guest and visiting artist arrangements, and presenting new work in a steady schedule of gallery exhibitions. By 1992 he was entering a new collaboration, with the poet Robert Pinsky, on a series of monotypes for Pinsky's new translation of Dante's *Inferno.*[26]

Much of 1992 was spent working on the black-and-white monotypes that were used as illustrations for Pinsky's *Inferno of Dante* (figs. 53–67). In many ways, the collaboration brought Mazur full circle. Having created illustrations for books and other publications over the years, Mazur's collaboration with his good friend Pinsky gave the artist the opportunity to return to the epic that had fascinated him since his school days. The give and take between him and Pinsky was a new kind of collaboration that forced them both to reexamine preconceived notions about Dante's work and about their own frames of reference in regard to the classic.[27] The monotypes display the range of Mazur's talents, this time in a variety of treatments from expressionistic to formal. The thirty-eight monotypes that were included in *The Inferno,* and countless studies that the artist created in marathon sessions, were made in random order and then edited for the final selection. Ever prolific, the studies explore different viewpoints and interpretations for each canto, making one wish that all could have been included in the book. Following the book's publication, the University of Iowa Museum of Art mounted a traveling exhibition based on the monotypes and studies,[28] and for three years Mazur and Pinsky visited the many venues to talk about the work and their collaboration. Mazur finally felt that he had "done right by Dante" and was ready to move on. The journey brought Mazur back to the natural world, as he returned to many of the themes and ideas of the late 1980s, this time in a very different frame of mind.

By the early 1990s it became clear that Mazur's malaise was as much physical as psychological. In January 1993 coronary catheterization revealed heart disease, and Mazur underwent a balloon angioplasty procedure. He watched the procedure on a monitor and was struck by the hidden networks and rhythms of his own body. A new inward focus on body and state of mind followed and was soon reflected in his work. A small painting made soon after his recovery, a pulsating web of arterylike lines in blood-red colors, was quickly followed by more works that began to merge the internal landscape of the body with the natural landscape Mazur had already returned to in the recent tree images (colorplates 32, 33, and 34). With renewed vigor, Mazur consciously sought to simplify, to trust his instincts, and to let the developing image dictate the next steps. In letting go, Mazur gave himself the opportunity to enter a new phase, to permit himself to enter new territories.

Since the mid-1990s, Mazur's paintings and prints have opened up and become almost impressionistic in their highly personal viewpoint and abstracted vision of the natural world. Combining a deeper understanding of Chinese landscape composition and philosophy, based on Chinese scrolls he had studied and territories and gardens he had visited in China, with his own long involvement with representing nature in more traditional Western ways, Mazur in his recent works uses landscape as a mere departure point for explorations that take on a life of their own. In his *Mind Landscape* pieces (colorplates 38 and 39), which include paintings, monotypes, and other types of prints, forms float from top to bottom without horizon or any specific landscape reference. The prints range from light and airy layers drawn on litho plates to densely printed and layered intaglios. Part of the richness of the recent intaglio prints stems from Mazur's use of multiple hand and power tools on the copper plate and the multiple-color *à la poupée* inking that make the prints seem more complicated than they actually are. In some cases, a slight offsetting of plates in printing creates a vibrating tension. The *Pond Edge* series (colorplates 40, 41, and 42) demonstrates this effect, with its heightening of the illusion of light and movement at water's edge.

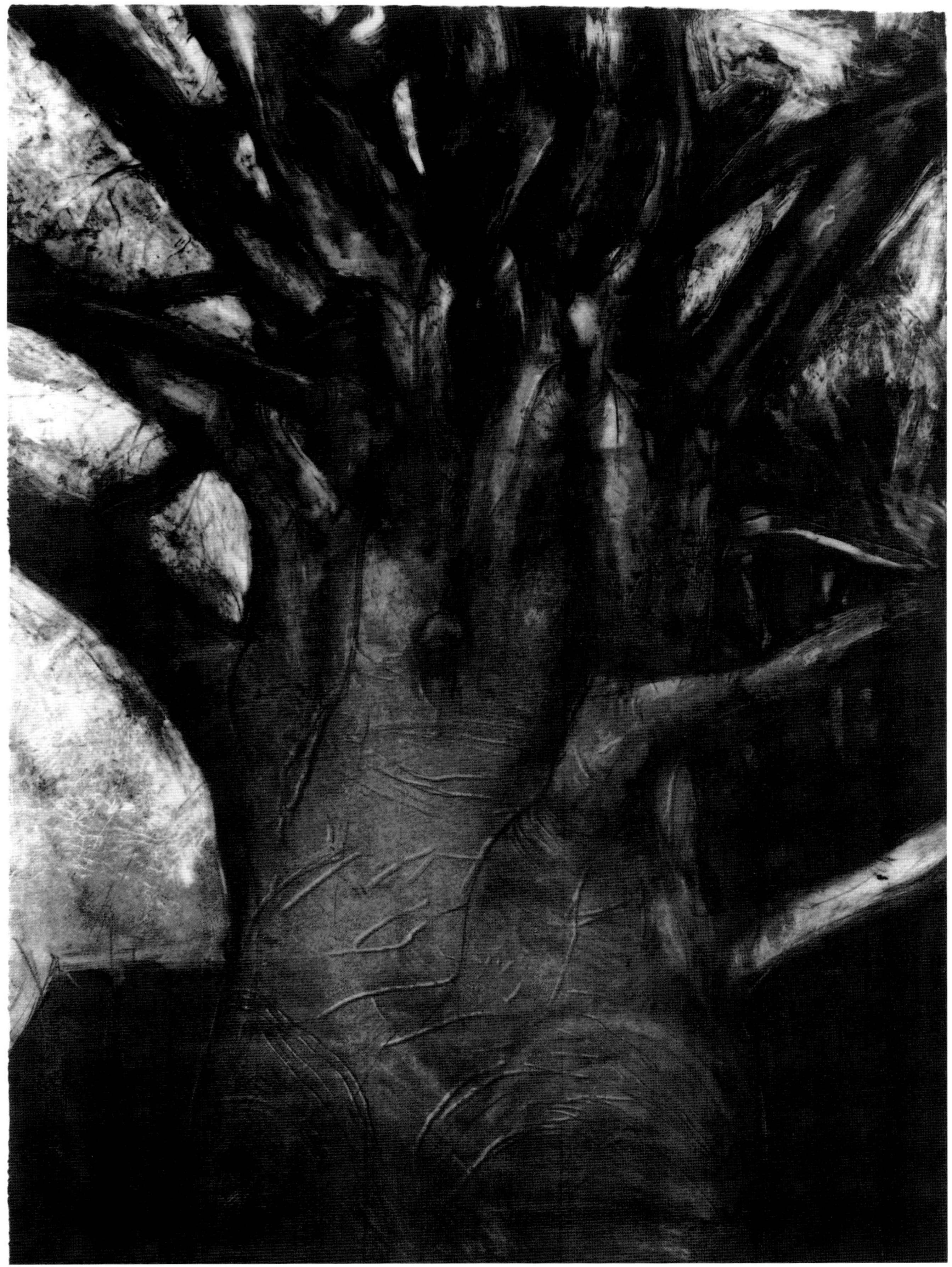

Fig. 13 *Copper Beech,* 1987, trace monotype, 47¾ × 34¾ in. (121.3 × 88.3 cm). Collection of the artist.

Discussion of Mazur's art has at times focused on the sheer beauty of his forms and surfaces. Beauty is a word that Mazur has no time for, finding the word to be "too loaded, too full of negative associations." In describing his work, Mazur prefers to think of finding "elegant solutions" in representing subjects and solving perceptual challenges.[29] The elegance of his solutions often makes his accomplishment appear deceptively simple, in the same way that a poem, a dance, a literary classic, or a haunting melody grasps one's imagination.

Quite predictably, Michael Mazur has continued to experiment and explore new printmaking horizons. For two recent commissions, he employed digital technologies and possibilities to create monumental printed works, and he is embracing this new set of tools and techniques with the same enthusiasm with which he mastered and then expanded traditional techniques. While most of the artist's recent exhibitions have focused on new paintings, Mazur actively works across boundaries, returning often to his graphic home base. In his career, Mazur has provided a strong example of artistic integrity and a romantic ideal that is in short supply in our times. In his work he has demonstrated new possibilities for graphic expression and created a wealth of unforgettable images. Mazur has also shown us his humanity and given us cause to think about our own.

NOTES

1. Quoted in Jeffrey Coven, *Baudelaire's Voyages: The Poet and His Painters* (Huntington, N.Y.: Heckscher Museum, 1993), 41. "La Fanfarlo," published in 1847, was Baudelaire's only short story and is generally considered to be highly autobiographical.

2. Conversation with the author, 8 July 1998.

3. A formative influence occurred at age eight, when Mazur's parents hired Gretchen Hanske, a young German woman, as a live-in babysitter. Hanske took regular art classes and she often arranged still-life compositions and taught Mazur how to draw from life.

4. From an audiotaped interview with Robert Brown, Archives of American Art, 12 January 1993 (tape 1).

5. Mazur had met Ullman through family connections. Mazur describes Davidson as "a sort of synthetic cubist" (audiotape interview with Barry Walker, 7 May 1998, Cambridge, Mass.).

6. This experience in printing for Baskin also provided Mazur with his first introduction to variable printing, as the plates were selectively inked and wiped to create variations among each impression of an image. *Horned Beetles and Other Insects,* an album of etchings and engravings, was published by Baskin's Gehenna Press in 1958.

7. Daniel Mazur was born in 1959 and daughter Kathe in 1961. Gail helped Mazur print *An Image of Salomé* shortly after they met; printed images of Gail and the children are well documented in the catalogue raisonné herein as well as in paintings, pastels, and other works.

8. See Paul J. Sachs, *Modern Prints and Drawings: A Guide to a Better Understanding of Modern Draughtsmanship* (New York: Alfred A. Knopf, 1954); José Ortega y Gasset, *The Dehumanization of Art and Other Writings on Art and Culture* (Garden City, N.Y.: Doubleday, 1956); and Wassily Kandinsky, *Concerning the Spiritual in Art and Painting in Particular* (New York: Wittenborn, 1947).

9. *It Is: A Magazine for Abstract Art* was published by Second Half Publishing Company in New York between spring 1958 and autumn 1965 (nos. 1–5 were published 1958–60 and no. 6 was published in 1965). These six issues included contemporary art criticism and the writings of American abstract artists, focusing on the New York School, and featured large black-and-white illustrations.

10. Michael Mazur, "An Introduction to the Book 'An Image of Salomé,'" honor's thesis, Amherst College, 1958, 14. A copy of the thesis is available in the Archives and Special Collections, Frost Library, Amherst College.

11. In addition to teaching, Peterdi published *Printmaking: Methods Old and New* (New York: Macmillan, 1959). Ten years earlier, Stanley William Hayter, director of the important Atelier 17, had written *New Ways of Graveur,* and in 1958 Jules Heller published *Printmaking Today: An Introduction to the Graphic Arts* (New York: Henry Holt).

12. In late 1959 Peterdi was given a retrospective exhibition, *Gabor Peterdi: Twenty-five Years of His Prints, 1934–1959,* at the Brooklyn Museum, and his print *Triumph of the Weed* received the first prize of $2,500 in the Associated American Artists 25th Anniversary National Fine Print Competition. Earlier that year Peterdi's landscape *Cathedral* was selected for *American Prints Today/1959,* the first exhibition organized by the Print Council of America.

13. Peter Selz, curator of paintings and sculpture at the Museum of Modern Art, organized the *New Images of Man* exhibition, which included the work of Karel Appel, Kenneth Armitage, Francis Bacon, Leonard Baskin, Reg Butler, Cosmo Campoli, César, Richard Diebenkorn, Jean Dubuffet, Alberto Giacometti, Leon Golub, Balcomb Greene, Willem de Kooning, Rico Lebrun, James McGarrell, Jan Müller, Nathan Oliveira, Eduardo Paolozzi, Jackson Pollock, Germaine Richter, Theodore J. Roszak, H. C. Westermann, and Fritz Wotruba.

14. Conversation with the author, 8 July 1998.

15. See the Chronology.

16. Thirteen of Mazur's work journals and one sketchbook, dating from May 1974 to March 1998, have been microfilmed and are on file at the Archives of American Art. The Archives has recorded 10¼ hours of taped interviews with the artist, conducted by Robert Brown in sessions between 12 January 1993 and 3 February 1995.

17. *The Artist and the Model* was published by Associated American Artists, New York, whose director at the time was the legendary print dealer Sylvan Cole.

18. Edward Bryant, introduction to *Michael Mazur,* exh. cat. (Hamilton, N.Y.: Picker Art Gallery, Colgate University, 1973), n.p.

19. The exhibition *Edgar Degas: Monotypes* was organized by curator Eugenia Parry Janis and included seventy-eight monotypes by the artist. More than three hundred prints were reproduced in the exhibition catalogue, *Degas Monotypes: Essay, Catalogue, and Checklist* (Cambridge: Fogg Art Museum, Harvard University, 1968).

20. For detailed accounts of the history of monotype, see Sue Welsh Reed et al., *The Painterly Print: Monotypes from the Seventeenth to the Twentieth Century,* exh. cat. (New York: Metropolitan Museum of Art, 1980), and Joann Moser, *Singular Impressions: The Monotype in America,* exh. cat. (Washington, D.C.: Smithsonian Institution Press for the National Museum of American Art, 1997).

21. Throughout his career, Mazur has collaborated at numerous printmaking workshops and presses, including Impressions Workshop, Drum Litho, Tamarind Lithography Workshop, Fox Graphics–Merrimac Editions, Pace Editions, Solo Press (now Solo Impression), Experimental Workshop, Smith Andersen Editions, R. E. Townsend Studio, Muskat Studios, Jungle Press Editions, and the New Provincetown Print Project.

22. Richard Howard's translation of *Les Fleurs du Mal* was published by David R. Godine, Boston, in 1982.

23. For a complete account of Mazur's work on the *Wakeby* project, see *Wakeby Day/Wakeby Night: Monumental Monotypes by Michael Mazur: A Documentation of the Commission for MIT,* exh. cat. (Cambridge: Hayden Gallery, Massachusetts Institute of Technology, 1983).

24. Boston photographer Greg Heins shot documentary black-and-white photographs of several of the *Wakeby* sessions, while Mazur's son, Daniel Mazur, produced the videotape for MIT (with additional camera work by Susan Chasen). The video is available through the Committee on the Visual Arts at MIT.

25. For a listing of artists Mazur collaborated with at the New Provincetown Print Project, see the Chronology.

26. *The Inferno of Dante,* a new verse translation by Robert Pinsky, was published by Farrar, Straus and Giroux, New York, 1994.

27. For interviews and conversations with both Mazur and Pinsky regarding their collaboration on *The Inferno of Dante,* see *Image and Text: A Dialogue with Robert Pinsky and Michael Mazur* (Berkeley: Townsend Center for the Humanities, University of California, 1994), and *Monotypes by Michael Mazur for the Inferno,* exh. cat. (Iowa City: University of Iowa Museum of Art, 1994).

28. *Monotypes by Michael Mazur for the Inferno* was organized by the University of Iowa Museum of Art in 1994 and traveled to other venues.

29. Conversation with the author, 26 July 1995.

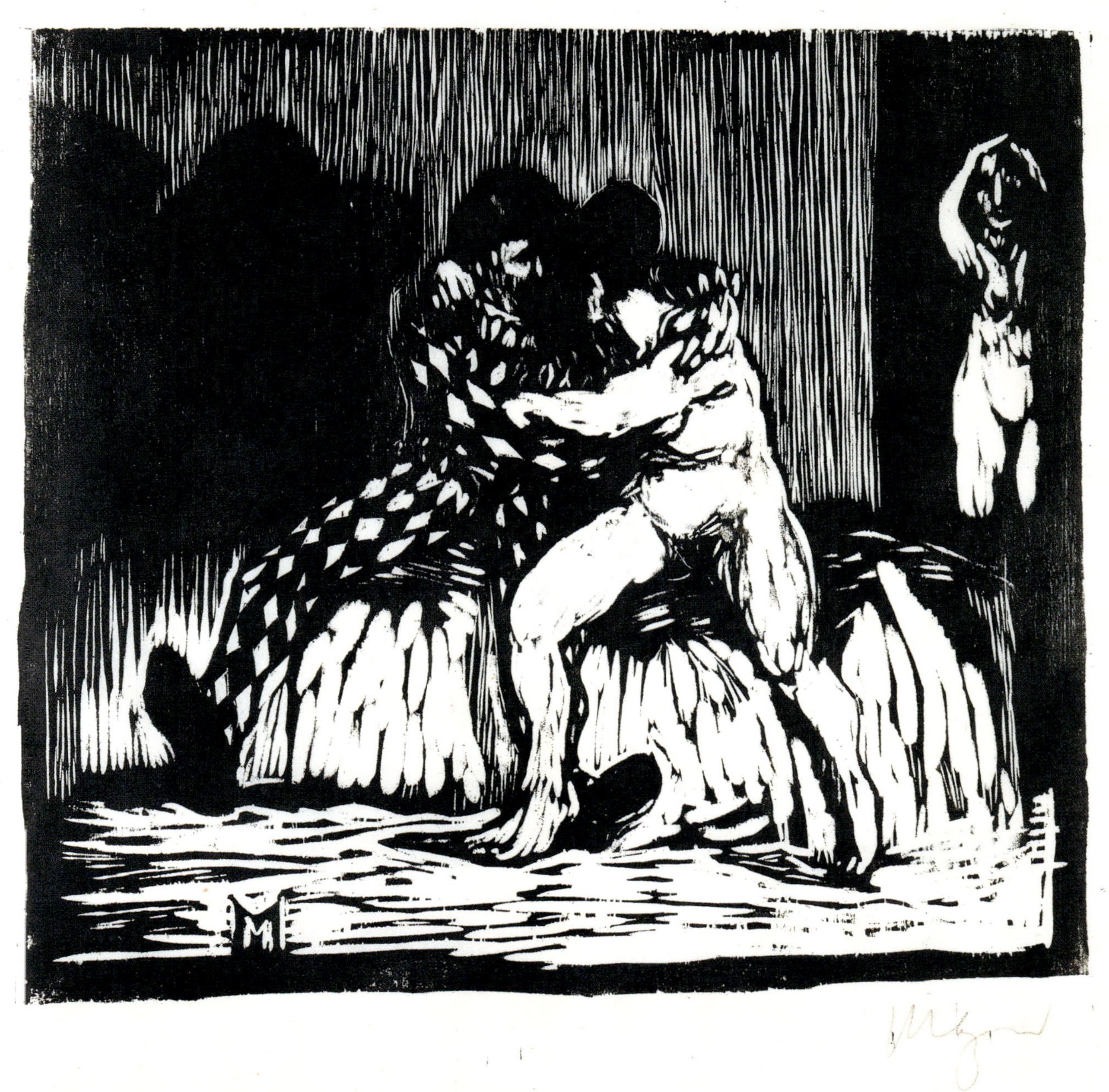

Colorplate 1 *Untitled (Embracing Couple),* 1957, wood relief, 18⅞ × 18⅛ in. (48.0 × 46.1 cm). Collection of the artist. (Catalogue raisonné 18)

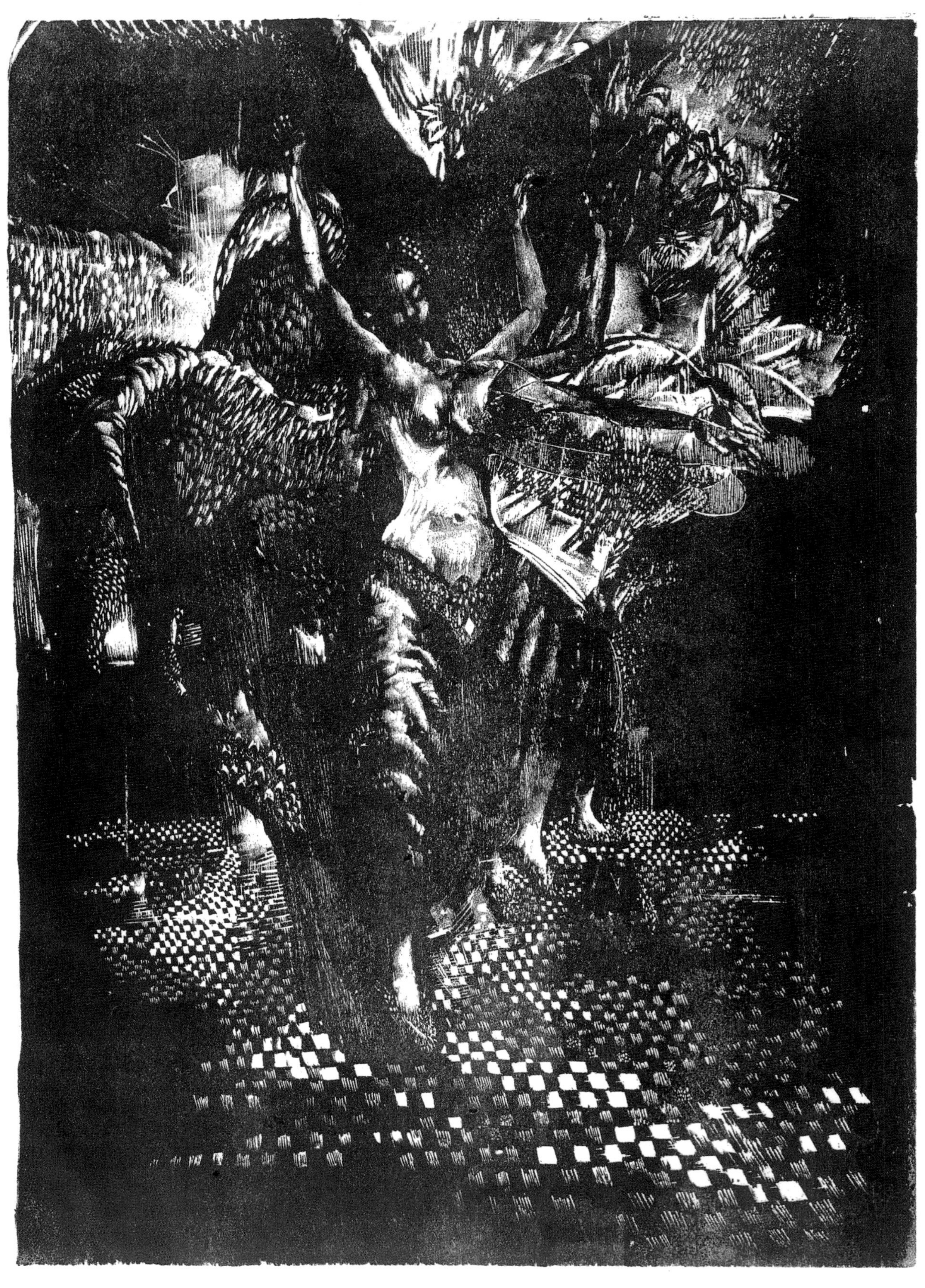

Colorplate 2 *The Dance of Salomé,* from *An Image of Salomé,* 1958, wood relief, 23½ × 17 in. (59.7 × 43.2 cm). Jane Voorhees Zimmerli Art Museum (82.017.069.12). (Catalogue raisonné 30)

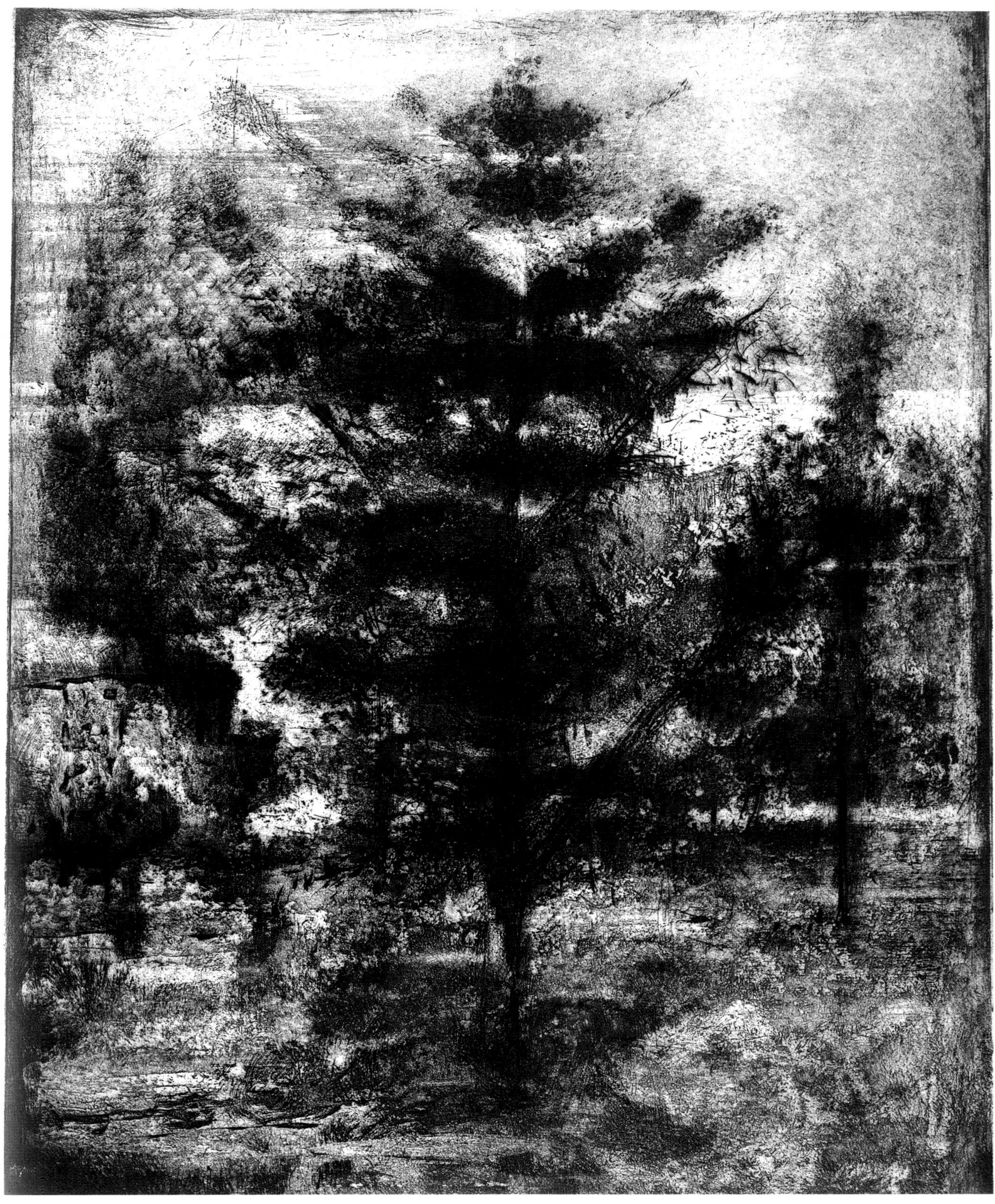

Colorplate 3 *Night Pine, Norfolk,* 1963, etching and aquatint, 26¾ × 21⅛ in. (68.0 × 53.7 cm). Jane Voorhees Zimmerli Art Museum, Museum Purchase (82.017.037). (Catalogue raisonné 113)

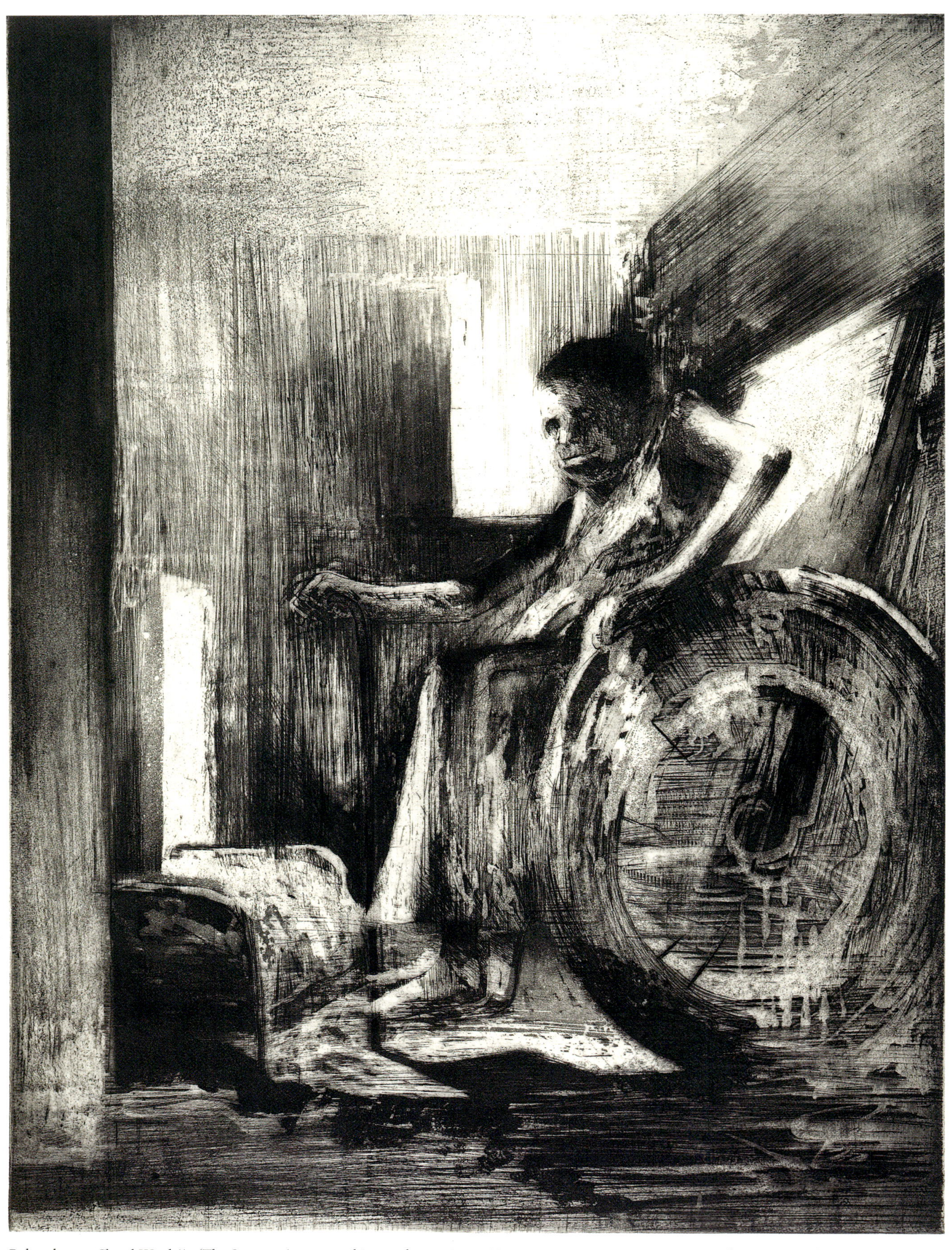

Colorplate 4 *Closed Ward #9 (The Occupant),* 1962, etching and aquatint, 27¼ × 21 in. (69.3 × 53.4 cm). Jane Voorhees Zimmerli Art Museum, Museum Purchase (82.017.033). (Catalogue raisonné 108)

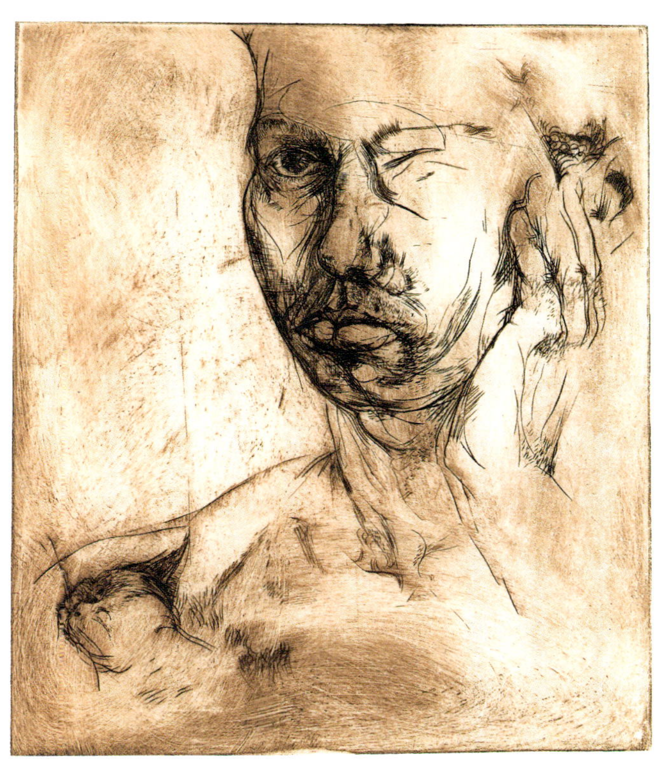

Colorplate 5 *Self-Portrait (State I),* 1959, engraving, 10¼ × 6¾ in. (26.0 × 17.2 cm). Collection of the artist. (Catalogue raisonné 48)

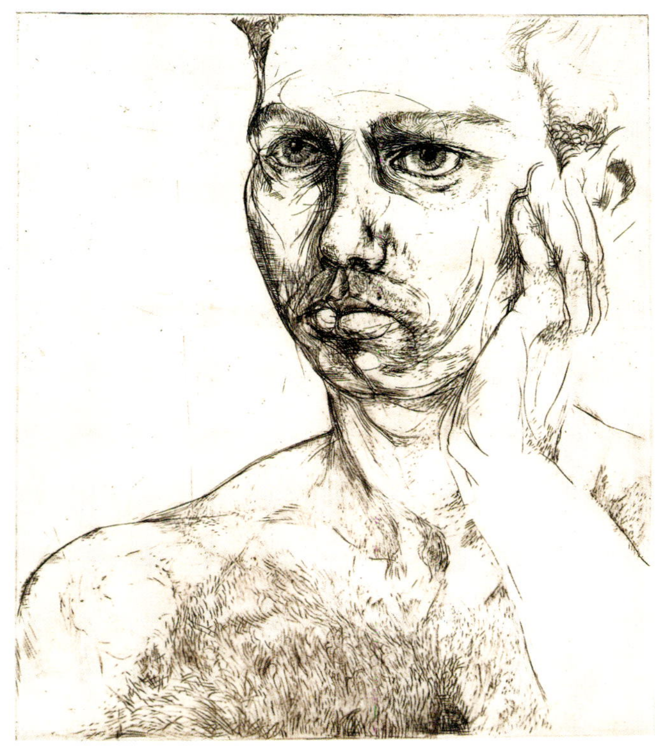

Colorplate 6 *Self-Portrait (State II),* 1959, engraving, 13 × 10¼ in. (33.0 × 26.0 cm). Collection of the artist. (Catalogue raisonné 49)

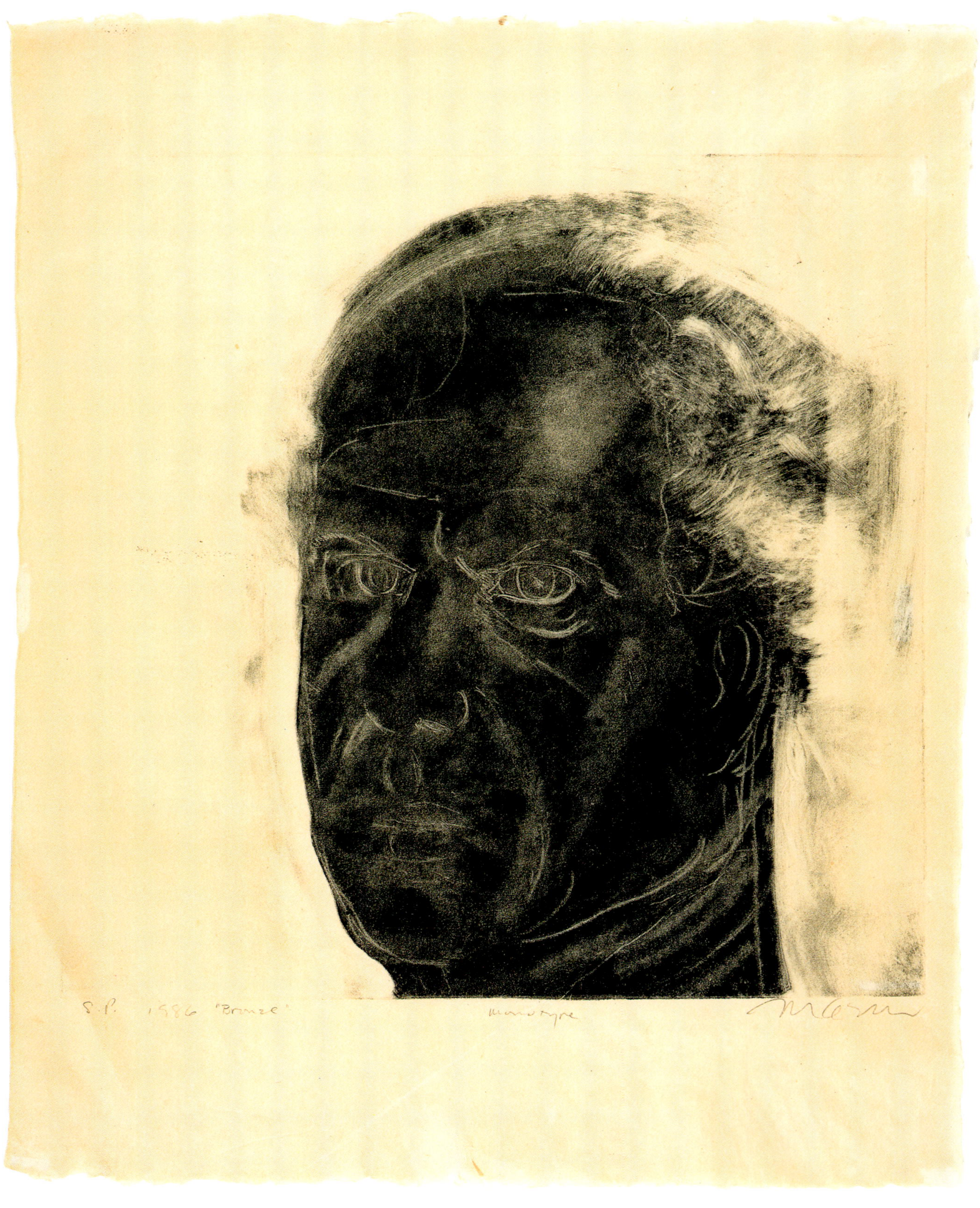

Colorplate 7 *Self-Portrait (Bronze),* 1986, trace monotype, 18 × 18 in. (45.8 × 45.8 cm). Private Collection.

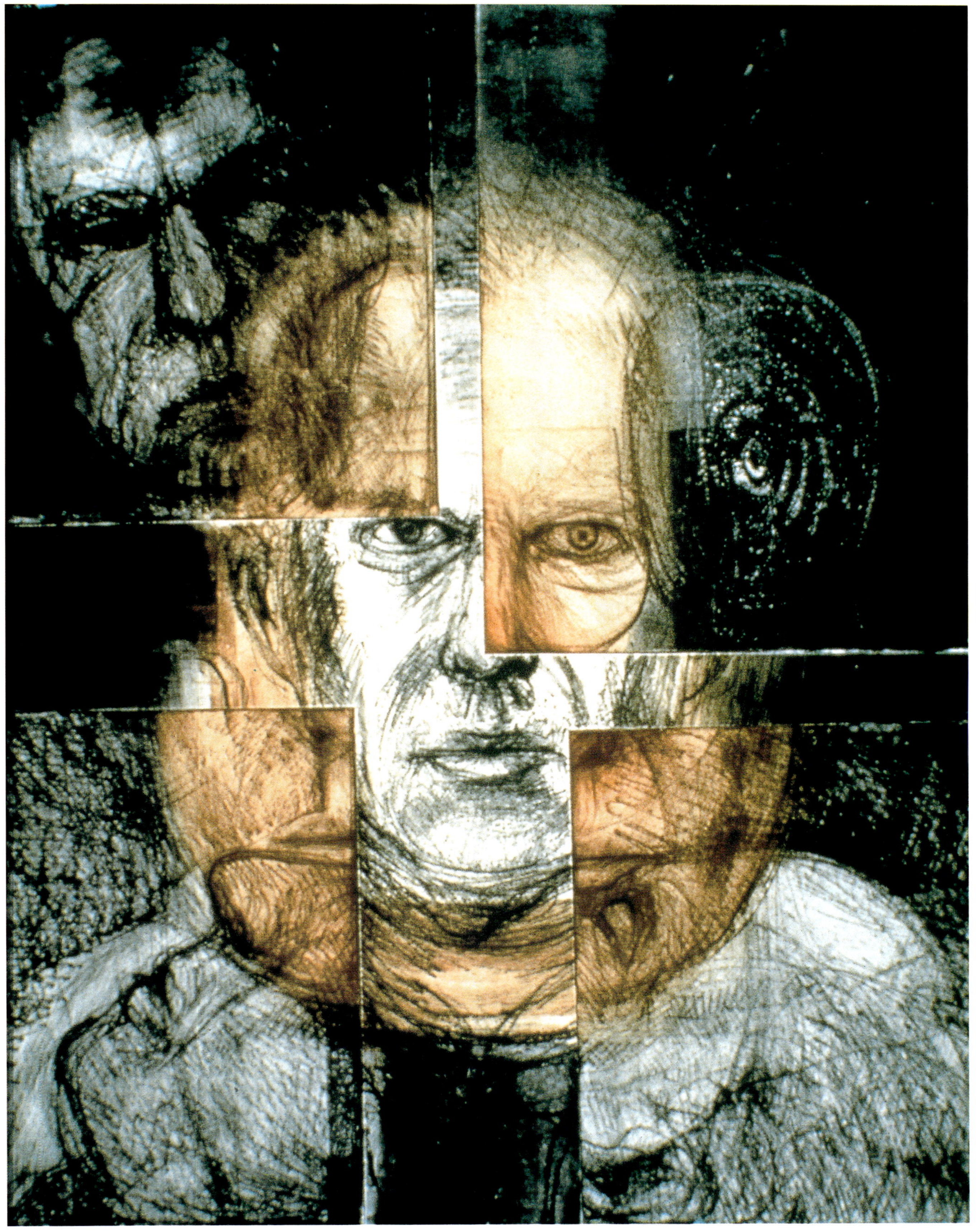

Colorplate 8 *Self-Portrait with Cut Plates,* 1985, drypoint monoprint, 45⅛ × 34½ in. (114.6 × 87.6 cm). Collection of the artist. (Catalogue raisonné 250)

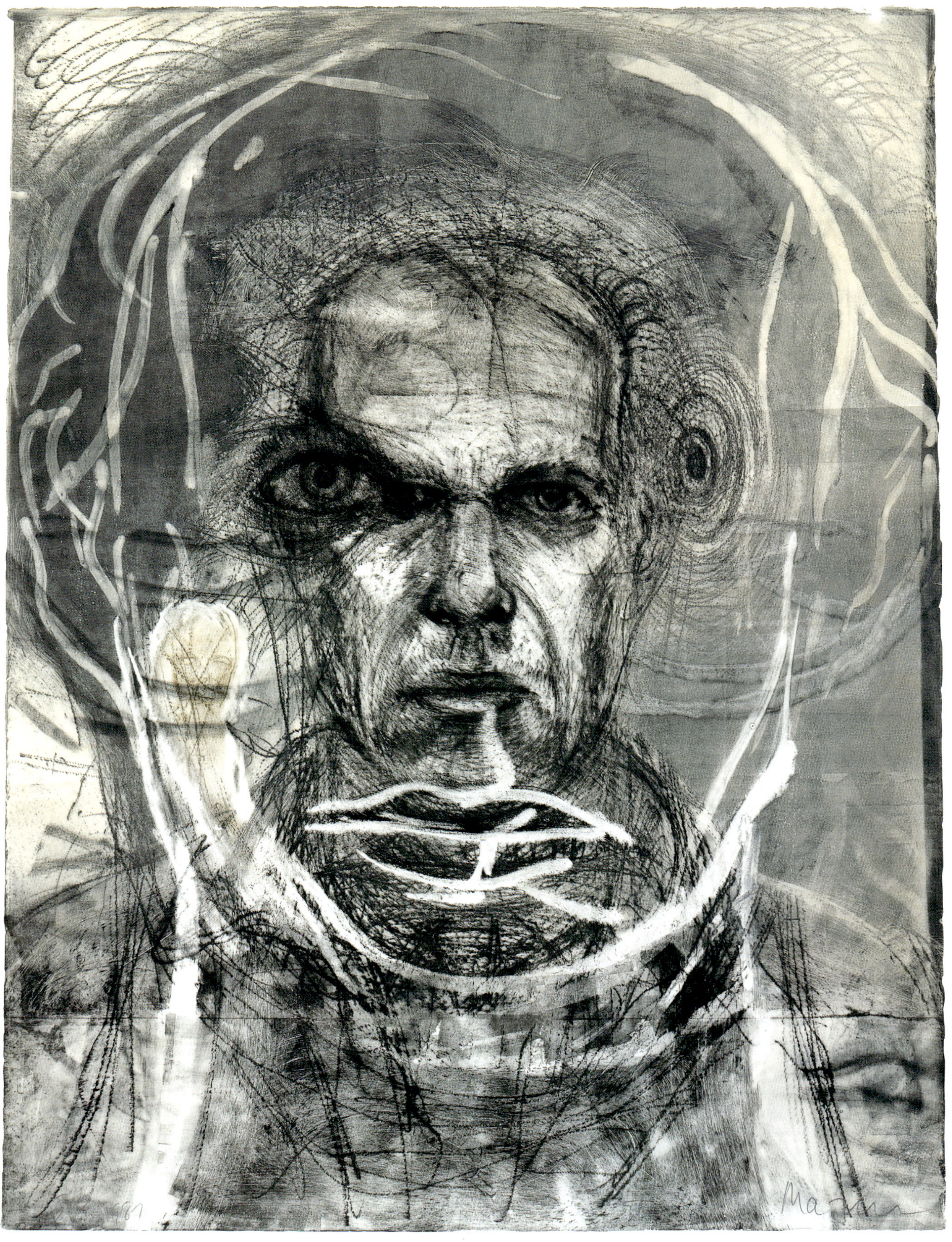

Colorplate 9 *The Unknown Region IV (Self-Portrait),* 1987, etching with monotype, 47⅝ × 35½ in. (121.0 × 90.2 cm). Collection of the artist. (Catalogue raisonné 259)

Making Marks: The Edition Prints

Barry Walker

What remains constant over the years is the surprise of each proof as it emerges from under the roller and yields its image.

— Michael Mazur[1]

PRINTMAKING, more than any other visual art form, offers a limitless range of choices and possibilities. As with any medium, mastery of technique can be judged only in conjunction with the image — the marriage of mark, meaning, and emotion that results in a successful work. Perhaps the most satisfying aspect of Michael Mazur's graphic oeuvre is that he always keeps that equation in perfect balance. His technique is so skilled that it never intrudes on the image. Mazur's prints, like all significant works of art, engage the viewer intellectually and emotionally in their content. Even the earliest prints from Mazur's forty-year career are as strong and fresh today as when he first pulled them. The means by which he realized the image, though fascinating to deconstruct for the print specialist, are, in the end, peripheral.

In looking back at Mazur's career as a printmaker, a clear progression can be seen as the artist refined his skill with each process that captured his imagination. Mazur's explorations in printmaking have gone beyond making and effacing marks to manipulating the inking of plates and blocks, experimenting with various papers and other supports for printing, and utilizing formats ranging from single sheet prints, portfolios, and books, to prints incorporated into three-dimensional screens (colorplate 28) and, most recently, large-scale digital prints. As Mazur mastered new techniques, he freely combined processes and/or added handwork at will. While some prints are pure examples of, for instance, a line engraving or a black-and-white lithograph, others feature complex blends of aquatint, etching, wood relief, and monoprinting that confound even the best of print scholars trying to dissect Mazur's process. In many cases the prints that appear to consist of multiple layers and a diversity of marks are often quite simple, in the way that only a truly experienced hand can achieve. Just as his imagery has constantly evolved, so have the subtleties of his vocabulary of marks.

Through a succession of more or less serendipitous decisions, Mazur's early choices led him to study with teachers who were involved primarily in the graphic arts. He was always attracted to drawing and printmaking, and his natural skills gravitated toward a sensitivity to line and a remarkable ability to master linear variety using the materials of both draftsman and printmaker. Although he took a painting course his freshman year at Amherst, a college in western Massachusetts, he did not become artistically focused until the following year. Through an arrangement that Amherst had with nearby Smith College, Mazur was able to enroll in classes at Smith during his sophomore year, and it was there that he came under the influence of his first important mentor, Leonard Baskin.

Although primarily a sculptor, Baskin was best known at the time for his prints, particularly his woodcuts and wood engravings, a medium he almost single-handedly rescued from oblivion. Mazur studied with Baskin because, he says, "I wanted to work with the best artist around, and he was the best."[2] Baskin was one of the most important and ambitious printmakers of the 1950s. His 1952 woodcut *Man of Peace* (fig. 3) was a benchmark of American graphic work of the decade. In the remoteness of rural New England, Baskin created an enclave for his students, completely ignoring the work of the Abstract Expressionists, the dominant avant-garde movement of the day. As Mazur describes it:

> When you studied with Leonard, he rarely showed you the work of his contemporaries, perhaps Rico Lebrun, Ben Shahn, and a few others, but mostly it was those artists from the past who he felt were most important — Rembrandt, Goya, Bresdin, and Degas. There was hardly anyone later in the twentieth century other than Ernst Barlach and other German Expressionists whom Baskin embraced as part of an "embattled" humanist tradition with himself as its contemporary voice. It was the work of those artists that I studied initially.

After taking a year off to study and live in Italy, Mazur returned to Amherst to complete his studies with Baskin. For his thesis project he worked in his teacher's preferred media of wood engraving and wood relief as well as in one of Baskin's favorite formats, the artist's book. He incorporated his interest in literature for his thesis, *An Image of Salomé,* which drew on texts by Gustave Flaubert, Stéphane Mallarmé, and Oscar Wilde. Although they were in the same medium, Mazur's block prints bore little resemblance to Baskin's. Mazur's work in *An Image of Salomé* is far more painterly, relying for its effects on Baroque chiaroscuro, with the figure of Salomé emerging in stark relief from dark but ornately patterned backgrounds. In such images as *The Dance of Salomé* (colorplate 2), the white-on-black patterning produced a cloying, claustrophobic feeling, fully appropriate to the source in symbolist poetry. Mazur

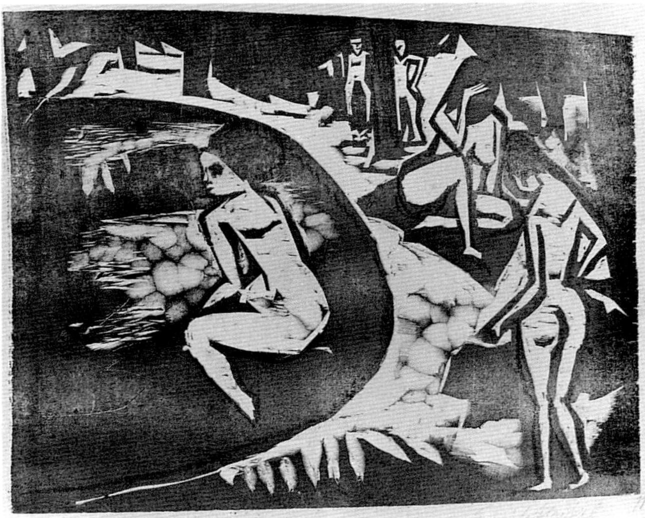

Fig. 14 Erich Heckel (German, 1883–1970), *At the Pond in the Woods,* 1911, woodcut, 10¼ × 13¾ in. (25.8 × 35.1 cm). The Brooklyn Museum of Art, New York (38.326).

allowed the gouges in the backgrounds to maintain their individual identities, reflecting the influence of Erich Heckel's wood-cutting style (fig. 14). The prints of the sculptor Bernard Reder (fig. 4), whose studio Mazur had visited in Italy, also showed Mazur ways to create volume and atmosphere in his woodcuts. In the *Salomé* woodcuts, Mazur made his cuts at different depths and varied the amount of ink applied to the block so that some areas of the block would print more lightly than the solid blacks of other areas. He says:

> My *Salomé* started with wood engravings, an homage of sorts to Baskin's mastery of that difficult medium, but I tried a different mark or line. Then I proceeded toward cruder cutting, chiaroscuro techniques, subtractive color printing, and masked-off reprinting. I see the thesis now as an early attempt to challenge myself with the notion of change and development, something I think characterizes a less self-conscious or "low" style.

In 1958 Mazur graduated from Amherst, married the poet Gail Beckwith, and enrolled in a one-year B.F.A. program at Yale University's School of Art and Architecture, followed by a two-year M.F.A. program. It was not his first contact with the Yale art faculty; in the summer after his sophomore year at Amherst, he had studied at the Yale Summer School of Music and Art in Norfolk, Connecticut. In choosing Yale for his graduate work, he was choosing Peterdi, again seeking out the best artist/teacher in his discipline.

The Hungarian-born Peterdi had worked at Stanley William Hayter's famous Atelier 17 in Paris, starting in 1933. When Hayter moved Atelier 17 to New York in 1940, Peterdi, who had also immigrated, continued his alliance with the studio. After the war Peterdi began to teach printmaking, first at the Brooklyn Museum art school and later at Yale. Mazur found Peterdi's printmaking to be straightforward and mark-oriented, providing solid technical examples (fig. 5). His earliest prints after he began studying with Peterdi were engravings, one of the most physically demanding forms of printmaking. Works such as *Self-Portrait* of 1959 (colorplates 5 and 6) show Mazur creating the swelling lines and staccato gouged marks made possible using a sharp burin on a bare copper plate. Studies of shoes, pipes, and all manner of everyday objects became swirling webs of undulating line as Mazur's skill and coordination grew. Although Mazur's last pure engravings were made in

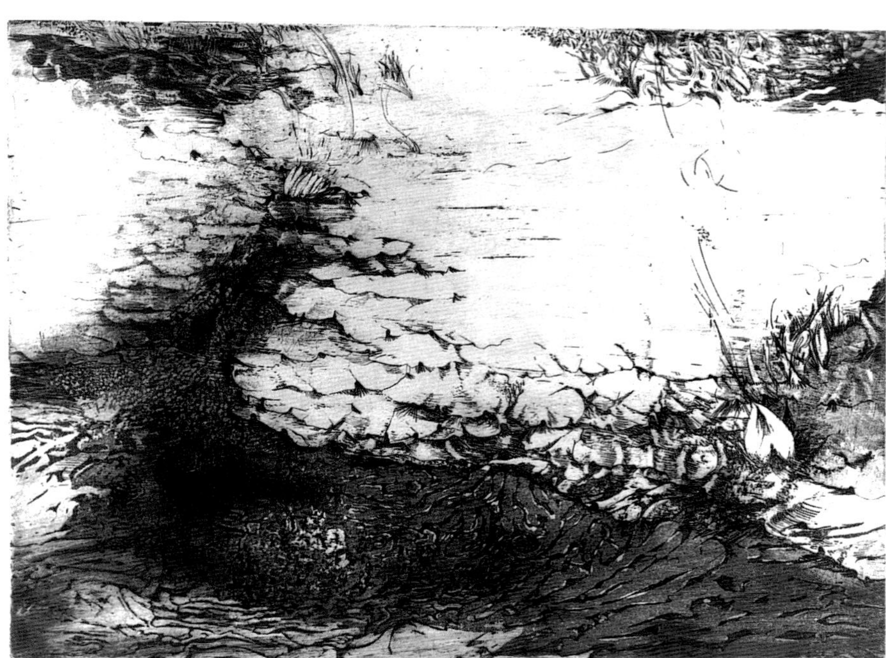

Fig. 15 *Lily Growths #1,* 1958, etching and aquatint, 17⅝ × 23¾ in. (44.7 × 60.3 cm). Jane Voorhees Zimmerli Art Museum (83.54.21). (Catalogue raisonné 42)

Fig. 16 *Lily Growths #2*, 1958, etching, 16⅜ × 22⅛ in. (41.6 × 56.3 cm). Collection of the artist. (Catalogue raisonné 43)

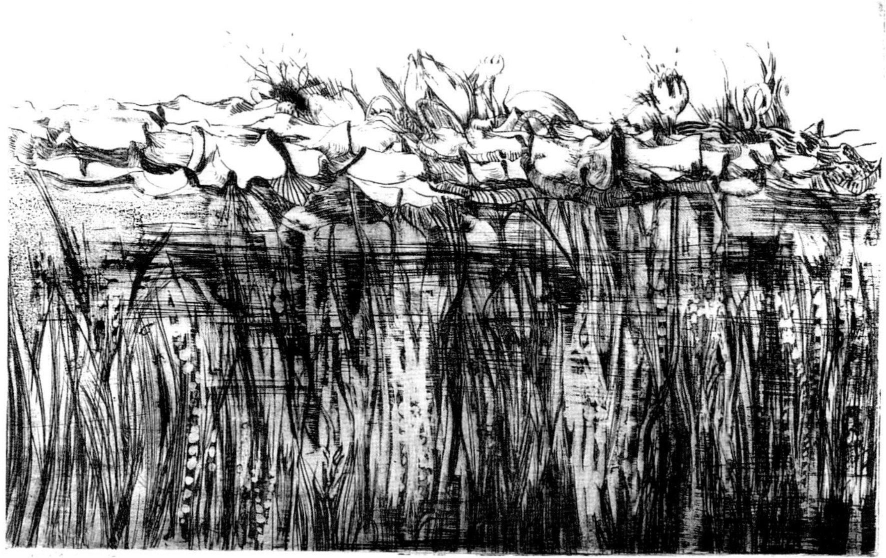

Fig. 17 *Lily Growths #4*, 1958, etching, 15⅞ × 18½ in. (40.3 × 47.0 cm). Collection of the artist. (Catalogue raisonné 45)

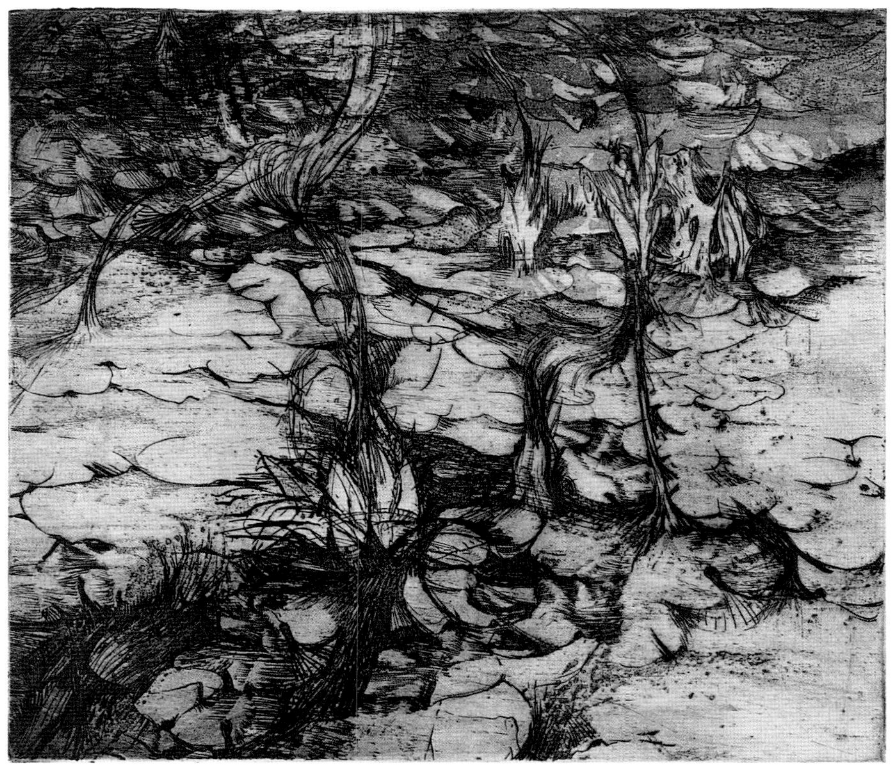

1959, these early prints that combined the skills of draftsman and printmaker already show a multifaceted nature and a dedication to mastering print processes.

In terms of technique, Peterdi had a far more profound influence on Mazur than did Baskin. In his *Lily Growths* series of 1958 (figs. 15, 16, and 17), Mazur adapted Peterdi's device of horizontally striated layering, although his composition is more irregular and open than Peterdi's generally were. It is in these prints that Mazur first evinced his interest in mirroring that is so apparent in the most recent water garden images. By this time Mazur had fully explored intaglio processes and was beginning to experiment widely with combinations of line etching and aquatint to create the volume and atmosphere he was interested in achieving. Like such artist/etchers as Rembrandt and Whistler who sought variation within an edition, Mazur also experimented with selective wiping, the practice of leaving some ink on the plate rather than wiping it perfectly clean before printing. This practice of leaving ink on the surface of the plate creates what is

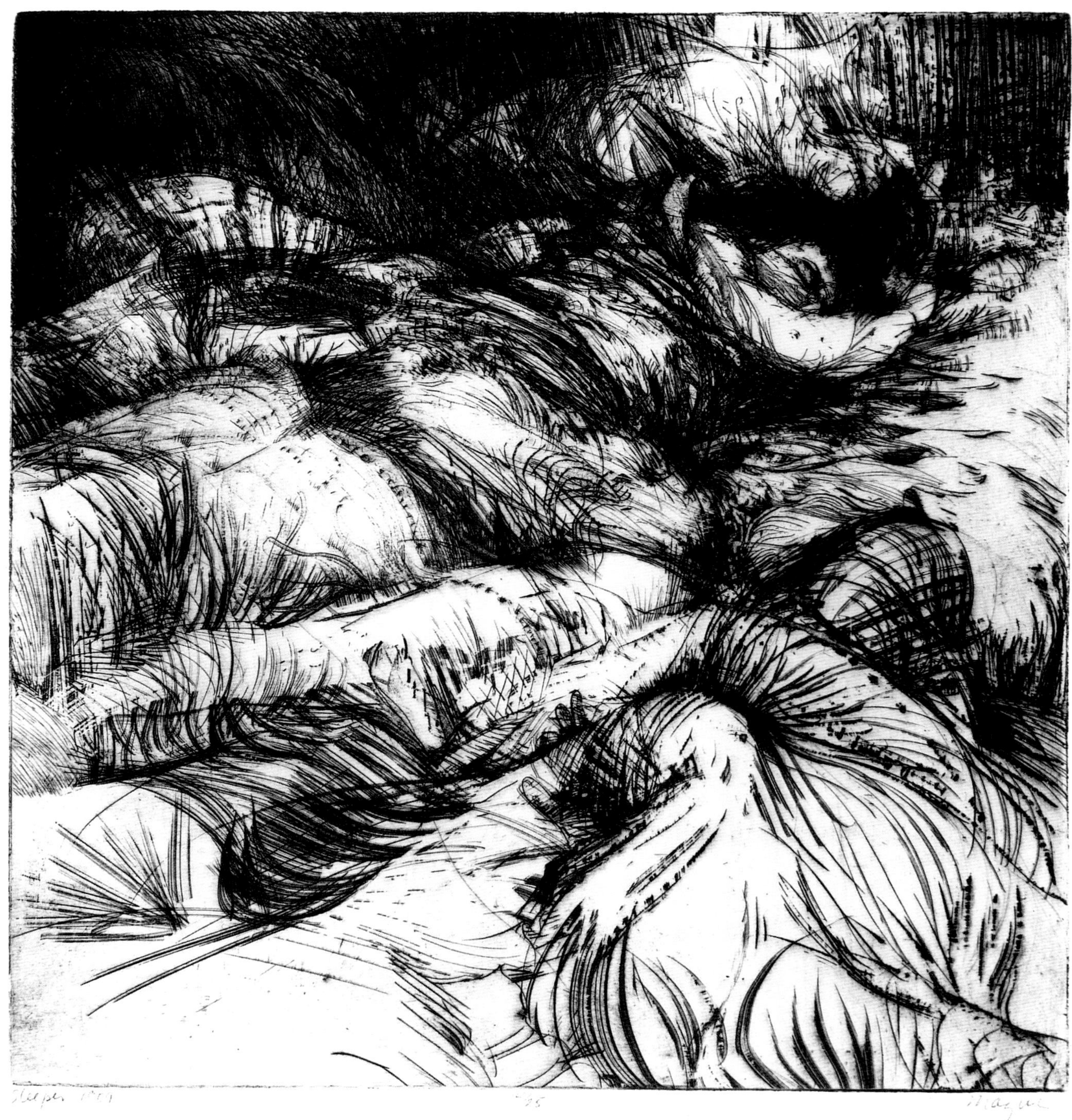

Fig. 18 *The Sleeper,* 1959, etching with plate tone, 23 × 19⅞ in. (58.4 × 50.5 cm). Jane Voorhees Zimmerli Art Museum, Gift of the Class of 1956, 25th Anniversary (81.042.29). (Catalogue raisonné 68)

known as plate tone. He also capitalized on imperfections in the metal plates themselves, often incorporating these random marks and tonal areas in his compositions.

As a member of the generation that came to artistic maturity in the late 1950s and early 1960s, Mazur was squarely within the group of artists in all media reacting against the largely nonrepresentational painting of the Abstract Expressionists. By 1960 the new avant-garde was imagistic, while gestural abstraction and Color Field painting were coming to be considered the new academy. While Mazur was never associated with Pop art, the most extreme manifestation of the renewed interest in image painting, his work until the 1990s was representational and, in varying degrees, realistic. Mazur's other instructors at Yale — Bernard Chaet, Neil Welliver, William Bailey, and Lebrun — were decidedly representational in their own work and in their teaching. He recalls Chaet and Lebrun as his greatest influences. Lebrun, though not well known today, had a considerable reputation in the 1950s. He was one of six artists representing the United States in Alfred Barr's 1950

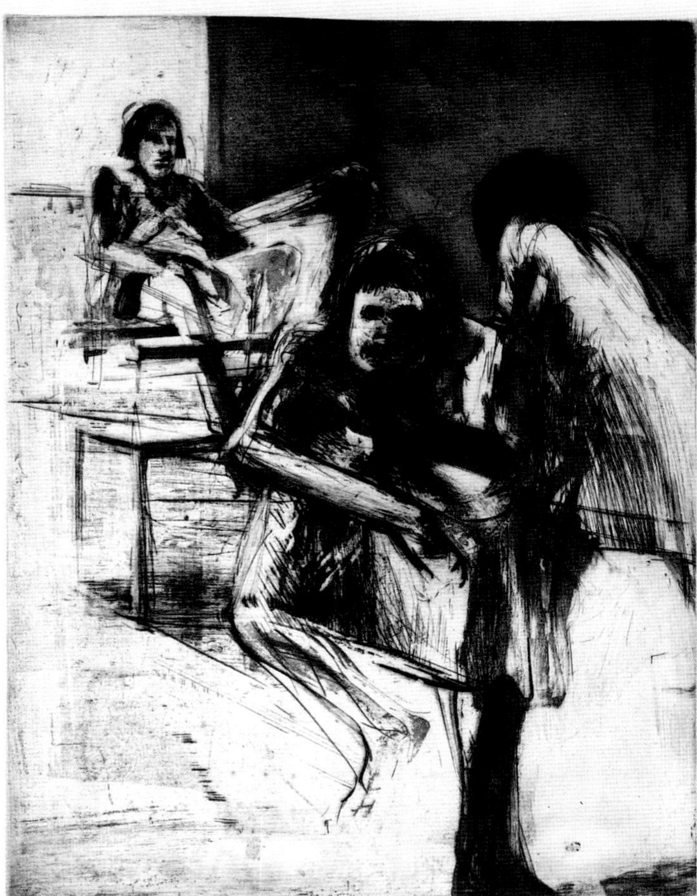
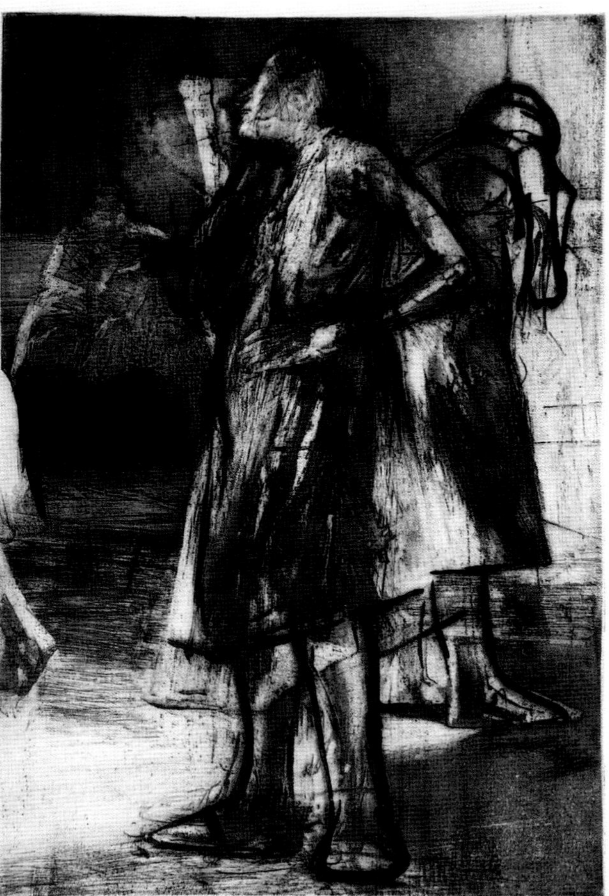

Fig. 19 *Closed Ward #12 (Untitled),* 1962–63, etching and aquatint, 27⅝ × 39¼ in. (70.2 × 99.7 cm). Jane Voorhees Zimmerli Art Museum (82.017.011). (Catalogue raisonné 111)

installation at the Venice Biennale. Mazur recalls: "He was a powerful figurative expressionist."

Mazur's first fully mature body of work, and still one of his most important, was his *Closed Ward* series of etchings and aquatints begun in 1962. He was first inspired to do this work, he says, by an experience he had as a visitor to a mental hospital during his Amherst years: "At Amherst a singing group that I had joined sophomore year — I was the comedian — was entertaining in the closed ward of the Veterans' Administration Hospital in Northampton, Massachusetts. It was an inappropriate place for us and deeply unsettling for me. After a chaotic episode we were led away." By the time he began working on *Closed Ward,* he was teaching at the Rhode Island School of Design in Providence and serving as a volunteer art therapist at the Howard State Mental Facility. He recalls: "My memory of the Amherst event haunted me until, after Yale, I had learned to draw from memory well enough to revisit a similar facility near Providence, do volunteer tasks, and work from memory back in my studio." The profound effects of this experience dominated his work for four years. *Closed Ward* is brooding and depressing, yet deeply humanistic. One must look back to Goya's *Caprichos* to find such effective use of aquatint to create mood through tonal inflection. Mazur brilliantly captured the isolation of each patient, especially the isolation within groups. Mazur describes how the *Closed Ward* series developed from earlier projects:

> Like the *Salomé,* this series evolved through several stages and includes various approaches to the material within the same series. The hospital series follows a group of sleeping figures [fig. 18], etchings and engravings that I started in 1959. The beds and recumbent figures investigate the bed as a landscape — which in turn come out of the *Lily Growths.* The first *Closed Ward* print relates to prints like *Nightmare* or *Sickbed,* both in their expressive content and in their mark making. They share the use of a razorblade as a drawing tool and rely on the speed of the mark. In *Closed Ward #1* the striations made by the notched blade play a horizontal composition against the organic curvaceousness of generalized figures. There is a growing specificity in the *Closed Ward* series as it develops. Images are fairly general until the characters at the hospital become better known as part of a specific grouping. This starts about *Closed Ward #8* and *Closed Ward #9 (The Occupant)* [colorplate 4] and builds to *Closed Ward #12 (Untitled)* [fig. 19], where the figures are those of real patients on the ward.

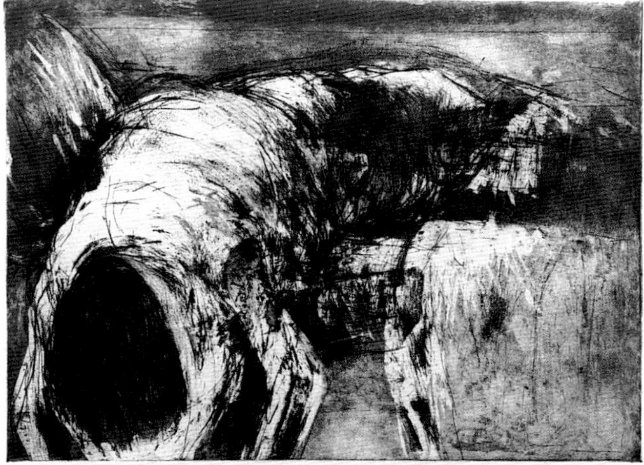

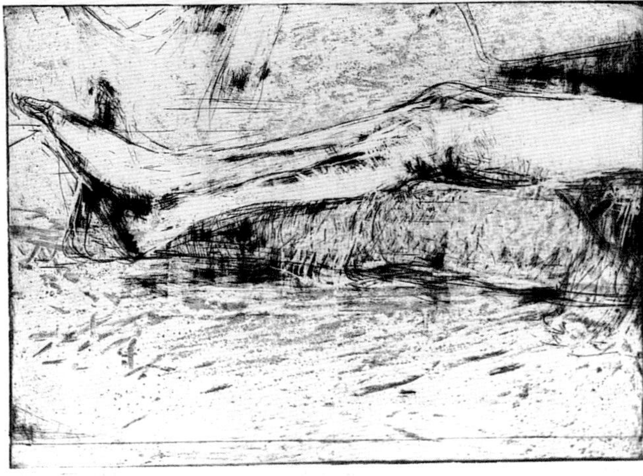

Fig. 20 *Closed Ward #16 (The Visit),* 1965, etching and aquatint, first state proof, 34½ × 25¾ in. (87.6 × 65.4 cm). Collection of the artist.

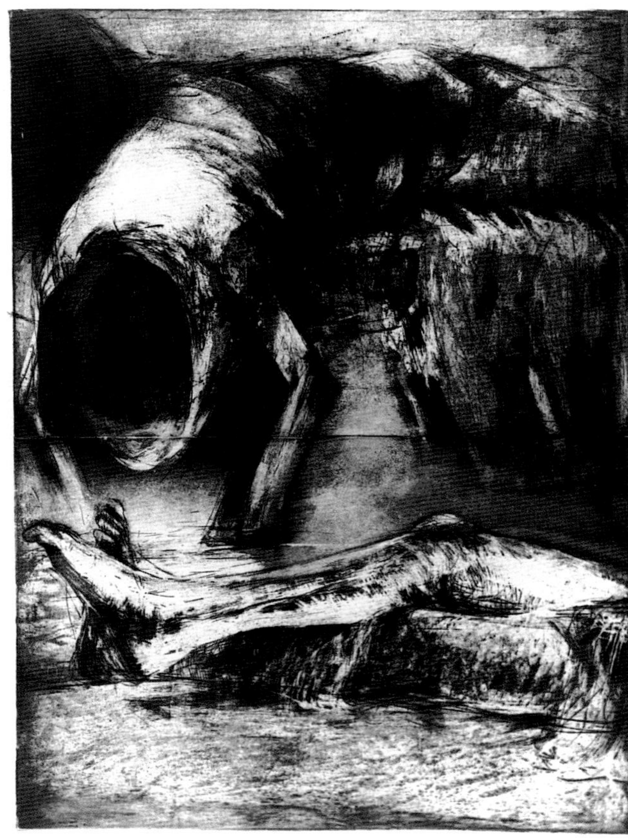

Fig. 21 *Closed Ward #16 (The Visit),* 1965, etching and aquatint, fourth state proof, 34½ × 25¾ in. (87.6 × 65.4 cm). Collection of the artist.

Closed Ward #12 evolves into a diptych of uneven proportions, the right side narrower than the left. The bar between the two plates printed on the same sheet emphasizes the caged condition of the unfortunate subjects while it stresses the inherent artificiality of the image-making process. The figure in the foreground of the right plate recalls the total lack of sentimentality in Degas's backstage dancer images, somewhat awkward and far from the illusory beauty produced on the stage. The figure in the left foreground jerks spastically in what seems a pathetic parody of dance. The figure between these two bridges the plates in a thrusting diagonal. The faces of all the figures are either averted or in partial shadow so that the drama of the scene is expressed by movement rather than by expression. In this haunting dance-in-the-madhouse image, each figure occupies a hermetic space, impervious to the outside world.

In the later part of the series, around *Closed Ward #16 (The Visit)* (figs. 20–25), "the series begins to move toward greater formality, alienation, and invention," says Mazur. This time Mazur used the diptych format vertically. The lower image depicts crossed legs in a recumbent position, while the upper shows a reclining figure lying crosswise on a bed, her hands continuing into the lower half. By the fourth state (fig. 21) the figures are clearer and the union of the abutted plates more cohesive. In the next state (fig. 22) Mazur cropped the upper plate at the bottom and the lower plate at the top, eliminating the integrity of the overall image so that the two plates seem arbitrarily juxtaposed except for the lower figure's knee that extends slightly into the upper plate. By the seventh state (fig. 24) Mazur had completely redrawn the upper figure, now depicting a seated female, cropped at the top to just below the shoulders, her legs cropped below the knees by the patient's bed. In the editioned state (fig. 25) the composition is identical, but highlights on the visitor's dress have been burnished for more contrast. Her hands are folded on her knees. Paradoxically, by reintegrating the two parts, making it a seamless image, Mazur established more disjunction between the two figures. Although both faces and considerable parts of both bodies are outside the picture plane, the psychological intensity of the total lack of communication between the two figures is fully captured.

In *Images from a Locked Ward* of 1965 (figs. 10, 26, and 47), the lithographic version of *Closed Ward* done concurrently with the etchings, Mazur continued his troubling evoca-

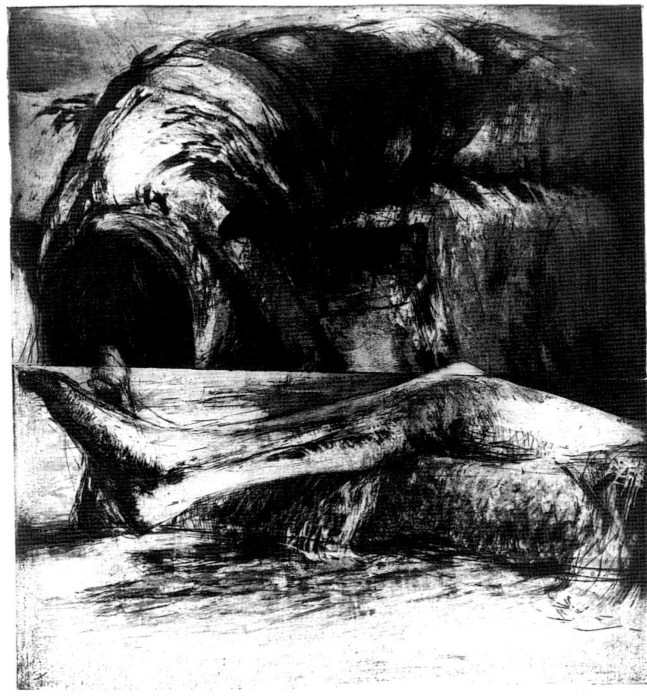

Fig. 22 *Closed Ward #16 (The Visit),* 1965, etching and aquatint, fifth state proof, 34½ × 25¾ in. (87.6 × 65.4 cm). Collection of the artist.

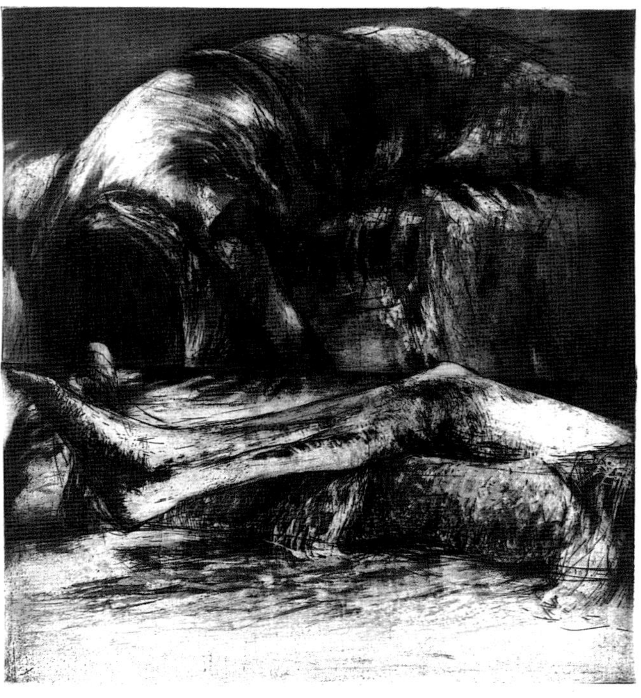

Fig. 23 *Closed Ward #16 (The Visit),* 1965, etching and aquatint, sixth state proof, 34½ × 25¾ in. (87.6 × 65.4 cm). Collection of the artist.

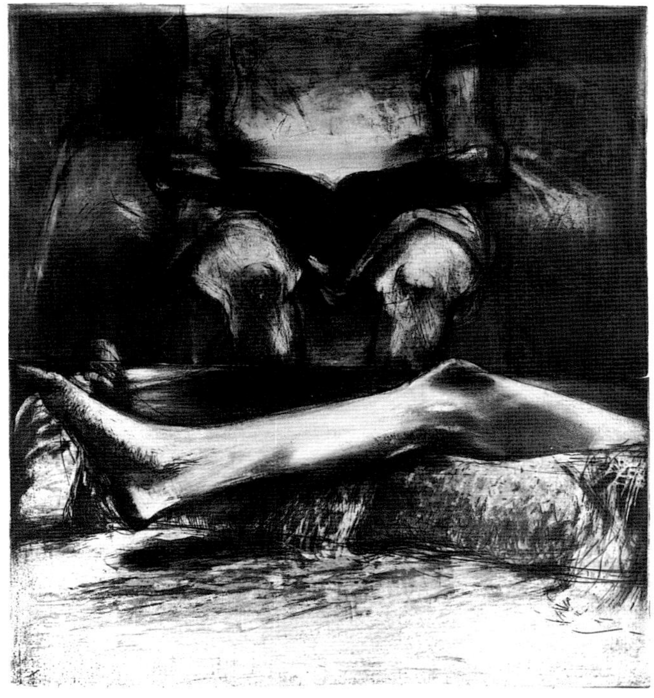

Fig. 24 *Closed Ward #16 (The Visit),* 1965, etching and aquatint, seventh state proof, 34½ × 25¾ in. (87.6 × 65.4 cm). Collection of the artist.

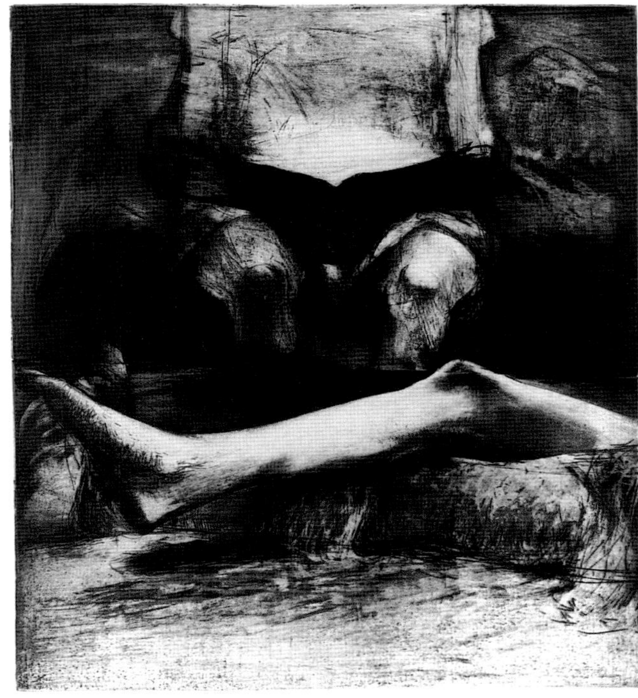

Fig. 25 *Closed Ward #16 (The Visit),* 1965, etching and aquatint, 34½ × 25¾ in. (87.6 × 65.4 cm). Collection of the artist. (Catalogue raisonné 127)

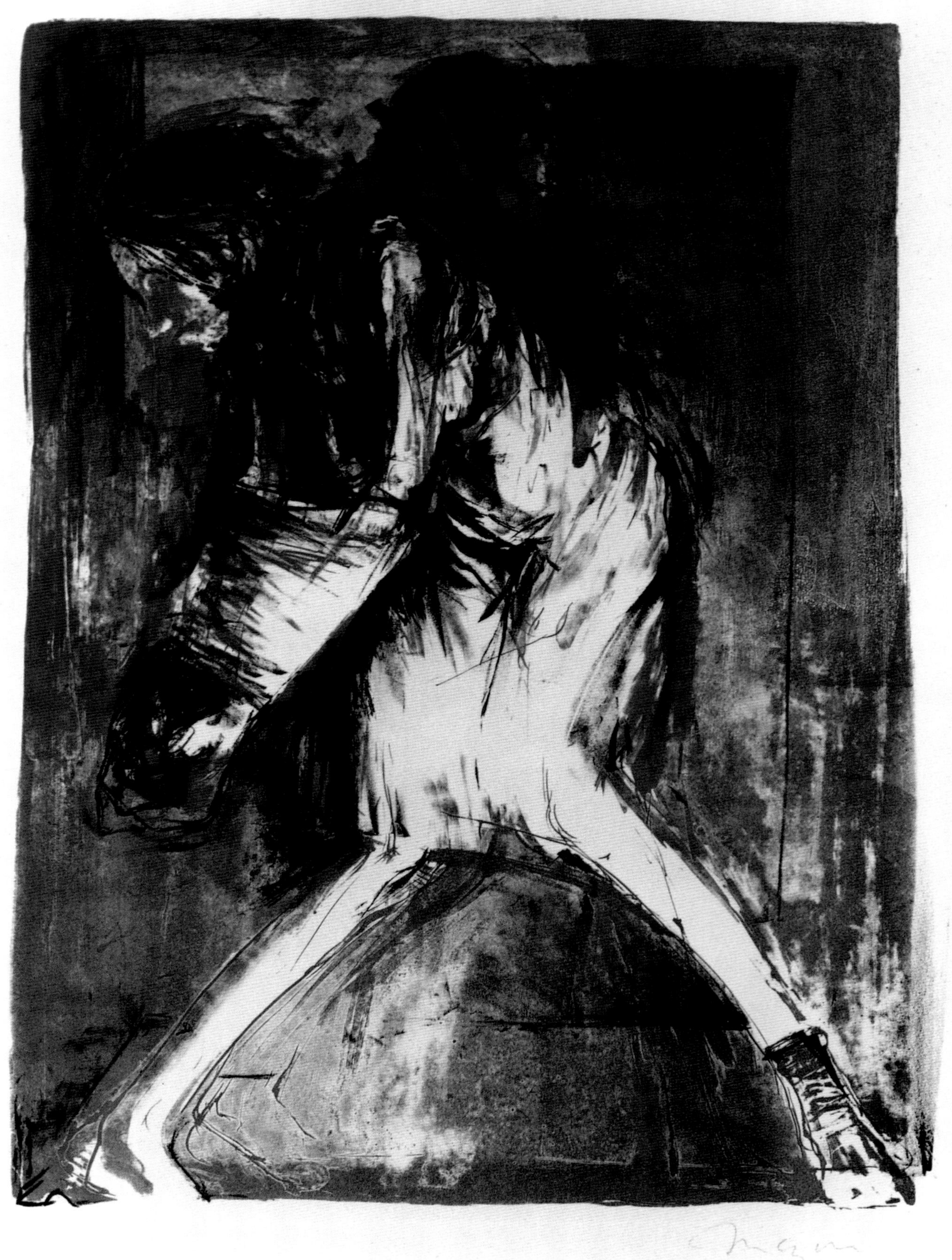

Fig. 26 *Images from a Locked Ward #10 (Bound Hands Swing),* 1965, lithograph, 26 × 20 in. (66.1 × 50.8 cm). Jane Voorhees Zimmerli Art Museum (82.017.052). (Catalogue raisonné 141)

tions of the isolation of the mentally handicapped. It was his first significant body of work in lithography, and it was the first time he worked with a collaborator — George Lockwood, founder of Impressions Workshop in Boston, whom he had met when the printer/publisher was Baskin's assistant. Lockwood, a master lithographer, showed Mazur many of the nuances of the lithographic medium. It was also the first time in his professional career that anyone other than Mazur himself had published his prints. "I loved the collaboration with George," he recalls.

> We were always trying out new ideas and techniques, and we had a lot of fun doing it. Not everything went smoothly, however, and we eventually took three years and some forty stones to complete the suite of fourteen. I made the portfolio to keep the narrative quality of the hospital prints together as I had with *Salomé*. I repeated some of the images in the etchings, but most are other ideas that developed in the course of the project.

The *Artist and the Model* series, published by Associated American Artists in New York in 1968, is the only body of work in Mazur's oeuvre that seems dated — locked in its particular era. At the time Mazur was experimenting with cut plates, one a nude model and the other an artist that can be read simultaneously as a self-portrait and "the artist" in general. In *Confrontation across Two Shadows* from the series (fig. 27), Mazur dealt with positive and negative shapes and, once again, his interest in mirroring.

In 1964 a grant from the Guggenheim Foundation had freed him from his teaching duties and allowed him to focus almost exclusively on sculpture for a year. He says of the *Artist and the Model* series:

> The series came out of a sculpture project started during my Guggenheim year that resulted in a "tableau" or setup with two life-sized direct plaster figures, the model and the artist, a self-portrait. I added still-life and studio objects, as well as a freestanding window with a painted view and shadows cut from masonite. The prints were made from the tableau, the cut plates as stand-ins for the sculpture that could be moved around. If you look at the end of the *Closed Ward* series, you see that the prints there, notably *Back View, Corner Figure,* and *White Nude* from 1965 and 1966, develop directly into the *Artist and the Model* series.

The same year he completed the *Artist and the Model* series, Mazur was involved in two other significant activities. He says of 1968:

> It was an important and unforgettable year for me. I was very much an antiwar activist. I designed a large anti–Vietnam War installation piece, *The American Way Room* [fig. 71], a collaboration with Fred Stone, an early reprographics specialist in Cambridge, and some other friends. Martin Luther King was killed the day *The American Way Room* opened to the public in Boston, and in that trauma, racism and war seemed inevitable. So Gail and I helped to initiate an antiwar event — Artists against Racism and the War — with other writers and artists in Boston later that spring.
>
> In May I went to Los Angeles to work at Tamarind Lithography Workshop on a two-month fellowship. The second month I was there, Andy Warhol was shot, and a day or so later Bobby Kennedy was assassinated.
>
> In the fall I returned to Brandeis — to sit-ins, explosive faculty meetings, sanctuaries for AWOL soldiers, and the impossibility of an orderly academic schedule or much time in the studio! The sixties were defined by 1968, an incredible year to have lived through.

Mazur's Tamarind fellowship enabled him to work with several printers (Lockwood's Impressions Workshop had been a one-man operation). He recalls:

> I felt I was invited there to experiment rather than do finished work, but I found out rather quickly that there was pressure to come up with work for the printers who needed material with which to learn the craft. I was privileged to work with some great printers there — Serge Lozingot (who had worked for Jean Dubuffet in Paris), Maurice Sánchez, and Jean Milant among others.
>
> I treated each print as a formal and technical question. *Studio Views I* [fig. 28], for example, utilized a then new German-made transfer paper for a cut-and-paste problem, creating a kaleidoscopic image — very sixties! I was there to work and also to experience the rhythms and demands of a big print shop. I learned some things, but I do not think of it as a formative experience. I should have deep-sixed most of the work, especially the color lithographs of figurative subjects that are so hard to pull off convincingly. I have always loved [Henri de Toulouse] Lautrec in this area, but few others do it well.

Another benefit of Mazur's stint at Tamarind was his being partnered with the Los Angeles painter Billy Al Bengston and, in his second month, Ed Moses. According to Mazur,

> Billy Al was doing a lot of work with airbrush, and to me it was like aquatint. So I thought, here is a way. Maybe I can airbrush things in — get into painting that way. The first painting I did on canvas after many years of not painting was an installation of large airbrush paintings [fig. 72].

To create tonal effects normally achieved using aquatint, Mazur experimented with airbrushing onto Mylar in preparing his printing plates. He also tried out a variety of new tools, such as the electric engraver.

In 1970 Mazur moved his family to New York. Until that time he had resisted the urging of his then New York dealer Jill Kornblee and others to locate in the center of the art world. In New York Mazur did some work using architectural imagery and subjects drawn from everyday life. His work in the early to mid-1970s was the most realistic of his career. He started several print projects while in New York, often using the facilities at Robert Blackburn's cooperative Printmaking Workshop. But after two years he decided to move back to Massachusetts. He says of that decision:

> I knew working outside New York would not be the best for my career. Everyone told me — I got told that so much. It may have put me at a disadvantage, but I was, and still am, doing the work my way and showing it in the city. I

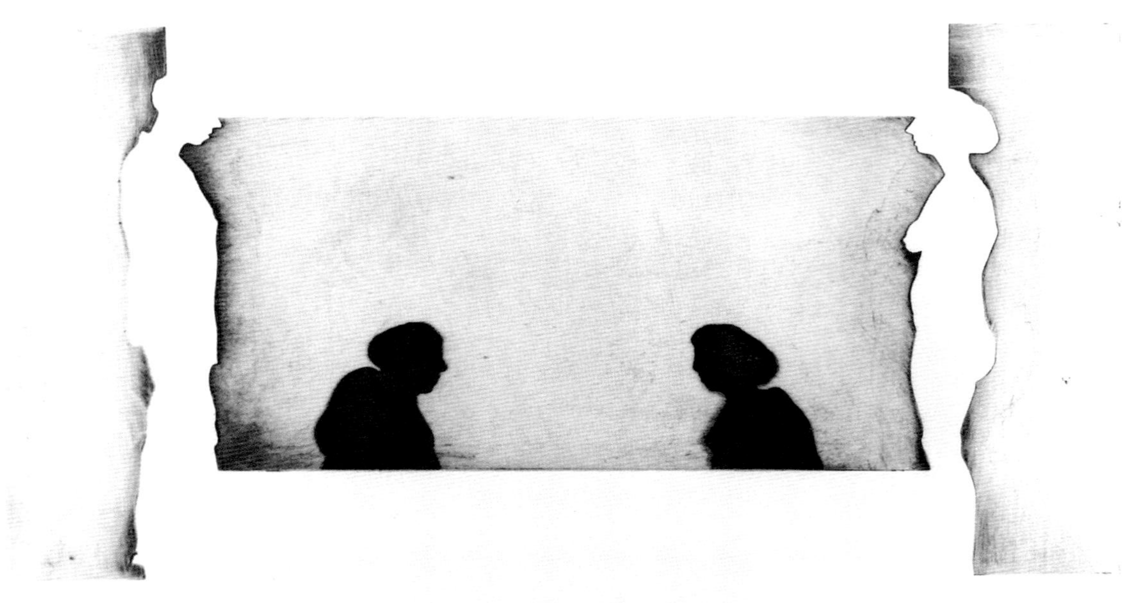

Fig. 27 *Confrontation across Two Shadows*, from *The Artist and the Model*, 1968, aquatint with plate tone, 24⅞ × 38⅛ in. (63.2 × 96.9 cm). Jane Voorhees Zimmerli Art Museum (82.017.057.03). (Catalogue raisonné 158)

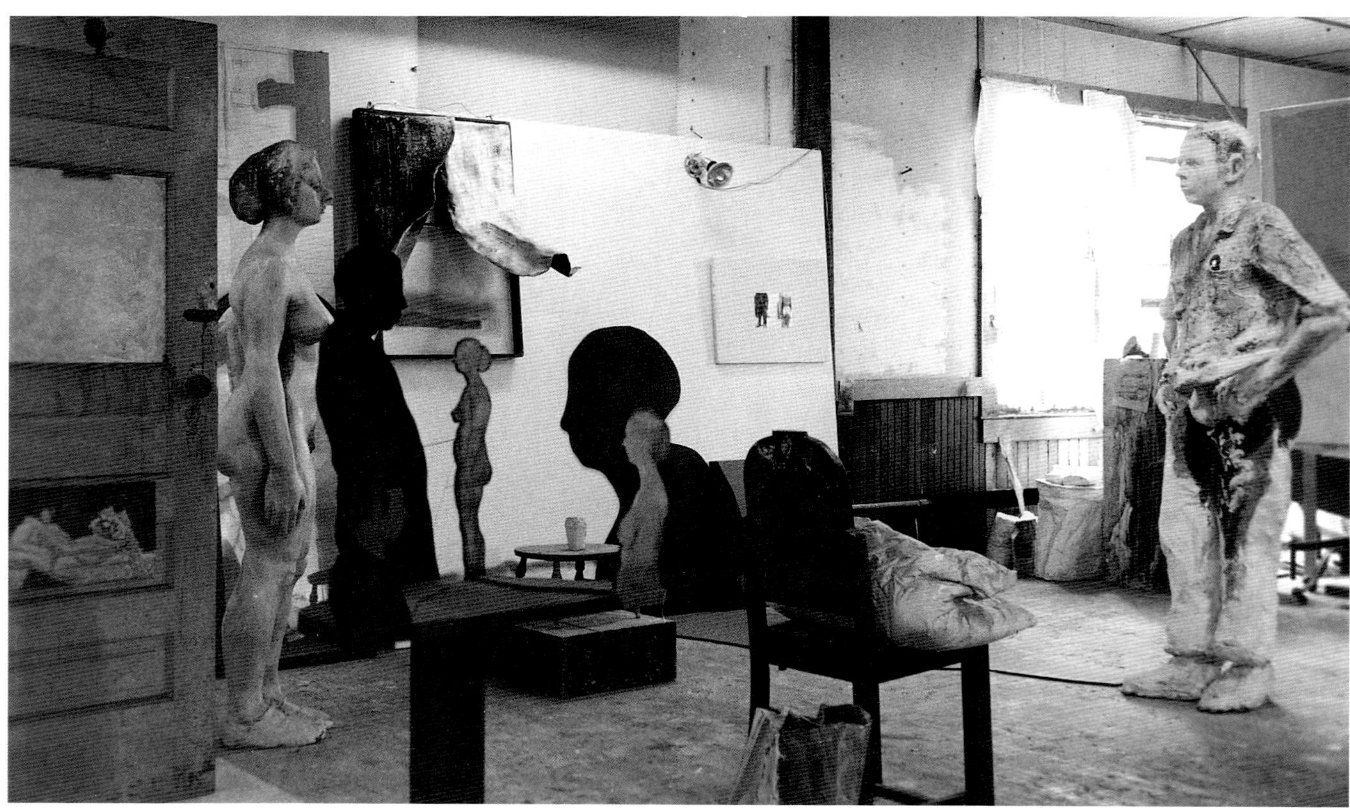

Tableau vivante installation created for *The Artist and the Model* in the artist's Harvey Street studio in Cambridge, Massachusetts, 1968

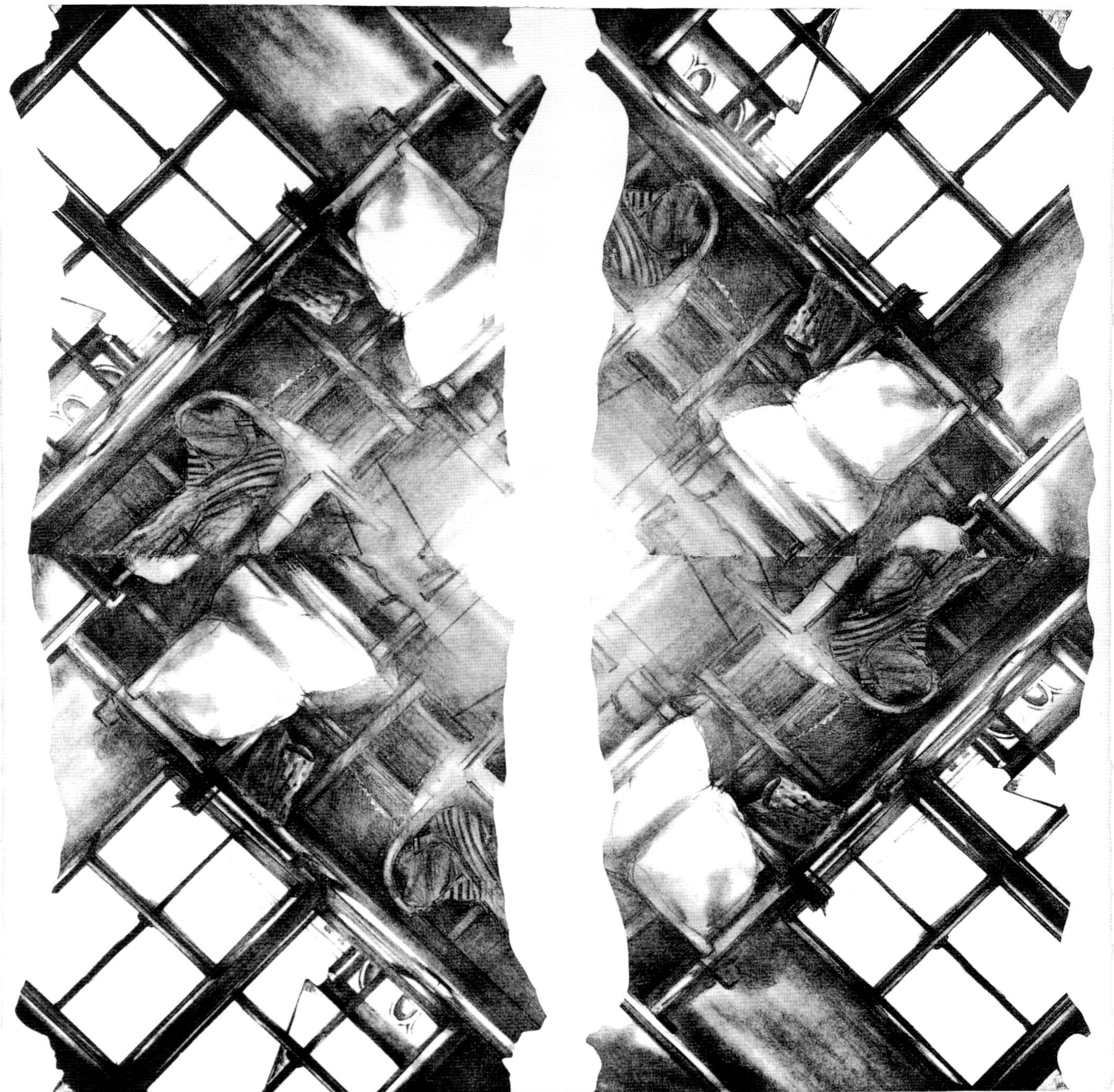

Fig. 28 *Studio Views I,* 1968, lithograph, 20 × 20 in. (50.8 × 50.8 cm). Collection of the artist. (Catalogue raisonné 183)

love where I live — Cambridge and Provincetown. If I had stayed I might have enjoyed the "romance" of being a "New York painter," but that no longer means what it did in the fifties or sixties.

During the 1970s a strong realist movement was a component of a growing pluralism in the art world. Back in Cambridge in 1972, Mazur began to depict simple, straightforward subjects in his studio. Indeed, throughout the 1970s and 1980s his work could perhaps be described by the French term *intimiste* — scenes from his studio and its exterior, his and his neighbors' gardens, a nearby tree — things he could see from his house or studio. Mazur's imagery of the early 1970s, as in such prints as *Easel and Chair* (fig. 29), *Glass on Table* (fig. 30), *Chair and Bench* (colorplate 11), and *Smoke* (colorplate 13), conceptually recalls the *intimiste* interiors of the 1890s by Edouard Vuillard and Pierre Bonnard — even though no figures inhabit Mazur's spaces. His style, however, embraces none of the flattening and patterning of the *intimiste* aesthetic, just as it avoids the gimmickry of the short-lived photorealist movement of the early 1970s.

In *Easel and Chair,* an early studio interior, Mazur combined etching with engraving with a dremel, an electric engraving tool that, according to Mazur, "can be used to

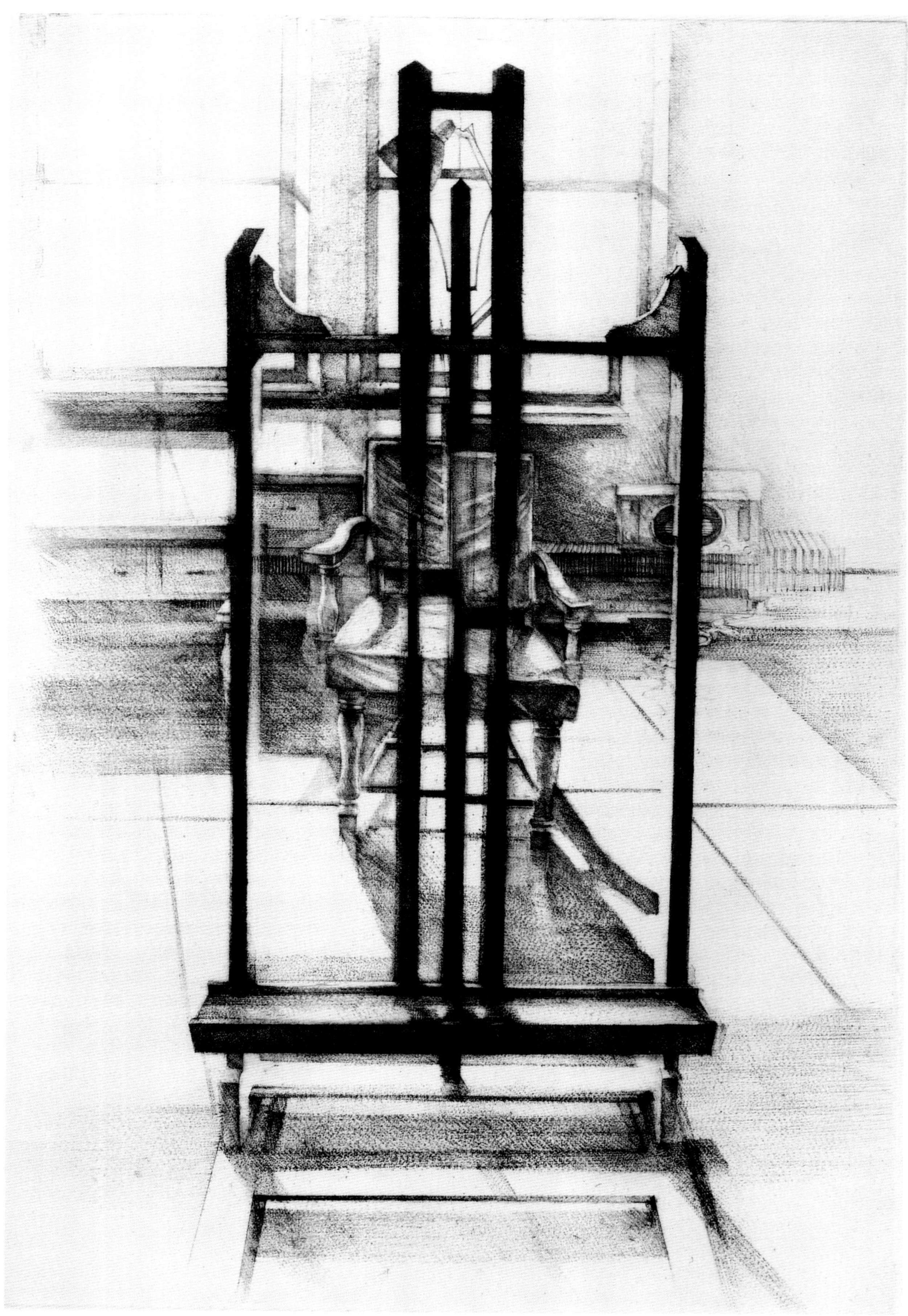

Fig. 29 *Easel and Chair,* 1972, etching and engraving with electric engraving tool, 40⅜ × 27¾ in. (102.6 × 70.5 cm). Jane Voorhees Zimmerli Art Museum, Gift of Dr. Lois Steinberg (83.054.012). (Catalogue raisonné 214)

imitate the texture and photo quality of the airbrush. I wanted to eliminate as far as possible the manmade mark. The airbrush turned into a dremel, creating a dot configuration, so those prints tended to be built up with dots rather than line." Whereas *Easel and Chair* is compositionally traditional, in that the two objects depicted establish scale for each relative to the other, the other three intaglio prints of the period represented here are so tightly focused that the objects depicted have no spatial context. The tables in both *Glass on Table* and *Smoke* are cropped much as a photograph might be cropped. The viewer is forced to contemplate the wood grain in each, which becomes an abstract component. As Mazur moved closer to literal realism, he simultaneously moved toward the most abstract work of his career.

In this group of early 1970s intaglio prints, Mazur, as had always been his habit, worked from detailed preliminary drawings. Although he had composed a few drypoints directly on the plate, this was not, according to Mazur, his usual working method.

> It is a strange admission, thinking where my work went, but I tended then to plan my prints in advance. Of course, I let them change during the process if it was needed, but they started as if they were already locked into a concept. The irony, of course, is that the monotypes served the purpose of direct response. I never made a drawing for a monotype. So the monotype was a reaction against the planning of prints, against the whole modus operandi of traditional printmaking. It was spontaneity, it was opening up.

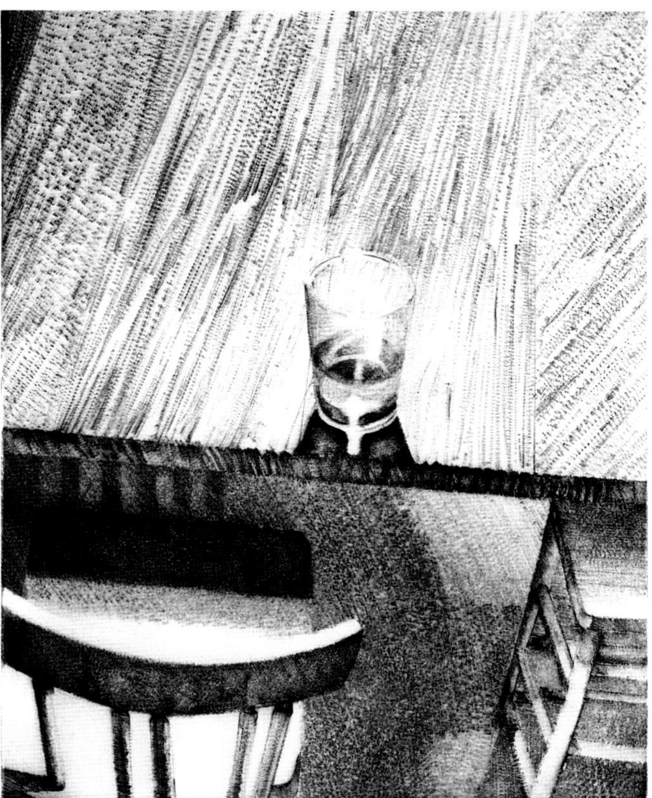

Fig. 30 *Glass on Table,* 1973, engraving with electric engraving tool, 27⅝ × 20¾ in. (70.2 × 52.7 cm). Collection of the artist. (Catalogue raisonné 220)

There is a chronological gap of seven years between *Smoke* of 1975 and the next editioned prints, the *Carriage House* series (colorplates 20, 21, and 22). This hiatus reflects Mazur's intense involvement during that period with painting, monotype printing, and pastel drawings. The *Carriage House* series, depicting Mazur's studio in Cambridge, represents a conscious attempt to bring some of his interest in narrative, the passage of time, and seriality into his traditional printmaking. He recalls:

> I kept planning but began to build variation into the printing of the plates. Pastel had become an important medium for me, and the monotypes and paintings were providing the spontaneity that I wanted. The *Net* prints from 1977 were like a monoprint sequence. They were editioned as two or three separate states from the plate as it developed. I was taken with the idea of having the plate change as light or seasons change a particular view. These led to the *Carriage House* images and eventually into the *Red Roller* works and the *Amaryllis-Calla* monoprints published by Pace Editions in 1982.

The next editioned print, *Wakeby Night* of 1986, was also an editioned monoprint.[3] In this three-sheet image, working with master printer Judith Solodkin and four assisting printers at Solo Press in New York, Mazur combined lithography and woodcut with monotype by overprinting with a monotyped Plexiglas plate, creating impressions in the edition that range from slightly to very different from one another. "What interested me by that time," he says, "was putting together different media. What would the combination of a woodcut and a monotype, or an etching and a monotype, or an etching and a woodcut — what would these feel like?" *Wakeby Night* is Mazur's most painterly print up to that time — lush, complex, and mystical in a Redon-like way.

Mazur acknowledges that the realist work of the 1970s and 1980s is hardly as straightforward as it seems.

> I look on my work as expressive concerns tempered by or explained by formal solutions. During its more "realist" stage, I was fascinated by the contradictions of perception, so I built my work around that. The so-called realism of the seventies was not one but many things, from faithful representation to, for instance, the stylized formalism of Alex Katz. I admired Catherine Murphy and Harry Roseman, Yvonne Jacquette, Sylvia Plimack Mangold, and Rackstraw Downes for their use of realism to question how we see things. Making objects or landscapes look real was not the point. I chose everyday objects and places around me because they defined my life somewhat and were convenient.
>
> Then, at the end of the eighties, I felt that I had had about as much image making as I ever wanted to do and that the whole realist endeavor had become deeply stressful. I wanted to get rid of all that dependence on delineation, and the monotypes helped me find the way. A lot of the *Palette Still Life* monotypes [colorplate 14] were an

> excuse for essentially abstractly expressionist imagery. The painterly qualities of the work came to dominate my practice.

Two Ideas about a Garden of 1990 (colorplate 24) and *Portrait* of 1990 (colorplate 10), a collaboration with the photographer Nicholas Nixon, further exemplify Mazur's ongoing interest in combining media while working in a representational mode. As in the *Wakeby* series (colorplates 18, 26, and 27), an overlaid image in *Two Ideas about a Garden* acts as a window into another reality. At the same time, the window draws the viewer's attention to the artificiality of two-dimensional representation of three-dimensional space. While the woodcut insets in the *Wakeby* prints led Mazur to the inset in *Two Ideas about a Garden,* the inset in *Memory and Distance,* 1992 (colorplate 23), reverses the order, with an etched inset over a woodcut. *Memory and Distance* employs the inset to represent two different locations central to Mazur's life, his backyard in Cambridge and the view from his studio on Cape Cod. Mazur created the image, with an easel representing the artist straddling the two worlds, after a freak storm in December 1991 destroyed his Provincetown studio. Mazur's memory of the studio, the storm brewing in the background, and the complexity of layers and marks mirror a period of unrest and transition in Mazur's life.

In the early 1990s Mazur's work took another radical turn, this time toward gestural, landscape-based abstraction. The genesis of the imagery, however, is the landscape of the body. In January 1993 Mazur underwent an emergency balloon angioplasty procedure. Though heavily sedated, he followed the procedure on a video monitor that showed the veins and arteries of his torso, which, of course, resemble a tree. Appreciating the duality of the imagery, he chose *Branching* as the title of the resulting series. *Ice Glen,* 1993–94 (colorplate 33), is representative of the series. Over its irregularly gridded background, curvilinear lines create a staccato pattern, some creating vegetative, leaflike forms, others creating forms that are more gestural and general. As the artist responded to the structure and organic anomalies of his own interior landscape, he created similarities and references to his early *Lily Growths* prints. He says that he was not immediately aware of the relationship to *Lily Growths.*

> In fact I was both attracted to and repulsed by the first small experiments that would be called the *Branching* series. The first prints, *Black Branching* [colorplate 34] and *Ice Glen,* are raw in their way. *Canyon* [colorplate 37] becomes more lush and subtle and begins to predict the *Mind Landscapes* [colorplate 39] based on the Chinese scroll. Of course later I realized that these forms had been with me from the beginning.

Mazur's latest work, both in painting and in prints, consists of highly abstracted garden imagery growing out of the *Mind Landscape* series and his interest in Chinese landscape paintings, particularly the work of Chao Meng-fu, a Yuan dynasty painter. This body of work is Mazur's lushest, most beautiful to date. As many of the images are of water gardens, the comparison to Claude Monet, particularly the work near the end of his life, is inevitable. In the mirroring of the reflected water flowers, however, Mazur revisits his early work at Yale. In many of his pre-*Wakeby* prints, color, when it appeared at all, often seemed incidental and arbitrary. These recent paintings and prints possess a strong, unexpected gift for color as the forms become less realistic, nonspecific studies in color relationships.

Printmaking is now, as ever, a constant if not intensive activity and a counterpoint to Mazur's painting. "Starting in about 1985," he says, "when I was doing the self-portrait series, I would escape back into printmaking when I was having trouble with the painting because it was a kind of home . . . back to basics." He still, clearly, returns to printmaking as if by second nature. Recently Mazur has returned to lithography. *Untitled* (colorplate 38), his first print at Jungle Press with master printer Andrew Mockler, and later *Thaw I, Thaw II* (colorplate 43), and *Summer Cascade* will be included in a portfolio with the working title *Seasons.* Still, most of his recent editioned prints are color intaglio. In these new prints, including *Pond Edge* (colorplates 40 and 42) and *Storm Warning* (colorplate 41), Mazur has made an effort to let go of the impulse to plan each move in advance by creating detailed drawings. The prints take on a rich painterliness as he uses a power sander to grind away marks and create new textures. For some prints the plates are printed deliberately off register, creating a vibrating double image that imparts added depth. Speaking of his recent prints, Mazur says:

> Clement Greenberg said somewhere that in order to change your work, you must change your habits. I think that happened. I work more directly on my plates than ever before, no drawing as preparation. I make plates now as I start my paintings, without any idea where they will end up. I draw on Mylars that get etched onto plates and add supporting Mylars that do not necessarily register. *Pond Edge I* and *II* were made from a number of plates in a nearly "blind" fashion and were made to work with each other as time went on. These six to eight plates are still creating new images as they get recombined.

Mazur has achieved virtuoso status in every major form of the graphic arts except screenprinting, which has never particularly interested him. Since almost every museum in the country that collects prints has acquired and exhibited his work, his reputation seems secure. Yet Mazur is beguilingly modest about his place in art history:

> I tend to see myself relatively clearly in terms of my weaknesses. I fully expect — I know this sounds self-conscious — to be forgotten, like those artists people suddenly rediscover and say, "Hey, this guy was interesting in his own right." I do not think of my life in prints as being so different from many of the other artists of my generation and earlier who patterned themselves on the painter-engraver tradition exemplified by many European and

> American modernists. The exception, I think, is that they began as painters. I began as a printmaker, and to this day I still make many of my prints in my own studio.

Perhaps the career of Camille Pissarro, the Impressionist artist who, along with Edgar Degas, was greatly involved in printmaking, would make a fitting historical comparison. Pissarro's constant experimentation and innovation resulted in a significant body of printed work, while his openness to new ideas and willingness to pursue new directions make his career, like Mazur's, difficult to classify. Mazur's contribution to contemporary printmaking lies in his flexibility, both technical and stylistic, and in the spirit of experimentation with which he approaches each project. His example has proved an important impetus for other artists to work within the graphic tradition.

NOTES

1. Work journal, spring 1987, p. 208 (in the artist's possession).
2. Quotations are from an interview with the artist, 7 May 1998, Cambridge, Mass., and follow-up conversations.
3. For more on the *Wakeby* prints, see the essay by Clifford Ackley in this volume.

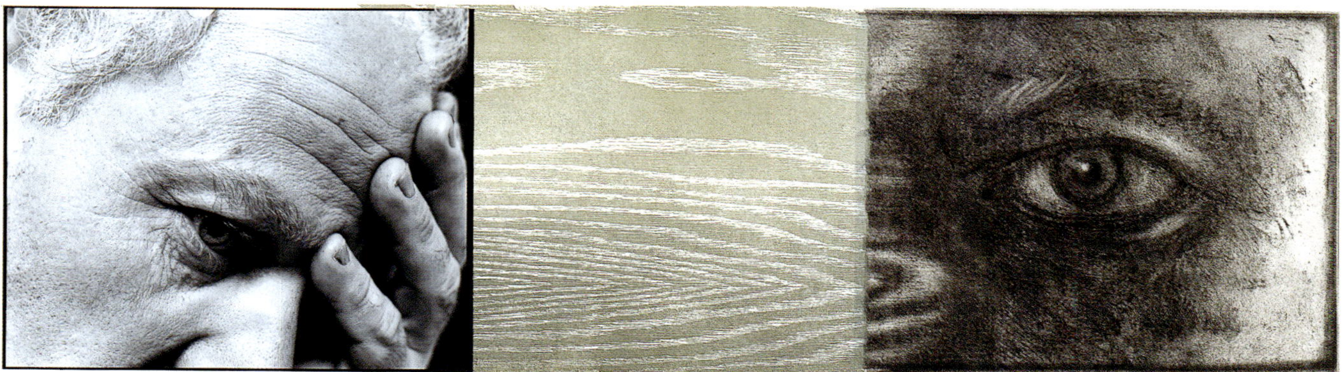

Colorplate 10 *Portrait* (collaboration with photographer Nicholas Nixon), 1990, etching with wood relief, *chine collé,* and collaged photograph, image 7¾ × 28 in., sheet 20 × 40 in. (image 19.7 × 71.1 cm, sheet 50.8 × 101.6 cm). Jane Voorhees Zimmerli Art Museum, Gift of the artist (1996.C117). (Catalogue raisonné 267)

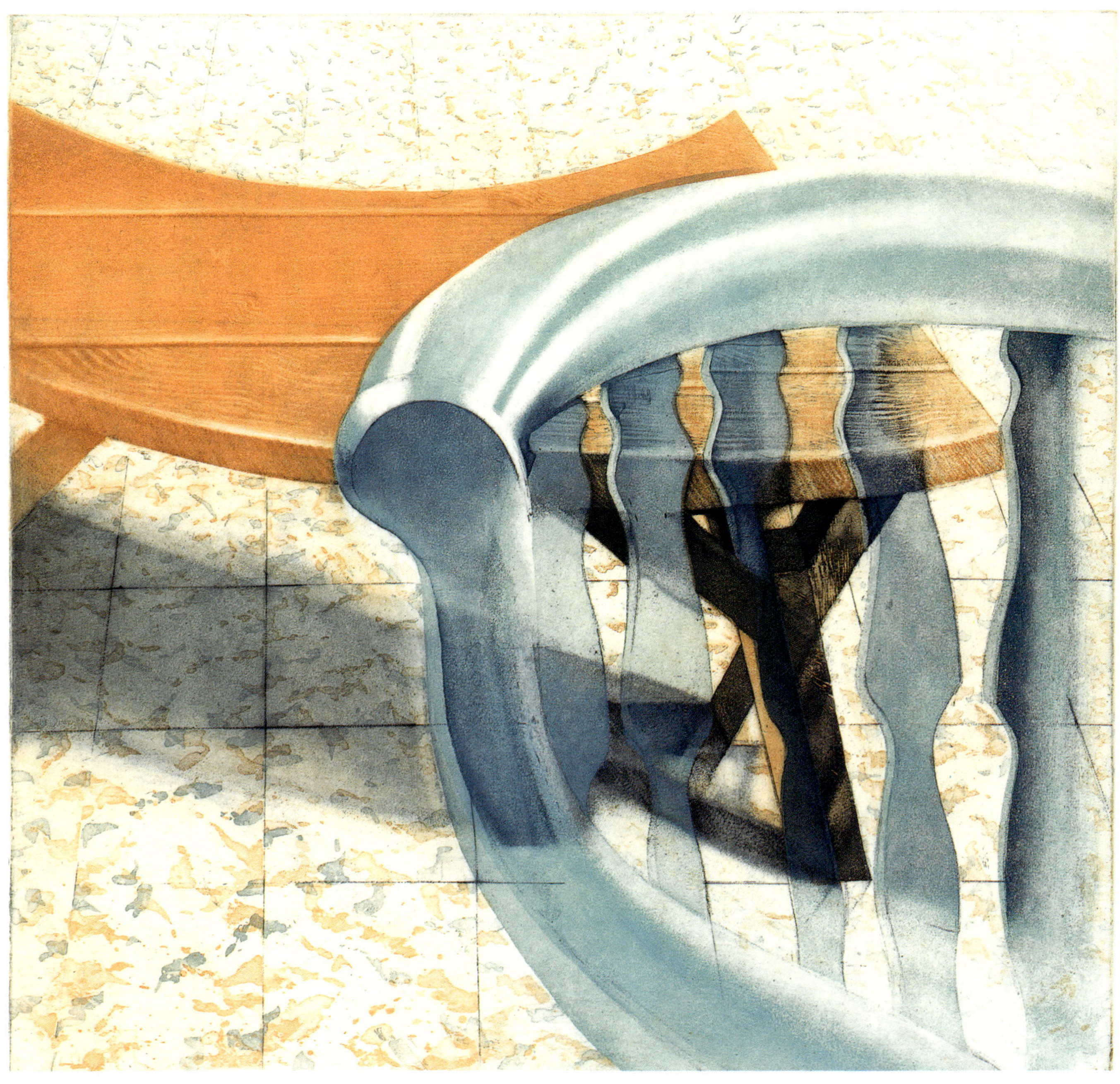

Colorplate 11 *Chair and Bench,* 1972, etching and aquatint with sugar lift, 25⅛ × 22 in. (63.8 × 55.9 cm). Jane Voorhees Zimmerli Art Museum, purchased in part with a grant from the National Endowment for the Arts (75.029.002). (Catalogue raisonné 213)

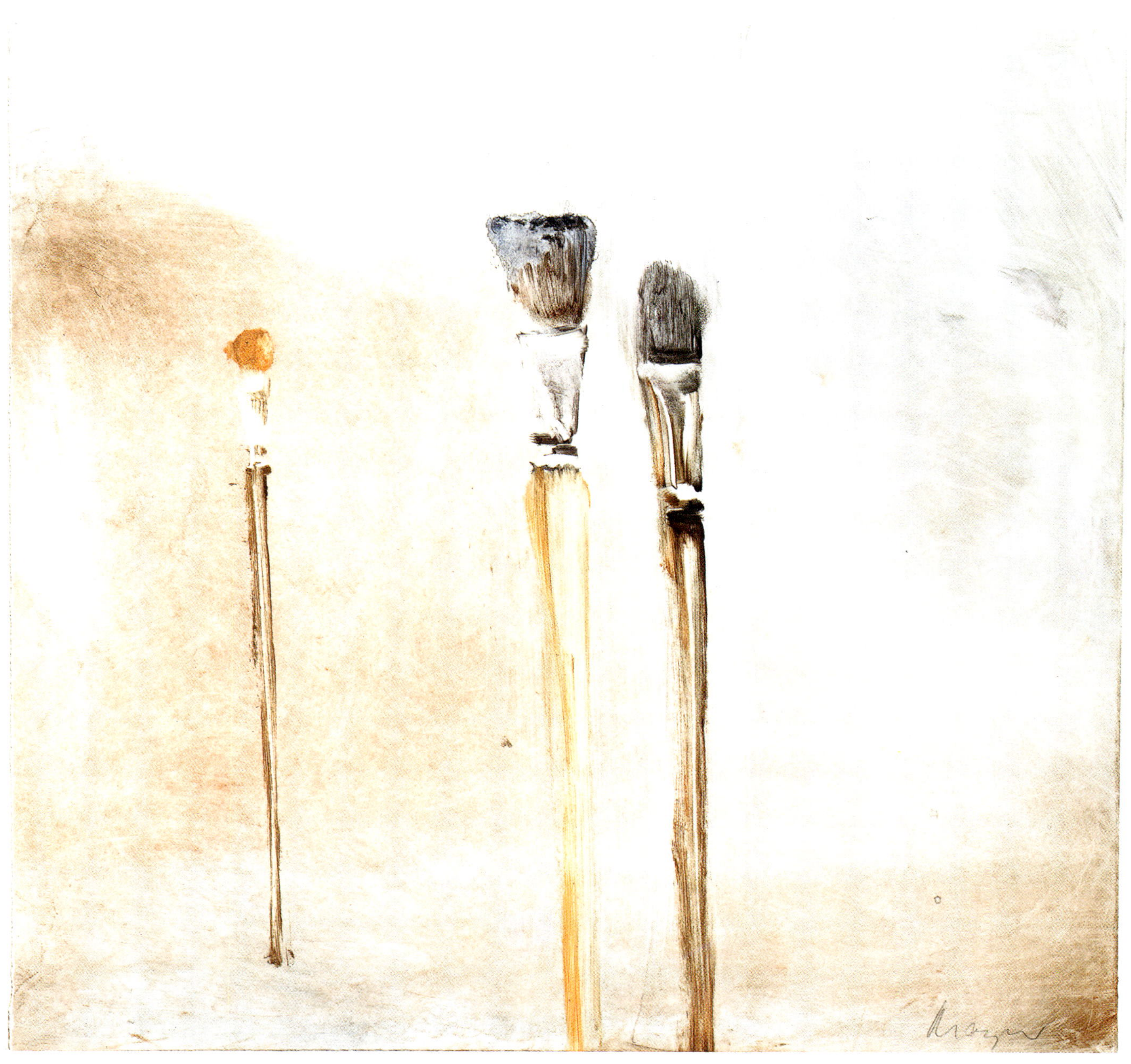

Colorplate 12 *Three Brushes,* ca. 1974, monotype, 19¾ × 20½ in. (50.2 × 52.1 cm). Jane Voorhees Zimmerli Art Museum, Museum Purchase (82.017.024).

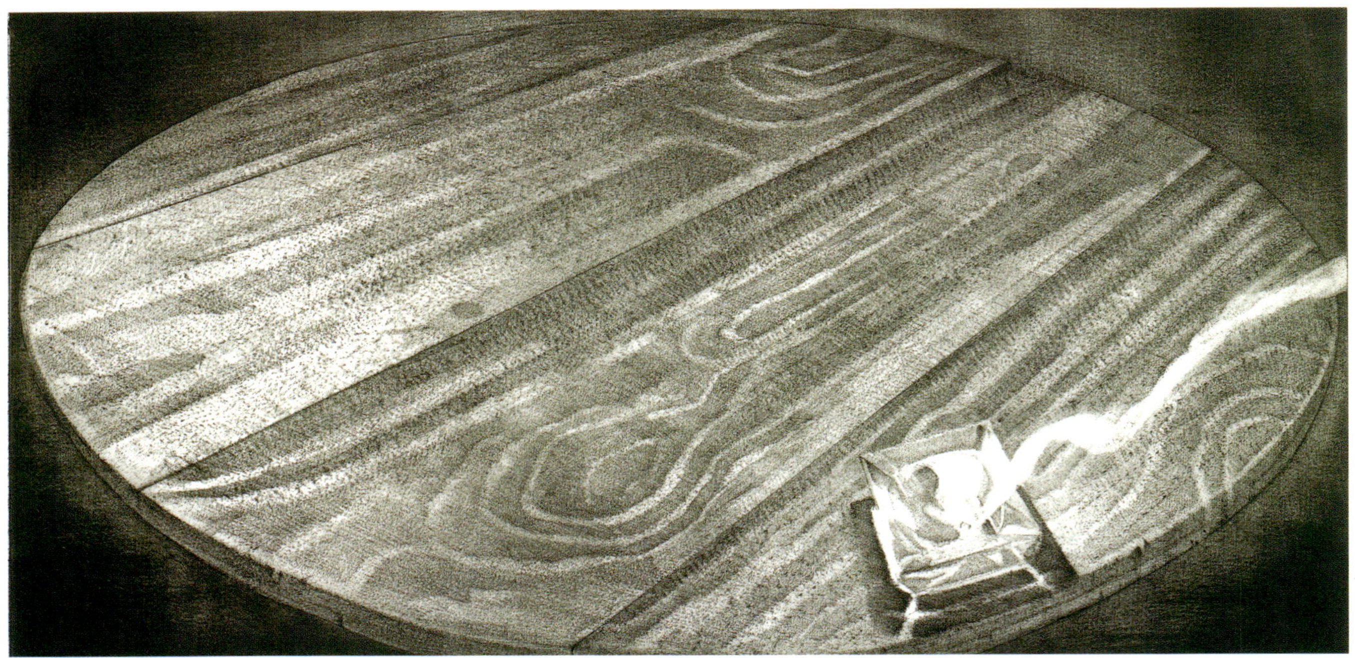

Colorplate 13 *Smoke,* 1975, engraving and aquatint, 21½ × 39½ in. (54.6 × 100.4 cm). Jane Voorhees Zimmerli Art Museum (75.029.003). (Catalogue raisonné 221)

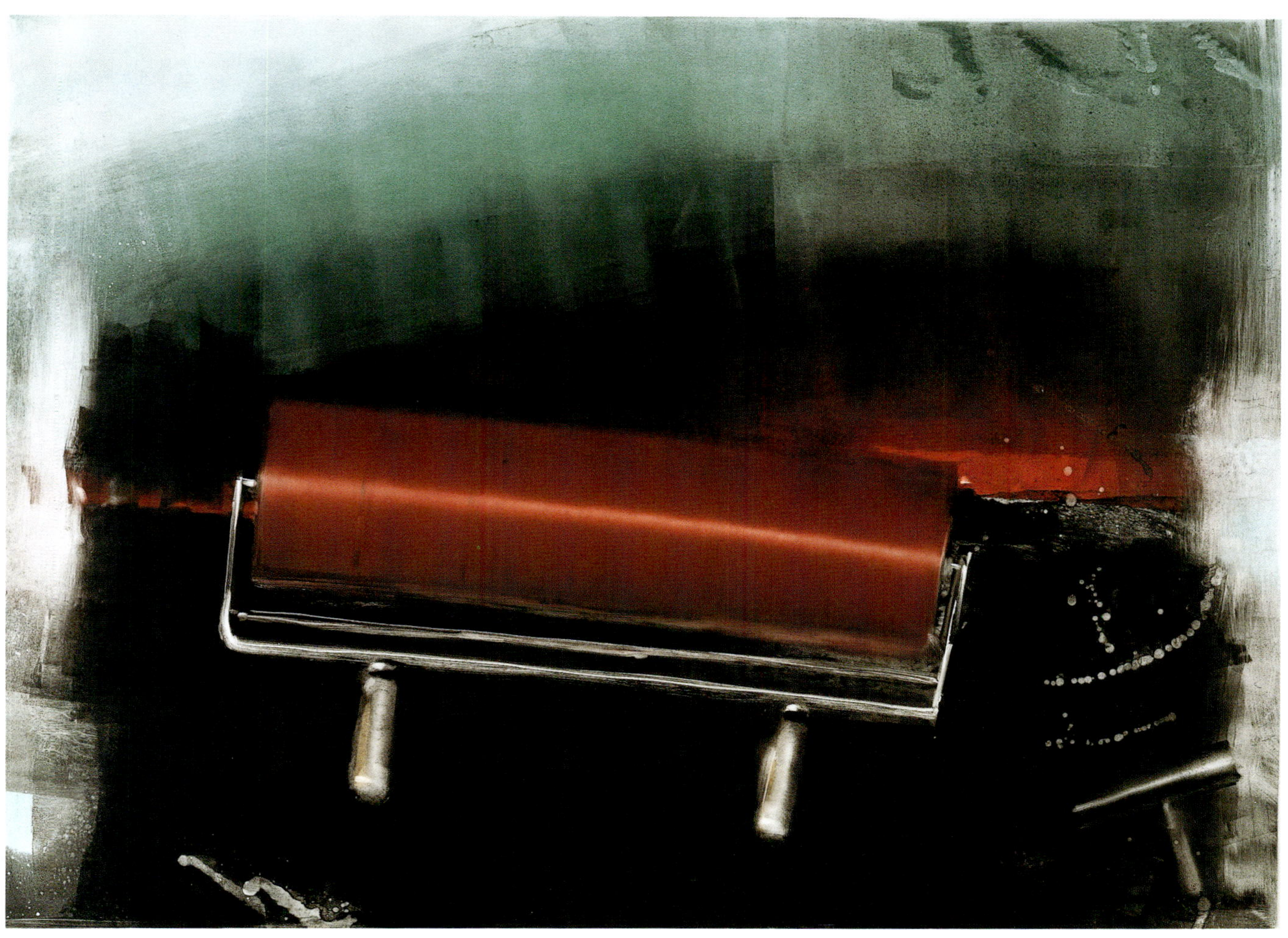

Colorplate 14 *Red Roller,* from the *Palette Still Life* series, 1977, monotype, 35⅝ × 47¹⁵⁄₁₆ in. (90.5 × 121.8 cm). The Museum of Modern Art, New York, John B. Turner Fund (631.78).

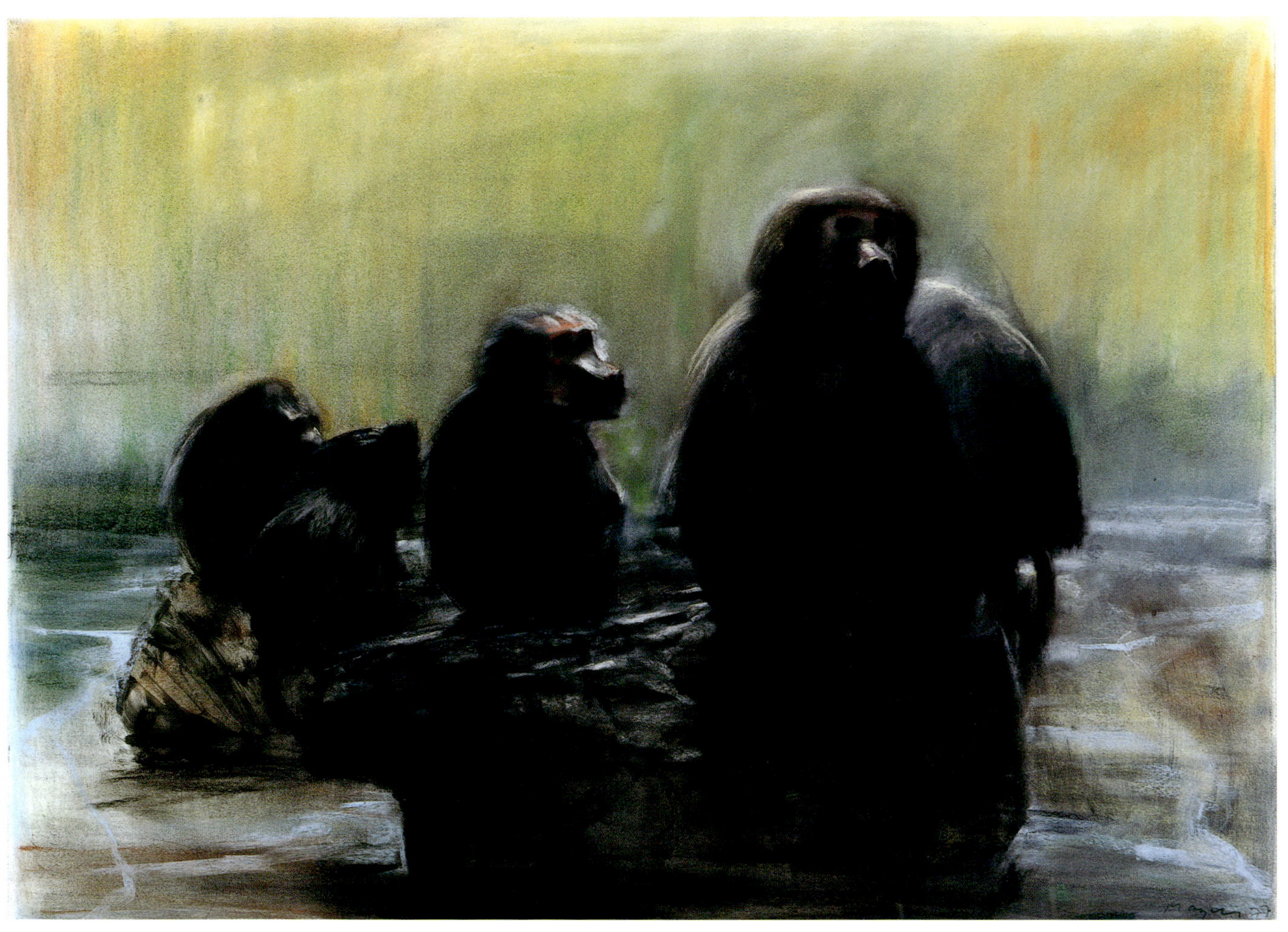

Colorplate 15 *Stoneham Cage #19*, 1977, monotype with pastel, 36 × 48 in. (91.4 × 121.9 cm). Jane Voorhees Zimmerli Art Museum (81.042.039).

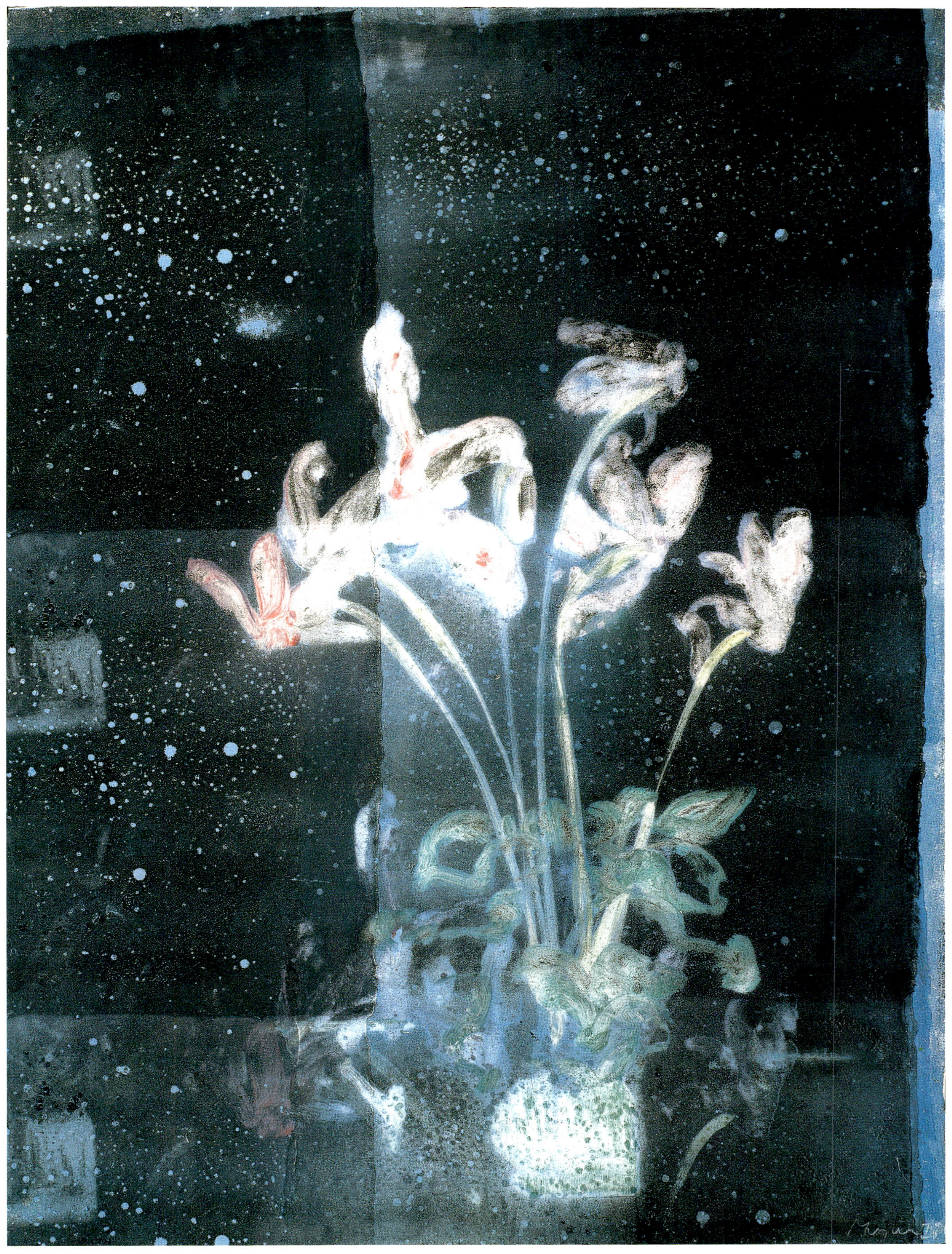

Colorplate 16 *Night Cyclamen,* 1980, monotype, 31¼ × 23½ in. (79.4 × 59.7 cm). Collection of Patricia Brown Specter.

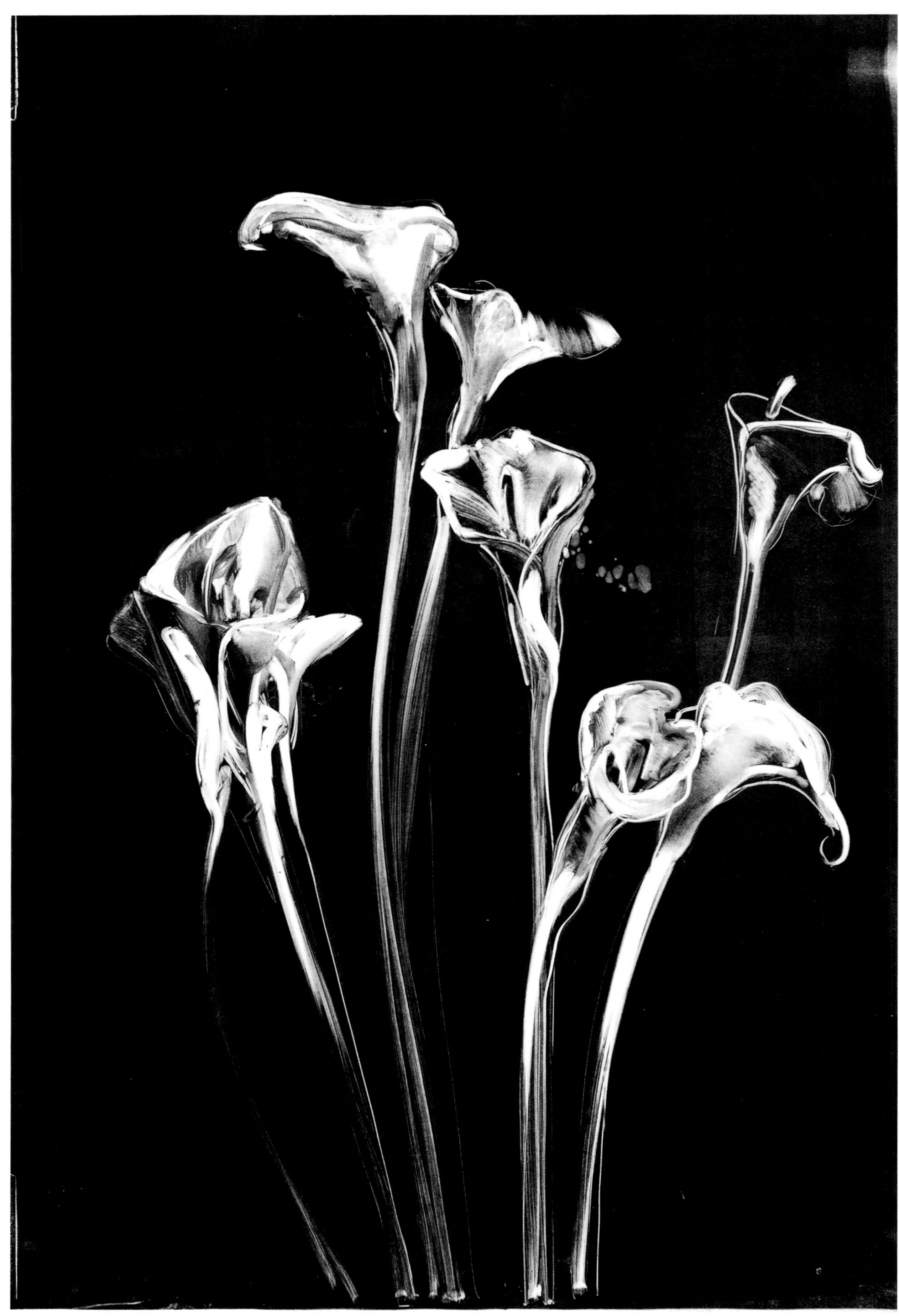

Colorplate 17 *Calla Lily #1 and #2*, 1980, monotype (diptych), 47½ × 31¼ in. (120.7 × 79.4 cm) each. Collection of the artist.

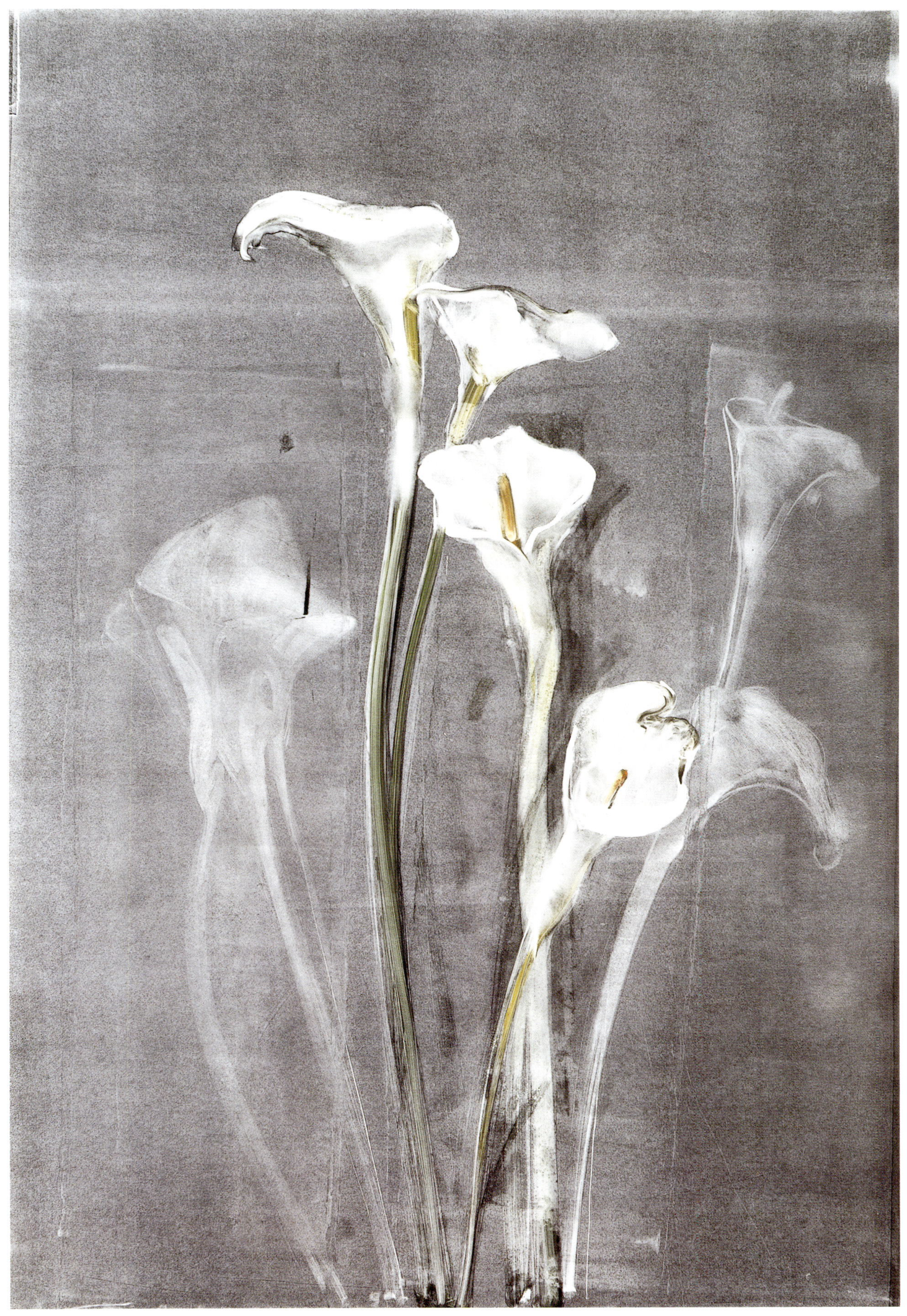

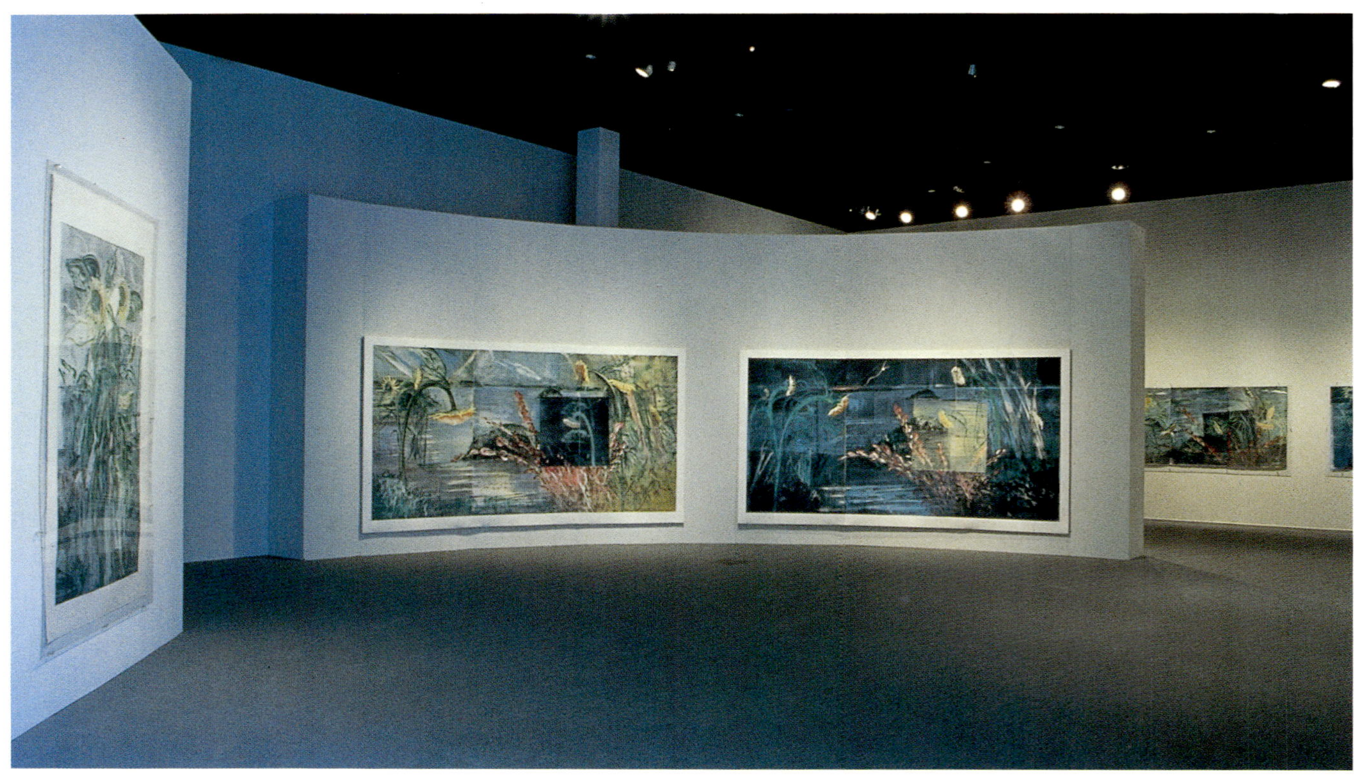

Colorplate 18 The *Wakeby Day/Wakeby Night* triptychs exhibited at the Hayden Gallery, Massachusetts Institute of Technology, Cambridge, 1983, prior to their permanent installation at 500 Memorial Drive, MIT.

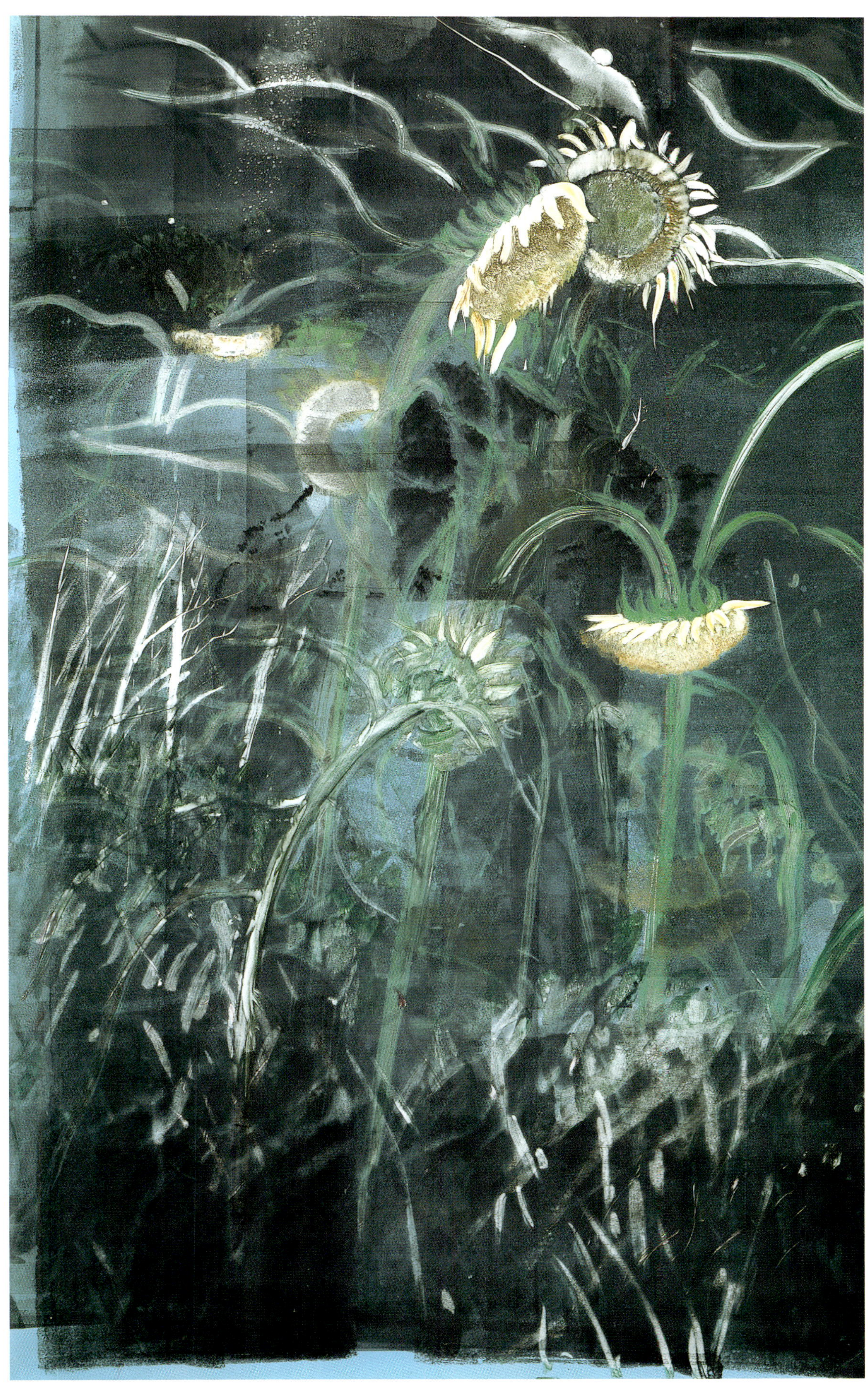

Colorplate 19 *Wakeby Night Study (Storm),* 1983, monotype, 78 × 49½ in. (198.1 × 125.7 cm). Collection of the artist.

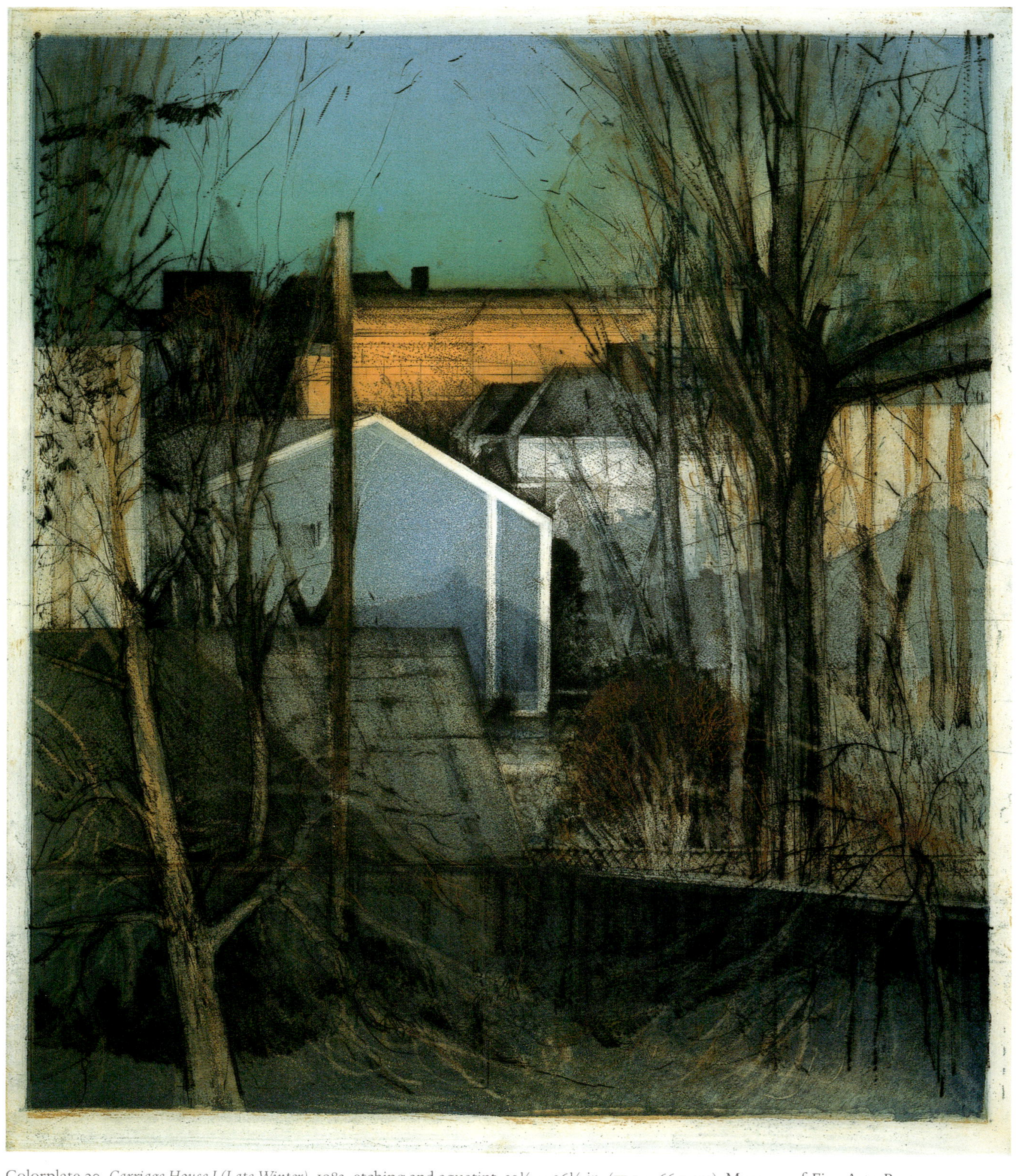

Colorplate 20 *Carriage House I (Late Winter),* 1983, etching and aquatint, 30½ × 26¼ in. (77.5 × 66.7 cm). Museum of Fine Arts, Boston, Gift of the Artist in Memory of His Framer, David Zacepitzky (1983.743). (Catalogue raisonné 243)

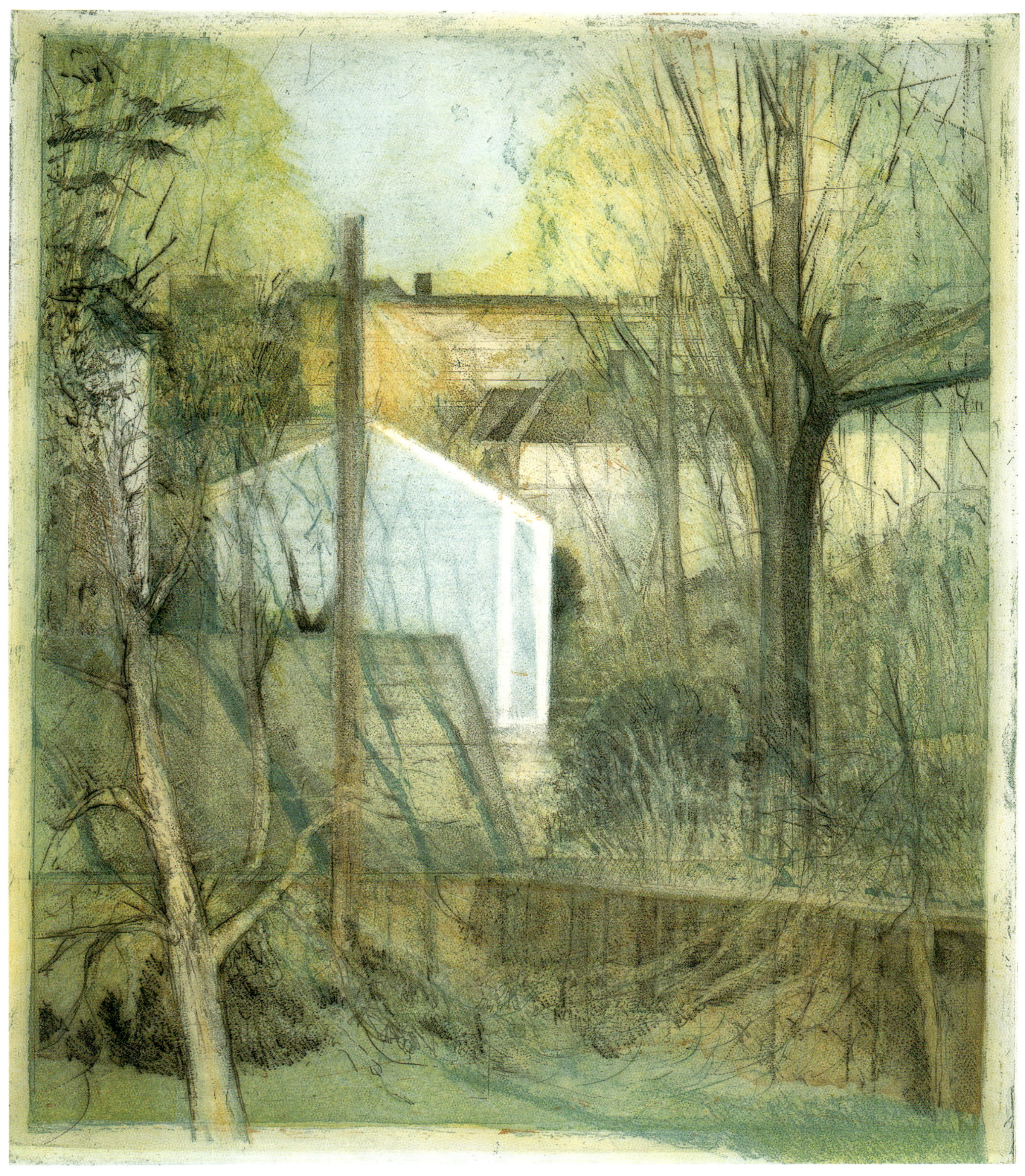

Colorplate 21 *Carriage House II (Spring),* 1983–84, etching and aquatint, 30¼ × 26¼ in. (76.9 × 66.7 cm). Museum of Fine Arts, Boston, Gift of the Artist in Memory of Frank Smullen, Artist (1983.744). (Catalogue raisonné 244)

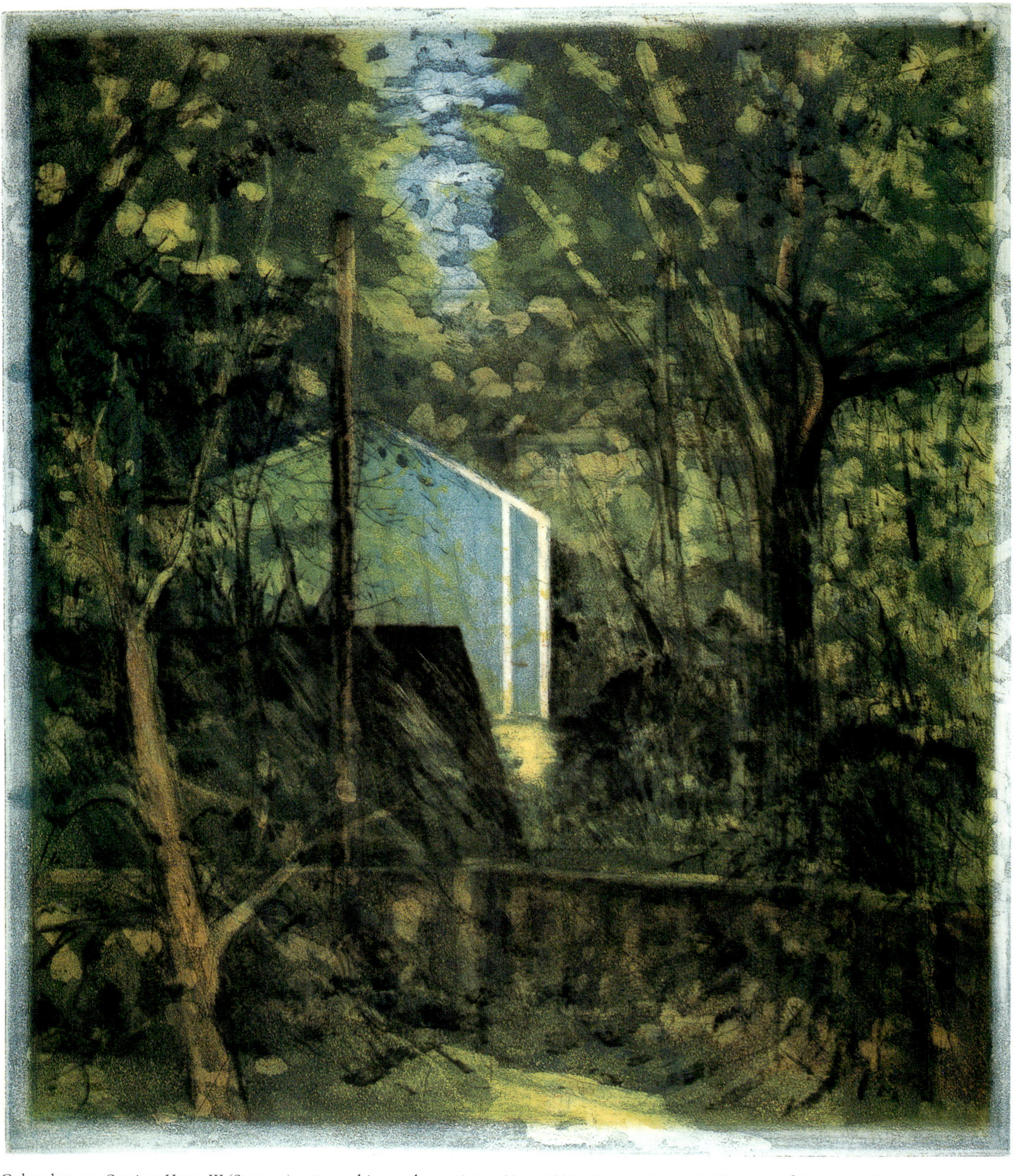

Colorplate 22 *Carriage House III (Summer),* 1984, etching and aquatint, 30¼ × 26¼ in. (76.9 × 66.7 cm). Museum of Fine Arts, Boston, Gift in Honor of Harold Isaacs (1986.418). (Catalogue raisonné 245)

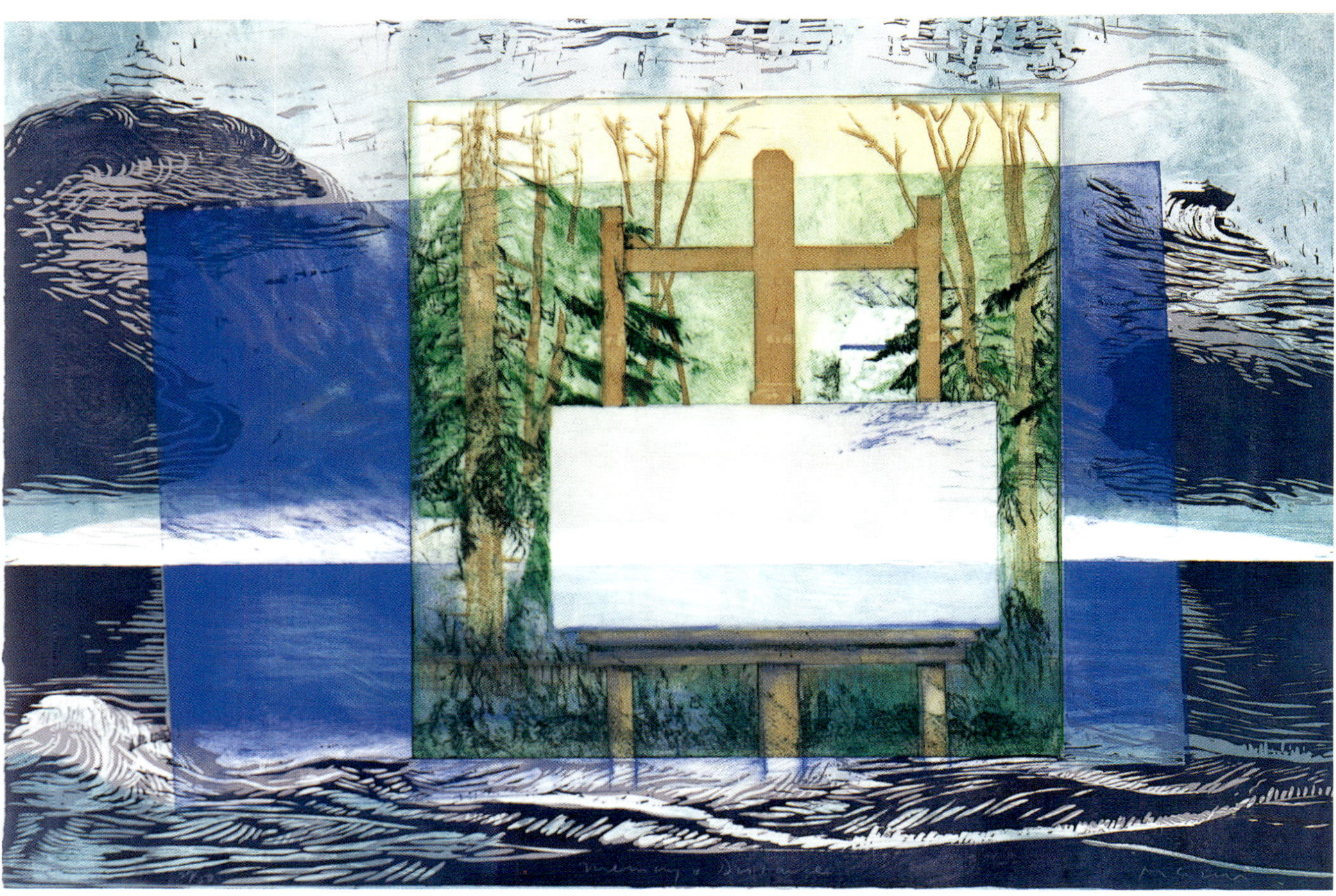

Colorplate 23 *Memory and Distance,* 1992, etching, aquatint, and wood relief, 31⅝ × 47 in. (80.3 × 119.4 cm). Jane Voorhees Zimmerli Art Museum (1995.0202). (Catalogue raisonné 271)

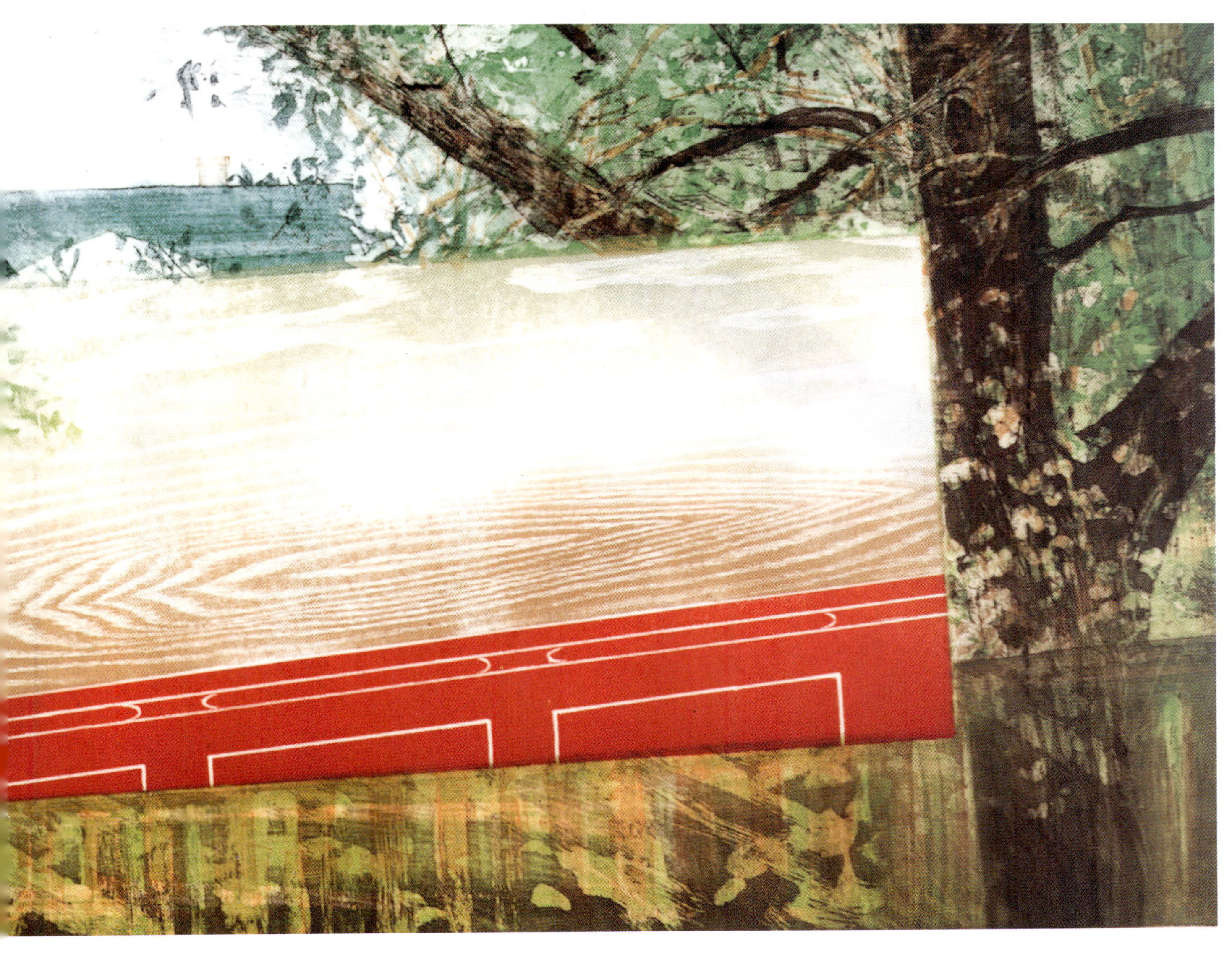

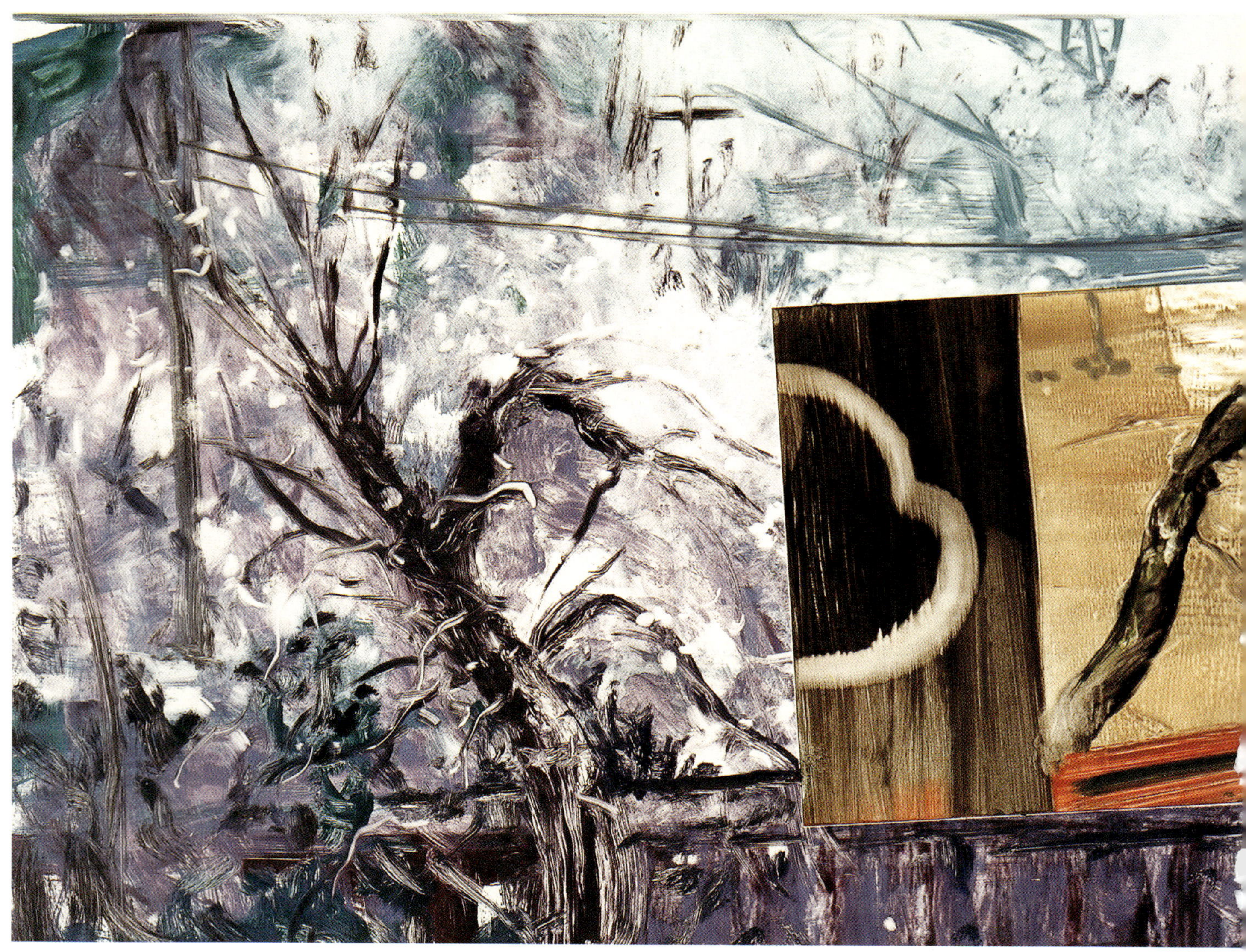

Colorplate 25 Study for *Two Ideas about a Garden,* 1990, monotype, 27½ × 63 in. (69.9 × 160.0 cm). Collection of the artist.

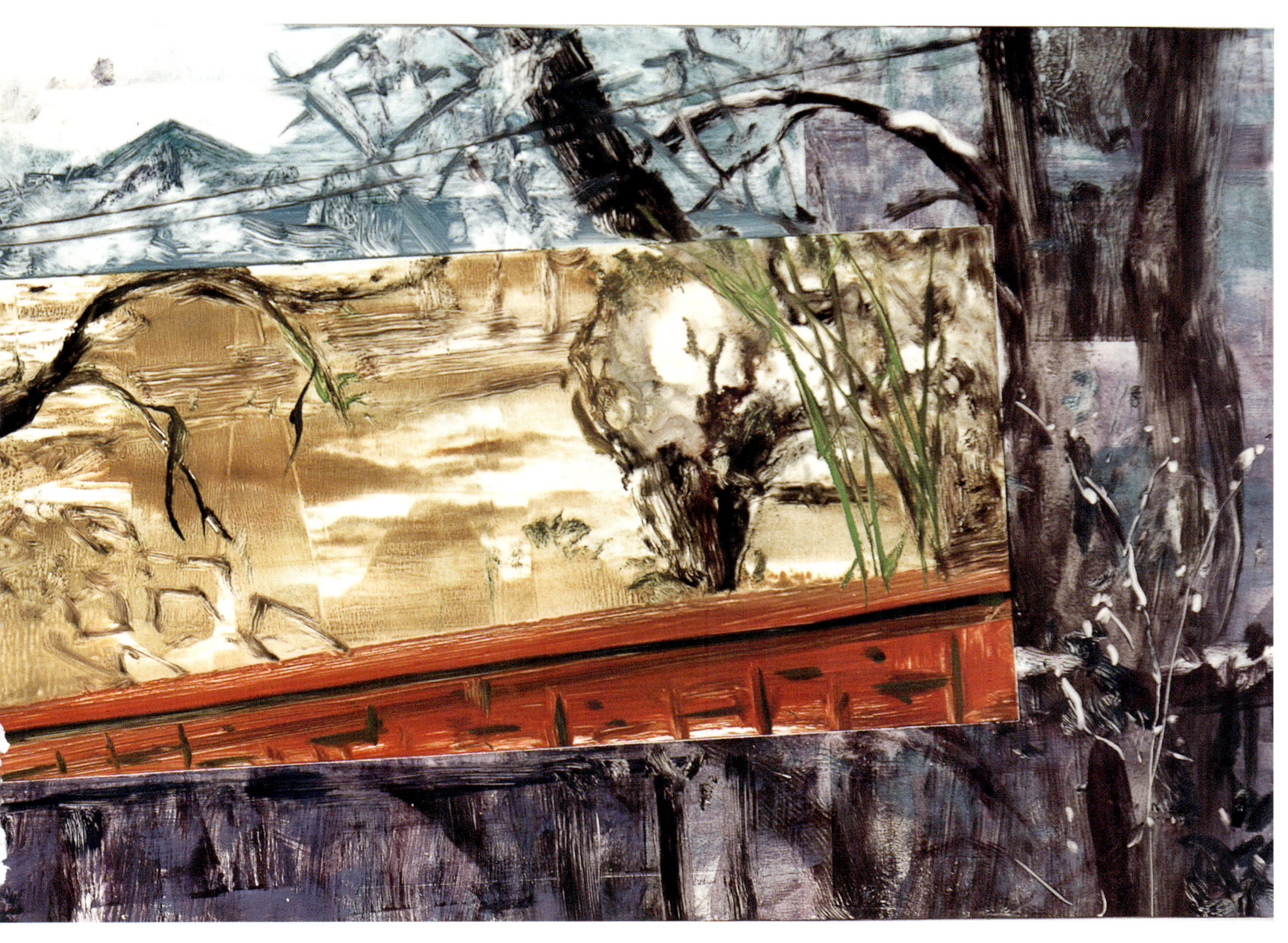

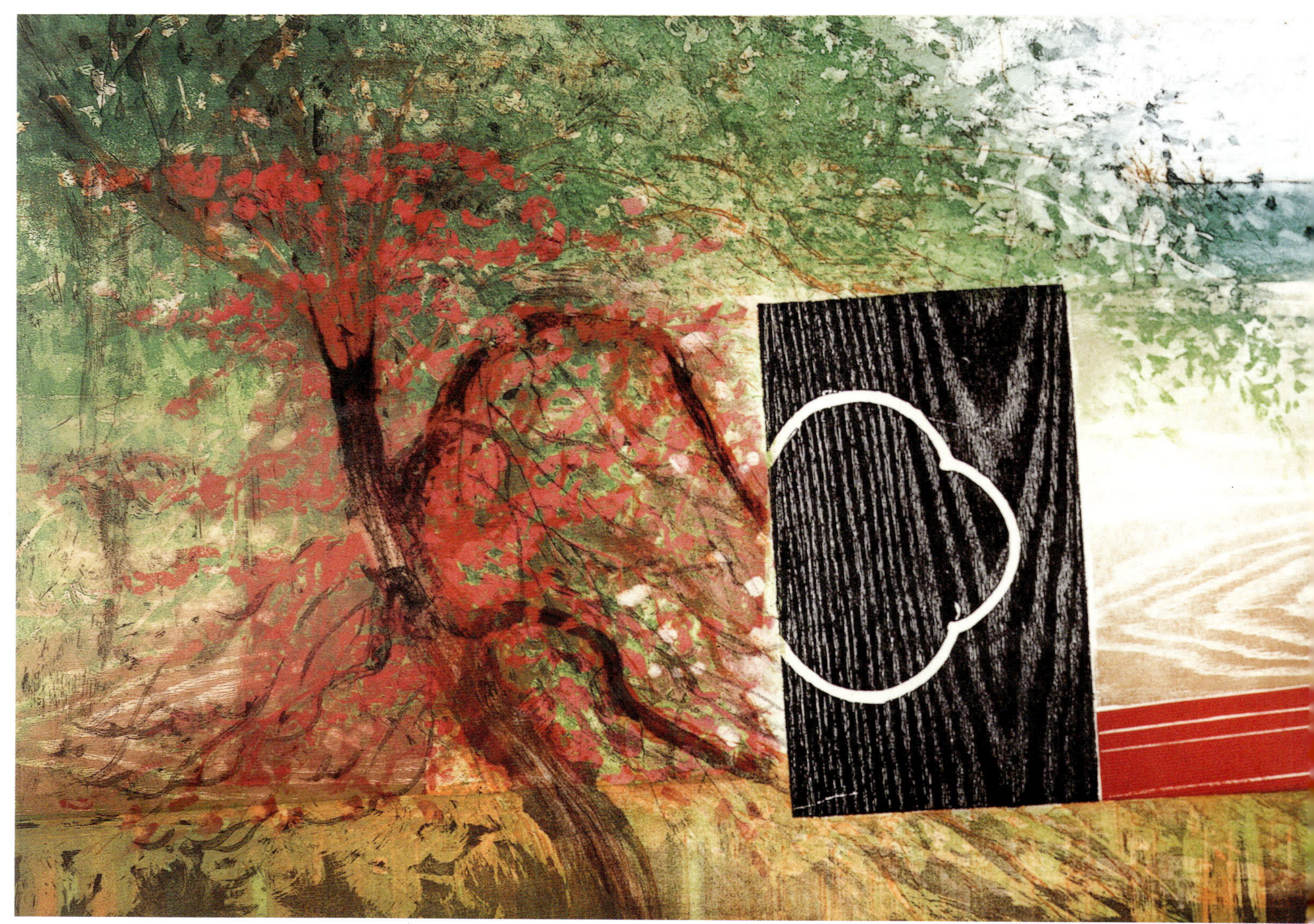

Colorplate 24 *Two Ideas about a Garden,* 1990, etching and aquatint with wood relief *chine collé,* 27½ × 63 in. (69.9 × 160.0 cm). Collection of David and Ruth Eisenberg. (Catalogue raisonné 269)

Mazur's Monotypes: The Medium with a Memory

Clifford S. Ackley

THE monotype, often regarded in the past as a minor medium or viewed with suspicion as being too quick and too easy, has been and continues to be a major means of expression for Michael Mazur. It occupies a central place in his work and has played a critical role in his development as a painter.

What is a monotype? This hybrid medium with an erratic history has been variously characterized as a "printed drawing" or a "painterly print." Its rather clinical-sounding name was invented about 1880–81 by the American monotype artist Charles Alvah Walker.[1] The compound term "mono-type" literally means "one print," indicating that the monotype generally yields only one strong impression. To make a traditional monotype, an artist paints or draws with — or manipulates with fingers and rag — printer's ink or paint on an unworked surface, often the smooth surface of a metal printing plate. The image is then printed onto a sheet of paper in a press or by hand pressure. The first pull, or impression, is strong; the subsequent impressions, the "ghosts" or cognates, are paler, but the artist has the option of working back into the ghost image on the plate, altering it and extending its life. The monotype, when compared with other methods of printmaking, which require step-by-step planning, is exceptionally direct, fluid, and flexible.

The monotype first emerged in the mid-seventeenth century, about 1645. It appears to have been a product of the seventeenth-century artist's two-fold interest in broad tonal effects, particularly dark tonalities, and in the spontaneous freehand sketch as a finished work of art, whether oil sketch or pen and wash drawing.

The artist generally conceded to be the inventor of the monotype is the Genoese painter and etcher of historical and allegorical subjects Giovanni Benedetto Castiglione (fig. 31).[2] His first monotypes, the "dark field" ones, appear to have been suggested by the act of inking his etching plates. When making a dark field monotype Castiglione apparently covered an untouched copper plate with a film of black printer's ink and then freely picked out the lights with a blunt point. The resulting monotypes were much more dramatic in their contrasts and effects of illumination than were Castiglione's etchings, with their delicate tonal webs or meshes of etched lines.

Castiglione's dark field monotypes are roughly contemporary with the beginning of Rembrandt van Rijn's experiments with the painterly inking of individual impressions of his etchings. Rembrandt left a veil of ink over certain parts of the image and wiped it away in others, creating variant painterly patterns of darkness and light. Surprising as it may seem in retrospect, Rembrandt never produced a pure monotype; however, in the later 1640s and 1650s he did ink many impressions of his etched plates in a monotype fashion. Rembrandt had been influenced by the experiments of the eccentric seventeenth-century Dutch painter

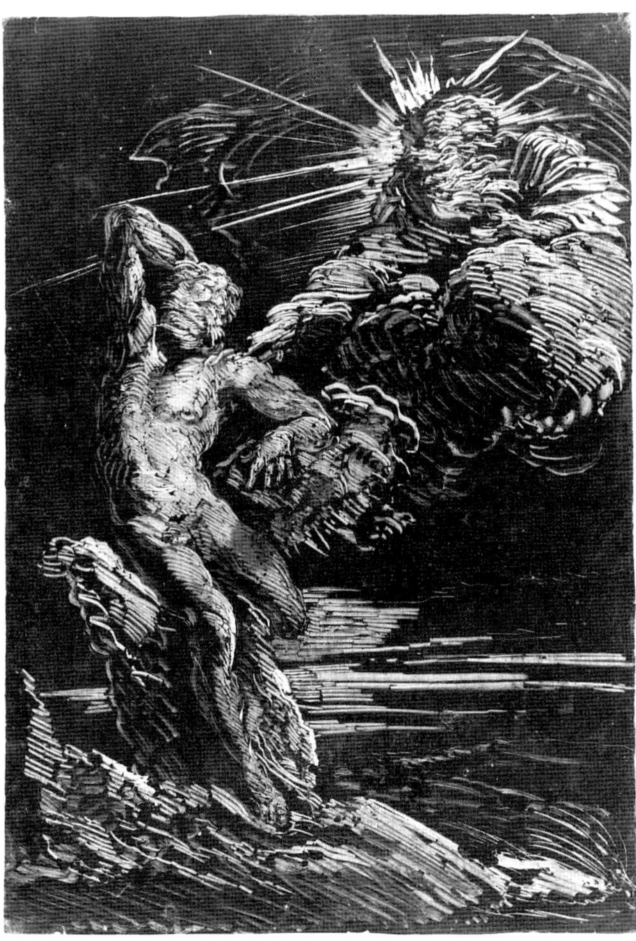

Fig. 31 Giovanni Benedetto Castiglione (Italian, 1609–1664), *God Creating Adam,* ca. 1645, monotype, 11⅞ × 8⅓ in. (30.2 × 20.5 cm). The Art Institute of Chicago, Restricted Gift of Dr. and Mrs. William D. Shorey and promised Gift of an anonymous donor (1985.113).

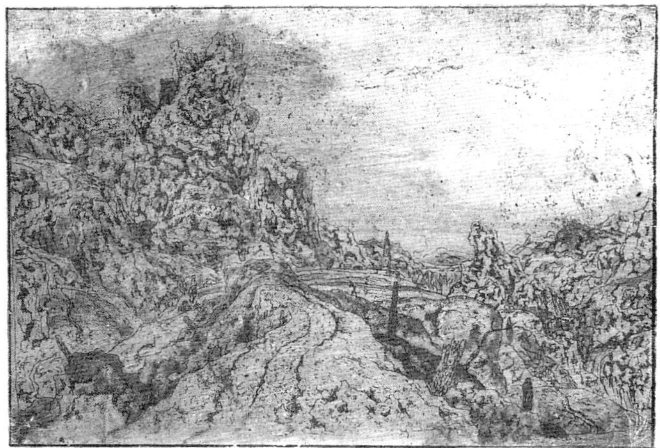

Fig. 32 Hercules Seghers (Dutch, ca. 1590–1645), *Rocky Landscape, a Church Tower in the Distance,* etching and drypoint printed in blue on paper prepared with a pink ground, with olive green wash, 5¼ × 7⅜ in. (13.3 × 18.7 cm). Museum of Fine Arts, Boston, Gift of Kate D. Griswold, Ernest Longfellow, Jessie Wilkinson, Katherine Eliot Bullard in memory of Francis Bullard, and M. and M. Karolik Funds (1973.208).

and etcher Hercules Seghers (fig. 32). Seghers not only printed his etchings on prepared colored grounds and on cloth, he also achieved original tonal effects through the use of granular bitten tone, bundles of drypoint scratches, or a tone of ink left on the plate.[3]

Although there is visual evidence that Castiglione knew Rembrandt's early prints (late 1620s – early 1630s), it is less certain that Castiglione was inspired by Rembrandt's later experiments with the painterly inking of plates; his invention of the monotype was most likely a parallel phenomenon spontaneously generated by similar interests. Castiglione also made drawings with brush and oil paint on paper, and there is another group of Castiglione monotypes that are essentially transfer drawings or counterproofs from brush drawings in oil paint, dark printed lines on a ground of light paper (figs. 33 and 34).

Until recent decades, the history of the monotype has been a relatively spotty, discontinuous one.[4] It seems primarily to have been a medium for private experiment and play, shared by artists but not known to the broader art public. In our time, many previously ignored monotype works are coming to light, filling in missing pieces of the mosaic.[5]

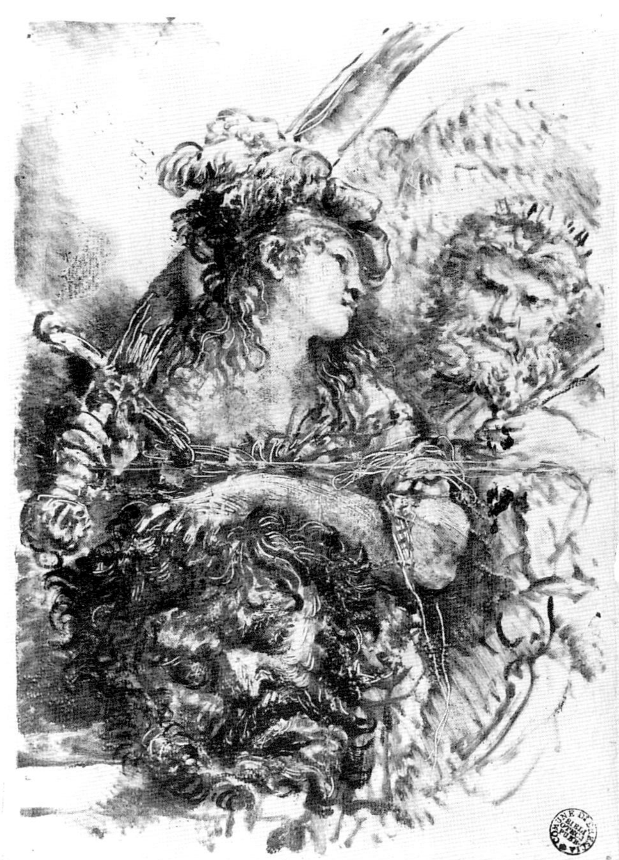

Fig. 33 Giovanni Benedetto Castiglione, *David with the Head of Goliath,* ca. 1650–55, monotype in brown oil pigment with hand additions (first pull), 14⅝ × 10 in. (37.1 × 25.4 cm). Pinacoteca Civica Tosio Martinengo, Brescia, Italy.

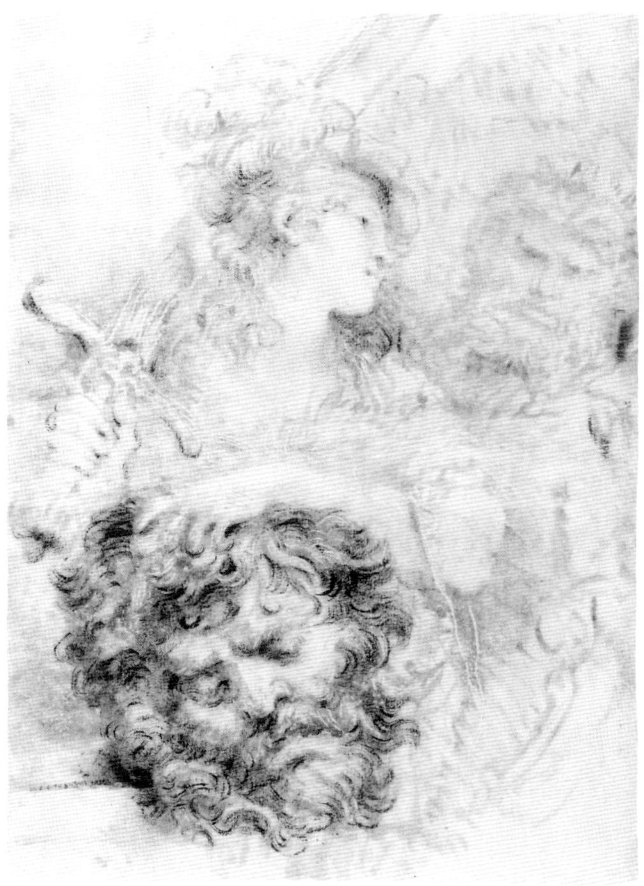

Fig. 34 Giovanni Benedetto Castiglione, *David with the Head of Goliath,* ca. 1650–55, monotype (second pull), 13¾ × 9¾ in. (34.8 × 24.8 cm). National Gallery of Art, Washington, D.C., Andrew W. Mellon Fund (1977.30.1.PR).

Many of these monotypes had been, not surprisingly, mistaken for drawings. From the 1870s on a more continuous tradition of monotype activity began to emerge, stimulated in part by the Rembrandt-inspired tonal inking experiments of the international Etching Revival that began in France and later spread to America. In France significant bodies of work in monotype were produced by the painters Edgar Degas, Camille Pissarro, and Paul Gauguin, and in America by the painters Frank Duveneck, William Merritt Chase, Maurice Prendergast, and John Sloan, among others.

The most significant nineteenth-century body of work in monotype was produced from the late 1870s to the early 1890s by Degas. Only a few of these private experiments were exhibited in the artist's lifetime. The full revelation of the originality and inventiveness of Degas's over three hundred monotypes had to wait for Eugenia Parry Janis's groundbreaking exhibition at the Fogg Art Museum in 1968.[6] Not only scholars and art lovers were galvanized by the exhibition and its catalogue, but also many artists as well.

Nothing better captures Mazur's sense of excitement and discovery on the occasion of the exhibition than his description of a small Degas monotype of a *café-concert* singer (fig. 35):

> This tiny explosive image, a spontaneous gift of the artist's spirit, seemed to have been breathed directly on the paper in one magical gesture. A closer look reveals Degas's labor. His fingers pushed in ink like modeling clay. His painter's cloth wiped out the black ink for luminous whites. His brush added telling contours. At just the right moment he printed his constellation of tones, not much more than a cluster of smudges. But when the paper emerged from the press, still damp and pliant, those little marks became flesh, hair, fabric: a nose and mouth in one line, a gloved hand, corrected and redrawn. They became a spotlighted café singer, bawdy and as aggressive as the strokes that made her. The spontaneity and energy in that little print lifts the medium into art.[7]

As the interview that follows makes clear,[8] Mazur has worked inventively with the monotype medium in a multitude of ways. One of the principal lessons he took away from the Degas exhibition was derived less from the exhibition itself than from the catalogue's checklist, which listed and reproduced all of Degas's known monotypes, including in particular second pulls or ghosts and cognates. These ghost images demonstrated to Mazur that the monotype had a memory, a fact of great significance for his later serial monotypes with their dimension of time and narrative. Mazur has produced an unusually large and vital body of work in monotype, a virtuoso medium that is both appealing and treacherous because of the speed and gestural freedom that it encourages. It is surely because Mazur brings such an instinctive, disciplined sense of drawing to the medium that his monotypes are characterized by coherence and firm structural backbone as well as a seemingly effortless fluidity of gesture.

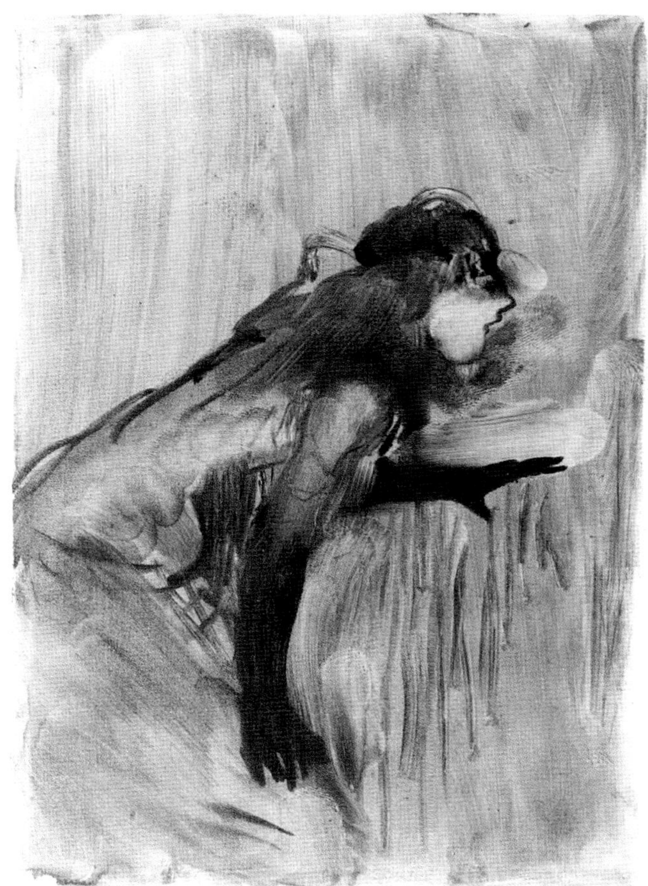

Fig. 35 Edgar Degas (French, 1834–1917), *Café-Concert Singer,* ca. 1877–78, monotype, 7¼ × 5¹⁄₁₆ in. (18.5 × 12.8 cm). Collection E.W.K., Bern.

The Interview

Clifford Ackley *When did you first become involved with the idea of the unique print?*

Michael Mazur I used to think it was Eugenia Parry Janis's Degas monotype show at the Fogg in 1968. In subsequent years it became clear to me that my first contact with the idea came from several sources. The first was when I was an Amherst undergraduate working with Leonard Baskin at Smith College. I began talking with the printmaker George Lockwood, who was also teaching at Smith, about different ways in which one could make or vary a print. The second source, I think, was the sculptor Naum Gabo [fig. 36], whom I assisted with printing for three months in 1961. It was my attraction to his monoprints, the variant printings of his wood engravings, that was the beginning of an interest in making a different kind of print, a print that would be more responsive to change and that would not be stuck in the traditional, consistent edition format. My cut plate etchings of 1968 were another attempt to vary the composition of a print by actually rearranging pieces of the plate. The very first monotypes I did after seeing the

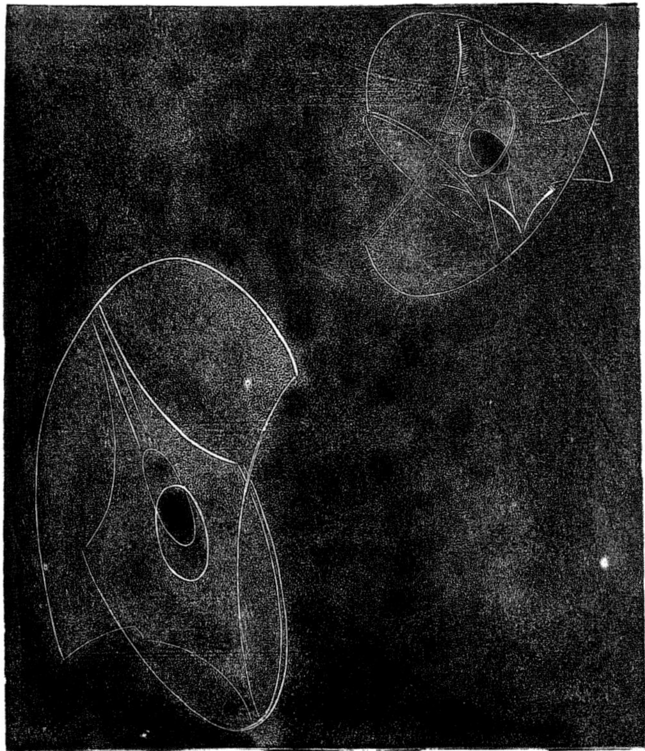

Fig. 36 Naum Gabo (American, born Russia, 1890–1977), *Opus 5*, from the series *The Constellations*, 1950, wood engraving (monoprint), 9⅝ × 8⅛ in. (24.4 × 20.6 cm). Museum of Fine Arts, Boston, Lee M. Friedman Fund (1976.148).

Degas show were made on the back of those cut plates [fig. 37], which links the two bodies of work — the variable cut plates and the first monotypes. I think the basic source of the fascination that I had with the monoprint and the monotype — which came to fruition when I saw the Degas show — was this need to break with the seamless consistency of the typical fifties and sixties prints that tended to be very clean, very meticulous, very edition oriented.

CA *I remember that in the print market of the 1960s if there was the slightest variation in a print, the customer would not buy it.*

MM Right, and the rules for all the print competitions — which were much more frequent then than now — excluded monotypes or monoprints. I believe that when I juried the Library of Congress show in the early seventies, I forced the first monotype into that show by submitting one of mine, which I was allowed as artist/juror.

CA *It was considered neither fish nor fowl.*

MM So, apart from the 1968 Degas show, I must have already been mentally prepared to respond quickly because my first monoprints were made in the summer of 1968, not more than a month or two after seeing the show. I had just returned from the Tamarind Lithography Workshop, also a contributing factor.

Because the Tamarind printers were so hungry for material to work with, at least 50 percent of the editions they printed for you were variations on previous editions; they would change colors, they would add something. In the case of Tamarind it wasn't really organic to the artist but came out of the nature of the shop.

CA *They were training printers. The monoprint/monotype attitude emerges in the middle of the seventeenth century. We have Castiglione in Genoa and in Holland we have Rembrandt and, before him, Seghers. You mentioned being exposed to the Dutch artists in Egbert Haverkamp-Begemann's class at Yale.*

MM Yes. Baskin was also an influential teacher and, above all, a very smart collector. In a way that may have been his greatest contribution for me. In his house there were many unusual prints, and I first encountered some of the more obscure printmakers there. Seghers was actually introduced to me before I went to graduate school; I heard about him through Baskin [fig. 3]. When I got to Yale I took a course with Begemann, and we did a study of Seghers's techniques [fig. 32]. I was well aware by the time — that was 1960 or 1961, almost fourteen years before you and I looked together at original Seghers prints in Holland.

My interest in monotype extended from 1968 to the early 1980s, and then it started to switch toward monoprint. I think 1983 would have been the height of the *Wakeby* series, the height of my interest in the absolutely unique image. And then from 1983 on, in the last fifteen years, I've been more interested in the variable print with a matrix than in the pure monotype. I obviously had been thinking about the differences between those two processes when the Metropolitan Museum of Art and the Museum of Fine Arts did the catalogue for the *Painterly Print* show [1980]. In my essay for the catalogue, I struggled to define the difference between monotype and monoprint in terms of that matrix orientation. Previous to that time the terms had been pretty much interchangeable, but to me they mean something very specific.

CA *I think it's a useful distinction, the idea that the monoprint is a print with an existing matrix that is printed monotype fashion, whereas the monotype has no matrix and is an absolutely unique image.*

You started with the classic monotype attitude — that is, Castiglione and Degas — the kind of monotype that arises in part out of the experience of manipulating ink on the smooth surface of an etching plate, although in the case of Castiglione it also grew out of drawing with oil paint and brush on paper. Seghers, on the other hand, apparently wanted to print paintings. He not only printed on paper but also on cloth, as you've done.

MM What, in retrospect, interested me most about the Degas show was the narrative implications of his use of the monotype. It was the ghosts and the cognates that made the biggest impression. His process was very interesting, white out of black and black onto white — those opposite dark and light field effects. I think the print that I wrote about, the *café-concert* singer [fig. 35], was one of the most

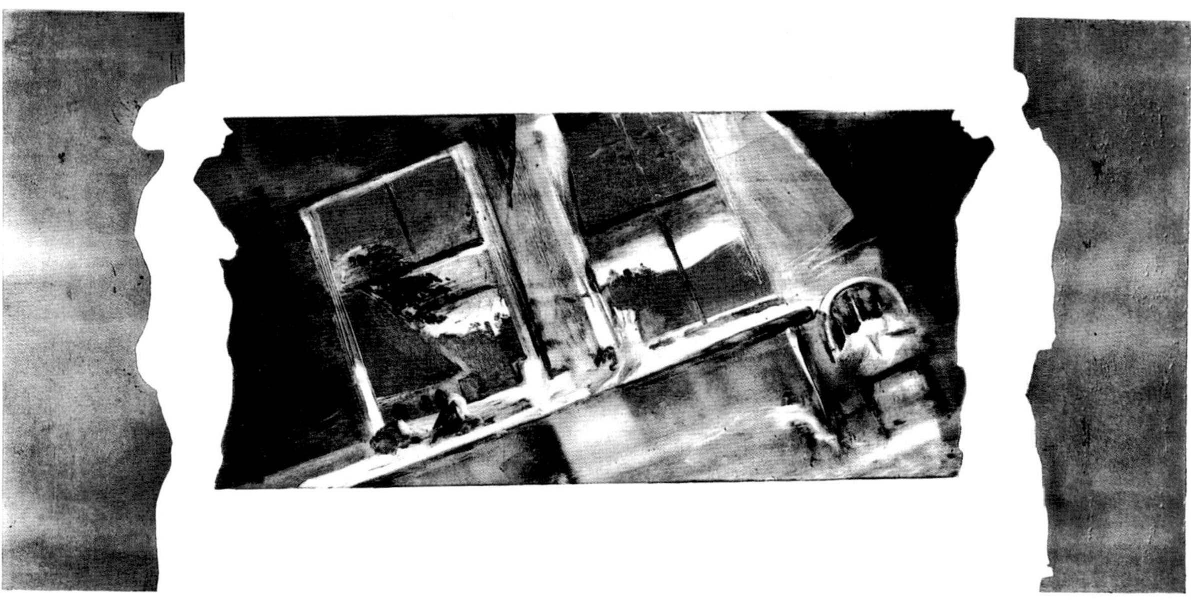

Fig. 37 *Artist and Model and Studio View,* 1968, monoprint, 24¾ × 37⅞ in. (62.9 × 96.2 cm). Collection of the artist.

energetic painterly drawings that I had ever seen. It dovetailed with my own yearning for painterliness, something that took years to truly happen but that I wasn't yet able to realize.

CA *Because you were a "line" man.*

MM I was a line man who wanted to make tone, and so a lot of my experiments in printmaking consisted of building tone out of line. Here was a more direct, immediate way to achieve tone.

CA *I think many other artists of your generation — whether it directly affected their work or not — responded to the Degas show. Wasn't the whole gestural aspect meaningful for those artists who emerged from Abstract Expressionism?*

MM I was born too late to be involved in the Abstract Expressionist movement. I graduated the year that one could say Pop art reared its head and made a major impression on the scene and actually began to remove the Abstract Expressionists from the galleries. My interest in monotype was as a narrative artist, as an artist who was interested mainly in the figure. Pop was a welcome change because it brought back the figure, it brought back representational ideas. Degas's monotypes linked him to the painterly, gestural tradition, but also to the new interest in narrative and figuration. His interest in using the print as a way of telling a story was very influential for me; it came at a critical point in my development.

The rollers became more important to me — even the act of rolling out the black ground created its own variations — and I began to play with the rollers, with the varying viscosities of ink, gaining greater and greater control over viscosity of ink so that I could pick an image up with the roller and lay it down again with the roller. I began experimenting — different tools became important to me at different times. Castiglione starts with the tip of a brush handle or what might have been a kind of Q-tip, a stick wrapped with a little rag.

CA *His black field monotypes.*

MM Degas, of course, clears away tone with turpentine, giving him greater flexibility, a whole new way of removing ink or pushing it around — because that's essentially what you're doing, pushing ink around. It began to emerge as a different medium for me technically. The rollers became very important. As they did, the growing complexity, the use of double images, of secondary plates and overlays, deepened my process with the medium, introduced my own particular approach. It was the fact that you could evolve with the medium by means of technical discoveries that intrigued me — monotype seemed inexhaustible. It seemed as inexhaustible as painting.

I was tired of the same image repeated over and over again. I wanted to move on with an image, within the same day, within the same hour. That was my artistic personality then, and monotype fed that personality. I settled down at some point to using certain tools — the rag, the brush, the rollers — that has been pretty much my stock-in-trade. One has to limit oneself to a repertoire of tools that you really feel comfortable with.

CA *In some people's minds and eyes, the monotype has been all too successful. We're now dealing with a veritable deluge.*

MM I think the nice thing is that the monotype has finally become just another way of making an image, and in a print shop it no longer is at all radical. In fact, I think that in most print shops around the country now, including student print shops, the monotype probably accounts for at least half the work that's being done. It's been totally assimilated into printmaking, and like any medium, it's going to have its stronger practitioners as well as a lot of mediocrity. When I started making monotypes I wasn't making them to make a statement about a medium. I started making them because they answered a need in my own development.

CA *Monotypes, I think, have always been, to some degree, about play — serious play. In the late nineteenth century artists had monotype parties just as they had tile painting parties. I'm talking about American artists such as Frank Duveneck and William Merritt Chase.*

MM I've worked on monotypes together with a lot of artists. When you're working with monotype, teaching is an unusually collaborative experience.

CA *The ease and instantaneous quality of monotype, and being able to get an image so quickly, makes it very useful in teaching, in breaking the ice.*

MM When I worked with Mary Frank or Jim Dine, the speed of what was being produced was very, very stimulating. It was a matter of surprise, of play. The fact that you could make a lot of these images meant that you could also throw a lot of them away, so there was a kind of irreverence. Only a few would work out, but you knew that there was always something else on its way. So there's a tremendous momentum that's built up in the development of a monotype that's nothing like the development of a print. The development of a print is slow and contemplative.

CA *Of course some artists, initially, have a terrible time getting into traditional printmaking because of all the planning and the collaboration that's involved.*

MM What was unique to my own development is that I went into it ass backwards. Basically I was trained in traditional printmaking, and so I knew as much as most people my age at the time about how to make a print — and then I discovered this painterly aspect in myself that liberated me and made it possible for me to get back into painting. So in a way the monotype was for me a bridge between printmaking and painting, a very rich transition and maybe the core of my work.

CA *I was trying to remember if, like Degas, you sometimes used a monotype image as a base for working up in pastel or some other medium.*

MM Yes, that movement from a wet medium to a dry medium, from a less controlled medium to a more controlled medium — I did a lot of that. Of the *Wakeby* series, for example, we did, I think, six sets, and at least three of them were heavily pasteled over [colorplate 27]. There is a great deal of pastel over monotype in the *Greenhouse* series. I did many images based on the Stoneham Zoo — monkey images that were pastel over monotype [colorplate 15].

There's something about printmaking that brings artists together. That sounds like a corny togetherness thing, but basically the collaboration between printers and artists, or printmakers and printmakers, has a rich tradition. The interdependency and camaraderie that exist between a printer and a painter who work together a great deal are unique.

CA *In our time there's been a fashion on the part of scholars of printmaking to stress the collaborative aspect of printmaking. A scholar such as Pat Gilmour is sometimes almost more interested in the printer's contribution than in the artist's.*

MM I think that not enough has been said about the printer's contribution — when, for example, you see an artist going from one print shop to another and producing prints with very different qualities.

CA *I remember when Robert Rauschenberg and Jasper Johns first shifted from Universal Limited Art Editions to Gemini G.E.L. There was quite a difference in the look of the prints that resulted.*

MM That's true with my own work. I know from working with various shops how subtly things can change. Thankfully, my own extensive experience as a printmaker contributes to a greater degree of control over the quality of work from one shop to the next than is the case with artists who don't have as much of a handle on printmaking and who are therefore more dependent. For a lot of artists starting to make prints, it takes a long time to understand what they're trying to get, and it can drive the printers crazy.

CA *One of the things we haven't really talked about in relation to your work in monotype is your involvement with the serial image. In our time there is an obsession with serial imagery and sometimes almost more interest in the process than in the results — a sensibility that goes back to the Impressionist era, basically.*

MM A serial work is based on the concept that the journey is more interesting than the destination, an attitude opposed to what one might call the masterpiece attitude, where everything is geared to perfection and completion.

CA *Transformation versus perfection — I think of the various serial images that you've made, the multipart monotypes you've produced.*

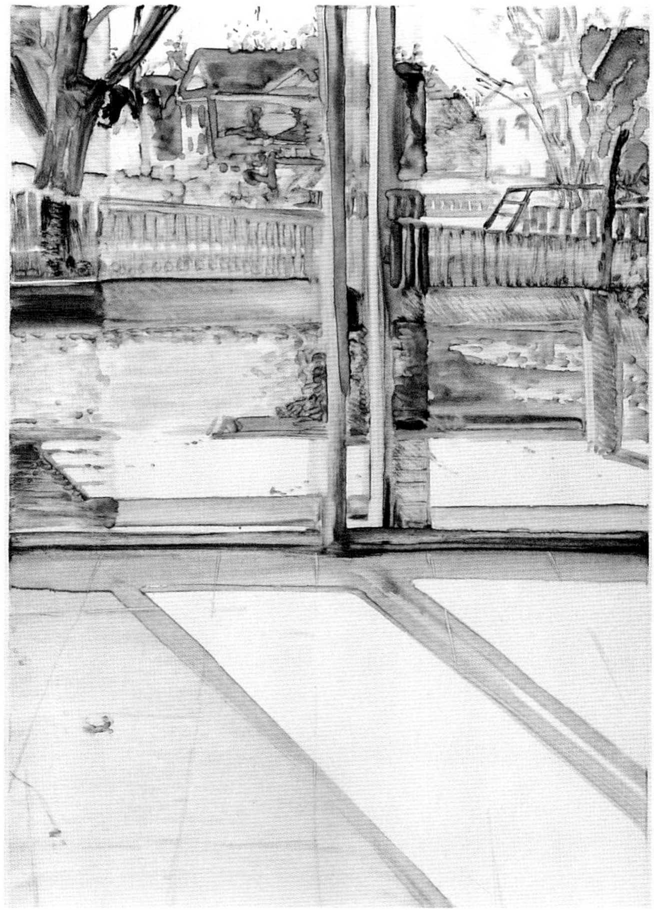

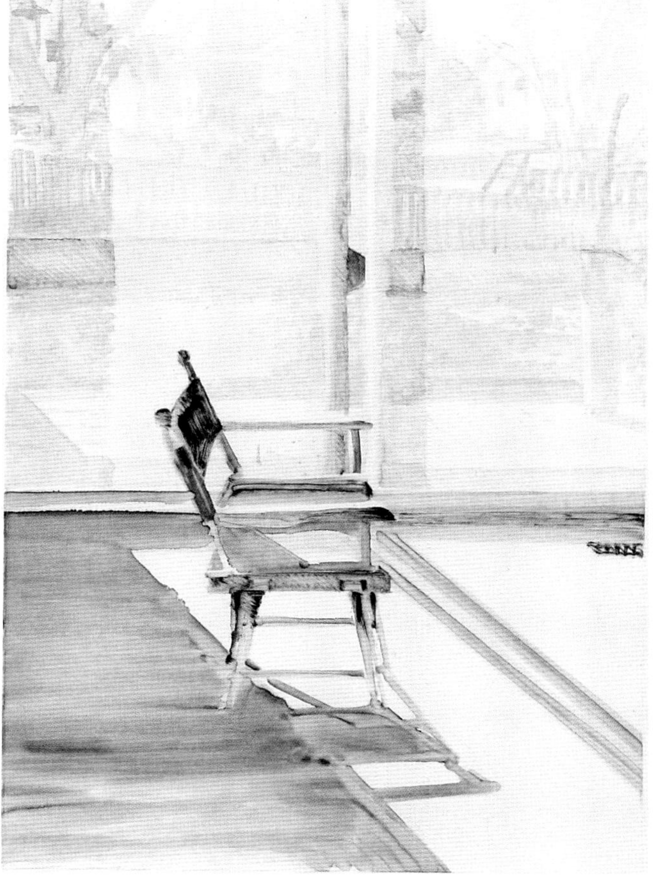

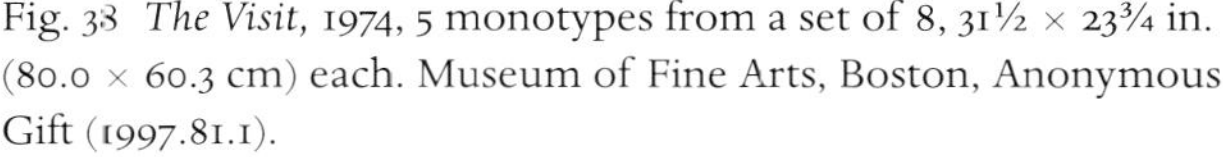

Fig. 38 *The Visit,* 1974, 5 monotypes from a set of 8, 31½ × 23¾ in. (80.0 × 60.3 cm) each. Museum of Fine Arts, Boston, Anonymous Gift (1997.81.1).

MM That was the mind-blowing aspect of the Degas show for me, that he could extend the life of the cognates or ghosts by adding a little material to them. No one else in the history of monotype had done that. Well, I take that back. The first two examples I show in my lecture on the history of monotype are the pair of Castiglione prints, *David with the Head of Goliath* [figs. 33 and 34]. In the second cognate ghost image, the head of Goliath is actually reworked by Castiglione, and so you've this ghosted David, very light and delicate, and this blacker, more intense head, which is thrust into the foreground by the change in tonality. That probably was one of the earliest examples of the use of narrative in monotype. My long series called *The Visit* [fig. 38], which the Museum of Fine Arts now owns — it's eight sheets — was an all-day narrative of what was going on in the studio, as if you had put a camera in there and let it run — in the Warholian sense — for eight hours.

CA *I was wondering about the relationship between trying things out in monotype and how that has or has not fed into your painting.*

MM When I got out of art school, the attempt to somehow connect printmaking and painting and the question as to what kind of painting I wanted to do was a real conundrum. I had a hard time with it and actually did not paint seriously for ten years after I got out of art school. So I found my home in the print during that time when I didn't feel at home with painting. Around 1971, when I began painting, I started with a kind of back-to-basics idea that I would paint directly from nature. My first paintings were studio views — doors, windows, tables, chairs, anything that was around the studio — small panel paintings, some of which still look very fresh to me but which I've never showed. The very first monotypes were also studio views, just like the paintings, even before the paintings: chairs, tables, still lifes.

As the monotypes began to loosen up and my confidence in the surface and the accidental grew, the paintings followed suit. Prior to the monotypes, prints always followed drawings for paintings in the sequence of things. There were very few prints that were without a source. The monotypes, on the other hand, created their own absolutely unique organic thing and didn't need a model. The paintings then began to follow the monotypes, until the paintings reached a point where they didn't need that kind of underpinning. It's only been in the last ten or fifteen years that I've felt at

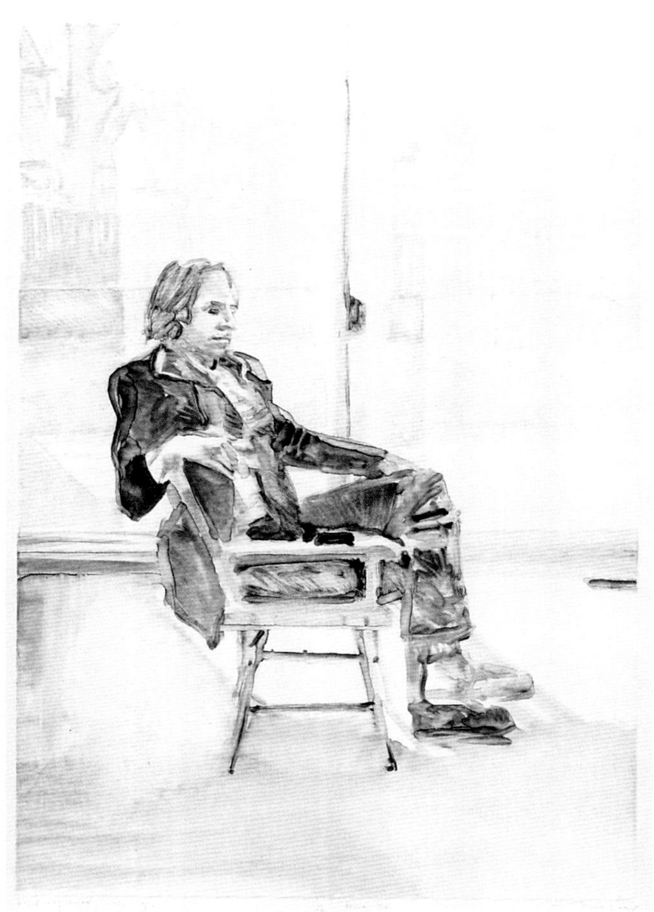

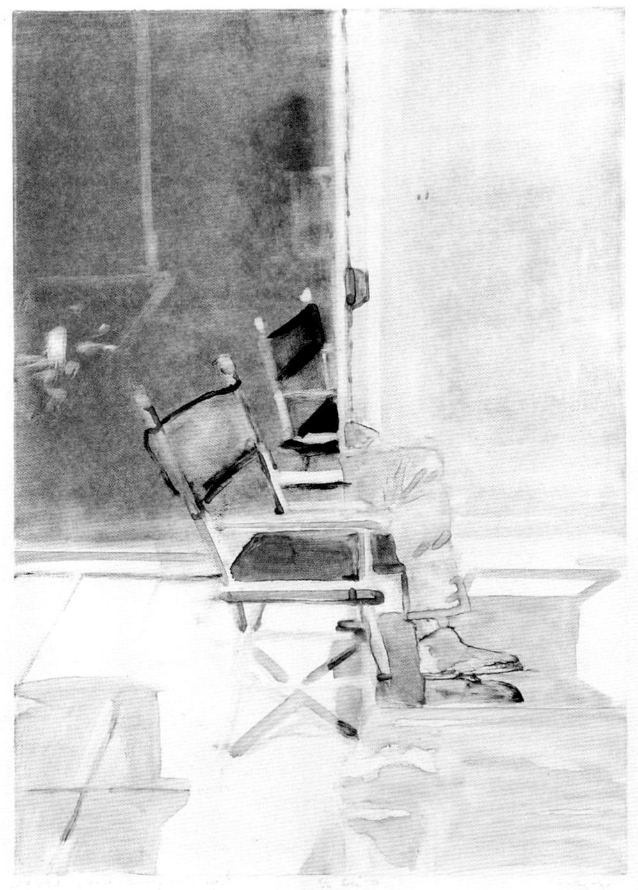

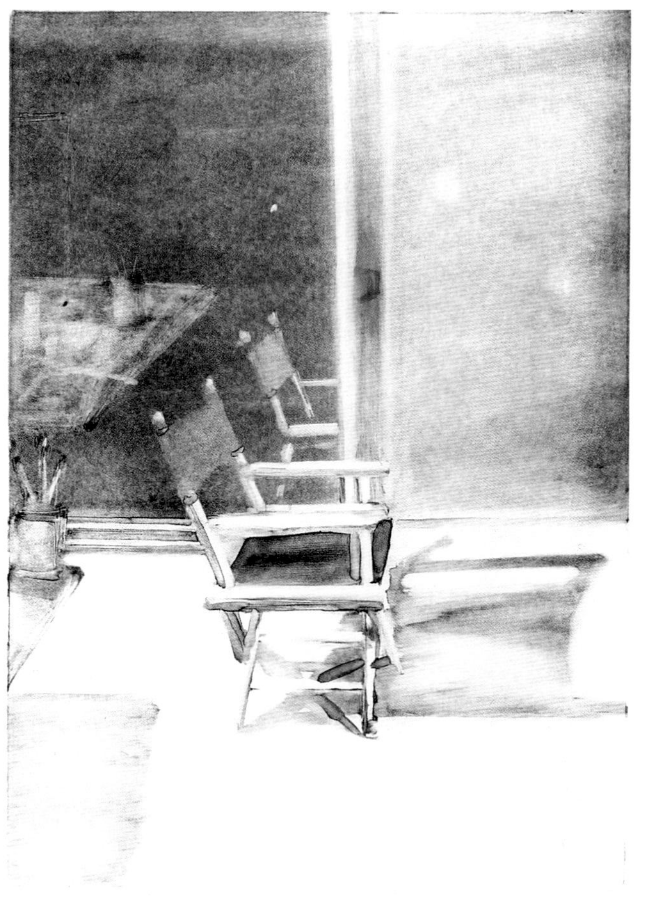

home enough with painting to achieve the painterly qualities that I wanted. Then there was consequently less production of monotypes. During the height of my production in monotype, I would make eight to ten prints a day for weeks at a time. Now, in the last year, I think, I've only made maybe thirty or forty monotypes and an equal number or more of paintings. So the monoprint, and actually the editioned print — the type of relatively complex editioned print that I'm making now — is a return to a different balance between printmaking and painting and no longer needs the monotype as a transition between them.

CA *I'd like to hear more about narrative and storytelling in your monotypes.*

MM We talked a little bit about how the ghost makes for narrative possibilities. There are several kinds of narratives that have interested me. In the late sixties right through the middle of the seventies, I was very interested in perception: how I see the world — a series of events that get reexamined as the context around them changes. In the *New York Memory Sequence* [fig. 39] I'm talking about distance and time and moving from looking out a window — the window, for any artist, no matter how unselfconscious they

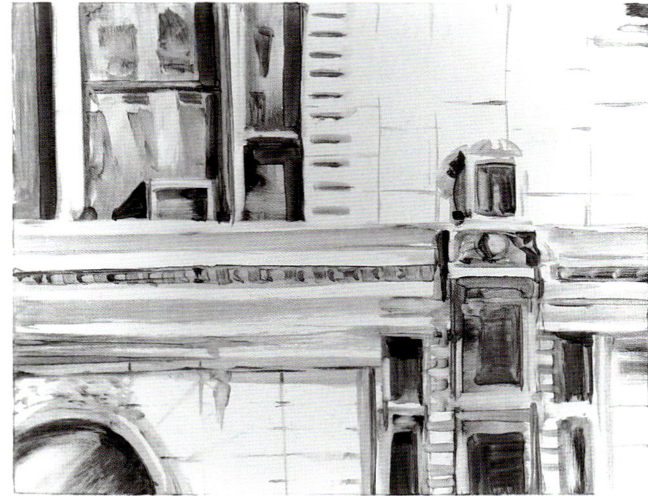

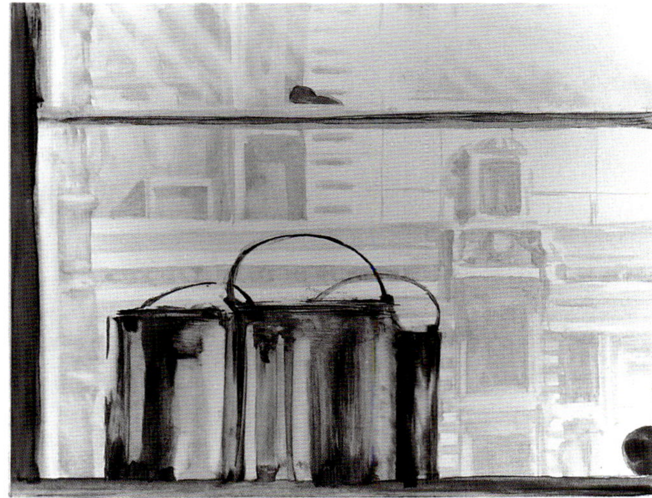

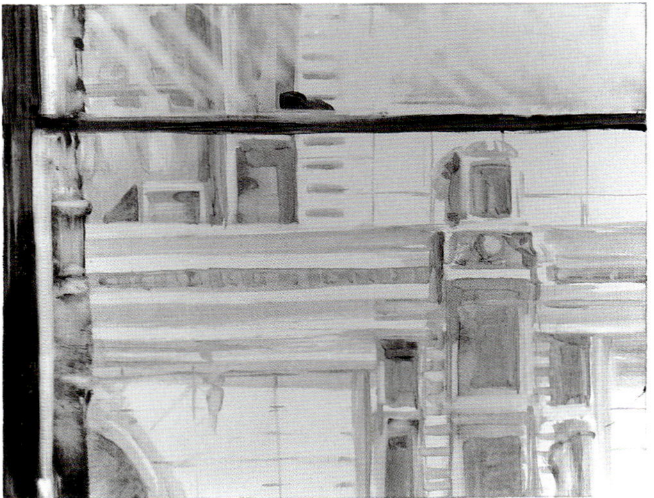

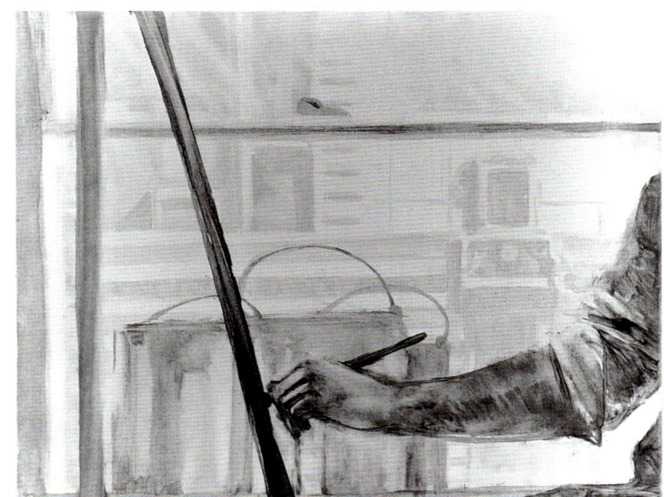

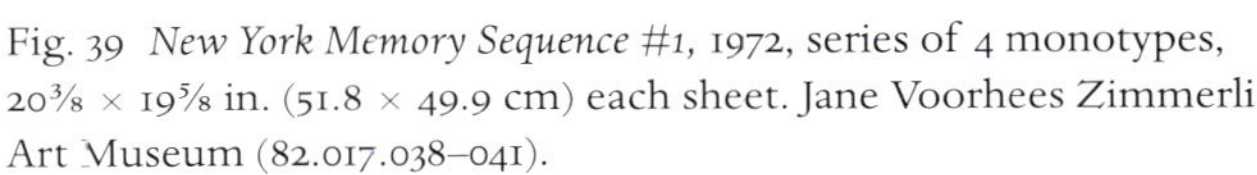

Fig. 39 *New York Memory Sequence #1*, 1972, series of 4 monotypes, 20⅜ × 19⅝ in. (51.8 × 49.9 cm) each sheet. Jane Voorhees Zimmerli Art Museum (82.017.038–041).

are, is a metaphor for looking at the world — and then I add a can of paint, which introduces the painter and the activity of the painter. The view out the window is not as sharply focused in the ghost image, and the added can of paint is sharper. The focus changes from the view itself to the medium that's going to translate that view, and then it finishes with the artist's hand and brush in the immediate foreground. So there's this passage of time between the first and last image, and it tells a very minimal story, but basically it deals with this issue of perception.

In *The Visit* I also started with a window image [fig. 38]. I enter the studio at eight in the morning. I'm affected by the light outside, the way the shadows form inside the studio and the view of my garden and backyard. So that becomes the first image, without any plan as to where it's going. And then a second image diffuses the quality of light in the view out the window. The next view is of a chair inside the studio. The window becomes less important and the chair more important, and it implies the presence of the artist or a sitter. This gets us to about eleven o'clock in the morning, and a visitor comes into the studio, unannounced, unexpected, and sits down in the chair, not knowing that the chair is part of a still life. So the visitor becomes part of this image, and I place the figure in the chair, as if the chair were waiting for something to happen. And then as the sequence develops, the visitor slowly disappears, the light outside changes to night, and you're left in conclusion with the empty chair and the artificial light of the studio. It's as if I made a rule, as conceptual artists do, that I'm going to start the image and that I'm going to continue it for a full day and take it wherever it wants to go. The monotype has this unique potential for being able to go on almost indefinitely as changes occur.

The *Window Sequence* started similarly. In this case it's not a window but a mirror. I wake up in the morning, and I see the reflection of a window in a standing mirror, which is

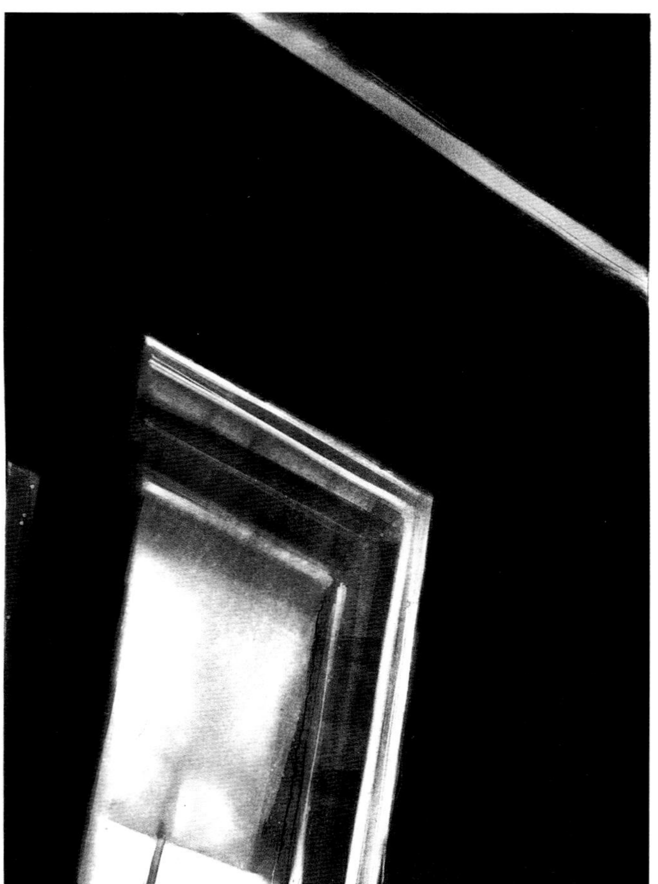
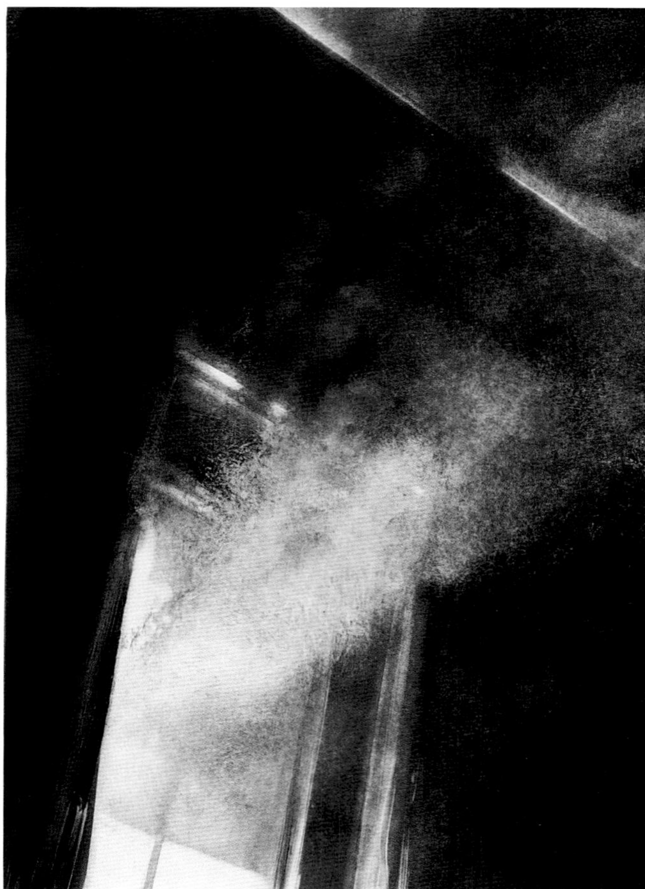

Fig. 40 *Window Sequence (Fire)*, 1974, monotype (diptych), 30¾ × 22¾ in. (78.1 × 57.8 cm) each. The Metropolitan Museum of Art, New York, John B. Turner Fund (1978.664.1–2).

slightly angled, and it interests me as an image. I had not planned to do it. I walk into the studio, and I start to make that image. Again, the advantage of monotype is that I'm not walking into the studio to complete the work of the day before. As a printmaker, my habit would have been to walk into the studio, pick up the plate that had been started weeks or days earlier, and continue to work on it, looking at the proofs and so forth. The monotype gave me the freedom of the empty plate that could be the vessel for whatever had happened five or ten minutes earlier. So it emerges, and it's white on black, and there's a strange light inside the window, which seems to have a life of its own. So the next image that I work with is a quick take on what that light is, and I decide that it's a fire, and it comes out of my own experience of having my studio in Cambridge on fire and going at three in the morning and seeing the window lit somewhat like that. So the second image becomes smoke coming out of that window. And then I actually did a third image in which fish are moving through what no longer looks like smoke but like bubbles. The *Aquarium* series [figs. 1 and 2] was done about the same time, and just for the fun of it I threw in these swimming fish, a very surreal idea. It didn't work. So the third image gets trashed, and so I stick with the diptych that's now called *Window Sequence (Fire)* [fig. 40].

In *The Chase* [fig. 41], which comes out of the series of paintings of the late seventies known as *Incident at Walden Pond* [fig. 77], I had done the image in different media — pastel, oil. I used the triptych format in a narrative way. A running man at the center is being chased by other men at the left, and on the right another figure is pointing toward the running man — a self-portrait, the artist himself as witness inside the image pointing at the running person — and underneath him the body of someone who has presumably been assaulted. So the sequences developed into a multiple format.

With many of the flower images, I used a diptych format in which I printed the first image, usually a dark field monotype, and then included the second ghost image alongside it. I believe that it grew directly out of a collaboration at the time with Mary Frank in which we were interested in combining sequences, and she made a remarkable print of three cognates shown together, so that they created at once a narrative in time and space and a record of the process. We would combine the first printings and second printings to make a sequence that was really a narrative about process itself. I think this also came out of the roller monotypes — the roller series was often sequenced. There was one major roller series in which the roller fades out and

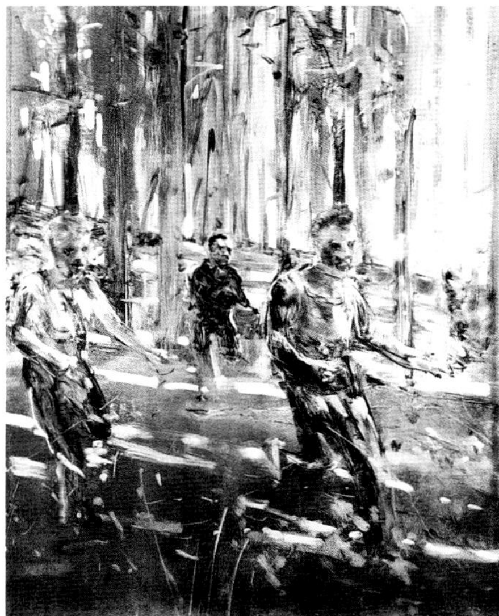
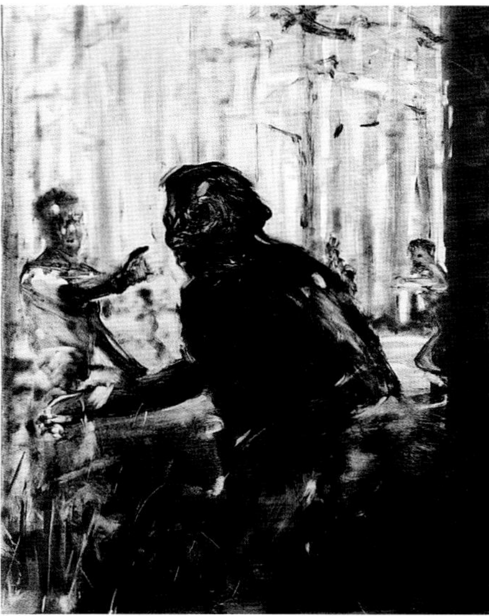
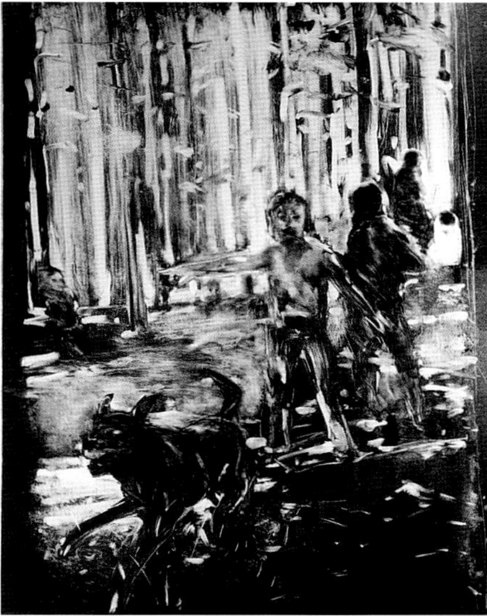

Fig. 21 *The Chase II,* 1979–80, monotype (triptych), 38⅛ × 29⅝ in. (96.9 × 75.3 cm) each. Jane Voorhees Zimmerli Art Museum, Gift of Arthur and Carol Goldberg (84.43.6.1–3).

then you have brushes. So I think that the sequences have a lot to do with my way of looking at the world and with the way the world changed as I looked at it and as the work represented it.

CA *It strikes me that the flower and tree images are unusually appropriate to the organic fluidity of the monotype.*

MM I've always been, as you know, interested in natural forms — flowers, trees, landscape material of one sort or another. I think it was something deeper and more important for me, having been a New York kid who grew up with relatively little nature, except in Central Park. It was a clarification of my own personality when I moved away from that into a suburban or country setting. However this came about — maybe through experiencing nature in summer camps as a kid — it was definitely a reaction against the city. Some people really love urban life and can't stand nature. You could say about the twentieth century that it substituted the city for the country, in art and in every other way.

CA *Some of your best work comes out of nature, obviously, particularly much of the tree imagery.*

MM The monotypes of the flowers allow me to work not just with natural images but with arm and hand gestures that are freer and more spontaneous. The figure also allows that kind of gestural imagery, but one is freer with natural forms because they still have anonymity compared to the figure. If you did those things to the figure it would inevitably be seen as a kind of expressionist statement. The flower is often an excuse for gestural images, and many of the calla lily images are in fact called *Gestures.* They allowed me to experiment with something that's more or less peculiar to the way I make monotypes, which is to draw with turpentine or with a very loose oil and turpentine mix. I allow the turpentine to dissolve the ink, the black ink covering the metal plate, and then I pick that dissolved or loosened material up with a roller. I want to see what happens if I pick that gesture up and lay it down on another plate or move it around on the same plate. The roller picks up these arclike gestures — made with a hand governed by elbow, not by wrist. The roller picks them up and puts them down elsewhere, and the kind of profusion that floral or natural growth seems to imply is maintained without the connotation of distortion. It allows me to focus on an aspect of nature — its density and its profusion.

CA *The scale change in the MIT mural commission encouraged you to explore a greater gestural freedom. How did this come about?*

MM The *Wakeby* prints [colorplates 18, 26, and 27] were the result of Kathy Halbreich, then director of exhibitions at MIT, commissioning me to do a mural for a particular interior space in an MIT dormitory at 500 Memorial Drive, an Alvar Aalto – like interior with a large curved wall. This was the spring of 1982, and she didn't dictate the medium. At the time I was interested in expanding monotype to a more monumental scale, and so I decided that I would do a large work in monotype for this room. A press was available that had belonged to George Lockwood's studio, and it had the potential to be expanded in size. Bob Townsend, who was then working at the Impressions Stanhope Street studio, and I devised a way to make it one of the largest presses in the country by doubling its size. So we had a press that could print a 67-by-100-inch image. Bob and I had begun working together earlier, but this project was still early in our collaborative history, which has continued over the last fifteen or so years. The subject matter that I chose was the summer experience of the landscape around Wakeby Lake, which is in the Sandwich-Mashpee area of Cape Cod. My wife's family had had a second house there since the forties, and Gail and I had spent a great deal of time there. The lake has three islands. We were high up over those islands, and we had a flower garden, and my perception of the lake changed with the passage of day and night. I wanted to play with this narrative that was about time and light, and also about the process of monotype, working light into dark and dark on top of light.

With this raw material in place, the scale and the subject matter, I started a series of small monotypes in order to work myself up to the process of making a large one. The problem of making a large monotype does not involve simply the size of the press — that's a relatively easy thing to solve if you have the machinery — but it involves the amount of time that it takes to make a print that big. It has to be made all in one shot. So you're dealing with a "run" — what abstract painters used to call the time in which they kept a painting going until they could finish it — the length of time of the run and the way in which the paint or ink would dry. I started with small images to practice, to rehearse, because I knew that doing these large monotypes would be an almost athletic event. It would have a quality of performance because it all had to be done at once. And because it had to be done all at once, the various aspects of the print had to be memorized, so that you moved through a sequence of steps like a dancer. So I practiced on smaller ones and finally on a few full-scale images, parts or fragments of them. The full scale would be three plates, each six by four feet. Each plate would take approximately two hours or more to complete, so that all three plates would involve a six-hour run, and if you also worked with the cognate it would be a twelve-hour run. The idea was to use a night image with a day inset.

Working all of that out meant separate studies for the flowers. I had large sunflowers that were like figure stand-ins, witnesses to the landscape — trees balancing them, and then this view of the lake, the water, the night sky. Each image was rehearsed. The print called *Night Cyclamen* [colorplate 16] had been done a year earlier and was the key to figuring out how to do these nocturnal images. I was working in the studio one day and I had an image in blue ink, and I had an imperfect roller that I had asked Gaby [Gabor] Peterdi for, which had lots of pockmarks in it, and I wanted to experiment with the roller. I had done a small image of the cyclamen, which was okay, but it wasn't that interesting, and I thought, what will this roller do if it's rolled up in black and simply rolled over the whole plate? I had some instinct about what might happen in terms of the viscosities, but the roller created this image that was so luminous and so surprising that I didn't quite know what to do with it at the time, and I put it away. A year later, when I began the studies for the new image, I remembered this print and used the same process.

The first day of working in full size, everything went perfectly. I had memorized the sequence, I knew what I wanted, I went bit by bit. Bob handled his end of it beautifully, being experienced in handling large sheets of paper. The only problem was that it wasn't the print that I finally wanted, even though both prints, the night and the day, had really interesting qualities. I found that I could work for eleven hours or so sustained, but the first run wasn't satisfactory so I went into a second version, and indeed into two more versions before the final image was made. It was approximately three to four sessions of making these prints and the cognates. It was a thrilling experience — one that I don't think I could physically cope with again — and it proved that you could push the monotype up to a significant scale without losing the qualities — even a certain kind of intimacy — that make the monotype so beautiful.

CA *You've worked with monotype in other ways — trace monotype, printing on silk charmeuse, woodcut monotype.*

MM I think I'm a natural experimenter. In the case of the silks, we have already talked a bit about the fascination that Seghers had with the idea of making printed paintings. It was also the interest I had in increasing the scale and complexity of the image and making it hold the wall as a painting would. But the problem of course was that they always had to be behind glass and you lose that direct relationship to the surface that you have in a painting. I saw some prints on silk that my friend David True had done with a printer in New York for Crown Point Press in San Francisco. They were aquatints that he had printed on silk. I called the printer, because I had come back from China and was interested in doing something with screens and didn't want any glass involved. He said, "Never print on silk, it's the hardest thing to do, it's tedious, takes eight people to hold the silk down so it won't bunch up," etc. He thought he was putting me off, but instead he was challenging me to come up with a solution. Between myself and a printer at the Experimental Workshop in San Francisco, Will Foo, we came up with a system of prestretching the silk so that it would come out of the press as a finished piece without having to be dried [colorplate 28]. It could simply go right on the wall. I enjoyed the idea of being able to put together constellations of stretched silk forms so that I could build a larger piece out of smaller sections that could be printed on my own press, therefore getting around the issue of having to have an outsize press. The charmeuse silk loves ink [colorplates 29 and 30]. It's already a synthetic so it's made of oil and attracts oil beautifully, and it sometimes fools the eye into thinking you're looking at the plate rather than the print because it has that direct quality.

My friend Mary Frank would often let the monotype image stay on the plate, not print it, and simply frame the plate, because the quality of the image on the plate was so beautiful that she didn't want to lose it by printing on paper. Sometimes the ghost on the plate would be very seductive and beautiful, and you would want to just keep it because the light inside the metal plate, the aluminum plate, would be this kind of silver light that the material would be reacting to. And so I wanted to play with that with the silk, sometimes using satin surfaces that would reflect light. These were experiments and not everything worked, but for a period of time when I was still not quite sure of what I wanted to do next as a painter, these became a kind of substitute painting. Of course there is an established history of printed paintings. Andy Warhol was making his paintings with silkscreen. You could say of Warhol that he really did carry the Seghers idea to fruition by essentially printing his paintings and making multiples of those paintings. So the work on silk was part of a much larger picture of painters and printmakers blurring the boundaries between what is a print and what is a painting. One could also say that the monotype is a form of painting printed on paper.

The trace monotypes and the woodcuts come out of another kind of inventive need. I had gone down to Philadelphia in 1973 to see the Gauguin monotype [fig. 42] show that Richard Field had put together, and I took some students with me.[9] I was then teaching at Queens College in New York. I went down to Philly and saw this show, which for me was a bookend to the Degas show that Nia Parry [Eugenia Parry Janis] had done. In the mid-seventies I experimented with my first trace monotypes. They were the kind of thing that Paul Klee did: they were transfer drawings.

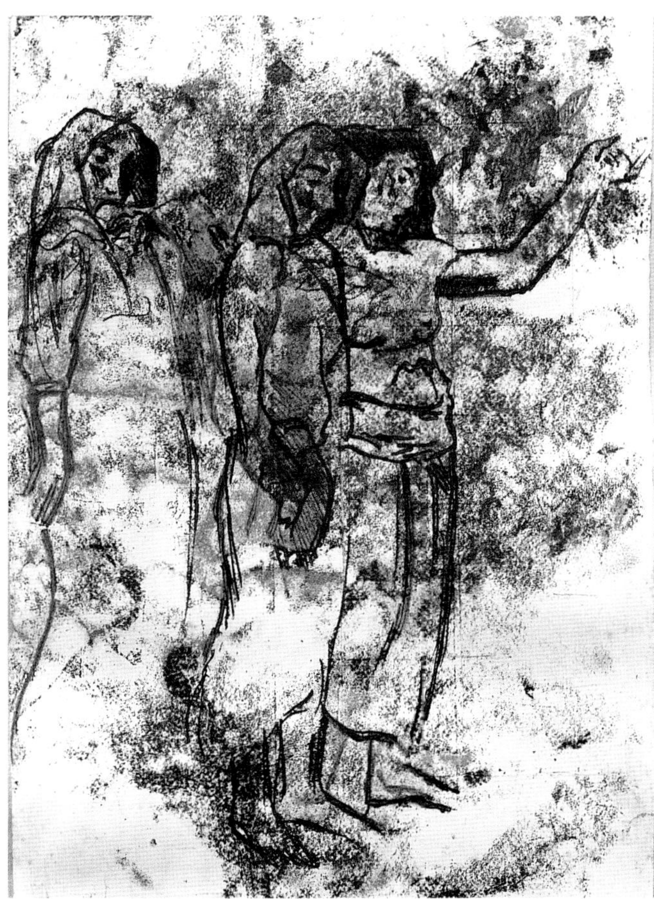

Fig. 42 Paul Gauguin (French, 1848–1903), *"Three Native Women" (Study for "The Call")*, ca. 1902–3, trace monotype, 17⅛ × 12 in. (43.5 × 30.5 cm). Museum of Fine Arts, Boston, Otis Norcross Fund (56.106).

CA *What was involved in this process?*

MM It's the simplest of all the monoprint media. You have an ink plate that you roll up in black ink, and you place a thin piece of paper — the thinness is very important — such as a Japanese woodcut paper, on top of the black ink. You either draw directly onto the back of the paper, or take another drawing, which is what Gauguin did, and place it on top of the paper and trace it. The pressure of the pencil on the drawing creates an ink transfer onto the back of the paper. So you pick up the paper and you see the image. You can do it with finger pressure, you can do it with fingernails, you can do it by rubbing an object over it. It creates a surface that's very different from a drawn surface.

CA *Granular and randomly blotchy.*

MM Right. The pressure of your hand is the press that actually creates the impression. After I did the first group of them I realized that there was a ghost left on the black plate. For the ink transfers I imagine Klee used a piece of glass, but if you use a metal plate you can print the metal plate with its ghost. So I began, almost from the beginning, printing the ghost of the trace monotype. Then I began to work over the ghosts with more tracing and began to combine ink transfer with monotype so that you could get a line, which was the one thing that monotype couldn't do. Monotype, as I originally experimented with it, could not produce a delicate line. So by combining line and tone I made quite a few large-scale pieces. I did some tree pieces using the trace monotype and monotype combination.

The last category is the woodcut. These were the first kind of prints I made, on my own in Italy in 1958. I started independently with woodcut, and then working with Baskin created an opportunity for me to learn more about wood engraving and woodcut. I didn't work with woodcut again until the late eighties. I was interested in the possibility of relief printing in monotype and the combinations that could produce. In the *Texas Tree* series [figs. 43 and 44] there are some experiments in which the woodcut image is transferred to the metal plate during the process of printing.

So there are endless possibilities. Of course, in the end, you're only as good as the image is, and how the image is produced is not the most important thing. On the other hand, the way images come into being is very often the reason why images exist — so the process is inextricably connected with the product.

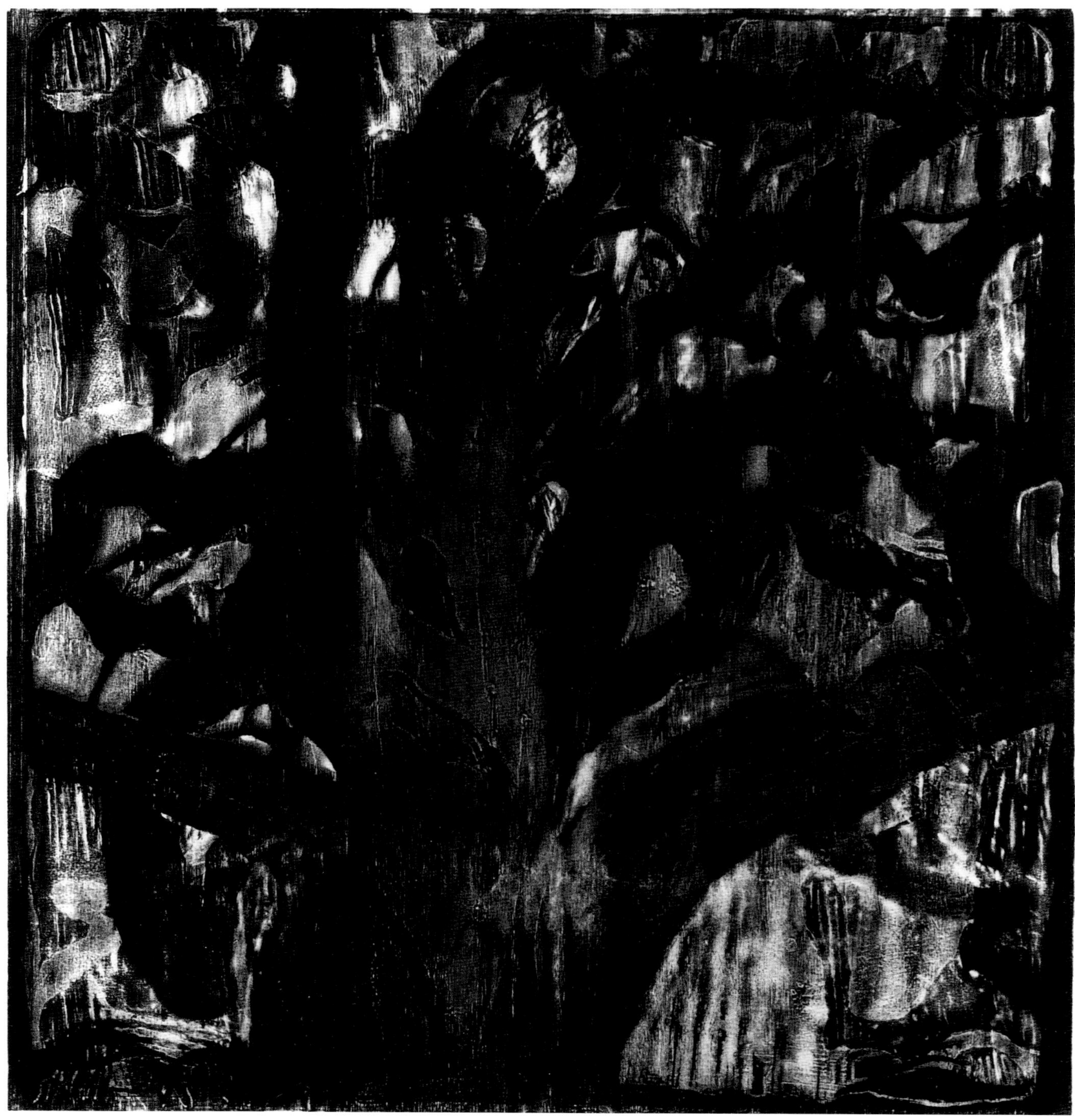

Fig. 43 *Texas Tree,* 1988, monoprint with transfer wood relief and metal plate offset, 35 × 31½ in. (88.9 × 80.0 cm). Collection of the artist. (Catalogue raisonné 261)

CA *It seems to be a very American idea in our time, the image emerging in the process, whether it's Abstract Expressionist painting or the movie* Apocalypse Now.

MM Maybe because we don't think as well as we make. The fact is that printmaking has always been bound up with process, and it was often a process that was meant to replicate more spontaneous media. It's interesting that when aquatint was developed in order to mimic brush and wash drawings, it also immediately became a process in which someone like Goya could create a completely new body of work.

CA *A new visual vocabulary.*

MM A new visual vocabulary that didn't even particularly relate to wash drawing after it was made because it had such different qualities.

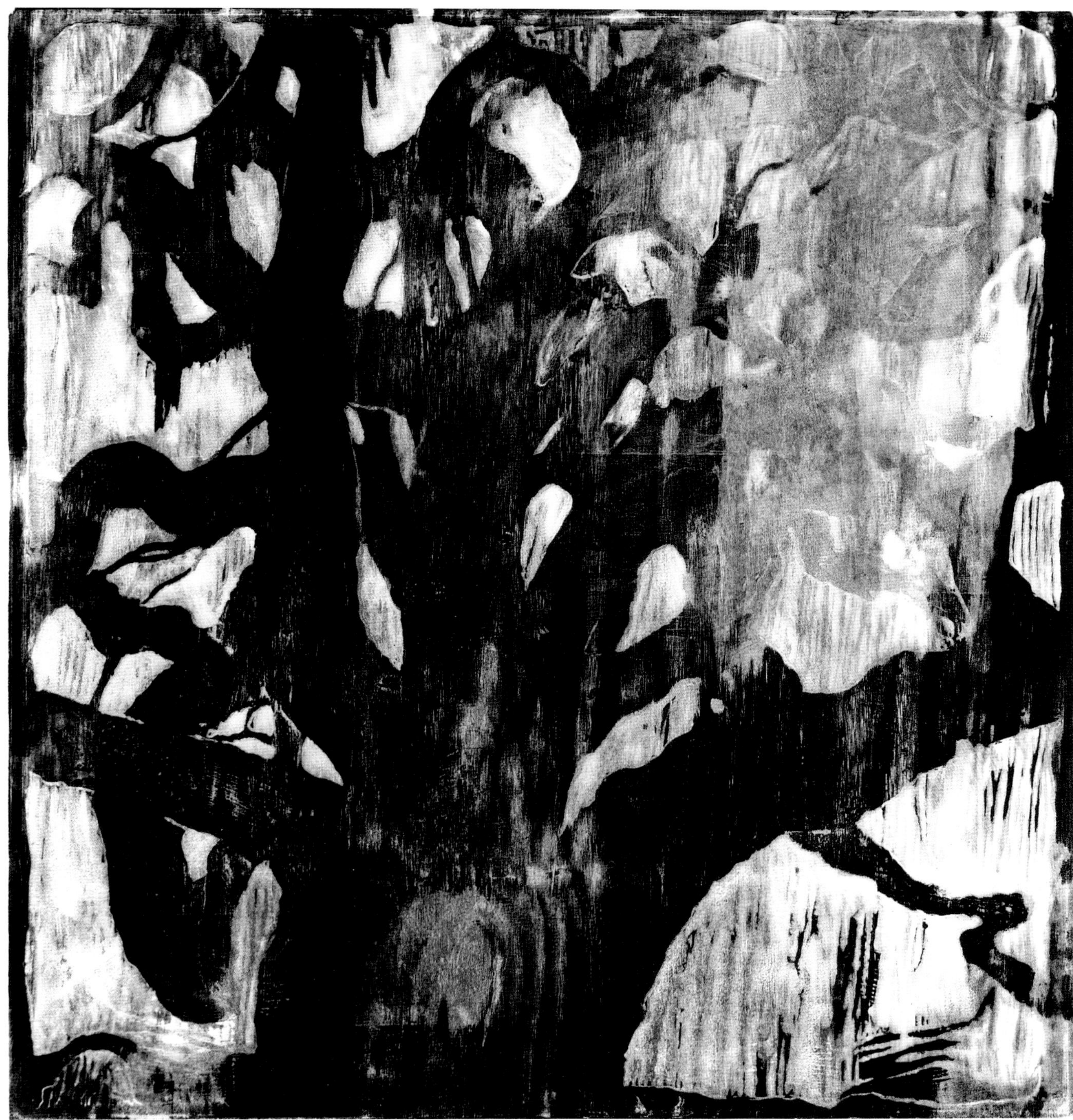

Fig. 44 *Texas Tree,* 1988, monoprint with transfer wood relief and metal plate offset, 35 × 31½ in. (88.9 × 80.0 cm). Collection of the artist. (Catalogue raisonné 261)

CA *Could you talk about the last six years of work, the* Branching *series and the* Mind Landscapes?

MM When I was in art school in the fifties and sixties there was this sort of war between figuration and abstraction. It was an argument that in a way had been solved many, many decades earlier with the clear transition from figuration into abstraction that you see in the work of Piet Mondrian or Arthur Dove.

CA *In the second half of the twentieth century we have a figure such as Richard Diebenkorn who flips back and forth between what we call abstraction and what we call figuration.*

MM I think the line between abstraction and figuration is completely destroyed. The war is over. An artist can choose abstraction as a medium just as he can switch from watercolor to oil. There's no reason why he has to be labeled as one thing or another. Another aspect of the late work is that I recognized — as part of a heart problem that I was experiencing — that the paintings of a realist or a figurative nature I was doing seemed to be bogging down. I didn't seem to have as much reason for doing them as I had had in the past. I was getting to a point where the paintings had reached a real low in terms of their creative energy, just as I was reaching a real low in physical energy, not able to walk up a hill without gasping for breath. Finally I developed an unstable angina situation that ultimately led to the angioplasty procedure. In the process of going through that I saw images of the heart or of the body that were like landscape images. Another factor was the realization that the kind of gesture that I was using with the flowers or the tree images could loosen up and have its own qualities as invented or imagined landscape.

CA *The encounter with Chinese painting and calligraphy was important too.*

MM Calligraphy and Chinese painting and the trip to China — all of these things connected at one point around 1992, and they changed the work. The work began to develop first into the *Branching* series [colorplates 32, 33, and 34], which was simply about letting the gestures move along the page, as a tree limb would move, invented calligraphy with a kind of life of its own that would lead me on a trip that I couldn't predict any more than I could predict those early sequential monotypes. It was almost as if I had started to teach myself to paint from scratch again, and the major change that occurred mentally was that I relaxed a great deal, that the paintings became full of promise rather than a chore — and full of surprise, like the monotypes. Teaching myself how to paint in a different kind of way opened up new territory for me. It may not be new territory for other artists, but it was for me.

The Chinese images developed after years of attempting to somehow find my way through this Chinese garden imagery that so intrigued me and made me want to go to China. When I saw a detail of a scroll painting by Chao Meng-fu [1280–1368], a Yüan dynasty painter, there was a connection with my own work that led to a group of pieces based on deconstructing and reconstructing his images and making them my own, just as he might have done with the work of a predecessor in China. Even some of the earlier imagery, like the islands from *Wakeby,* came back in the new work, reasserting themselves as the kinds of spaces I was working with. So rather than being about "abstraction," this new material [colorplates 38 and 39] refers back to earlier work.

CA *While you were talking, I realized that there's a layering in these paintings that comes out of the monotypes.*

MM Right, repositioning and allowing things to happen, and ghosts and spaces — all of that material finds its way into the paintings. Even though they look different, and they're somewhat — I suppose you could use the word shocking — to those people who want to see my work in terms of figuration, they are to me very natural and explicable extensions of the work I've done before.

CA *In addition to your own extensive contribution to the recent history of monotype, you've also gotten involved in encouraging other artists to make monotypes and monoprints through the New Provincetown Print Project.*[10]

MM It was a convenient way to combine raising some money for the Fine Arts Work Center, where I'm an active participant on the board, with working with other artists, which I really enjoy. The Provincetown project started as a suggestion that Bob Townsend and I would work with a third artist who would create over a short period of time — a week, two weeks — a small body of work that they could keep part of and that we could keep part of to raise money. The three of us would work together, as a kind of team. The idea was to bring in artists who had not made monotypes and who interested me and Bob as artists. Over a period of five years we worked with about twenty-five artists, very different kinds of artists, from Expressionists like George McNeil to Minimalists like Fred Sandback. We didn't hold to any particular school. The challenge to someone like Fred of having to make a single unique image and then to vary it was a big one for artists who were not used to thinking in those terms. George McNeil, who had never made a monotype before, had been making prints, lithographs, for years, and felt so freed up by monotypes. To see him working on a print as he would work on a painting — which he didn't know he could do — was wonderful. He was in his eighties when we worked with him, but he was a natural. It was great fun. I'd often share techniques that I had developed with the artists [colorplates 35 and 36].

CA *"Why don't you try this?"*

MM "Why don't you try this, let me show you how to do this." My way of working with the artists was to say: Well, it's your imagery, but you might be interested in using this technique to develop that imagery. In the case of John Walker, I initially stayed out of his way because he had made many monotypes but in very different ways. However, I had an idea for something that might intrigue him. At the end of the first week he said: "Well, Mike, show me your magic." And so we made an image in which he made the gestures, and then I lifted them with the roller and I showed him how he could develop that kind of thing. He was very excited and worked the following days almost entirely with that process.

Since then I've worked with lots of other artists. I do a kind of monotype marathon now. I did one last summer with thirty artists over two days in which we worked in groups of ten for three hours. It's a return to what you mentioned earlier, the monotype party, and you would be surprised how extraordinary some of the prints are. Many of the artists are looking forward to doing it again or have done more on their own. I'm not doing this with the idea of becoming King Monotype. I have no interest in the proselytizing of monotype versus other media, because I'm equally interested in all media. I remember there was an artist early on — when there were only five or six of us in this country working seriously with this medium — who said to me "Why are you telling everyone your secrets?" As if this was a Cold War undercover activity. And I replied that if you tell someone how to do something, it just means that they have another tool. We share brushes, we share rags, we share rollers — that doesn't mean anybody's work looks like anybody else's. I think the spread of the monotype is simply due to the fact that this is an age — maybe a whole century — in which experimentation and freedom are the norm.

CA *The breaking down of barriers between media.*

MM The breaking down of barriers is perhaps the most typical cultural drive of our time. I don't know how it's going to look in the future, but it obviously has a kind of energy that will cause people to want to know who these crazy inventors were.

NOTES

1. See Joann Moser, *Singular Impressions: The Monotype in America,* exh. cat. (Washington, D.C.: Smithsonian Institution Press for the National Museum of American Art, 1997), 1.

2. Another seventeenth-century artist who made brush monotypes about the same time (or earlier?) was the Flemish artist Anthonis Sallaert (ca. 1590–1650). See Martin Royalton Kisch, "A Monotype by Sallaert," *Print Quarterly* 5, no. 1 (March 1988): 60–61.

3. For Castiglione and Rembrandt, see Sue Welsh Reed, "Monotypes in the Seventeenth and Eighteenth Centuries," pp. 3–8, and catalogue entries 1–15, in *The Painterly Print: Monotypes from the Seventeenth to the Twentieth Century,* exh. cat. (New York: Metropolitan Museum of Art, 1980). For Hercules Seghers, see Clifford Ackley, *Printmaking in the Age of Rembrandt,* exh. cat. (Boston: Museum of Fine Arts, 1981), 58–60.

4. The enthusiasm for monotypes in this country seems to have first peaked two decades ago, as evidenced by the November–December 1978 (vol. 9, no. 5) issue of the *Print Collector's Newsletter* specially devoted to the monotype. For contemporary monotypes and monoprints, see Clifford Ackley, *The Unique Print,* exh. cat. (Boston: Museum of Fine Arts, 1990).

5. See, for example, the group of earlier twentieth-century British monotypes published in Garton and Company, *British Printmakers, 1855–1955: A Century of Printmaking from the Etching Revival to St. Ives* (Aldershot, Great Britain: Scolar Press, 1992), 287–304.

6. Eugenia Parry Janis, *Degas Monotypes,* exh. cat. (Cambridge: Fogg Art Museum, Harvard University, 1968).

7. Michael Mazur, "Monotype: An Artist's View," in *The Painterly Print,* 54–62.

8. The interview took place on 15 May 1998 at the artist's home in Cambridge, Mass. I would like to thank Stephanie Stepanek for her help in preparation of the manuscript.

9. Richard Field, *Paul Gauguin: Monotypes,* exh. cat. (Philadelphia: Philadelphia Museum of Art, 1973).

10. The New Provincetown Print Project was initiated by Mazur in 1990 at the Fine Arts Work Center in Provincetown, Mass. The Fine Arts Work Center was founded in 1968 by writers, including the poets Stanley Kunitz and Alan Dugan; painters, including Robert Motherwell, Myron Stout, and Jack Tworkov; and the patron Hudson D. Walker. Its mission is to provide studio and living space annually for up to twenty emerging artists and writers. The FAWC acquired the Days Lumber Yard in 1972, a property that had been home to artists since the turn of the century, including Charles Hawthorne, Edwin Dickinson, Hans Hofmann, Motherwell, and Helen Frankenthaler. Mazur set up a print workshop there in 1990 and began inviting artists to collaborate on monotypes and monoprints with him and master printer Robert Townsend (see Chronology for listing of yearly collaborations). These collaborations led to the annual publication of a portfolio of monoprints. In 1995 Mazur brought an end to the program of collaborating with artists at the print shop and has instead each year since conducted a series of monotype workshops, or "marathons."

The Wakeby Monotypes: A Photo Diary

Michael Mazur

OVER a period of three weeks in January 1983, I printed six large-scale monotype triptychs and numerous smaller-scale monotypes comprising revisions and adjustments leading up to the printing of the final monumental pair, *Wakeby Day* and *Wakeby Night*. This photographic diary documents a representative day of printing with master printer Robert Townsend at the R. E. Townsend Studio in Georgetown, Massachusetts, captured in the photographs of Boston photographer Greg Heins.

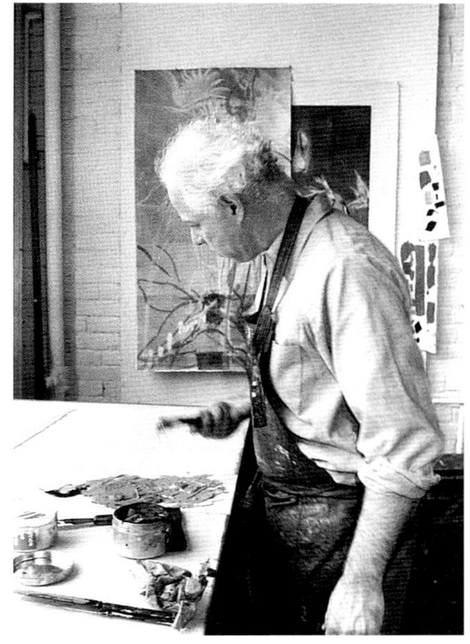

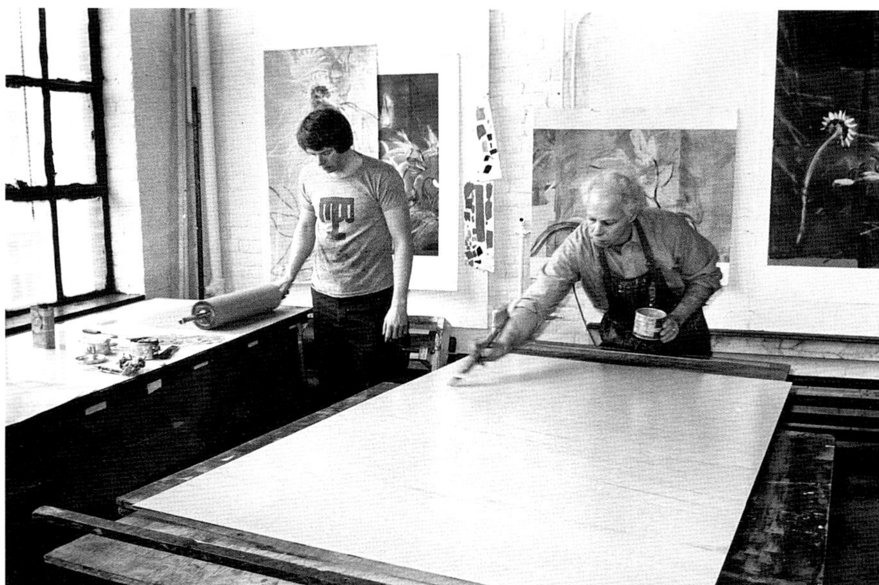

Above
Work on the 6-by-12-foot monotype triptych *Wakeby Day* begins at 9:00 A.M. with mixing two blue inks for the striated background color. "Draw downs," or color tests, are kept nearby so they can be matched for each plate.

Above right
After the light blue "flat" is rolled over the entire plate, lines are painted in a deeper but less viscous blue over the surface. On the wall behind us are studies and part of the first full-size triptych.

Right
Townsend and I work a large roller back and forth to pick up and displace thinner and deeper blues, creating watery striations.

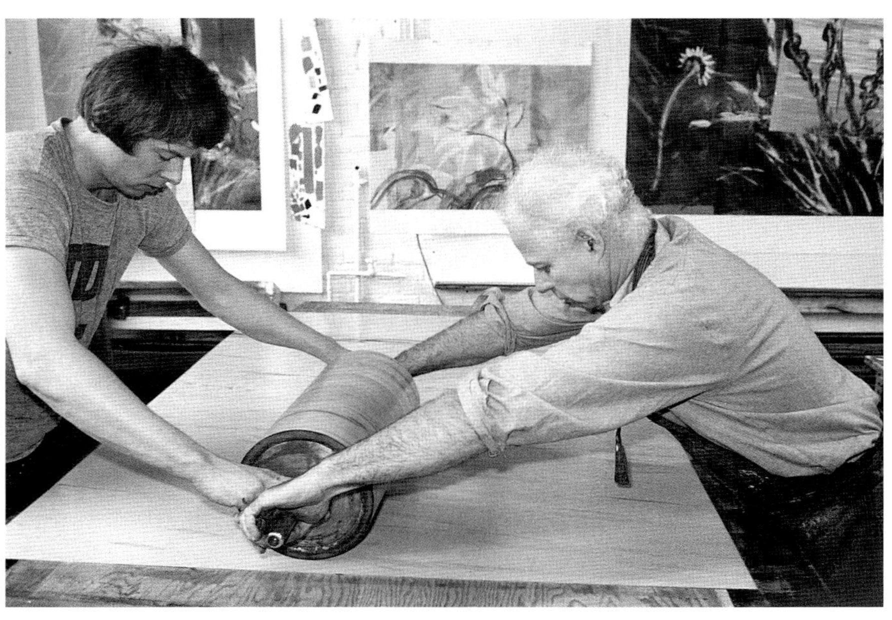

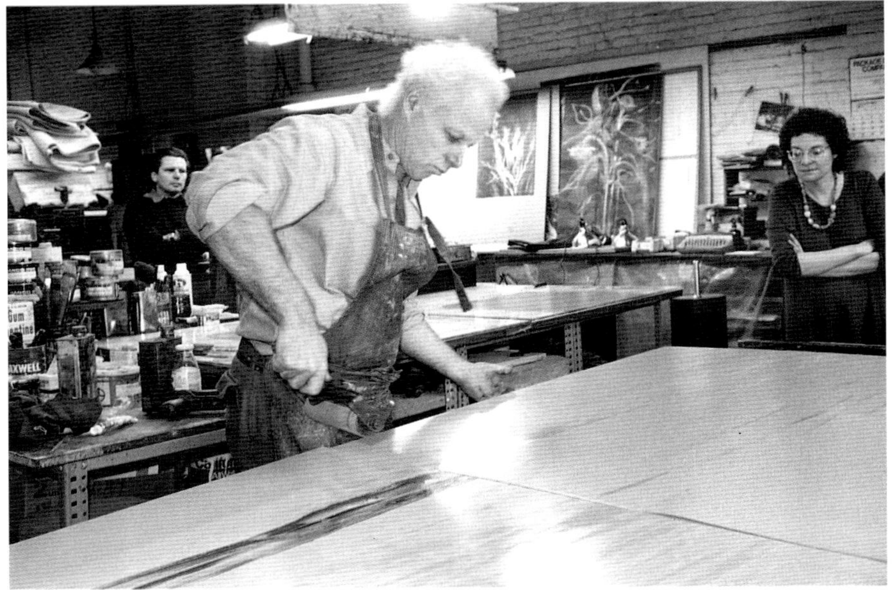

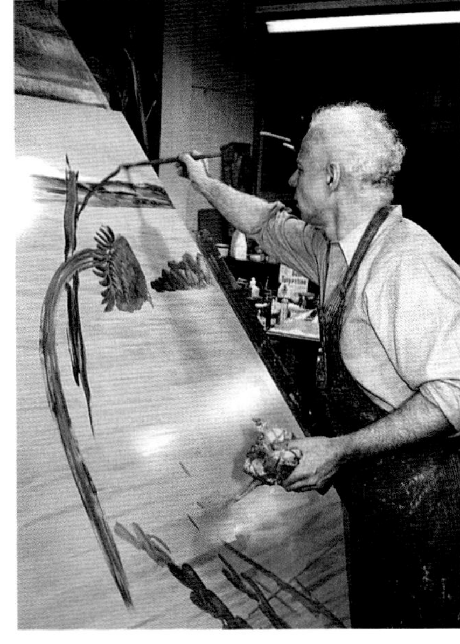

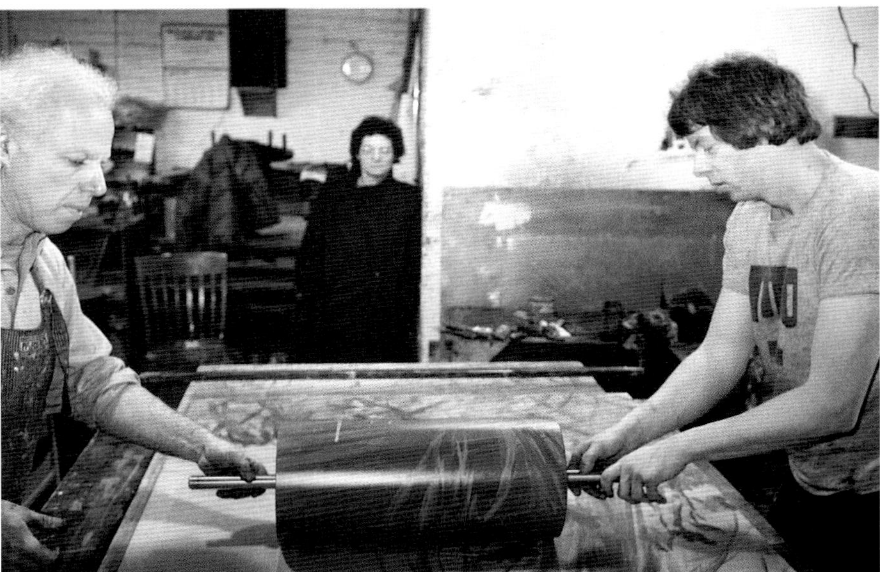

Above left
I then work with a small roller over the right and center plates, which are lined up for proper registration.

Above right
The right-side plate, which measures 72 by 48 inches, is lifted on a moveable tabletop into a vertical position for easel-height painting with brushes.

Left
When the painting reaches a certain point, Townsend and I use rollers to pick up, move, and offset parts of the painting (notice the offsetting that can be read on the roller surface).

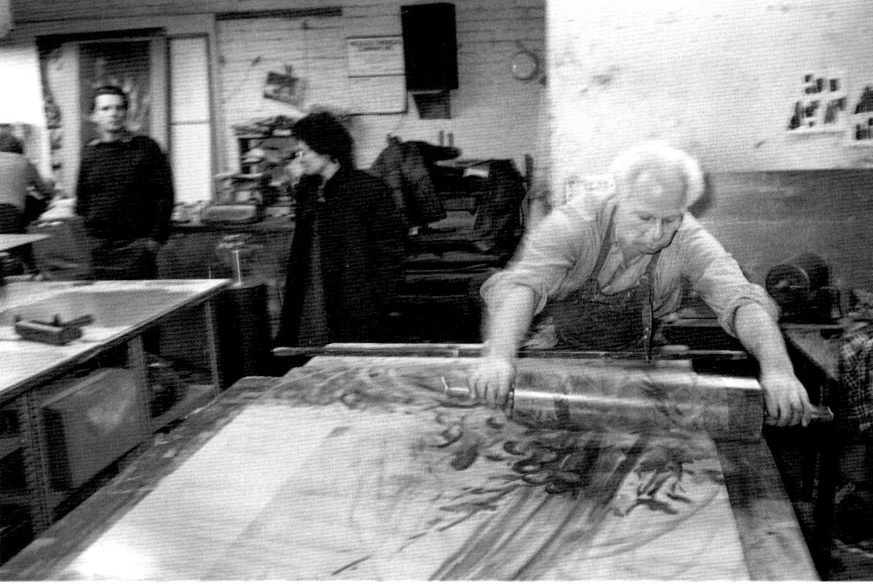

The roller is used as a tool with which to paint the image as well as lay out color.

Right
I begin work on the inset plate, a thin sheet of aluminum that will lie on the surface and be printed at the same time as the plate upon which it is placed. It will be worked separately from the large plates, but I will place it from time to time to see how it works with the rest of the image. In the print it will function as a palimpsest of the same area, seen at another time of day.

Far right
Again, the roller is used with inks of differing viscosities to add new colors to the inset plate.

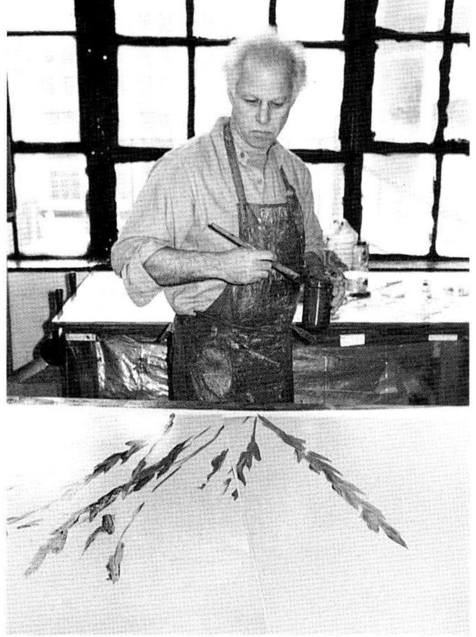

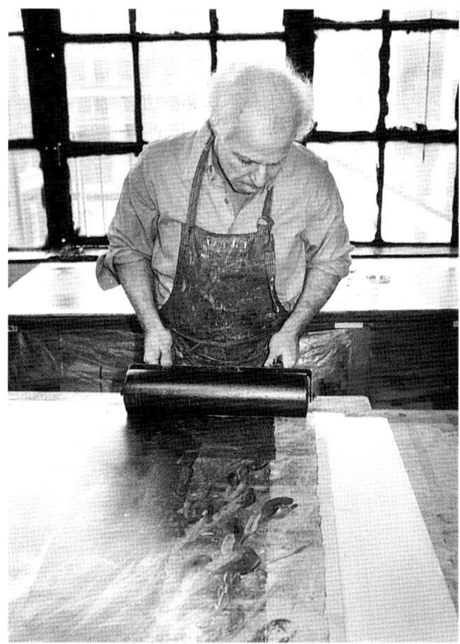

It is now noon. I have nearly completed working on the inset plate.

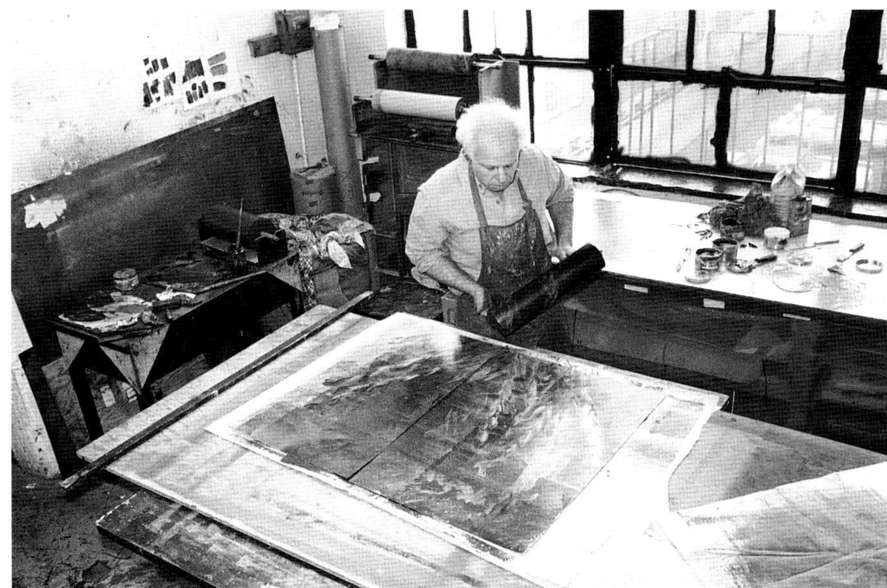

After lunch, I continue to work on both the plate and the inset plate, integrating them with small rollers, or brayers.

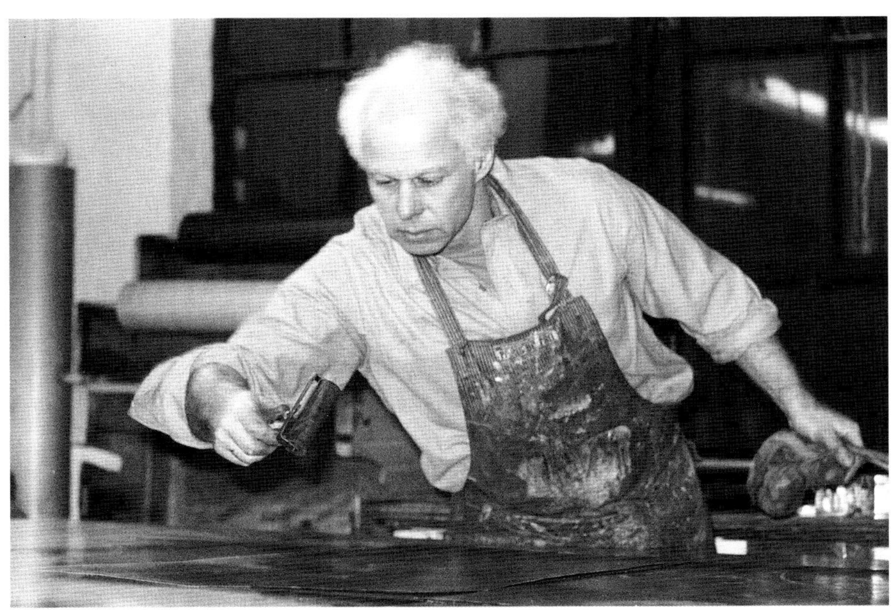

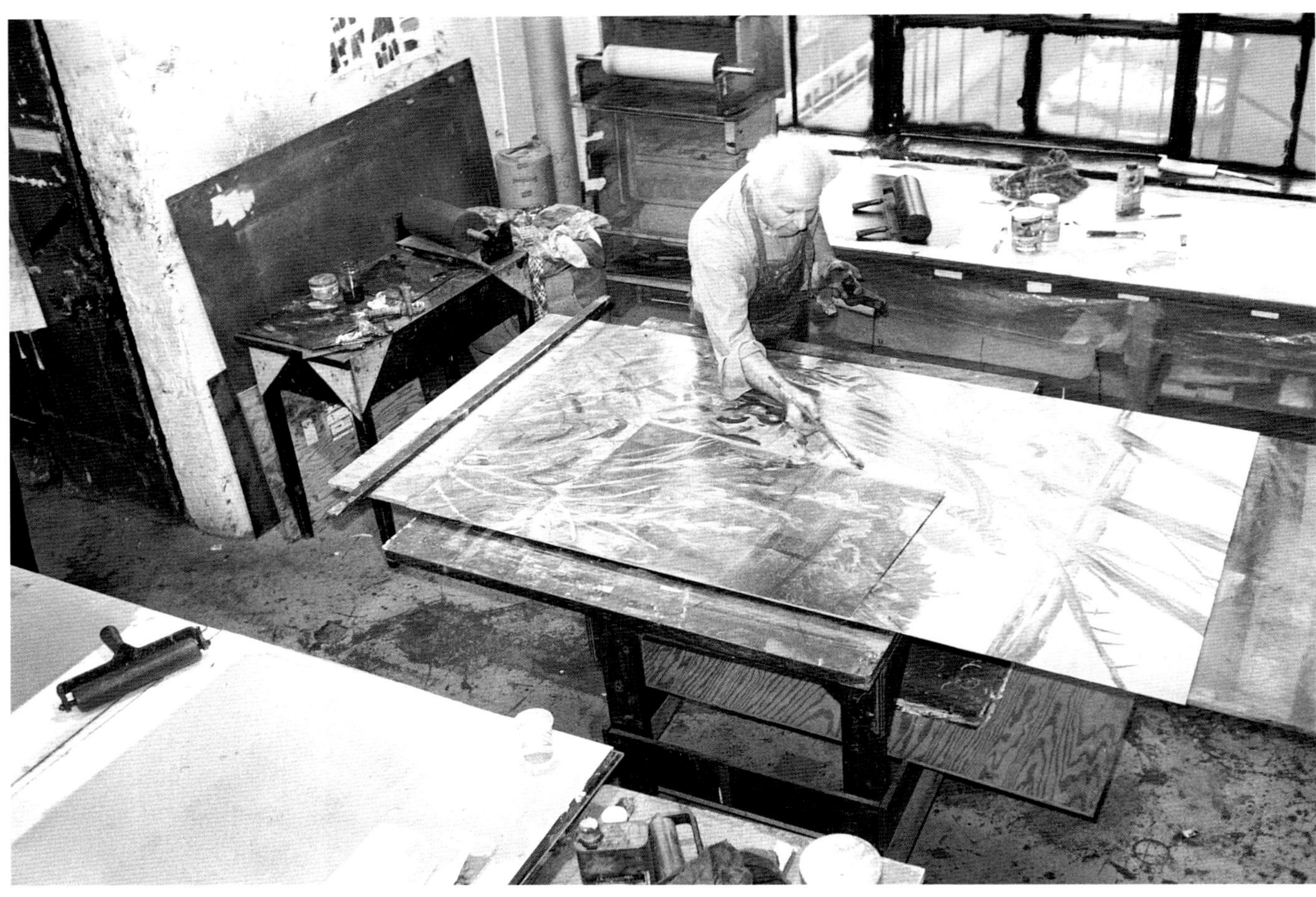

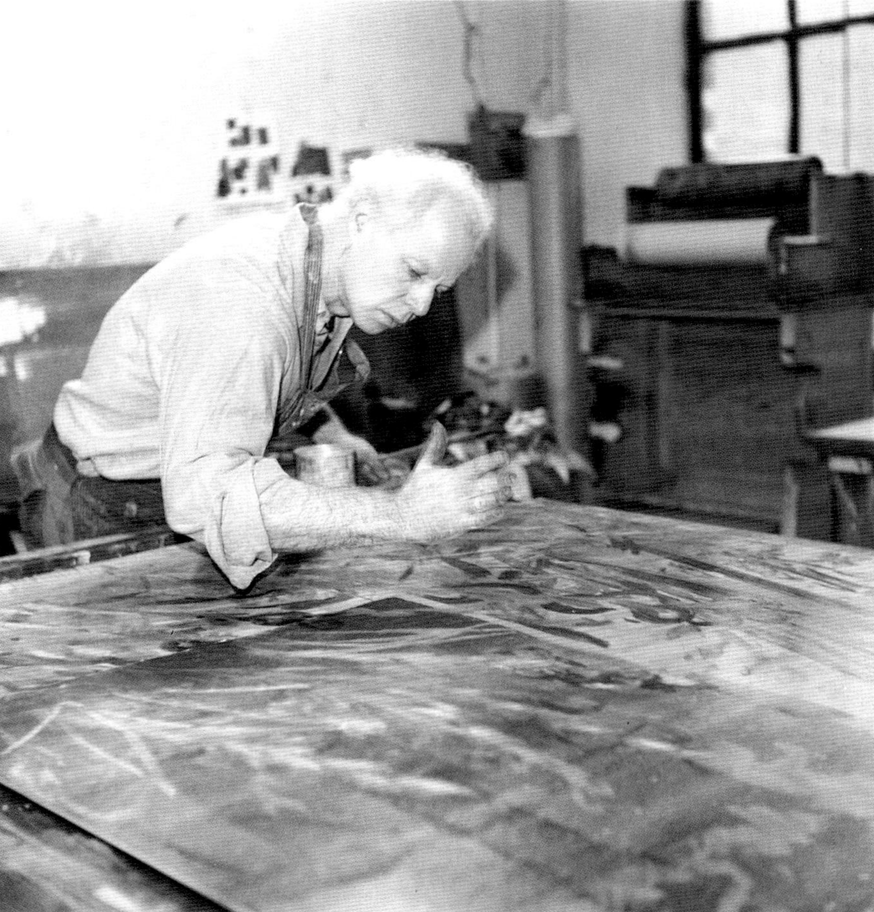

Above
I also use brushes.

Left
I use my hand.

After Townsend and I move the plate onto the bed of the press, we reposition the inset plate, which has been divided to span the center and right plates of the triptych.

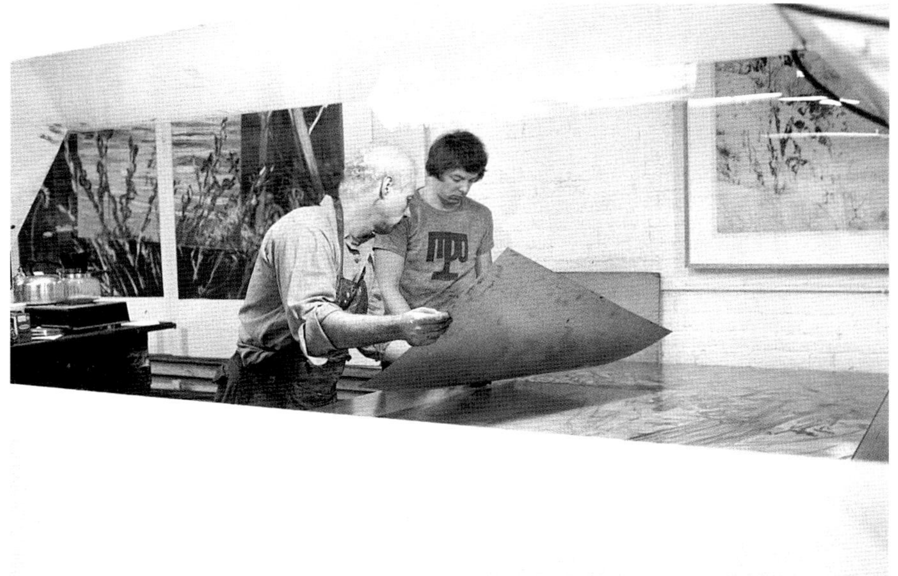

I stand over the press bed to get a better view of the image. The left-side plate will be at the right side of the final image, as it will be reversed in printing. Each of the three plates takes three to fours hours of painting. All three plates must be finished before any one of them can be printed in order to ensure proper integration and resolution of the triptych. Oils are added to the inks and the thinners to retard drying, but there is always the risk that delicate areas will dry out before they can be printed.

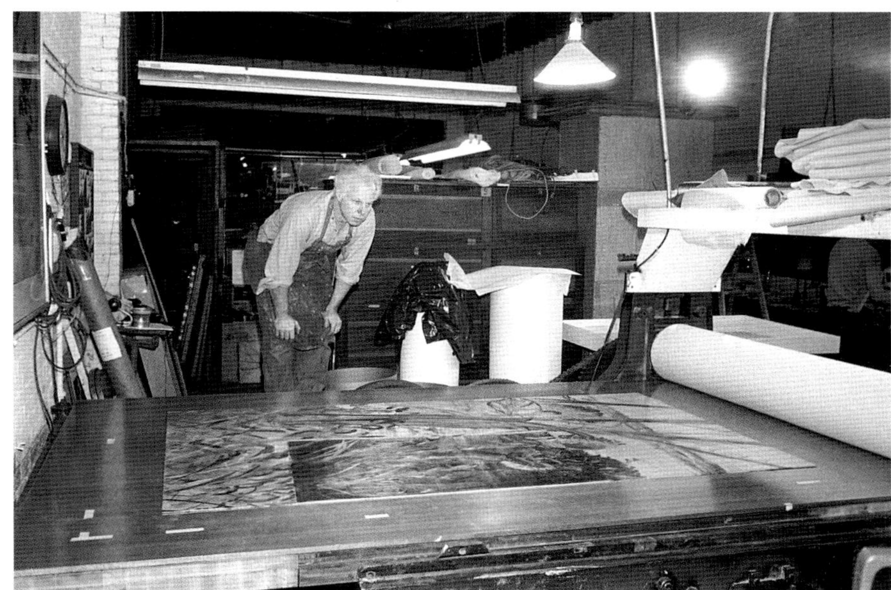

9:00 P.M. I finish work on the right-side plate while Townsend prepares the paper, which is about 84 by 60 inches. He sprays it with water to make the fibers softer, more "ink-loving," and rolls it up to make it easier to bring to the press.

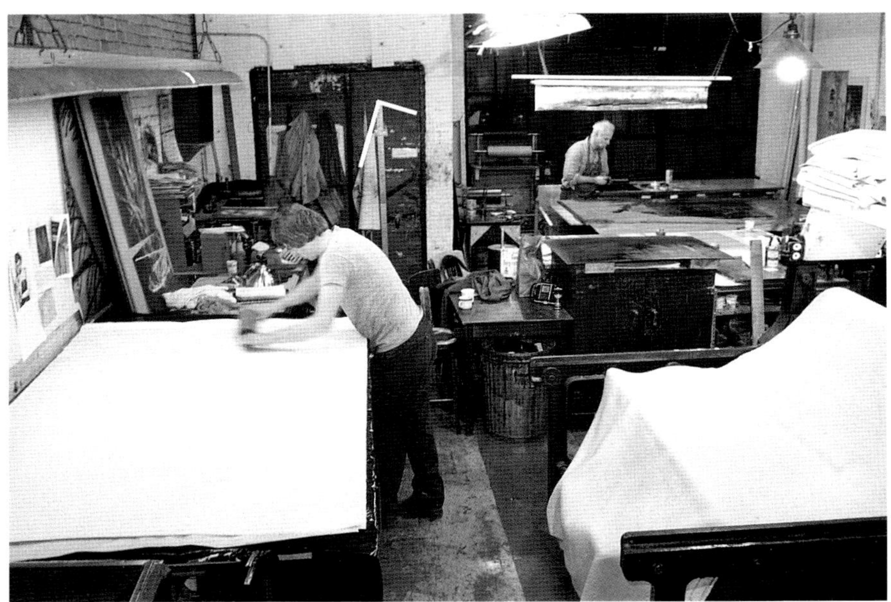

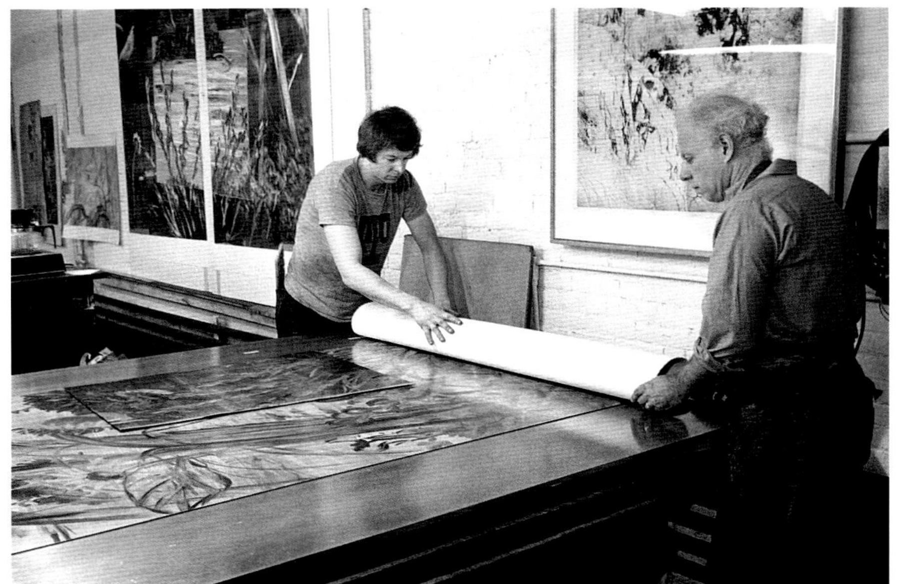

Left
We unroll the damp paper onto the plate. The bed of the press, originally used for gluing plywood veneers, measures 67 by 100 inches. It was redesigned and refitted for this project. Its hydraulic and manually adjusted pressure provides about two thousand pounds of weight per square inch.

Below
The right and center panels are attached to the wall for viewing.

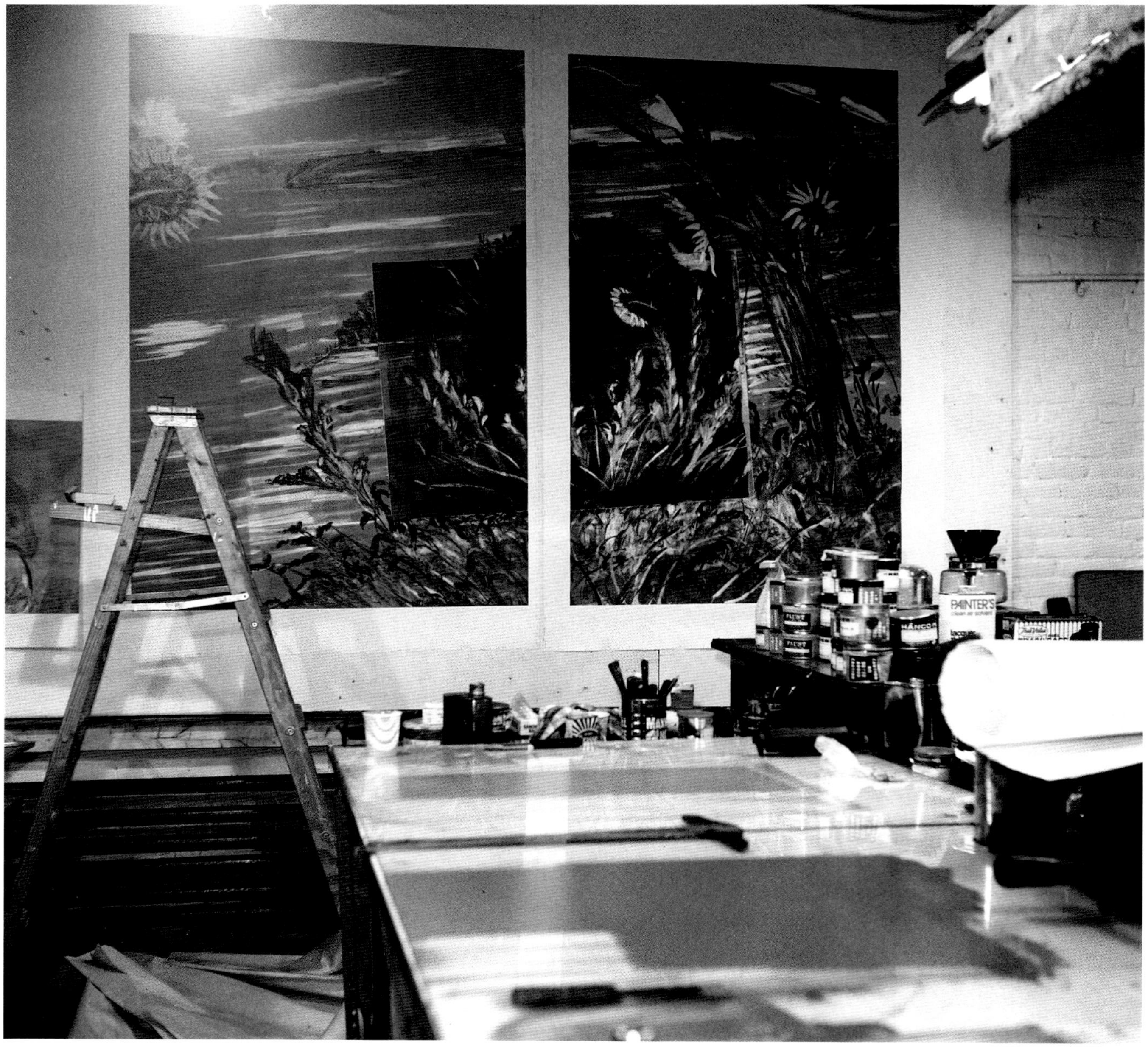

Right
After printing, Townsend and I remove the paper from the plate and get a first indication of the quality of the print. At this point, about 11:00 P.M., while the ink is still workable, I make additions to the residue left on the plates after printing and reprint a full-size cognate (called the ghost image) of the previous print *(Wakeby Day II,* colorplate 26).

Below
I study the results. Work stops and we clean up at 1:00 A.M.

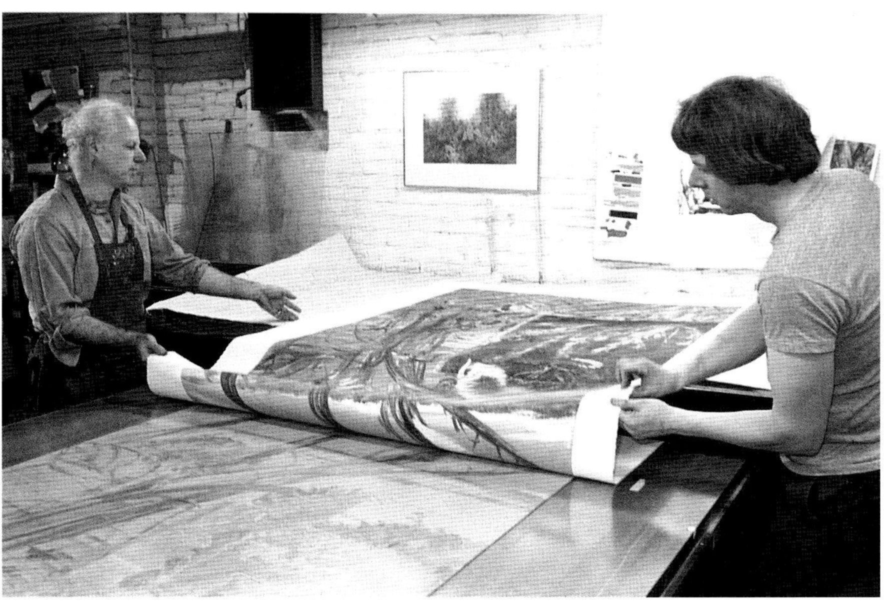

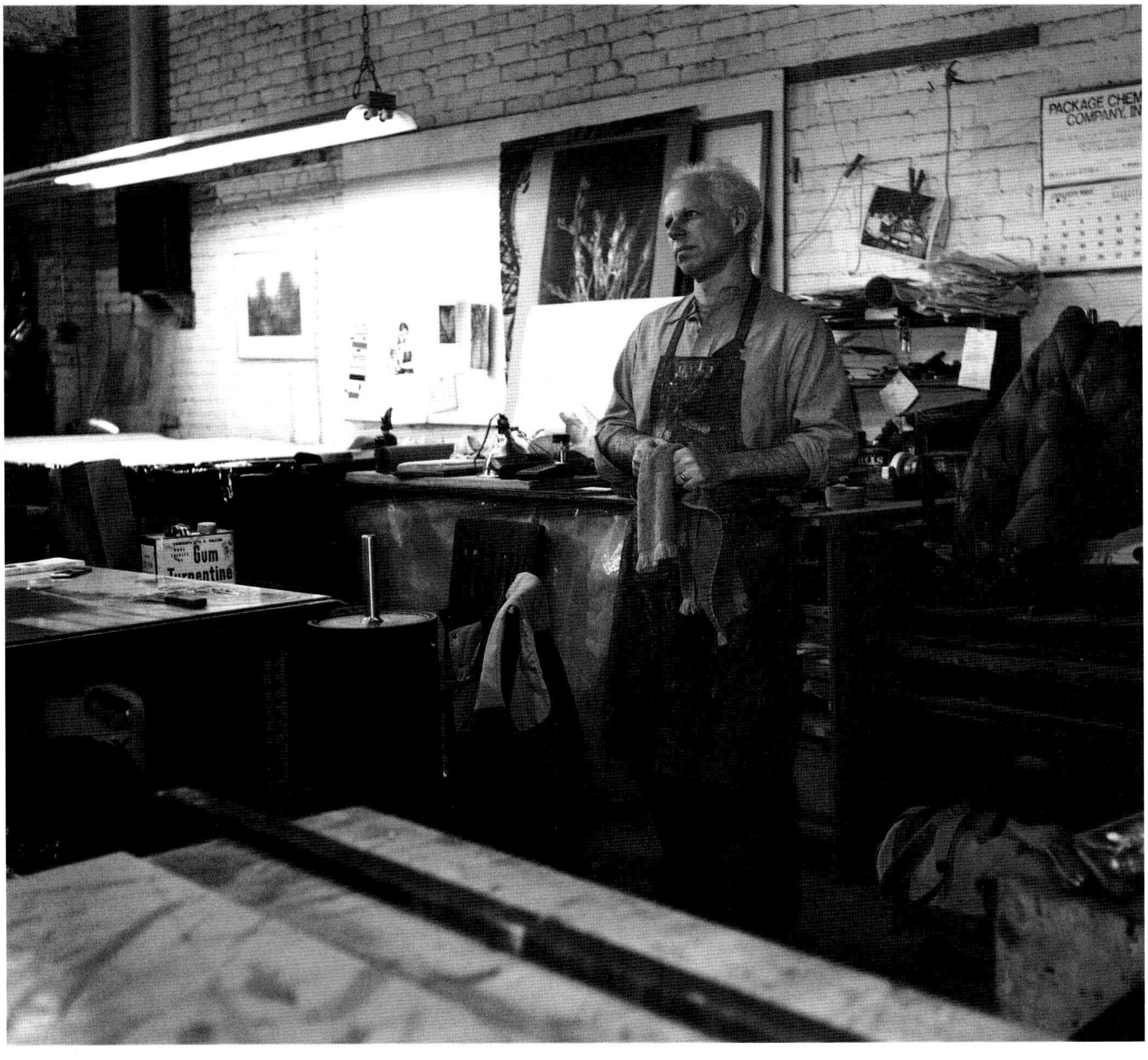

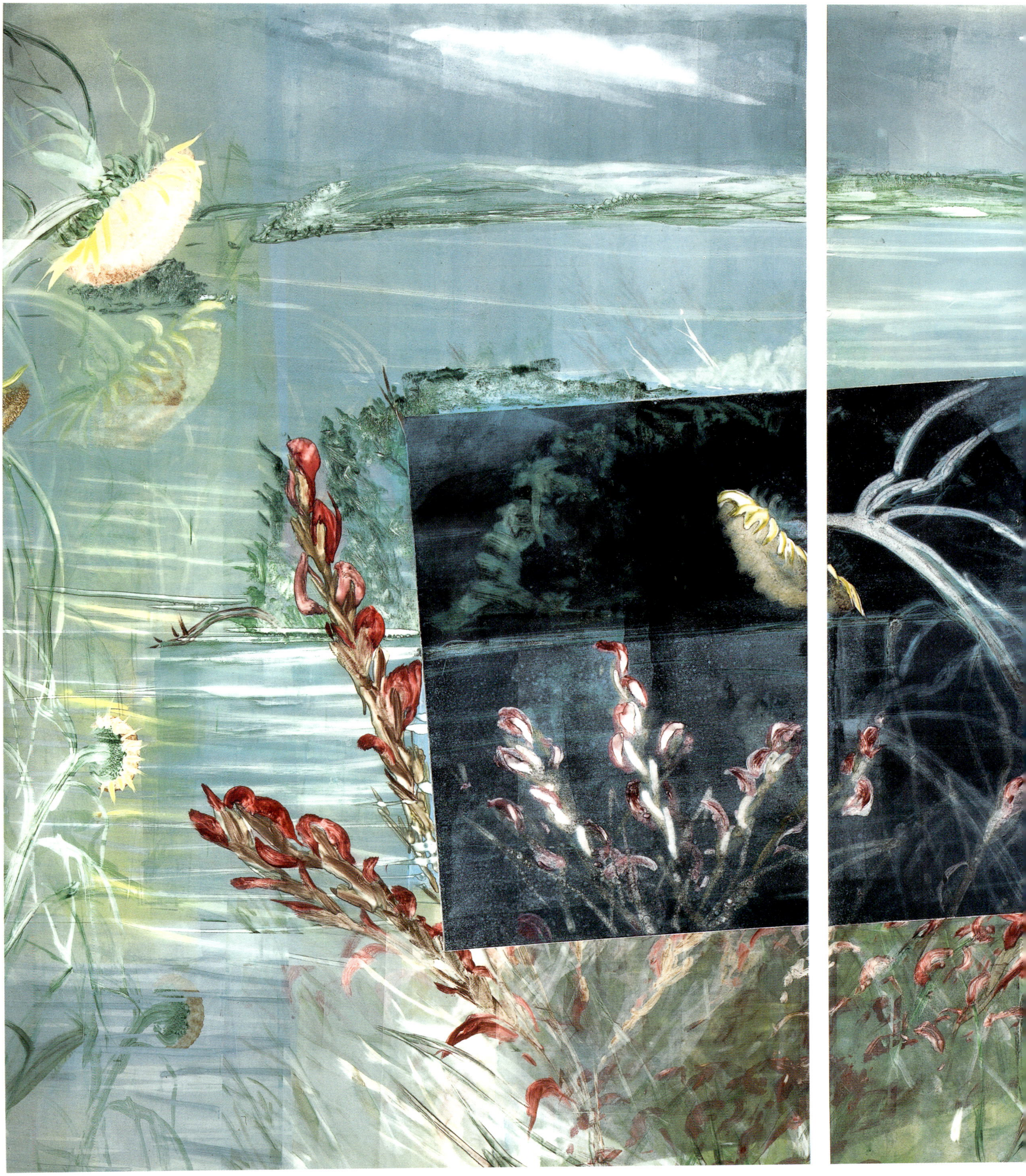

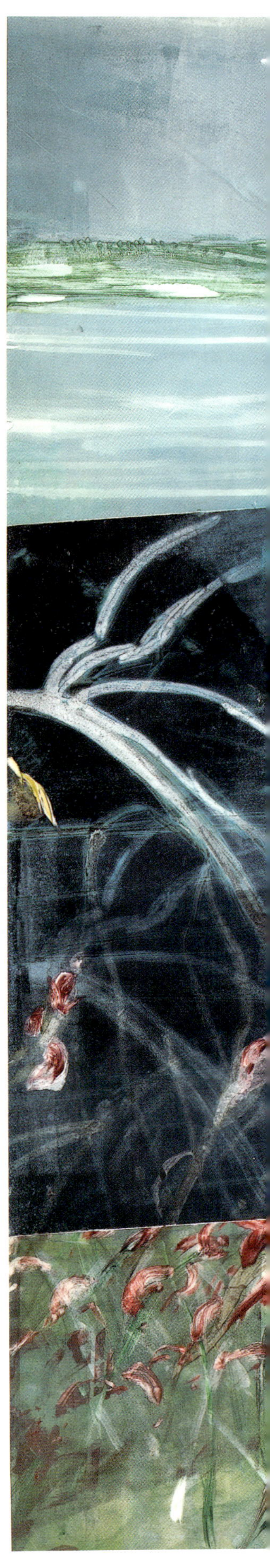

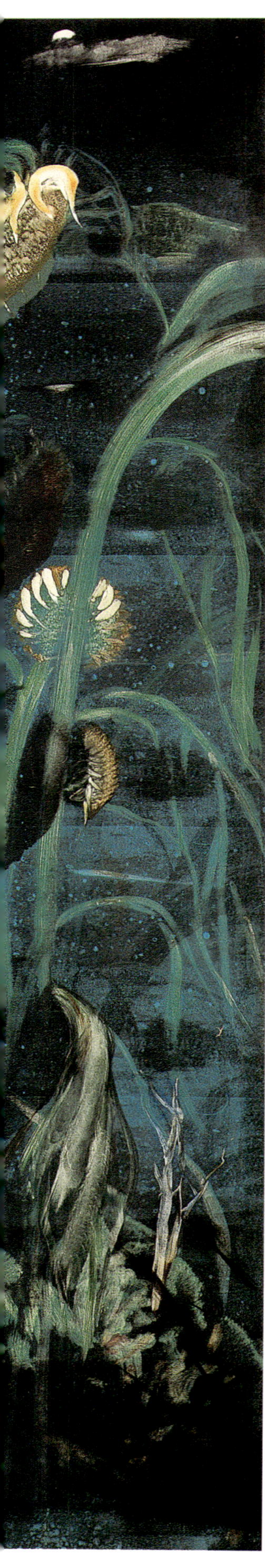

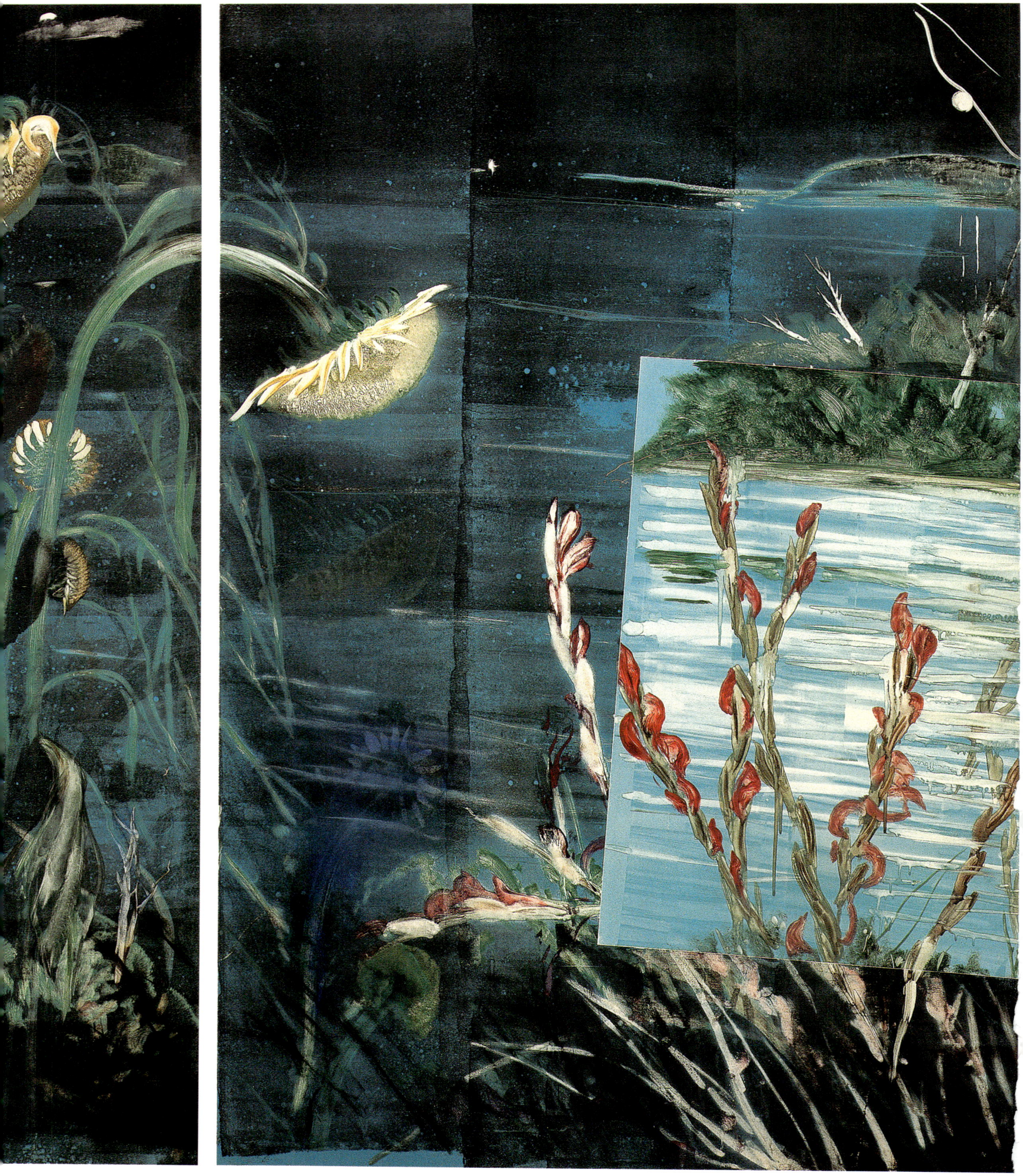

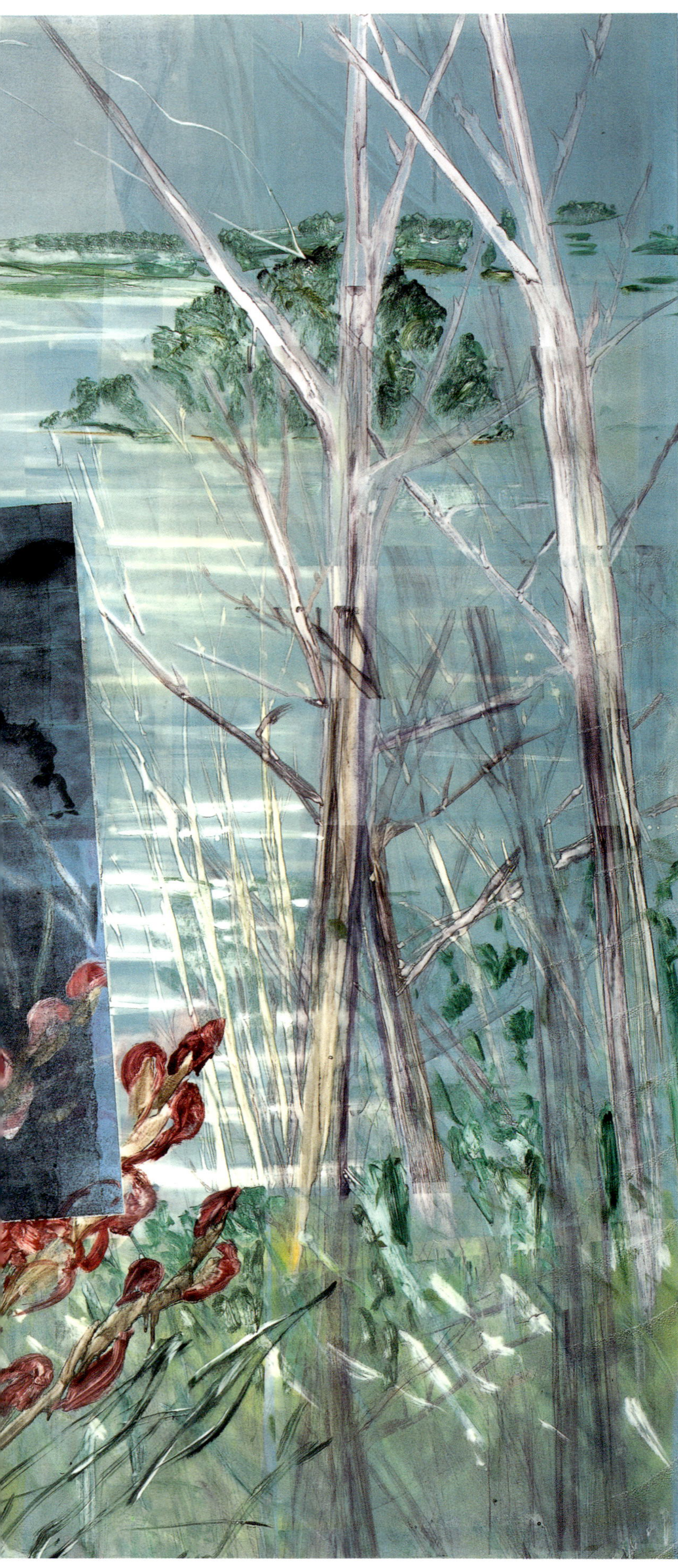

Colorplate 26
Wakeby Day II, 1983, monotype (triptych),
left panel: 71½ × 43½ in. (181.5 × 110.5 cm);
center panel: 71½ × 47⅜ in. (181.5 × 120.2 cm);
right panel: 71¼ × 43¼ in. (181.1 × 110.2 cm).
Brooklyn Museum of Art, New York,
Gift of the artist (87.43 a – c).

Colorplate 27
Wakeby Night, 1983, monotype and pastel (triptych), 72 × 136½ in. (182.9 × 346.7 cm). National Museum of American Art, Smithsonian Institution, Washington, D.C., Gift of Mr. and Mrs. Hugh Halff, Jr., Judith Ross, and Kurt and Kim Butenhoff, and Museum purchase through the Luisita L. and Franz H. Denghausen Endowment (1996.46a – c).

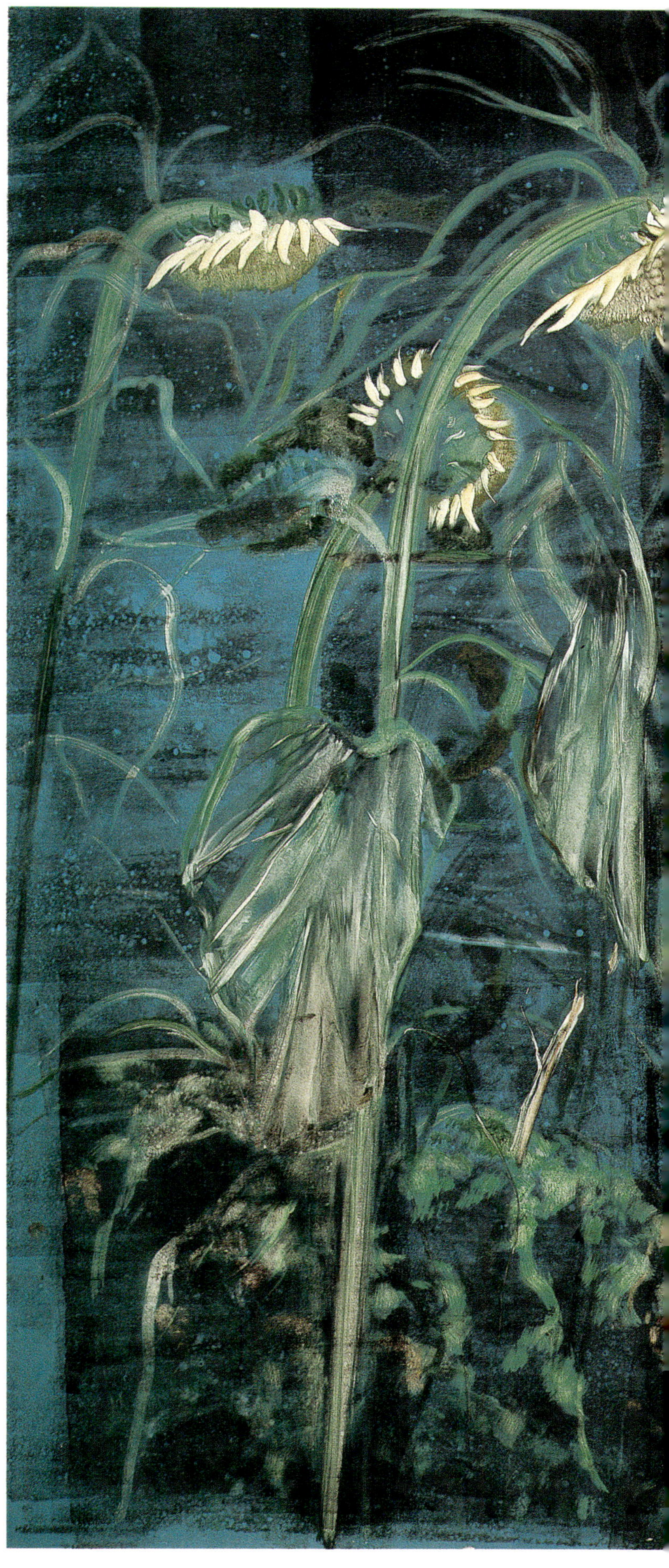

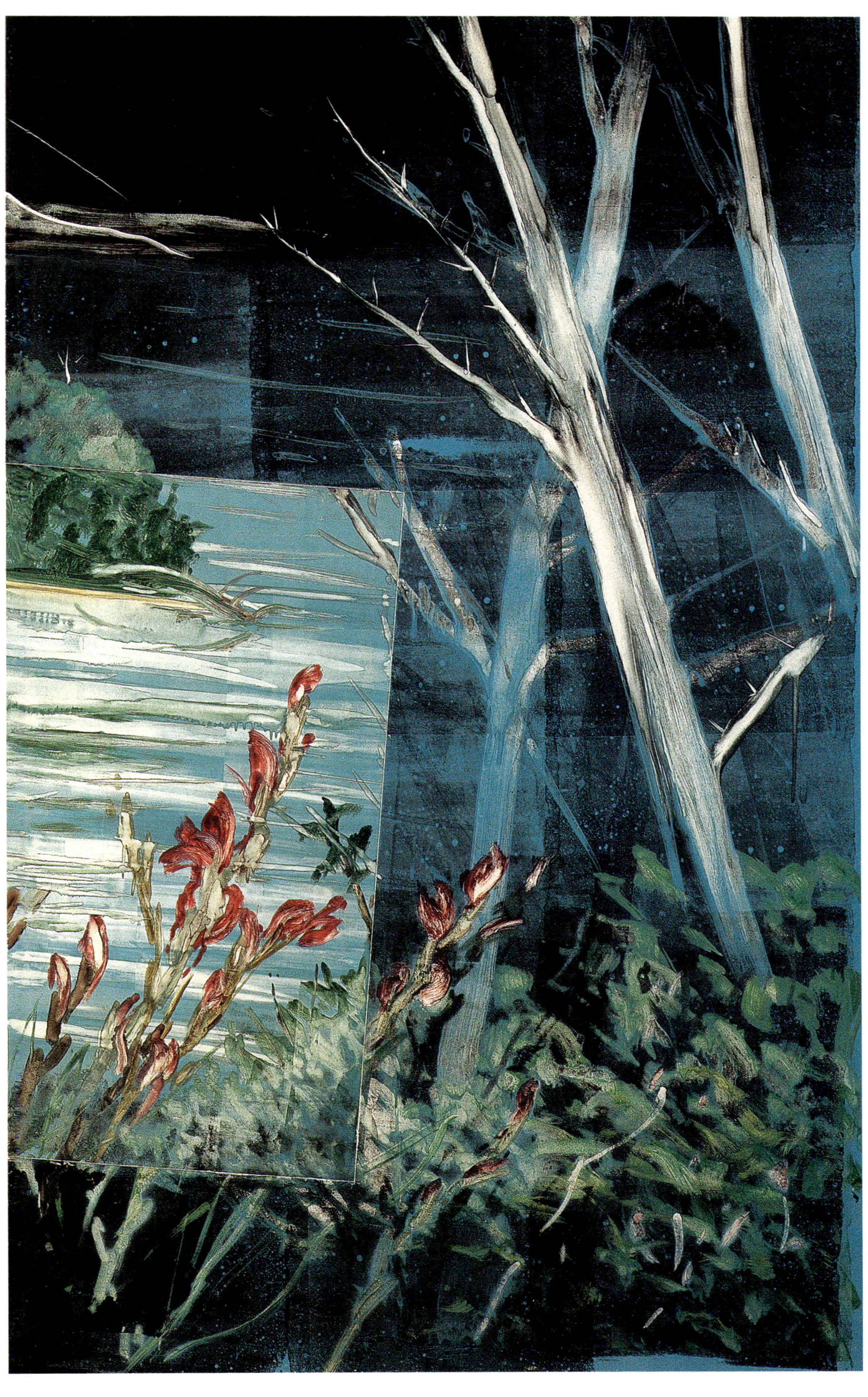

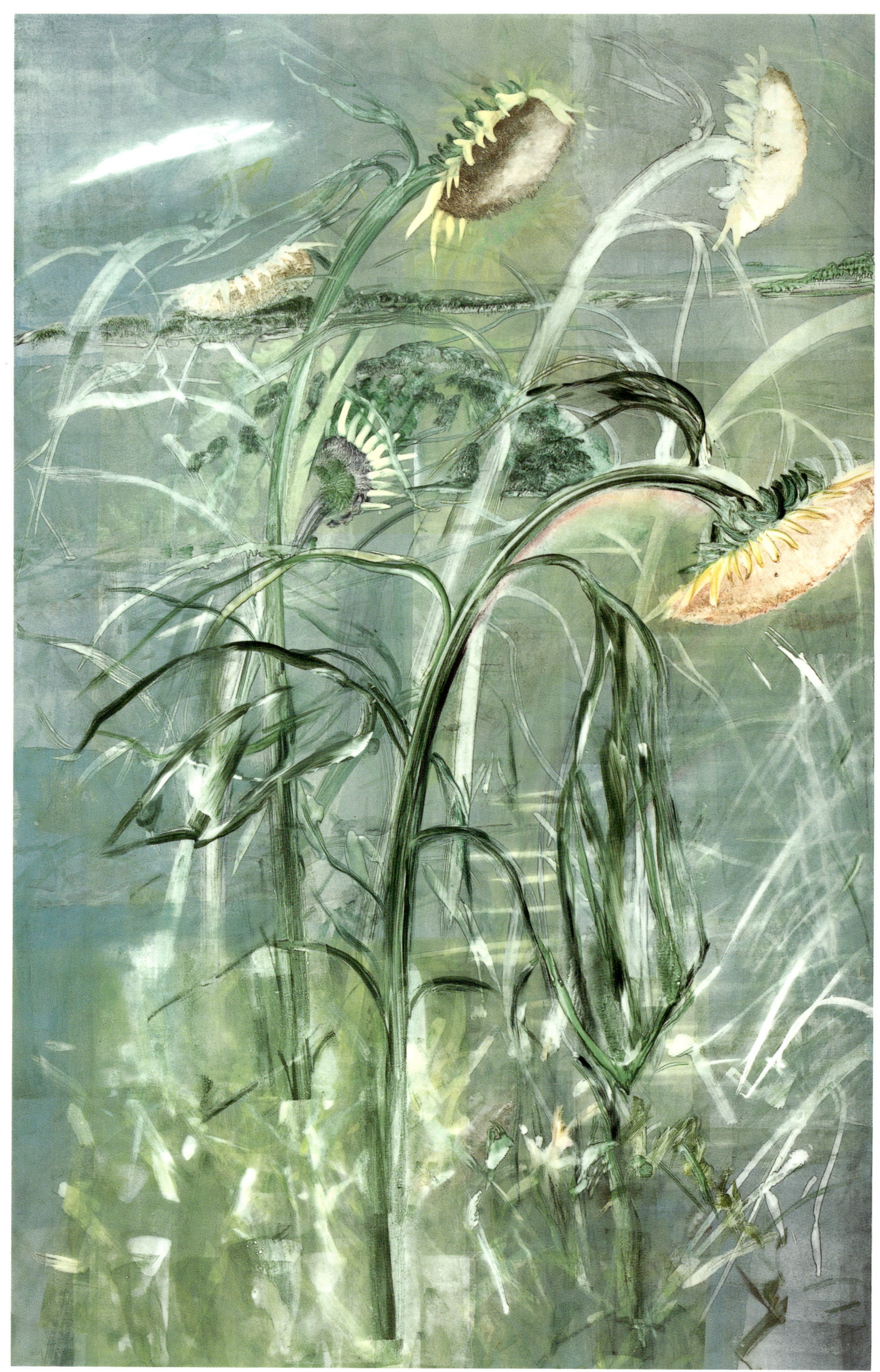

Michael Mazur: The Poetry of Illustration

Lloyd Schwartz

I'M looking at several books spread out on and near my desk — poetry books with covers by Michael Mazur. It's impossible for me not to think of Michael Mazur in relation to poetry. This is partly because Gail Mazur, his wife, is an extraordinary poet, and since she's also the director of the most prestigious and longest-running poetry reading series in Cambridge, I often see Michael (in fact, I see him most often) at poetry readings. Also because I've always admired the poetry in his work. Clouds and horizons, both of which he's done so evocatively, are subjects with their own poetry built in. He's also incorporated a mysterious sense of narrative: moving and painful scenes in a mental hospital (colorplate 4; figs. 8, 9, and 19–25); the poignant activity of monkeys in a zoo (colorplate 15; figs. 11 and 76); a strangely cinematic series involving a violent incident in the woods, perhaps a shooting (fig. 41) — explicitly narrative, but can we ever know the precise nature of the event? ("The lesson is from Brueghel," Mazur said, "bad things can happen on beautiful days.")[1] Isn't the very ambiguity of his recent series *Branchings* (are these tree branches or amplifying veins and arteries?) a kind of poetry?

A number of his monotypes, oil paintings, and pastels (several among his largest works) are scenes of Wakeby Lake, on Cape Cod, where the Mazurs used to spend their summers. These are like the "picture-within-a-picture" feature on TV monitors, in which a square or rectangular "insert," sometimes a close-up or enlarged detail, like a captured moment or a memory, creates an exciting tension or complication in relation to the larger image — the way a metaphor or simile within a poem also does.

The book covers compel my eye in a similar way. The pastels on the covers of Gail Mazur's two most recent volumes were clearly not first intended for these particular books. *Wing Chair, Martha's Vineyard,* 1972 (fig. 45), was made fourteen years before *The Pose of Happiness* was published,[2] yet it's nevertheless a powerful evocation of both the courage (that determined solidity, the broad stride of those curvaceously squat chair legs) and the fear (the chair itself in shadowy silhouette against a background of windows ablaze with sunlight) that the title of the book embodies. *Carriage House* (created in 1979), on the cover of *The Common,*[3] depicts a lovely, tranquil backyard scene. Because many of the trees are bare, they and the squarely, unavoidably intruding telephone pole and the low stockade fence don't exactly block our view of the neighboring carriage house; still they interfere with it, blur it, make what we thought we were looking at harder to distinguish. It's a "common" scene, just as the poems seem to be about (in Gail Mazur's phrase) the "inexhaustible reality" of the everyday. But like these poems themselves, that reality turns out to be more complex than what first meets the eye.

The monotype *The Want Bone* (1989), Mazur's first cover designed specifically for a new book of poems, is a more literal response to the title — and the title poem — of Robert Pinsky's fourth volume.[4] Against a dark, watery blue-green with a red-and-purple–layered sunsetlike "sky" above it, Mazur inserts into a rectangular box an image of

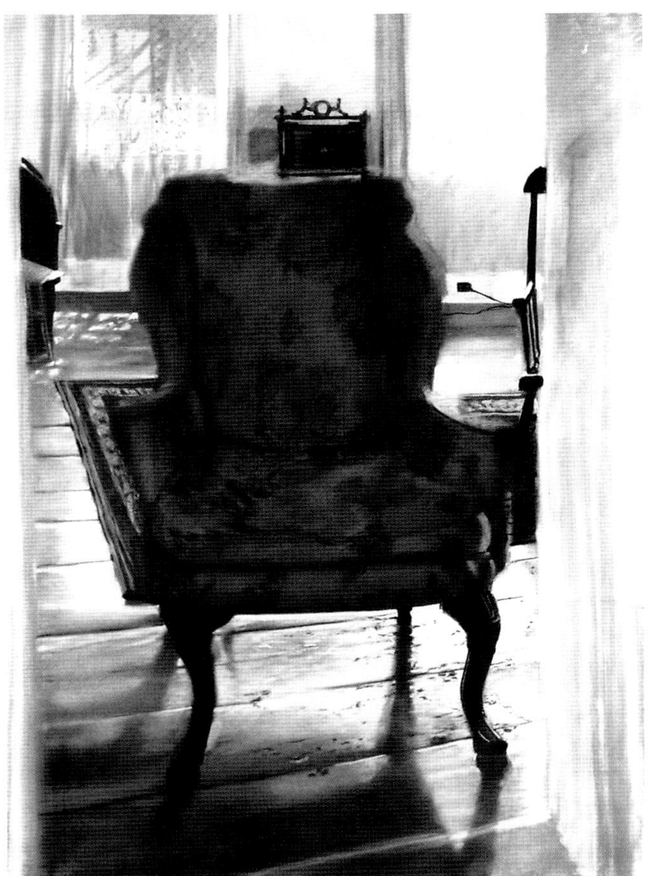

Fig. 45 *Wing Chair, Martha's Vineyard,* 1972, pastel, 40 × 30 in. (101.6 × 76.2 cm). Collection of the artist.

the "scrubbed and etched and pickled" shark bone of Pinsky's title. It's as if within or beneath the abstractly cosmic, painterly suggestions of sea and firmament, if we'd only look closely enough, microscopically perhaps, we'd find that perpetual, sensual, open-mouthed "O" of astonishment and desire that keeps recurring in Pinsky's poem.

Mazur traces his artistic interest in literature to his student days. At Horace Mann School, in New York, he was co-editor of the school literary magazine. At Amherst, he developed an interest in poetry, and he became associate editor of the Amherst College magazine. Leonard Baskin, his art teacher, was extremely well read, with "a high level of erudition." Mazur spent the year before his senior year of college, 1956–57, in Italy, where he was planning his final honors project — a book that he first thought might be an illustrated version of the Pagliacci story. He says he became interested in both opera, or at least the operatic impulse, and the *commedia dell'arte.* He was looking at Venetian images of carnivals; *commedia dell'arte* figures by Giandomenico Tiepolo; Watteau's sad clown, Gilles; and Picasso's clowns. He recalls a satirical idea of presenting a sorrowing *commedia dell'arte* Harlequin in front of the Duomo in Florence. Later his themes became more specifically concerned with jealousy. In Florence, he says, "I was very much in a decadent, 'jealousy' world of British and American expatriates — a world of post-adolescent Sturm und Drang, loneliness, longing, and unrequited love." He worked on dark, distressed images of Harlequin with a model and a mysterious third figure (colorplate 1).

At the end of his Italian year, Mazur turned away from *commedia dell'arte* and did his first images from Dante's *Divine Comedy,* drawings of Dante and Geryon, from canto XVII. He'd read *The Divine Comedy* in bits and pieces in Italian, in Italy. When he returned to Amherst, he took a Dante course, in Italian, with the comparative literature scholar Reginald French. But he began to realize that a Dante project would be impossible to complete in a few months. His fascination with decadence in Italy had led him to *The Yellow Book,* Huysmans's *A Rebours,* Poe, and Wilde's *Salomé,* and his senior thesis took its final shape in a project he called *An Image of Salomé,* a series of literal images for texts from the Bible, Wilde, Flaubert *(Hérodias),* and Mallarmé:

I feel how vertebrae
in the dark give way
all of them together
in a shudder

but, thanks to a baptism
shining from the chrism
of that consecration
my head bows salutation.[5]

Mazur responds to such extravagances of language with dramatic, expressionistic images, high contrasts of black

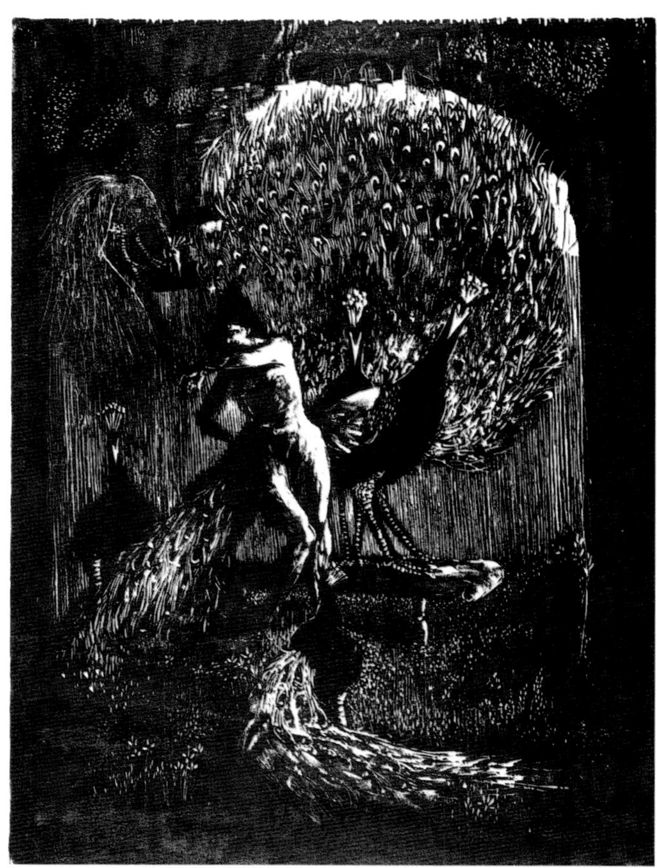

Fig. 46 *Princess with Peacock,* from *An Image of Salomé,* 1958, wood relief, 23½ × 17 in. (59.7 × 43.2 cm). Jane Voorhees Zimmerli Art Museum (82.017.069). (Catalogue raisonné 32)

on white and white on black, as in *Princess with Peacock* (fig. 46), where he creates a teasing ambiguity between positive and negative. He says the style was more influenced by the woodcuts of Bernard Reder (fig. 4), who was living in Florence when Mazur was there, than by Baskin's greater delicacy of line. But you can also see, in the several small vignettes, the influence of the extreme technical finesse, the refined shadings and fine lines, of the early-nineteenth-century British woodcut artist and engraver Thomas Bewick, whose subtle medium of wood engraving had been revived by Baskin. And there were portrait faces of Wilde, Flaubert, and Mallarmé, the Mallarmé based on a Gauguin etching. Mazur told me he did all the work for this volume himself; he even printed it himself: "It was my own book."

Between 1962 and 1965 he worked on a series of forty lithographs in what he calls "tonal" black and white, which, pared down to fourteen images, resulted in *Images from a Locked Ward,* 1965 (figs. 10, 26, and 47), a striking and powerful portfolio, not an actual book, but what Mazur describes as having the "feeling of a book," with an implied narrative inspired by Rouault's *Miserère.* You don't need to know Dante to see the progress through the mental hospital as a journey through Hell. Figures in torment move, or flee, down a deep central corridor, past the patients' rooms

("Like rings or 'bolge,'" Mazur says). He recalls his wife saying in her sleep: "This trip has walls."

He was also returning more explicitly to Dante. Near his studio in North Cambridge, Massachusetts, in 1968, he witnessed a series of fires, which first resulted in an etching of a church fire. Thinking about Dante again, he was trying to connect *The Divine Comedy* with his own personal experience. His idea was to combine the fire scene with the scene from the mental hospital of women in hospital johnnies. He was also reading Joyce and thinking about cities — his own city — as an image of Hell. He thought about a Dante series that would be organized like *Ulysses* — two men walking through the city of Dis, with figures on view in department store windows. Some of these *Inferno* studies would be hard to tell apart from the mental hospital images. In 1968 he published one Dante image (fig. 48), from canto VIII (misnamed canto XI), in an Impressions Workshop portfolio used to raise money for an anti–Vietnam War group, Artists against Racism and the War. This etching was an image from the first ring of the seventh circle, depicting black-and-white horizontal strips with figures plunging down into and surfacing up from the Stygian Lake, "where men, violent toward other men, fight submerged in a river of blood."

Mazur maintained his involvement with the literary world. He did a line-drawing portrait of the Greek poet Constantine Cavafy for the cover of Stratis Haviaras's magazine *Arion's Dolphin*. For *Ploughshares* he did cover portraits of the poets and guest editors Bill Knott, Michael Harper, and Seamus Heaney, and two spectacular full-color covers — one, a dazzling red calla lily against a white background — for the two issues Gail Mazur edited. His monoprint for a broadside of Gail's poem "Next Door," produced by Copper Canyon Press (1980), may be the first broadside edition made up of a series of unique prints. Mazur provides haunting visions of a front window and what can be seen through it — the evanescent life outside passing by. The poem ends: "I want to know / nothing less than I know."

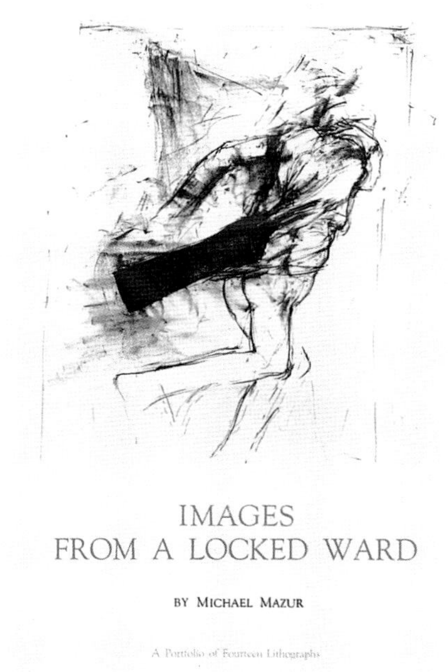

Fig. 47 *Images from a Locked Ward* (title page), 1965, lithograph and letterpress, 26 × 20 in. (66.1 × 50.8 cm). Jane Voorhees Zimmerli Art Museum (82.017.043). (Catalogue raisonné 132)

Mazur's next big literary project, in 1982, at the request of the publisher David R. Godine, was a series of illustrations for Richard Howard's new translation of Baudelaire's *Les Fleurs du Mal* (fig. 49). The frontispiece, like the fron-

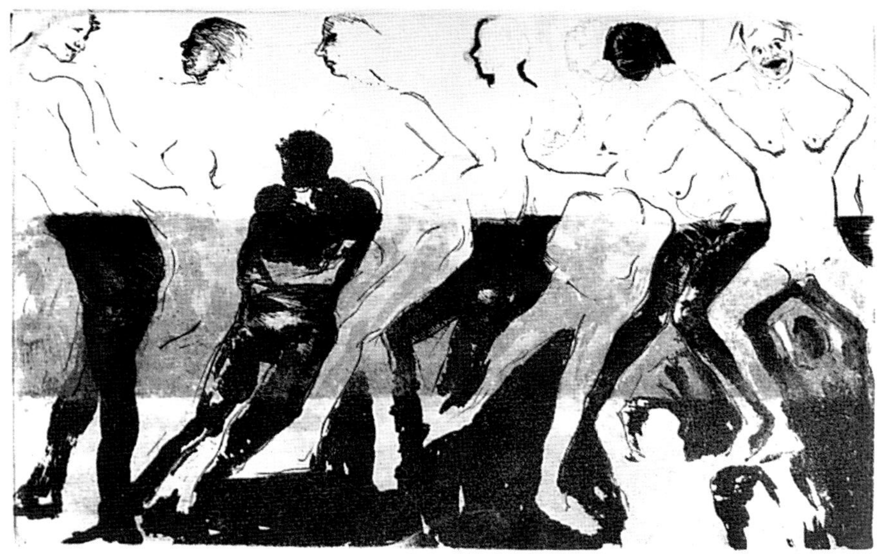

Fig. 48 *Study for a Dante's Inferno, Canto VIII,* 1968, etching and aquatint, $14\frac{3}{4} \times 20\frac{1}{4}$ in. (37.5 × 51.5 cm). Jane Voorhees Zimmerli Art Museum (81.42.31). (Catalogue raisonné 173)

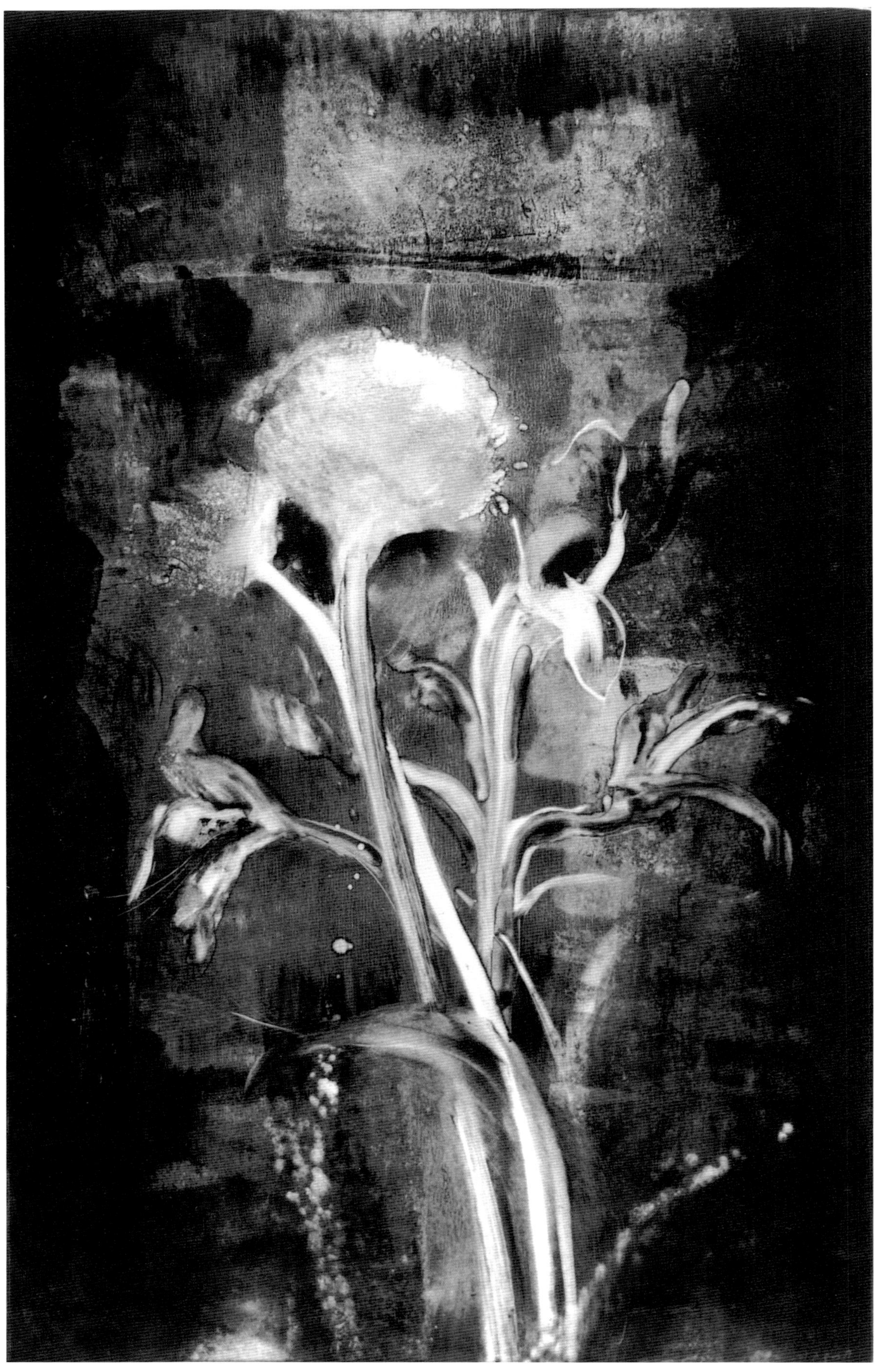

Fig. 49 *Flowers of Evil*, from *Les Fleurs du Mal*, 1981, monotype, 37¾ × 25⅞ in. (95.9 × 65.7 cm). The New York Public Library, Gift of Michael Mazur and David R. Godine, in memory of Morton Godine.

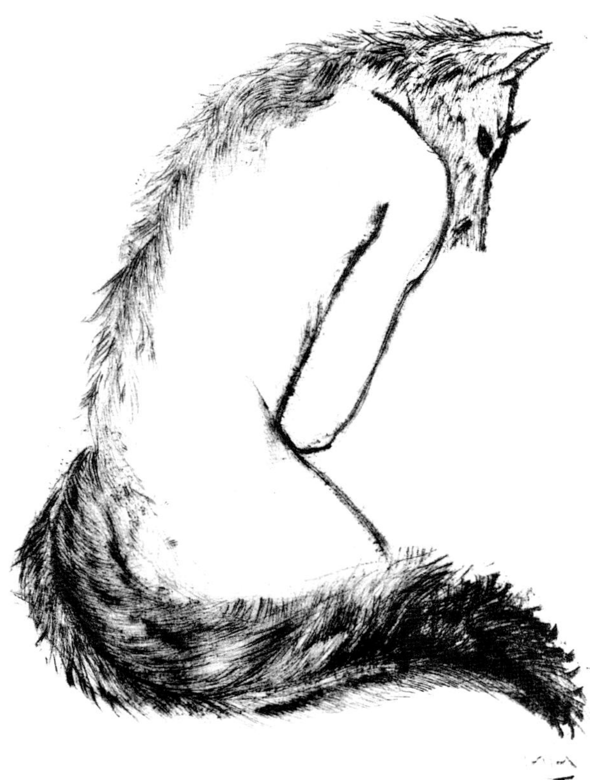

Fig. 50 *Herna: A Story* (frontispiece), 1993, drypoint, 10 × 8 in. (25.4 × 20.3 cm). Jane Voorhees Zimmerli Art Museum, Gift of the artist (1995.0336.001). (Catalogue raisonné 273)

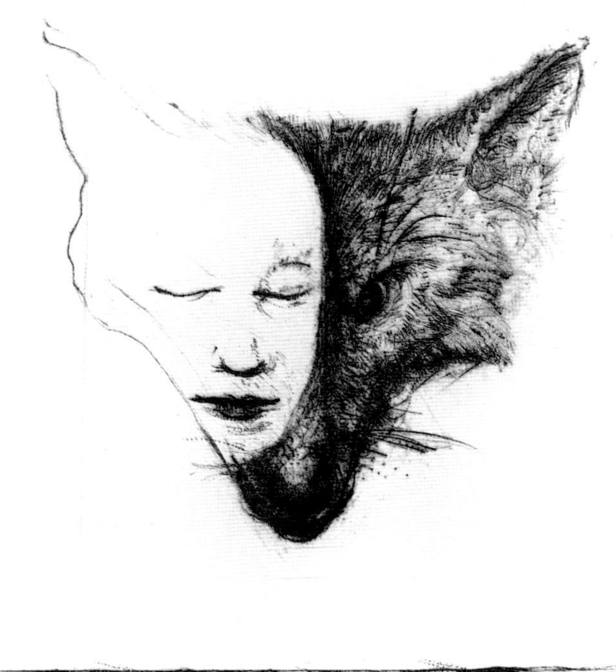

Fig. 51 *Herna: A Story* (endpiece), 1993, drypoint, 10 × 8 in. (25.4 × 20.3 cm). Jane Voorhees Zimmerli Art Museum, Gift of the artist (1995.0336.002). (Catalogue raisonné 274)

tispiece for the *Salomé,* was a portrait of the author taken from a Rodin portrait. What he came up with for the body of the book were images he'd already begun working on — dark flowers (calla lilies, cyclamen, irises, tulips), emblems that had less to do with poetry than with mood and were not specifically related to the individual poems. Mazur calls these images "intimations of destruction" (Richard Howard referred to them as "adornments," says Mazur). If he were to do them again now, he says, he'd study the text thoroughly and try to respond more immediately. Yet, in their *fin-de-siècle,* quasi-Victorian elegance and dark sense of menace, their inextricable combination of beauty and decadence captures the ambiguous spirit of the poems superbly. These funerary flowers parallel Baudelaire's relentless suggestions of mortality: the blossoms almost exploding; the fretwork of spiky leaves; a tulip cut off by one of its leaves — the leaf almost a threat to the flower.

More recently, there were two eerie fine-line drypoints, a Rackham-like fox / woman frontispiece (fig. 50) and an overlapping fox face and human face (fig. 51), bracketing Melinda Marble's contemporary psycho–fairy tale *Herna* (in a sumptuous small-press edition by the Bow and Arrow Press, 1993). In 1996 Mazur made a swirling image of the Creation (fig. 52) in brownish purple for Robert Alter's translation of *Genesis* for Arion Press. An image of dovetailing fingers for the cover of poet Steven Cramer's *Dialogue for the Left and Right Hand* (Lumen, 1997), in muted, intersecting shades of rose and blue, embodies the fluid, almost abstract style Mazur now favors in his paintings.

Mazur's most ambitious literary collaboration, of course, is his extraordinary series of illustrations for Robert Pinsky's contemporary translation of Dante's *Inferno* (Pinsky calls it *The Inferno of Dante* — suggesting, underlining, the autobiographical midlife crisis and breakdown that Dante was living through).[6] This project was the culmination of Mazur's longtime ambition, tying together his experience in Italy with the recurring dark impulse throughout his career — Pagliacci, Salomé, images of fire, and of course, the living Hell of the locked ward.

Mazur completed more than two hundred black-and-white monotypes for what would be only thirty-four final choices (one illustration for each canto), plus a frontispiece, a concluding-yet-forward-looking vision of the stars after the last page of the poem, double-page endpapers, and a searing red-and-black wraparound cover showing a limp victim impaled on a pitchfork in silhouette against a background of flaming fireworks (colorplate 31). "I wanted to make as many images as I could," Mazur says, "then I picked the one I liked best" (although some of the "rejects" work extremely well as independent images and have been successfully exhibited). Gustav Doré used different engravers, but each image of his famous set is exactly the same size. Mazur didn't want all the pages to have the same look, so he kept varying the scale. Some of the images represent general scenes and take a full page, bleeding off the

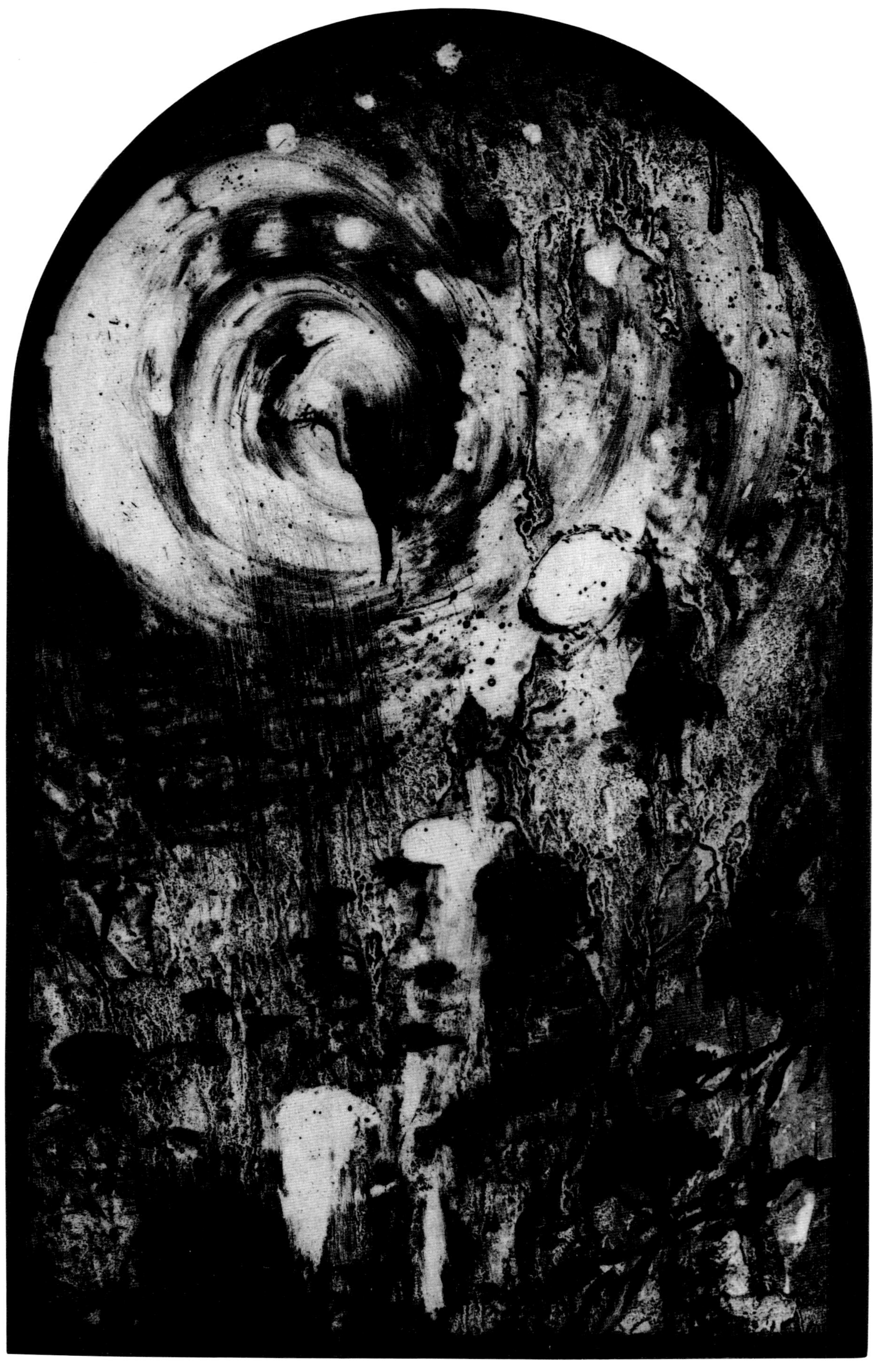

Fig. 52 *Genesis,* 1996, etching, 16¼ × 11⅜ in. (41.3 × 28.9 cm). Collection of the artist. (Catalogue raisonné 315)

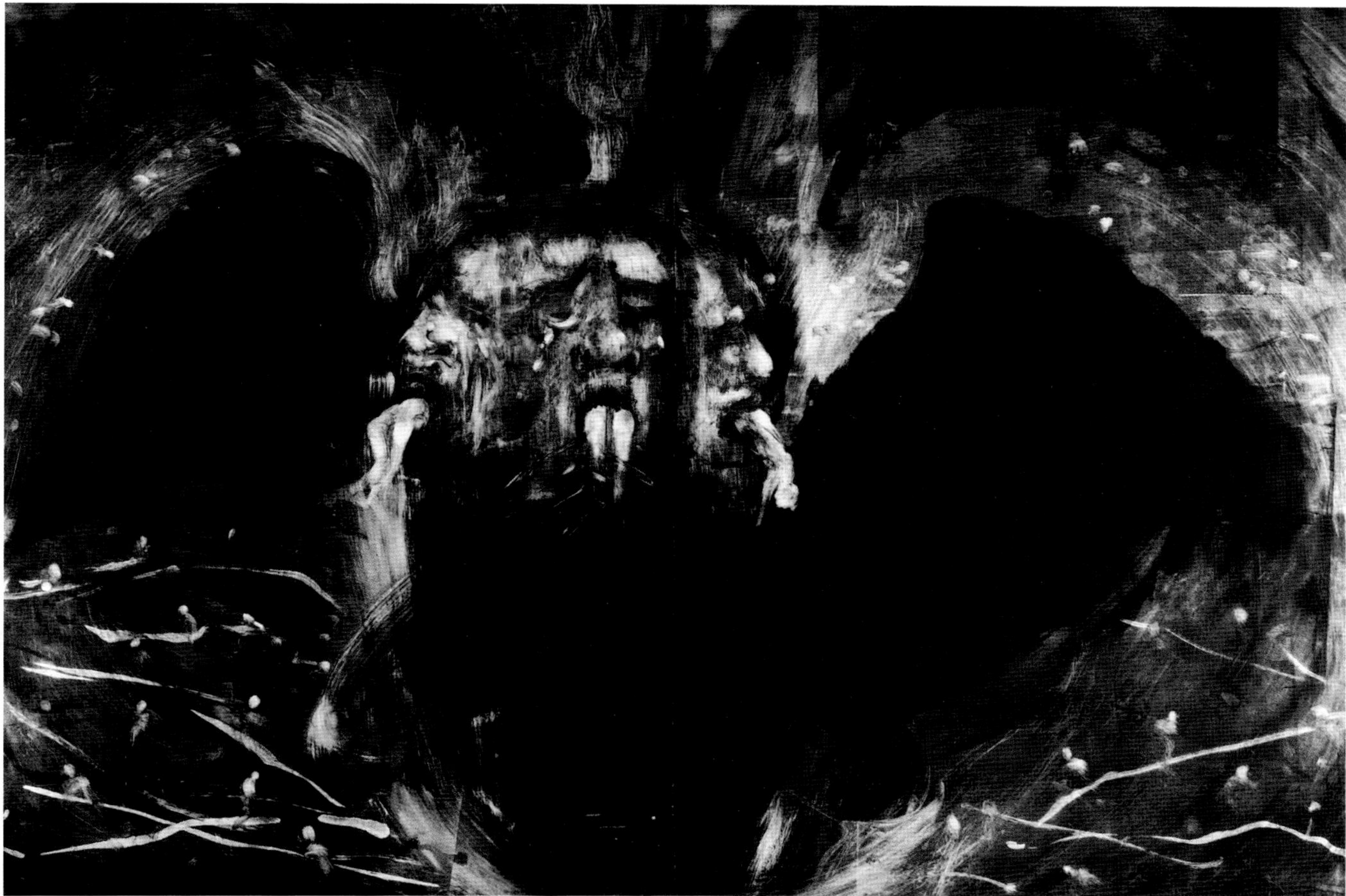

Fig. 53 *Canto XXXIV,* from *The Inferno of Dante,* 1993, monotype, 30 × 44 in. (76.2 × 111.8 cm). Collection of the artist.

edge of the paper. The other cantos are illustrated with details, "inserts," with white borders. The final canto erupts in a startling, literally overwhelming double-page image of the three-headed Lucifer chewing on Dante's three greatest sinners: the betrayers Brutus, Cassius, and Judas Iscariot (fig. 53).

If Doré is the most theatrical of Dante's illustrators, and Blake the most visionary, Mazur is the most dreamlike. He never depicts either the first-person protagonist, Dante, or Virgil, Dante's guide through Hell. Everything we see is, as it were, through their eyes. Mazur's images compel us to identify with the poet's primary experience: the bewildering sense of space — swirling, often mysteriously dislocated; the stupendous grandeur of the Infernal architecture; the grotesque tortures (often literally tortuous) of the sufferers and their profound pain.

The frontispiece (fig. 54) is one of Mazur's most beautiful and evocative images. Facing the title page, it's a depiction of Charon's boat at "Acheron's dismal shore." The image really belongs in canto III, and it's fascinating to compare it with the Charon image Mazur later uses for that canto. The frontispiece is an image of calm — a foreshortened rowboat skimming silently over a dark, glassy surface. We can barely make out the figures, though closer inspection reveals the hulking silhouette of the rower and a blur of smaller figures within the approaching boat, as well as some blurry figures on the shore. In the distance is a dark, ambiguous sky — cloudy, mysterious. Is this a dawn or a sunset? Directly overhead is a brightly glowing arch, like a rainbow, and another, darker arch joining it above, its foot planted on the far shore, the shore of Hell. There are ghosts of other rainbow-arches, too. The image is deceptively seductive and welcoming, practically beckoning us into the poem: "I come to ferry you across / Into eternal dark on the opposite side, / Into fire and ice!"

Then at the beginning of canto III, we're confronted with a much more unsettling, disturbing version of this same image (fig. 55). We see the inside of Charon's boat from overhead, and it fills the entire page. It looms. The tip of the rowboat is cut off by the top border of the monotype. We see the wide thwarts and blurred figures beginning to crowd the hull. We can barely make out the dark waves surrounding the bow. We're thoroughly disoriented. The verticality of the image suggests a Gothic window or a ladder with broad rungs. For a moment we don't know how to look at this image: which end is up? It's not precisely what Dante in the poem perceives, but the image comes astonishingly close to letting us feel the disorientation he feels.

The first canto proper begins another element that runs through Mazur's *Inferno* illustrations: the underworld

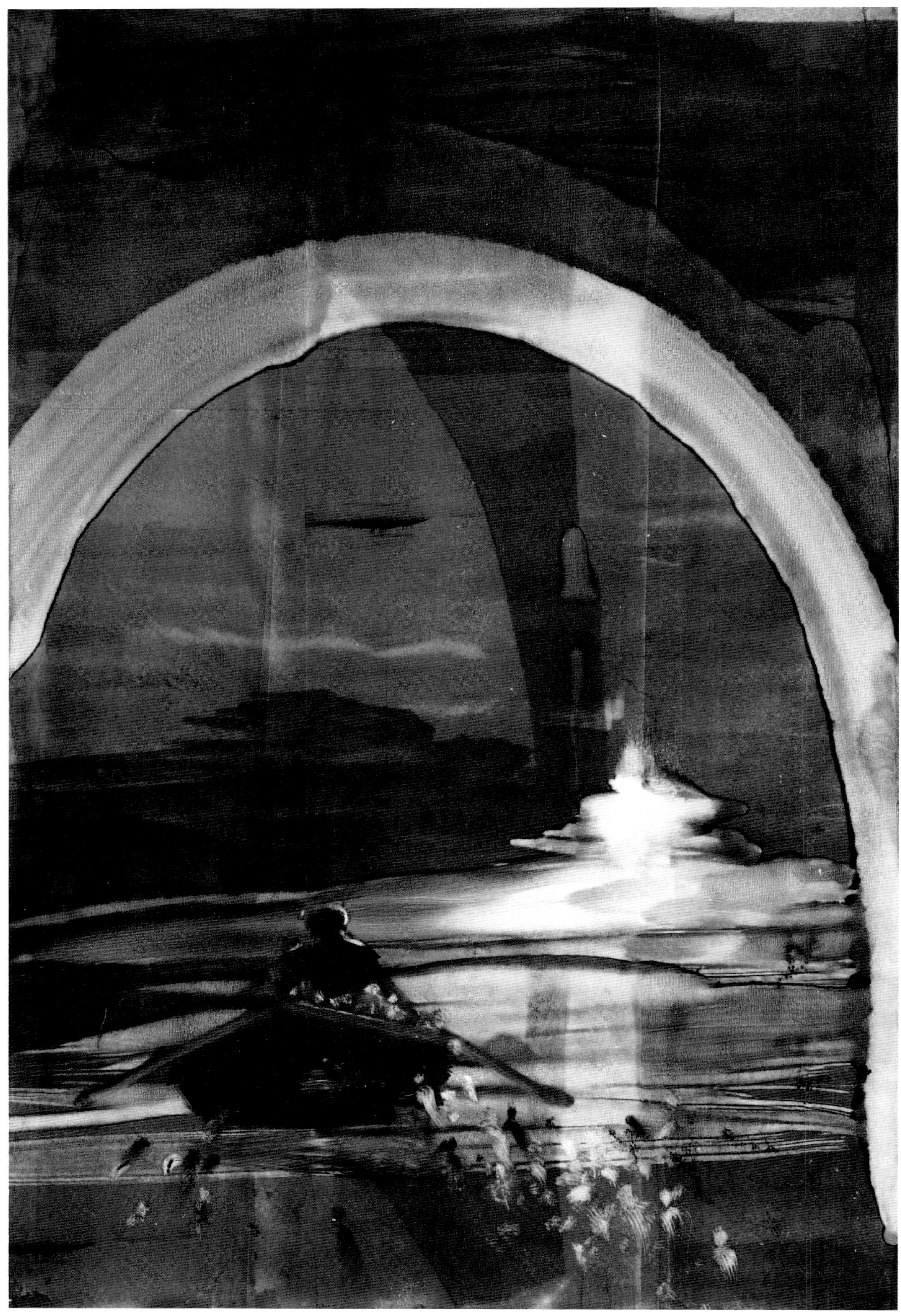

Fig. 54 *Canto III* (frontispiece), from *The Inferno of Dante,* 1993, monotype, 23¾ × 15¾ in. (60.3 × 40.0 cm). Collection of the artist.

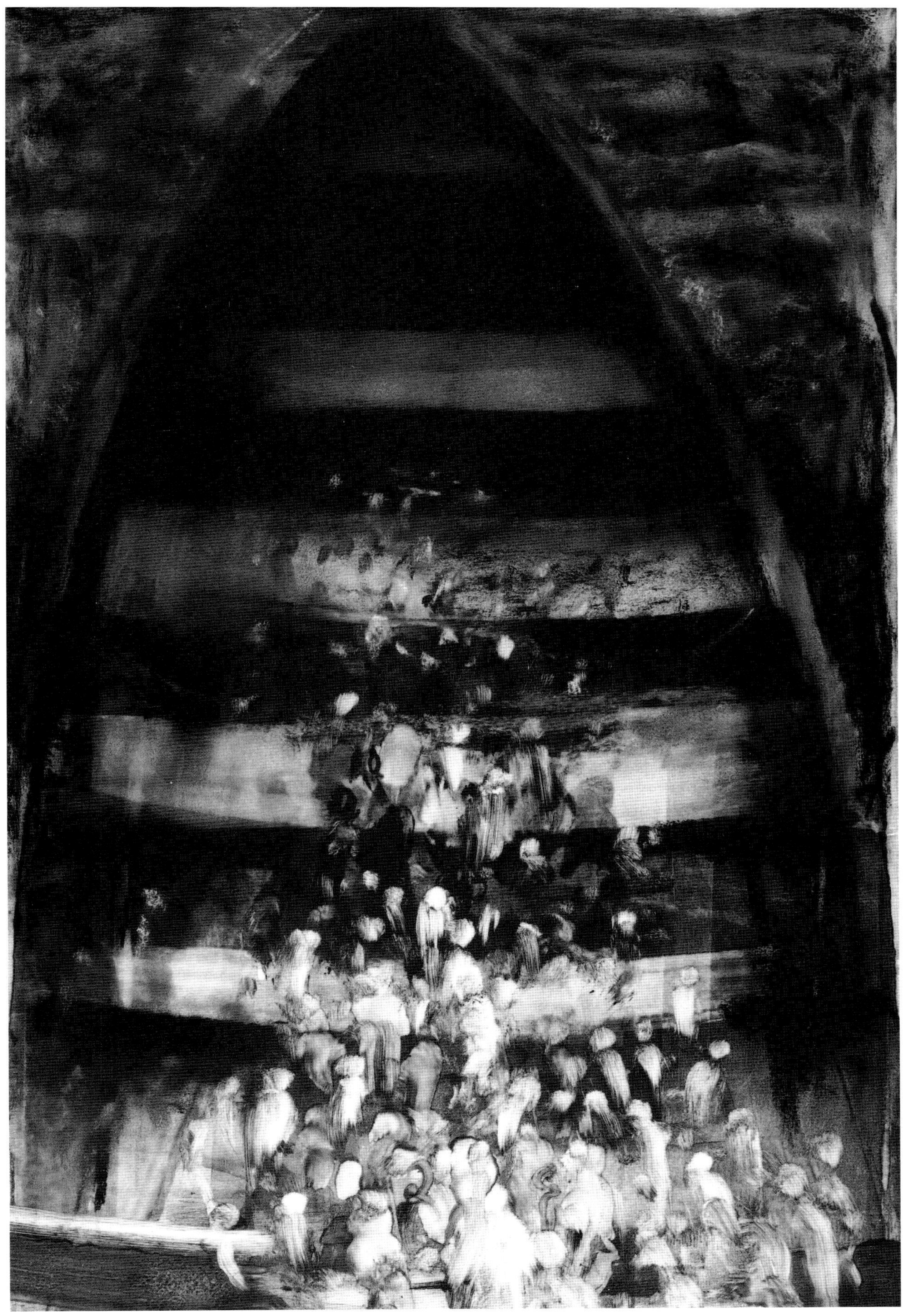

Fig. 55 *Canto III*, from *The Inferno of Dante*, 1992, monotype, 23¾ × 15¾ in. (60.3 × 40.0 cm). Collection of the artist.

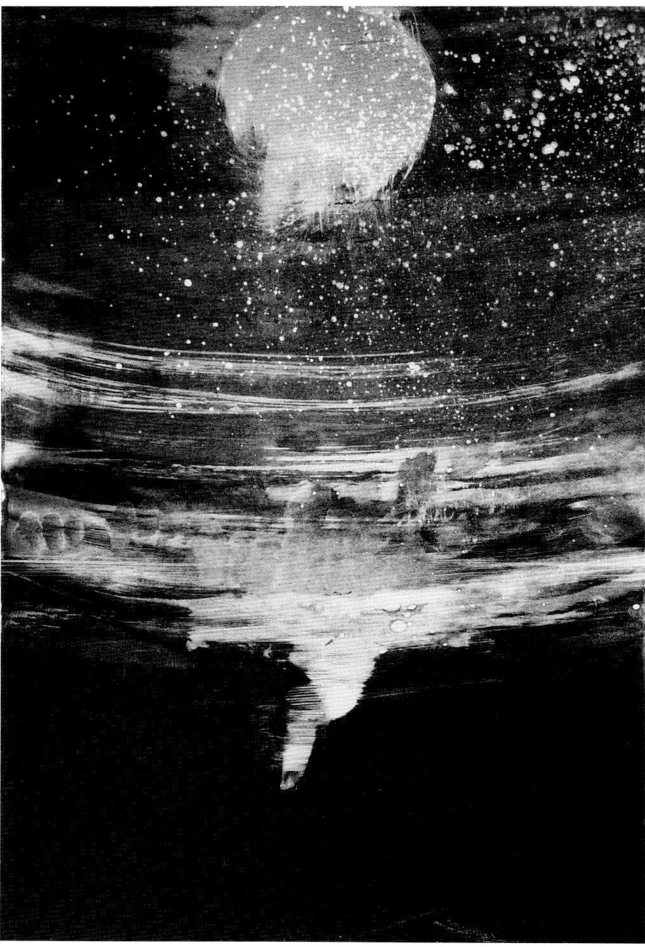

Fig. 56 *Canto II,* from *The Inferno of Dante,* 1992, monotype, 23¾ × 15¾ in. (60.3 × 40.0 cm). Collection of the artist.

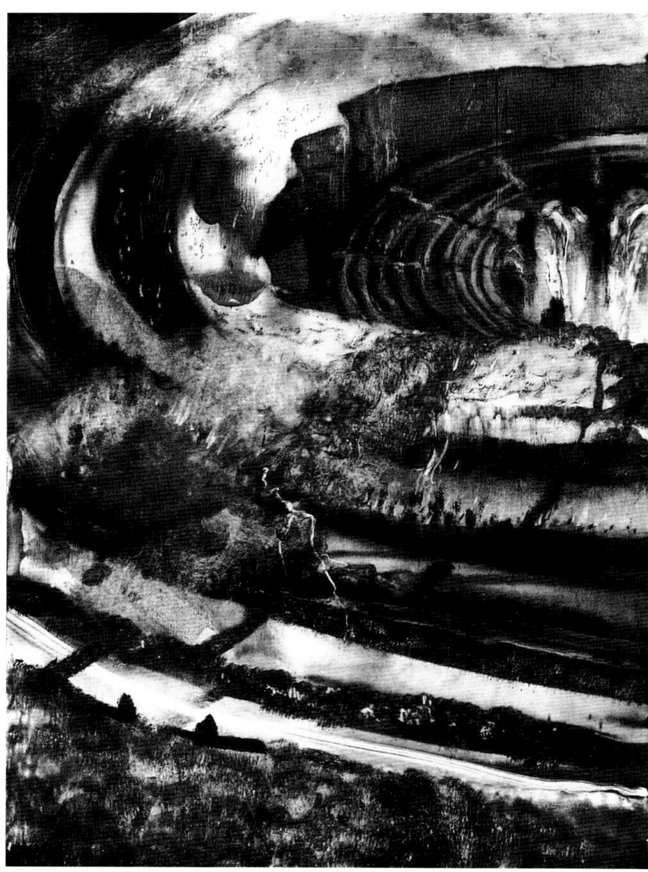

Fig. 57 *Canto XI,* from *The Inferno of Dante,* 1993, monotype, 30 × 22 in. (76.2 × 55.9 cm). Collection of the artist.

landscape. These are among his most abstract and volatile images, and most of these are intimately related to Mazur's exciting etching for the Arion Press *Genesis.* Mazur writes in some detail about his decision to picture the hill that Dante sees in the first canto — not the hill of Purgatory, which is on the opposite side of the earth, but a "hallucination":

> I felt more and more that Dante was using the hill as a mirage, a way to dash the pilgrim's hopes for an easy way out of his crisis and to show him his own vulnerability before his deeper journey. As a mirage its form would be indistinct, a misreading perhaps of a road (in modern perspective) or the very entrance to the pit of Hell that would yawn open in Medieval illuminations.
>
> It occurred to me, as I printed one image after another, that what I wanted was an image that would be all three at once — a form that could be read as a road, a hill, or a pit.[7]

Mazur's high-contrast black and whites are at their most striking here. The dark triangle (or tall, narrow trapezoid) could be vertical (a hill in shadow?) or, in ambiguous "modern perspective," horizontal (a road disappearing into the distance?). The foreground is filled with gnarled trees and slithery foliage — Dante's "dark woods." Far off, beyond the hill (or road), there's an explosion of light — heavenly? fiery? Are these stars or volcanic eruptions from a hellish bonfire? A similar image begins canto II (fig. 56), though it seems more benign ("Day was departing, and the darkening air / Called all earth's creatures to their evening quiet"). We get our first sense here of the circularity of the underworld landscape, with Mazur's swirling streaks interrupted only by sudden declivities.

The climactic image of this series comes at the beginning of canto XI (fig. 57). Dante has crossed the River Styx into the city of Dis, and in canto XI he gets his first Infernal geography lesson. Mazur's image is his first large perspective of the circles of Hell, a spectacular downward look into the funnel of a tornado. The page with this image is immediately followed by a page in which a key to the circles and the rivers is "superimposed" over the muted image. This key wittily suggests the tracing paper in old books upon which a key to a map or an illustration might be found.

The final "landscape" is the very last image, where we see in the distance the hill of Purgatory as if through the far end of a telescope (fig. 58). Of course it looks very

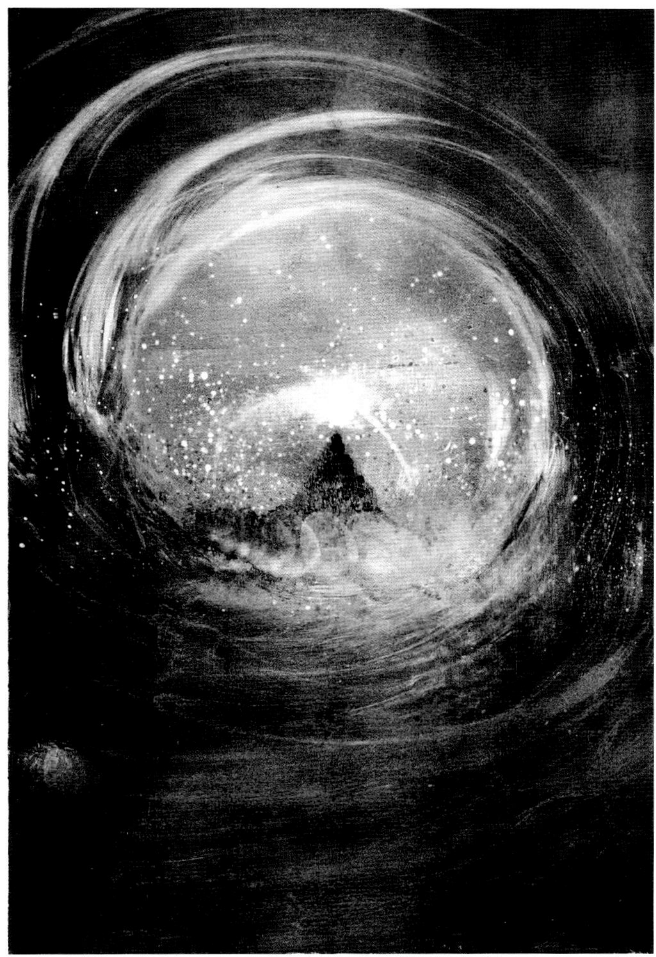

Fig. 58 *Canto XXXIV*, from *The Inferno of Dante* (afterpiece), 1993, monotype, 23¾ × 15¾ in. (60.3 × 40.0 cm). Collection of the artist.

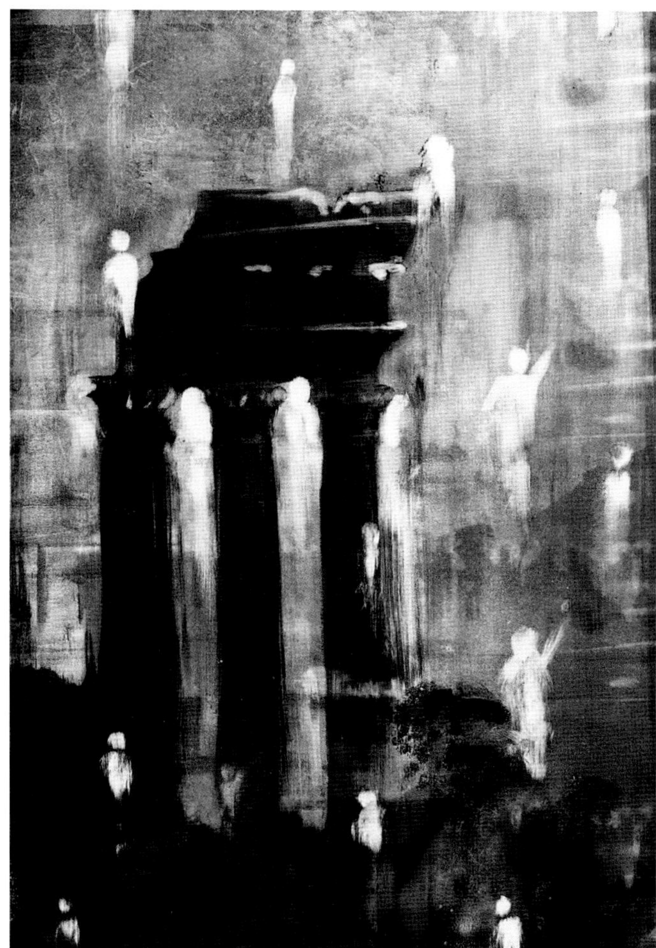

Fig. 59 *Canto IV*, from *The Inferno of Dante*, 1992, monotype, 23¾ × 15¾ in. (60.3 × 40.0 cm). Collection of the artist.

much like the false hill of ascent in canto II. But this time the image through the lens is heavenly — stars swimming in the firmament.

> *Through a round aperture, I saw appear*
>
> *Some of the beautiful things that Heaven bears,*
> *Where we came forth, and once more saw the stars.*

The last stanza of the *Inferno* is a couplet, so in turn Mazur's image closes the "couplet" that began with the parallel image in canto II.

Equally remarkable are Mazur's renderings of the architecture of doom. Limbo of canto IV, for example (fig. 59), seems the ruin of some Roman temple from the Foro Romano — three looming Corinthian columns supporting the fragment of an architrave, with ghostly ectoplasms floating about:

> *"We are lost, afflicted only this one way:*
> *That having no hope, we live in longing." I heard*
> *These words with heartfelt grief that seized on me*
>
> *Knowing how many worthy souls endured*
> *Suspension in that Limbo.*

It's not entirely clear whether the spaces between the columns are just spaces or are ghostly apparitions. This classical ruin (and it's precisely pre-Christian heroes — like Virgil — who are condemned to Limbo) becomes the background against which these doomed souls play out their eternal uncertainty.

In canto VIII (fig. 60) the image of the tower on the bank of the Styx is instantly identifiable — or is it? Surely, through the palpable atmosphere, it's the Palazzo Vecchio of Florence ("Dante's town," Mazur calls it — and Mazur's).[8] A double flame leaps up from the parapet; the river flows by beyond it. This is one of the images that most directly embodies Mazur's determination to coalesce his own experience and Dante's. The tower, he says, was also suggested by the Pilgrims' Memorial Tower in Provincetown, where the Mazurs now spend their summers (this tower itself modeled on the towers in Florence and Siena).[9] He could see the Palazzo Vecchio from his hotel room in 1957; from his back porch in Provincetown he can see the Pilgrims' Tower (Dante, Mazur is eager to point out, called himself a pilgrim).[10] The very next image is of the gate to the city of Dis (fig. 61). It's another classical structure, a Roman

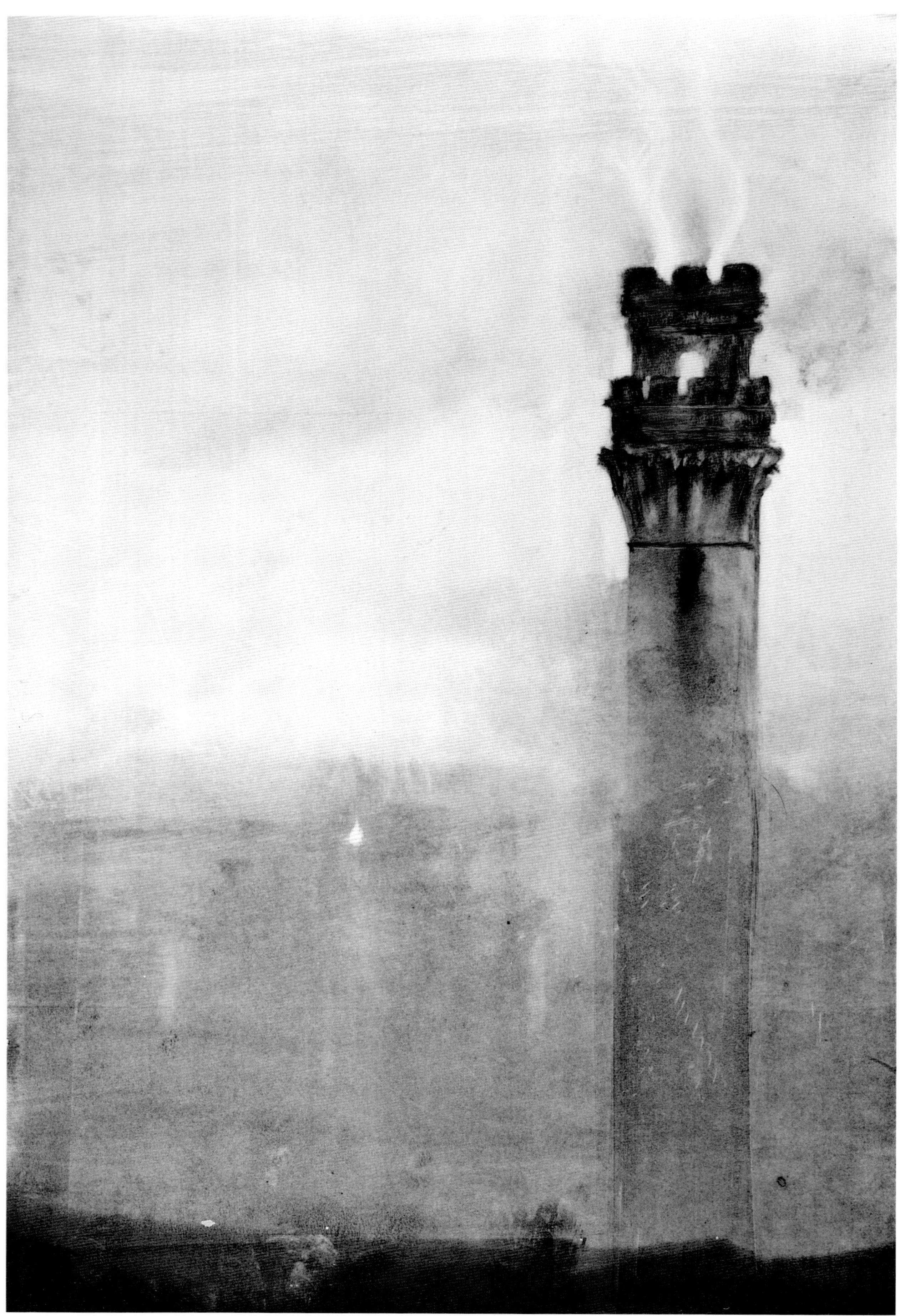

Fig. 60 *Canto VIII,* from *The Inferno of Dante,* 1992, monotype, 23¾ × 15¾ in. (60.3 × 40.0 cm). Collection of the artist.

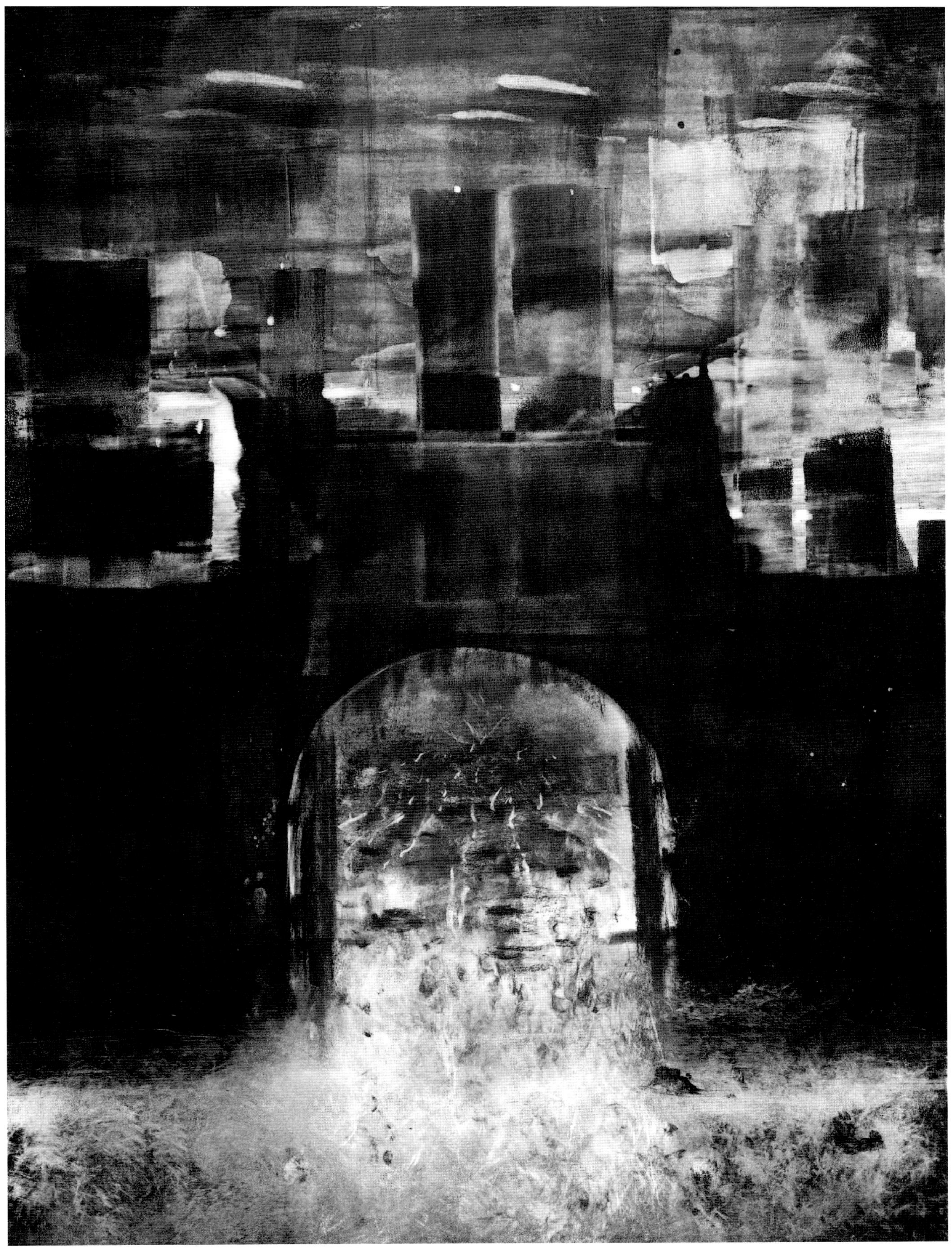

Fig. 61 *Canto IX,* from *The Inferno of Dante,* 1992, monotype, 30 × 22 in. (76.2 × 55.9 cm). Collection of the artist.

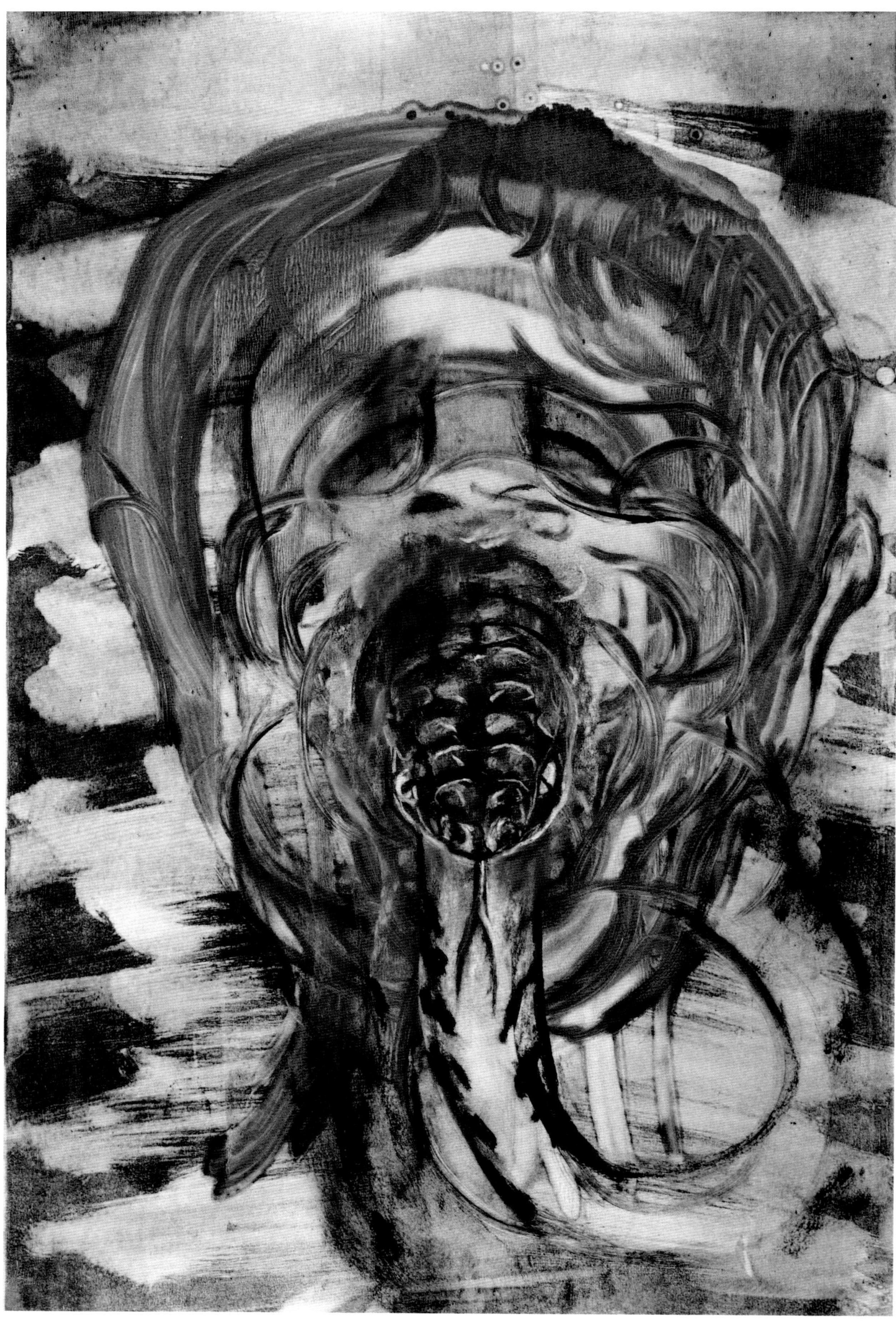

Fig. 62 *Canto XXV*, from *The Inferno of Dante*, 1993, monotype, 23¾ × 15¾ in. (60.3 × 40.0 cm). Collection of the artist.

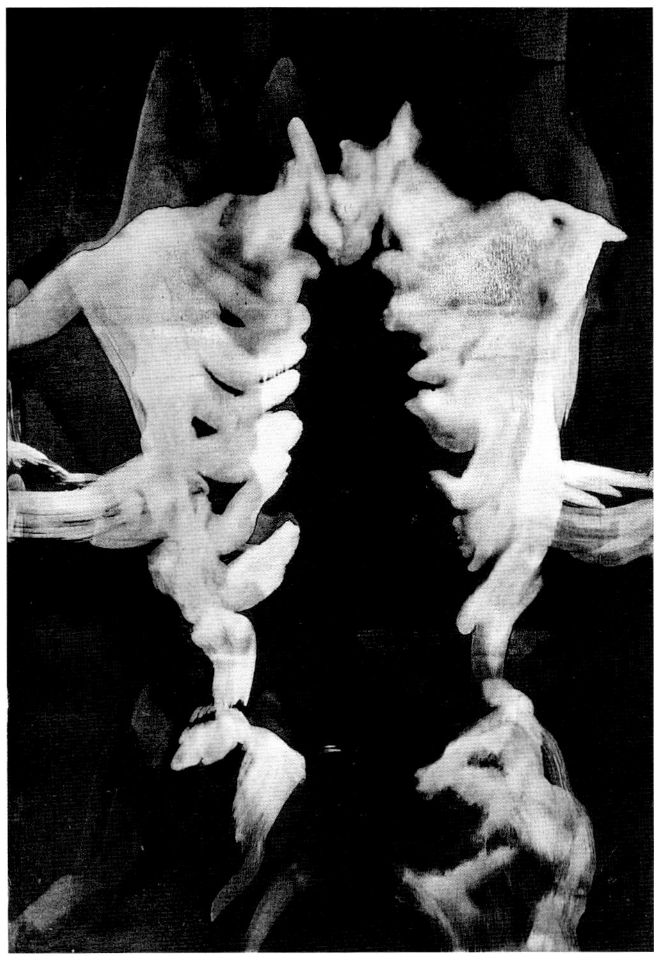

Fig. 63 *Canto XXVIII,* from *The Inferno of Dante,* 1993, monotype, 23¾ × 15¾ in. (60.3 × 40.0 cm). Collection of the artist.

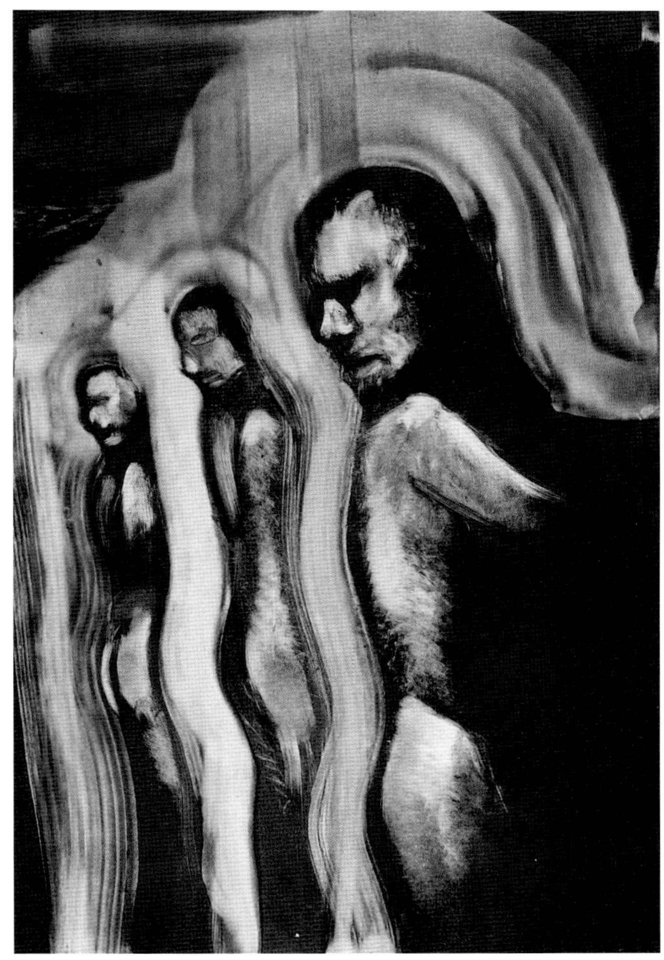

Fig. 64 *Canto XX,* from *The Inferno of Dante,* 1993, monotype, 23¾ × 15¾ in. (60.3 × 40.0 cm). Collection of the artist.

arch — massive, darkly lumbering, with flickering splashes of energy visible through the great aperture: a victory arch through which captive slaves would have been led. Mazur's first impulse, he says, was to depict the Auschwitz gate, but finally he had a severe reaction against the association of the inhabitants of Auschwitz with sinners.[11] This great gate then was inspired by Rodin's *Gates of Hell.* And since this is a city gate, it's not only Rome but also New York — Washington Square. We can even see the twin towers of the World Trade Center in the background. Pilgrims' Tower. World Trade Center. Isn't any — every — modern city an Inferno?

More important even than the architecture and geography of *The Divine Comedy* are the characters. The heart of the *Inferno* is Dante's confrontation with suffering souls and the devils and devilish creatures (the three-headed fanged and reptilian monster/dog, Cerberus; the repellent, serpentine Geryon) who torment them. Mazur usually blurs and distorts these figures. Few of them have a distinct identity. Instead of showing us Paolo and Francesca seducing themselves as they read together about Lancelot, Mazur gives us the entire whirlwind of lustful spirits, in the circle of those who can't restrain their feelings — on a page that has no border. It's a startling image, a train of windswept souls, appearing as if they're being swept through the labyrinth of a giant ear. Dante is their ear as well as their voice.

The tyrants, like Alexander, are literally up to their eyeballs in blood — those pained, hollow eyes. Or later, the close-up of the figure in the Malebolge, with the shit he's submerged in coming out of his mouth and eyes. There are the blasphemers, hard to tell apart from the confetti of fire that attacks them. There's the writer Brunetto Latini, among the sodomites, Dante's mentor and friend, one of the most moving figures in the *Inferno,* whom — in his characteristic refusal to settle for the obvious, predictable, or traditional illustration — Mazur depicts here as Latini's fearful projection of the punishment he will receive if he stops to talk to Dante — a figure broken, naked, on his knees, besieged by fire. This image, which Mazur says was taken from a nineteenth-century French academic picture of a slave, has the heartbreaking eloquence of Goya's war victims. There are the grotesques: the limp, beforked barrator (a black-and-white version of the image on the cover, a pitchfork pushing him under the boiling pitch, Mazur here

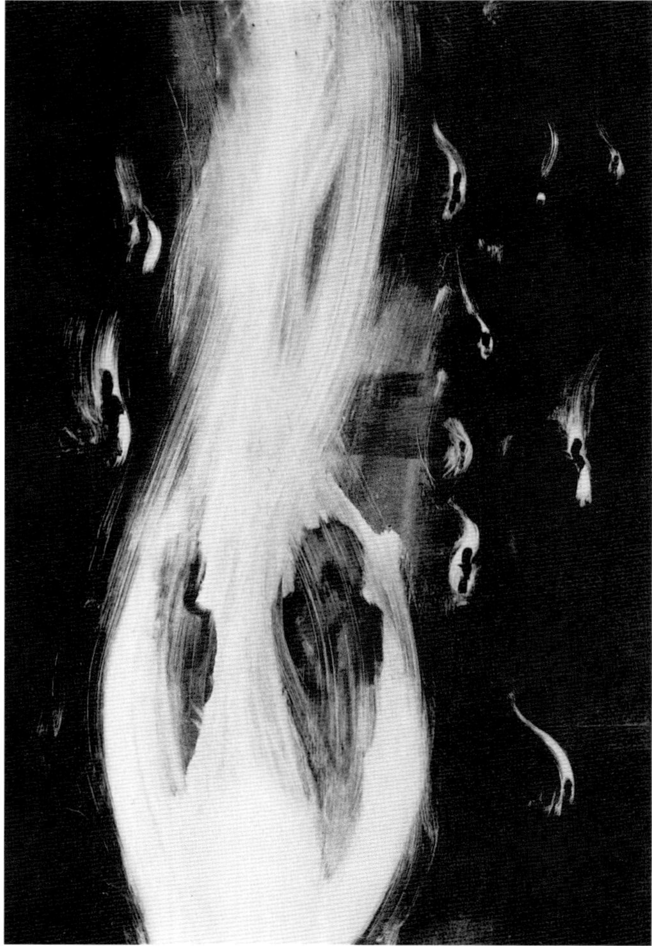

Fig. 65 *Canto XXVI,* from *The Inferno of Dante,* 1993, monotype, 23¾ × 15¾ in. (60.3 × 40.0 cm). Collection of the artist.

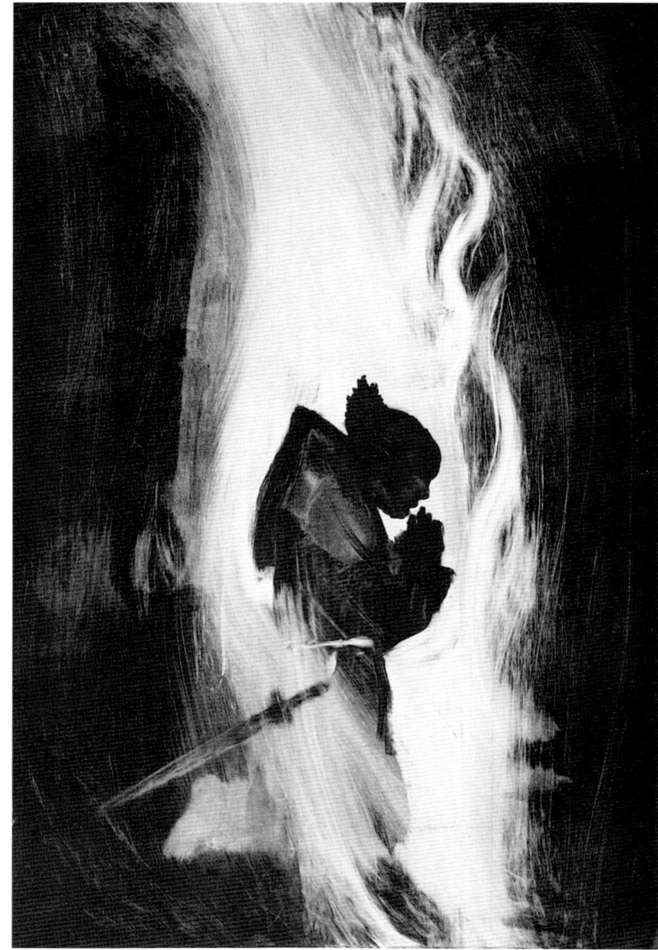

Fig. 66 *Canto XXVII,* from *The Inferno of Dante,* 1993, monotype, 23¾ × 15¾ in. (60.3 × 40.0 cm). Collection of the artist.

capturing the pain rather than merely the satire of Dante's merciless description). The horrible image of Agnello (fig. 62), another of the Malebranche, reminds me of the monster in the movie *Alien,* who emerges by piercing through the body of his victim from within. There's the skeletal schismatic (fig. 63), "split open from his chin / / Down to the farting place," and the horrifyingly distorted image of the diviners (such as Tiresias), with their heads literally twisted on backwards (fig. 64).

Some figures are treated with awe. "Tormented Ulysses and Diomedes," the mythical Greeks who conspired against the Trojans, are trapped, as if in their own Trojan horse, in a single flame sizzling against a flame-speckled darkness that reminds us of the flickering shades in Limbo (fig. 65). In the next canto we see another figure trapped in flames — the violent militarist Guido de Montefeltro, who sought absolution at the end of his life by entering a monastery (fig. 66). Mazur depicts him with his monk's tonsure and cowl, a solitary silhouette against the stark white glare of the surrounding hellfire, his sword surreptitiously still at his side — a subtle embodiment of Dante's (radical?) idea that mere lip service to Church doctrine (confession, last-minute conversion) is no guarantee of final forgiveness for an evil life. Like Goya's Colossus, the monolithic (virtually megalithic) monster Nimrod (the architect of the Tower of Babel, condemned never to be understood) towers over the world of doom, almost Neanderthal in his blank, inarticulate agony. "Little by little," Dante says, "vision starts picking out / Shapes that were hidden in the misty air." Over and over again, Mazur allows us — forces us — to relive the way the pilgrim Dante must work to decipher the figures, dim or burning, isolated or cramped, wrenching and twisting in the impenetrable dark.

Some of these figures have an almost cartoonlike linearity — this is Mazur the conscious illustrator, half mocking the whole idea of illustration. Yet he gives even the most sketchlike of these images an edge of menace. There's no image in which we don't feel the subject's pain or desire to inflict pain.

Mazur says Doré's greatest illustration is his image of the frozen world at the center of Hell. These images are Mazur's crowning achievements as well, his most heartrending and tragic in the poem. "I think that the most overrid-

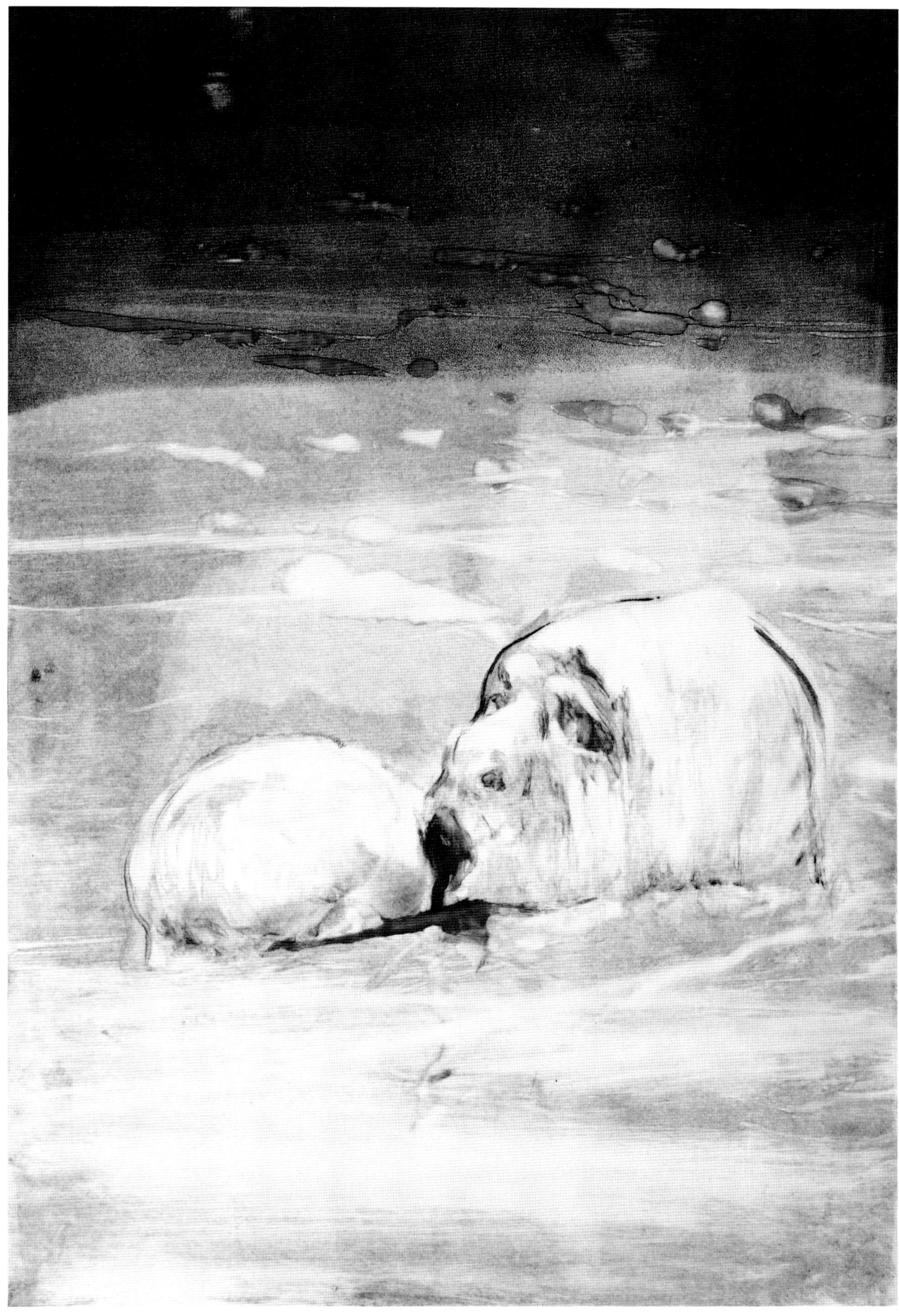

Fig. 67 *Canto XXXIII,* from *The Inferno of Dante,* 1993, monotype, 23¾ × 15¾ in. (60.3 × 40.0 cm). Collection of the artist.

ing element of the whole *Inferno* is not the horror of the *Inferno,* it is, in fact, the sadness of the *Inferno,*" he says.[12] This is profound literary criticism, and is the central spirit of what Mazur himself calls his "parallel translation."

The horrendous narrative of the death of Count Ugolino and his children in cantos XXXII and XXXIII (fig. 67) is the only place in the *Inferno* where the story of one soul continues into a second canto. This inspires Mazur's most cinematic (or at least montagelike) treatment. His illustration for canto XXXII is the big picture, overflowing the borders of the page.

> *. . . I turned and saw before me and underfoot*
> *A lake that ice made less like water than glass.*

Under the vast night of Hell is the translucent frozen lake, through which what seem to be small bumps of stones buried in the ice are poking up. These protrusions turn out to be human heads — the heads of the betrayers of country and party (for Dante among the most cardinal of sins). And one of the protrusions is really two heads. In canto XXXIII we see the ghastly but sublime close-up of these heads, one head submerged in the ice, the other gnawing on its skull.

The story of Ugolino is a complex one of multiple betrayals — betrayals and counterbetrayals among the rival Guelphs and Ghibellines. Ugolino conspired against both sides, making sure the Ghibelline archbishop Ruggieri took power in Pisa. Ruggieri, in turn, turned against Ugolino and had him sealed in a prison tower with two of his sons and two grandsons, ultimately starving them all to death. In the antepenultimate canto of the *Inferno,* Ugolino tells Dante the story of his imprisonment and the deaths of his sons. When the children see their father biting his own hand in his grief over their pain, they mistake the gesture for an expression of hunger and offer to feed him with their own flesh.

> "*. . . 'Father: our pain,' they said.*
> *'Will lessen if you eat us — you are the one*
>
> *Who clothed us in this wretched flesh: we plead*
> *For you to be the one who strips it away.'*"

Ugolino goes blind from hunger as his children one by one die of starvation. "And then," Ugolino says, in one of the most horrifying moments of understated indirection in Western literature, "the hunger had more / Power than even sorrow had over me."

As in several of the greatest episodes of the *Inferno* (Paolo and Francesca, Brunetto Latini, Ulysses), Dante here transcends his own moral judgments. This is what wrong-doers deserve, he wants to insist. Yet these extraordinary passages are so moving because underlying — undermining — the judgment is the tragic sense that no one on earth deserves such suffering. Mazur pictures not the scene in the tower, but what Dante actually witnesses before Ugolino's narration:

> *Pausing in his savage meal, the sinner raised*
> *His mouth and wiped it clean along the hair*
> *Left on the head whose back he had laid waste. . . .*

After the narration, Ugolino resumes his punishment/revenge:

> *He gripped the skull again in his teeth, which ground*
> *Strong as a dog's against the bone he tore.*

Every detail of Mazur's monotype contributes to the tragic insight. Ugolino is in semiprofile. His head is tilted slightly back. His mouth is open in a wide O, pressed against the back of the archbishop's skull. We focus on his eyes, glancing sidelong at his interlocutors, Dante and Virgil. And at us. The look combines guilt, suspicion, and the desire for exoneration, with the depths of sorrow and helplessness. This is his fate — there's nothing else he can do. He's looking at us — challenging us — to understand that none of us is exempt from this condition. Are those tears streaming down his cheek or just lines in his face? In the distance is endless darkness. Mazur has risen to one of an artist's greatest challenges. This is one of the most graphic embodiments of the tragic vision by any artist — Aristotelian "pity and terror" — a devastating visualization of Dante's words that is finally also (and must be) beyond words.

NOTES

1. Quotations from Michael Mazur are from a series of conversations we had during the winter and spring of 1998, unless otherwise cited.
2. Gail Mazur, *The Pose of Happiness* (Boston: David R. Godine, 1986).
3. Gail Mazur, *The Common* (Chicago: University of Chicago Press, 1995).
4. Robert Pinsky, *The Want Bone* (Hopewell, N.J.: Ecco Press, 1990).
5. Mallarmé, "The Canticle of Saint John" from *Hérodiade,* in *Stéphane Mallarmé: Selected Poems,* trans. C. F. Macintyre (Berkeley: University of California Press, 1957), 43, 45.
6. Robert Pinsky, *The Inferno of Dante* (New York: Farrar, Straus and Giroux, 1994).
7. Michael Mazur, "Illustrating Dante's *Inferno,*" in *The Monotypes by Michael Mazur for the Inferno,* exh. cat. (Iowa City: University of Iowa Museum of Art, 1994), 10.
8. *Image and Text: A Dialogue with Robert Pinsky and Michael Mazur* (Berkeley: Townsend Center for the Humanities, University of California, 1994), 3.
9. Ibid., 23.
10. Ibid.
11. Ibid., 45.
12. Ibid., 37.

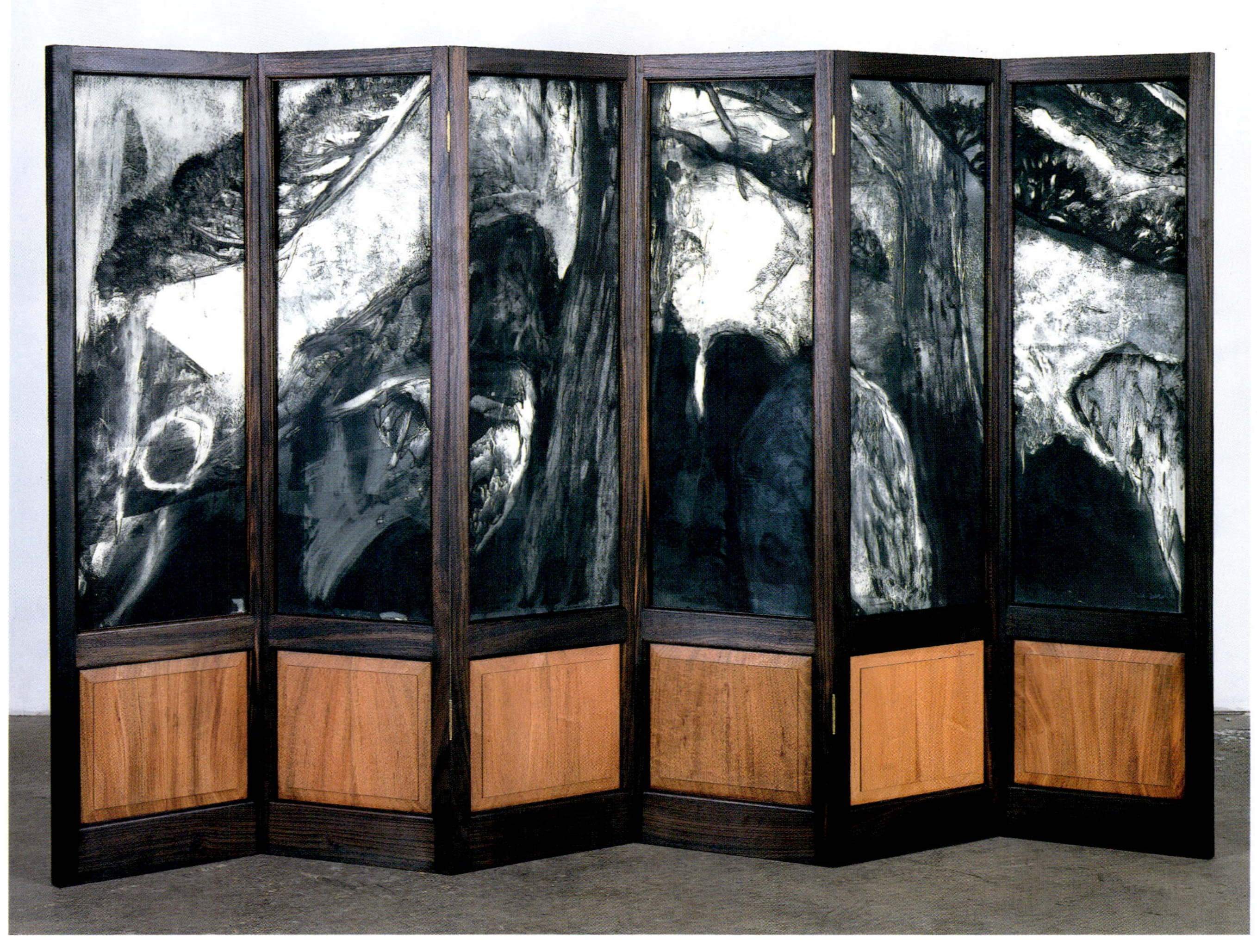

Colorplate 28 *Trees and Rocks in Western Hills,* 1988, folding screen with 6 silk monotype panels, 72 × 98 in. (182.9 × 248.9 cm). Courtesy of Experimental Workshop, Emeryville, California.

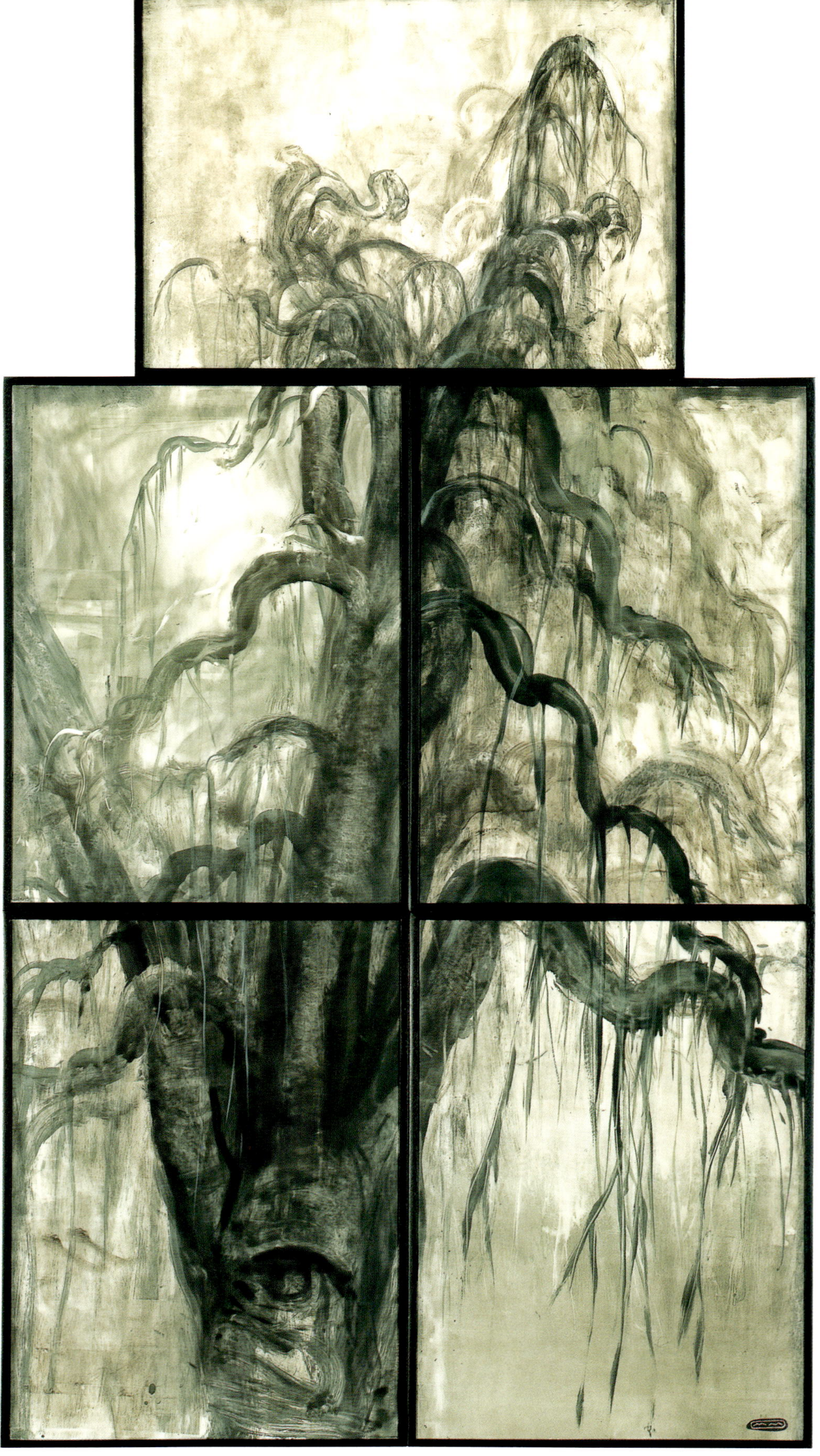

Colorplate 29 *Weeping Beech,* 1988, monotype on silk charmeuse (5 panels), 84½ × 45½ in. (214.6 × 115.6 cm) overall. Museum of Fine Arts, Boston, Gift of the artist (1990.305a–e).

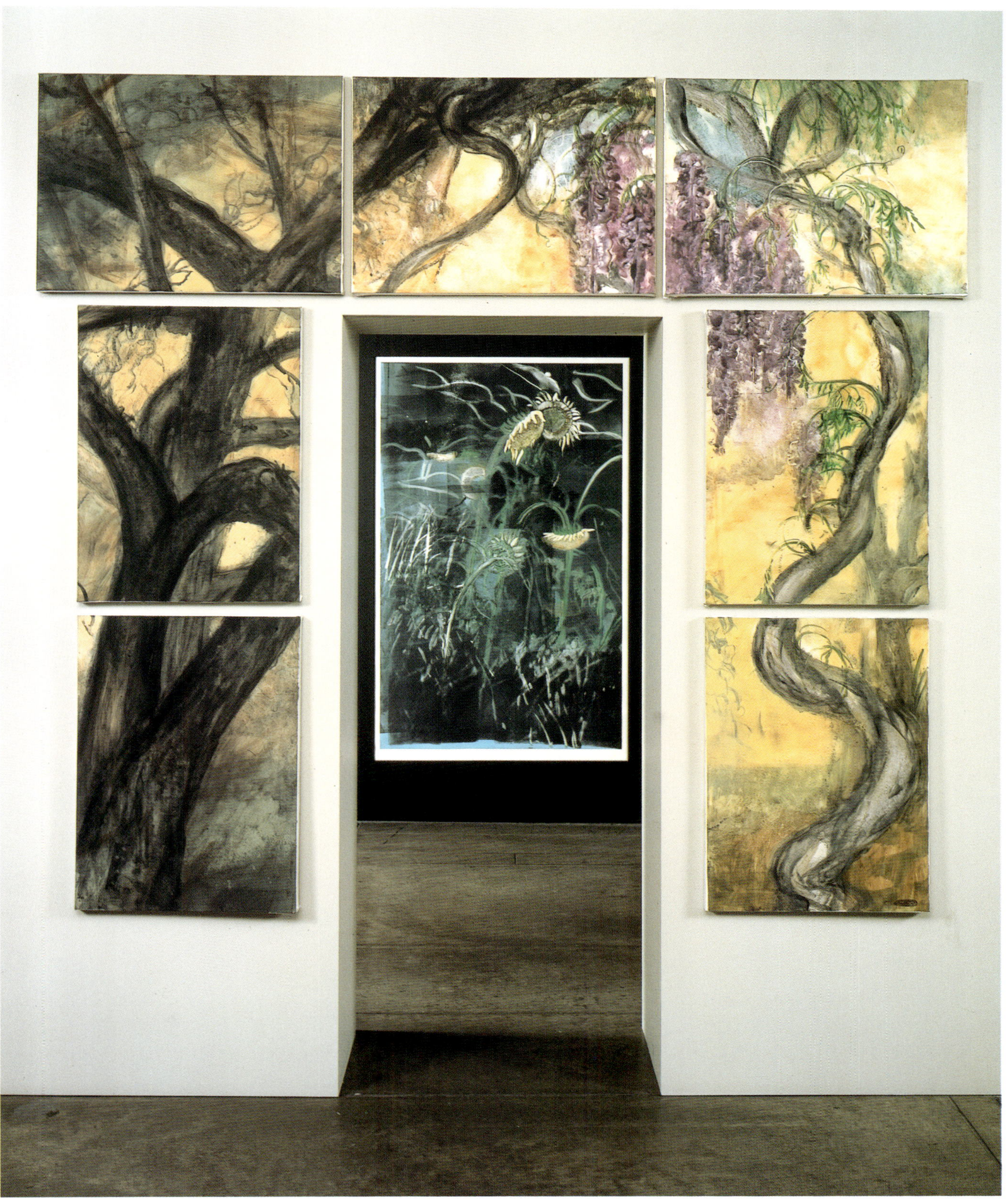

Colorplate 30 *Wisteria Door,* 1988, monotype on silk charmeuse (7 panels), 30¼ × 22¼ in. (76.9 × 56.5 cm) each (four panels), 22¼ × 30¼ in. (56.5 × 76.9 cm) each (three panels), Collection of the artist. Note: *Wakeby Night Study (Storm)* is in background.

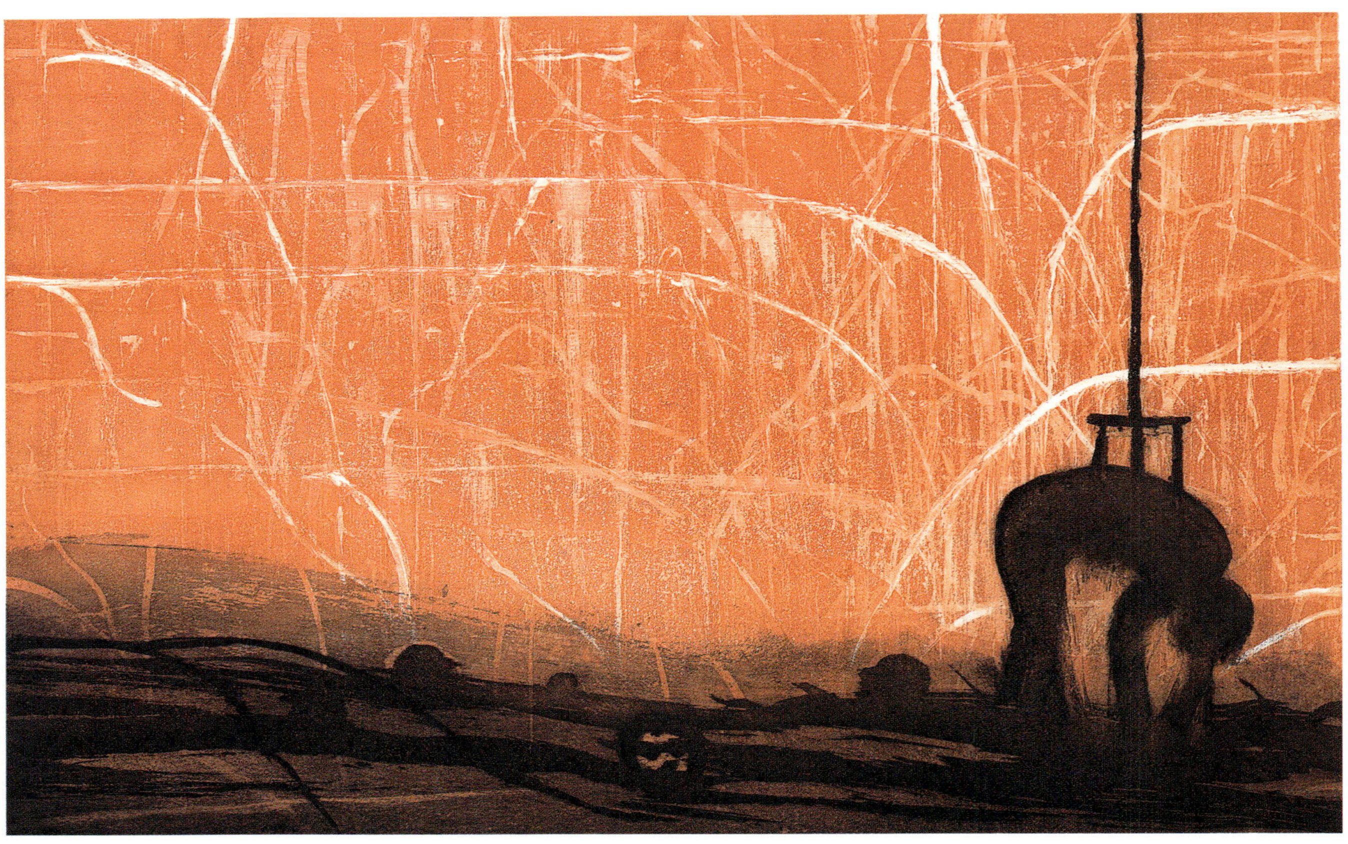

Colorplate 31 *Canto XXI (The Lawyers),* from *The Inferno of Dante,* 1992, etching and aquatint, 22⅛ × 30⅝ in. (56.2 × 77.8 cm). Collection of the artist. (Catalogue raisonné 272)

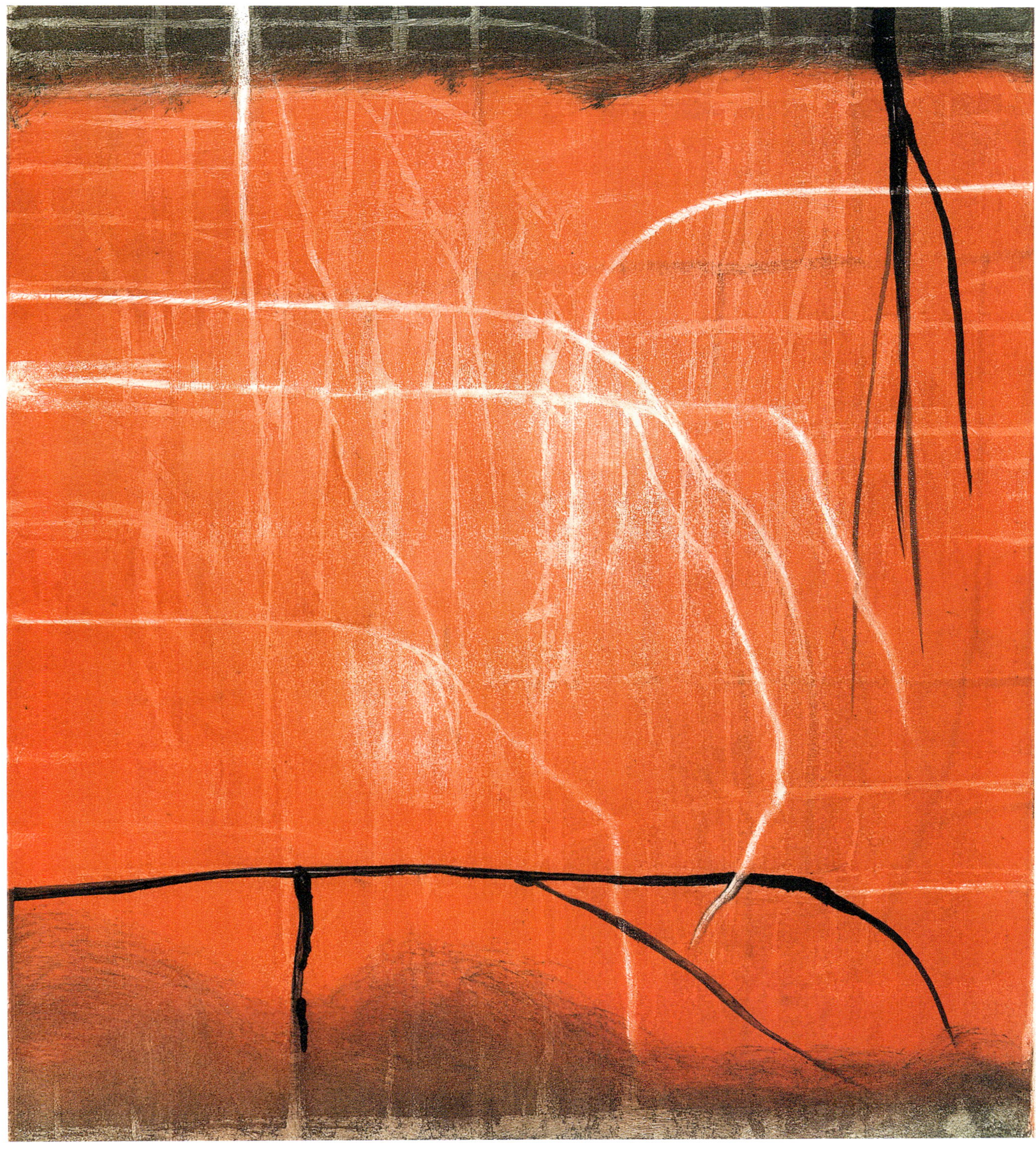

Colorplate 32 *Fall Branching,* 1992, monotype, 30 × 22½ in. (76.2 × 57.2 cm). Collection of the artist.

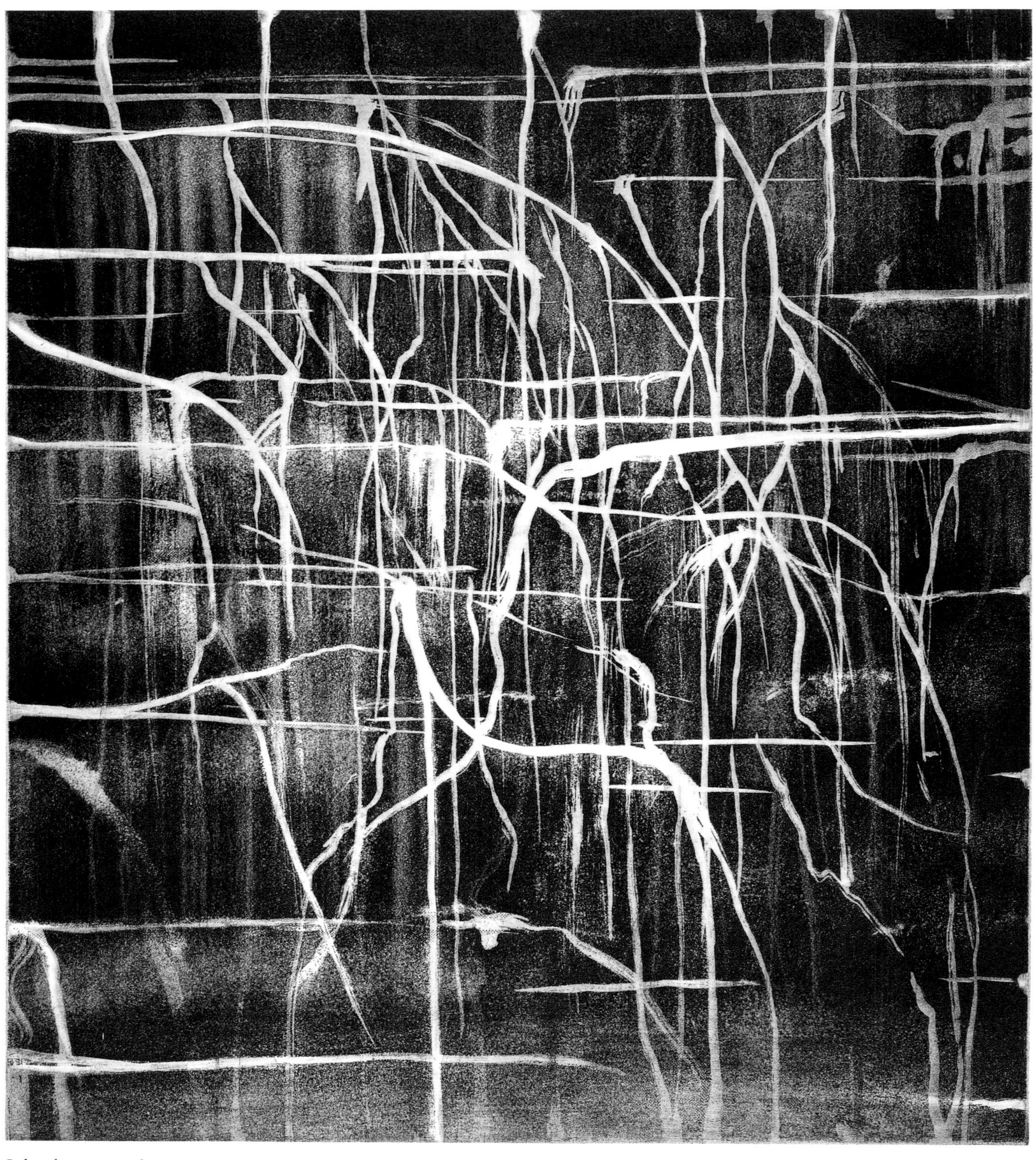

Colorplate 33 *Ice Glen,* 1993–94, aquatint, 30 × 22½ in. (76.2 × 57.2 cm). Collection of the artist. (Catalogue raisonné 276)

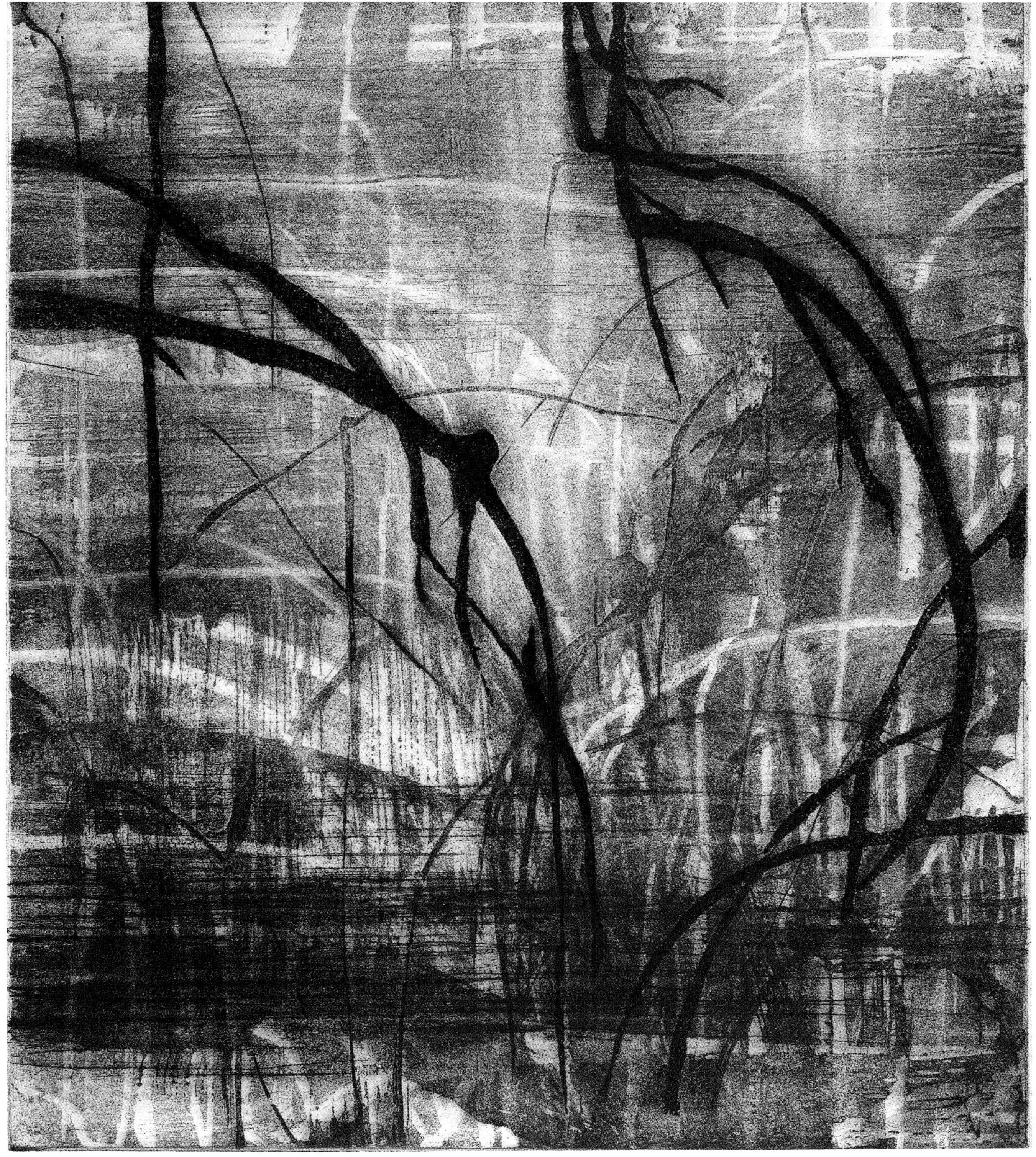

Colorplate 34 *Black Branching*, 1994, etching and aquatint, 27¾ × 23¾ in. (70.5 × 60.3 cm). Collection of the artist. (Catalogue raisonné 277)

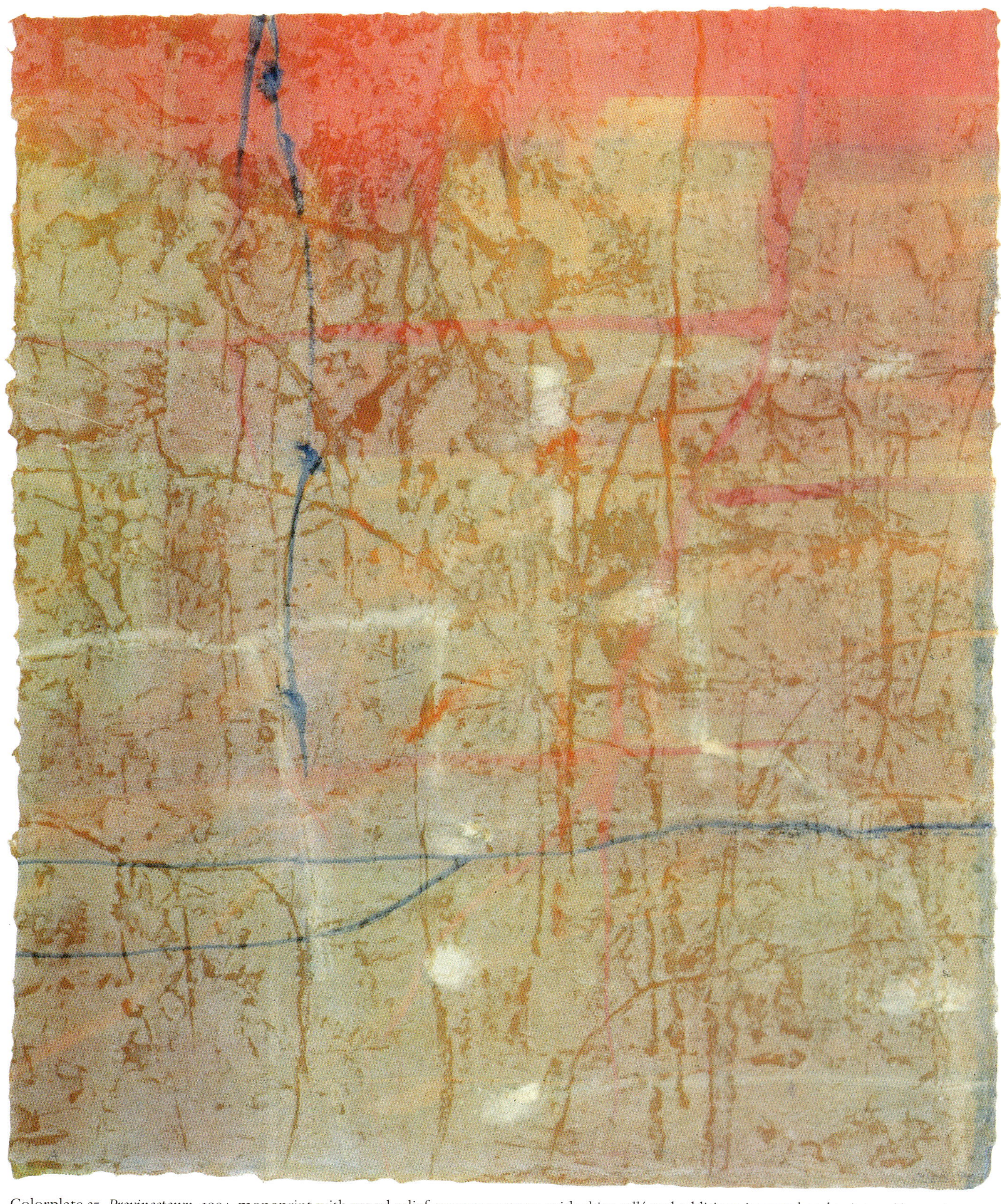

Colorplate 35 *Provincetown,* 1994, monoprint with wood relief over monotype, with *chine collé* and additions in pastel and paint, 20½ × 17 in. (52.1 × 43.2 cm) image. Collection of Robert and Ellen Pinsky. (Catalogue raisonné 279)

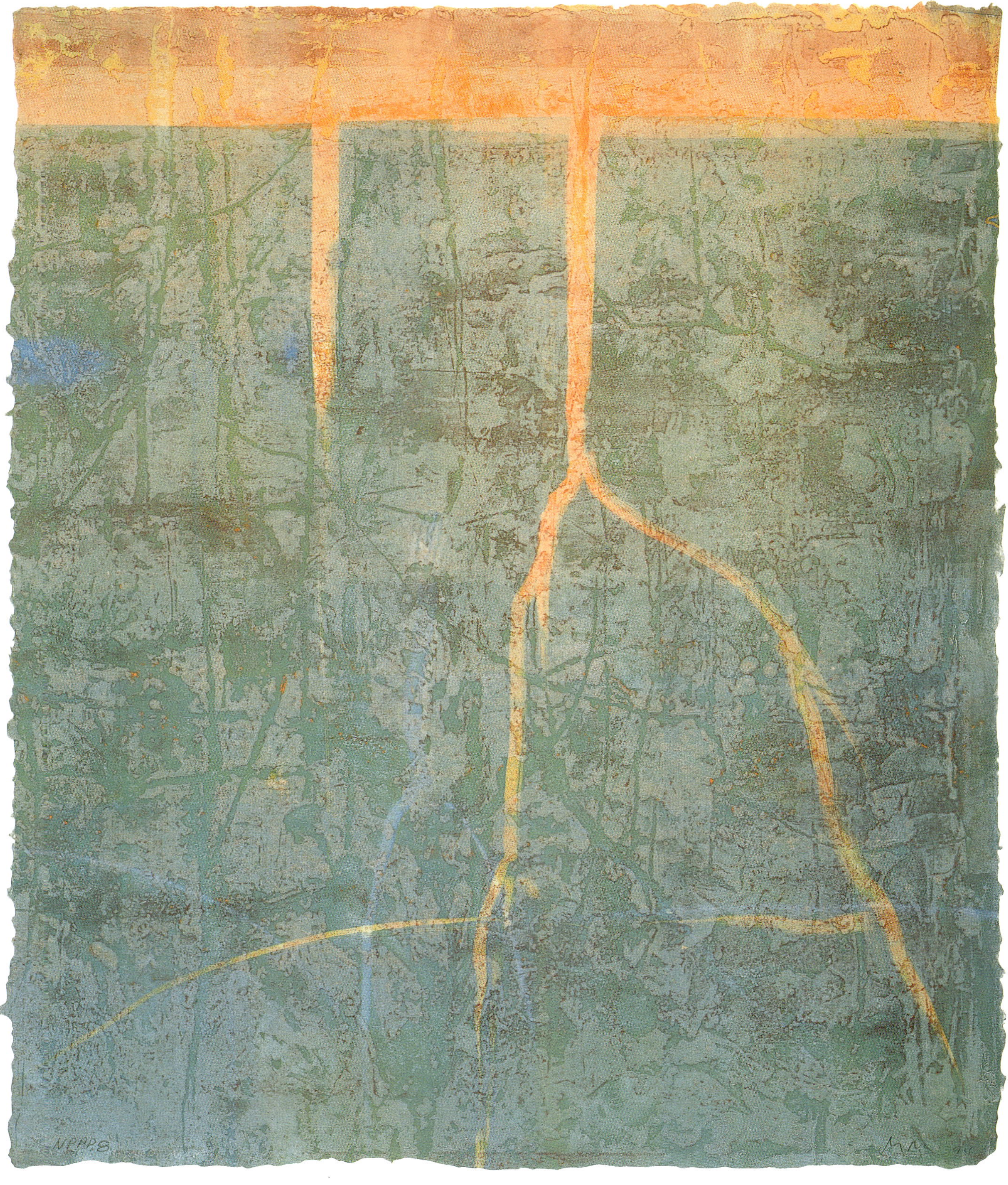

Colorplate 36 *Provincetown,* 1994, monoprint with wood relief over monotype, with *chine collé* and additions in pastel and paint, 20½ × 17 in. (52.1 × 43.2 cm) image. Museum of Fine Arts, Boston, Gift of Virginia Herrick Deknatel (1995.14.6). (Catalogue raisonné 279)

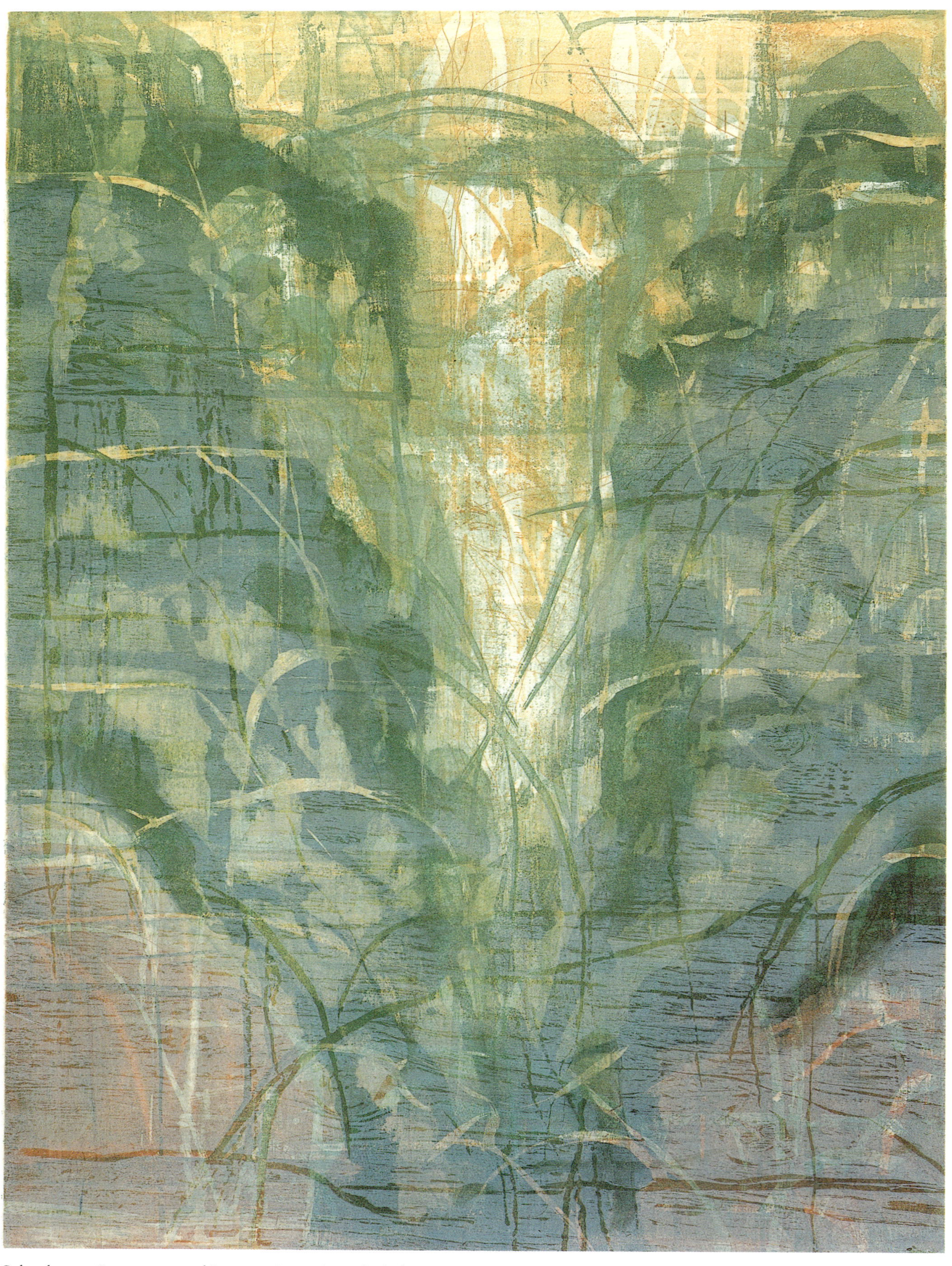

Colorplate 37 *Canyon,* 1994, etching, aquatint, and wood relief, 41⅞ × 29½ in. (106.4 × 75.0 cm). Collection of the artist. (Catalogue raisonné 280)

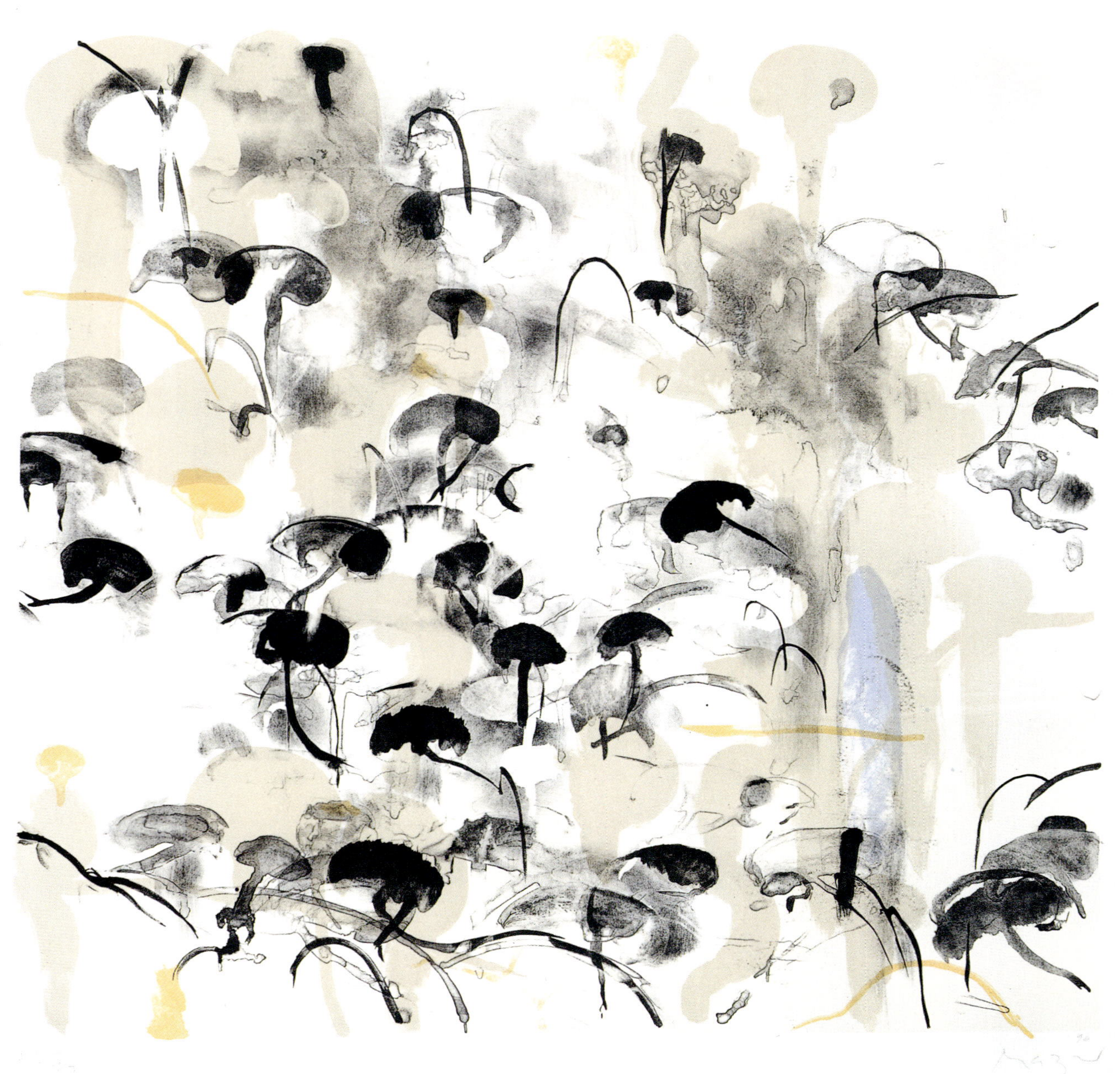

Colorplate 38 *Untitled,* 1996, lithograph, 26⅜ × 26¾ in. (67.0 × 68.8 cm). Collection of the artist. (Catalogue raisonné 314)

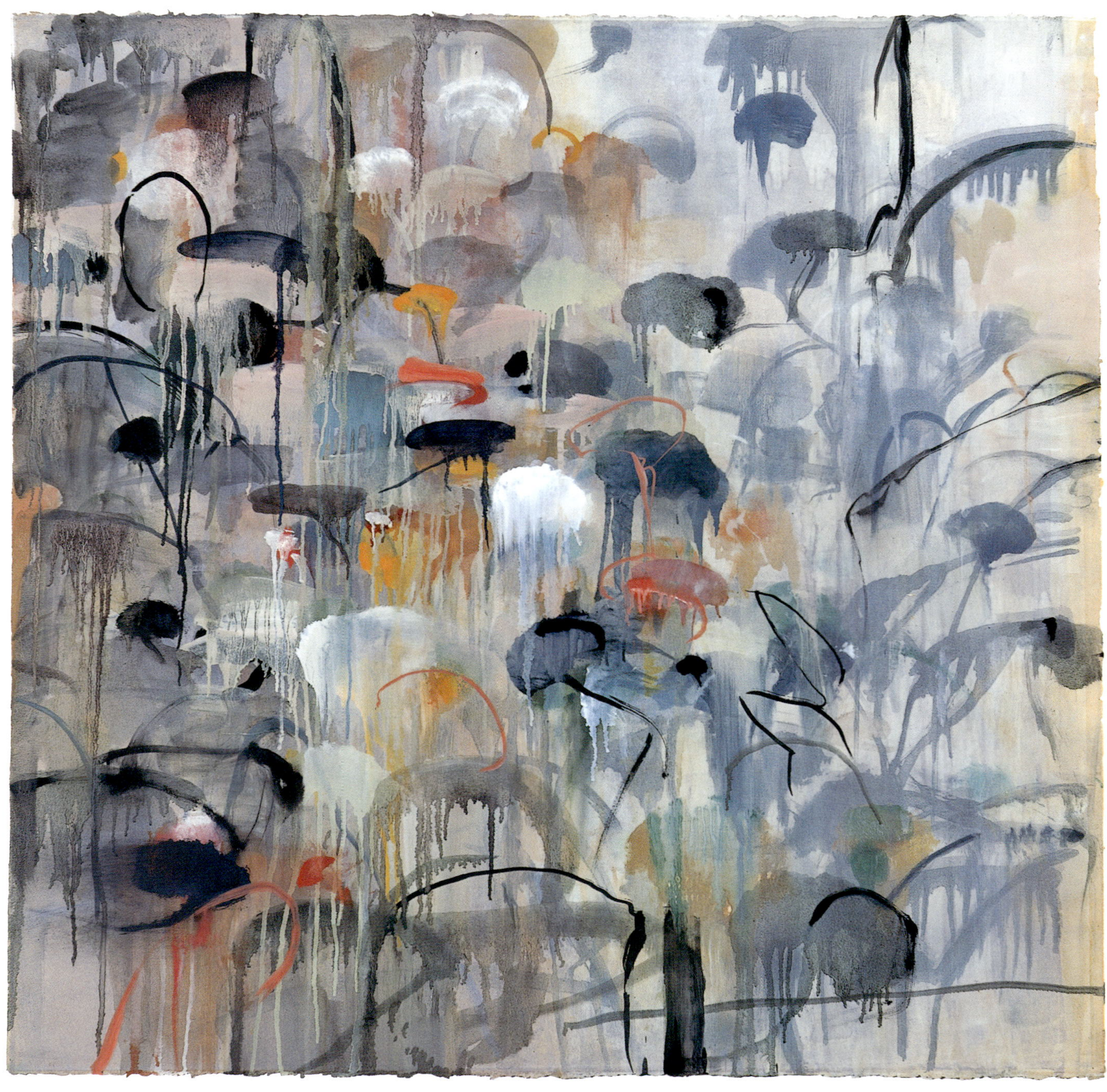

Colorplate 39 *Untitled,* from the *Mind Landscapes (Series I),* 1996, monotype with hand painting, 43 × 42⅝ in. (109.2 × 108.3 cm). Collection of the artist.

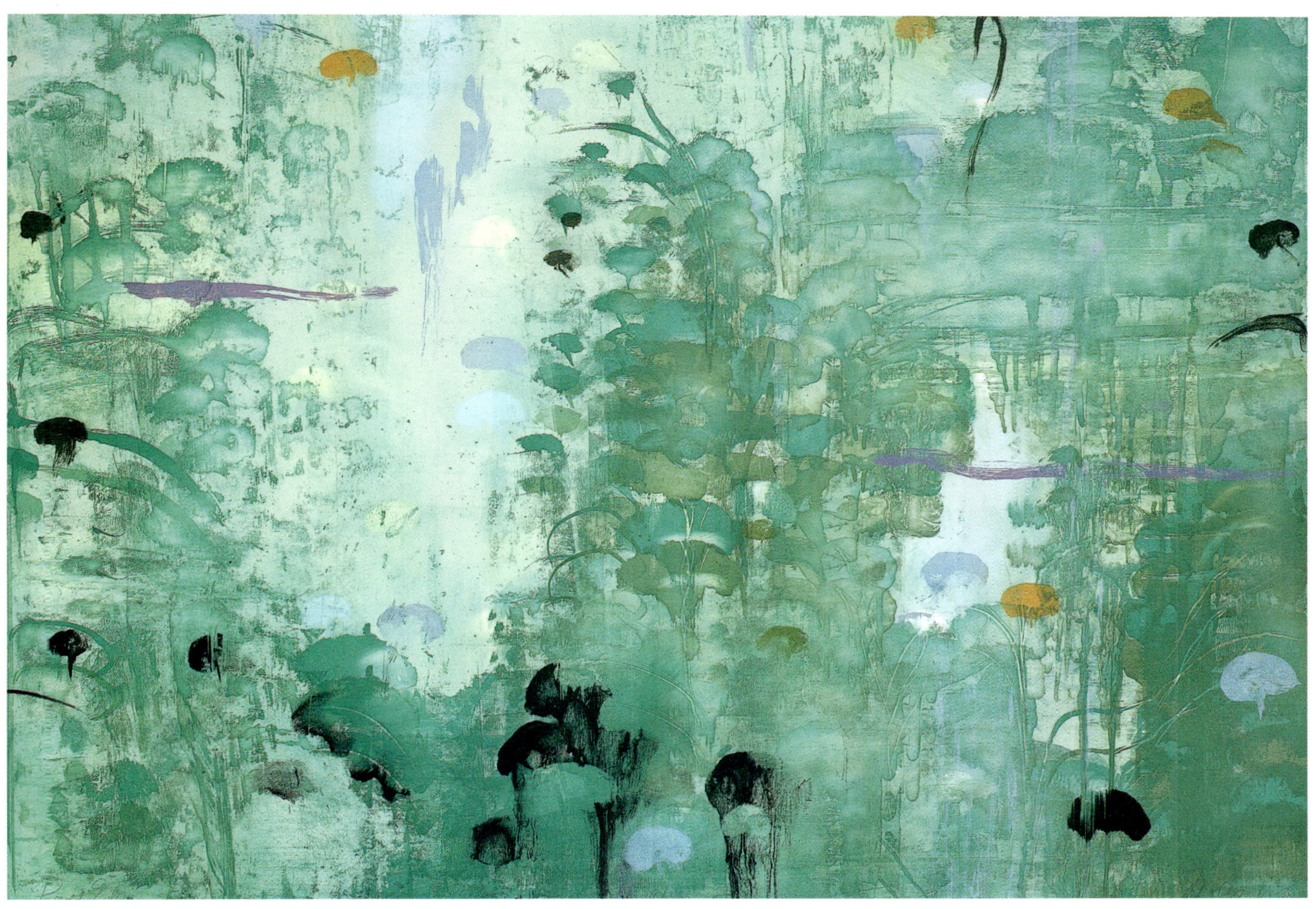

Colorplate 40 *Pond Edge,* 1997, etching and aquatint, 29¾ × 41¾ in. (75.6 × 106.1 cm). Courtesy Mary Ryan Gallery. (Catalogue raisonné 317)

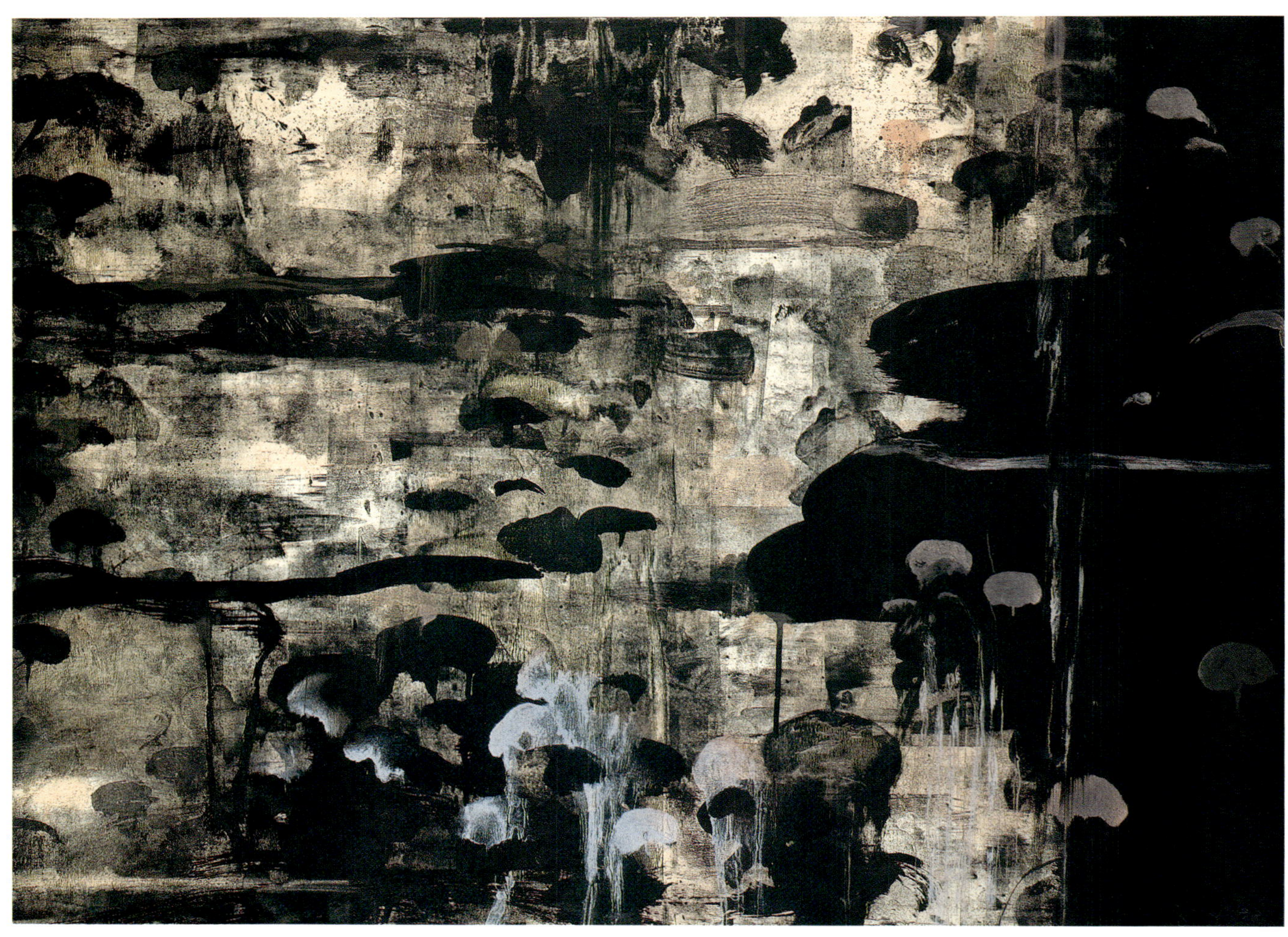

Colorplate 41 *Storm Warning*, 1997, etching and aquatint, 31¼ × 42 in. (79.4 × 106.7 cm). Courtesy Barbara Krakow Gallery. (Catalogue raisonné 318)

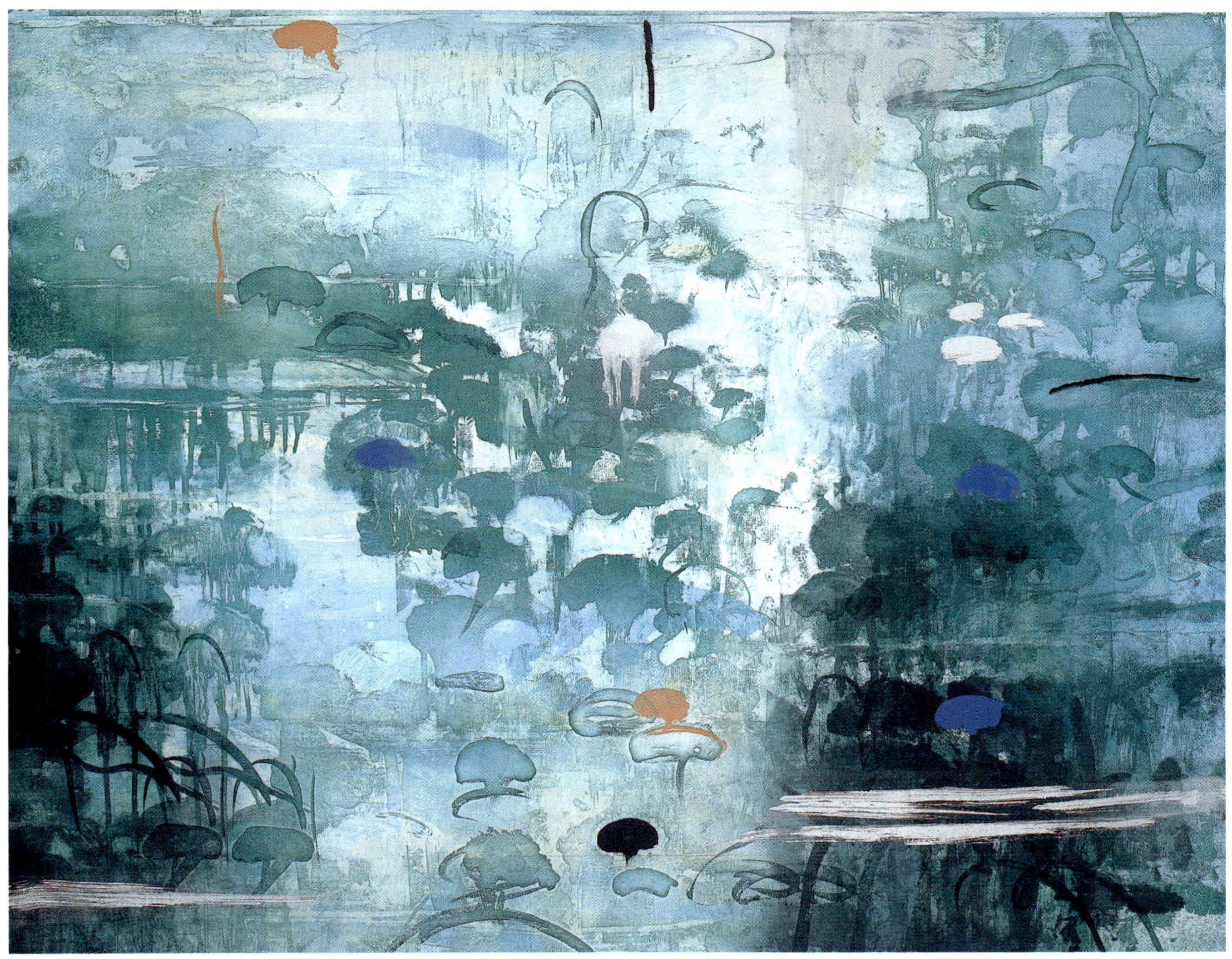

Colorplate 42 *Pond Edge II,* 1997–98, etching and aquatint, 32 × 39¾ in. (81.3 × 101.0 cm). Courtesy Mary Ryan Gallery. (Catalogue raisonné 319)

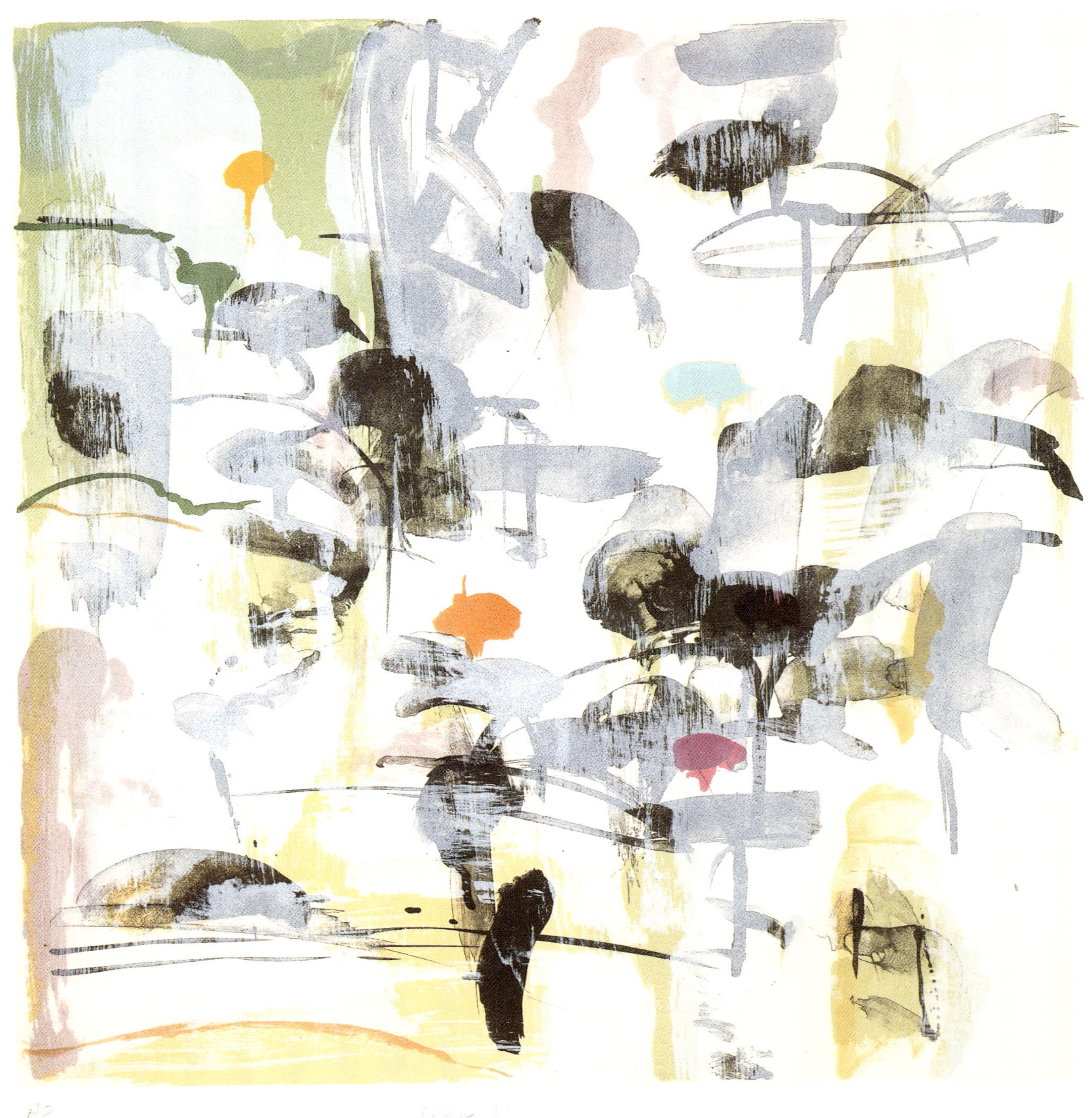

Colorplate 43 *Thaw II,* 1998, lithograph, 28½ × 26½ in. (72.4 × 67.3 cm). Collection of the artist. (Catalogue raisonné 324)

Chronology

THE work of Michael Mazur has been featured in numerous solo and group painting, print, and drawing exhibitions, nationally and internationally, since 1958. Only those exhibitions significant to Mazur's career as a printmaker are documented here. The artist's complete gallery and museum exhibition history is maintained by his current dealers, Barbara Krakow Gallery in Boston and Mary Ryan Gallery in New York. The Archives of American Art has 10¼ hours of taped interviews with Mazur, conducted by Robert Brown in sessions between 12 January 1993 and 3 February 1995. The Archives has also microfilmed thirteen bound work journals and one loose sketchbook kept by the artist between 1 May 1974 and 3 March 1998.

1935–53

Born Michael Burton Mazur on 2 November 1935 at Doctor's Hospital in New York, the only child of Burton and Helen (Isaacs) Mazur; spends summers at boys' camps in Maine; attends the Lincoln School in Manhattan and the Horace Mann School, located in the Riverdale section of the Bronx; while still in high school, spends Saturdays in 1949–50 assisting the artist Alan Ullman in his Greenwich Village studio and taking painting classes with Morris Davidson; high school art club friends include the art critic Henry Geldzahler and the artist/cartoonist Ed Koren, with whom Mazur worked on the school literary magazine, *Manuscript.*

1953–54

Attends Amherst College in Massachusetts; spends summer of freshman year traveling in Europe, including Venice and southern France.

1954–55

Under reciprocal arrangement between Amherst and Smith College, takes classes from Smith faculty member Leonard Baskin; in the summer of his sophomore year, works as an intern in the New York architectural offices of Ely Jacques Kahn and Robert Jacobs and also attends Yale Summer School of Music and Art, Norfolk, Connecticut.

1956

Takes a year off from studies at Amherst to live in Italy; takes drawing classes at the Accademia di Belle Arti in Florence; studies the work of Renzo Vespignani and other Italian neorealists as well as the Italian old masters; learns Italian; while in Florence, visits the studio of American sculptor Bernard Reder; buys his first prints, which include works by Georges Rouault, Käthe Kollwitz, Rodolphe Bresdin, and illustrations from the German periodical *Die Stürm;* on his return to the U.S., reads Dante's *Divine Comedy* in the original Italian.

1958

B.A., Amherst College; creates *An Image of Salomé* for his senior thesis project, which is published by the artist and printed at Apiary Press, run by Baskin's students at Smith College; meets and becomes good friends with Baskin's assistant George Lockwood, who would later found Impressions Workshop in Boston; marries Gail Beckwith (later, the poet Gail Mazur), who was then a student at Smith College; begins graduate study at School of Art and

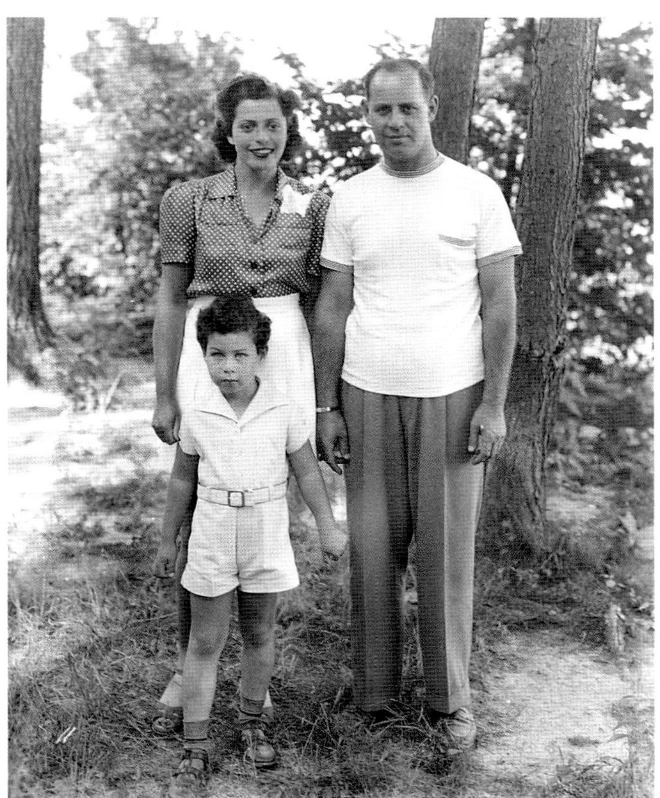

Mazur with parents, about 1939–40

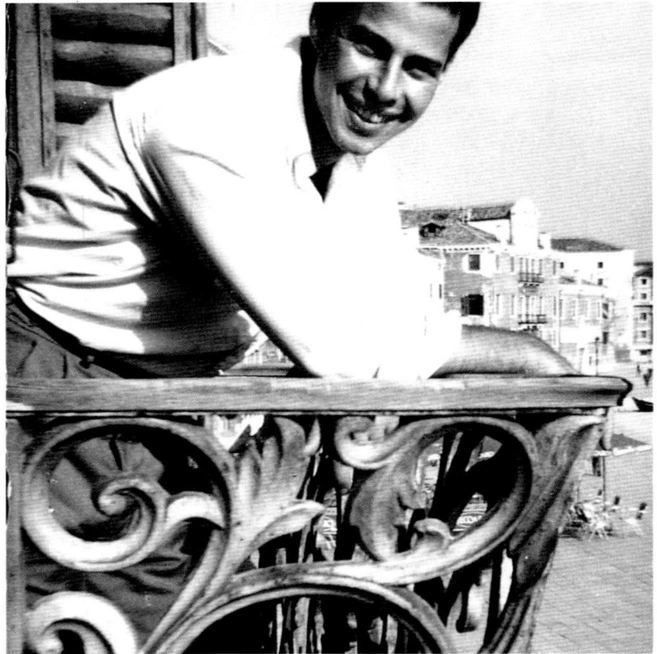

Mazur on balcony in Venice, 1956

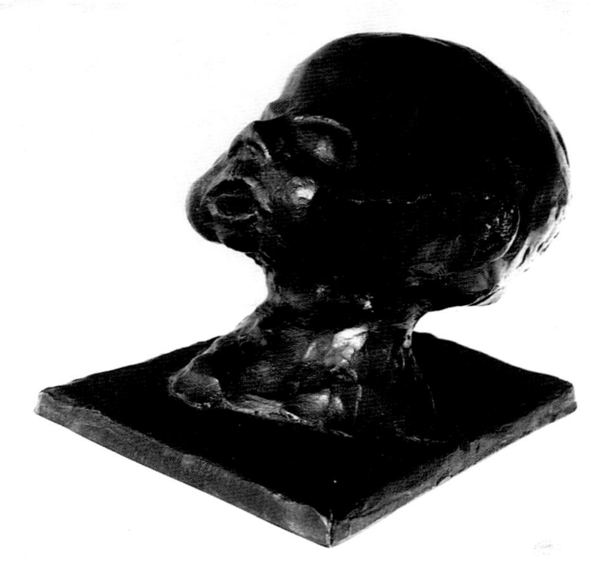

Fig. 68 *Head of Baby,* 1960, bronze, 6 × 6 × 6¼ in. (15.2 × 15.2 × 15.9 cm). Collection of the artist. Note: In Barone Gallery exhibition, 1960.

Architecture, Yale University, New Haven; studies with Gabor Peterdi, Bernard Chaet, William Bailey, Rico Lebrun, Sewell Sillman, Neil Welliver, art historian Egbert Haverkamp-Begemann, and Asian-art historian Nelson Wu, as well as with visiting artists Fairfield Porter and John Scheuler; makes regular Thursday trips with other students to Peterdi's home/studio; works as a teaching assistant for both Peterdi and Bailey.

1959

Receives B.F.A. from Yale University; son Daniel is born in New Haven.

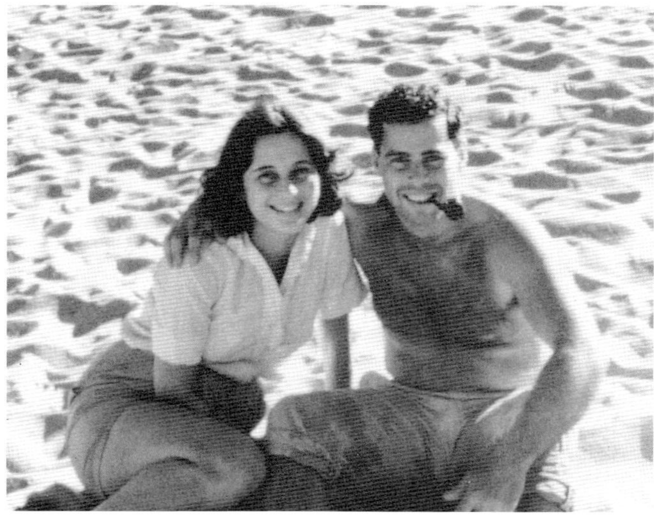

Gail and Michael Mazur in Provincetown, Massachusetts, 1959

1960

First solo exhibition: Barone Gallery, New York (prints, drawings, and sculpture [fig. 68]); group exhibitions: *18th National Print Exhibition,* Library of Congress, Washington, D.C.; *12th National Print Exhibition,* Brooklyn Museum, New York.

1961

In spring of his last semester at Yale, assists sculptor Naum Gabo for three months in printing two editions of etchings; Gabo shows Mazur the wood-engraved monoprints he is printing by hand; receives M.F.A., School of Art and Architecture, Yale University; begins teaching printmaking, life drawing, and anatomy at the Rhode Island School of Design, Providence; daughter Kathe is born in Providence; begins *Closed Ward* series (colorplate 4; figs. 8, 9, and 19–25), which is based on art therapy visits with student volunteers to the Howard State Mental Facility in Providence; solo exhibition: Jill Kornblee Gallery, New York (also 1963 and 1966).

1962

Receives Louis Comfort Tiffany Foundation grant; group exhibitions: *13th National Print Exhibition,* Brooklyn Museum, New York; *Boston Printmakers,* Museum of Fine Arts, Boston.

1963

Teaches at the Yale Summer School of Music and Art; exhibits first *Closed Ward* prints and drawings (fig. 69) at the Providence Art Club, where several works are purchased by the Fogg Art Museum at Harvard University, Cambridge, and the Museum of Modern Art, New York; group exhibitions: *19th Annual Print Exhibition,* Library of

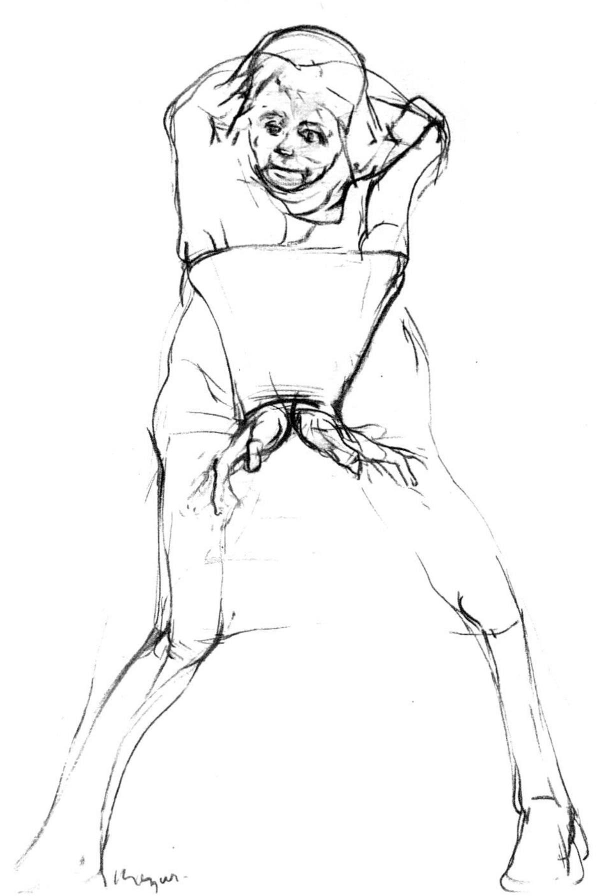

Fig. 69 *Mental Patient in Restraint,* 1962–63, charcoal (early *Closed Ward* drawing), 30 × 20 in. (76.2 × 50.8 cm). Private collection.

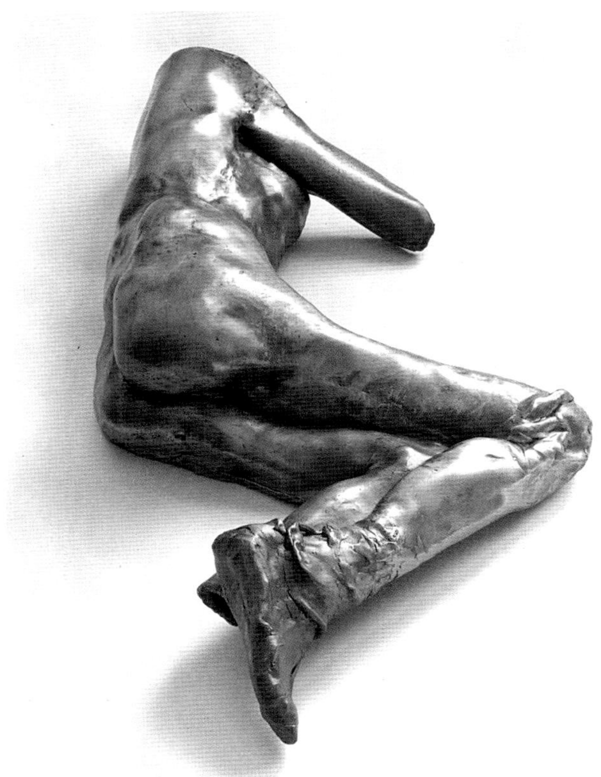

Fig. 70 *Torso,* 1964–65, bronze, 48 × 36 × 12 in. (121.9 × 91.4 × 30.5 cm). Picker Art Gallery, Colgate University, Hamilton, N.Y.

Congress, Washington, D.C.; *National Print Exhibition,* Brooks Memorial Art Gallery, Memphis, Tennessee.

1964

Receives a fellowship from the John Simon Guggenheim Foundation; moves family to Arlington Street in Cambridge, Massachusetts, for the year of his Guggenheim grant; though still drawing and experimenting with printmaking, his main activity is in making sculpture (fig. 70); receives

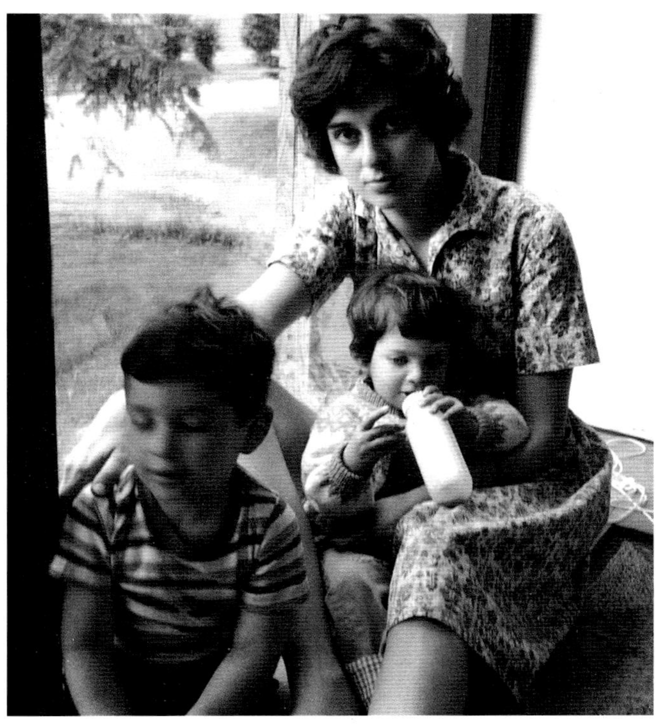

Gail Mazur with Daniel and Kathe, Norfolk, Connecticut, July 1963

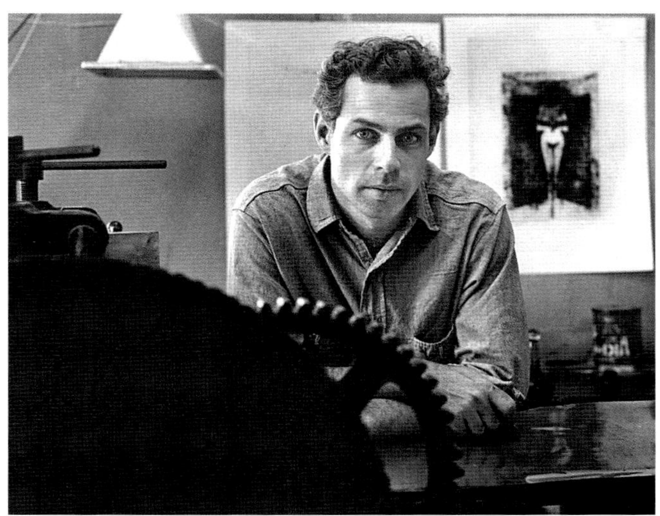

Mazur at press, 1964

an award from the American Academy of Arts and Letters and subsequently has a small solo exhibition in New York in conjunction with the award; solo exhibitions: Boris Mirski Gallery, Boston (also 1966); Philadelphia Print Club; Silvermine Guild of Artists, New Canaan, Connecticut; group exhibitions: *Painters and Sculptors as Printmakers,* Museum of Modern Art, New York; *14th National Print Exhibition,* Brooklyn Museum, New York.

1965

Moves to Fuller Place in Cambridge; completes the *Images from a Locked Ward* portfolio of fourteen lithographs (figs. 10, 26, and 47), which are printed at Impressions Workshop in Boston with images based on the *Closed Ward* etching series; begins teaching at Brandeis University in Waltham, Massachusetts, where he remains for the next ten years, except for a two-year leave to work in New York in 1970–71; is active in university politics and in the peace movement; solo exhibition: Alpha Gallery, Boston (also 1969 and 1974); group exhibitions: *A Decade of American Drawings,* Whitney Museum of American Art, New York; *Young Americans: 35 Artists under 35,* Whitney Museum of American Art, New York; *Print Biennial of the Americas,* Santiago, Chile.

1966

Group exhibitions: *15th National Print Exhibition,* Brooklyn Museum, New York; *Annual Exhibition: Sculpture and Prints,* Whitney Museum of American Art, New York.

1967

Group exhibitions: *Prints of Two Countries, Italy-America,* Tyler School of Art, Philadelphia; *The Helen W. and Robert M. Benjamin Collection,* Yale University Art Gallery, New Haven.

1968

The Artist and the Model, a portfolio of twelve intaglio prints, is published by Sylvan Cole at Associated American Artists, New York; receives a Tamarind Artist Fellowship and travels to the Tamarind Lithography Workshop in Los Angeles, where he produces thirty-four editions of primarily black-and-white lithographs that continue the *Artist and the Model* theme; begins using the airbrush, which he had learned from the artist Billy Al Bengston while at Tamarind; sees the exhibition *Edgar Degas: Monotypes* at the Fogg Art Museum and subsequently begins making monotypes; in Boston co-founds Artists against Racism and the War and collaborates with Fred Stone on *The American Way Room* (fig. 71), an antiwar installation piece that is shown throughout the Boston area and subsequently travels to New York, Atlanta, Syracuse, and Philadelphia; solo exhibitions: Associated American Artists, New York *(The Artist and the Model);* Comsky Gallery, Los Angeles; group exhibitions: *Contemporary American Graphic Artists,* Rijksakademie van Beeldende Kunsten, Amsterdam (travels); *New Expressions in Fine Printmaking,* National Collection of Fine Arts,

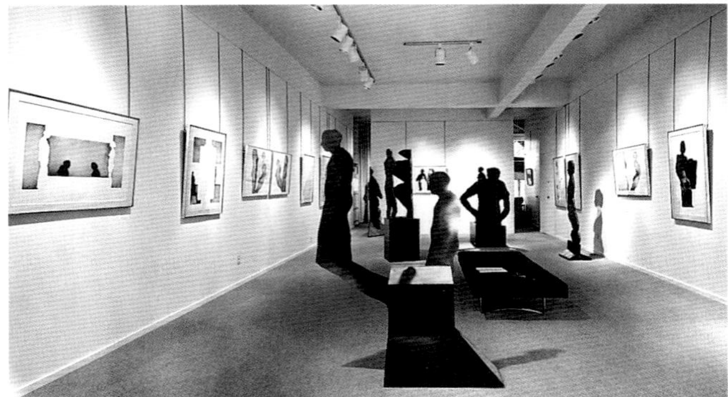

Exhibition of *The Artist and the Model* portfolio and sculpture at the Alpha Gallery, Boston, 1968

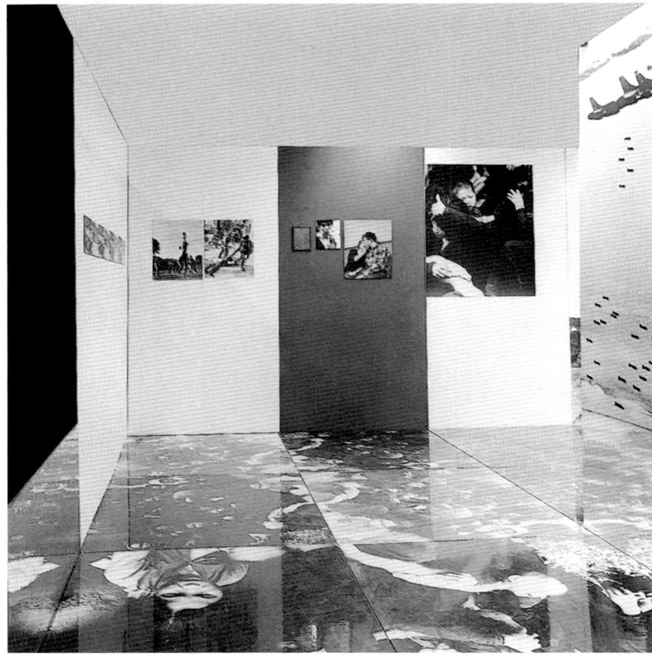

Fig. 71 *The American Way Room,* 1968 (collaboration with Fred Stone). Installation in a storefront on Central Square, Cambridge, Mass.

Washington, D.C. (travels in Germany and Belgium); *16th National Print Exhibition,* Brooklyn Museum, New York; *Annual Exhibition,* Whitney Museum of American Art, New York; *Graphics '68: Recent American Prints,* University of Lexington, Kentucky.

1969

Master printer and good friend George Lockwood dies in Boston; solo exhibition: *Prints by Michael Mazur,* Rose Art Museum, Brandeis University; group exhibitions: *Homage to Tamarind,* Museum of Modern Art, New York; *Prints of the 1960s,* Museum of Fine Arts, Boston; *Primero Biennale,* Cali, Colombia; *Big Prints,* Albright-Knox Art Gallery, Buffalo, New York; *Annual,* Pennsylvania Academy of the Fine Arts, Philadelphia.

1970

Mazur's father dies; he moves family to New York City and rents living and studio space (figs. 72 and 73) in the old Lord and Taylor Building at 901 Broadway that had formerly belonged to the sculptor Paul Manship; while in New York becomes active in the Art Workers Coalition; is selected as one of the American artists to exhibit at the Venice Biennale, but subsequently withdraws in protest with several other artists as part of an antiwar boycott of American foreign policy; solo exhibition: *"The Studio" and Other Works, 1969–70*, Institute of Contemporary Art, Boston (environmental installations); group exhibition: *Human Concerns, Personal Torment*, Whitney Museum of American Art, New York.

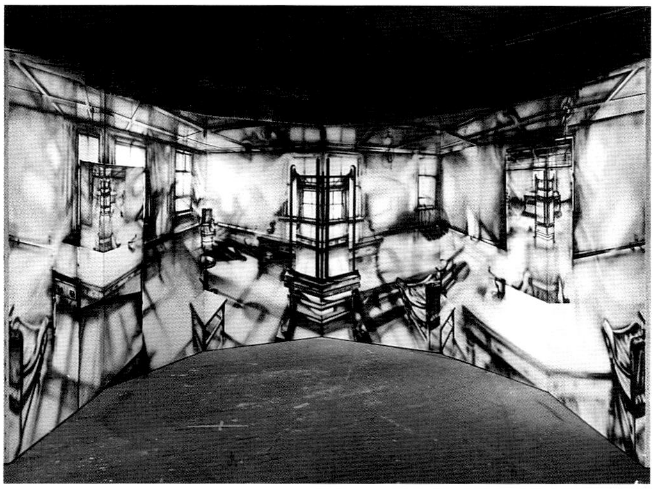

Fig. 72 *The Studio*, 1969–70, airbrushed ink on canvas, ca. 6 × 15 × 8 feet (182.9 × 457.2 × 243.8 cm). Installation in the artist's studio.

1971

Group exhibition: *Two Aspects of Illusion: Paul Gedeohn/ Michael Mazur*, Finch College Museum of Art, New York.

1972

Returns to Cambridge and purchases house on Walnut Avenue in the Porter Square neighborhood; converts carriage house into a studio (fig. 74); in spring semester, is visiting professor at Yale University School of Art and Architecture; solo exhibition: *"The Studio" and Other Works, 1969–70*, Finch College Museum of Art, New York (a revised and expanded version of the 1970 show); group exhibition: *Phases of New Realism*, Lowe Art Museum, University of Miami, Florida.

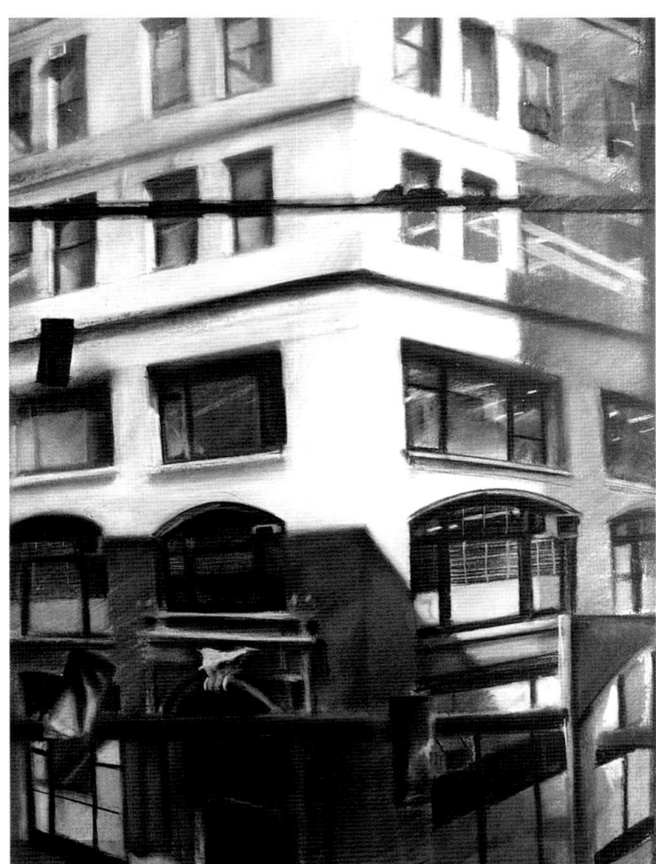

Fig. 73 *View from Studio, New York*, 1972, pastel, 28¾ × 21¼ in. (73.1 × 54.0 cm). Private collection.

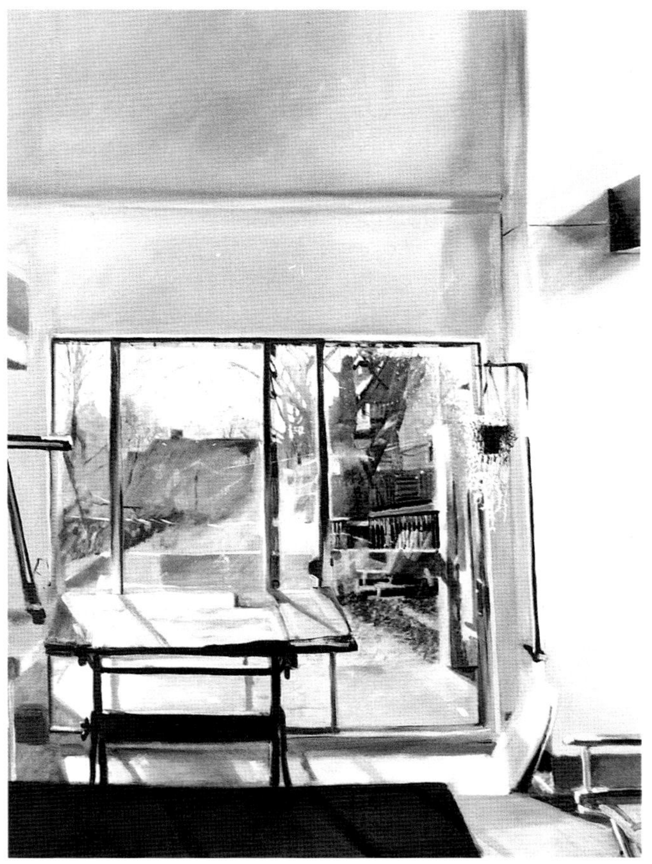

Fig. 74 *View from the New Studio*, 1972, oil on canvas, 28½ × 20½ in. (72.4 × 52.1 cm). Collection of the artist.

1973

In spring semester, is visiting professor, Queens College, Flushing, New York; solo exhibition: Picker Art Gallery, Colgate University, Hamilton, New York (paintings, prints, drawings, and sculpture); group exhibitions: *Michael Mazur and Robert Birmelin,* State University of New York, Cortlandt; *Segundo Bienal Americana de Artes Graficas,* Museo La Tertulia, Cali, Colombia.

1974

Meets the artist Mary Frank and begins a long friendship that often includes joint work sessions; is appointed to the board of the Artists' Foundation in Boston; joins the Terry Dintenfass Gallery, New York, and has regular solo exhibitions there; group exhibition: *Selections from the Permanent Collection,* Museum of Fine Arts, Boston.

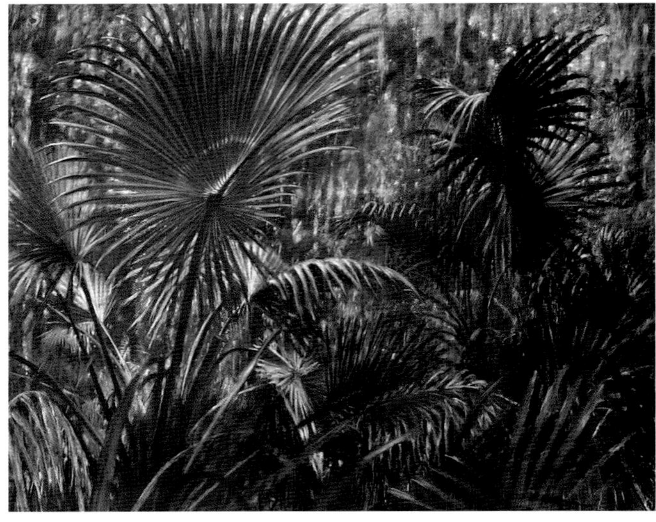

Fig. 75 *Palmetto Grove,* 1976, pastel, 71 × 89½ in. (180.3 × 227.3 cm). Los Angeles County Museum of Art.

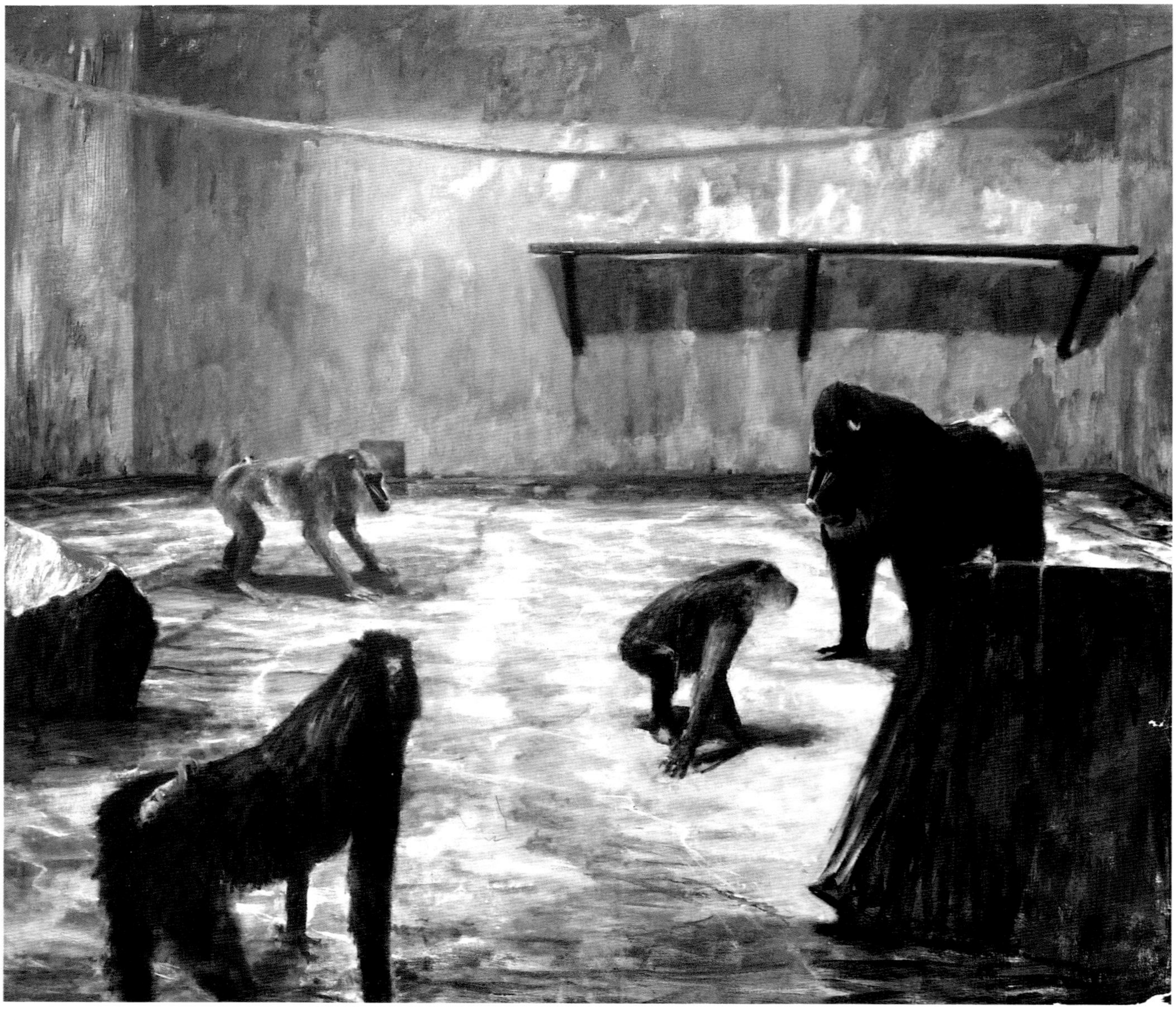

Fig. 76 *Cage at Stoneham #11,* 1977, oil on canvas, 69 × 80 in. (175.3 × 203.2 cm). Private collection.

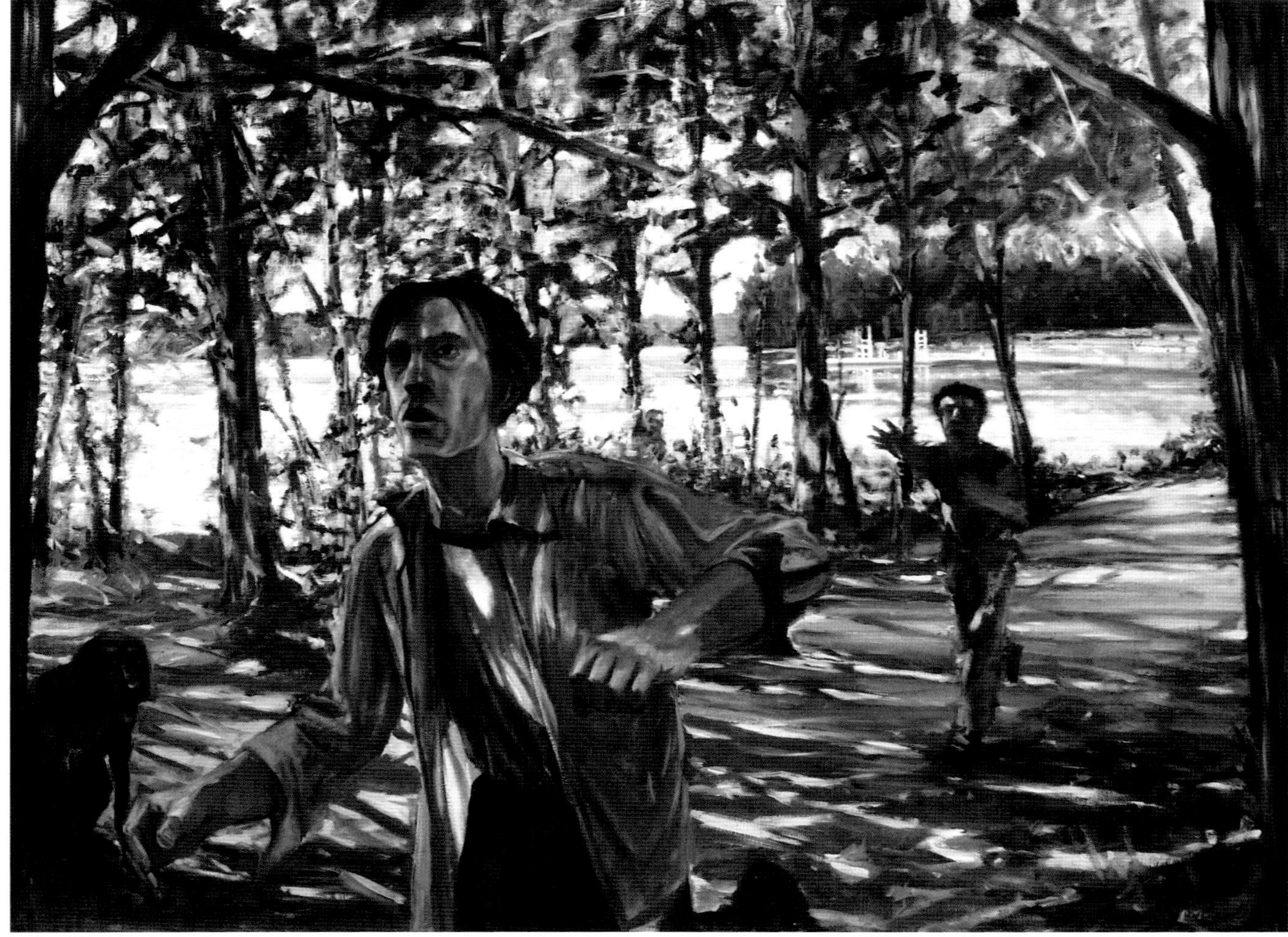

Fig. 77 *Incident at Walden Pond* (detail), 1977–78, oil on canvas, 48 × 74 in. (121.9 × 188.0 cm). Museum of American Art, Pennsylvania Academy of the Fine Arts, Philadelphia.

1975

Receives commission from the U.S. Department of the Interior to participate in a project and subsequent bicentennial-year traveling exhibition, *America 1976,* and in January goes to Ossabaw Island off the coast of Georgia to create a series of landscape oils, pastels, and monotypes (fig. 75); in April, is guest teacher at the College of Creative Studies, University of California, Santa Barbara; in July, teaches at the Yale Summer School of Music and Art; in November, travels in France, Austria, East Germany, and Holland, with particular interest in studying the landscape drawings of Pieter Brueghel; resigns from Brandeis University to devote full time to art; joins the Harcus-Krakow Gallery, Boston, and has regular solo exhibitions there; group exhibition: *60 Prints from 60 Years,* Philadelphia Print Club.

1976

In April, with Museum of Fine Arts print curators, visits Naum Gabo to view Gabo's wood-engraving monoprints; solo exhibitions: *Michael Mazur: Vision of a Draughtsman: A Twenty-Year Retrospective of Works on Paper,* Brockton Art Center, Massachusetts (organized by Marylin Hoffman; travels to Middlebury College, Vermont; Montreal Museum of Fine Arts; Delaware Art Museum, Wilmington; and the Jane Haslem Gallery, Washington, D.C.); *Michael Mazur: Prints and Drawings,* Widener Gallery, Trinity College, Hartford, Connecticut; group exhibitions: *American Prints, 1913–1963,* Museum of Modern Art, New York (travels); *Thirty Years of American Printmaking,* Brooklyn Museum, New York; *The Figurative Tradition: Nine Artists and Their Prints,* Williams College Museum of Art, Williamstown, Massachusetts; *America 1976: A Bicentennial Exhibition Sponsored by the Department of the Interior,* Corcoran Gallery of Art, Washington, D.C. (travels through 1978).

1977

Begins guest teaching printmaking classes at Harvard University, which continue regularly through 1997; works for the first time with master printer Robert Townsend, a relationship that continues today; group exhibitions: *Print Biennial,* National Collection of Fine Arts, Washington,

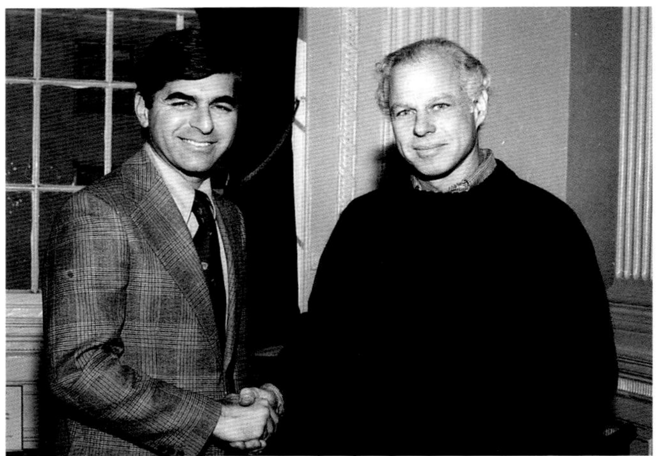

Michael Mazur with Massachusetts Governor Michael Dukakis, 1978

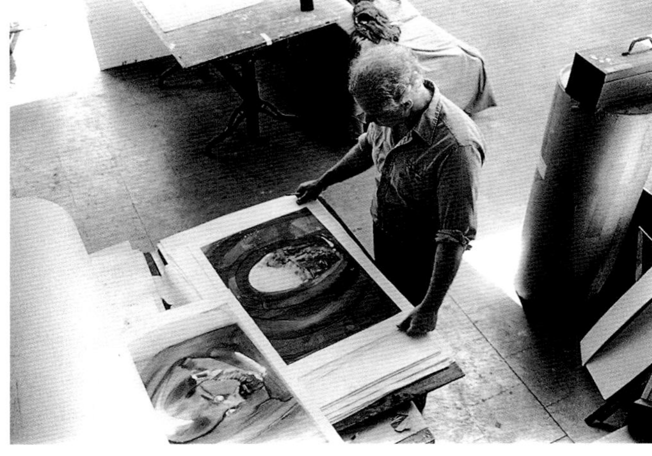

Mazur examining his series of portraits of artist Jim Dine, 1980

D.C.; *Wellesley Greenhouse: Janowitz, Kumler, Mazur,* Wellesley College Museum of Art, Massachusetts; *New England Works on Paper,* Museum of Fine Arts, Boston.

1978

In January, testifies before Senator John Brademas's congressional committee regarding government support for individual artists; travels to France and Barcelona; at the request of the Gabo estate, documents and organizes ten portfolios of Gabo's wood-engraving monoprints and writes article on Gabo's monoprints for the *Print Collector's Newsletter* special issue on monotype; on 11 December, is sworn in as a member of the Massachusetts State Art Council for a three-year term; is active in establishing the state's "New Works" program and artists' rights legislation.

1979

Curates exhibition at MIT's Hayden Gallery titled *The Narrative Impulse,* which opens on 16 November and includes the work of Mazur, Mary Frank, Robert Birmelin, and Irving Petlin; joins the Robert Miller Gallery, New York (exhibits the Stoneham Zoo series of paintings, drawings, monotypes, and pastels); group exhibitions: *Grafica Contemporanea Americana,* Galleria Bevilacqua, La Massa, Venice, Italy; *Nouvelle Sujectivité,* Palais des Beaux-Arts, Brussels; *Fifty American Works on Paper from the Collection of Mr. and Mrs. Stephen D. Paine,* Williams College Museum of Art, Williamstown, Massachusetts.

1980

Meets Jim Dine and introduces him to monotype techniques; writes catalogue essay for *The Painterly Print: Monotypes from the Seventeenth to the Twentieth Century,* Metropolitan Museum of Art, New York (travels to the Museum of Fine Arts, Boston, 1981); the monotype *Window Sequence (Fire)* (fig. 40) is included in that exhibition; solo exhibition: Pace Editions, New York; group exhibitions: *Aspects of the '70s: Directions in Realism,* Danforth Museum, Framingham, Massachusetts; *Three Decades,* DeCordova Museum and Sculpture Park, Lincoln, Massachusetts; *Realist Works on Paper,* Virginia Museum of Fine Arts, Richmond.

1981

Travels to Washington on 3 May for march to the Pentagon in protest of Reagan foreign policy; teaches at Yale Summer School of Music and Art; Mazurs build a summer home overlooking Wakeby Pond in Mashpee on Cape Cod after Gail Mazur's family summer home there is destroyed by fire (1979); after dissolution of the Harcus-Krakow Gallery, continues regular solo exhibitions at the Barbara Krakow Gallery, Boston (also 1984, 1987, 1989, 1990, 1993, 1995, 1996, and 1998); solo exhibitions: Rutgers University Art Gallery (now the Jane Voorhees Zimmerli Art Museum), New Brunswick, New Jersey (in conjunction with a large acquisition of the artist's work); John Stoller Gallery, Minneapolis; Greenberg Gallery, St. Louis; Andrews Gallery, College of William and Mary, Williamsburg, Virginia; group exhibition: *American Prints: Process and Proofs,* Whitney Museum of American Art, New York.

1982

Begins the *Wakeby Day, Wakeby Night* series of monumental monotypes, commissioned by MIT; creates monotype series to illustrate Richard Howard's translation of *Les Fleurs du Mal* by Charles Baudelaire (Boston: David R. Godine, 1982); in spring semester, is guest teacher at Cornell University and at SUNY Purchase; in fall semester, teaches a class in the Graduate School of Art, Boston University; begins planning for the Artists for a Nuclear Weapons Freeze project that he co-directs with his Boston dealer Barbara Krakow; solo exhibitions: Smith Andersen Gallery, Palo Alto, California; *The Cyclamen Dance Series* (fig. 78), Janus Gallery, Los Angeles; Gustavus Adolphus College, St. Peter, Minnesota; group exhibitions: *Perspectives on Contemporary American Realism: Works on Paper from the Collection of Jalane and Richard Davidson,* Pennsylvania Academy of the Fine Arts, Philadelphia; *A Private Vision: Contemporary Art from the Graham Gund Collection,* Museum of Fine Arts, Boston;

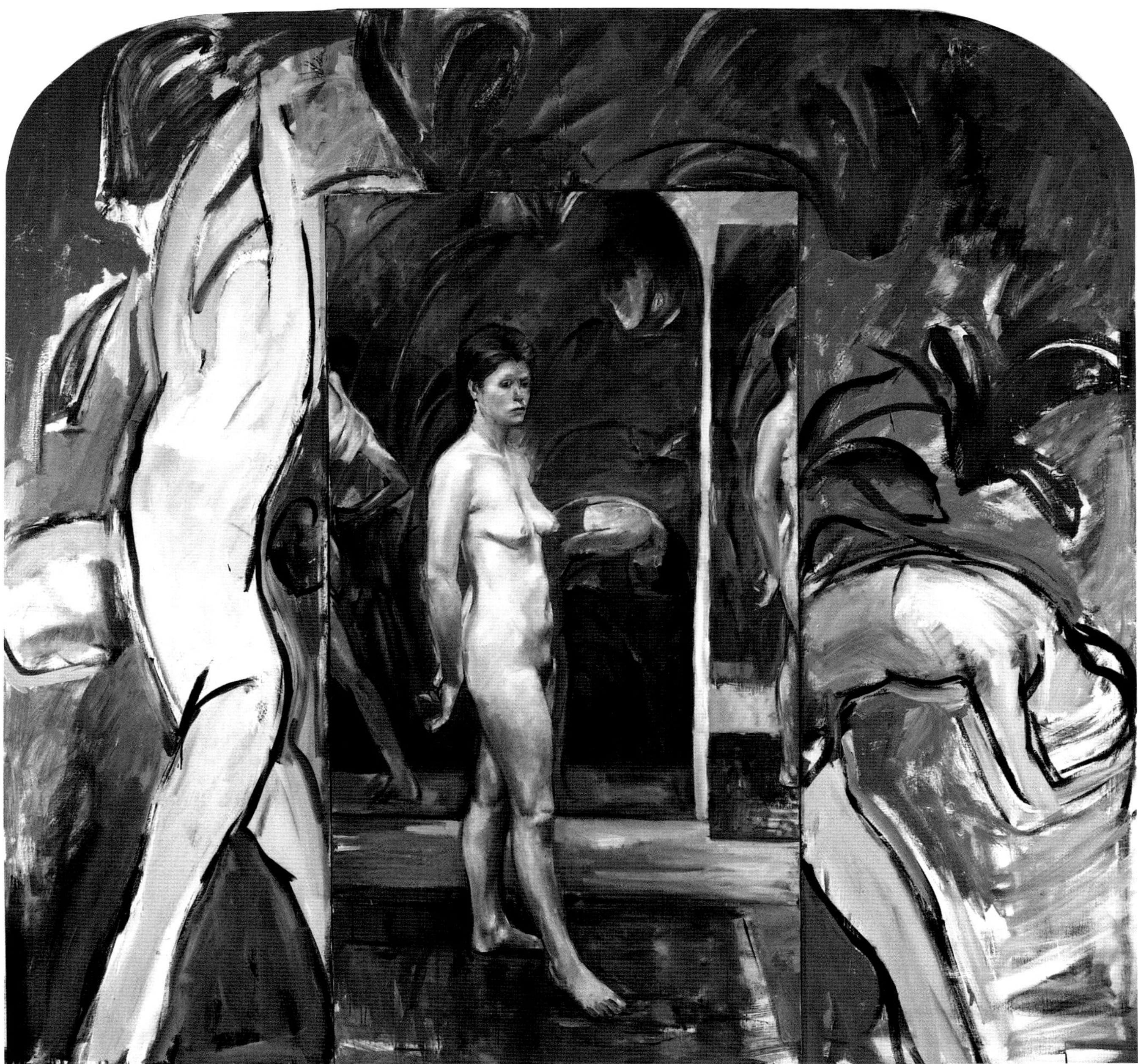

Fig. 78 *The Dancer or the Dance,* 1981–82, oil on canvas, 84 × 86 in. (213.4 × 218.4 cm). Private collection.

A Close Look at the Human Figure in Contemporary Art, Contemporary Arts Center, New Orleans.

1983

Serves as a member of the Pennell Committee at the Library of Congress until 1993, replacing Jim Dine; works first with Donald Saff and then with Yvonne Jacquette to select prints for the Library of Congress Pennell Print Collection; is guest teacher at Cornell University, SUNY Purchase, and University of Southern California, Los Angeles; sings in and designs a set based on Goya's prisoner figures for the "El Salvador" oratorio concert by the Back Bay Chorale under the direction of conductor Larry Hill, which takes place at Harvard's Sanders Theater on 18 May; exhibition *Wakeby Day/Wakeby Night: Monumental Monotypes by Michael Mazur* opens 11 March at the Hayden Gallery, MIT (colorplate 18), in conjunction with installation of *Wakeby* monotypes at the 500 Memorial Drive dormitory building.

1984

Organizes *Art for a Nuclear Weapons Freeze,* a national traveling exhibition and benefit auction for the antinuclear campaign; his "Art for Arm's Sake" satire is published by the *New York Times* on the Op-Ed page.

1985

Solo exhibition: Arts Club of Chicago; group exhibitions: *Contemporary American Monotype,* Chrysler Museum,

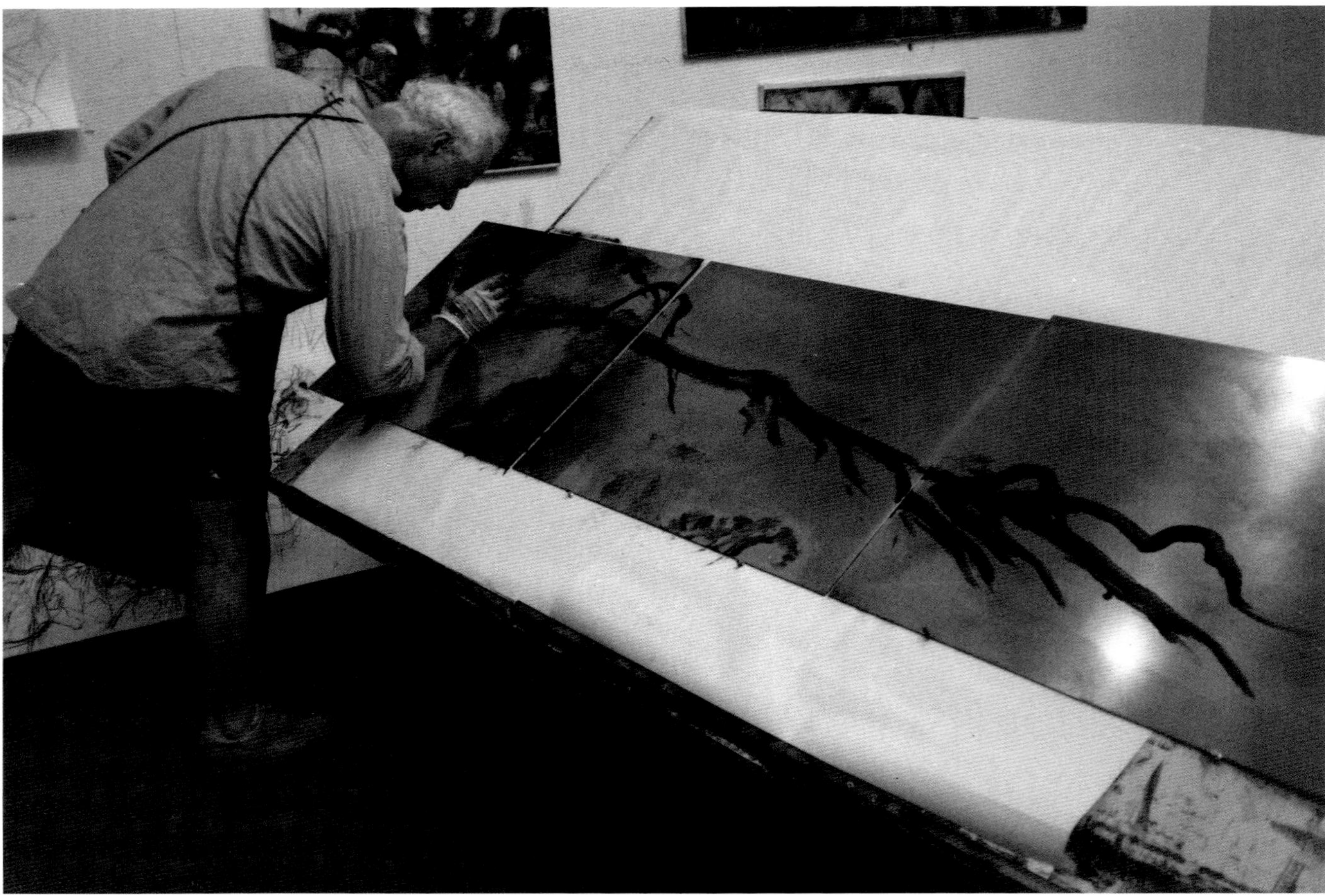

Mazur working on monotype plates, 1989

Norfolk, Virginia; *Contemporary Monotype: Six Masters,* De Saisset Museum, Santa Clara University, California.

1986

Designs screenprint poster for a Russell Sherman concert to benefit the nuclear weapons freeze campaign; begins spending part of each summer in Provincetown, Massachusetts, where he and Gail Mazur are visiting critics at the Fine Arts Work Center.

1987

Begins collaboration with New York master printer Judith Solodkin on *Wakeby Night* edition; in May and June, travels to Suchow, Shanghai, and Beijing in China with Gail and artist friends, including Catherine Murphy, Harry Roseman, Marianna Pineda, and Richard Rosenblum; visits Hong Kong, Shanghai, Beijing, Xian, and other cities and sites to study landscape and Chinese garden traditions; solo exhibition: *Michael Mazur's Self-Portraits,* Joe Fawbush Gallery, New York; group exhibitions: *The Monumental Image: Prints by Jennifer Bartlett, Chuck Close, Michael Mazur, Susan Rothenberg, Donald Sultan, Terry Winters,* California State University, Northridge; *Modern American Realism,* National Museum of American Art, Smithsonian Institution, Washington, D.C.

1988

Mazur's mother dies; travels to San Francisco to work at the Experimental Workshop on a series of silk monotype screens (colorplate 28); solo exhibitions: *Michael Mazur: Paintings, Prints, Drawings, Monotypes, 1962–1988,* Macalester College, St. Paul, Minnesota; Joe Fawbush Gallery, New York.

1989

Spends winter and spring in Houston, where Gail is visiting associate professor in the Graduate Writing Program at the University of Houston; purchases summer house in Provincetown.

1990

Founds the New Provincetown Print Project in conjunction with the Fine Arts Work Center; during summer, collaborates with master printer Robert Townsend and guest artists Mary Frank, George McNeil, Fred Sandback, and Gregory Gillespie on monoprint and monotype projects; at Harvard's Carpenter Center for the Visual Arts, attends weekly drawing and printmaking sessions with fellow faculty and teaching assistants, resulting in the continuing *Harvard Evenings* print series; solo exhibition: *Michael Mazur: Color Prints,* Mary Ryan Gallery, New York (also has solo exhibitions there in 1994, 1995, 1996, 1997, 1998, and 1999).

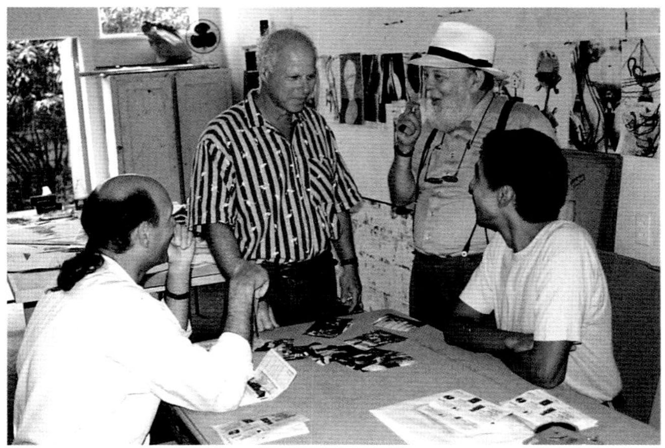

Donny Resnick and Michael Mazur with Henry Geldzahler and artist Roberto Juarez at the Fine Arts Work Center, Provincetown, Massachusetts, 1991

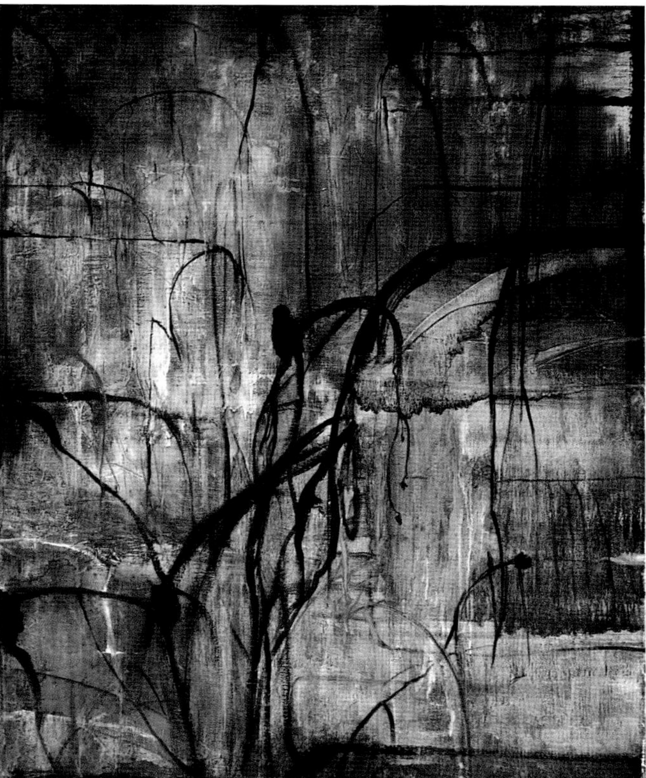

Fig. 79 *Fall Branching,* 1993, oil on canvas, 50 × 40 in. (127.0 × 101.6 cm). Barbara Krakow Gallery, Boston.

1991

In June and July, collaborates with Townsend and guest artists Yvonne Jacquette, Sylvia Plimack Mangold, Roberto Juarez, and David True at the New Provincetown Print Project; solo exhibition: *Reflected Self: Mazur Prints,* Kansas City Art Institute, Missouri.

1992

Begins collaboration with poet/translator Robert Pinsky, resulting in a series of monotype illustrations to accompany Pinsky's translation of *The Inferno of Dante* (New York: Farrar, Straus and Giroux, 1994); in June and July, collaborates with Townsend and guest artists Jacqueline Humphries, Nathan Oliveira, Therese Oulton, and John Walker at the New Provincetown Print Project; is appointed to the board of trustees of the Fine Arts Work Center.

1993

In January, after coronary catheterization reveals heart disease, undergoes balloon angioplasty procedure; during the summer months, collaborates with Townsend and guest artists Eric Avery, Sue Coe, Sam Messer, and Joan Snyder at the New Provincetown Print Project; the resulting portfolio is published to jointly benefit the Fine Arts Work Center and the Provincetown AIDS Support Group; joins U.F.O. Gallery in Provincetown; granddaughter Rebecca is born to son Daniel and his wife Susan Chasen.

1994

In January, addresses the Massachusetts Board of Education at the statehouse to request increased support for arts in the public school system and to propose several approaches to arts in the core curriculum; during summer, collaborates with Townsend and guest artists Richard Rosenblum, Richard Baker, Paul Bowen, James Balla, Georgia Marsh, and Varujan Baghosian at the New Provincetown Print Project; solo exhibition: *Monotypes by Michael Mazur for the Inferno,* University of Iowa Museum of Art, Iowa City (travels through 1997 with Mazur and Pinsky giving lectures on their collaboration at eight venues).

1995

Is visiting critic, Massachusetts College of Art, Boston, returning in 1996; begins teaching a summer workshop in monotype at the Fine Arts Work Center; group exhibition: *The Herbert W. Plimpton Collection of Realist Art: 18th Annual Patrons and Friends Exhibition,* Rose Art Museum, Brandeis University.

1996

Is invited to join the Longpoint Gallery, a cooperative gallery in Provincetown founded by Robert Motherwell, Leo Manso, Sidney Simon, and others.

1997

Is elected chair of the board of the Fine Arts Work Center; returns to Florence and Rome in the company of Dimitri and Cynthia Hadzi; collaborates on monotypes at Smith Andersen Editions, Palo Alto. Solo exhibition: *Branching: The Art of Michael Mazur,* Mead Art Museum, Amherst College, Massachusetts (travels to DeCordova Museum and Sculpture Park, Lincoln, Massachusetts, 1998); group exhibition: *Singular Impressions: The Monotype in America,*

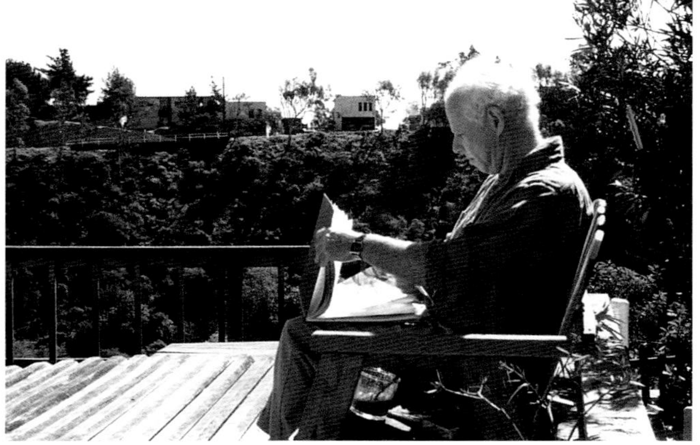

Mazur drawing in Los Angeles

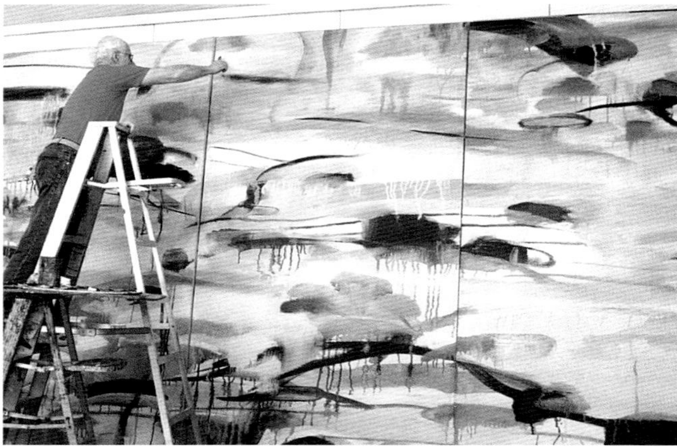

Mazur in his studio putting finishing touches on a monumental digital commission titled *The Variables* and *The Trade Winds,* for installation at Warburg Dillon Read, Stamford, Conn., 1999

National Museum of American Art, Smithsonian Institution, Washington, D.C.

1998–99

Collaborates on a set design for a staged adaptation of Dante's *Inferno,* with script by Pinsky, performed at the Unterberg Poetry Center, 92nd Street YMCA, New York; completes commissions for large-scale digital prints on canvas for the Federal Reserve Bank, Boston, and the Swiss Bank Warburg Dillon Read, Stamford, Connecticut.

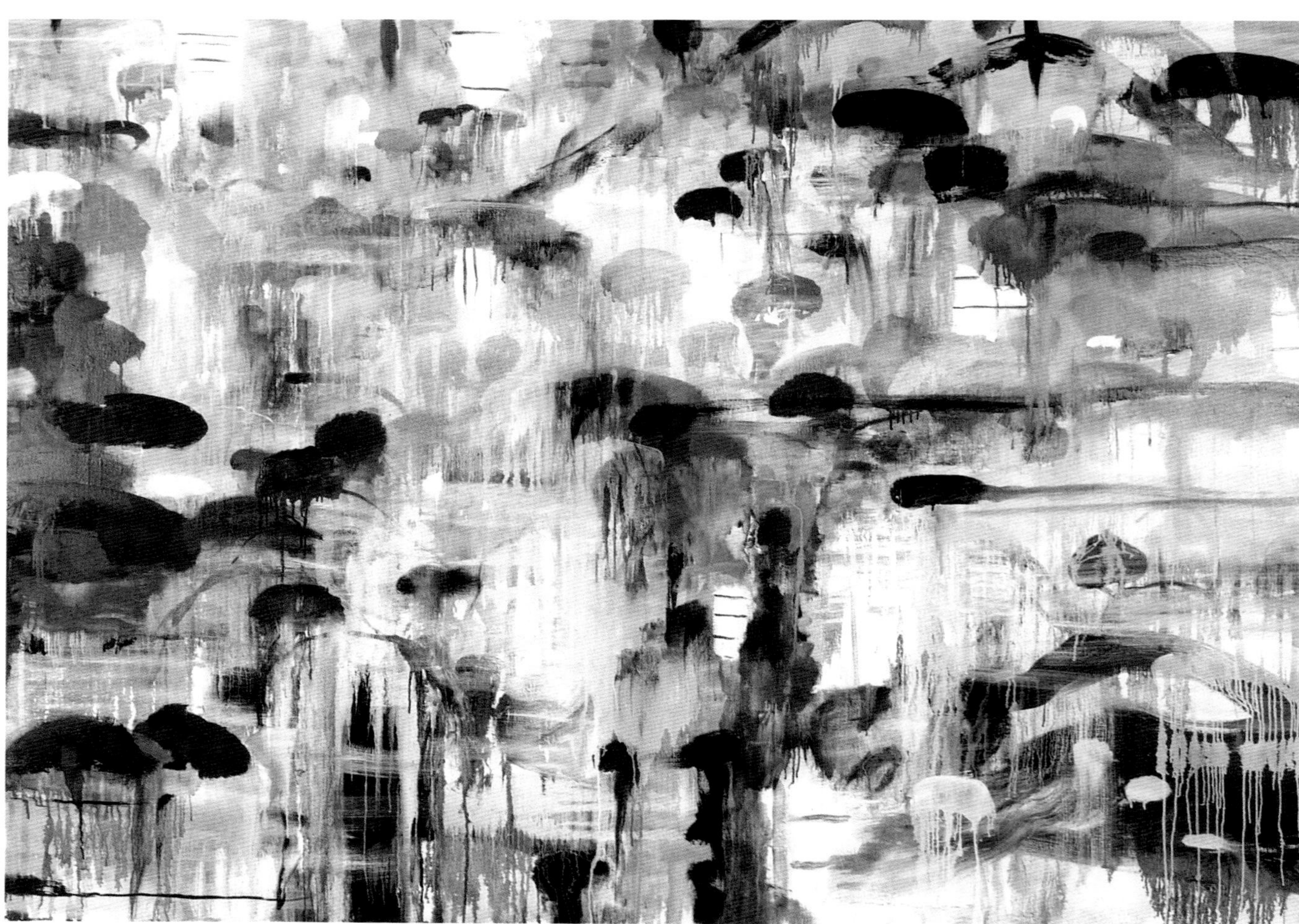

Fig. 80 *Storm Warning,* 1997–98, oil on canvas, 60 × 84 in. (152.4 × 213.4 cm). Mary Ryan Gallery, New York.

Catalogue Raisonné

THIS catalogue raisonné includes prints created by Michael Mazur between 1956 and the spring of 1999. Listed chronologically, only prints for which a fixed matrix was created are included, i.e., editioned prints, prints created from a fixed matrix that were not editioned, and monoprints that were printed and published in variant editions. Therefore, monotypes are not included. Many of Mazur's prints, especially prints made early in his career, were not formally editioned. The number, or estimated number, of impressions printed is given for these projects. For a small number of projects that the artist has intended to edition, the anticipated size of the complete edition is given. Mazur has followed a standard practice of signing and dating his prints in pencil in the lower right corner and noting edition number or proof at the lower left. He also notes the title of many of his prints along the bottom at lower left or center. In some of Mazur's early editions, which were printed over a period of time, slight variations in the title of a work or date are sometimes found. The research is based on prints that have been examined by the author; information was collected in consultation with the artist and his printers and publishers.

Unless otherwise noted, prints were printed and published by the artist.

Measurements are given in inches and in centimeters, height precedes width; inches precede centimeters. For prints that have a margin, both image size and sheet size are given. Prints that bleed to the edge of the sheet, with no margin, have one set of measurements only. Image size refers to the size of the printmaking matrix that carries the image, i.e., the plate size or block size.

The "Mazur" numbers noted under references refer to a master set of prints in the artist's collection. The letters preceding each number refer to size, i.e., small (S), medium (M), large (L), and oversize (X). Not all prints are represented in this master set. For prints that were created at the Tamarind Lithography Workshop in Los Angeles in 1968, the Tamarind catalogue raisonné numbers are given.

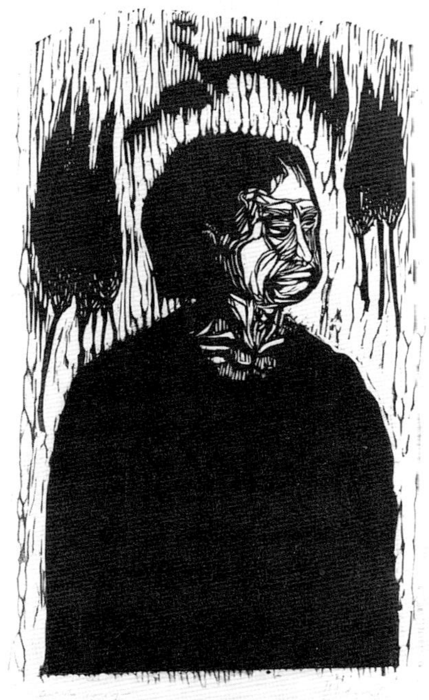

1

1
Untitled (Italian widow), 1956
Medium handprinted wood relief
Edition size not editioned; 3–4 impressions printed
Paper handmade Japanese
Plates/blocks 1 wood block
Inks black
Image size 21¼ × 12⅝ in. (54.0 × 32.1 cm)
Sheet size 33½ × 23¾ in. (85.1 × 60.3 cm)
Remarks made while Mazur was studying in Florence, Italy
Reference Mazur L-71

2
Untitled (Italian interior), 1956
Medium handprinted wood relief
Edition size not editioned; 3–4 impressions printed
Paper handmade Japanese
Plates/blocks 1 wood block
Inks black
Image size 28½ × 19½ in. (72.4 × 49.6 cm)
Sheet size 35¾ × 24½ in. (90.8 × 64.8 cm)
Remarks made while Mazur was studying in Florence, Italy
Reference Mazur L-76

3
Untitled (Italian view from interior), 1956
Medium handprinted wood relief
Edition size not editioned; 3–4 impressions printed
Paper handmade Japanese
Plates/blocks 1 wood block
Inks black

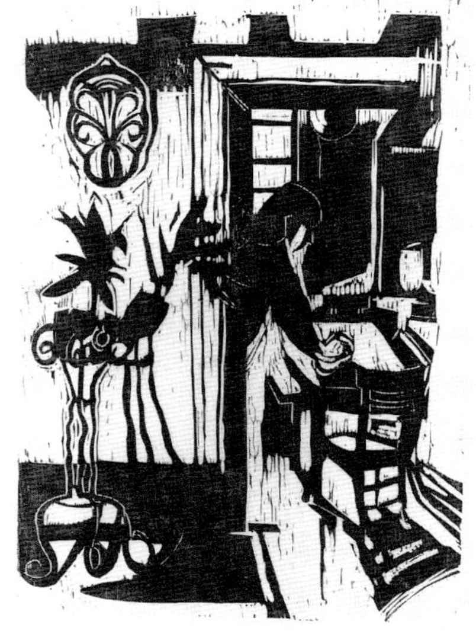

2

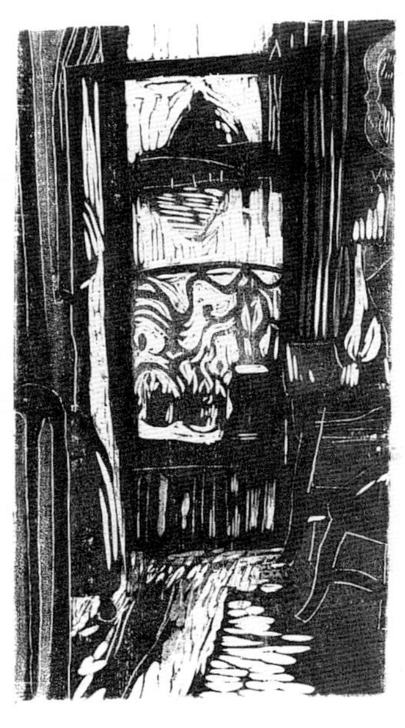

3

Image size 17½ × 9½ in. (44.5 × 24.2 cm)
Sheet size 27 × 17½ in. (68.6 × 44.5 cm)
Remarks made while Mazur was studying in Florence, Italy

4
Untitled (Italian church), 1956
Medium handprinted wood relief
Edition size not editioned; 1–2 impressions printed
Paper handmade Japanese
Plates/blocks 1 wood block
Inks black
Image size 11½ × 10¾ in. (29.2 × 27.3 cm)
Sheet size 18½ × 15¾ in. (47.0 × 40.0 cm)
Remarks made while Mazur was studying in Florence, Italy
Reference Mazur S-13

4

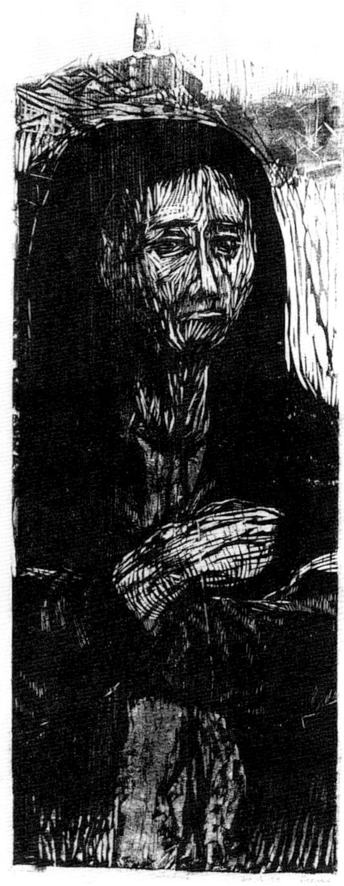

5

5
Contadina, 1956–57
Medium handprinted wood relief
Edition size 3
Paper handmade Japanese
Plates/blocks 2 wood blocks
Inks black and gray
Image size 26⅛ × 10⅛ in. (66.4 × 25.7 cm)
Sheet size 33⅜ × 19⅜ in. (84.8 × 49.2 cm)
Remarks made while Mazur was studying in Florence, Italy
Reference Mazur L-72

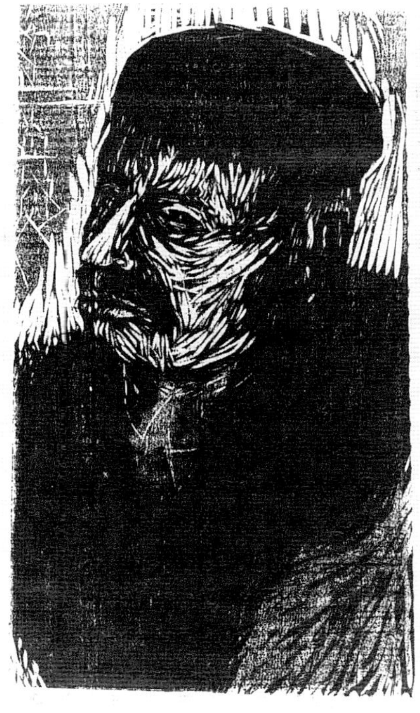

6

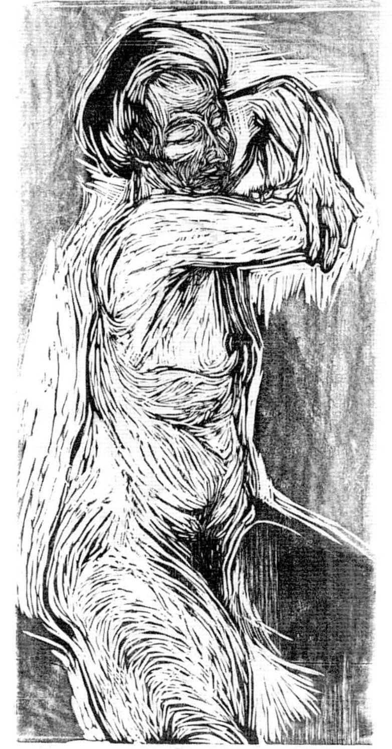

7

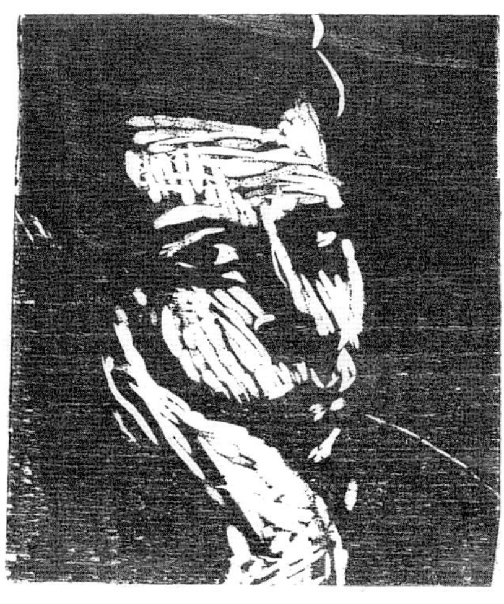

9

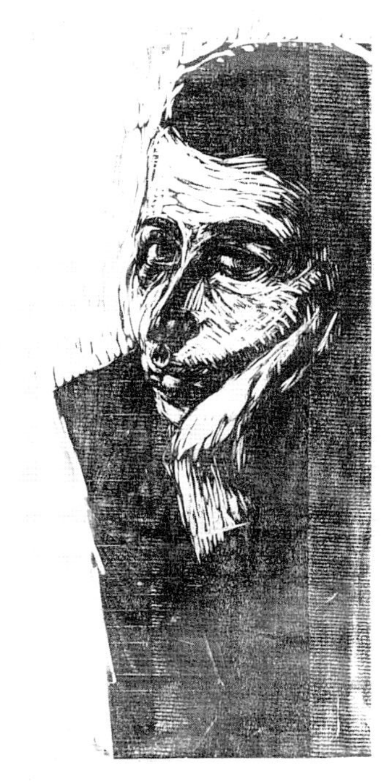

10

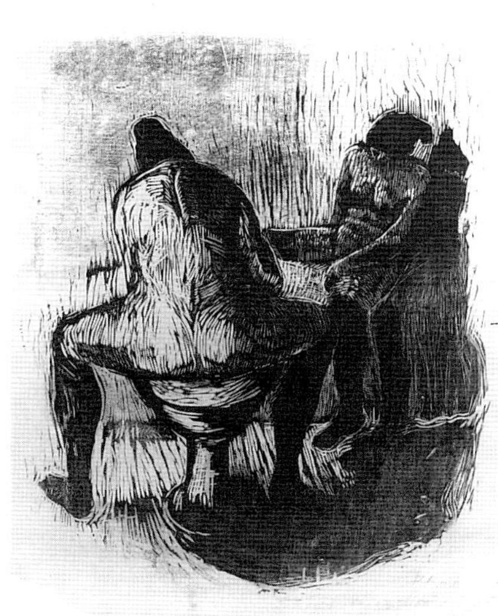

8

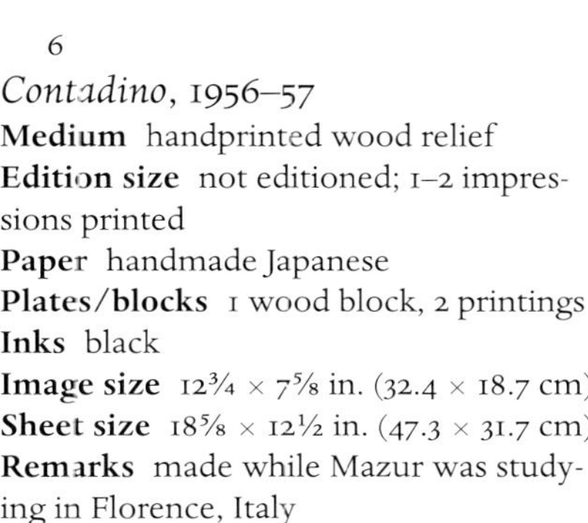

6
Contadino, 1956–57
Medium handprinted wood relief
Edition size not editioned; 1–2 impressions printed
Paper handmade Japanese
Plates/blocks 1 wood block, 2 printings
Inks black
Image size 12¾ × 7⅝ in. (32.4 × 18.7 cm)
Sheet size 18⅝ × 12½ in. (47.3 × 31.7 cm)
Remarks made while Mazur was studying in Florence, Italy
Reference Mazur S-12

7
Sketch for Nude, 1956–57
Medium handprinted wood relief
Edition size not editioned; 3–4 impressions printed
Paper handmade Japanese
Plates/blocks 1 wood block with selective rubbing
Inks black
Image size 23¼ × 10⅞ in. (59.1 × 27.7 cm)
Sheet size 28 × 15⅛ in. (71.2 × 38.4 cm)
Remarks made while Mazur was studying in Florence, Italy
Reference Mazur L-73

8
Two Nudes, 1956–57
Medium handprinted wood relief
Edition size not editioned; 3–4 impressions printed
Paper white wove
Plates/blocks 1 wood block
Inks black
Image size 24¼ × 19⅜ in. (61.6 × 49.2 cm)
Sheet size 33¾ × 23½ in. (85.8 × 59.7 cm)
Remarks made while Mazur was studying in Florence, Italy
Reference Mazur L-75

9
Self-Portrait (Small Italian), 1957
Medium handprinted wood relief
Edition size not editioned; 1–2 impressions printed
Paper handmade Japanese
Plates/blocks 1 wood block
Inks black
Image size 8 × 6⅜ in. (20.3 × 16.2 cm)
Sheet size 18 × 12⅜ in. (45.8 × 31.5 cm)
Remarks made while Mazur was studying in Florence, Italy
Reference Mazur S-12a

10
Self-Portrait (Italian), 1957
Medium handprinted wood relief
Edition size not editioned; 5 impressions printed
Paper handmade Japanese

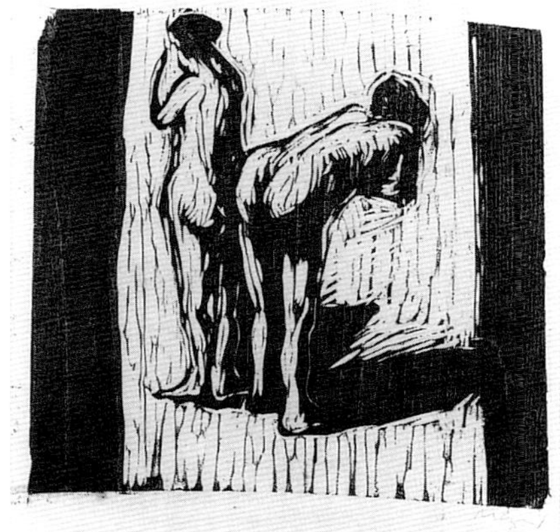

11

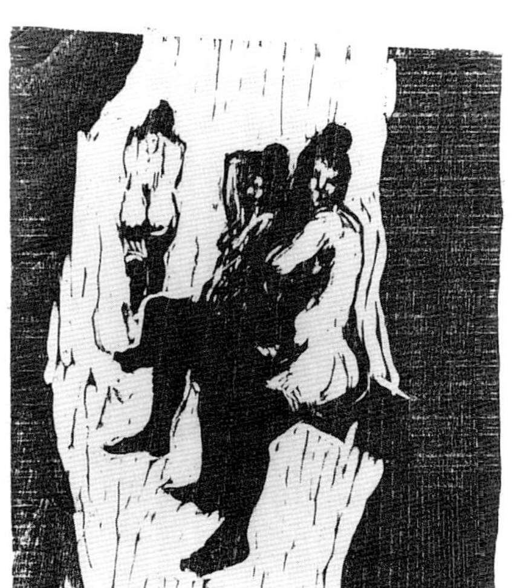

12

Plates/blocks 1 wood block
Inks black
Image size 20 × 8½ in. (50.8 × 21.6 cm)
Sheet size 33 × 24 in. (83.9 × 61.0 cm)
Remarks made while Mazur was studying in Florence, Italy; three of the impressions for this image are handprinted on one sheet of paper
Reference Mazur L-76a

11
Two Standing Women II, 1957
Medium handprinted wood relief
Edition size not editioned; 4–5 impressions printed with variant inking and wiping
Paper handmade Japanese
Plates/blocks 1 wood block
Inks black
Image size 9 × 9 in. (22.9 × 22.9 cm)
Sheet size 16⅛ × 12¼ in. (41.0 × 31.1 cm)
Remarks made while Mazur was studying in Florence, Italy
References Mazur S-8, S-9, and S-10

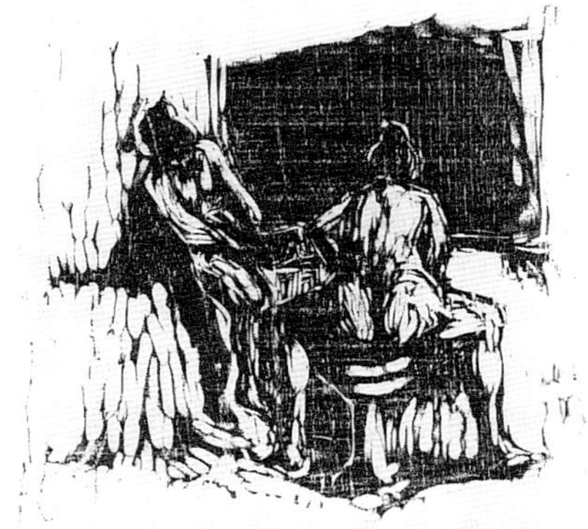

13

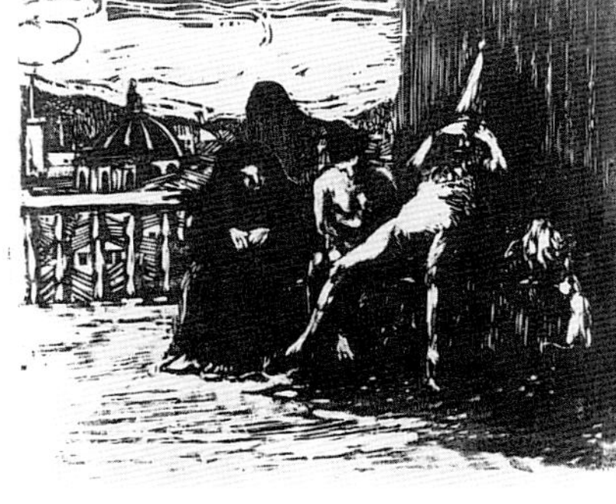

14

12
Three Women, 1957
Medium handprinted wood relief
Edition size not editioned; 4–5 impressions printed with variant inking and rubbing
Paper handmade Japanese
Plates/blocks 1 wood block
Inks black
Image size 9¼ × 7⅝ in. (23.5 × 19.3 cm) irregular
Sheet size 15¼ × 12⅜ in. (38.7 × 31.4 cm)
Remarks made while Mazur was studying in Florence, Italy
Reference Mazur S-11

13
Two Seated Women, 1957
Medium handprinted wood relief
Edition size not editioned; 4–5 impressions of two states printed with variant inking and wiping
Paper mulberry
Plates/blocks 1 wood block
Inks black
Image size 9 × 8 in. (22.9 × 20.3 cm)
Sheet size 18¼ × 12¼ in. (46.4 × 31.1 cm) approximate
Remarks made while Mazur was studying in Florence, Italy
References Mazur S-5, S-6, and S-7

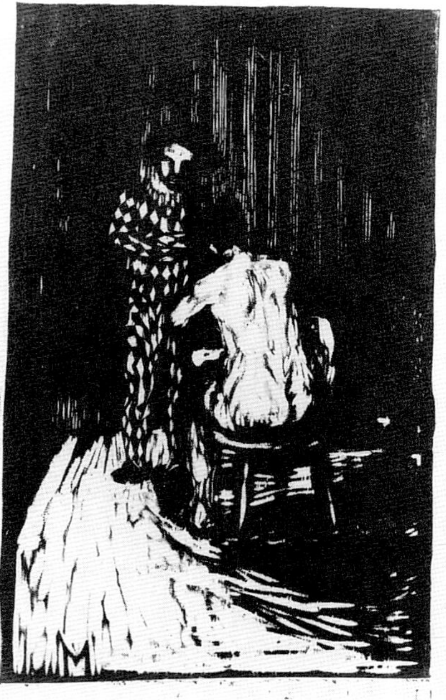

15

14
Untitled (*commedia dell'arte* study), 1957
Medium wood relief
Edition size not editioned; 3–4 impressions printed
Paper handmade Japanese
Plates/blocks 1 wood block
Inks black
Image size 9⅛ × 10¼ in. (23.2 × 26.0 cm)
Sheet size 12¾ × 17⅜ in. (32.4 × 44.2 cm) irregular
Remarks from a series of images based on the Italian opera *Pagliacci* and *commedia dell'arte* figures
Reference Mazur S-13d

15
Untitled (*commedia dell'arte* study), 1957
Medium wood relief
Edition size not editioned; 3–4 impressions printed
Paper handmade Japanese
Plates/blocks 1 wood block
Inks black
Image size 10⅛ × 6½ in. (25.7 × 16.5 cm)
Sheet size 14⅞ × 12¾ in. (37.8 × 32.4 cm)
Remarks from a series of images based on the Italian opera *Pagliacci* and *commedia dell'arte* figures
Reference Mazur S-13f

16
Untitled (Standing Couple — Harlequin), 1957
Medium wood relief

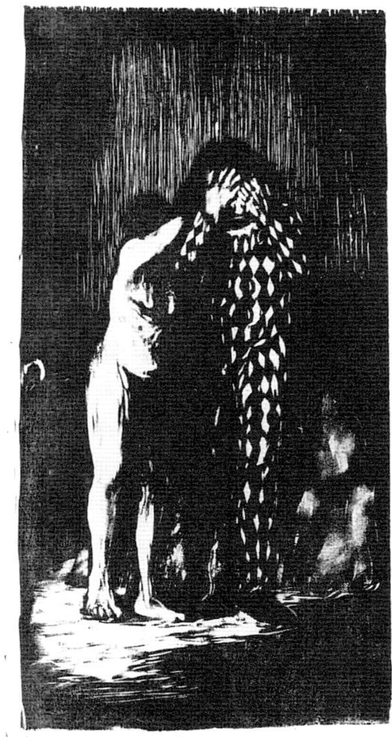

16

Edition size not editioned; 3–5 impressions printed
Paper handmade Japanese
Plates/blocks 1 wood block
Inks black
Image size 12⅝ × 6⅜ in. (32.1 × 16.2 cm)
Sheet size 19⅜ × 17 in. (32.7 × 31.8 cm)
Remarks from a series of images based on the Italian opera *Pagliacci* and *commedia dell'arte* figures
Reference Mazur S-13e

17
Untitled (Seated Harlequin with Pointed Cap), 1957
Medium wood relief
Edition size not editioned; 3–4 impressions printed
Paper handmade Japanese
Plates/blocks 1 wood block
Inks black
Image size 10¾ × 8¾ in. (27.3 × 22.2 cm)
Sheet size 12⅞ × 12½ in. (32.7 × 31.8 cm)
Remarks from a series of images based on the Italian opera *Pagliacci* and *commedia dell'arte* figures
Reference Mazur S-13b

18
Untitled (Embracing Couple), 1957
Medium wood relief
Edition size not editioned; 3–4 impressions printed
Paper handmade Japanese

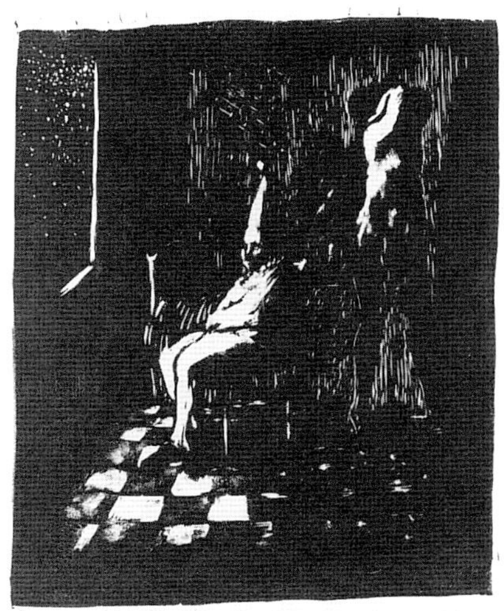

17

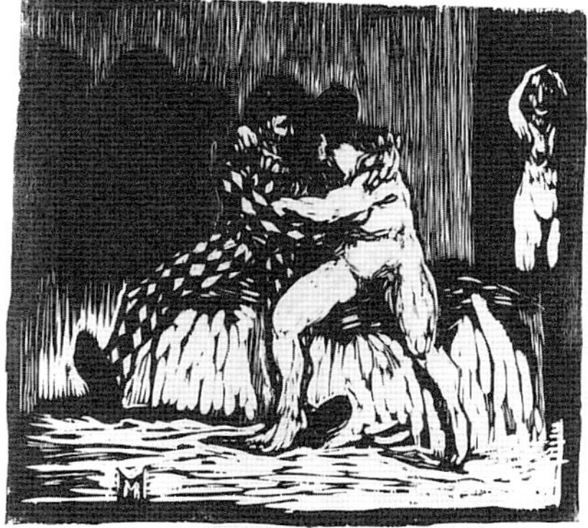

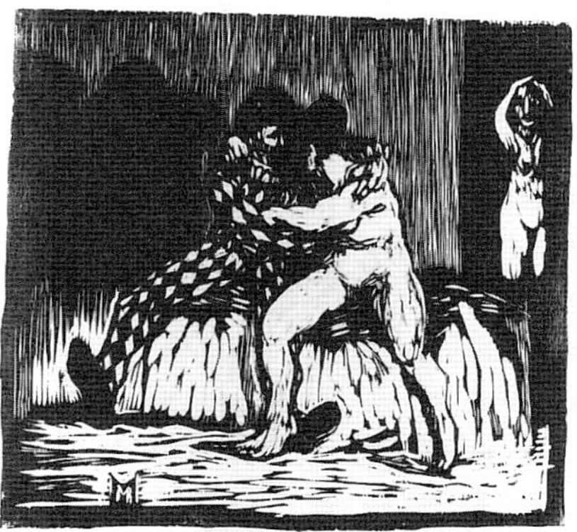

18

Plates/blocks 1 wood block
Inks black
Image size 10¾ × 11⅝ in. (27.3 × 29.5 cm)
Sheet size 18⅞ × 18⅛ in. (48.0 × 46.1 cm)
Remarks from a series of images based on the Italian opera *Pagliacci* and *commedia dell'arte* figures
Reference Mazur S-13a

19
Untitled (Harlequin and Nude Bending Over), 1957
Medium wood relief
Edition size not editioned; 3–4 impressions printed
Paper handmade Japanese
Plates/blocks 1 wood block
Inks black
Image size 11½ × 8½ in. (29.2 × 21.6 cm)
Sheet size 19¼ × 18¾ in. (48.9 × 47.7 cm)
Remarks from a series of images based on the Italian opera *Pagliacci* and *commedia dell'arte* figures
Reference Mazur S-13c

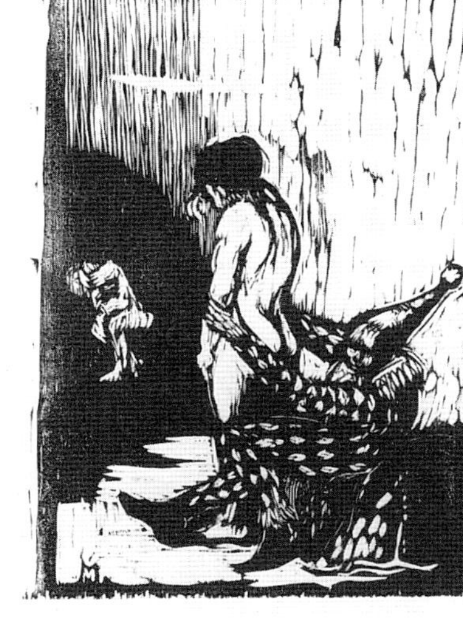

19

AN IMAGE OF
SALOME
THE STORY OF THE DEATH OF JOHN THE BAPTIST
EDITED FROM THE NEW TESTAMENT
AND FROM THE WORKS OF
GUSTAVE FLAUBERT, STEPHANE MALLARME
AND OSCAR WILDE
ILLUSTRATED BY
MICHAEL MAZUR

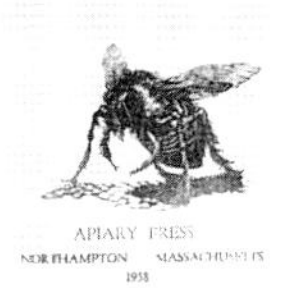

APIARY PRESS
NORTHAMPTON MASSACHUSETTS
1958

20

20
An Image of Salomé (title page), 1958
Medium wood engraving and letterpress
Edition size 34
Paper Troya
Printed by the artist at Apiary Press, Smith College, Northampton, Mass.
Plates/blocks 1 wood block
Inks black
Image and sheet size 23½ × 17 in. (59.7 × 43.2 cm)
Remarks Apiary Press was a student press run by Smith College art professor Leonard Baskin; this title page is in a bound book that was the artist's senior thesis project (Amherst College, 1958)
Reference Mazur S-71

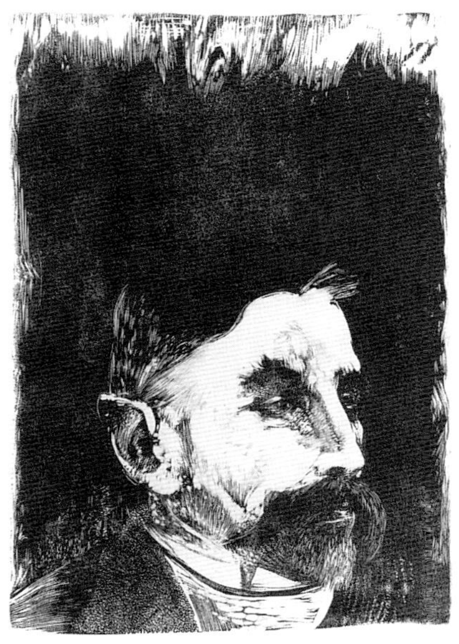

21

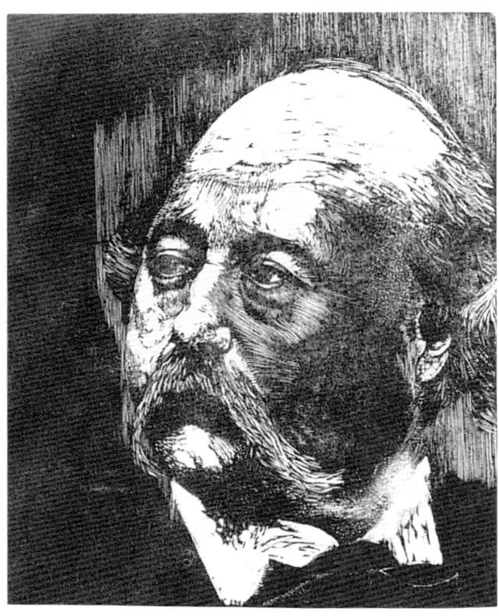
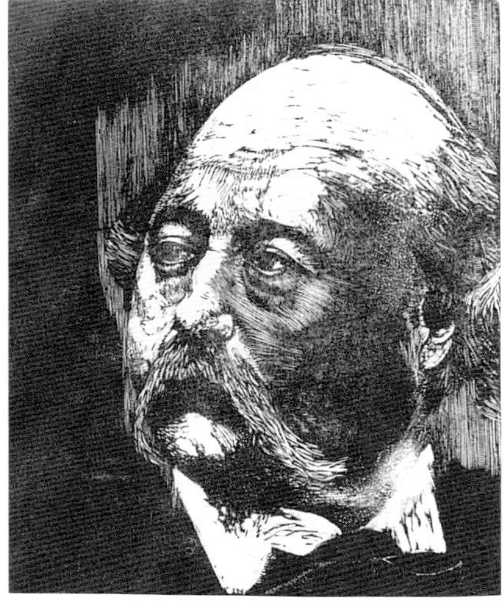

22

21
Stéphane Mallarmé, from *An Image of Salomé,* 1958
Medium wood engraving
Edition size 34
Paper Troya
Printed by the artist at Apiary Press, Smith College, Northampton, Mass.
Plates/blocks 1 wood block
Inks black
Image size 7⅛ × 4¾ in. (18.1 × 12.1 cm)
Sheet size 23½ × 17 in. (59.7 × 43.2 cm)
Reference Mazur S-67

22
Gustave Flaubert, from *An Image of Salomé,* 1958
Medium wood engraving
Edition size 34
Paper Troya

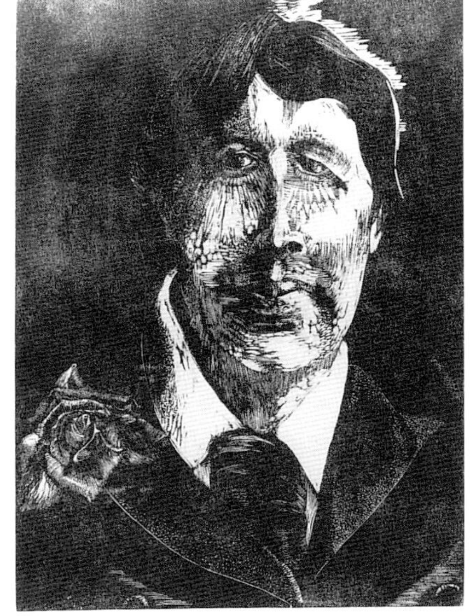

23

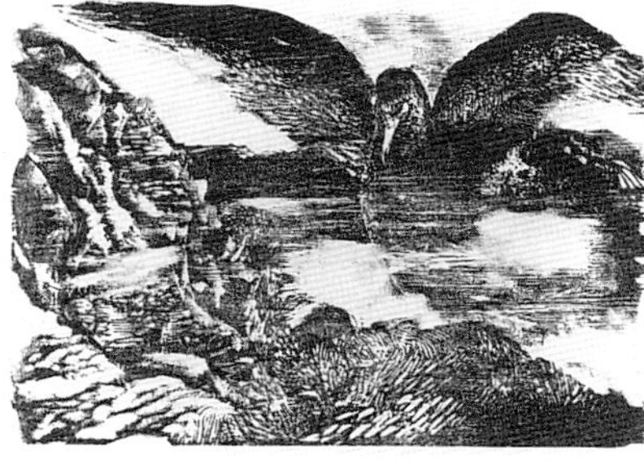

24

Printed by the artist at Apiary Press, Smith College, Northampton, Mass.
Plates/blocks 1 wood block
Inks black
Image size 5 × 4 in. (12.7 × 10.2 cm)
Sheet size 23½ × 17 in. (59.7 × 43.2 cm)
Reference Mazur S-68

23
Oscar Wilde, from *An Image of Salomé,* 1958
Medium wood engraving
Edition size 34
Paper Troya
Printed by the artist at Apiary Press, Smith College, Northampton, Mass.
Plates/blocks 1 wood block
Inks black
Image size 7 × 5 in. (17.8 × 12.7 cm)
Sheet size 23½ × 17 in. (59.7 × 43.2 cm)
Reference Mazur S-69

24
Overture, from *An Image of Salomé,* 1958
Medium wood relief
Edition size 34
Paper Troya

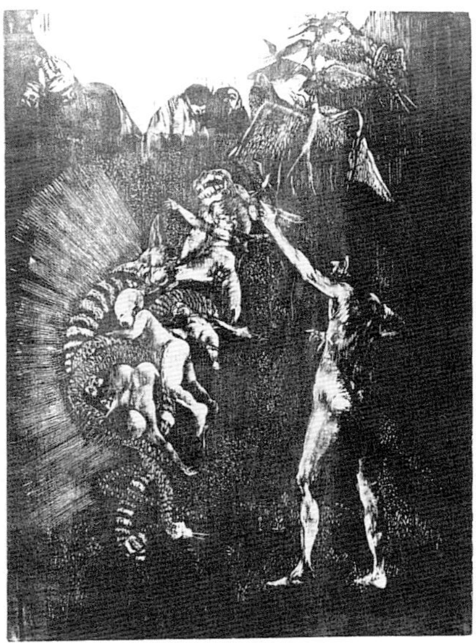

25

Printed by the artist at Apiary Press, Smith College, Northampton, Mass.
Plates/blocks 1 wood block
Inks black
Image size 5 × 7 in. (12.7 × 17.8 cm)
Sheet size 23½ × 17 in. (59.7 × 43.2 cm)
Reference Mazur S-70

25
The Curse of John, from *An Image of Salomé,* 1958
Medium wood relief
Edition size 34
Paper Troya
Printed by the artist at Apiary Press, Smith College, Northampton, Mass.
Plates/blocks 1 wood block
Inks black
Image size 18 × 13 in. (45.8 × 33.0 cm)
Sheet size 23½ × 17 in. (59.7 × 43.2 cm)
Reference Mazur M-66

26
Herodias, from *An Image of Salomé,* 1958
Medium wood relief (reduction printing)
Edition size 34
Paper Troya
Printed by the artist at Apiary Press, Smith College, Northampton, Mass.
Plates/blocks 1 wood block, 3 printings
Inks black, gray, and purple
Image size 16⅝ × 7⅜ in. (42.2 × 18.7 cm)
Sheet size 23½ × 17 in. (59.7 × 43.2 cm)
Reference Mazur M-69

27
Full Portrait of Herod, from *An Image of Salomé,* 1958
Medium wood relief
Edition size 34
Paper Troya

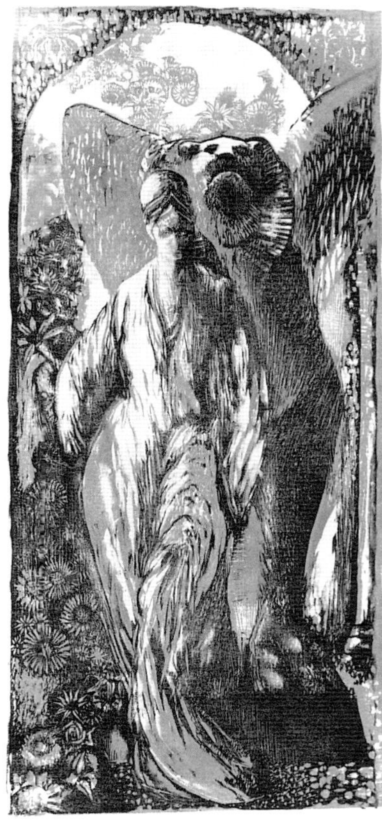

26

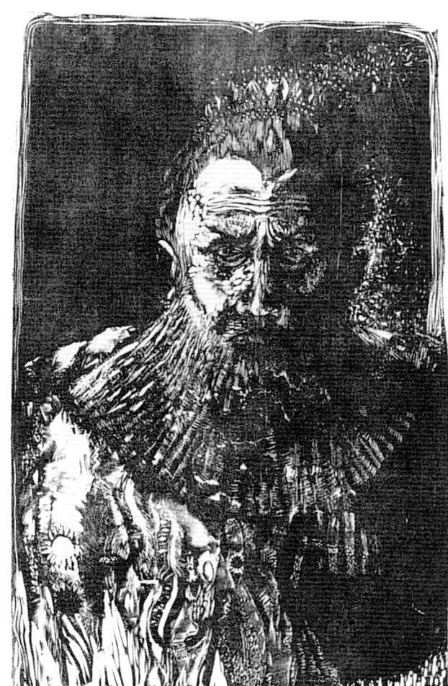

27

Printed by the artist at Apiary Press, Smith College, Northampton, Mass.
Plates/blocks 1 wood block
Inks black
Image size 14¾ × 9⅛ in. (37.5 × 23.2 cm)
Sheet size 23½ × 17 in. (59.7 × 43.2 cm)
Reference Mazur M-68

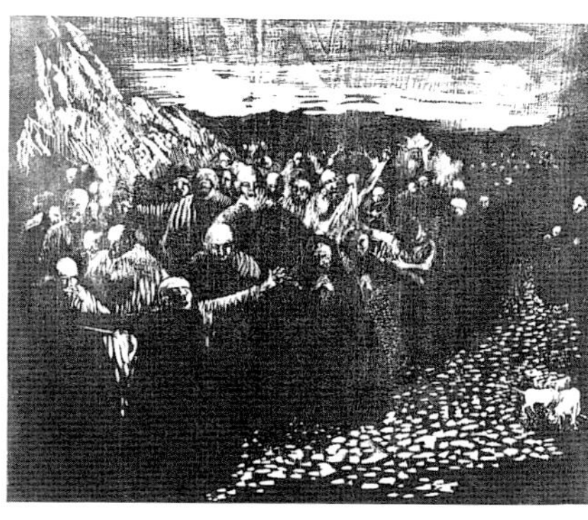

28

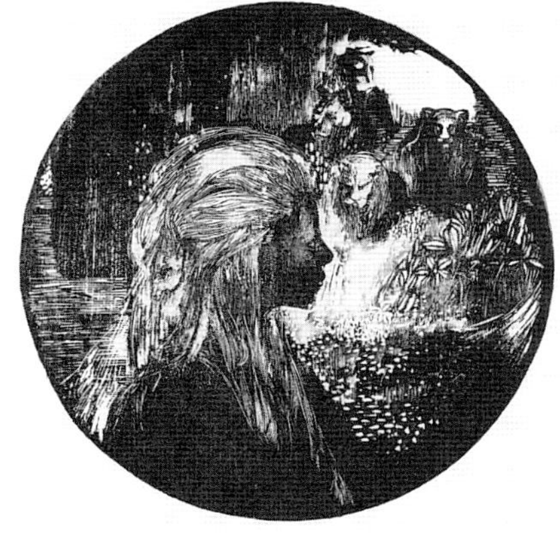

29

28
Multitude, from *An Image of Salomé,* 1958
Medium wood relief
Edition size 34
Paper Troya
Printed by the artist at Apiary Press, Smith College, Northampton, Mass.
Plates/blocks 1 wood block
Inks black
Image size 11⅛ × 13 in. (28.6 × 33.0 cm)
Sheet size 23½ × 17 in. (59.7 × 43.2 cm)
Reference Mazur M-64

29
The Princess with Lions, from *An Image of Salomé,* 1958
Medium wood relief
Edition size 34
Paper Troya
Printed by the artist at Apiary Press, Smith College, Northampton, Mass.
Plates/blocks 1 wood block
Inks black
Image size 10¾ in. (27.3 cm) diameter
Sheet size 23½ × 17 in. (59.7 × 43.2 cm)
Reference Mazur M-70

30
The Dance of Salomé, from *An Image of Salomé,* 1958
Medium wood relief
Edition size 34

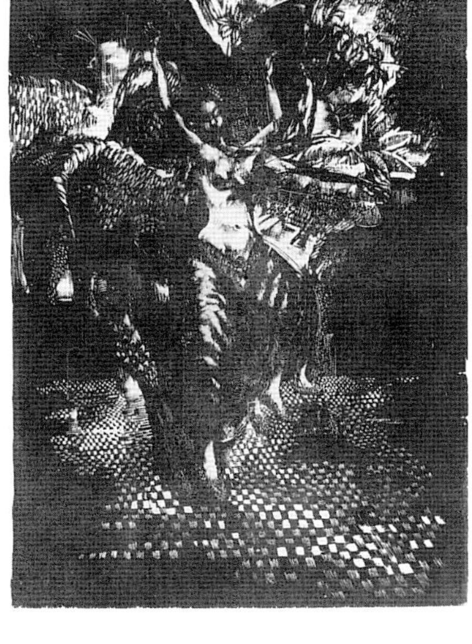

30

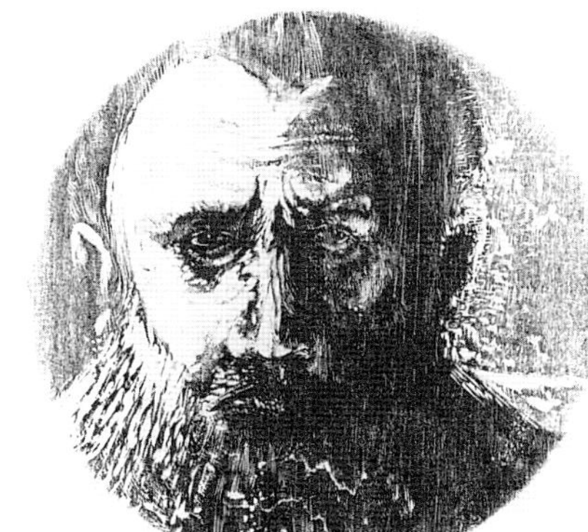

31

Paper Troya
Printed by the artist at Apiary Press, Smith College, Northampton, Mass.
Plates/blocks 1 wood block
Inks black
Image size 16¼ × 11½ in. (41.3 × 29.2 cm)
Sheet size 23½ × 17 in. (59.7 × 43.2 cm)
Reference Mazur M-65

31
Herod, from *An Image of Salomé,* 1958
Medium wood relief
Edition size 34
Paper Troya
Printed by the artist at Apiary Press, Smith College, Northampton, Mass.
Plates/blocks 1 wood block
Inks black
Image size 6⅜ in. (16.2 cm) diameter
Sheet size 23½ × 17 in. (59.7 × 43.2 cm)
Remarks the block used for *Full Portrait of Herod* (no. 27) was reworked for this image
Reference Mazur M-67

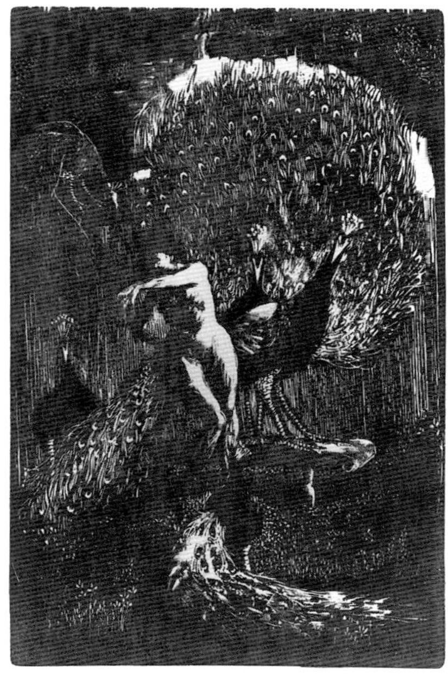

32

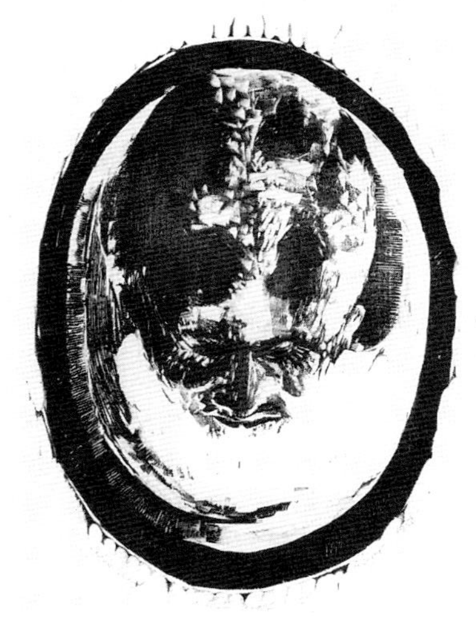

33

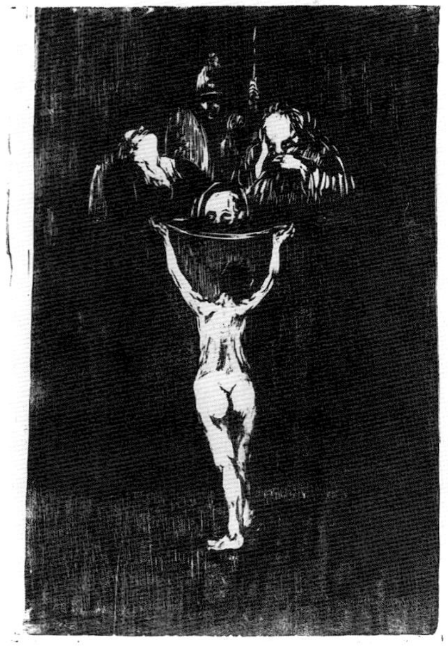

35

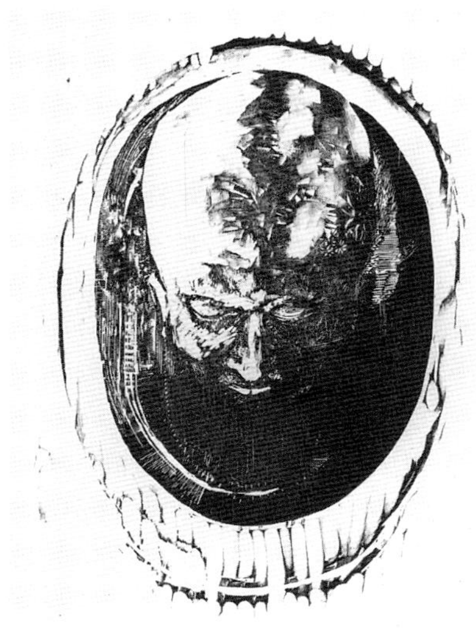

34

36

32
Princess with Peacock, from *An Image of Salomé,* 1958
Medium wood relief
Edition size 34
Paper Troya
Printed by the artist at Apiary Press, Smith College, Northampton, Mass.
Plates/blocks 1 wood block
Inks black
Image size 16⅞ × 10¾ in. (42.9 × 27.3 cm)
Sheet size 23½ × 17 in. (59.7 × 43.2 cm)
Remarks a separate edition of 35 from this block was printed in 1958; this edition was also printed using black ink on Troya paper, with the sheet size measuring 24⅛ × 18⅛ in. (61.3 × 46.1 cm)
Reference Mazur M-73a

33
Head of John the Baptist I, from *An Image of Salomé,* 1958
Medium wood relief
Edition size 34
Paper Troya
Printed by the artist at Apiary Press, Smith College, Northampton, Mass.
Plates/blocks 1 wood block
Inks black
Image size 12 × 8¼ in. (30.5 × 21.0 cm) oval
Sheet size 23½ × 17 in. (59.7 × 43.2 cm)

34
Head of John the Baptist II, from *An Image of Salomé,* 1958
Medium wood relief
Edition size 34
Paper Troya
Printed by the artist at Apiary Press, Smith College, Northampton, Mass.
Plates/blocks 1 wood block
Inks black
Image size 13¼ × 9⅛ in. (33.7 × 23.2 cm) oval
Sheet size 23½ × 17 in. (59.7 × 43.2 cm)
Remarks the block used for *Head of John the Baptist I* (no. 33) was reworked for this image
Reference Mazur M-71

35
Untitled, 1958
Medium wood relief
Edition size not editioned; 1 impression printed
Paper handmade Japanese
Plates/blocks 1 wood block
Inks black
Image size 15¾ × 10⅛ in. (40.0 × 25.7 cm)
Sheet size 20½ × 18¼ in. (52.1 × 46.4 cm)
Remarks related to prints created for *An Image of Salomé*
Reference Mazur M-71a

36
Untitled, 1958
Medium wood relief
Edition size not editioned; 3–4 impressions printed
Paper handmade Japanese
Plates/blocks 1 wood block
Inks black
Image size 7¼ × 6⅞ in. (18.4 × 17.5 cm)
Sheet size 11 × 8 in. (28.0 × 20.3 cm)
Remarks related to prints created for *An Image of Salomé*
Reference Mazur S-72

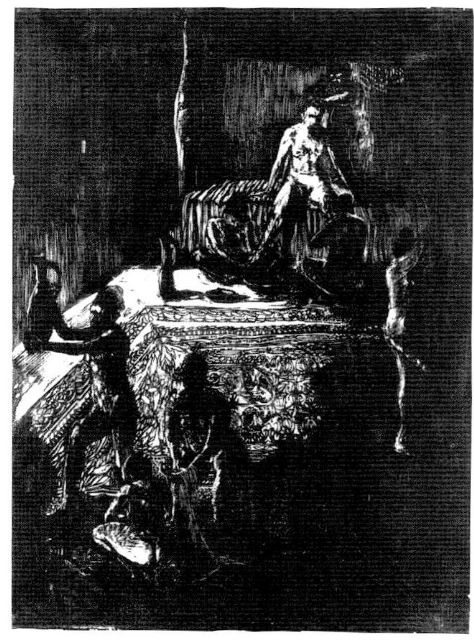
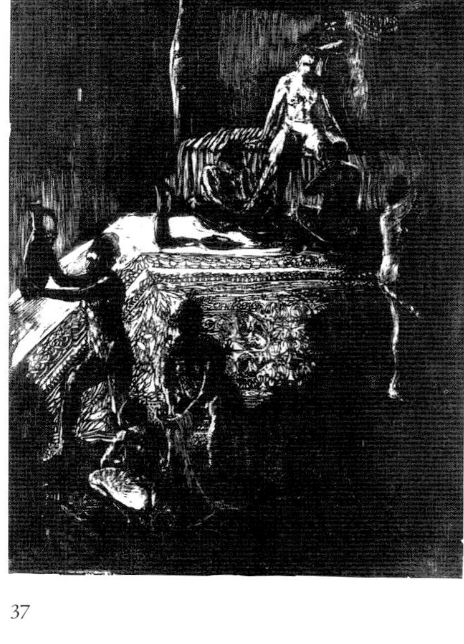

37

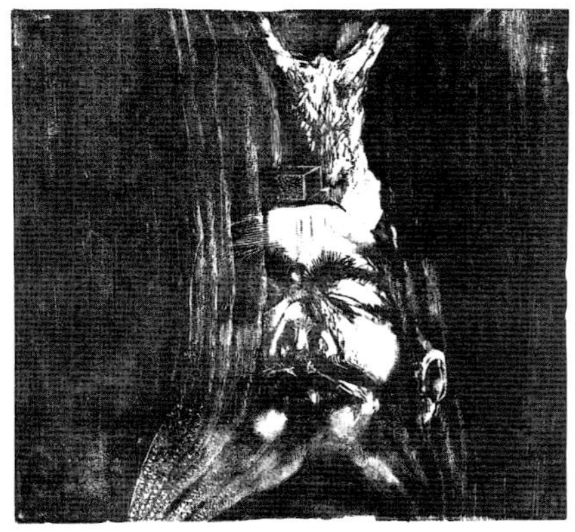

38

37
Salomé Attended, 1958
Medium wood relief
Edition size not editioned; 3–4 impressions printed
Paper Troya
Plates/blocks 1 wood block
Inks black
Image size 17¾ × 12¾ in. (45.1 × 32.4 cm)
Sheet size 23½ × 17 in. (59.7 × 43.2 cm)
Remarks related to prints created for *An Image of Salomé*
Reference Mazur M-63

38
Untitled, 1958
Medium wood relief
Edition size not editioned; 3–4 impressions printed
Paper handmade Japanese
Plates/blocks 1 wood block
Inks black
Image size 10 × 10⅜ in. (25.4 × 26.4 cm)

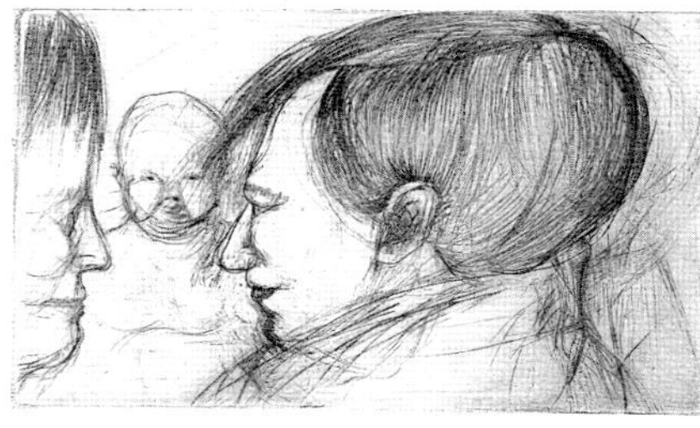

39

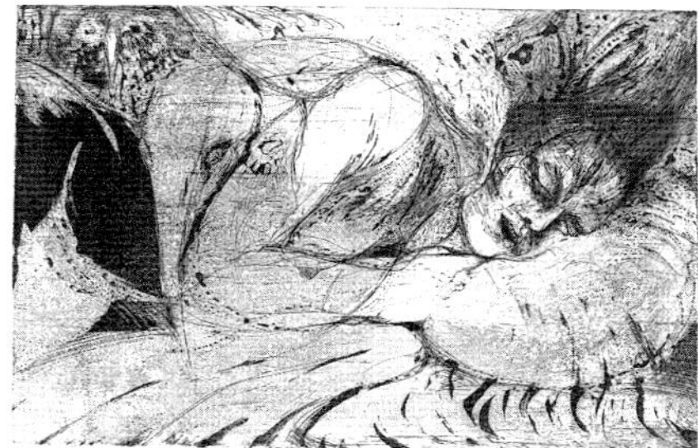
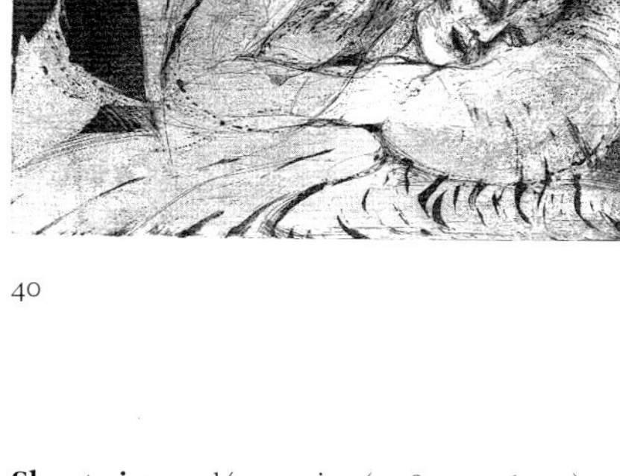

40

Sheet size 12½ × 14 in. (31.8 × 35.6 cm) irregular
Remarks related to prints created for *An Image of Salomé*
Reference Mazur S-73

39
Baskin and Family, 1958
Medium drypoint
Edition size not editioned; no more than 6 impressions printed
Paper laid
Plates/blocks 1 copper plate
Inks sepia
Image size 3¼ × 5¾ in. (8.3 × 14.6 cm)
Sheet size 6½ × 10⅜ in. (16.5 × 26.3 cm)
Remarks Mazur made this portrait of the artist Leonard Baskin, his wife, Hester, and their son, Tobias, while studying at Amherst College and with Baskin at Smith College
Reference Mazur S-16

40
Woman Dreaming (State 2), 1958
Medium etching and aquatint
Edition size not editioned; 3–4 impressions printed
Paper Rives BFK
Plates/blocks 1 copper plate
Inks sepia
Image size 7⅞ × 11⅞ in. (20.0 × 30.2 cm)
Sheet size 13⅞ × 19 in. (35.3 × 48.2 cm)
Reference Mazur S-27b

41
Flowers #3, 1958
Medium etching with plate tone

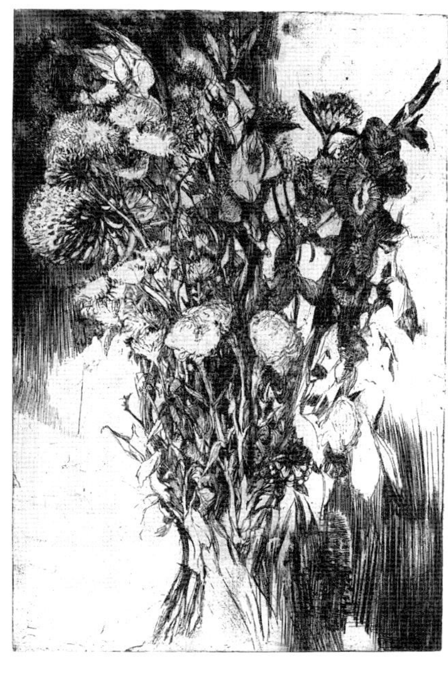

41

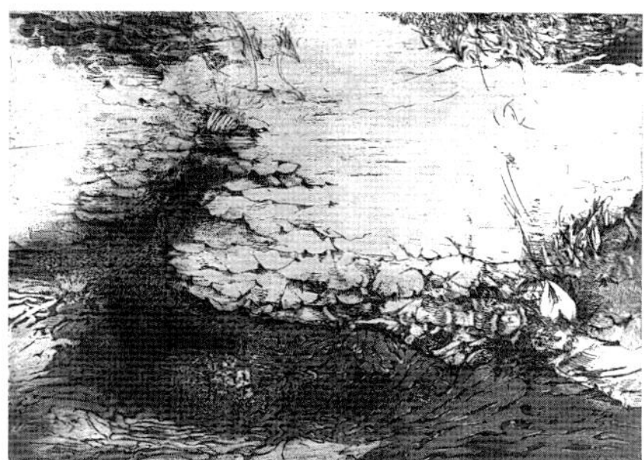

42

Edition size not editioned; 5–6 impressions printed
Paper white wove
Plates/blocks 1 zinc plate
Inks black
Image size 17¾ × 11¾ in. (45.1 × 29.9 cm)
Sheet size 22½ × 15¼ in. (57.2 × 38.7 cm)
Reference Mazur M-19e

42
Lily Growths #1, 1958
Medium etching and aquatint
Edition size 25
Paper A. Millbourn and Company
Plates/blocks 1 zinc plate
Inks bluish green-black
Image size 12¼ × 18⅛ in. (31.1 × 46.1 cm)
Sheet size 17⅝ × 23¾ in. (44.7 × 60.3 cm)
Remarks made while Mazur was a student at Yale; staining on the plate was incorporated into the composition; a few of the prints in the *Lily Growth* series were alternately titled by the artist *Water Lily Growths*
Reference Mazur M-7

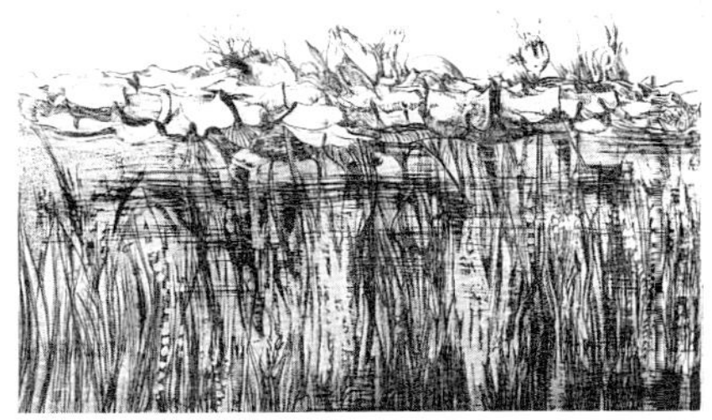

43

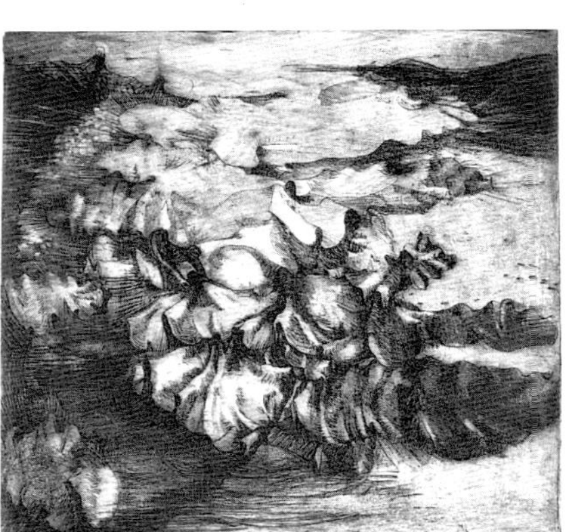

44

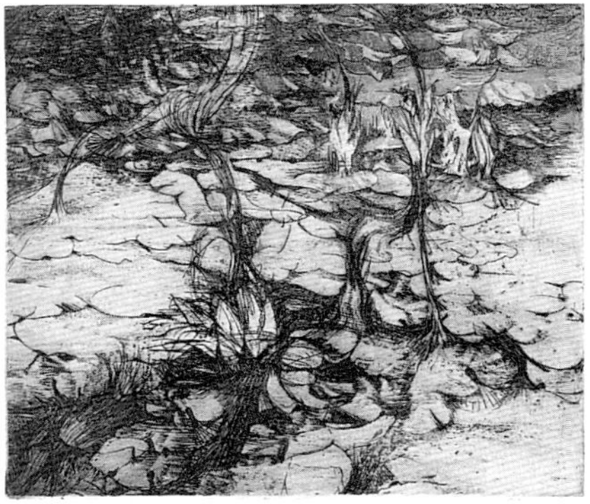

45

43
Lily Growths #2, 1958
Medium etching
Edition size 25
Paper white wove
Plates/blocks 1 zinc plate
Inks black
Image size 11⅞ × 17⅞ in. (30.2 × 45.4 cm)
Sheet size 16⅜ × 22⅛ in. (41.6 × 56.3 cm)
Reference Mazur M-13

44
Lily Growths #3, 1958
Medium etching and aquatint
Edition size 25

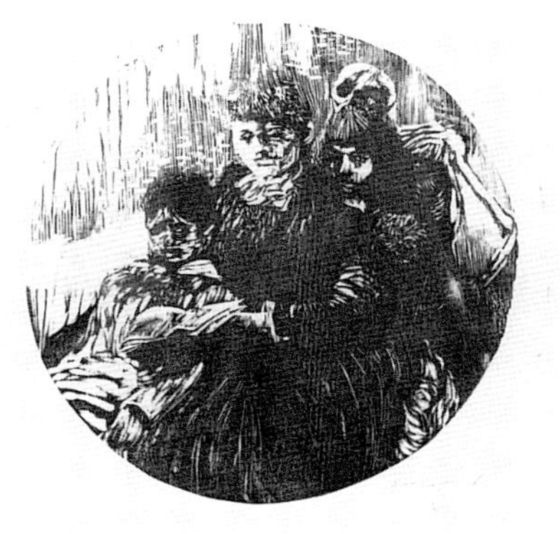

46

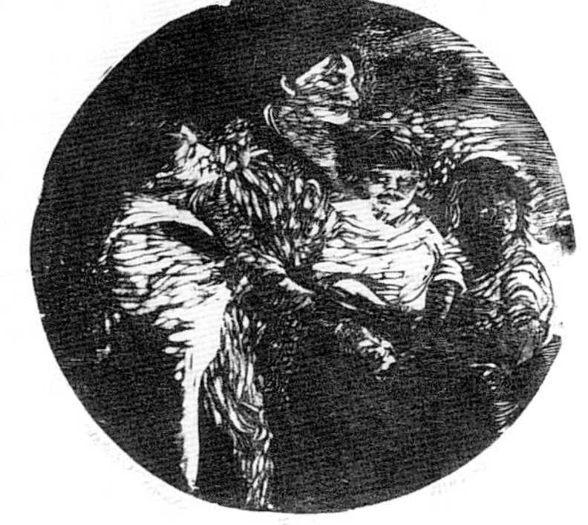

47

Paper white wove
Plates/blocks 1 zinc plate
Inks black
Image size 19¾ × 20⅛ in. (50.2 × 51.1 cm)
Sheet size 22¼ × 25⅜ in. (56.5 × 64.4 cm)
Reference Mazur M-12

45
Lily Growths #4, 1958
Medium etching
Edition size 25
Paper white wove
Plates/blocks 1 zinc plate
Inks green-black
Image size 11¼ × 12¾ in. (28.6 × 32.4 cm)
Sheet size 15⅞ × 18½ in. (40.3 × 47.0 cm)
Reference Mazur S-29

46
The Victorian Family, 1958
Medium handprinted wood relief
Edition size not editioned; 5–7 impressions printed
Paper handmade Japanese
Plates/blocks 1 wood block
Inks black
Image size 6¾ in. (17.1 cm) diameter

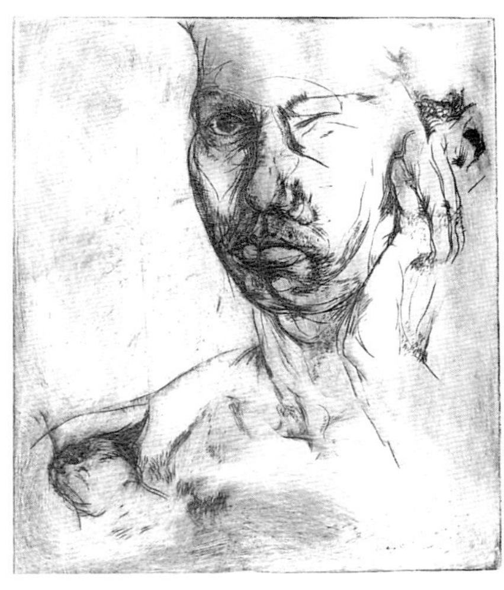

48

Sheet size 17 × 13¼ in. (43.2 × 33.7 cm)
Remarks the wood block was cut during 1958 while the artist was at his summer residence in Mashpee, Mass.; he had been studying a book of Victorian photographs with the intent of starting a series called *Death and the Victorians;* the project was never realized
Reference Mazur S-14

47
Theatrical Family, 1958
Medium handprinted wood relief
Edition size 25
Paper handmade Japanese
Plates/blocks 1 wood block
Inks black
Image size 6¾ in. (17.2 cm) diameter
Sheet size 13¼ × 12 in. (33.7 × 30.5 cm)
Reference Mazur S-15

48
Self-Portrait (State I), 1959
Medium engraving
Edition size not editioned; 2 impressions printed
Paper handmade Japanese
Plates/blocks 1 copper plate
Inks sepia
Image size 7 × 6 in. (17.8 × 15.2 cm)
Sheet size 10¼ × 6¾ in. (26.0 × 17.2 cm)
Remarks in this state, the artist cradles a cat in the lower left corner
Reference Mazur S-2

49
Self-Portrait (State II), 1959
Medium engraving
Edition size 8
Paper handmade Japanese
Plates/blocks 1 copper plate
Inks brown-black
Image size 7 × 6 in. (17.8 × 15.2 cm)

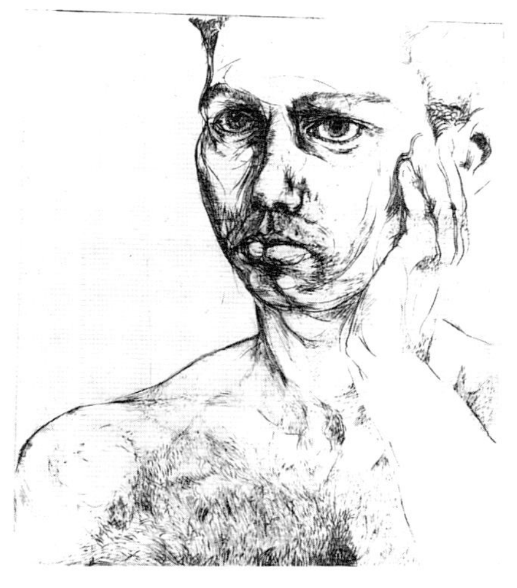

49

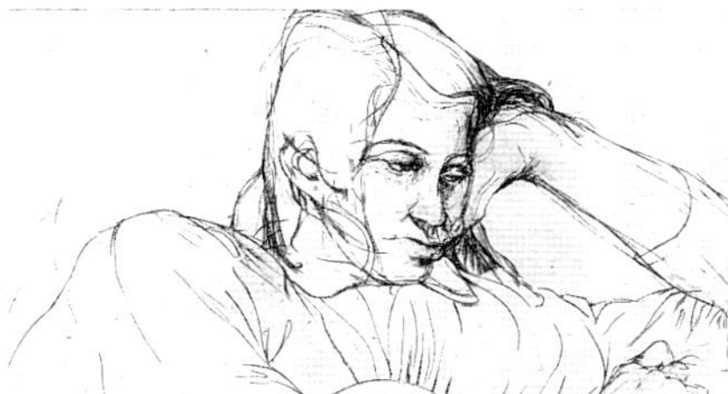

50

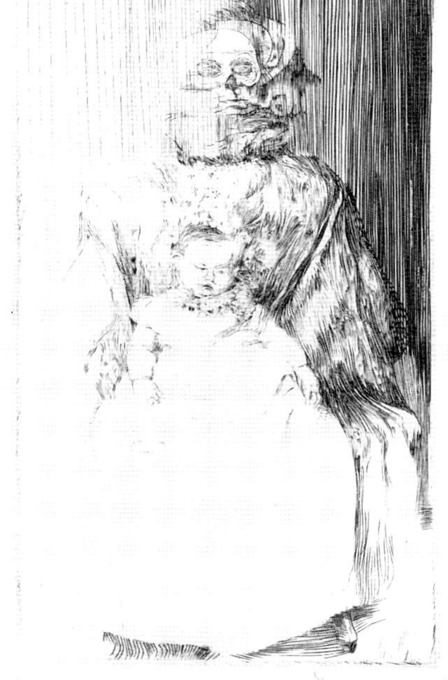

51

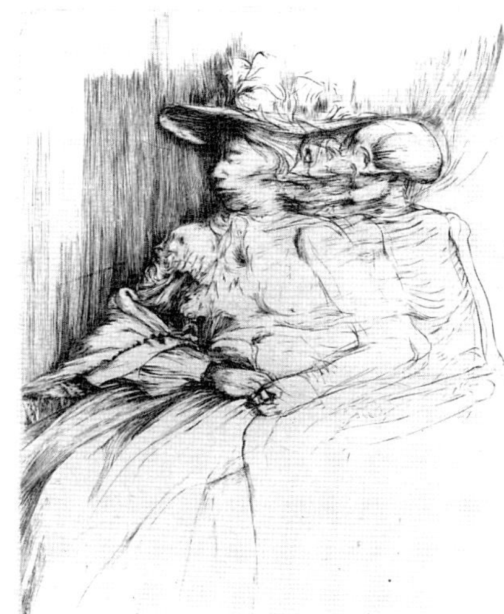

52

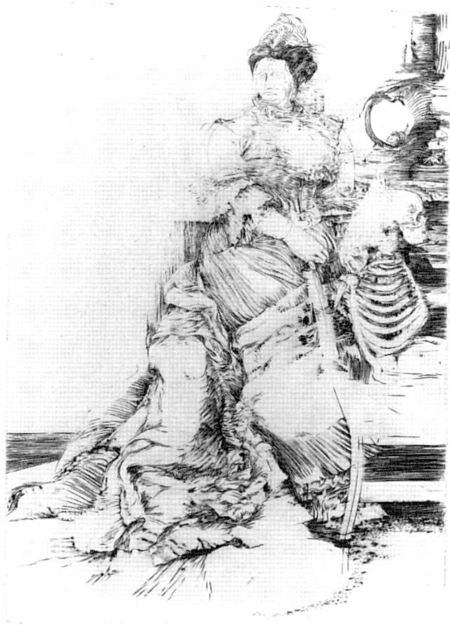

53

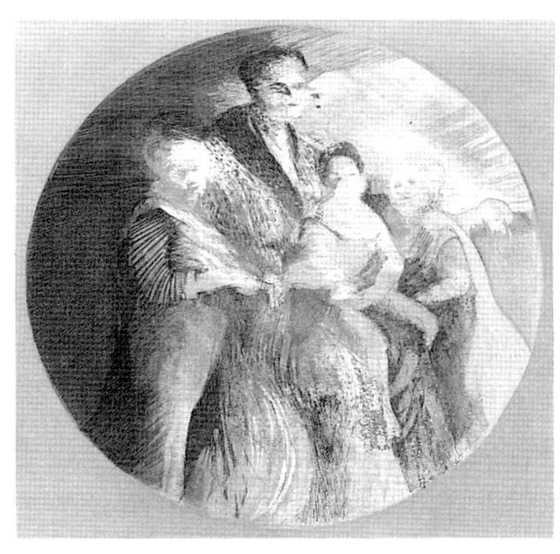

54

Sheet size 13 × 10¼ in. (33.0 × 26.0 cm)
Reference Mazur S-1

50
Gail, 1959
Medium engraving
Edition size not editioned; no more than 5 impressions printed
Paper various papers
Plates/blocks 1 copper plate
Inks varying browns and blacks
Image size 5 × 7 in. (12.7 × 17.8 cm)
Sheet size 6¾ × 10⅜ in. (17.2 × 26.4 cm)
Reference Mazur S-3

51
Victorian Baby III, 1959
Medium engraving
Edition size not editioned; 4–5 impressions printed
Paper white wove
Plates/blocks 1 copper plate
Inks black
Image size 7 × 4 in. (17.8 × 10.2 cm)
Sheet size 8⅝ × 5½ in. (21.9 × 14.0 cm)
Remarks from the unrealized *Death and the Victorians* series
Reference Mazur S-22b

52
Metamorphosis of the Victorian, 1959
Medium engraving
Edition size 20
Paper white wove
Plates/blocks 1 copper plate
Inks black
Image size 7⅞ × 6¼ in. (20.0 × 15.9 cm)
Sheet size 12⅜ × 9⅜ in. (31.5 × 23.8 cm)
Remarks from the unrealized *Death and the Victorians* series
Reference Mazur S-24

53
For A.T.B., Study for Death and the Victorians, 1959
Medium engraving
Edition size not editioned; 3–4 impressions printed
Paper white wove
Plates/blocks 1 copper plate
Inks black
Image size 8¾ × 6⅛ in. (22.2 × 15.6 cm)
Sheet size 13⅛ × 8¾ in. (33.4 × 22.2 cm)

54
Theatrical Family (large color), 1959
Medium etching and aquatint with soft ground
Edition size not editioned; 5–6 impressions printed
Paper white wove
Plates/blocks 3 zinc plates
Inks red, orange, and buff
Image size 16¾ in. (42.6 cm) diameter
Sheet size 19 × 20¾ in. (48.2 × 52.7 cm)
Reference Mazur M-11

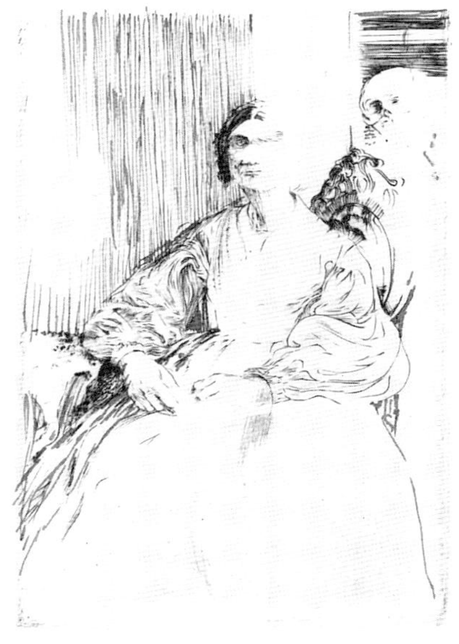

55

55
Victorian with Skull, 1959
Medium engraving
Edition size not editioned; 2–3 impressions printed
Paper white wove
Plates/blocks 1 copper plate
Inks black
Image size 4¼ × 2⅞ in. (10.8 × 7.3 cm)
Sheet size 7⅝ × 10½ in. (19.4 × 26.7 cm) maximum (proof sheets vary)
Remarks from the unrealized *Death and the Victorians* series
Reference Mazur S-22d

56
Study for Death and the Victorians, ca. 1959
Medium etching
Edition size not editioned; 3–4 impressions printed
Paper white wove
Plates/blocks 1 zinc plate
Inks black
Image size 10 in. (25.4 cm) diameter
Plate size 12 × 12 in. (30.5 × 30.5 cm)
Sheet size 18⅛ × 18⅛ in. (46.1 × 46.1 cm)
Remarks from the unrealized *Death and the Victorians* series

57
Baby, 1959
Medium etching
Edition size not editioned; 2–3 impressions printed
Paper white wove
Plates/blocks 1 zinc plate
Inks blue-black

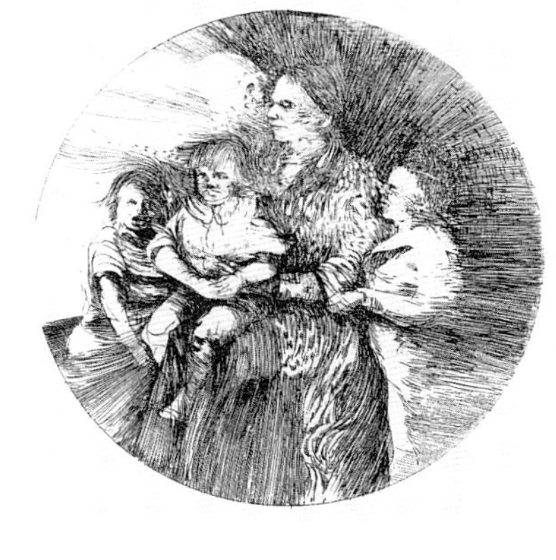

56

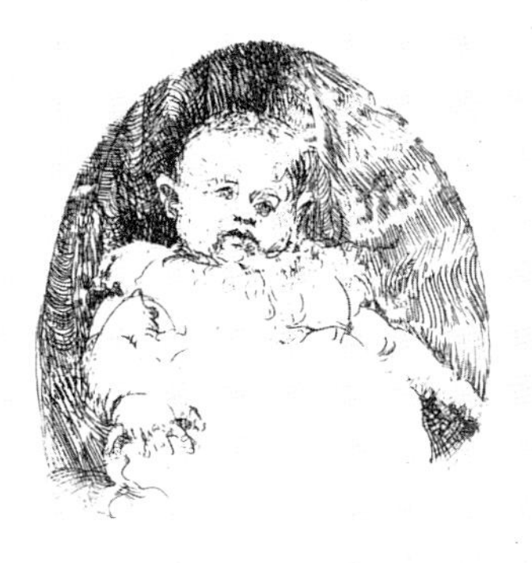

57

Image size 5⅛ × 3⅛ in. (13.0 × 7.9 cm)
Sheet size 9 × 6⅛ in. (22.9 × 15.6 cm)
Remarks from the unrealized *Death and the Victorians* series
Reference Mazur S-22c

58
Victorian Baby II, 1959
Medium wood relief
Edition size not editioned; 2–3 impressions printed
Paper handmade Japanese
Plates/blocks 1 wood block
Inks black
Image size 3½ × 2 in. (8.9 × 5.1 cm)
Sheet size 12⅛ × 7 in. (30.8 × 17.8 cm)
Remarks from the unrealized *Death and the Victorians* series
Reference Mazur S-22a

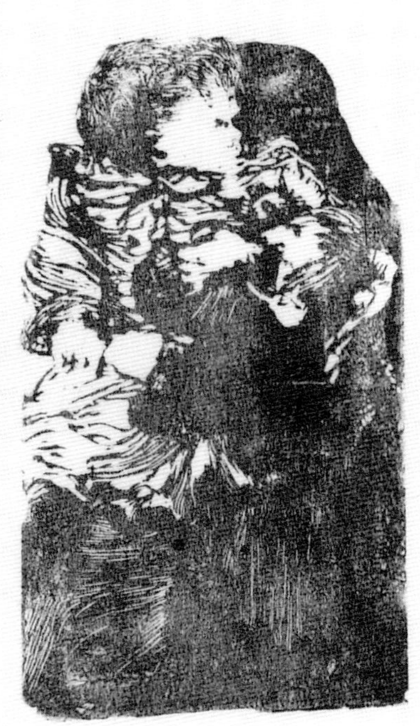

58

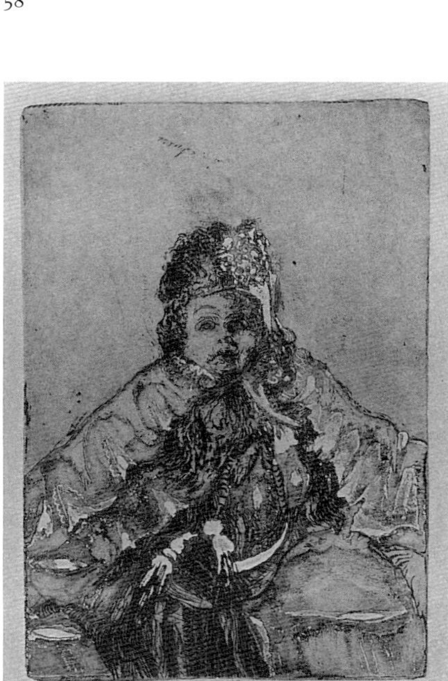

59

59
The Victorian Baby, 1959
Medium etching printed in relief and intaglio
Edition size 25
Paper Barchem green
Plates/blocks 1 zinc plate
Inks black
Image size 8⅞ × 6 in. (22.7 × 15.2 cm)
Sheet size 13 × 9⅝ in. (33.0 × 24.5 cm)
Remarks from the unrealized *Death and the Victorians* series
Reference Mazur S-22

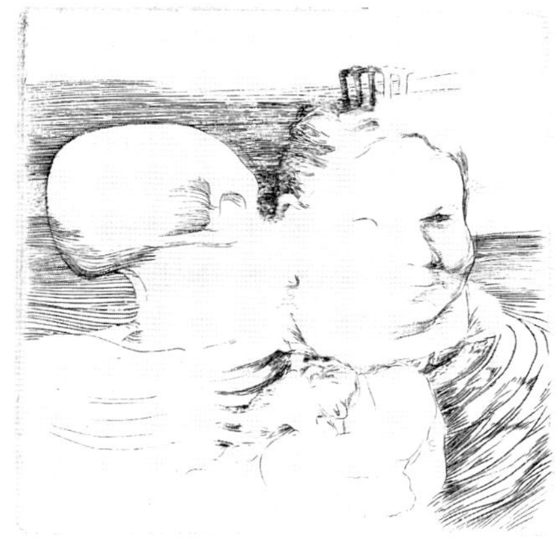

60

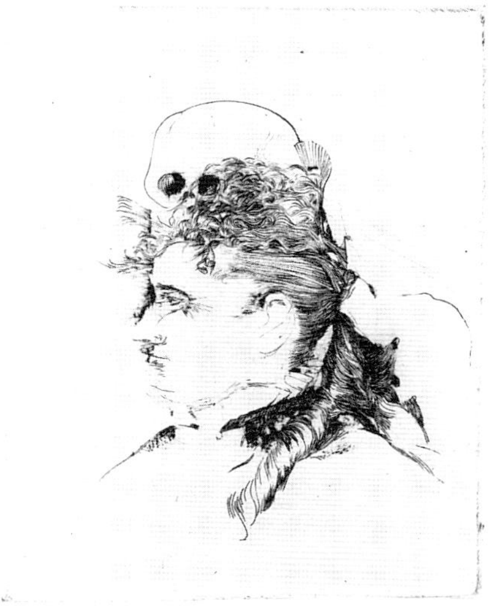

61

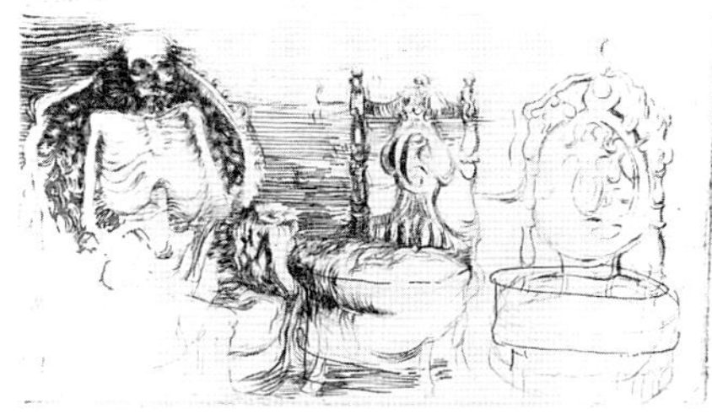

62

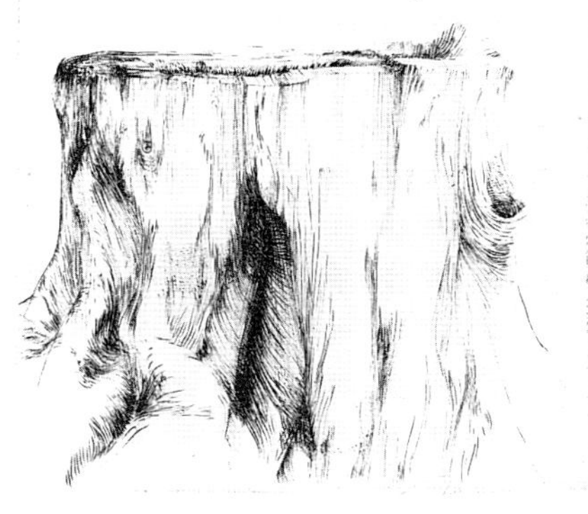

63

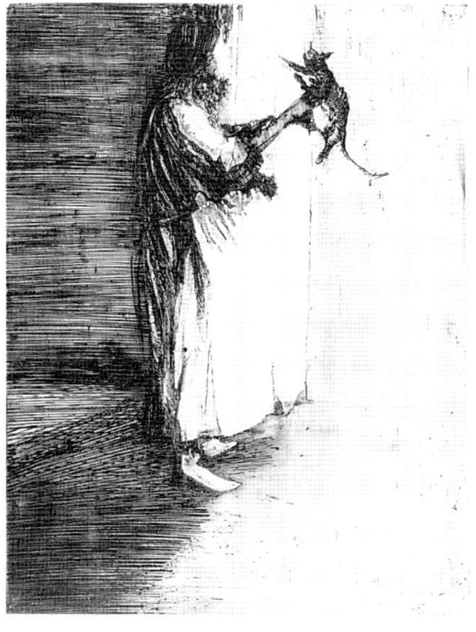

64

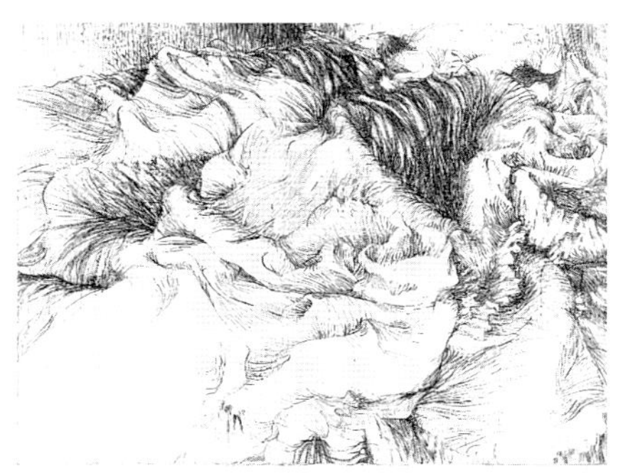

65

60
Untitled (Victorian Woman with Skull), 1959
Medium engraving
Edition size not editioned; 2–3 impressions printed
Paper white wove
Plates/blocks 1 zinc plate
Inks black
Image size 3⅞ × 5 in. (9.9 × 12.7 cm)
Sheet size 10 × 7¼ in. (25.4 × 18.4 cm)
Remarks from the unrealized *Death and the Victorians* series
Reference Mazur S-24c

61
Untitled (Victorian Woman with Skull)
Medium engraving
Edition size not editioned; 2–3 impressions printed
Paper white wove
Plates/blocks 1 zinc plate
Inks black

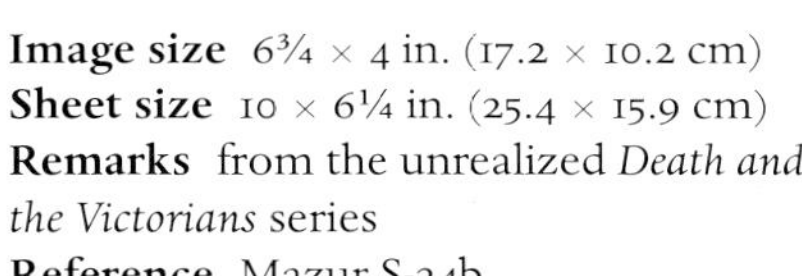
Image size 6¾ × 4 in. (17.2 × 10.2 cm)
Sheet size 10 × 6¼ in. (25.4 × 15.9 cm)
Remarks from the unrealized *Death and the Victorians* series
Reference Mazur S-24b

62
Victorian Furniture, 1959
Medium engraving
Edition size not editioned; 2–3 impressions printed
Paper Rives
Plates/blocks 1 zinc plate
Inks black
Image size 4¼ × 6 in. (10.8 × 15.2 cm)
Sheet size 9¾ × 13⅜ in. (24.8 × 34.0 cm)
Remarks from the unrealized *Death and the Victorians* series
Reference Mazur S-24a

63
Untitled (Stump), 1959
Medium drypoint
Edition size not editioned; 2–3 impressions printed
Paper white wove
Plates/blocks 1 zinc plate
Inks black
Image size 3⅞ × 4¼ in. (9.9 × 10.8 cm)
Sheet size 8¼ × 8½ in. (21.0 × 21.6 cm)
Reference Mazur S-29a

64
Gail with Cat, 1959
Medium etching printed in relief and intaglio
Edition size not editioned; 2–3 impressions printed
Paper white wove
Plates/blocks 1 zinc plate
Inks black
Image size 11¾ × 8⅝ in. (29.9 × 21.9 cm)
Sheet size 14½ × 11 in. (36.8 × 28.0 cm)
Remarks an early experiment in printing intaglio plates in relief
Reference Mazur S-4

65
In Bed, 1959
Medium etching
Edition size not editioned; 2–3 impressions printed
Paper white wove
Plates/blocks 1 zinc plate
Inks brown-black
Image size 11½ × 15¼ in. (29.2 × 38.7 cm)
Sheet size 16⅜ × 19⅜ in. (41.6 × 49.2 cm)
Reference Mazur S-28

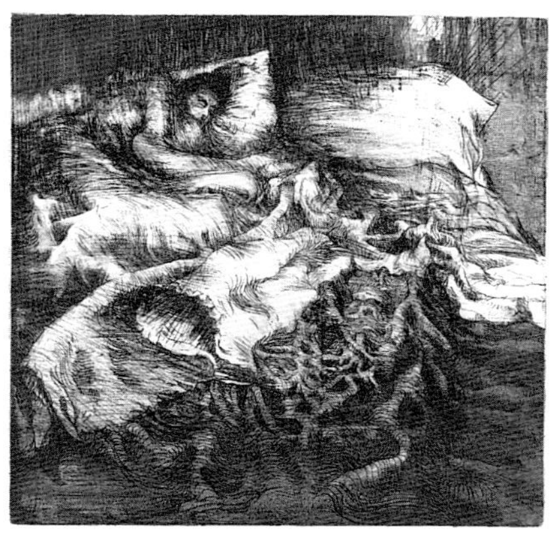

66

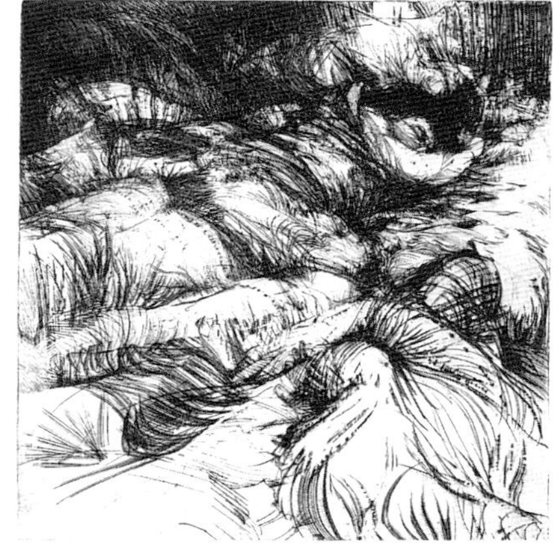

68

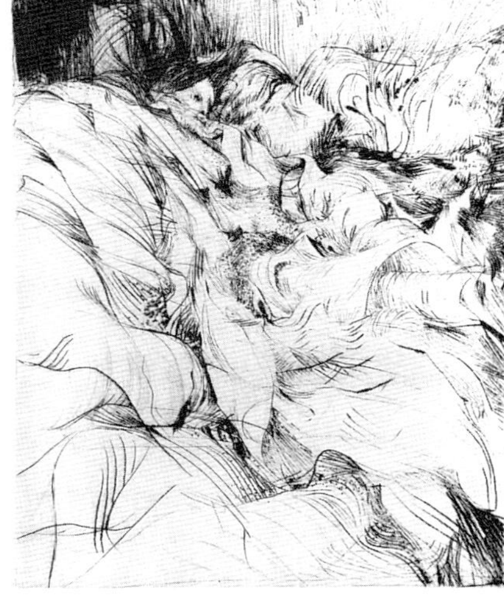

70

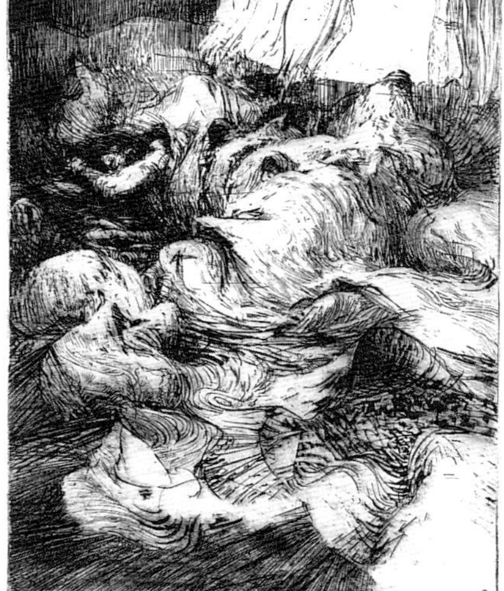

67

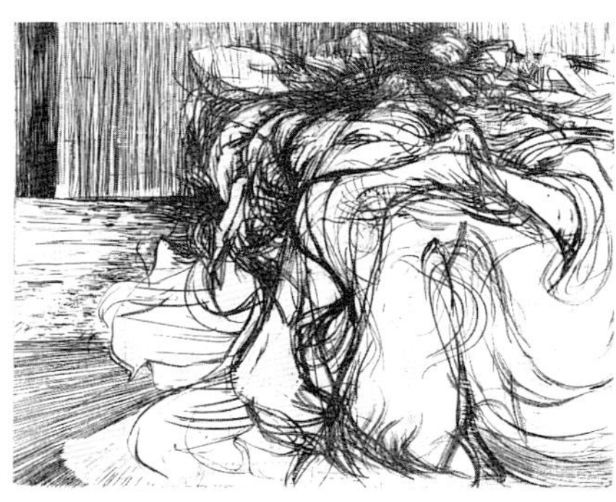

69

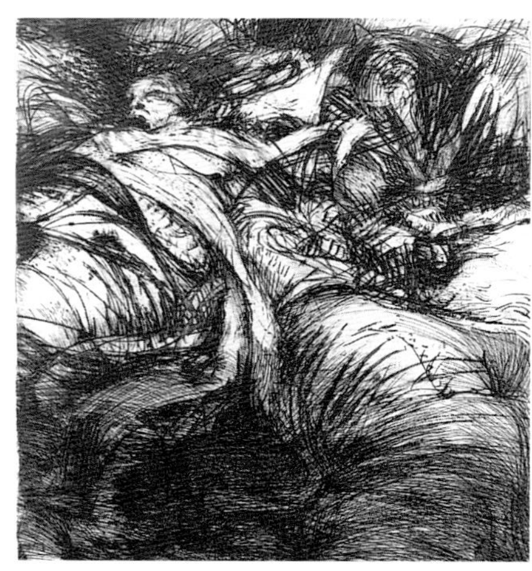

71

66
Sleeper, 1959
Medium etching and aquatint with soft ground
Edition size 10
Paper white wove
Plates/blocks 1 zinc plate
Inks black
Image size 17½ × 17¾ in. (44.5 × 45.1 cm)
Sheet size 20¼ × 21⅞ in. (51.5 × 55.6 cm)
Reference Mazur M-1

67
The Window Bed, 1959
Medium etching
Edition size 25
Paper white wove
Plates/blocks 1 zinc plate
Inks black
Image size 15 × 11¾ in. (38.1 × 29.9 cm)
Sheet size 20⅛ × 16⅛ in. (51.1 × 41.0 cm)
Reference Mazur S-31

68
The Sleeper, 1959
Medium etching with plate tone
Edition size 25
Paper white wove
Plates/blocks 1 zinc plate
Inks black
Image size 18½ × 17¾ in. (47.0 × 45.1 cm)
Sheet size 23 × 19⅞ in. (58.4 × 50.5 cm)
Reference Mazur M-5

69
Sick Bed, 1959
Medium etching
Edition size 25
Paper white wove
Plates/blocks 1 zinc plate
Inks black
Image size 11¾ × 14¾ in. (29.9 × 37.5 cm)
Sheet size 15⅞ × 18⅝ in. (40.4 × 47.3 cm)
Reference Mazur S-30

70
Sleeper, 1959
Medium drypoint
Edition size 25 (editioning not completed; about 8 impressions printed)
Paper Zerkall
Plates/blocks 1 copper plate
Inks black
Image size 7¼ × 5⅞ in. (18.4 × 15.0 cm)
Sheet size 9¾ × 8¾ in. (24.8 × 22.2 cm)
Reference Mazur S-26

71
Nightmare, 1959
Medium etching
Edition size 25
Paper white wove
Plates/blocks 1 zinc plate
Inks black
Image size 19¼ × 17½ in. (48.9 × 44.5 cm)
Sheet size 22¼ × 20¾ in. (56.5 × 52.7 cm)
Remarks the plate for *Nightmare* was lost; in 1987 the artist created a second, slightly larger plate for the same image and printed a second edition; see no. 258

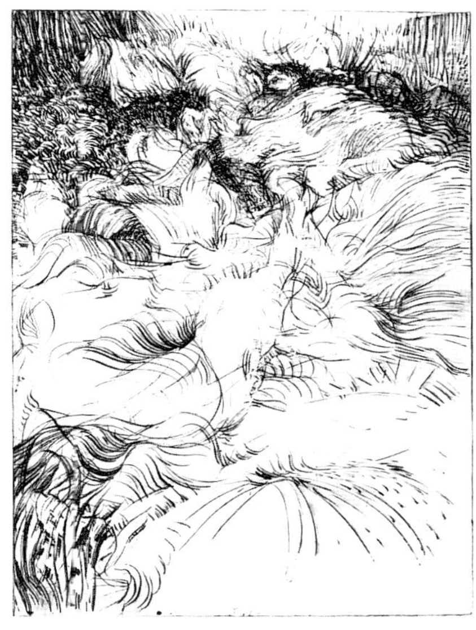

72

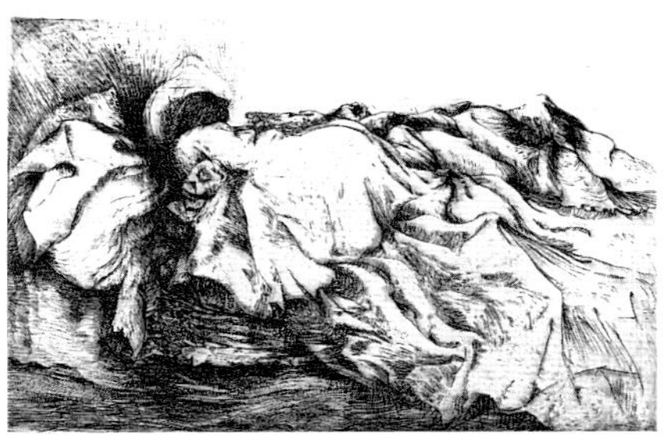

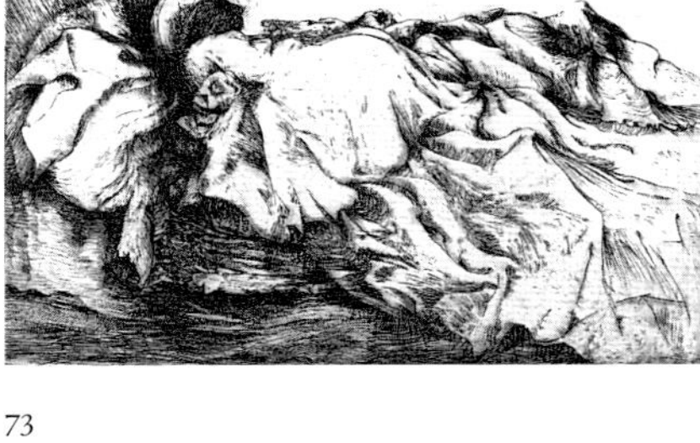

73

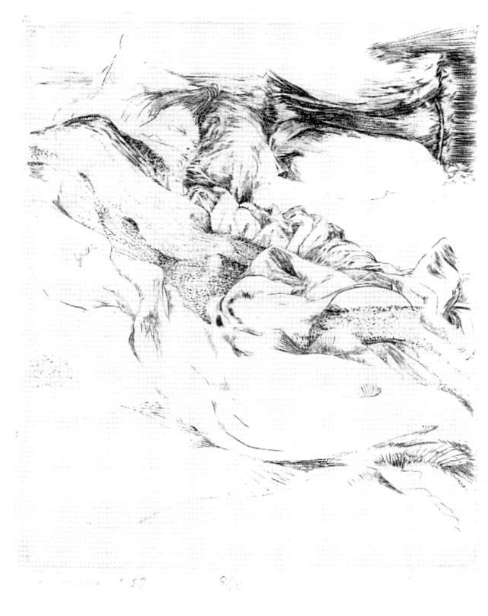

74

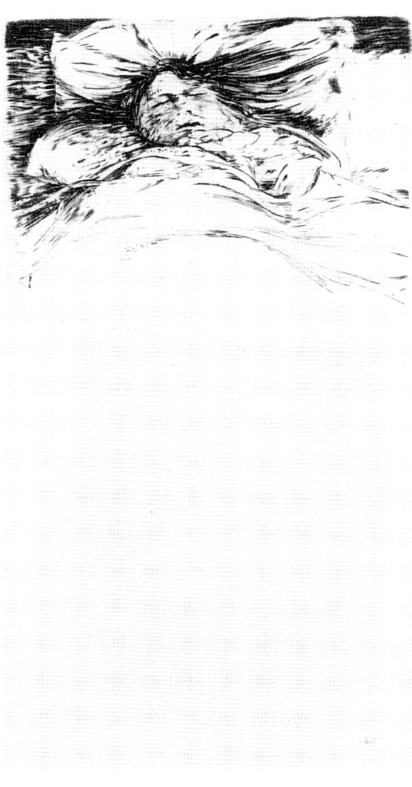

75

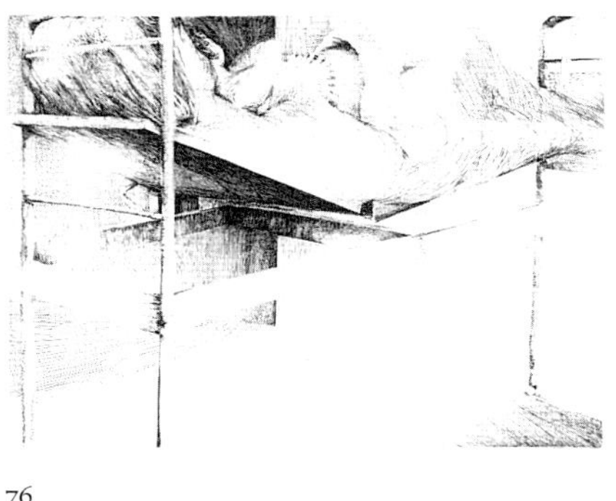

76

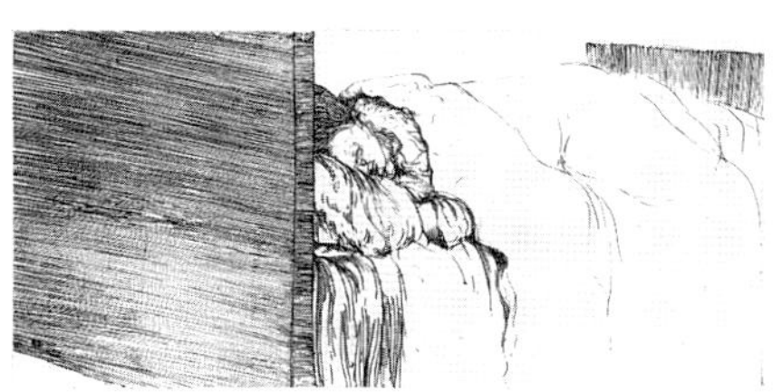

77

72
Sleeper, 1959
Medium etching with plate tone
Edition size not editioned; 3–4 impressions printed
Paper white wove
Plates/blocks 1 zinc plate
Inks black
Image size 23⅝ × 17½ in. (60.0 × 44.5 cm)
Sheet size 26¾ × 20½ in. (68.0 × 52.1 cm)

73
Reading in Bed, 1959
Medium etching with plate tone
Edition size 25
Paper white wove
Plates/blocks 1 zinc plate
Inks brown
Image size 11¾ × 17¾ in. (29.9 × 45.1 cm)
Sheet size 16¼ × 24⅛ in. (41.3 × 61.3 cm)
Remarks printed at Yale University; the prints in this edition were used as gifts for donors to its School of Art and Architecture
Reference Mazur M-2

74
The Sleeper, 1959
Medium engraving
Edition size 25
Paper white wove
Plates/blocks 1 copper plate
Inks blue-black
Image size 5 × 4 in. (12.7 × 10.2 cm)
Sheet size 8⅞ × 7⅝ in. (22.7 × 19.4 cm)
Reference Mazur S-27

75
Small Sleeper, 1959
Medium engraving
Edition size 100
Paper white wove
Plates/blocks 1 copper plate
Inks black
Image size 4⅜ × 2⅜ in. (11.2 × 6.0 cm)
Sheet size 6⅝ × 4⅝ in. (16.9 × 11.8 cm)
Reference Mazur S-25

76
The Hospital Bed, 1959
Medium etching
Edition size 25
Paper white wove
Plates/blocks 1 copper plate
Inks black
Image size 14¾ × 19¾ in. (37.5 × 50.2 cm)
Sheet size 19 × 25¾ in. (48.2 × 65.4 cm)
Remarks the artist's wife, Gail, in delivery
Reference Mazur M-3

77
Sleeper with Headboard, 1959
Medium etching
Edition size not editioned; 2–3 impressions printed
Paper white wove
Plates/blocks 1 zinc plate
Inks black
Image size 5⅞ × 11¾ in. (15.0 × 29.9 cm)
Sheet size 10 × 14 in. (25.4 × 35.6 cm)
Reference Mazur S-22e

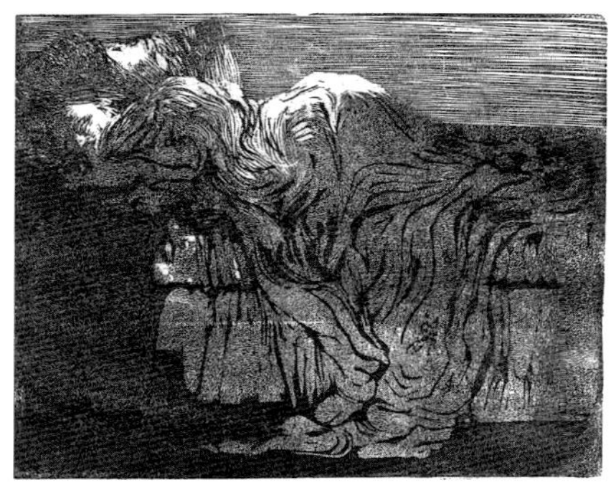

78

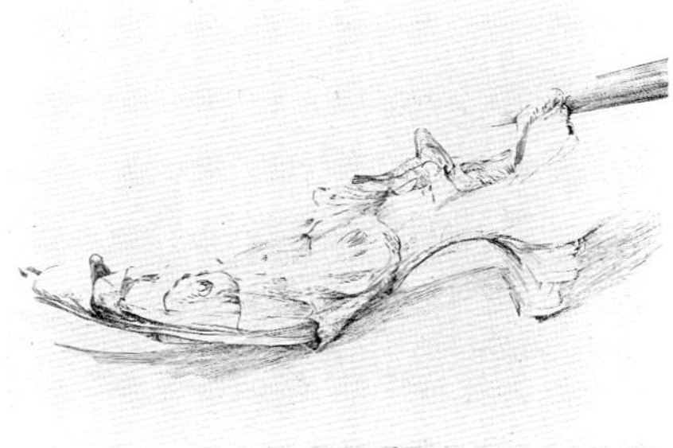

79

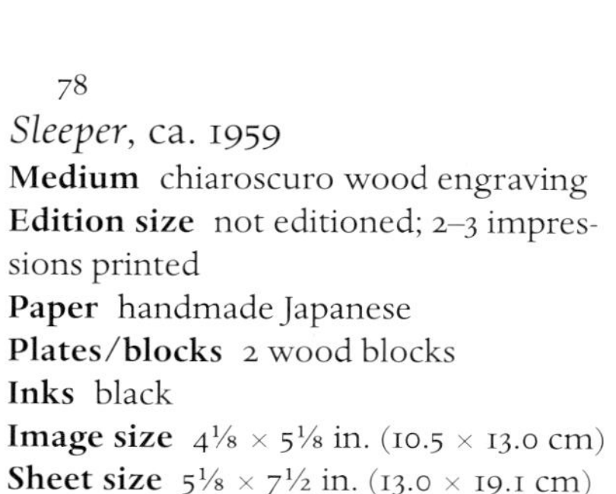

78
Sleeper, ca. 1959
Medium chiaroscuro wood engraving
Edition size not editioned; 2–3 impressions printed
Paper handmade Japanese
Plates/blocks 2 wood blocks
Inks black
Image size 4⅛ × 5⅛ in. (10.5 × 13.0 cm)
Sheet size 5⅛ × 7½ in. (13.0 × 19.1 cm)
Reference Mazur S-27a

79
Old Shoe, 1959
Medium engraving
Edition size not editioned; 5–6 impressions printed
Paper white wove
Plates/blocks 1 copper plate
Inks brown
Image size 8¾ × 12 in. (22.2 × 30.5 cm)
Sheet size 13⅜ × 16⅛ in. (34.0 × 41.0 cm) approximate (sheet sizes vary)
Reference Mazur S-23

80
Bed, 1960
Medium wood relief
Edition size not editioned; 3–4 impressions printed
Paper handmade Japanese
Plates/blocks 1 wood block
Inks black
Image size 15 × 15 in. (38.1 × 38.1 cm)
Sheet size 24 × 17⅝ in. (61.0 × 44.8 cm)
Reference Mazur L-74

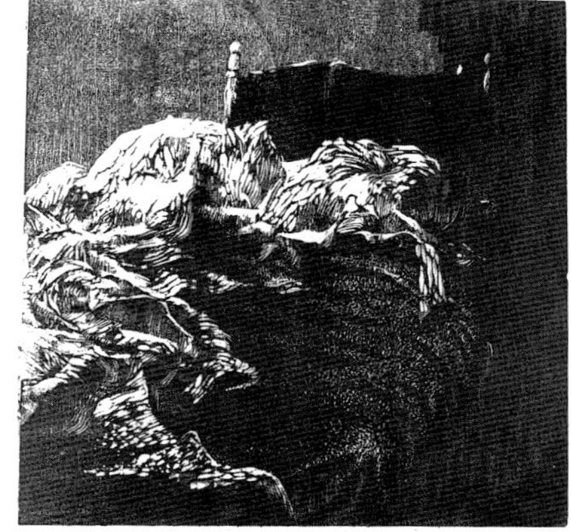

80

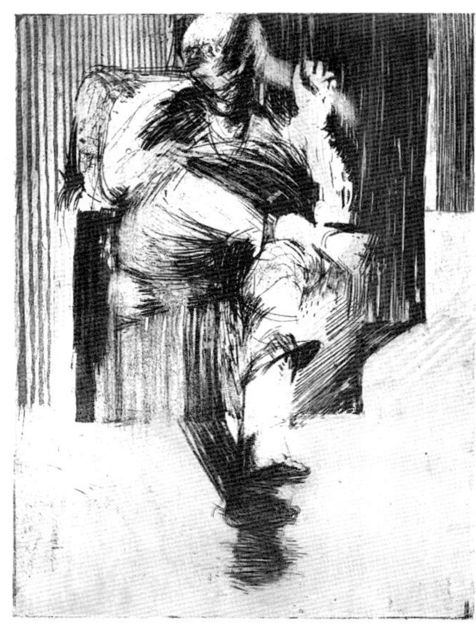

81

81
A Portrait of R. B., 1960
Medium etching and aquatint
Edition size not editioned; 5–6 impressions printed
Paper Rives and other papers
Plates/blocks 2 zinc plates
Inks 2 colors that vary with each impression
Image size 14½ × 10¾ in. (36.8 × 27.3 cm)
Sheet size 19⅜ × 15 in. (49.2 × 38.1 cm) approximate (proof sheets vary)
Remarks a portrait of the artist Robert Birmelin, made while Mazur and Birmelin were students at Yale; an early experiment in color printing
Reference Mazur S-19

82
Baby on Table, 1960
Medium etching
Edition size 25
Paper A. Millbourn and Company

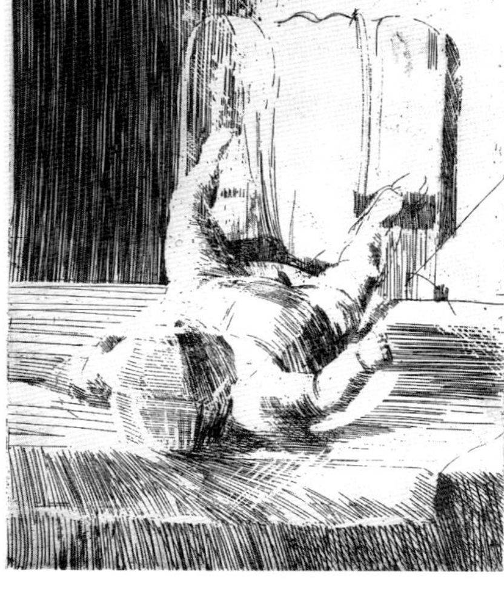

82

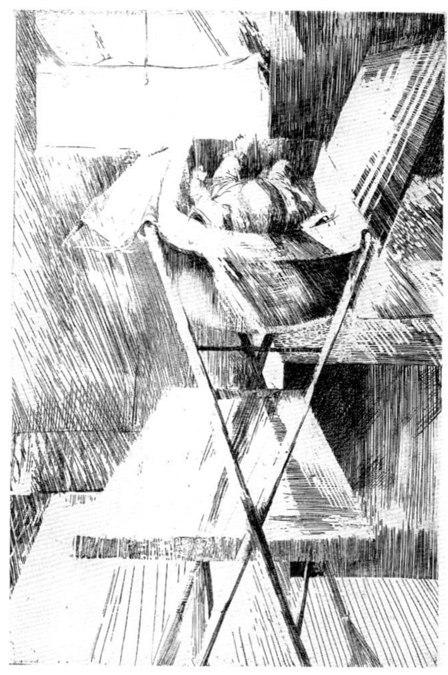

83

Plates/blocks 1 zinc plate
Inks black
Image size 17¾ × 14¼ in. (45.1 × 36.2 cm)
Sheet size 24⅝ × 20⅞ in. (62.6 × 53.0 cm)
Reference Mazur M-6

83
Baby in Bathinette, 1960
Medium etching
Edition size 25
Paper white wove
Plates/blocks 1 zinc plate
Inks blue-black
Image size 21⅝ × 13¾ in. (54.9 × 34.9 cm)
Sheet size 26½ × 18 in. (67.3 × 45.8 cm)
Reference Mazur M-4

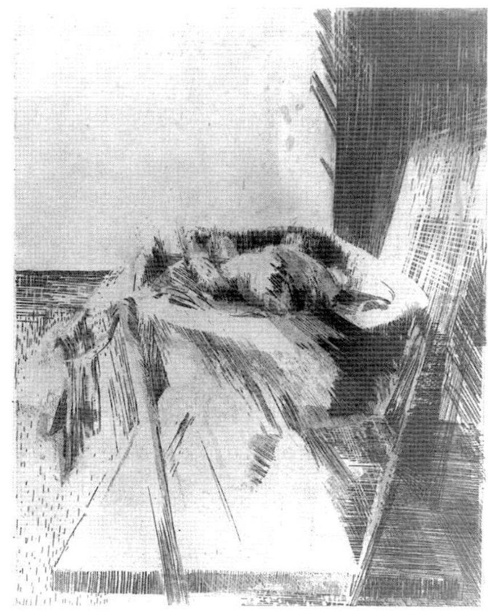

84

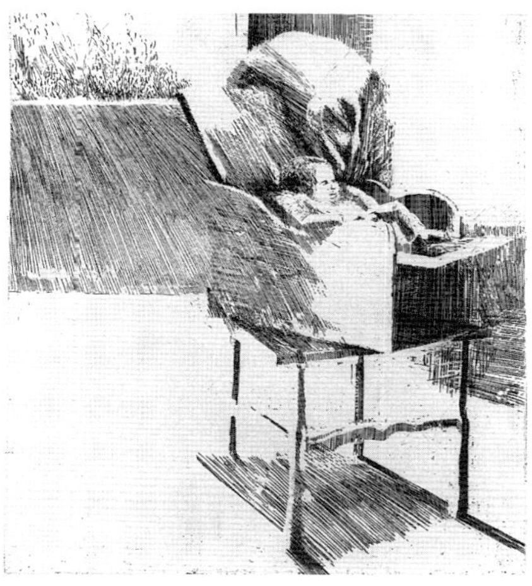

85

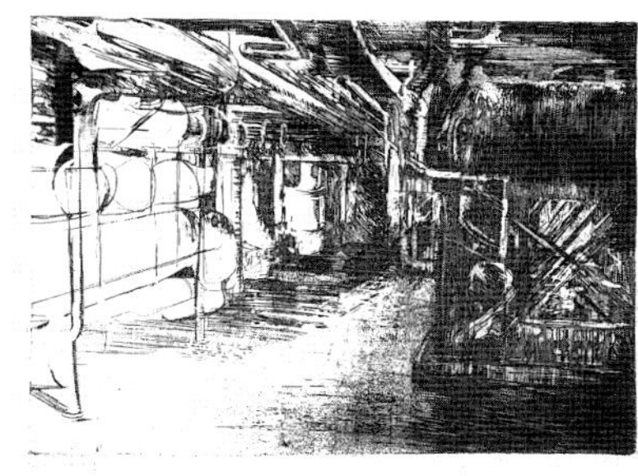

86

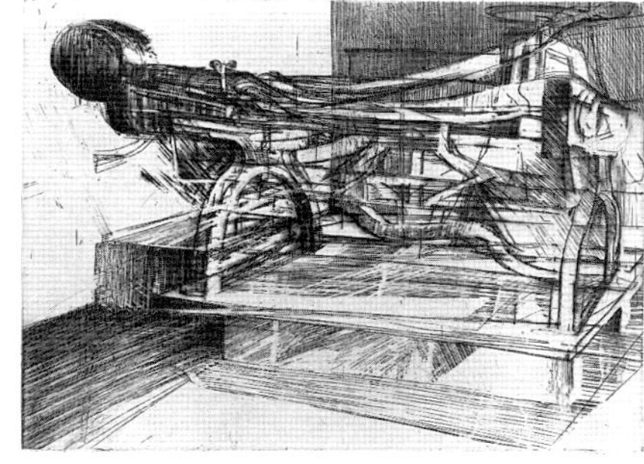

87

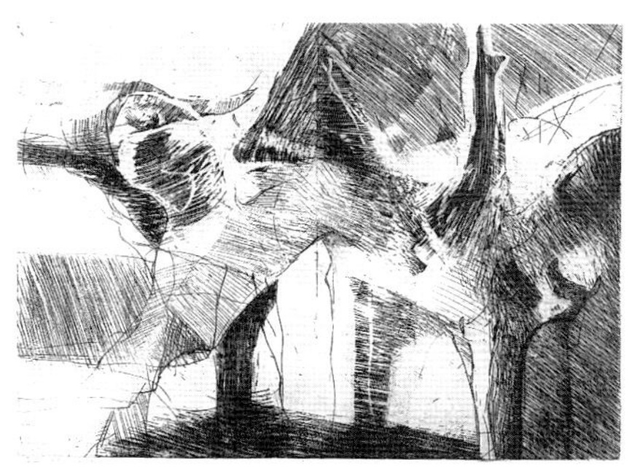

88

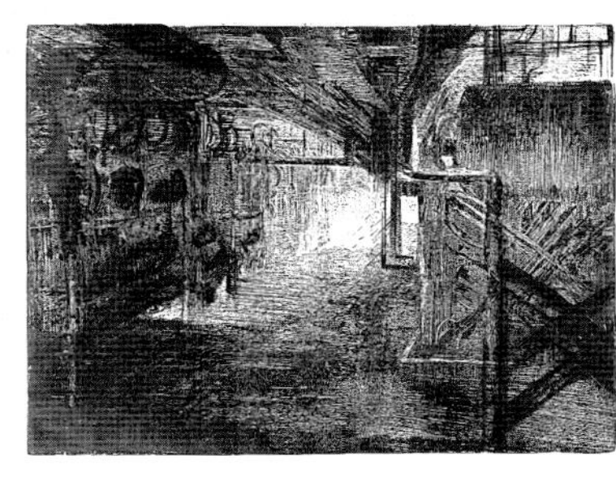

89

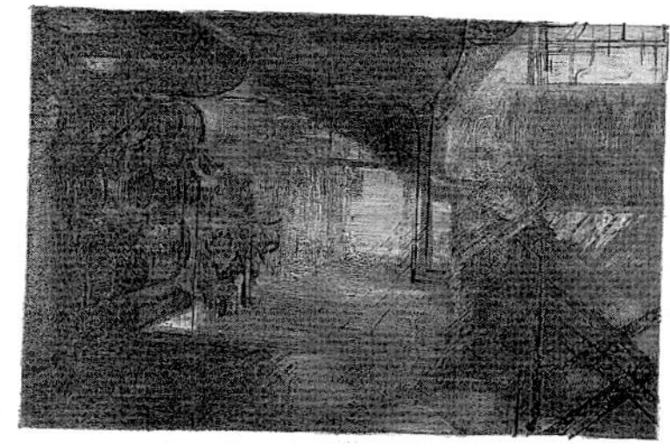

90

84
Baby in Bathinette, 1960
Medium etching
Edition size 25
Paper white wove
Plates/blocks 2 zinc plates
Inks green and orange
Image size 19¾ × 15¼ in. (50.2 × 38.7 cm)
Sheet size 24⅛ × 19¾ in. (61.3 × 50.2 cm)
Reference Mazur M-4a

85
Baby Furniture, 1960
Medium etching
Edition size not editioned; 2 impressions printed
Paper white wove
Plates/blocks 1 zinc plate
Inks black
Image size 16 × 14¼ in. (40.7 × 36.2 cm)
Sheet size 26½ × 20¼ in. (67.3 × 51.5 cm)
Reference Mazur M-4b

86
Boiler Room #1, 1960
Medium etching
Edition size 20
Paper white wove
Plates/blocks 1 zinc plate
Inks black
Image size 17⅝ × 23⅝ in. (44.8 × 60.0 cm)
Sheet size 19⅜ × 26¾ in. (49.2 × 68.0 cm)
Reference Mazur M-10

87
Paper Cutter, 1960
Medium etching
Edition size 25
Paper white wove
Plates/blocks 1 zinc plate
Inks brown
Image size 17¾ × 23¾ in. (45.1 × 60.3 cm)
Sheet size 21⅝ × 27¼ in. (54.9 × 69.2 cm)
Remarks an old large paper cutter at Yale University
Reference Mazur M-17

88
The Animal Stump, 1960
Medium etching
Edition size 25
Paper white wove
Plates/blocks 1 zinc plate
Inks blue-black
Image size 17¾ × 23¾ in. (45.1 × 60.3 cm)
Sheet size 20⅜ × 26⅝ in. (51.8 × 67.7 cm)
Reference Mazur M-15

89
Boiler Room #2, 1960–61
Medium etching printed in relief and intaglio
Edition size 20
Paper white wove
Plates/blocks 2 zinc plates
Inks black and gray-black
Image size 17⅝ × 23⅝ in. (44.8 × 60.0 cm)
Sheet size 21¼ × 27⅜ in. (54.0 × 69.5 cm)
Remarks a boiler room at Yale University
Reference Mazur M-9

90
Boiler Room #3, 1960–61
Medium etching printed simultaneously in relief and intaglio
Edition size 10
Paper Fabriano Murillo
Plates/blocks 1 zinc plate
Inks orange with blue surface roll
Image size 16 × 23⅝ in. (40.7 × 60.0 cm)
Sheet size 20¾ × 26½ in. (52.7 × 67.3 cm)
Reference Mazur M-8

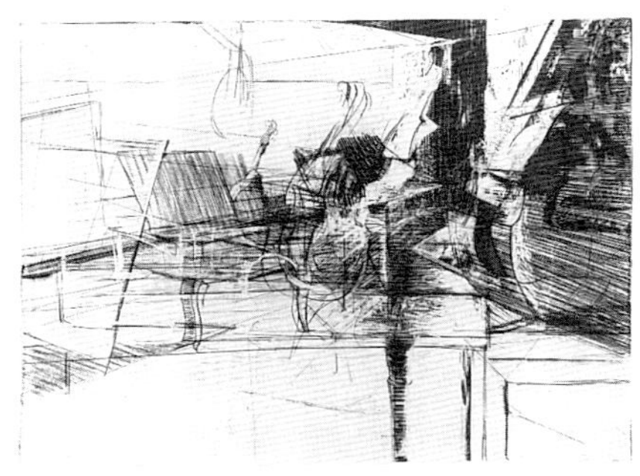

91

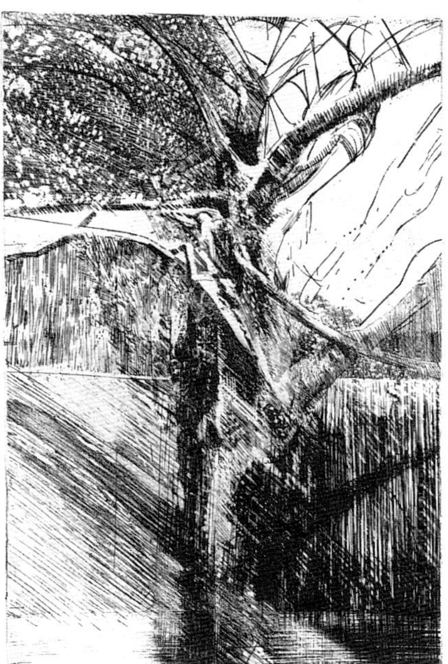

92

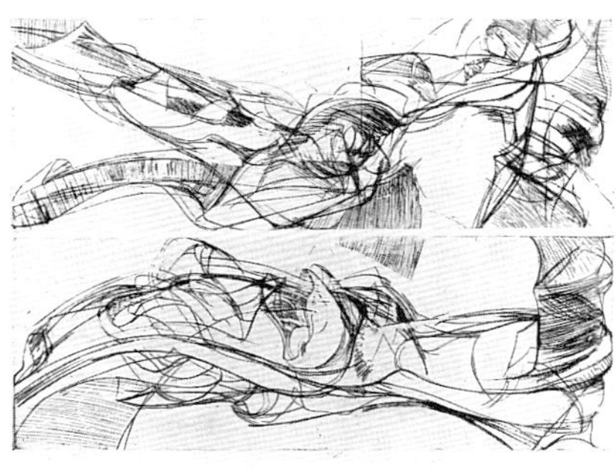

93

91
Musical Instruments, 1961
Medium etching
Edition size not editioned; 3–4 impressions printed
Paper white wove
Plates/blocks 1 zinc plate
Inks black
Image size $17\frac{5}{8} \times 23\frac{3}{4}$ in. (44.8×60.3 cm)
Sheet size $20\frac{1}{2} \times 27$ in. (52.1×68.6 cm)
Reference Mazur M-18

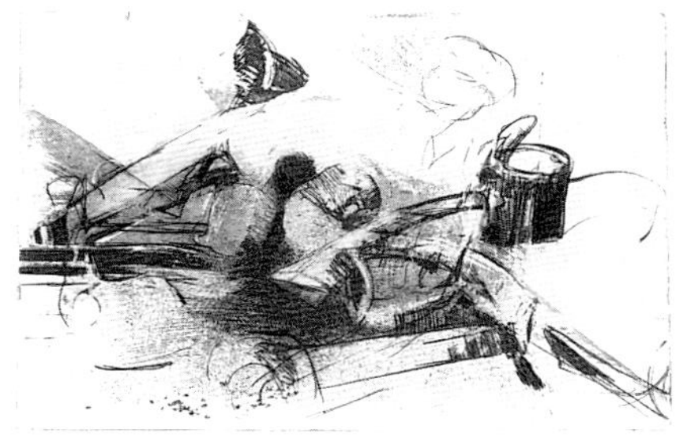

94

95

92
Tree (State 4), 1961
Medium etching
Edition size not editioned; 5–6 impressions printed
Paper white wove
Plates/blocks 1 zinc plate
Inks black
Image size $17\frac{7}{8} \times 11\frac{1}{2}$ in. (45.5×29.2 cm)
Sheet size $22\frac{1}{4} \times 15\frac{7}{8}$ in. (56.5×40.4 cm)
Reference Mazur M-19b

93
Studies of an Old Shoe (diptych), 1961
Medium etching
Edition size not editioned; 5–6 impressions printed
Paper white wove
Plates/blocks 2 zinc plates
Inks black
Plate size $8\frac{7}{8} \times 23\frac{3}{4}$ in. (22.6×60.3 cm) each
Image size $17\frac{3}{4} \times 23\frac{3}{4}$ in. (45.1×60.3 cm)
Sheet size $19\frac{5}{8} \times 27$ in. (49.9×68.6 cm)

94
Study of Pipes, 1961
Medium etching and aquatint

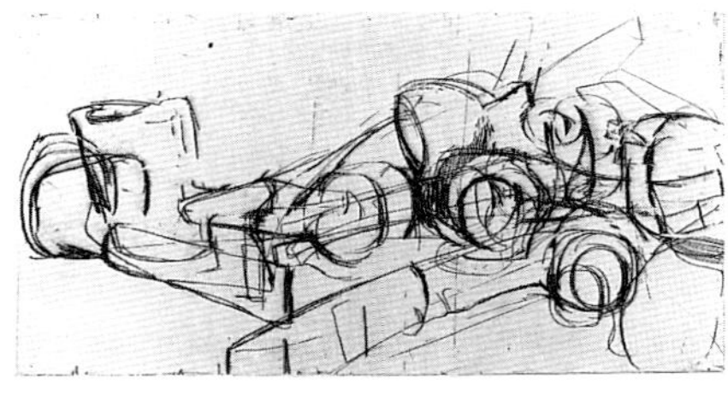

96

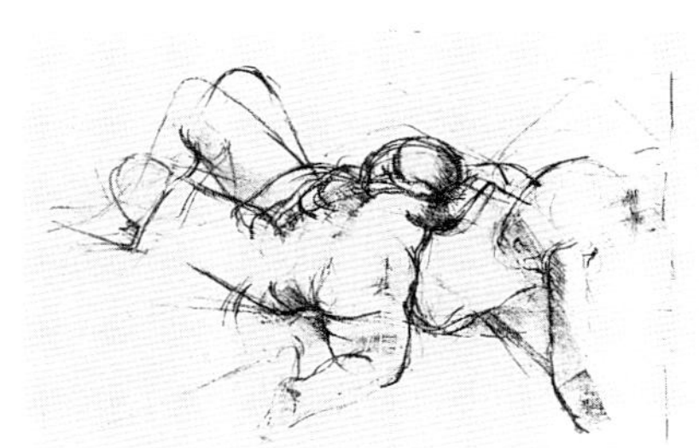

97

Edition size not editioned; 4–5 impressions printed
Paper white wove
Plates/blocks 1 zinc plate
Inks sepia
Image size $11\frac{7}{8} \times 17\frac{7}{8}$ in. (30.2×45.5 cm)
Sheet size $15\frac{3}{4} \times 23\frac{1}{8}$ in. (40.0×58.8 cm)

95
Study of Pipes, 1961
Medium etching
Edition size not editioned; 4–5 impressions printed
Paper white wove
Plates/blocks 1 zinc plate
Inks brown
Image size $15\frac{1}{8} \times 10\frac{5}{8}$ in. (38.4×27.0 cm)
Sheet size $17\frac{1}{2} \times 12\frac{5}{8}$ in. (44.5×32.1 cm)
Reference Mazur S-31c

96
Study of Pipes, 1961
Medium etching
Edition size not editioned; 4–5 impressions printed
Paper white wove
Plates/blocks 1 zinc plate
Inks sienna
Image size $7\frac{1}{4} \times 14$ in. (18.4×35.6 cm)
Sheet size $11\frac{5}{8} \times 16\frac{1}{8}$ in. (29.5×41.0 cm)

97
Mother and Child, State 1, 1961
Medium lithograph
Edition size 6
Paper white wove
Plates/blocks 1 stone
Inks black
Image and sheet size $12\frac{1}{2} \times 19$ in. (31.8×48.2 cm)
Reference Mazur S-20

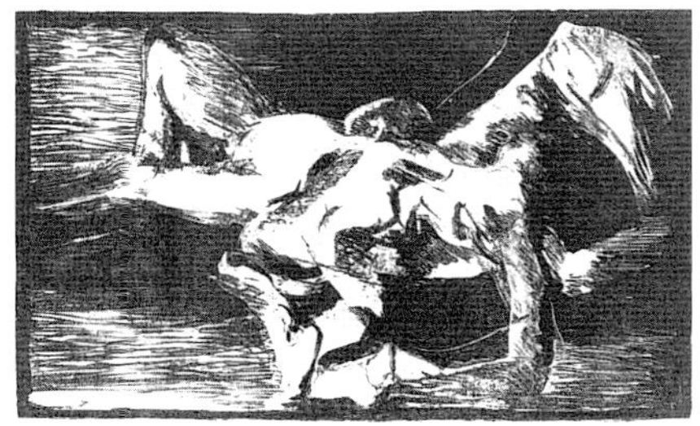

98

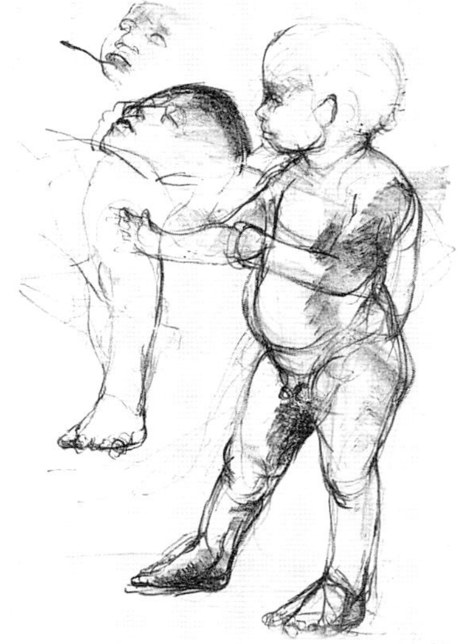

99

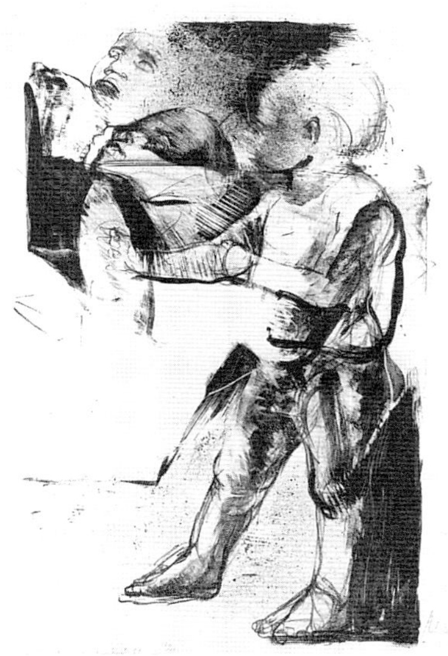

100

98
Mother and Child, State 5, 1961
Medium lithograph
Edition size not editioned; 2–3 impressions printed
Paper white wove
Plates/blocks 1 stone
Inks black
Image size 10½ × 16¾ in. (26.7 × 42.6 cm)

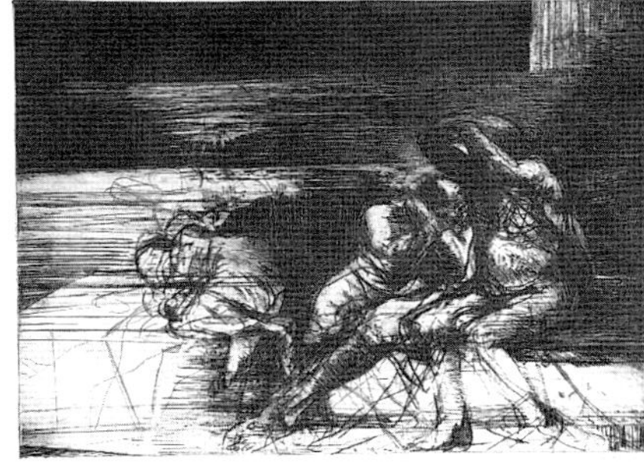

101

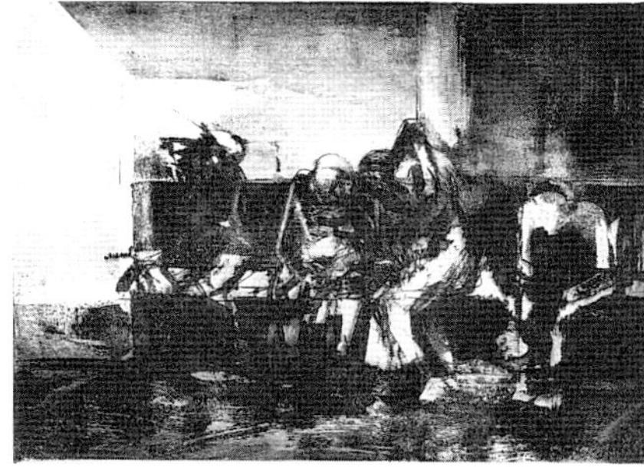

102

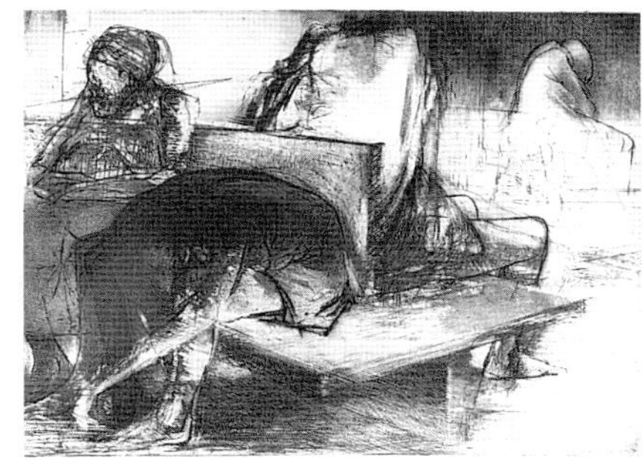

103

Sheet size 13 × 19¾ in. (33.0 × 50.2 cm)
Reference Mazur S-21

99
Standing Child, State 1, 1961
Medium lithograph
Edition size 4
Paper Arches
Plates/blocks 1 stone
Inks black
Image and sheet size 17⅝ × 12¾ in. (44.8 × 32.4 cm)
Reference Mazur S-17

100
Standing Child, State 2, 1961
Medium lithograph
Edition size 4
Paper Arches
Plates/blocks 1 stone
Inks black
Image and sheet size 16⅞ × 12⅝ in. (42.9 × 32.1 cm)
Reference Mazur S-18

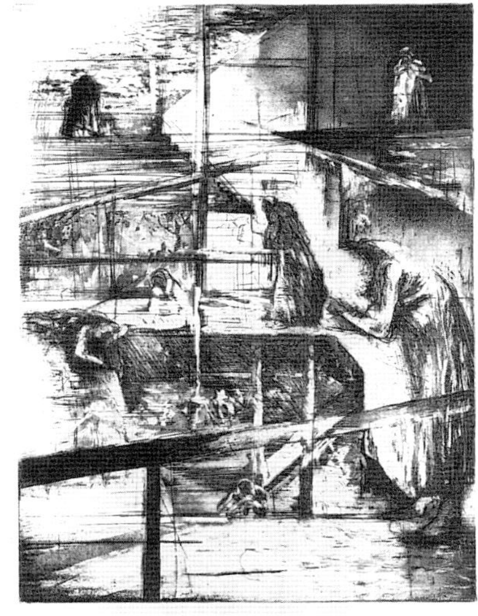

104

101
Closed Ward #1 (Asylum), 1962
Medium etching and aquatint
Edition size 30
Paper Fabriano Murillo
Plates/blocks 1 zinc plate
Inks black
Image size 17¾ × 23¾ in. (45.1 × 60.3 cm)
Sheet size 21 × 26¾ in. (53.4 × 68.0 cm)
Reference Mazur M-20

102
Closed Ward #2 (Untitled), 1962
Medium etching and aquatint
Edition size 30
Paper Fabriano Murillo
Plates/blocks 1 zinc plate
Inks black
Image size 17¾ × 23¾ in. (45.1 × 60.3 cm)
Sheet size 21 × 26⅝ in. (53.4 × 67.7 cm)
Reference Mazur M-21

103
Closed Ward #3 (Positions), 1962
Medium etching and aquatint
Edition size 30
Paper Fabriano Murillo
Plates/blocks 1 zinc plate
Inks black
Image size 17¾ × 23¾ in. (45.1 × 60.3 cm)
Sheet size 21⅛ × 27⅛ in. (53.7 × 68.9 cm)
Reference Mazur M-22

104
Closed Ward #5 (Levels), 1962
Medium etching and aquatint
Edition size 30
Paper Fabriano Murillo
Plates/blocks 1 zinc plate
Inks black
Image size 23¾ × 17¾ in. (60.3 × 45.1 cm)
Sheet size 26½ × 21¼ in. (67.3 × 54.0 cm)
Reference Mazur M-23

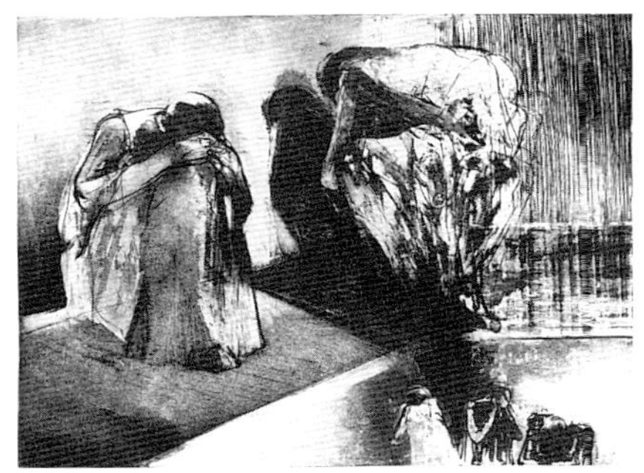

105

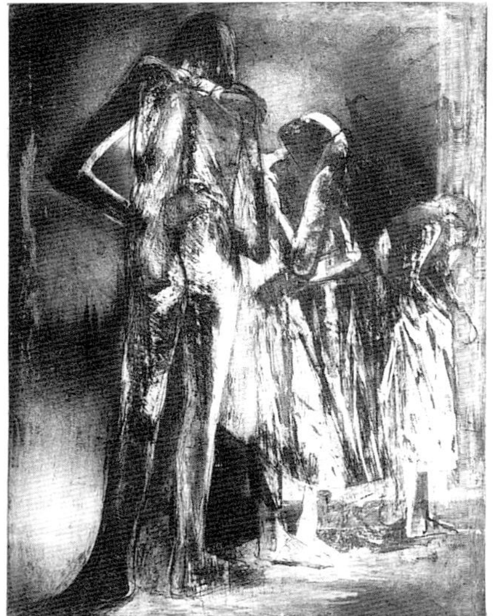

106

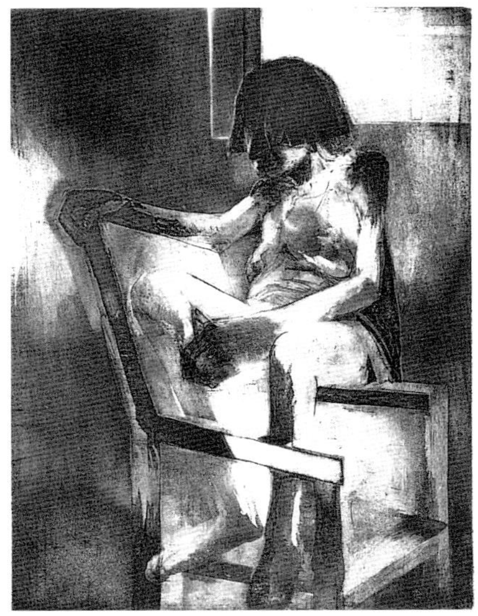

107

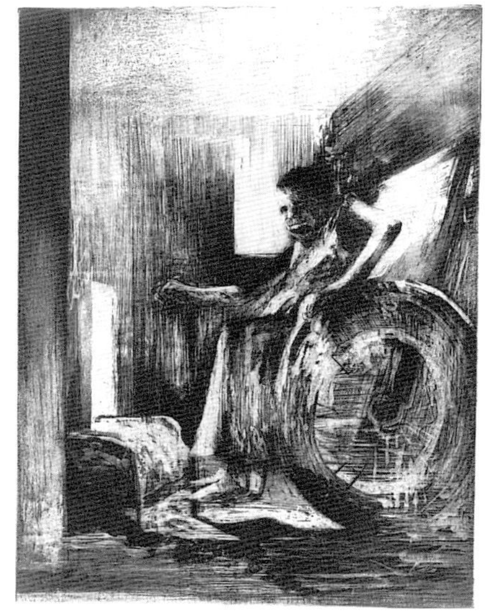

108

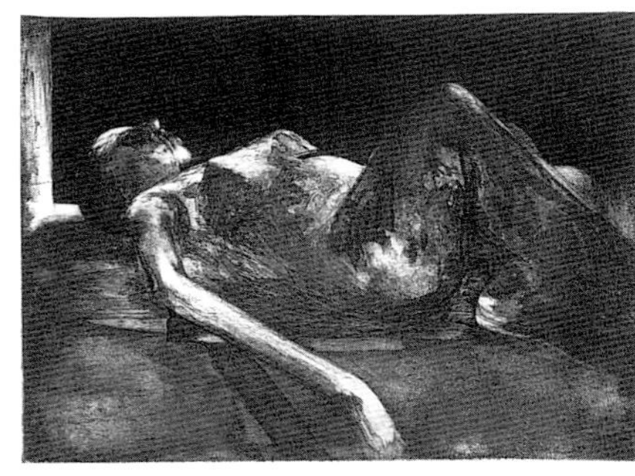

109

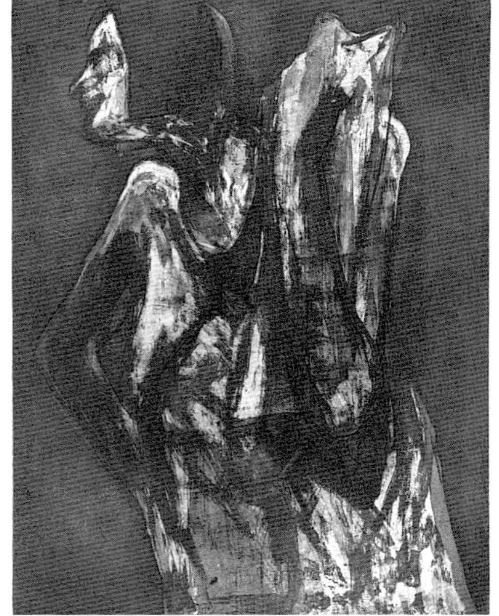

110

105
Closed Ward #6 (A Still and Rocking Figure — Below the Restless), 1962
Medium etching and aquatint
Edition size 30
Paper Fabriano Murillo
Plates/blocks 1 zinc plate
Inks black
Image size 17¾ × 23¾ in. (45.1 × 60.3 cm)
Sheet size 20¾ × 26⅞ in. (52.7 × 68.3 cm)
Reference Mazur M-24

106
Closed Ward #7 (Processional), 1962
Medium etching and aquatint
Edition size 30
Paper Fabriano Murillo
Plates/blocks 1 zinc plate
Inks black
Image size 23¾ × 17¾ in. (60.3 × 45.1 cm)
Sheet size 26⅞ × 20 in. (68.3 × 50.7 cm)
Reference Mazur M-25

107
Closed Ward #8 (Her Place), 1962
Medium etching and aquatint
Edition size 30
Paper Fabriano Murillo
Plates/blocks 1 zinc plate
Inks black
Image size 23¾ × 17¾ in. (60.3 × 45.1 cm)
Sheet size 27¼ × 21 in. (68.3 × 54.0 cm)
Reference Mazur M-26

108
Closed Ward #9 (The Occupant), 1962
Medium etching and aquatint
Edition size 30
Paper Fabriano Murillo
Plates/blocks 1 zinc plate
Inks black
Image size 23¾ × 17¾ in. (60.3 × 45.1 cm)
Sheet size 27¼ × 21 in. (69.3 × 53.4 cm)
Reference Mazur M-27

109
Closed Ward #10 (Untitled), 1962
Medium etching and aquatint
Edition size 30
Paper Fabriano Murillo
Plates/blocks 1 zinc plate
Inks black
Image size 17¾ × 23¾ in. (45.1 × 60.3 cm)
Sheet size 21½ × 26¾ in. (54.6 × 67.9 cm)
Reference Mazur M-28

110
Closed Ward #11 (She Carries a Magazine), 1962
Medium etching and aquatint
Edition size 30
Paper Fabriano Murillo
Plates/blocks 1 zinc plate
Inks brown-black
Image size 23¾ × 17¾ in. (60.3 × 45.1 cm)
Sheet size 26¾ × 20⅜ in. (67.9 × 51.8 cm)
Reference Mazur M-29

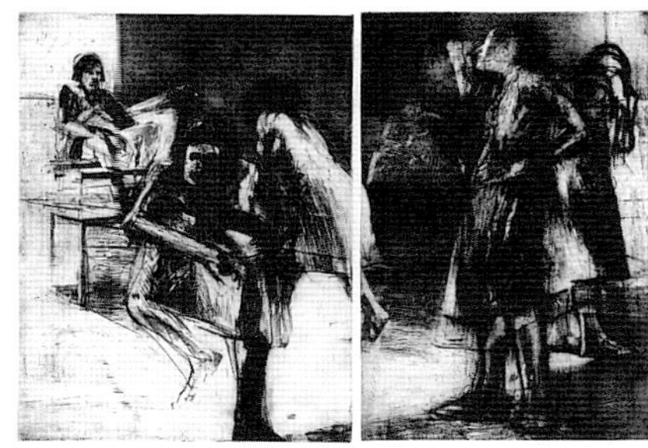

111

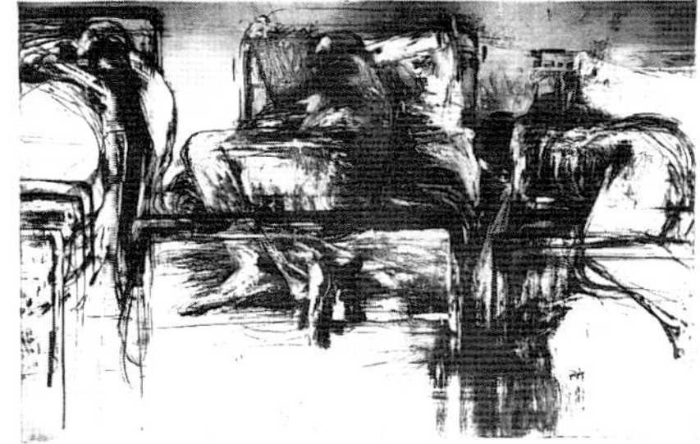

112

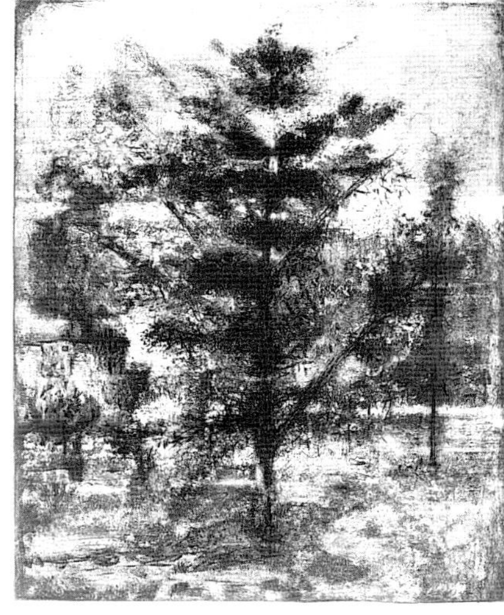

113

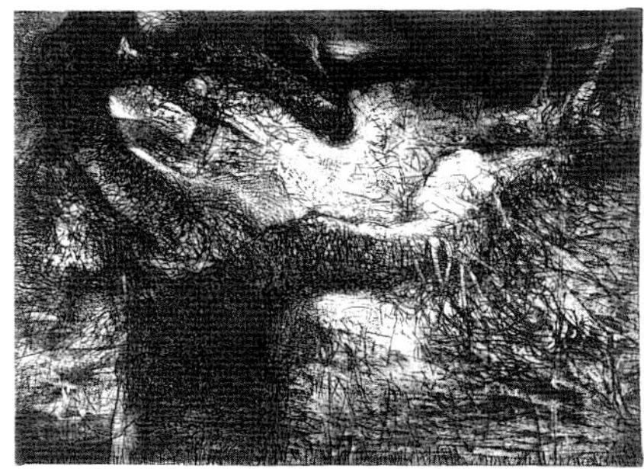

114

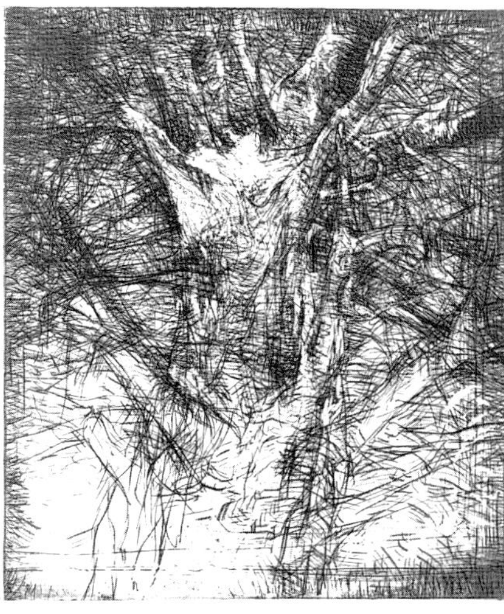

115

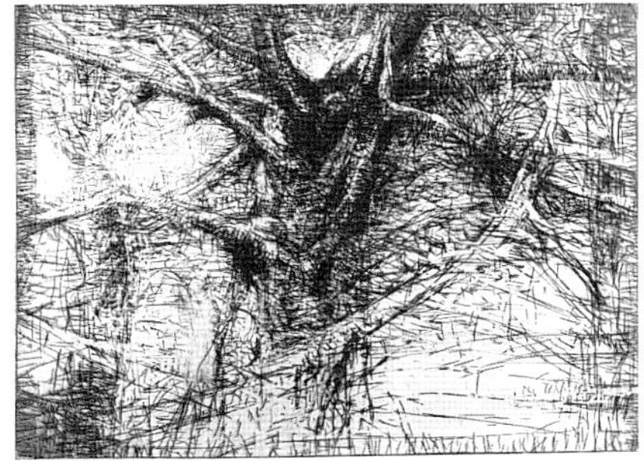

116

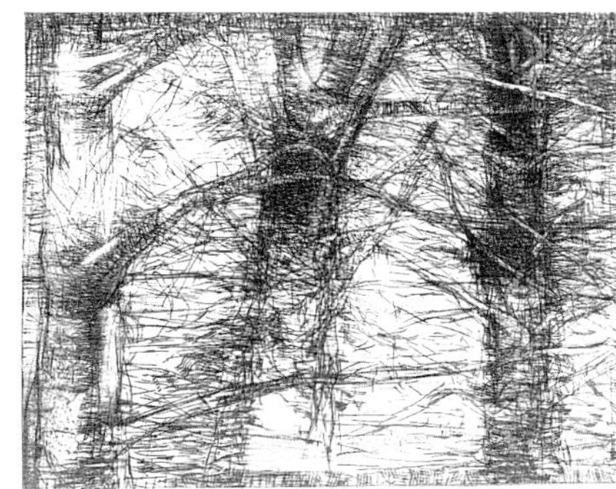

117

111
Closed Ward #12 (Untitled) (diptych), 1962–63
Medium etching and aquatint
Edition size 30
Paper Fabriano Murillo
Plates/blocks 2 zinc plates
Inks black
Image size (left) 23⅜ × 17¾ in. (59.4 × 45.1 cm)
Image size (right) 23⅜ × 15⅝ in. (59.4 × 39.7 cm)
Sheet size 27⅝ × 39¼ in. (70.2 × 99.7 cm)
Reference Mazur L-1

112
Closed Ward #14 (The Three Beds), 1963
Medium etching and aquatint
Edition size 30 (editioning not completed; about 15 impressions printed)
Paper Fabriano Murillo
Plates/blocks 1 zinc plate
Inks black
Image size 23¾ × 35½ in. (60.3 × 90.2 cm)
Sheet size 27½ × 38⅛ in. (69.9 × 96.9 cm)
Reference Mazur L-2

113
Night Pine, Norfolk, 1963
Medium etching and aquatint
Edition size 50 (editioning not completed; about 20 impressions printed)
Paper Fabriano Murillo
Plates/blocks 1 zinc plate
Inks black
Image size 22⅛ × 17⅝ in. (56.2 × 44.8 cm)
Sheet size 26¾ × 21⅛ in. (68.0 × 53.7 cm)
Reference Mazur M-19

114
Dark Tree, Norfolk, 1963
Medium etching and aquatint
Edition size 30
Paper white wove
Plates/blocks 1 zinc plate
Inks black
Image size 17⅝ × 23⅝ in. (44.8 × 60.0 cm)
Sheet size 20⅞ × 27⅛ in. (53.0 × 68.9 cm)
Reference Mazur M-14

115
Tree-Hand — Norfolk, 1963
Medium etching
Edition size not editioned; 4–5 impressions printed
Paper Fabriano Murillo
Plates/blocks 1 zinc plate
Inks blue-black
Image size 17¾ × 14¾ in. (45.1 × 37.5 cm)
Sheet size 22½ × 18⅜ in. (57.2 × 46.7 cm)
Remarks made while at Yale Summer School of Music and Art, Norfolk, Conn.
Reference Mazur M-16

116
Tree, Norfolk, 1963
Medium etching
Edition size not editioned; 4–5 impressions printed
Paper white wove
Plates/blocks 1 zinc plate
Inks black
Image size 17¾ × 23¾ in. (45.1 × 60.3 cm)
Sheet size 19⅞ × 25¾ in. (50.5 × 65.4 cm)
Reference Mazur M-19c

117
Three Trees, Norfolk, 1963
Medium etching
Edition size not editioned; a few impressions printed
Paper white wove
Plates/blocks 1 zinc plate
Inks black
Image size 14¾ × 17⅞ in. (37.5 × 45.5 cm)
Sheet size 17⅞ × 24 in. (45.5 × 61.0 cm)
Reference Mazur M-19d

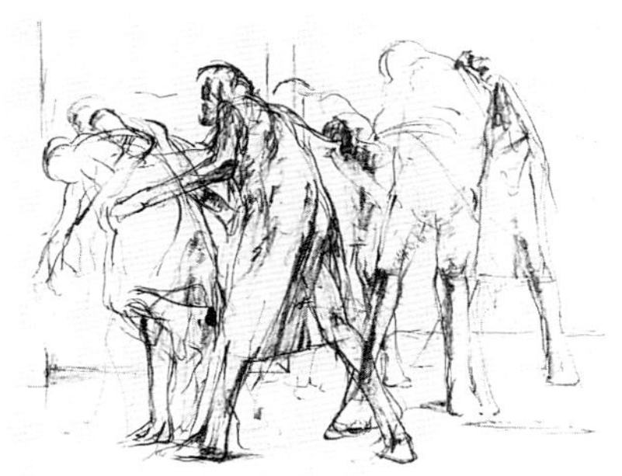

118

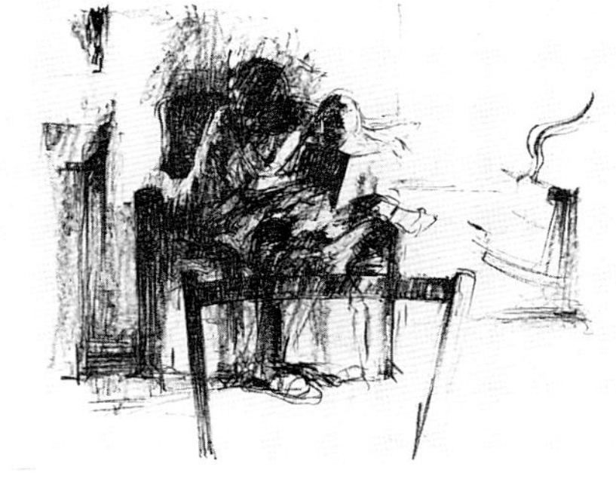

120

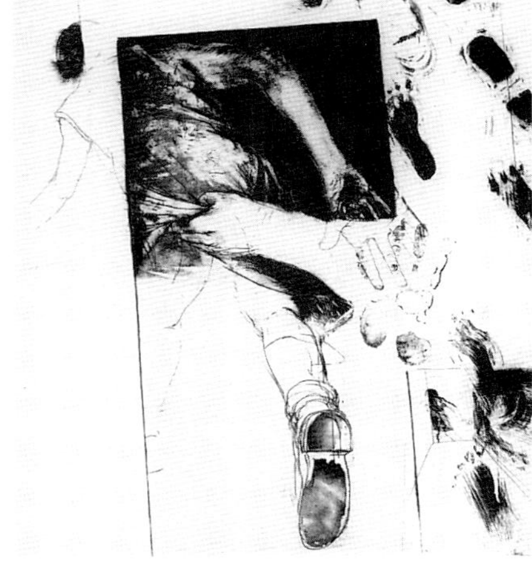

122

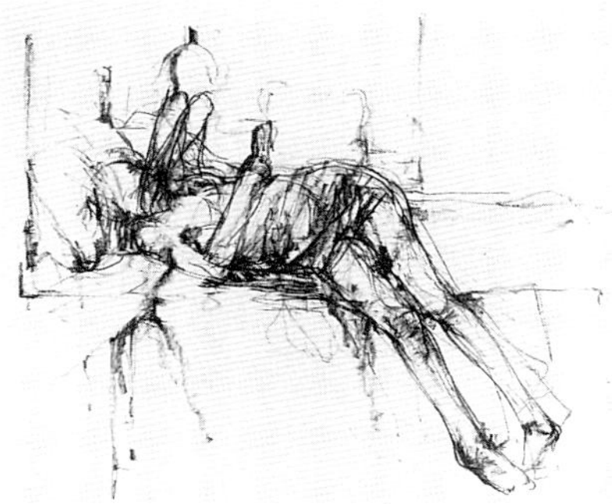

119

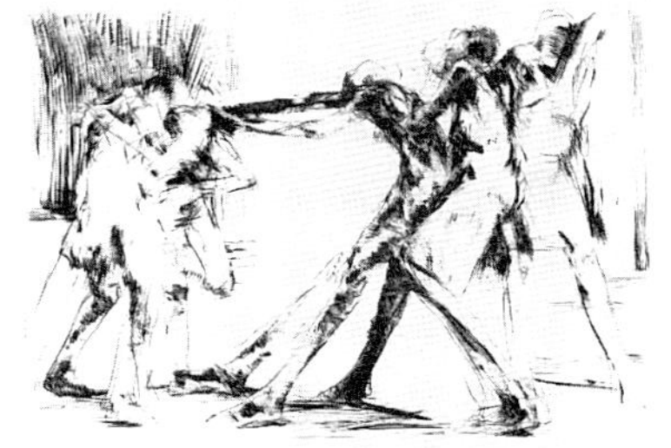

121

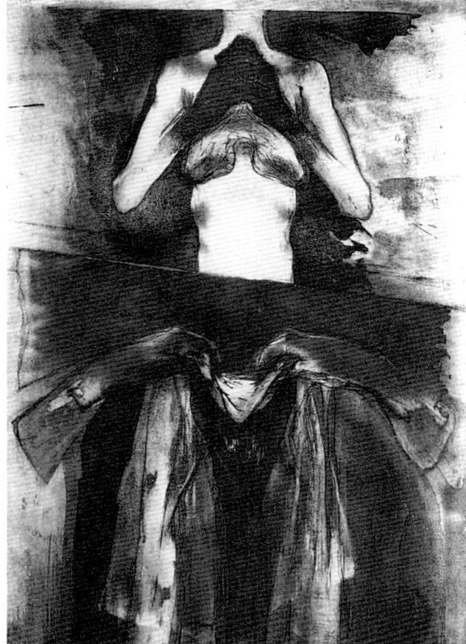

123

118
Figure Group, 1963
Medium paper plate lithography
Edition size 88 plus a few artist's proofs
Paper Arches laid
Printed at Drum Litho, New York
Published by Collector's Graphics, Inc., in conjunction with Peridot Gallery, New York
Plates/blocks 1 paper plate
Inks black
Image and sheet size 22⅞ × 28¾ in. (58.1 × 73.1 cm)
Reference Mazur M-37

119
Figure Study, 1963
Medium paper plate lithography
Edition size 97 plus a few artist's proofs
Paper Arches wove
Printed at Drum Litho, New York
Published by Collector's Graphics, Inc., in conjunction with Peridot Gallery, New York
Plates/blocks 1 paper plate
Inks black
Image and sheet size 23 × 28 in. (58.4 × 71.2 cm)
Remarks commissioned by Peridot Gallery
Reference Mazur M-38

120
Untitled (Adult Holding a Child with Book), 1963
Medium paper plate lithography
Edition size 85 plus a few artist's proofs
Paper Arches laid
Printed at Drum Litho, New York
Published by Collector's Graphics, Inc., in conjunction with Peridot Gallery, New York
Plates/blocks 1 paper plate
Inks blue
Image and sheet size 23 × 28⅞ in. (58.4 × 73.4 cm)

121
They Stopped the Hair Pulling, 1964
Medium drypoint
Edition size not editioned; 7 artist's proofs
Paper white wove
Plates/blocks 1 zinc plate
Inks black
Image size 17¾ × 24 in. (45.1 × 61.0 cm)
Sheet size 21½ × 28½ in. (54.6 × 72.4 cm)
Remarks related to the *Closed Ward* series
Reference Mazur M-31

122
Escape, 1964
Medium etching and aquatint
Edition size 30 (editioning not completed; about 10 impressions printed)
Paper white wove
Plates/blocks 1 zinc plate
Inks black
Image size 27⅜ × 23¾ in. (69.5 × 60.3 cm)
Sheet size 32 × 26¾ in. (81.3 × 68.0 cm)
Remarks related to the *Closed Ward* series
Reference Mazur L-4

123
Closed Ward #15 (A Towel for Edith S.), 1964–65
Medium etching and aquatint
Edition size 30
Paper white wove
Plates/blocks 1 zinc plate
Inks black
Image size 28½ × 19⅜ in. (72.4 × 49.2 cm)
Sheet size 32¾ × 24⅞ in. (83.2 × 63.2 cm)
Reference Mazur L-5

124
Closed Ward (Figure Fixed on Figure Falling), 1965
Medium etching and aquatint
Edition size 50 (editioning not completed; about 15 impressions printed)
Paper white wove
Plates/blocks 1 zinc plate
Inks black

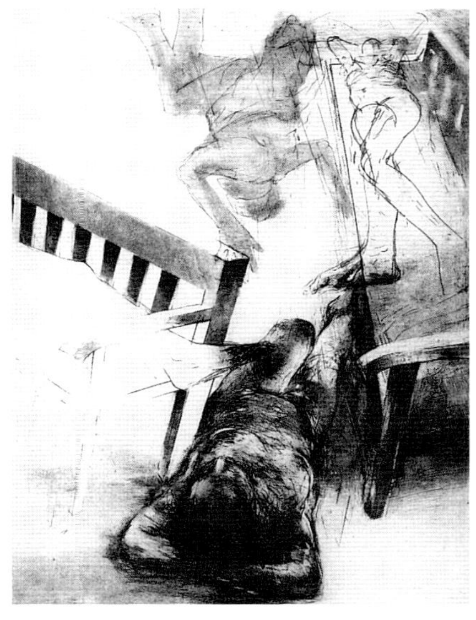

124

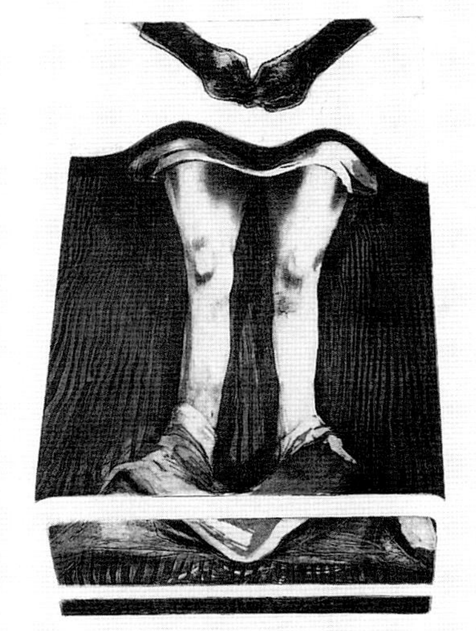

126

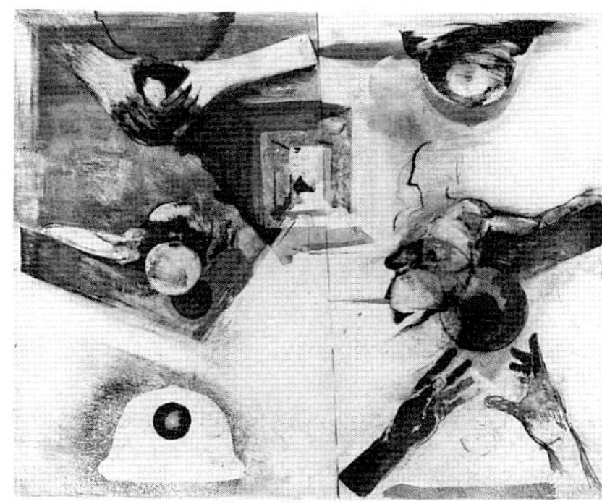

128

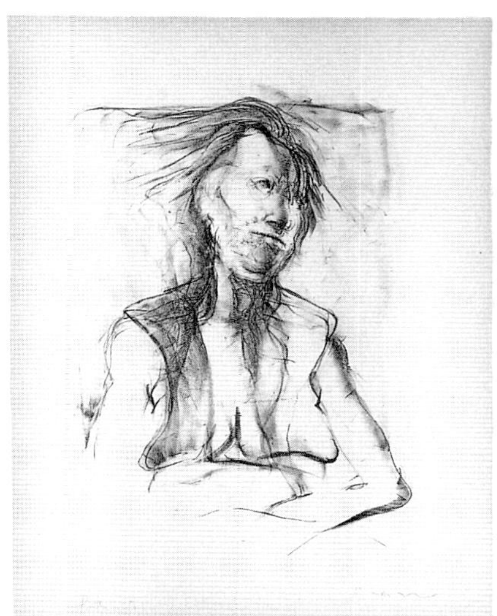

125

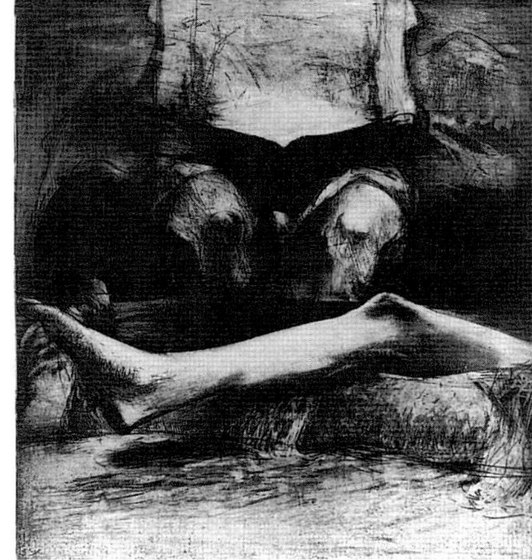

127

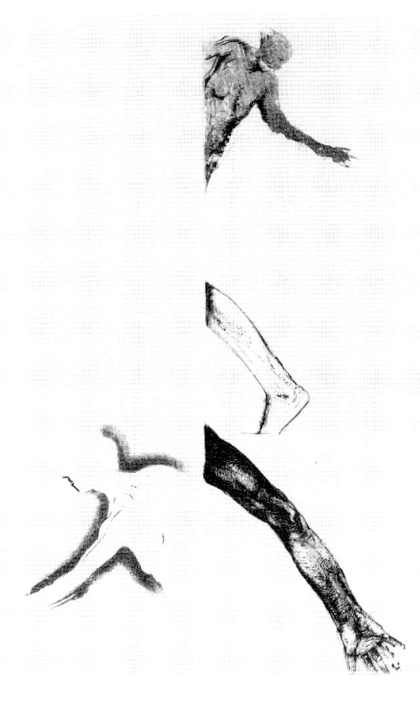

129

Image size 30⅜ × 23¾ in. (77.2 × 60.3 cm)
Sheet size 35½ × 26¾ in. (90.2 × 68.0 cm)
Reference Mazur L-3

125
Portrait 2, 1965
Medium lithograph
Edition size 25 plus 5 artist's proofs
Paper Arches
Plates/blocks 1 stone
Inks black
Image and sheet size 25⅞ × 19⅞ in. (65.7 × 50.5 cm)
Remarks related to the *Closed Ward* series
Reference Mazur M-52

126
Hands — Legs on Bed, 1965
Medium etching and aquatint
Edition size 30
Paper white wove
Plates/blocks 3 zinc plates
Inks black
Image size 27⅝ × 18⅝ in. (70.2 × 47.3 cm) overall
Sheet size 32⅜ × 22⅞ in. (82.3 × 58.1 cm)
Remarks related to the *Closed Ward* series
Reference Mazur L-6

127
Closed Ward #16 (The Visit), 1965
Medium etching and aquatint
Edition size 30
Paper white wove
Plates/blocks 2 zinc plates
Inks black
Image size 26 × 23¼ in. (66.1 × 59.1 cm)
Sheet size 34½ × 25¾ in. (87.6 × 65.4 cm)
Remarks originally a diptych (vertical); the plate was cut and joined
Reference Mazur L-7

128
Institutional Ballgame, 1965
Medium etching and aquatint
Edition size 50 (editioning not completed; about 10 impressions printed)
Paper white wove
Plates/blocks 1 zinc plate
Inks black
Image size 23½ × 28¼ in. (59.7 × 71.8 cm)
Sheet size 26⅜ × 32½ in. (67.0 × 82.6 cm)
Remarks related to the *Closed Ward* series
Reference Mazur L-8

129
Around a Corner, 1965
Medium etching
Edition size 20
Paper white wove
Plates/blocks 1 copper plate
Inks black
Image size 15⅞ × 9⅞ in. (40.4 × 25.1 cm)
Sheet size 20⅛ × 14⅛ in. (51.1 × 35.9 cm)
Remarks related to the *Closed Ward* series; made for the announcement of an exhibition at the Kornblee Gallery, New York
Reference Mazur S-32

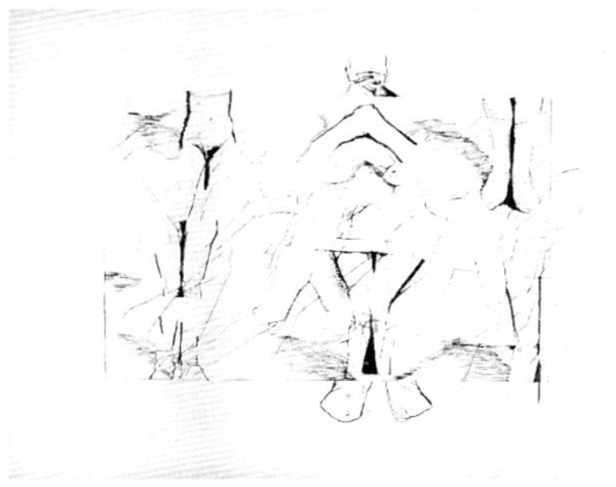

130

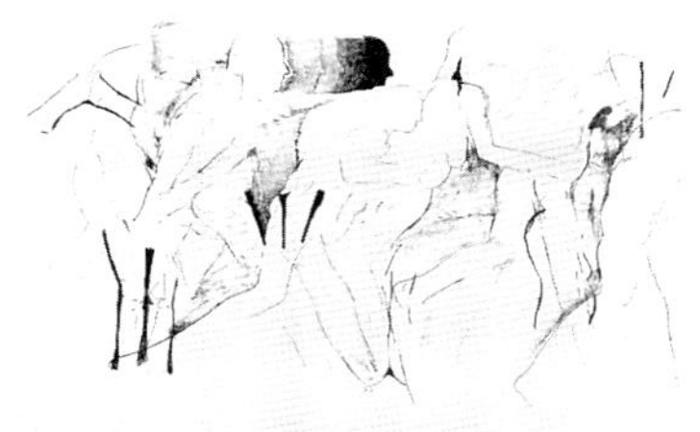

131

130
Running — Standing — Sitting, 1965
Medium drypoint
Edition size 25
Paper Arches
Plates/blocks 1 zinc plate
Inks black
Image size 17⅝ × 23¾ in. (44.8 × 60.3 cm)
Sheet size 22¼ × 29⅞ in. (56.5 × 75.9 cm)
Remarks related to the *Closed Ward* series
Reference Mazur M-32

131
Large Running, 1965
Medium etching and aquatint
Edition size 25
Paper white wove
Plates/blocks 1 zinc plate
Inks black
Image size 19⅛ × 30⅝ in. (48.6 × 77.8 cm)
Sheet size 24¾ × 35¾ in. (62.9 × 90.8 cm)
Remarks related to the *Closed Ward* series
Reference Mazur L-9

132
Images from a Locked Ward #1 (The Frustrated) (title page), 1965
Medium lithograph and letterpress
Edition size 75
Paper Rives Heavyweight white; housed in a Rives Lightweight white folio
Printed at Impressions Workshop, Inc., Boston, under the supervision of George Lockwood; portfolio slipcase fabricated by Harcourt Bindery, Boston
Published by Impressions Workshop, Inc.

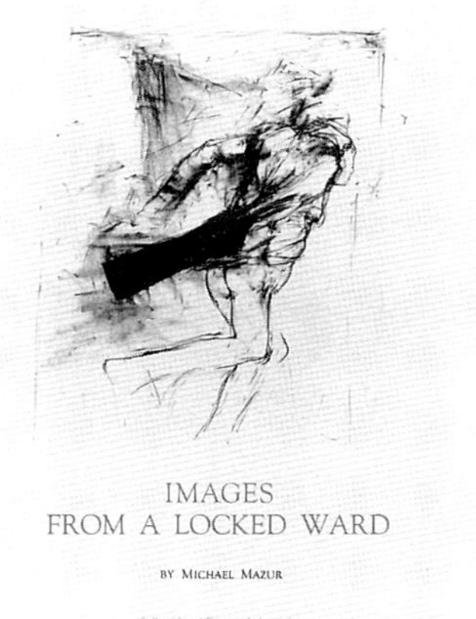

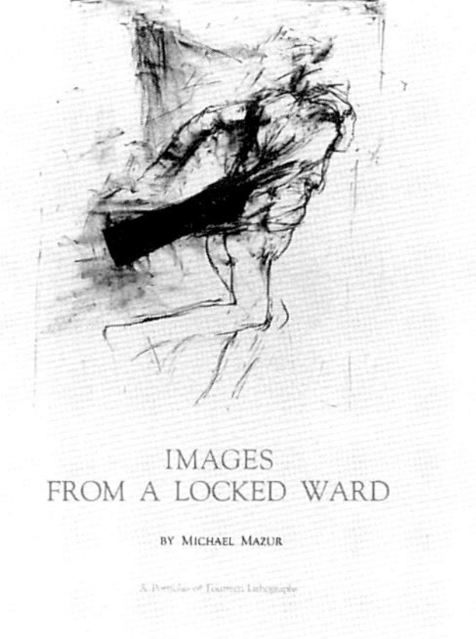

132

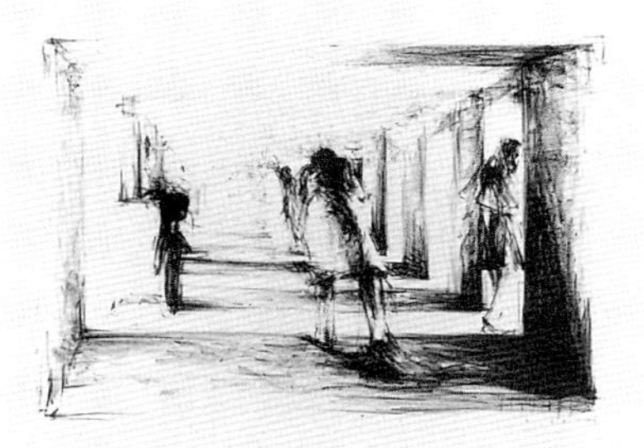

133

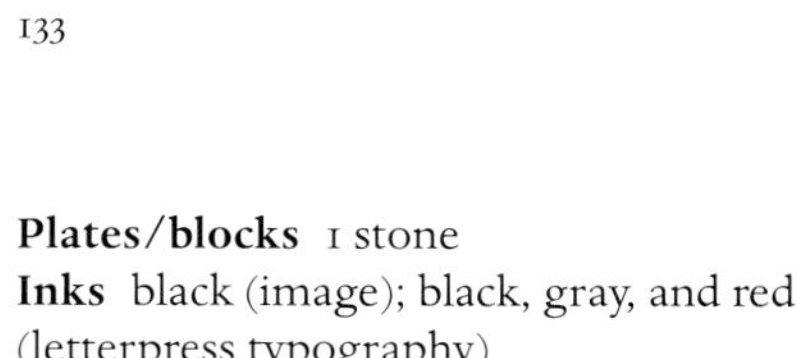

Plates/blocks 1 stone
Inks black (image); black, gray, and red (letterpress typography)
Image and sheet size 26 × 20 in. (66.1 × 50.8 cm)
Reference Mazur M-42

133
Images from a Locked Ward #2 (The Corridor), 1965
Medium lithograph
Edition size 75 plus 2–3 artist's proofs
Paper Arches Cover buff; housed in a Rives Lightweight white folio
Printed at Impressions Workshop, Inc., Boston, under the supervision of George Lockwood
Published by Impressions Workshop, Inc.
Plates/blocks 1 stone
Inks black
Image and sheet size 20 × 26 in. (50.8 × 66.1 cm)
Reference Mazur M-43

134
Images from a Locked Ward #3 (The Occupant), 1965
Medium lithograph
Edition size 75

134

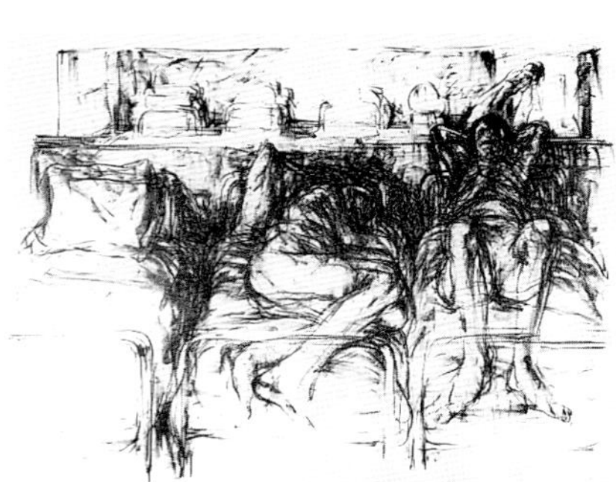

135

Paper Arches Cover buff; housed in a Rives Lightweight white folio
Printed at Impressions Workshop, Inc., Boston, under the supervision of George Lockwood
Published by Impressions Workshop, Inc.
Plates/blocks 1 stone
Inks black
Image and sheet size 26 × 20 in. (66.1 × 50.8 cm)
Reference Mazur M-52b

135
Images from a Locked Ward #4 (The Room for Sleeping), 1965
Medium lithograph
Edition size 75
Paper Arches Cover buff; housed in a Rives Lightweight white folio
Printed at Impressions Workshop, Inc., Boston, under the supervision of George Lockwood
Published by Impressions Workshop, Inc.
Plates/blocks 1 stone
Inks black
Image and sheet size 20 × 26 in. (50.8 × 66.1 cm)
Reference Mazur M-46

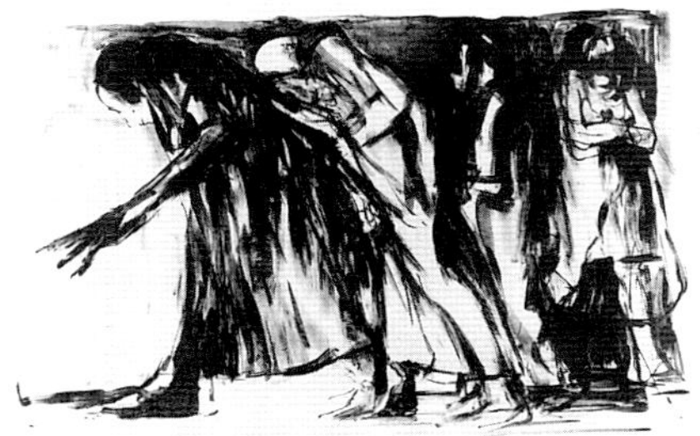

136

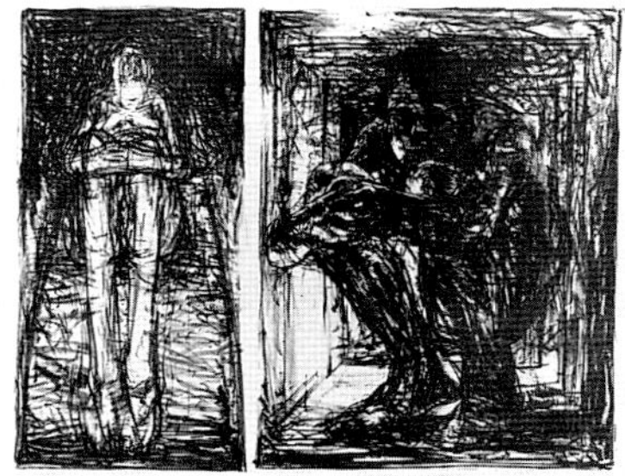

138

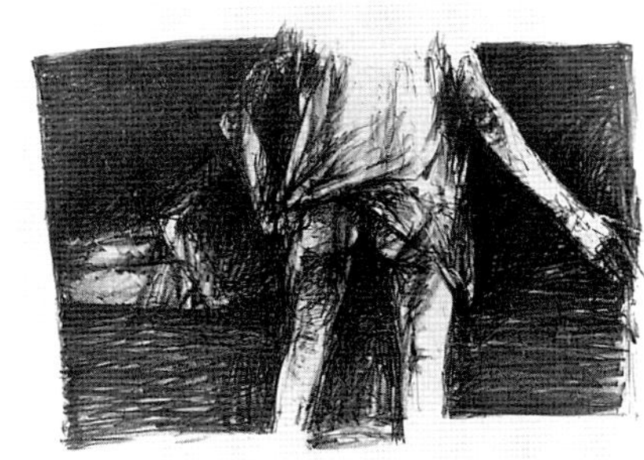

140

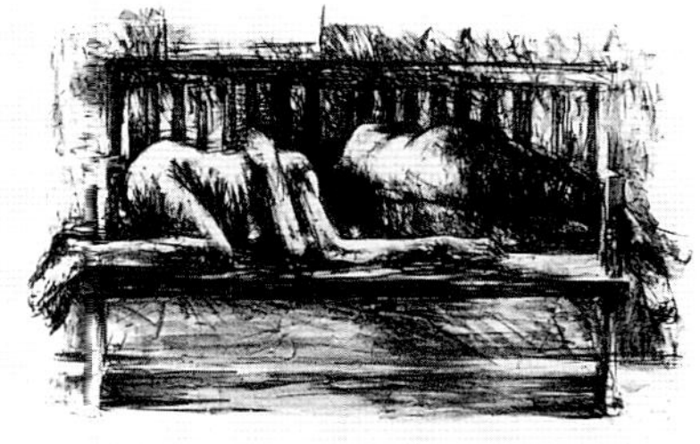

137

139

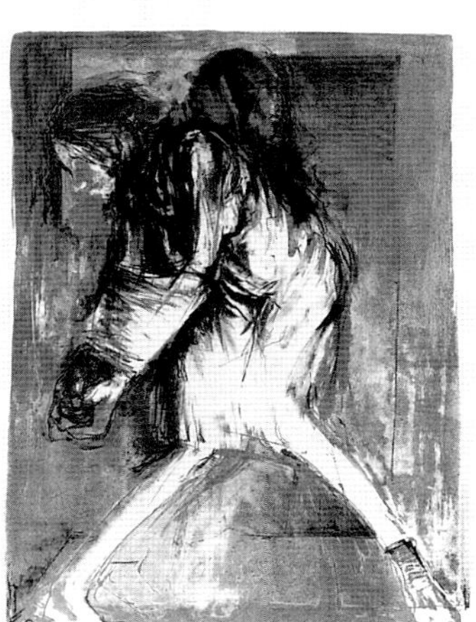

141

136
Images from a Locked Ward #5 (This Trip Has Walls), 1965
Medium lithograph
Edition size 75 plus 12 artist's proofs
Paper Arches Cover buff; housed in a Rives Lightweight white folio
Printed at Impressions Workshop, Inc., Boston, under the supervision of George Lockwood
Published by Impressions Workshop, Inc.
Plates/blocks 1 stone
Inks black
Image and sheet size 20 × 26 in. (50.8 × 66.1 cm)
Reference Mazur M-44

137
Images from a Locked Ward #6 (The Bench), 1965
Medium lithograph
Edition size 75 plus 16 artist's proofs
Paper Arches Cover buff; housed in a Rives Lightweight white folio
Printed at Impressions Workshop, Inc., Boston, under the supervision of George Lockwood
Published by Impressions Workshop, Inc.
Plates/blocks 1 stone
Inks black
Image and sheet size 20 × 26 in. (50.8 × 66.1 cm)
Reference Mazur M-45

138
Images from a Locked Ward #7 (Modules of Madness I), 1965
Medium lithograph
Edition size 75 plus 13 artist's proofs
Paper Arches Cover buff; housed in a Rives Lightweight white folio
Printed at Impressions Workshop, Inc., Boston, under the supervision of George Lockwood
Published by Impressions Workshop, Inc.
Plates/blocks 1 stone
Inks black
Image and sheet size 20 × 26 in. (50.8 × 66.1 cm)
Reference Mazur M-49

139
Images from a Locked Ward #8 (The Swing), 1965
Medium lithograph
Edition size 75 plus 10 artist's proofs
Paper Arches Cover buff; housed in a Rives Lightweight white folio
Printed at Impressions Workshop, Inc., Boston, under the supervision of George Lockwood
Published by Impressions Workshop, Inc.
Plates/blocks 1 stone
Inks black
Image and sheet size 20 × 26 in. (50.8 × 66.1 cm)
Reference Mazur M-50

140
Images from a Locked Ward #9 (Guardian of a Corner), 1965
Medium lithograph
Edition size 75
Paper Arches Cover buff; housed in a Rives Lightweight white folio
Printed at Impressions Workshop, Inc., Boston, under the supervision of George Lockwood
Published by Impressions Workshop, Inc.
Plates/blocks 1 stone
Inks black
Image and sheet size 20 × 26 in. (50.8 × 66.1 cm)
Reference Mazur M-52c

141
Images from a Locked Ward #10 (Bound Hands Swing), 1965
Medium lithograph
Edition size 75 plus 11 artist's proofs
Paper Arches Cover buff; housed in a Rives Lightweight white folio
Printed at Impressions Workshop, Inc., Boston, under the supervision of George Lockwood

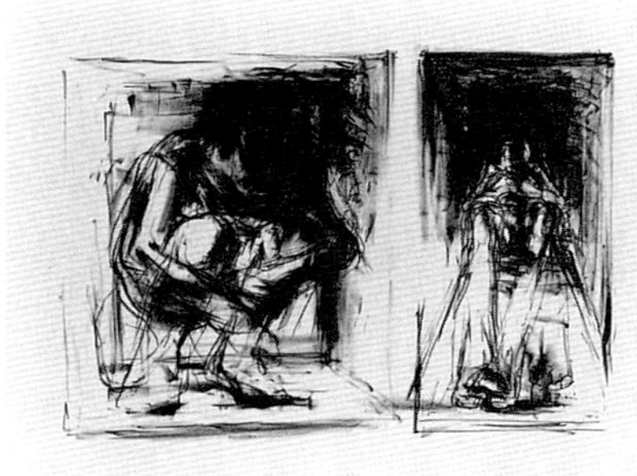

142

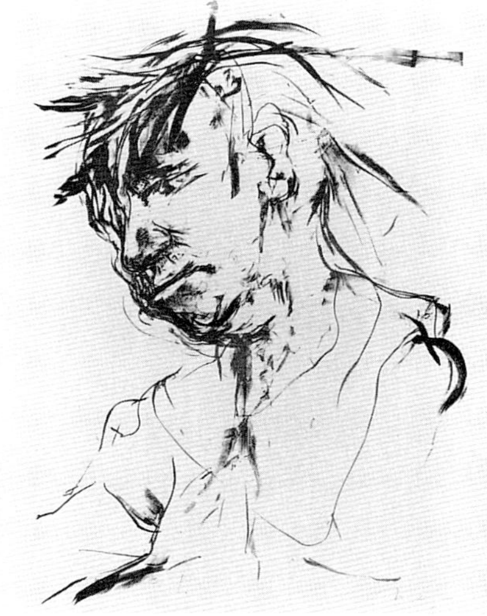

143

Published by Impressions Workshop, Inc.
Plates/blocks 1 stone and 2 aluminum plates
Inks black and green-gray
Image and sheet size 26 × 20 in. (66.1 × 50.8 cm)
Reference Mazur M-48

142
Images from a Locked Ward #11 (Modules of Madness II), 1965
Medium lithograph
Edition size 75 plus 10 artist's proofs
Paper Arches Cover buff; housed in a Rives Lightweight white folio
Printed at Impressions Workshop, Inc., Boston, under the supervision of George Lockwood
Published by Impressions Workshop, Inc.
Plates/blocks 1 stone
Inks black
Image and sheet size 20 × 26 in. (50.8 × 66.1 cm)
Reference Mazur M-47

143
Images from a Locked Ward #12 (Portrait), 1965
Medium lithograph

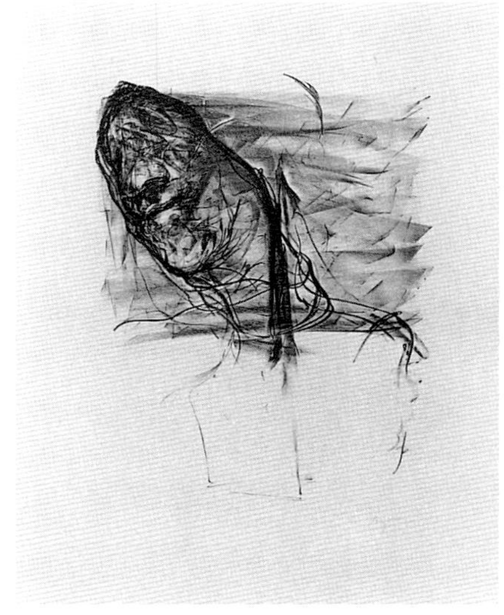

144

Edition size 75 plus 5 artist's proofs
Paper Arches Cover buff; housed in a Rives Lightweight white folio
Printed at Impressions Workshop, Inc., Boston, under the supervision of George Lockwood
Published by Impressions Workshop, Inc.
Plates/blocks 1 stone
Inks black
Image and sheet size 26 × 20 in. (66.1 × 50.8 cm)
Reference Mazur M-51

144
Images from a Locked Ward #13 ("All the Work I Do Is in My Neck"), 1965
Medium lithograph
Edition size 75
Paper Arches Cover buff; housed in a Rives Lightweight white folio
Printed at Impressions Workshop, Inc., Boston, under the supervision of George Lockwood
Published by Impressions Workshop, Inc.
Plates/blocks 1 stone
Inks black
Image and sheet size 26 × 20 in. (66.1 × 50.8 cm)
Reference Mazur M-52a

145
Images from a Locked Ward #14 (Companions), 1965
Medium lithograph
Edition size 75
Paper Arches Cover buff; housed in a Rives Lightweight white folio

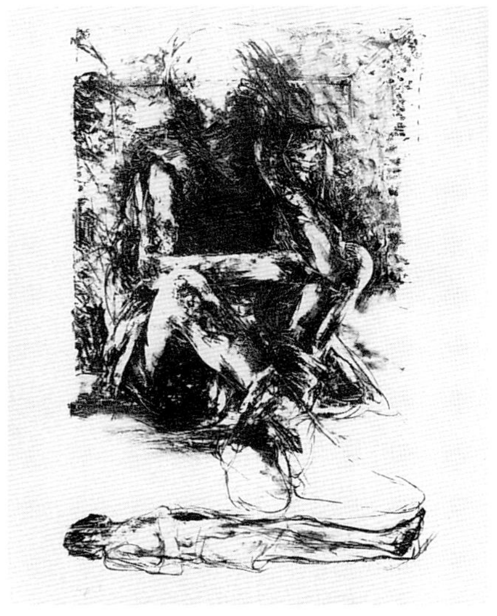

145

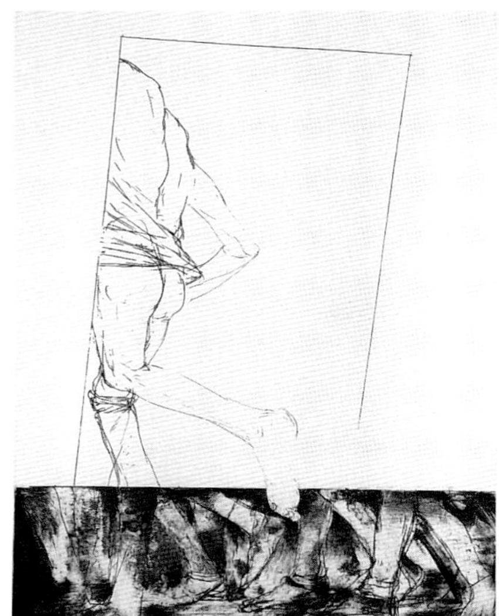

146

Printed at Impressions Workshop, Inc., Boston, under the supervision of George Lockwood
Published by Impressions Workshop, Inc.
Plates/blocks 1 stone
Inks black
Image and sheet size 26 × 20 in. (66.1 × 50.8 cm)
Reference Mazur M-54

146
Running, 1965
Medium etching and aquatint
Edition size 50
Paper white wove
Plates/blocks 1 zinc plate
Inks black
Image size 23⅞ × 17⅞ in. (59.4 × 45.5 cm)
Sheet size 29⅛ × 22⅞ in. (74.0 × 58.1 cm)
Reference Mazur M-30

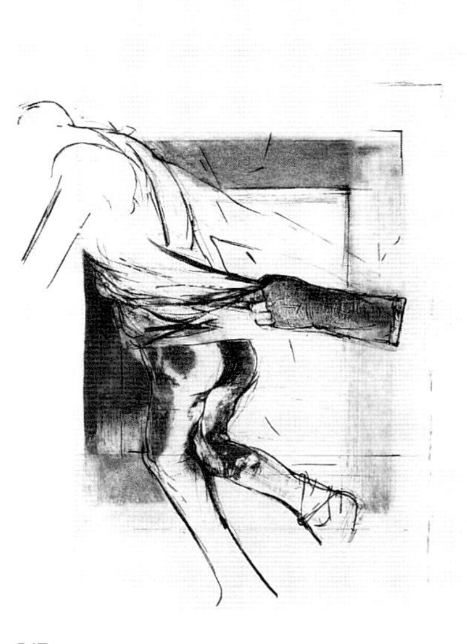

147

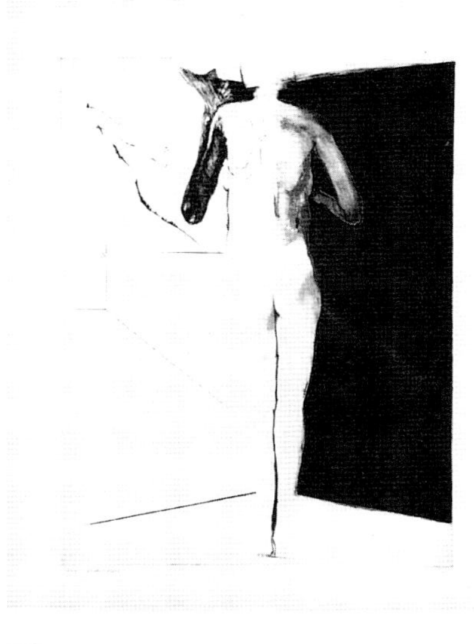

149

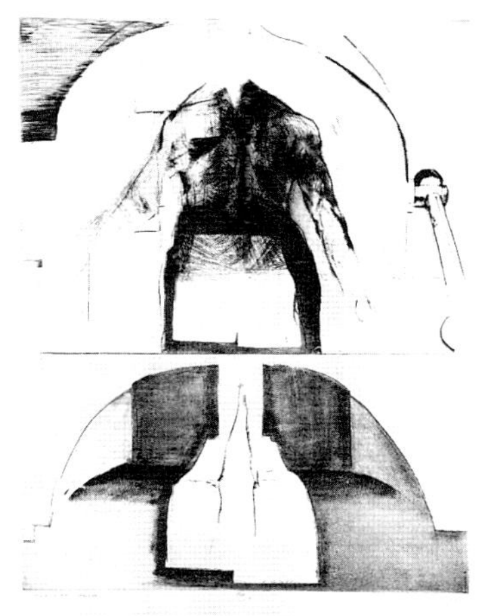

151

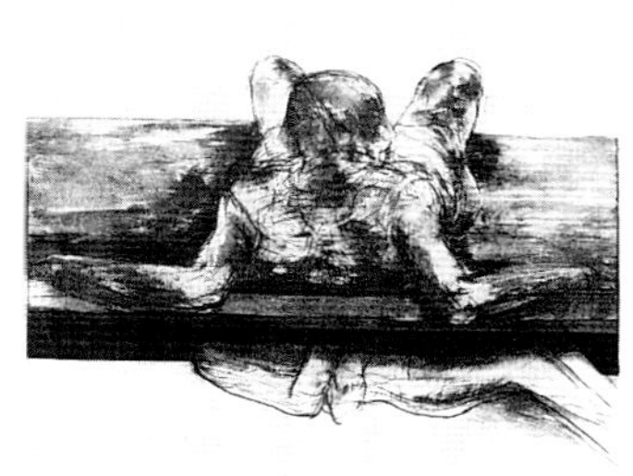

148

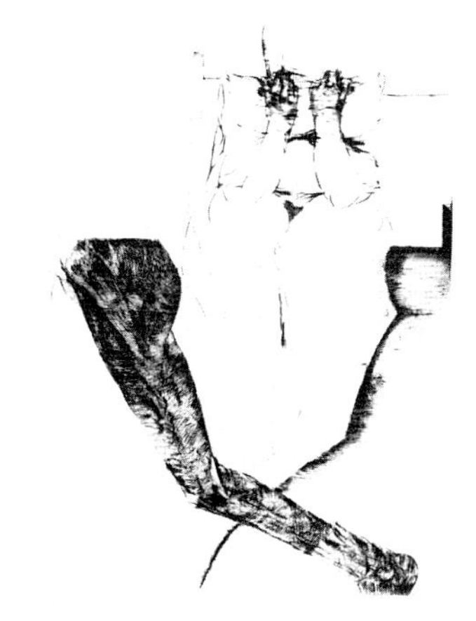

150

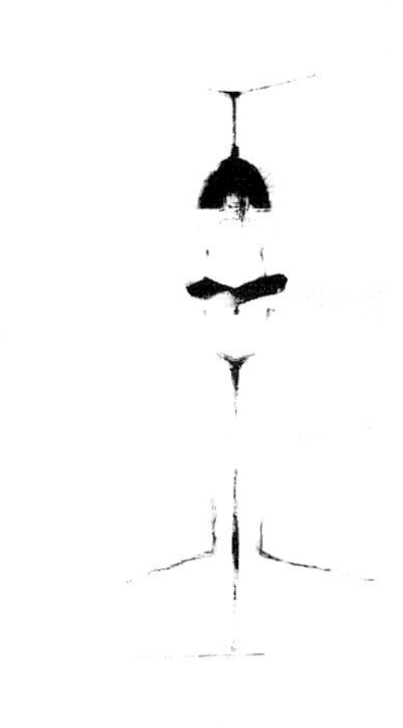

152

147
Frustration Symbol, 1965
Medium etching and aquatint
Edition size 30
Paper white wove
Plates/blocks 1 zinc plate
Inks black
Image size 23¾ × 17⅝ in. (60.3 × 44.8 cm)
Sheet size 28⅝ × 22 in. (72.7 × 55.9 cm)
Remarks related to the *Closed Ward* series
Reference Mazur M-35

148
On the Bench and under It, 1965
Medium etching and aquatint
Edition size 50
Paper white wove
Plates/blocks 1 zinc plate
Inks black
Image size 23½ × 17¾ in. (59.7 × 45.1 cm)
Sheet size 29⅞ × 22⅛ in. (75.9 × 56.2 cm)
Remarks related to the *Closed Ward* series
Reference Mazur M-36

149
Back View, 1965
Medium etching and aquatint
Edition size 30
Paper white wove
Plates/blocks 1 copper plate
Inks black
Image size 23⅝ × 17¾ in. (60.0 × 45.1 cm)
Sheet size 29¼ × 22⅛ in. (74.3 × 56.2 cm)
Remarks related to the *Closed Ward* series
Reference Mazur M-39

150
Legs — Hands — Pillow, 1965
Medium drypoint
Edition size 30
Paper white wove
Plates/blocks 1 copper plate
Inks black
Image size 23½ × 17⅞ in. (59.7 × 44.8 cm)
Sheet size 30⅜ × 23 in. (77.2 × 58.4 cm)
Remarks related to the *Closed Ward* series
Reference Mazur M-40

151
Bench Vise — Back, 1965
Medium etching, aquatint, and drypoint
Edition size 30
Paper white wove
Plates/blocks 1 zinc plate
Inks black
Image size 23½ × 17⅞ in. (59.7 × 45.5 cm)
Sheet size 27⅝ × 23 in. (70.2 × 58.4 cm)
Reference Mazur M-41

152
Corner Figure, 1965
Medium drypoint
Edition size 30
Paper Arches
Plates/blocks 1 zinc plate
Inks black
Image size 23¾ × 17¾ in. (60.3 × 45.1 cm)
Sheet size 30 × 22¼ in. (76.2 × 56.5 cm)
Reference Mazur M-103

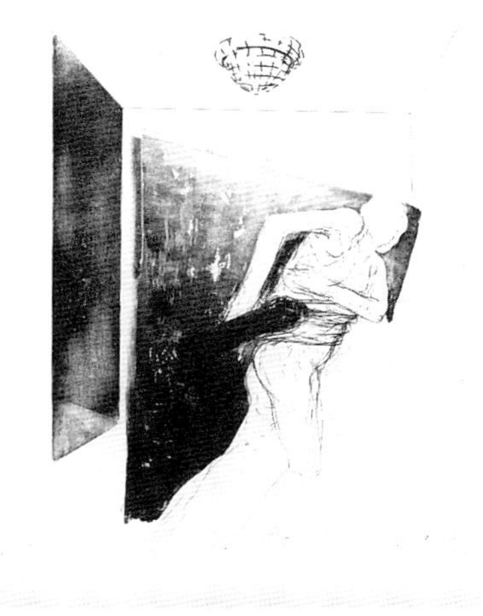

153

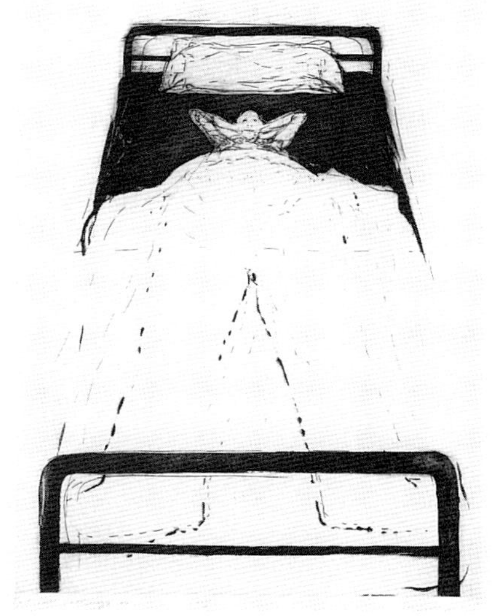

155

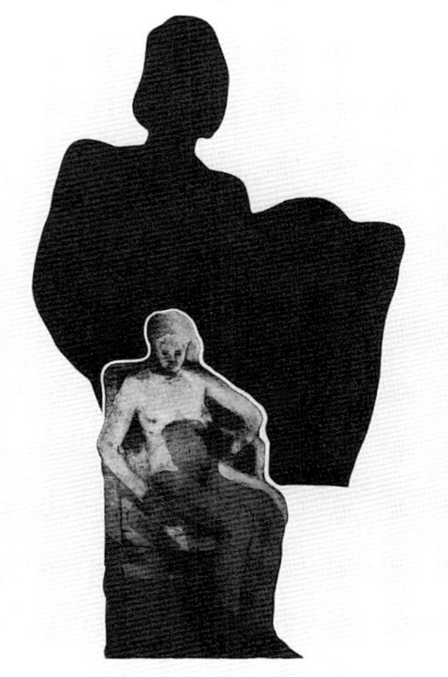

157

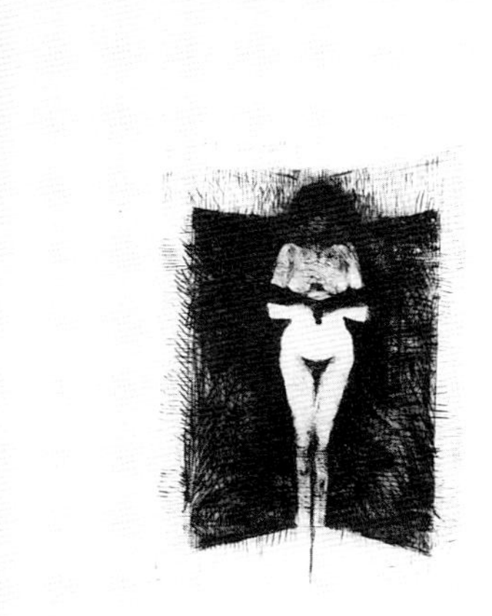

154

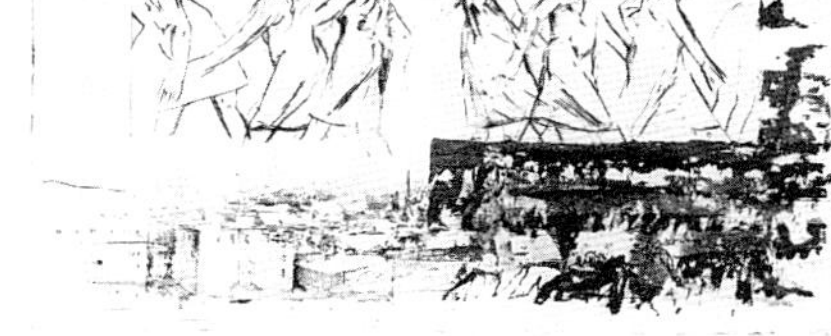

156

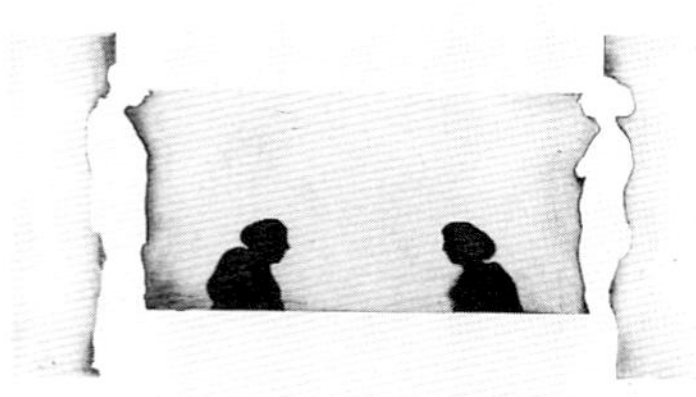

158

153
Frustration, 1966
Medium etching and aquatint
Edition size 50 (editioning not completed; about 20 impressions printed)
Paper white wove
Plates/blocks 1 zinc plate
Inks black
Image size 23⅝ × 17⅞ in. (60.0 × 45.5 cm)
Sheet size 29½ × 22 in. (75.0 × 55.9 cm)
Reference Mazur M-34

154
White Nude, 1966
Medium drypoint
Edition size 30
Paper Arches
Plates/blocks 1 zinc plate
Inks black
Image size 23¾ × 17⅝ in. (60.3 × 44.8 cm)
Sheet size 30 × 22¼ in. (76.2 × 56.5 cm)
Reference Mazur M-99

155
Bed Rest Feelings, 1966
Medium etching and aquatint
Edition size 30
Paper white wove
Plates/blocks 1 zinc plate
Inks black
Image size 23¾ × 17¾ in. (60.3 × 45.1 cm)
Sheet size 28⅜ × 22¼ in. (73.1 × 56.5 cm)
Remarks related to the *Closed Ward* series
Reference Mazur M-33

156
Study for a Dante's Inferno (2nd State), 1966–67
Medium etching, aquatint, and drypoint
Edition size not editioned; a few impressions printed
Paper white wove
Plates/blocks 1 zinc plate
Inks brown-black
Image size 9⅞ × 15¾ in. (25.1 × 40.0 cm)
Sheet size 16⅞ × 25¾ in. (42.9 × 65.4 cm)

157
The Model, Her Shadow, and Mine, from *The Artist and the Model*, 1968
Medium aquatint with plate tone
Edition size 50 with first 25 prints in each edition in boxed portfolio; 3 artist's proofs
Paper American Etching white
Printed by the artist assisted by Kenneth Helphand and Michel Durand
Published by Associated American Artists, New York
Plates/blocks 2 shaped zinc plates
Inks green-black
Image and sheet size 38⅛ × 24⅞ in. (96.9 × 63.2 cm)
Reference Mazur L-28

158
Confrontation across Two Shadows, from *The Artist and the Model*, 1968
Medium aquatint with plate tone
Edition size 50 with first 25 prints in each edition in boxed portfolio; 8 artist's proofs
Paper American Etching white
Printed by the artist assisted by Kenneth Helphand and Michel Durand
Published by Associated American Artists, New York
Plates/blocks 3 shaped zinc plates
Inks green-black
Image and sheet size 24⅞ × 38⅛ in. (63.2 × 96.9 cm)
Reference Mazur L-23

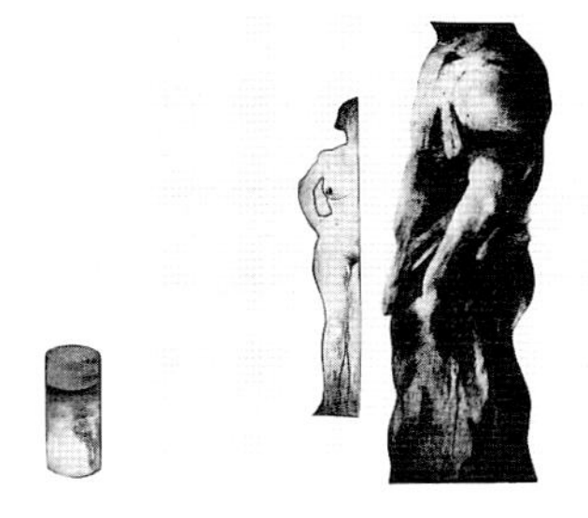

159

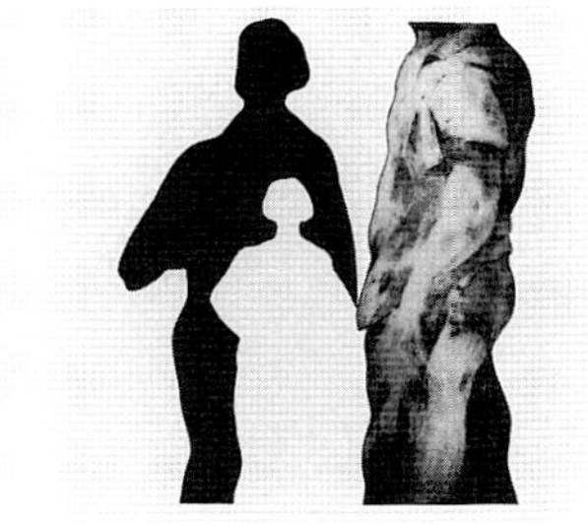

161

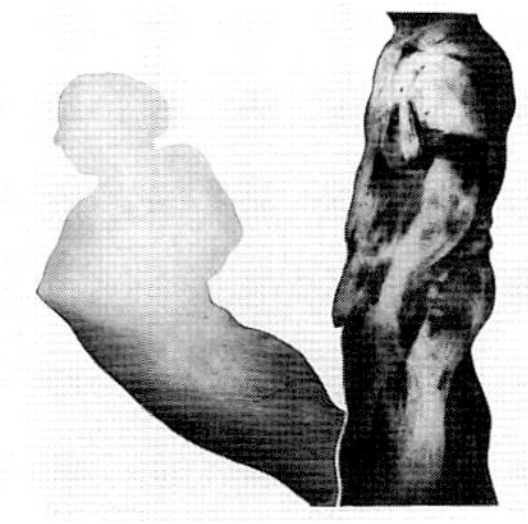

163

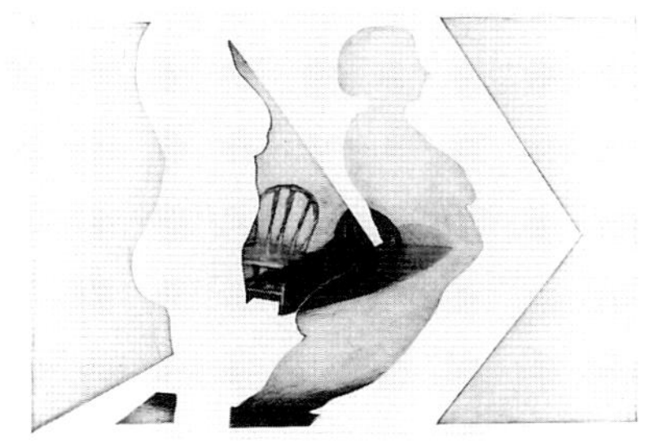

160

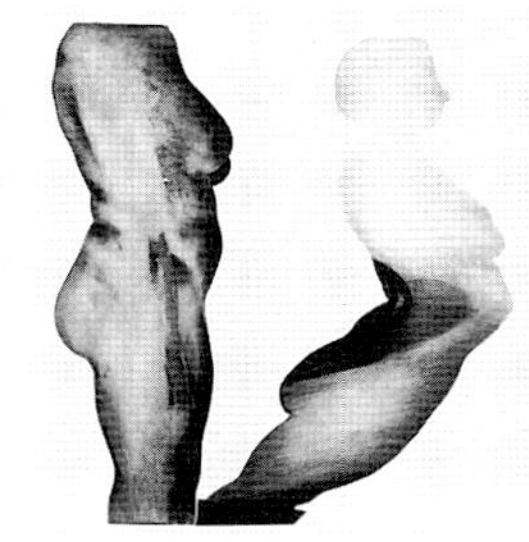
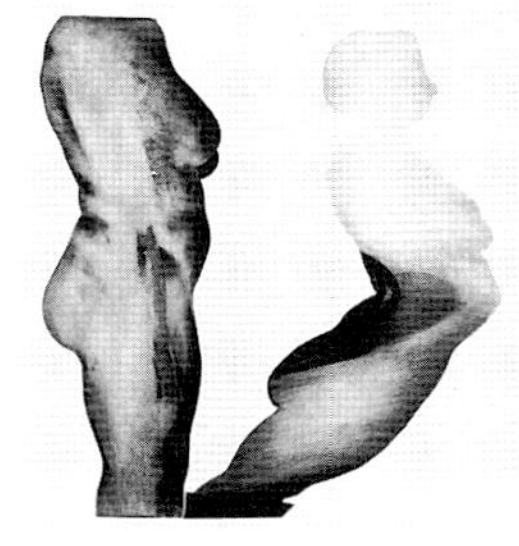

162

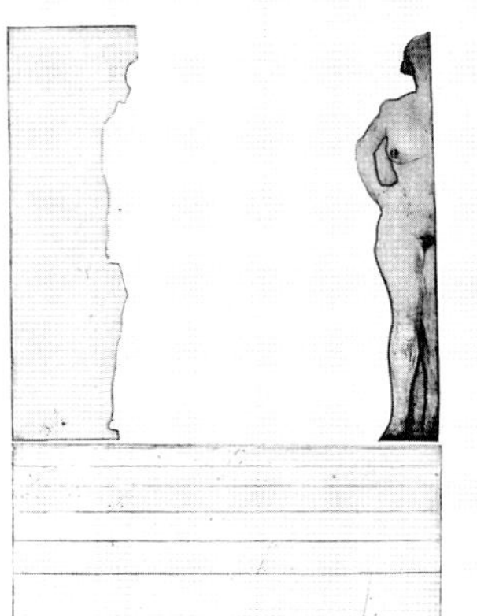

164

159
Artist Model Container,
from *The Artist and the Model*, 1968
Medium etching and aquatint
Edition size 50 with first 25 prints in each edition in boxed portfolio
Paper American Etching white
Printed by the artist assisted by Kenneth Helphand and Michel Durand
Published by Associated American Artists, New York
Plates/blocks 3 shaped zinc plates
Inks green-black
Image and sheet size 24⅞ × 38⅛ in. (63.2 × 96.9 cm)

160
The Chair,
from *The Artist and the Model*, 1968
Medium etching and aquatint with plate tone
Edition size 50 with first 25 prints in each edition in boxed portfolio
Paper American Etching white
Printed by the artist assisted by Kenneth Helphand and Michel Durand
Published by Associated American Artists, New York
Plates/blocks 5 shaped zinc plates
Inks green-black
Image and sheet size 24⅞ × 38⅛ in. (63.2 × 96.9 cm)
Reference Mazur L-33

161
The Artist and Her Shadow,
from *The Artist and the Model*, 1968
Medium aquatint with plate tone
Edition size 50 with first 25 prints in each edition in boxed portfolio
Paper American Etching white
Printed by the artist assisted by Kenneth Helphand and Michel Durand
Published by Associated American Artists, New York
Plates/blocks 2 shaped zinc plates
Inks green-black
Image and sheet size 24⅞ × 38⅛ in. (63.2 × 96.9 cm)
Reference Mazur L-25

162
Diptych #1 (The Model),
from *The Artist and the Model*, 1968
Medium etching and aquatint
Edition size 50 with first 25 prints in each edition in boxed portfolio
Paper American Etching white
Printed by the artist assisted by Kenneth Helphand and Michel Durand
Published by Associated American Artists, New York
Plates/blocks 2 shaped zinc plates
Inks green-black
Image and sheet size 24⅞ × 38⅛ in. (63.2 × 96.9 cm)
Reference Mazur L-22

163
Diptych #1 (The Artist),
from *The Artist and the Model*, 1968
Medium etching and aquatint
Edition size 50 with first 25 prints in each edition in boxed portfolio
Paper American Etching white
Printed by the artist assisted by Kenneth Helphand and Michel Durand
Published by Associated American Artists, New York
Plates/blocks 2 shaped zinc plates
Inks green-black
Image and plate size 24⅞ × 38⅛ in. (63.2 × 96.2 cm)
Reference Mazur L-22a

164
Composition with Floor,
from *The Artist and the Model*, 1968
Medium etching with plate tone
Edition size 50 with first 25 prints in each edition in boxed portfolio
Paper American Etching white
Printed by the artist assisted by Kenneth Helphand and Michel Durand
Published by Associated American Artists, New York
Plates/blocks 3 shaped zinc plates
Inks green-black
Image and sheet size 38⅛ × 24⅞ in. (96.9 × 63.2 cm)
Reference Mazur L-32

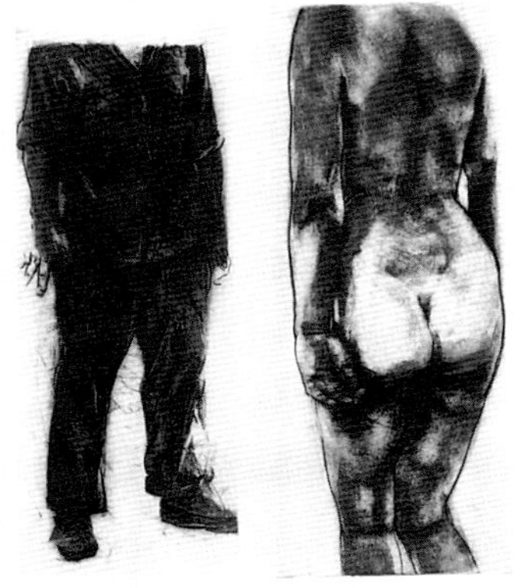

165

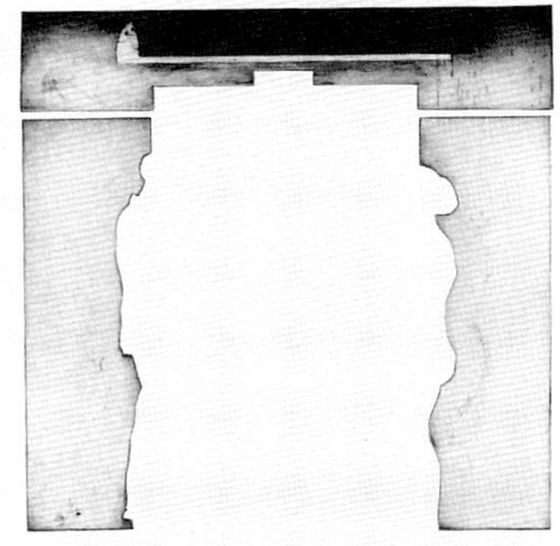

167

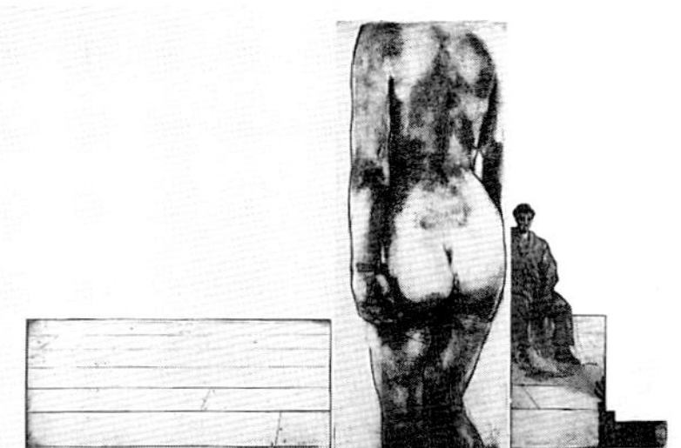

169

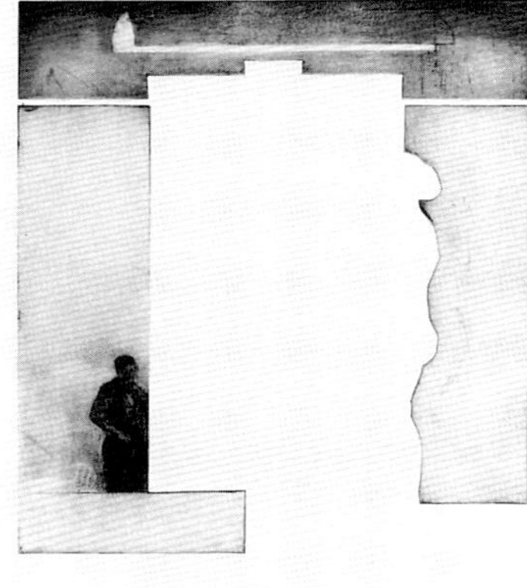

166

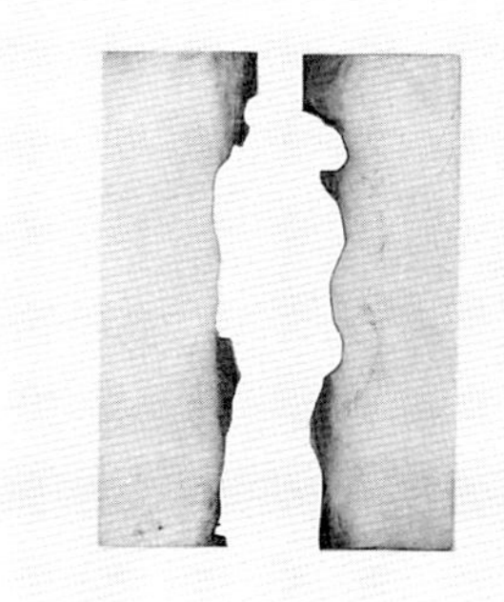

168

165
Confrontation,
from *The Artist and the Model*, 1968
Medium etching and aquatint with plate tone
Edition size 50 with first 25 prints in each edition in boxed portfolio
Paper American Etching white
Printed by the artist assisted by Kenneth Helphand and Michel Durand
Published by Associated American Artists, New York
Plates/blocks 2 zinc plates
Inks green-black
Image and sheet size 38⅛ × 24⅞ in. (96.9 × 63.2 cm)
Reference Mazur L-29

166
Small Composition with Easel,
from *The Artist and the Model*, 1968
Medium etching and aquatint with plate tone
Edition size 50 with first 25 prints in each edition in boxed portfolio
Paper American Etching white
Printed by the artist assisted by Kenneth Helphand and Michel Durand
Published by Associated American Artists, New York
Plates/blocks 3 shaped zinc plates
Inks green-black
Image and sheet size 38⅛ × 24⅞ in. (96.9 × 63.2 cm)
Reference Mazur L-26

167
Confrontation across Easel,
from *The Artist and the Model*, 1968
Medium etching and aquatint
Edition size 50 with first 25 prints in each edition in boxed portfolio
Paper American Etching white
Printed by the artist assisted by Kenneth Helphand and Michel Durand
Published by Associated American Artists, New York
Plates/blocks 3 shaped zinc plates
Inks green-black
Image and sheet size 38⅛ × 24⅞ in. (96.9 × 63.2 cm)
Reference Mazur L-27

168
End Game,
from *The Artist and the Model*, 1968
Medium etching with plate tone
Edition size 50 with first 25 prints in each edition in boxed portfolio
Paper American Etching white
Printed by the artist assisted by Kenneth Helphand and Michel Durand
Published by Associated American Artists, New York
Plates/blocks 2 shaped zinc plates
Inks black
Image and sheet size 38⅛ × 24⅞ in. (96.9 × 63.2 cm)
Reference Mazur L-31

169
Composition with Floor, 1968
Medium etching and aquatint with plate tone (pitted)
Edition size 25
Paper American Etching white
Plates/blocks 2 shaped zinc plates
Inks black
Image and sheet size 24¾ × 38¼ in. (62.9 × 97.2 cm)
Remarks related to *The Artist and the Model* portfolio
Reference Mazur L-24

170
Two Views, 1968
Medium etching and aquatint with plate tone
Edition size 25

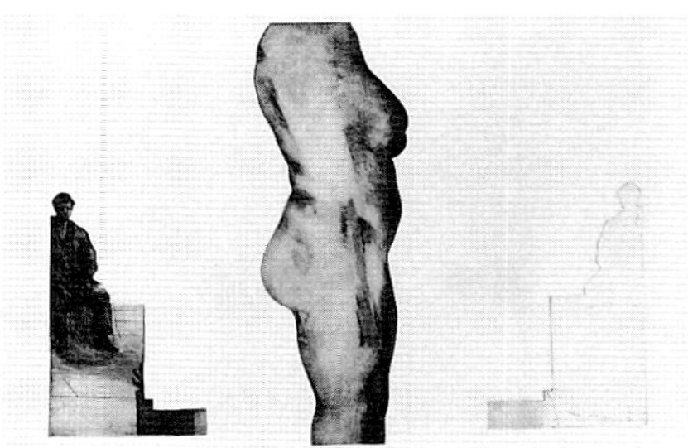

170

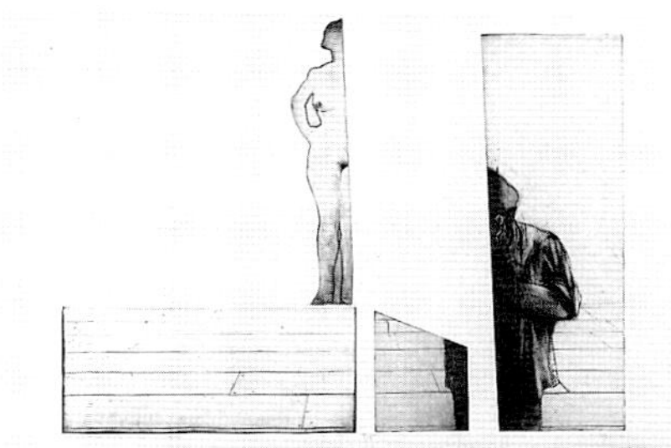

171

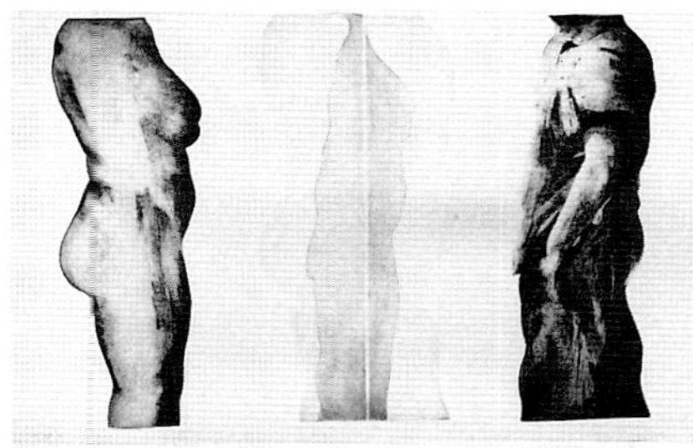

172

Paper American Etching white
Plates/blocks 3 zinc plates
Inks black
Image and sheet size 24¾ × 38⅛ in. (62.9 × 96.9 cm)
Remarks related to *The Artist and the Model* portfolio
Reference Mazur L-19

171
Composition with Artist at Easel, 1968
Medium etching and aquatint with plate tone
Edition size 25
Paper American Etching white
Printed by the artist assisted by Kenneth Helphand and Michel Durand
Plates/blocks 4 zinc plates
Inks black
Image and sheet size 24¾ × 38¼ in. (62.9 × 97.2 cm)
Remarks related to *The Artist and the Model* portfolio
Reference Mazur L-21

172
Overlap, ca. 1968
Medium etching and aquatint with plate tone

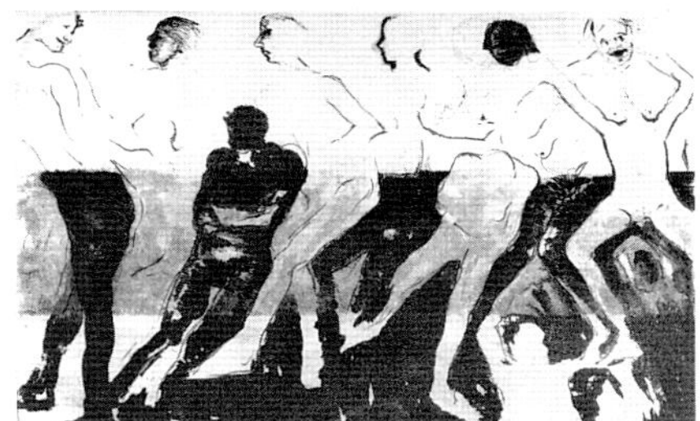

173

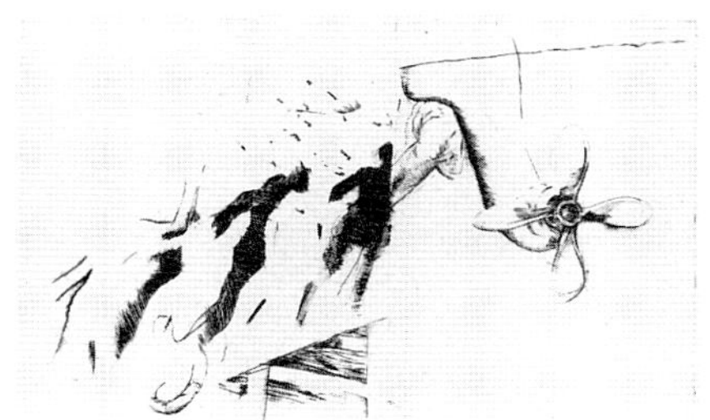

174

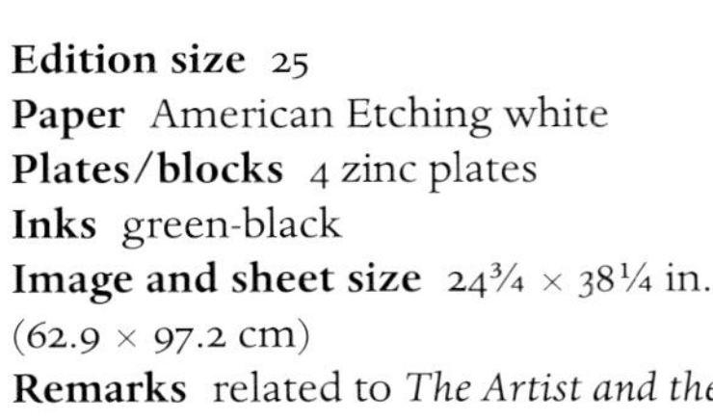

Edition size 25
Paper American Etching white
Plates/blocks 4 zinc plates
Inks green-black
Image and sheet size 24¾ × 38¼ in. (62.9 × 97.2 cm)
Remarks related to *The Artist and the Model* portfolio
Reference Mazur L-30

173
Study for a Dante's Inferno, Canto VIII, 1968
Medium etching and aquatint
Edition size 50
Paper white wove
Inks black
Printed by George Lockwood at Impressions Workshop, Inc., Boston
Published by Artists against Racism and the War, Boston
Plates/blocks 1 zinc plate
Image size 9⅞ × 15½ in. (25.1 × 39.4 cm)
Sheet size 14¾ × 20¼ in. (37.5 × 51.5 cm)
Remarks part of the portfolio *Artists against Racism and the War*, published in spring 1968
Reference Mazur S-41

174
For a Dante's Inferno, Canto III, 1968
Medium etching
Edition size not editioned; 2–3 impressions printed
Paper white wove
Plates/blocks 1 copper plate
Inks brown-black
Image size 9⅞ × 15⅞ in. (25.1 × 40.4 cm)
Sheet size 15½ × 20 in. (39.4 × 50.8 cm)
Reference Mazur S-40

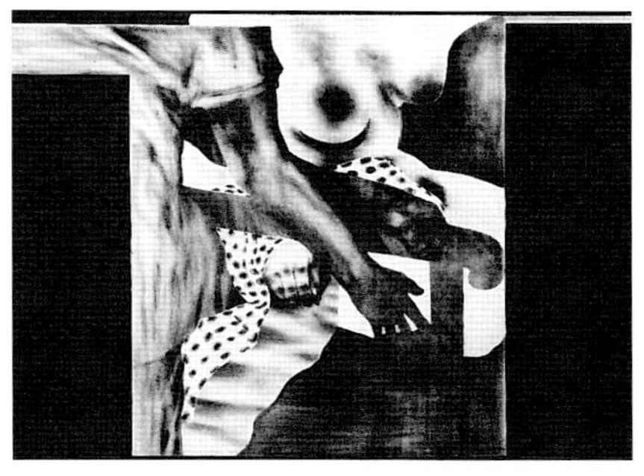

175

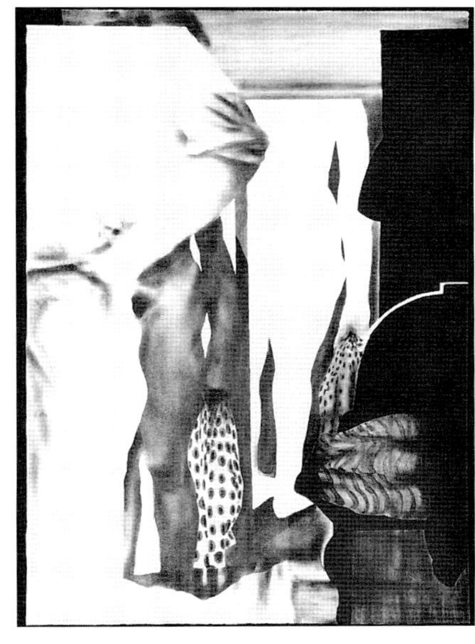

176

175
Melrose Avenue, 1968
Medium lithograph
Edition size 20
Paper Rives BFK
Printed by Serge Lozingot at Tamarind Lithography Workshop, Inc., Los Angeles
Published by Tamarind Lithography Workshop, Inc.
Plates/blocks 1 stone
Inks black
Image and sheet size 22 × 30⅛ in. (55.9 × 76.6 cm)
References Mazur M-75, Tamarind 2316

176
The Mirror, 1968
Medium lithograph
Edition size 20
Paper Rives BFK
Printed by Manuel Fuentes at Tamarind Lithography Workshop, Inc., Los Angeles
Published by Tamarind Lithography Workshop, Inc.
Plates/blocks 1 stone
Inks black
Image and sheet size 30 × 22⅝ in. (76.2 × 57.5 cm)
References Mazur M-74, Tamarind 2317

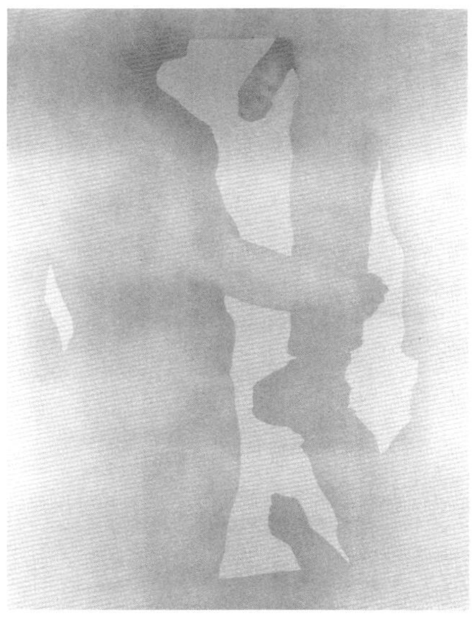

177

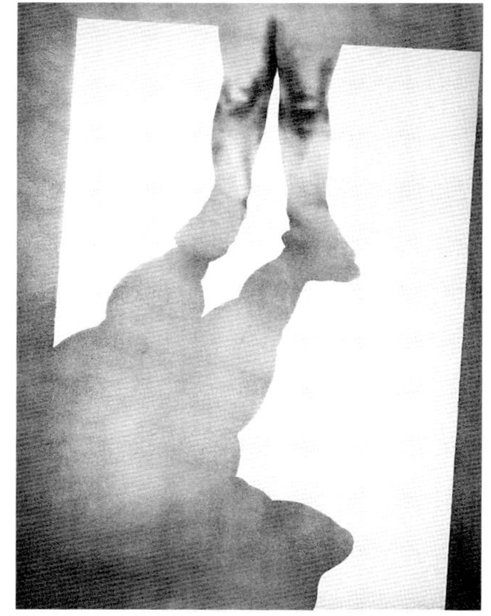

178

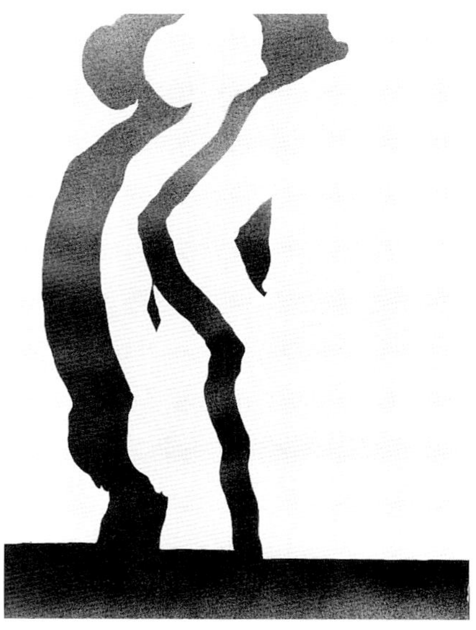

180

177
Venice Boulevard, 1968
Medium lithograph
Edition size 16
Paper Rives BFK
Printed by Fred Akers at Tamarind Lithography Workshop, Inc., Los Angeles
Published by Tamarind Lithography Workshop, Inc.
Plates/blocks 1 stone and 1 zinc plate
Inks light gray and pink
Image and sheet size 30 × 22⅛ in. (76.2 × 56.2 cm)
References Mazur M-78, Tamarind 2318

178
Griffith Park #1, 1968
Medium lithograph
Edition size 20
Paper Rives BFK
Printed by Theo Wujcik at Tamarind Lithography Workshop, Inc., Los Angeles
Published by Tamarind Lithography Workshop, Inc.
Plates/blocks 1 stone
Inks black
Image and sheet size 30 × 22½ in. (76.2 × 57.2 cm)
References Mazur M-76, Tamarind 2319

179
Griffith Park #2, 1968
Medium lithograph
Edition size 20
Paper Rives BFK
Printed by Theo Wujcik at Tamarind Lithography Workshop, Inc., Los Angeles
Published by Tamarind Lithography Workshop, Inc.
Plates/blocks 2 aluminum plates and 1 stone

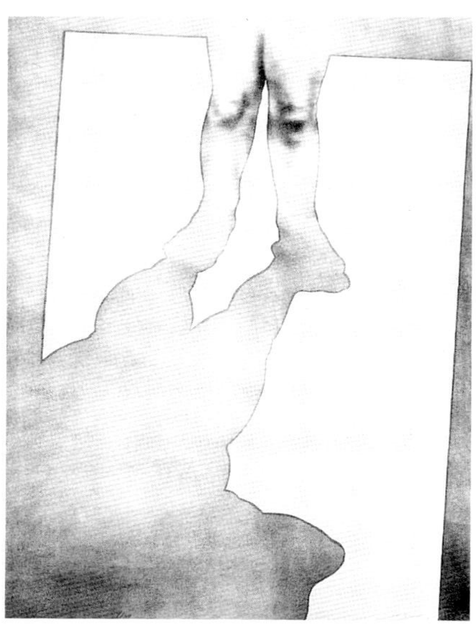

179

Inks orange, pink, and black
Image and sheet size 30⅛ × 22¼ in. (76.6 × 56.5 cm)
Remarks the stone from *Griffith Park #1* (no. 178) was used, with added color plates
References Mazur M-77, Tamarind 2319II

180
Shadow Game (1), 1968
Medium lithograph
Edition size 20
Paper Arches white (17) and Copperplate Deluxe (3)
Printed by Jean Milant at Tamarind Lithography Workshop, Inc., Los Angeles
Published by Tamarind Lithography Workshop, Inc.

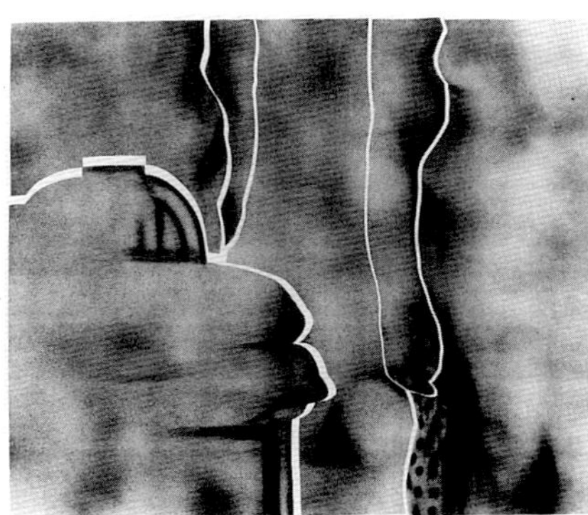

181

Plates/blocks 2 aluminum plates
Inks light violet and black
Image and sheet size 30 × 21¾ in. (76.2 × 55.2 cm)
Remarks the artist destroyed his impressions from this project in 1973
References Mazur M-79, Tamarind 2320

181
White Division #1 (1), 1968
Medium lithograph
Edition size 20
Paper Rives BFK
Printed by Anthony Stoeveken at Tamarind Lithography Workshop, Inc., Los Angeles
Published by Tamarind Lithography Workshop, Inc.
Plates/blocks 1 stone
Inks black
Image and sheet size 24¼ × 29½ in. (61.6 × 75.0 cm)
Remarks the artist destroyed his impressions from this project in 1973
Reference Tamarind 2321

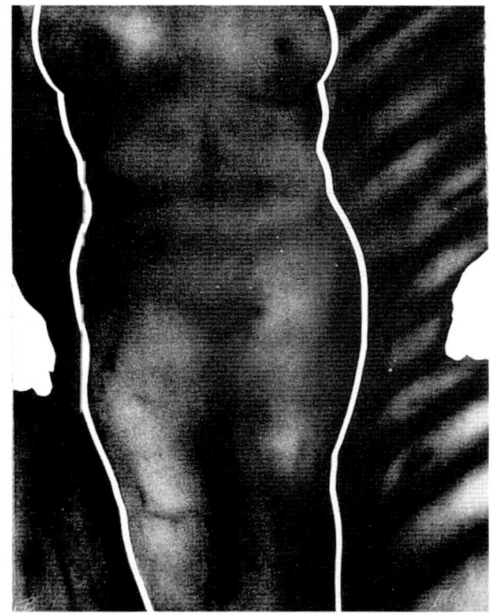

182

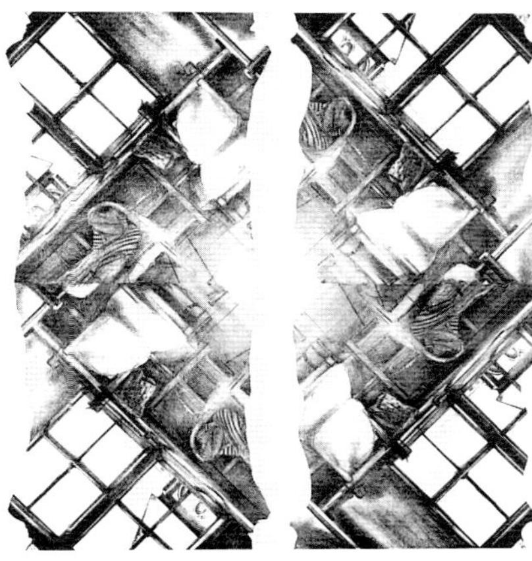

183

182
Untitled (1), 1968
Medium lithograph
Edition size 6
Paper Rives BFK
Printed by Maurice Sánchez at Tamarind Lithography Workshop, Inc., Los Angeles
Published by Tamarind Lithography Workshop, Inc.
Plates/blocks 1 stone
Inks black
Image and sheet size 23 × 17½ in. (58.4 × 44.5 cm)
Remarks the artist destroyed his impressions from this project in 1973
Reference Tamarind 2322

183
Studio Views I, 1968
Medium lithograph
Edition size 20
Paper Rives BFK
Printed by Robert Rogers at Tamarind Lithography Workshop, Inc., Los Angeles
Published by Tamarind Lithography Workshop, Inc.
Plates/blocks 1 stone

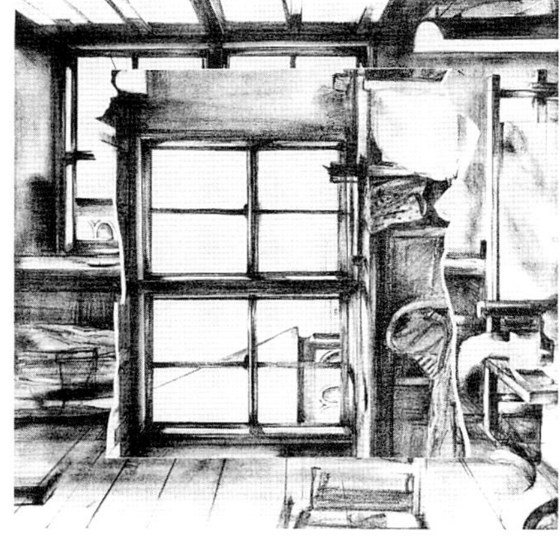

184

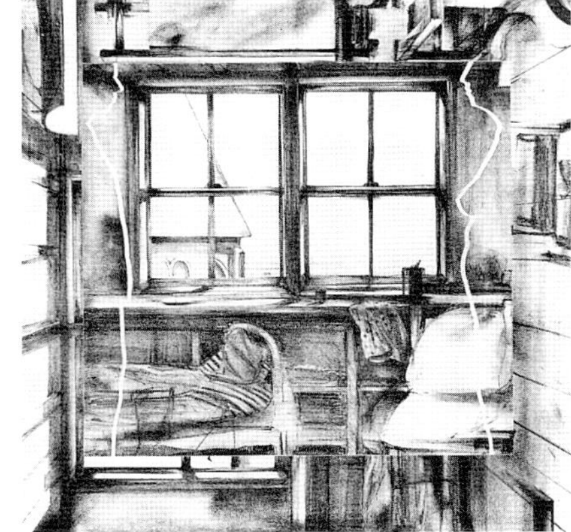

185

Inks black
Image and sheet size 20 × 20 in. (50.8 × 50.8 cm)
Remarks based on studies of the artist's Harvey Street studio
References Mazur M-84, Tamarind 2324

184
Studio Views II, 1968
Medium lithograph
Edition size 20
Paper Arches buff
Printed by Robert Rogers at Tamarind Lithography Workshop, Inc., Los Angeles
Published by Tamarind Lithography Workshop, Inc.
Plates/blocks 1 stone
Inks black
Image and sheet size 13 × 13 in. (33.0 × 33.0 cm)
References Mazur S-38, Tamarind 2324A

185
Studio Views III, 1968
Medium lithograph
Edition size 20
Paper Arches buff
Printed by Robert Rogers at Tamarind Lithography Workshop, Inc., Los Angeles
Published by Tamarind Lithography Workshop, Inc.

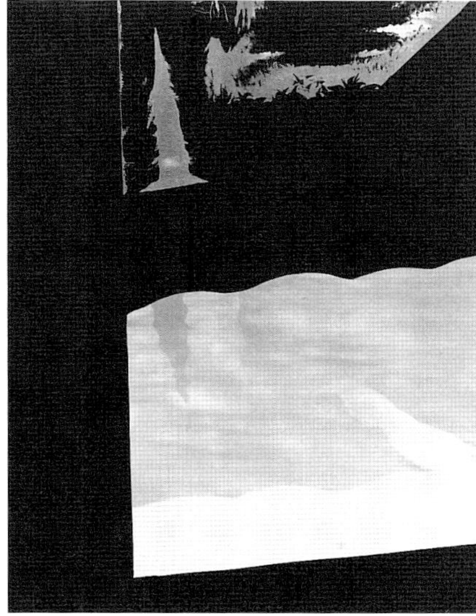

186

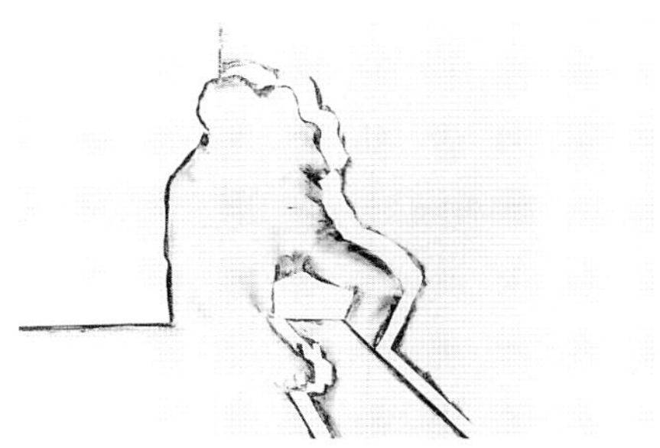

187

Plates/blocks 1 stone
Inks black
Image and sheet size 13 × 13 in. (33.0 × 33.0 cm)
References Mazur S-39, Tamarind 2324B

186
Untitled, 1968
Medium lithograph
Edition size 20
Paper Arches buff
Printed by E. Hughes at Tamarind Lithography Workshop, Inc., Los Angeles
Published by Tamarind Lithography Workshop, Inc.
Plates/blocks 1 stone and 2 aluminum plates
Inks dark pink, light blue, and black
Image and sheet size 30¼ × 22⅜ in. (76.9 × 56.8 cm)
References Mazur M-80, Tamarind 2325

187
Untitled (1), 1968
Medium lithograph
Edition size 20
Paper German Etching
Printed by Maurice Sánchez at Tamarind Lithography Workshop, Inc., Los Angeles
Published by Tamarind Lithography Workshop, Inc.

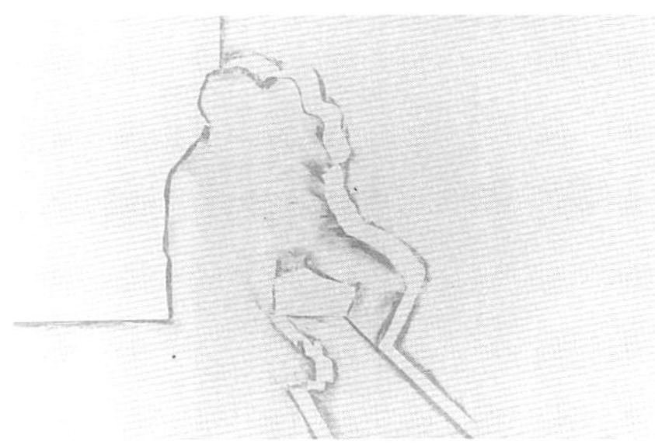

188

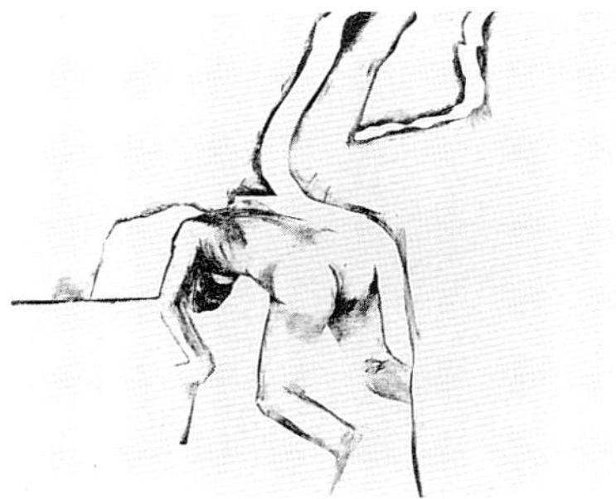

189

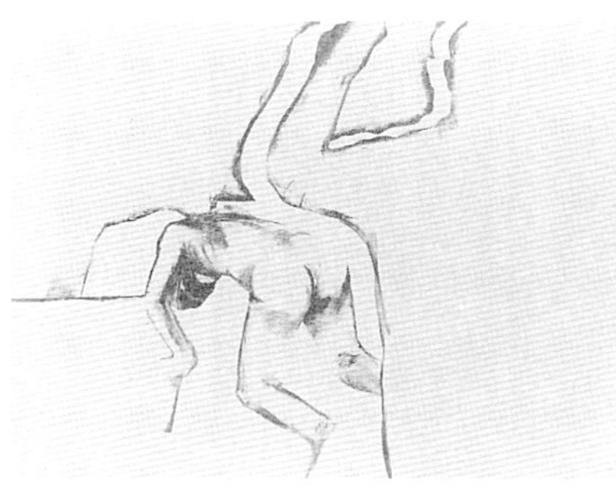

190

Plates/blocks 1 stone
Inks black
Image and sheet size 13⅞ × 20½ in. (35.3 × 52.1 cm)
Remarks the artist destroyed his impressions from this project in 1973
Reference Tamarind 2333

188
Untitled (1), 1968
Medium lithograph
Edition size 10
Paper German Etching
Printed by Maurice Sánchez at Tamarind Lithography Workshop, Inc., Los Angeles
Published by Tamarind Lithography Workshop, Inc.
Plates/blocks 1 stone
Inks dark beige
Image and sheet size 13¾ × 20½ in. (34.9 × 52.1 cm)

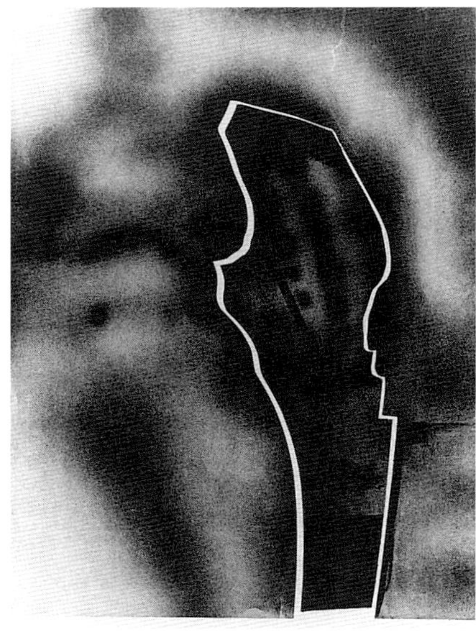
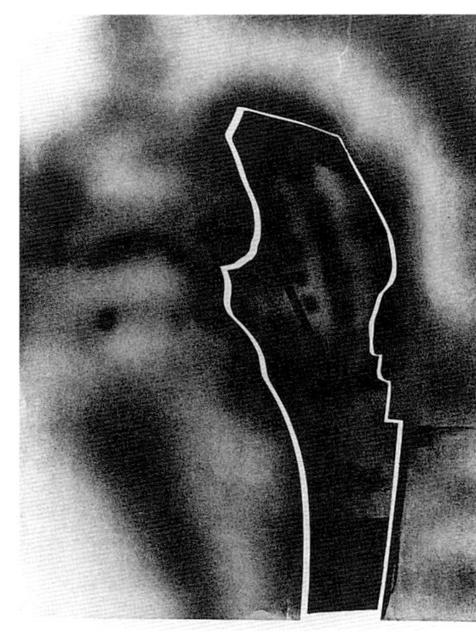

191

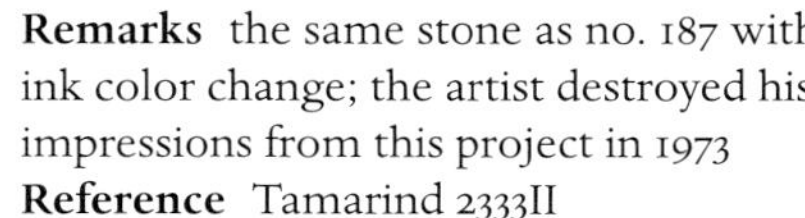

Remarks the same stone as no. 187 with ink color change; the artist destroyed his impressions from this project in 1973
Reference Tamarind 2333II

189
Untitled (1), 1968
Medium lithograph
Edition size 20
Paper German Etching
Printed by Maurice Sánchez at Tamarind Lithography Workshop, Inc., Los Angeles
Published by Tamarind Lithography Workshop, Inc.
Plates/blocks 1 stone
Inks black
Image and sheet size 13 × 18 in. (33.0 × 45.8 cm)
Remarks the artist destroyed his impressions from this project in 1973
References Mazur S-33, Tamarind 2334

190
Untitled (1), 1968
Medium lithograph
Edition size 20
Paper German Etching
Printed by Maurice Sánchez at Tamarind Lithography Workshop, Inc., Los Angeles
Published by Tamarind Lithography Workshop, Inc.
Plates/blocks 1 stone
Inks dark beige
Image and sheet size 13⅛ × 18 in. (33.4 × 45.8 cm)
Remarks the same stone as no. 189 with ink color change; the artist destroyed his impressions from this project in 1973
Reference Tamarind 2334II

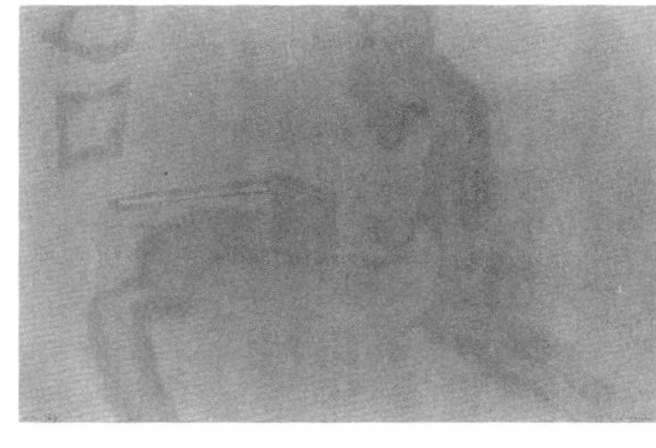

192

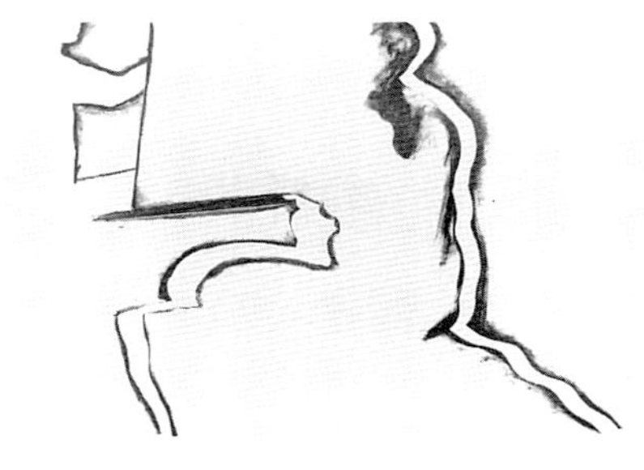

193

191
White Divisions #2, 1968
Medium lithograph
Edition size 20
Paper Rives BFK
Printed by Jean Milant at Tamarind Lithography Workshop, Inc., Los Angeles
Published by Tamarind Lithography Workshop, Inc.
Plates/blocks 1 stone
Inks black
Image and sheet size 24⅛ × 18 in. (61.3 × 45.8 cm)
Reference Tamarind 2335

192
Dark Division (1), 1968
Medium lithograph
Edition size 20
Paper German Etching
Printed by Manuel Fuentes at Tamarind Lithography Workshop, Inc., Los Angeles
Published by Tamarind Lithography Workshop, Inc.
Plates/blocks 1 stone
Inks yellow-brown
Image and sheet size 20 × 32 in. (50.8 × 81.3 cm)
Remarks the artist destroyed his impressions from this project in 1973
Reference Tamarind 2336

193
Van Ness Avenue, 1968
Medium lithograph
Edition size 20
Paper Arches buff

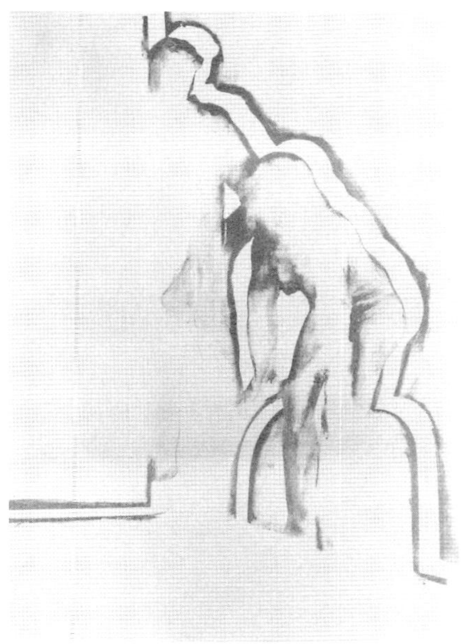

194

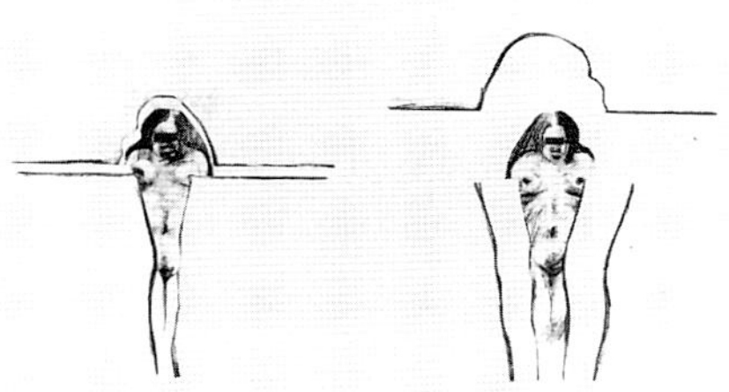

195

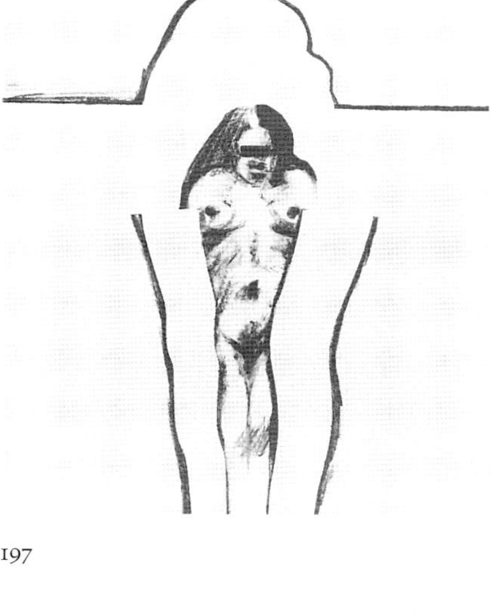

197

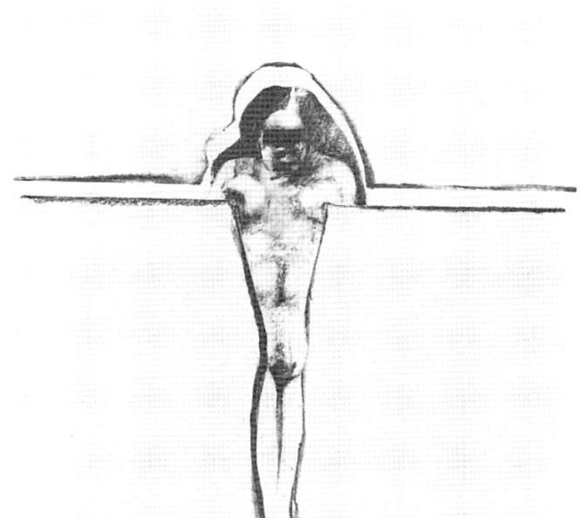

196

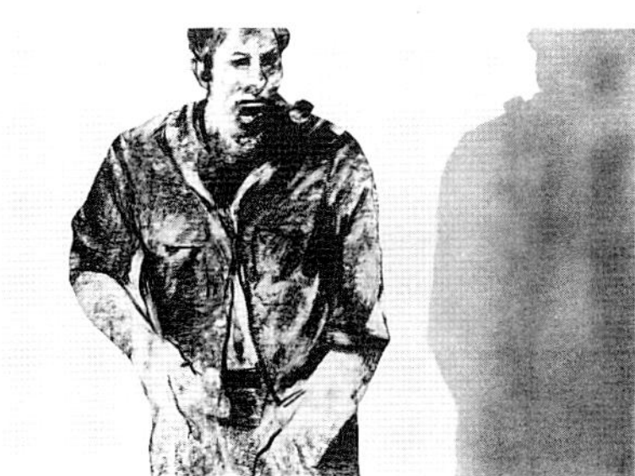

198

Printed by Manuel Fuentes at Tamarind Lithography Workshop, Inc., Los Angeles
Published by Tamarind Lithography Workshop, Inc.
Plates/blocks 1 stone, 1 aluminum plate, and 2 zinc plates
Inks light pearly orange, pearly green, light violet-pink, and pearly orange
Image and sheet size 20 × 30 in. (50.8 × 76.2 cm)
Remarks the stone from *Dark Division (1)* (no. 192) was reworked and printed in different colors
References Tamarind 2336II

194
Her Emergence, 1968
Medium lithograph
Edition size 20
Paper Arches buff
Printed by Serge Lozingot at Tamarind Lithography Workshop, Inc., Los Angeles
Published by Tamarind Lithography Workshop, Inc.
Plates/blocks 1 stone
Inks light red-violet
Image and sheet size 17⅞ × 12½ in. (45.5 × 31.8 cm)
References Mazur S-37, Tamarind 2337

195
Angelina's Legs (1), 1968
Medium lithograph
Edition size 10
Paper German Etching
Printed by Anthony Stoeveken at Tamarind Lithography Workshop, Inc., Los Angeles
Published by Tamarind Lithography Workshop, Inc.
Plates/blocks 1 stone
Inks black
Image and sheet size 20 × 30 in. (50.8 × 76.2 cm)
Remarks the artist destroyed his impressions from this project in 1973
Reference Tamarind 2339

196
Angelina's Legs A (1), 1968
Medium lithograph
Edition size 10
Paper German Etching
Printed by Anthony Stoeveken at Tamarind Lithography Workshop, Inc., Los Angeles
Published by Tamarind Lithography Workshop, Inc.
Plates/blocks 1 stone
Inks gray
Image and sheet size 15 × 13 in. (38.1 × 33.0 cm)
Remarks the artist destroyed his impressions from this project in 1973
References Mazur S-36, Tamarind 2339A

197
Angelina's Legs B (1), 1968
Medium lithograph
Edition size 10
Paper German Etching
Printed by Anthony Stoeveken at Tamarind Lithography Workshop, Inc., Los Angeles
Published by Tamarind Lithography Workshop, Inc.
Plates/blocks 1 stone
Inks gray
Image and sheet size 15⅛ × 13 in. (38.4 × 33.0 cm)
Remarks the artist destroyed his impressions from this project in 1973
References Mazur S-35, Tamarind 2339B

198
Self-Portrait, 1968
Medium lithograph
Edition size 20
Paper German Etching
Printed by Anthony Stoeveken at Tamarind Lithography Workshop, Inc., Los Angeles
Published by Tamarind Lithography Workshop, Inc.
Plates/blocks 1 stone
Inks black
Image and sheet size 23⅛ × 35 in. (58.8 × 88.9 cm)
References Mazur L-16, Tamarind 2340

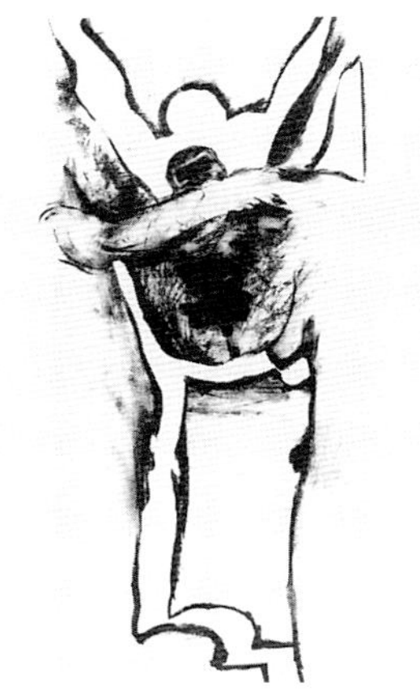

199

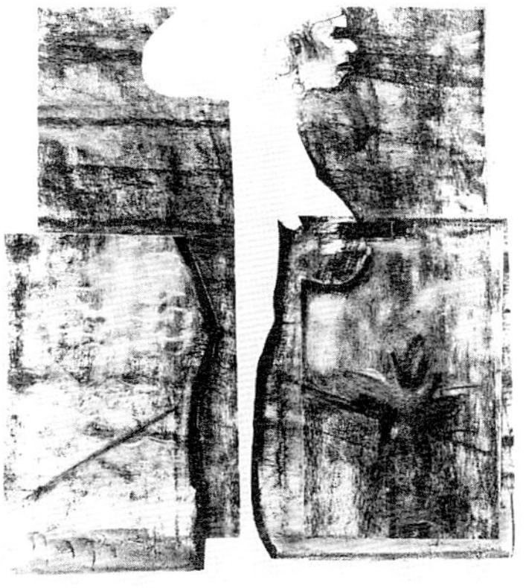

200

199
Untitled (1), 1968
Medium lithograph
Edition size 20
Paper German Etching
Printed by Fred Akers at Tamarind Lithography Workshop, Inc., Los Angeles
Published by Tamarind Lithography Workshop, Inc.
Plates/blocks 1 stone
Inks black
Image and sheet size 15 × 14½ in. (38.1 × 36.8 cm)
Remarks the artist destroyed his impressions from this project in 1973
Reference Tamarind 2341

200
Untitled (1), 1968
Medium lithograph
Edition size 20
Paper German Etching
Printed by Fred Akers at Tamarind Lithography Workshop, Inc., Los Angeles
Published by Tamarind Lithography Workshop, Inc.
Plates/blocks 1 stone

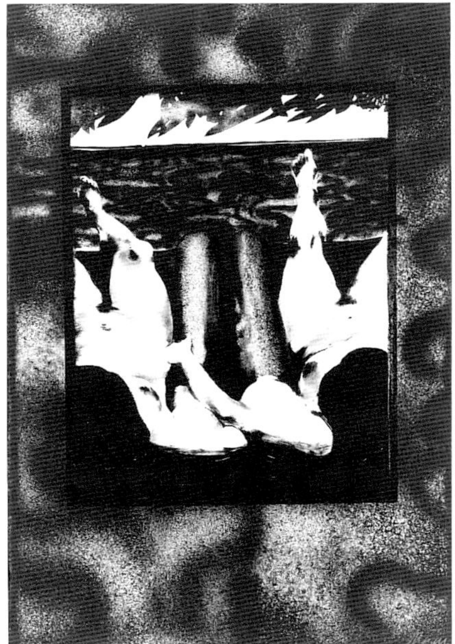

201

Inks black
Image and sheet size 15⅛ × 14½ in. (38.4 × 36.8 cm)
Remarks the artist destroyed his impressions from this project in 1973
References Mazur S-34, Tamarind 2342

201
Sunset Boulevard III, 1968
Medium lithograph
Edition size 20
Paper German Etching
Printed by Maurice Sánchez at Tamarind Lithography Workshop, Inc., Los Angeles
Published by Tamarind Lithography Workshop, Inc.
Plates/blocks 1 stone and 1 aluminum plate
Inks blue-black and black
Image and sheet size 29 × 19 in. (73.7 × 48.2 cm)
References Mazur M-82, Tamarind 2343

202
Untitled, 1968
Medium lithograph
Edition size 20
Paper Arches buff
Printed by Maurice Sánchez at Tamarind Lithography Workshop, Inc., Los Angeles
Published by Tamarind Lithography Workshop, Inc.
Plates/blocks 2 aluminum plates
Inks light beige and light blue
Image and sheet size 29 × 19¼ in. (73.7 × 48.9 cm)
Remarks incorporates the aluminum plate used for *Sunset Boulevard III* (no. 201)
References Mazur M-83, Tamarind 2343II

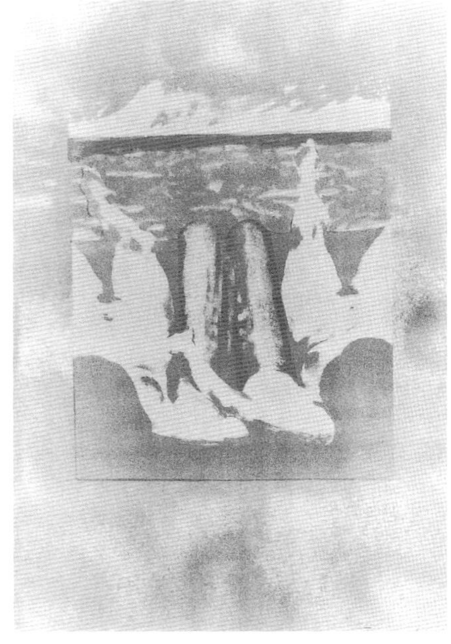

202

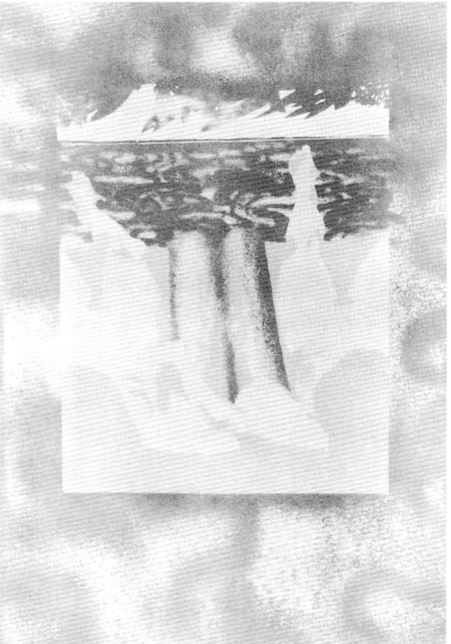

203

203
Untitled, 1968
Medium lithograph
Edition size 10
Paper Arches buff
Printed by Maurice Sánchez at Tamarind Lithography Workshop, Inc., Los Angeles
Published by Tamarind Lithography Workshop, Inc.
Plates/blocks 2 aluminum plates
Inks gray and blue
Image and sheet size 29 × 19 in. (73.7 × 48.2 cm)

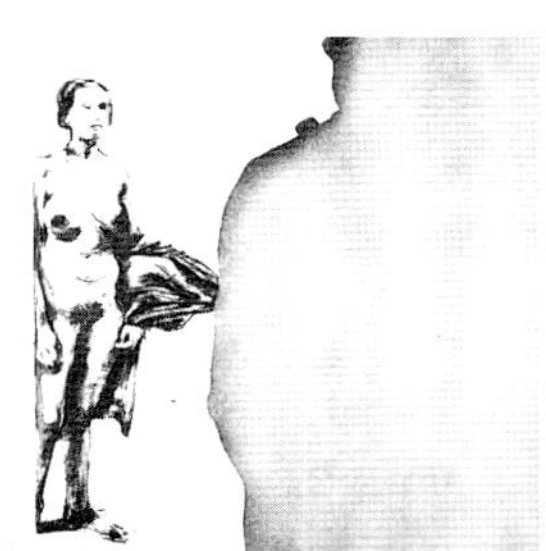

204

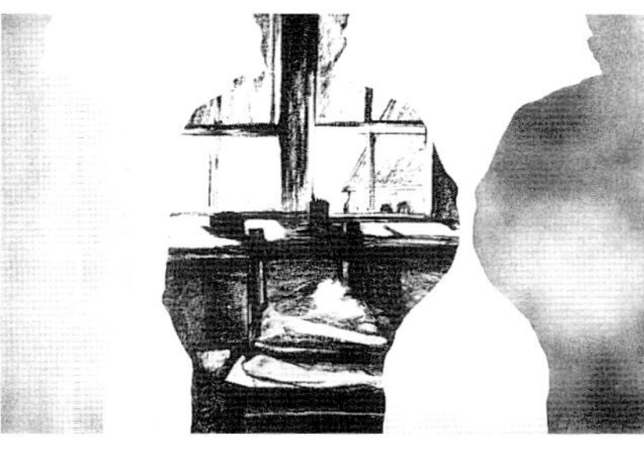

205

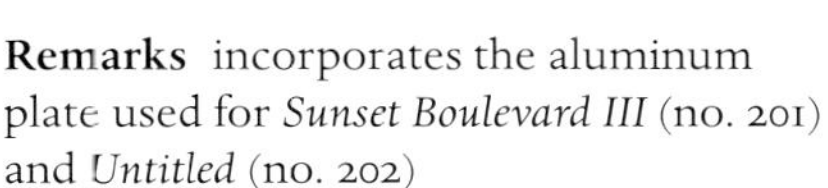

Remarks incorporates the aluminum plate used for *Sunset Boulevard III* (no. 201) and *Untitled* (no. 202)
Reference Tamarind 2343III

204
Model's Entrance, 1968
Medium lithograph
Edition size 20
Paper Magnani Italia (10) and German Etching (10)
Printed by Anthony Stoeveken at Tamarind Lithography Workshop, Inc., Los Angeles
Published by Tamarind Lithography Workshop, Inc.
Plates/blocks 1 stone
Inks black or yellow-gray
Image and sheet size $23 \times 34\frac{7}{8}$ in. (58.4×88.6 cm)
Remarks this edition was printed using two color variations: 10 impressions in black and 10 impressions in yellow-gray
References Mazur L-18, Tamarind 2360

205
Shadow Interior, 1968
Medium lithograph
Edition size 20
Paper Magnani Italia
Printed by Jean Milant at Tamarind Lithography Workshop, Inc., Los Angeles
Published by Tamarind Lithography Workshop, Inc.
Plates/blocks 1 stone
Inks black

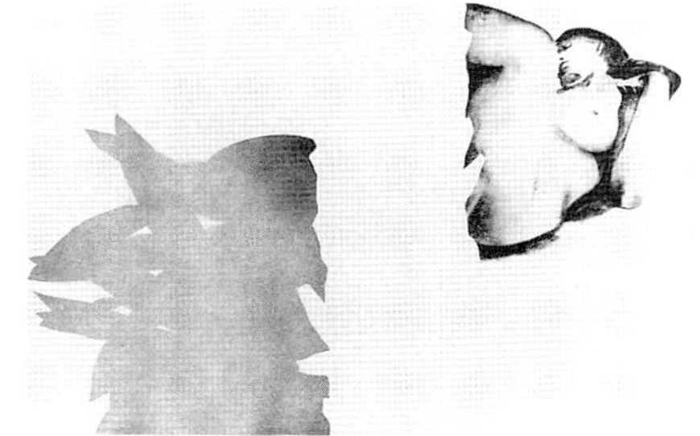

206

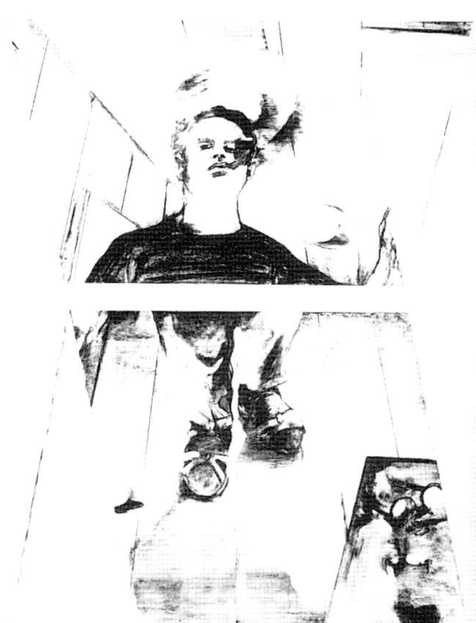

207

Image and sheet size $23 \times 34\frac{7}{8}$ in. (58.4×88.6 cm)
References Mazur L-15, Tamarind 2361

206
Tamarind Avenue, 1968
Medium lithograph
Edition size 20
Paper German Etching
Printed by Manuel Fuentes at Tamarind Lithography Workshop, Inc., Los Angeles
Published by Tamarind Lithography Workshop, Inc.
Plates/blocks 1 stone
Inks black
Image and sheet size $24\frac{1}{8} \times 36\frac{1}{4}$ in. (61.3×92.1 cm)
Reference Tamarind 2362

207
Self-Portrait II, 1968
Medium lithograph
Edition size 20
Paper German Etching
Printed by Theo Wujcik at Tamarind Lithography Workshop, Inc., Los Angeles

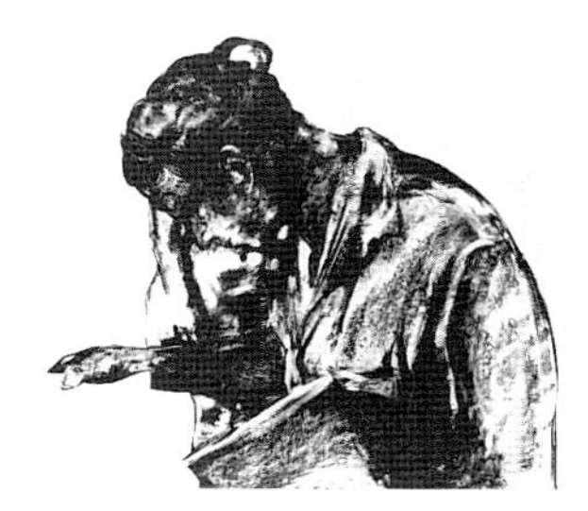

208

209

Published by Tamarind Lithography Workshop, Inc.
Plates/blocks 1 stone
Inks black
Image and sheet size $32\frac{1}{4} \times 23\frac{1}{8}$ in. (81.9×58.8 cm)
References Mazur L-14, Tamarind 2363

208
Self-Portrait III, 1968
Medium lithograph
Edition size 20
Paper German Etching (15) and Copperplate Deluxe (5)
Printed by Manuel Fuentes at Tamarind Lithography Workshop, Inc., Los Angeles
Published by Tamarind Lithography Workshop, Inc.
Plates/blocks 1 stone
Inks black
Image and sheet size 23×35 in. (58.4×88.9 cm)
References Mazur L-17, Tamarind 2364

209
4½ Poses, 1969
Medium drypoint
Edition size 25
Paper white wove
Plates/blocks 1 copper plate
Inks black
Image size $15\frac{1}{2} \times 23\frac{5}{8}$ in. (39.4×60.0 cm)
Sheet size $22\frac{1}{8} \times 30$ in. (56.2×76.2 cm)
Reference Mazur M-100

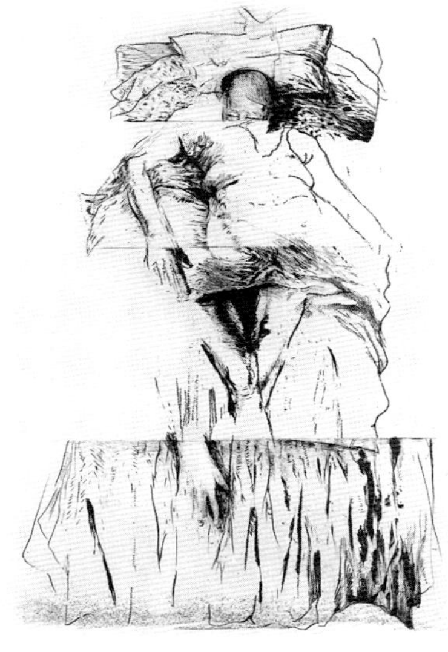

210

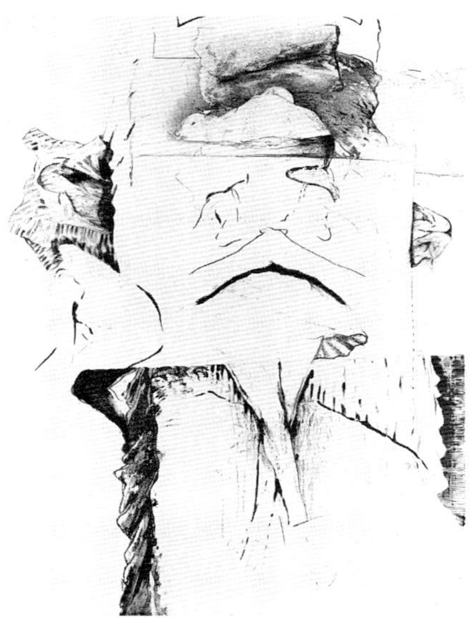

211

210
Bed Image, 1969
Medium etching and drypoint
Edition size 30
Paper Rives BFK
Plates/blocks 1 zinc plate
Inks black
Image size $23\frac{7}{8} \times 17\frac{7}{8}$ in. (60.6 × 45.5 cm)
Sheet size $29\frac{7}{8} \times 22\frac{1}{8}$ in. (75.9 × 56.2 cm)
Reference Mazur M-101

211
Morning Bed, 1969
Medium etching and drypoint
Edition size 30
Paper Rives BFK
Plates/blocks 1 zinc plate
Inks black
Image size $23\frac{5}{8} \times 17\frac{3}{4}$ in. (60.0 × 45.1 cm)
Sheet size $29\frac{1}{2} \times 21\frac{7}{8}$ in. (75.0 × 55.6 cm)
Reference Mazur M-102

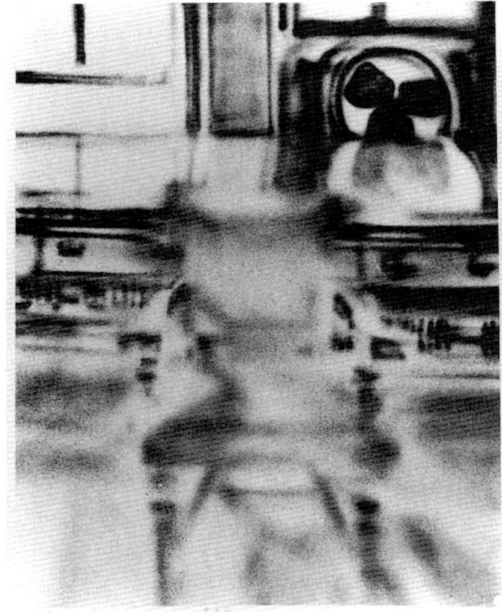

212

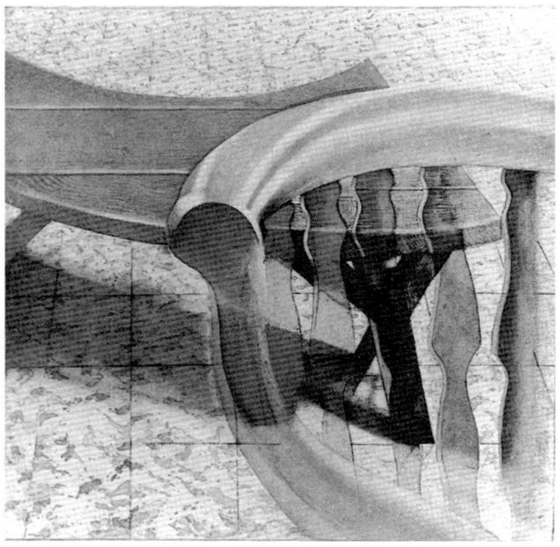

213

212
Chair at Harvey Street, 1971
Medium lithograph
Edition size not editioned; 7 impressions printed
Paper Rives BFK
Plates/blocks 1 aluminum plate
Inks black
Image size $22\frac{3}{4} \times 17\frac{3}{4}$ in. (57.8 × 45.1 cm)
Sheet size 30 × 22 in. (76.2 × 55.9 cm)
Remarks an experimental project in which the artist drew the image on a piece of Mylar with an airbrush and then exposed the image on a photo-sensitized aluminum plate
Reference Mazur M-98b

213
Chair and Bench, 1972
Medium etching and aquatint with sugar lift
Edition size 20 (editioning not completed; about 12 impressions printed)
Paper Fabriano Murillo
Printed by Robert Townsend and the artist; plate preparation by the artist
Plates/blocks 3 copper plates
Inks blue, green, and sepia
Image size $19\frac{3}{4} \times 19\frac{3}{4}$ in. (50.2 × 50.2 cm)
Sheet size $25\frac{1}{8} \times 22$ in. (63.8 × 55.9 cm)
Remarks the artist began editioning this project in his studio; additional impressions were later printed by Robert Townsend at his shop, which at that time was in Boston
Reference Mazur L-13

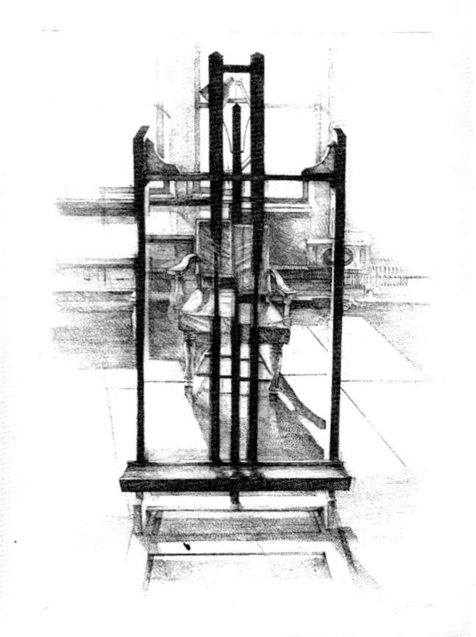

214

214
Easel and Chair, 1972
Medium etching and engraving with electric engraving tool
Edition size 25
Paper German Etching
Plates/blocks 1 copper plate
Inks black
Image size $35\frac{3}{8} \times 23\frac{1}{2}$ in. (89.9 × 59.7 cm)
Sheet size $40\frac{3}{8} \times 27\frac{3}{4}$ in. (102.6 × 70.5 cm)
Reference Mazur L-12

215
N.Y. Memory, 1972
Medium etching with soft ground and engraving with electric engraving tool
Edition size 20
Paper white wove
Plates/blocks 1 copper plate
Inks black
Image size $23\frac{3}{4} \times 17\frac{3}{4}$ in. (60.3 × 45.1 cm)
Sheet size $29\frac{7}{8} \times 23\frac{1}{4}$ in. (75.9 × 59.1 cm)
Reference Mazur M-97

216
Ladder, 1972
Medium etching with soft ground
Edition size 20
Paper Arches

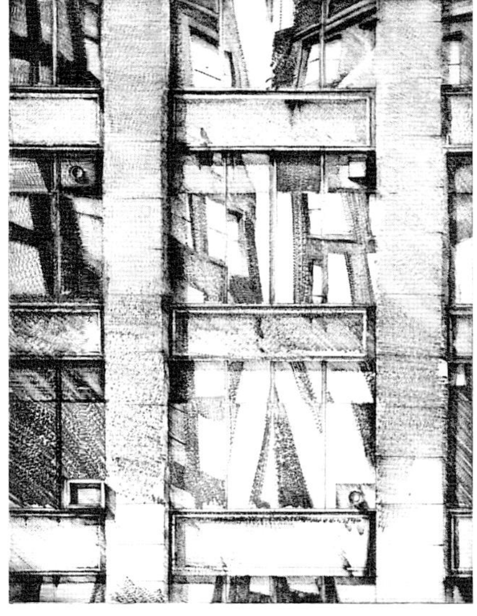

215

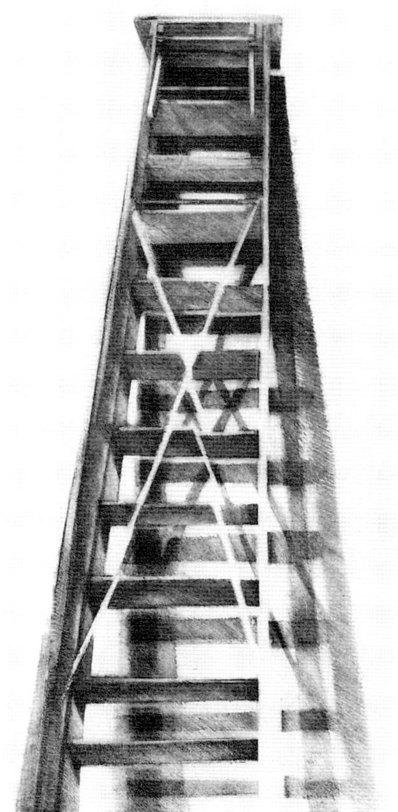

216

Plates/blocks 1 copper plate
Inks black
Image size 35½ × 17⅞ in. (90.2 × 45.5 cm)
Sheet size 41⅜ × 24 in. (105.1 × 61.0 cm)
Remarks proofs of a first state with a chair in the upper right corner also exist
Reference Mazur L-11

217
Studio Door, 1973
Medium engraving

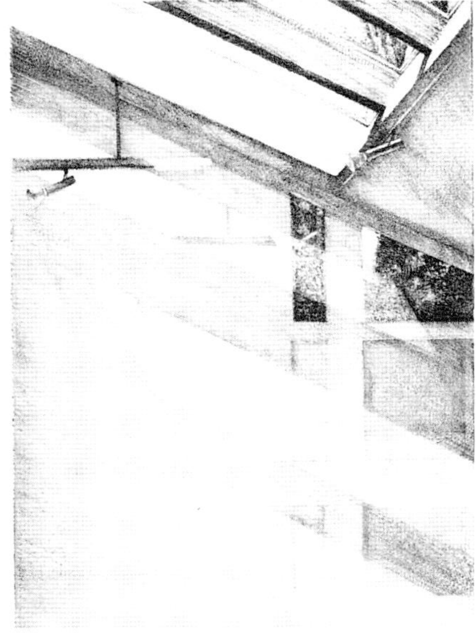

217

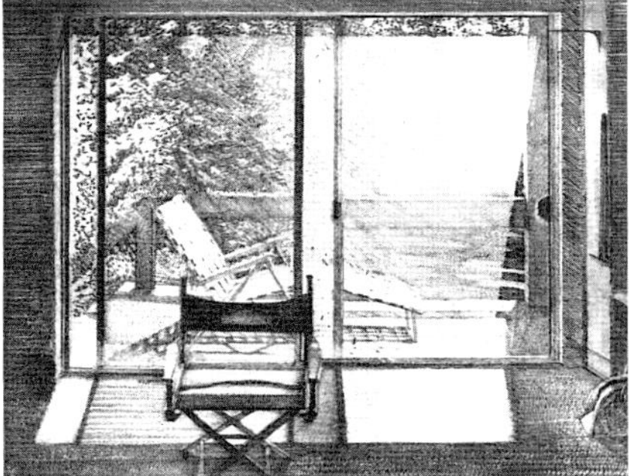

218

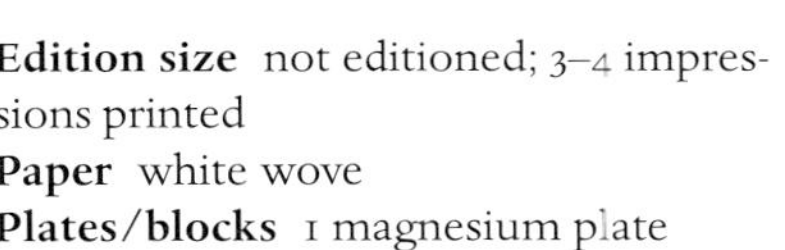

Edition size not editioned; 3–4 impressions printed
Paper white wove
Plates/blocks 1 magnesium plate
Inks black
Image size 20⅞ × 14¾ in. (53.0 × 37.5 cm)
Sheet size 28 × 20¾ in. (71.2 × 52.7 cm)
Reference Mazur M-94

218
View onto Porch (Light at 10 A.M.), 1973
Medium engraving with electric engraving tool
Edition size 20
Paper Rives BFK
Plates/blocks 1 copper plate
Inks black
Image size 17¾ × 22½ in. (45.1 × 57.2 cm)
Sheet size 20¾ × 26¾ in. (52.7 × 68.0 cm)
Reference Mazur M-96

219
Light Box, 1973
Medium engraving with electric engraving tool

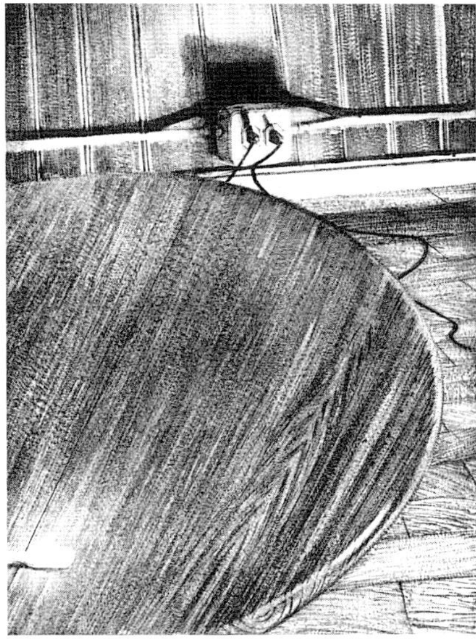

219

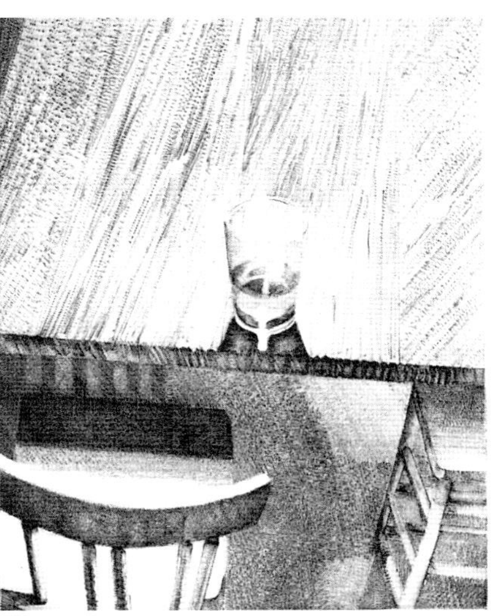

220

Edition size 20
Paper Rives BFK
Plates/blocks 1 copper plate
Inks black
Image size 21⅞ × 15⅞ in. (55.6 × 40.4 cm)
Sheet size 28⅝ × 20½ in. (72.7 × 52.1 cm)
Reference Mazur M-98

220
Glass on Table, 1973
Medium engraving with electric engraving tool
Edition size 20
Paper Rives BFK
Plates/blocks 1 copper plate
Inks black
Image size 19⅞ × 15⅝ in. (50.5 × 39.7 cm)
Sheet size 27⅝ × 20¾ in. (70.2 × 52.7 cm)
Reference Mazur M-95

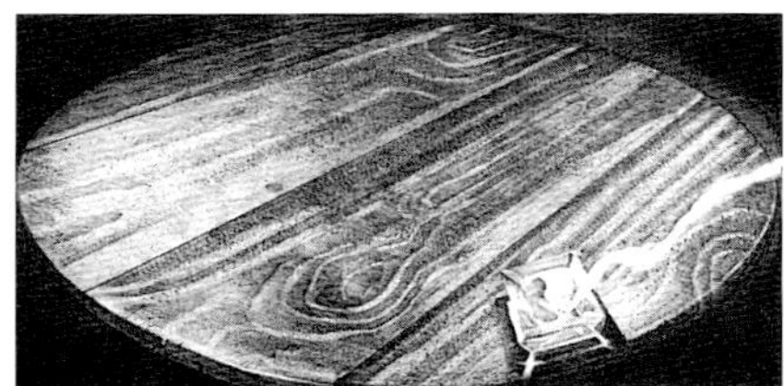

221

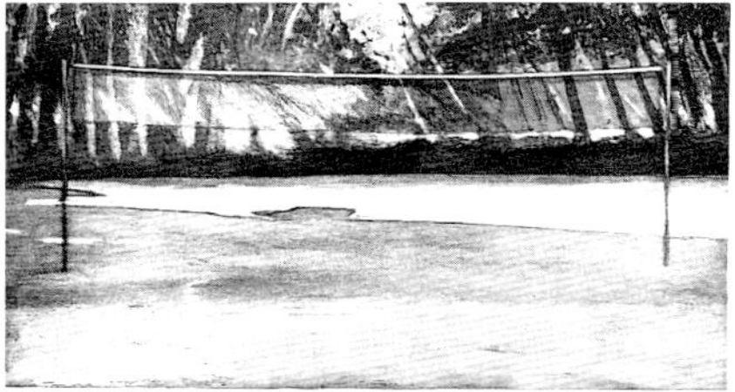

222

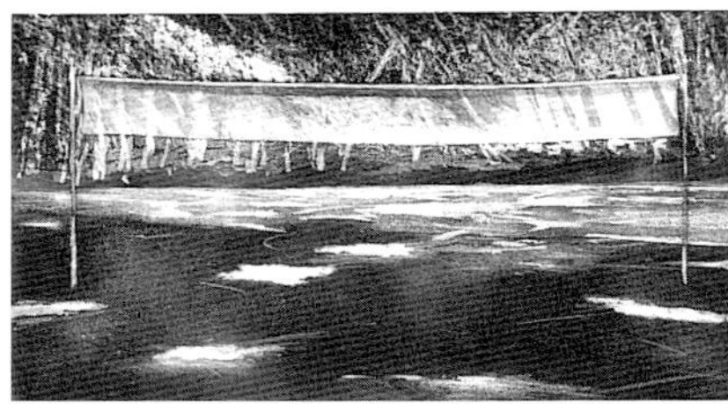

223

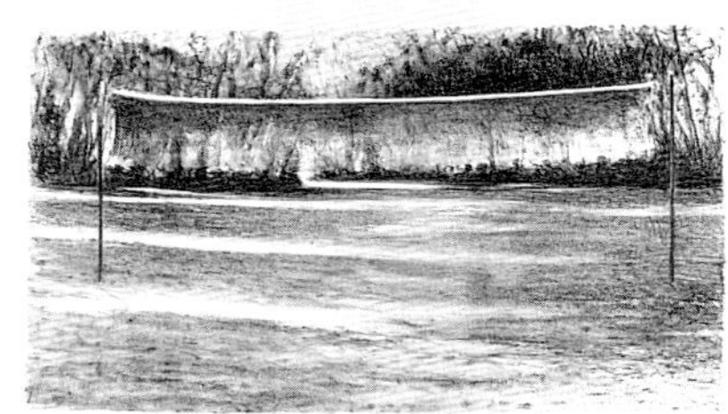

224

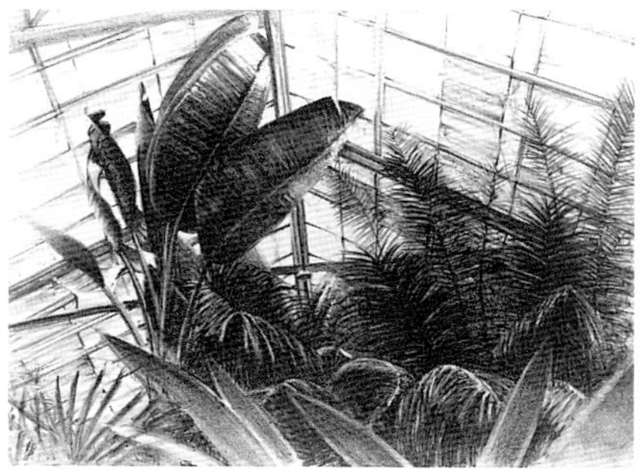

225

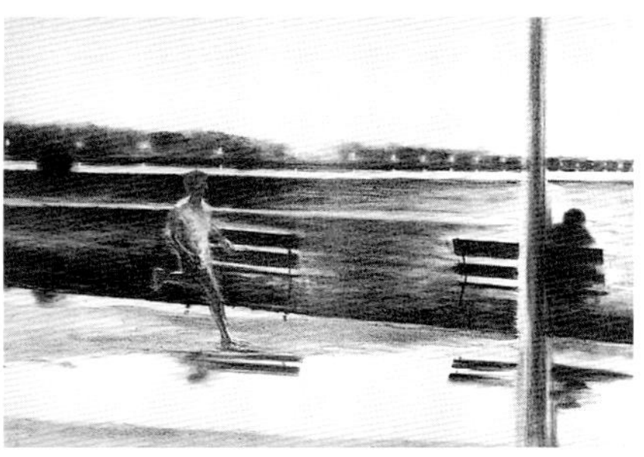

226

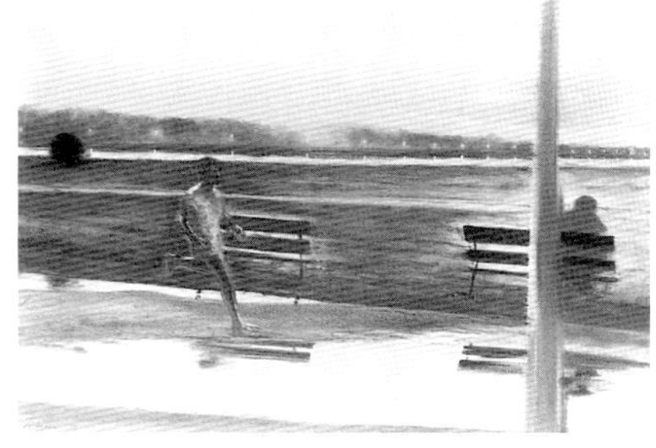

227

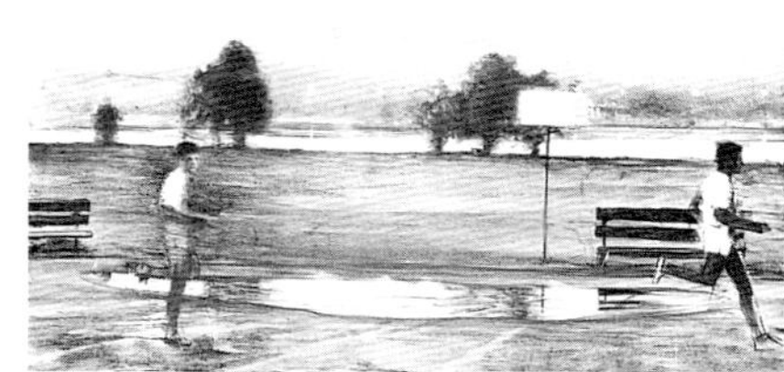

228

221
Smoke, 1975
Medium aquatint and engraving with electric engraving tool
Edition size 25
Paper German Etching
Plates/blocks 1 magnesium plate
Inks brown-black
Image size 17¾ × 35⅜ in. (45.1 × 89.9 cm)
Sheet size 21½ × 39½ in. (54.6 × 100.4 cm)
Reference Mazur L-10

222
The Net I (1st State), 1976
Medium etching and aquatint
Edition size 20
Paper Rives BFK
Plates/blocks 1 zinc plate
Inks green-black
Image size 17⅜ × 31⅜ in. (44.2 × 79.7 cm)
Sheet size 23¾ × 35¾ in. (60.3 × 90.8 cm)
Reference Mazur L-48

223
The Net I (2nd State), 1976
Medium etching and aquatint
Edition size 20
Paper Rives BFK
Plates/blocks 1 zinc plate
Inks black
Image size 17⅜ × 31⅜ in. (44.2 × 79.7 cm)
Sheet size 24 × 35⅝ in. (61.0 × 90.5 cm)
Reference Mazur L-48a

224
The Net, 1977
Medium lithograph
Edition size 50 plus 4 artist's proofs
Paper Rives gray, tan, or white
Printed by Herb Fox at Fox Graphics – Merrimac Editions, Merrimac, Mass.
Plates/blocks 1 zinc plate
Inks black
Image and sheet size 26 × 40⅞ in. (66.1 × 103.8 cm)
Remarks this edition was printed using three different papers
References Mazur L-46 and L-47

225
Greenhouse, 1977
Medium lithograph
Edition size 50
Paper Arches
Printed by Herb Fox at Fox Graphics – Merrimac Editions, Merrimac, Mass.
Plates/blocks 1 stone
Inks black
Image and sheet size 26½ × 35¼ in. (67.3 × 89.6 cm)
Remarks several impressions were subsequently hand-colored with pastel
Reference Mazur L-34

226
Runner, 1977
Medium lithograph
Edition size 6
Paper Rives BFK
Printed by Herb Fox at Fox Graphics–Merrimac Editions, Merrimac, Mass.
Plates/blocks 1 stone
Inks black
Image and sheet size 21 × 29⅞ in. (53.4 × 75.9 cm)
Reference Mazur M-85

227
Runner, 1977
Medium lithograph
Edition size 50
Paper Arches
Printed by Herb Fox at Fox Graphics – Merrimac Editions, Merrimac, Mass.
Plates/blocks 4 aluminum plates
Inks black, yellow, green, and blue
Image and sheet size 22 × 30 in. (55.9 × 76.2 cm)
Reference Mazur M-85a

228
Two Runners (My Running, His Running), 1978
Medium lithograph
Edition size 40
Paper Arches
Printed by Herb Fox at Fox Graphics – Merrimac Editions, Merrimac, Mass.

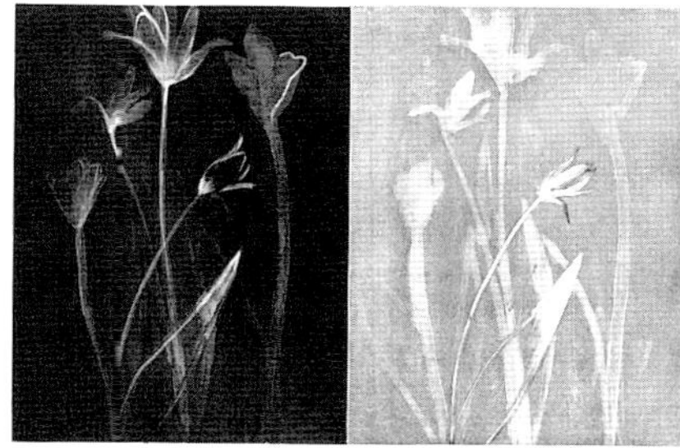

229

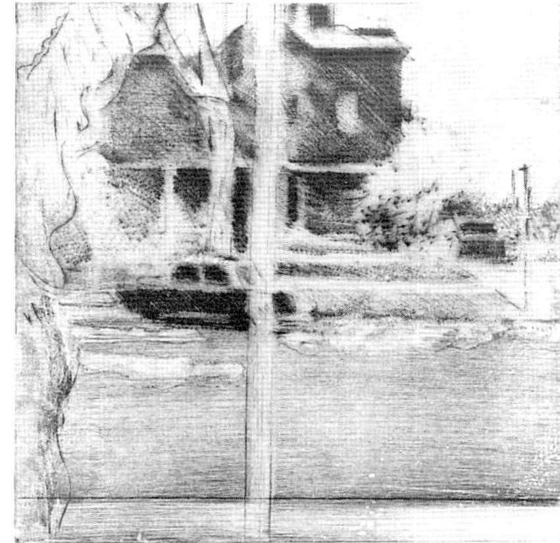

230

Plates/blocks 2 stones and 4 aluminum plates
Inks black, transparent blue, medium blue, sienna, green, and gray
Image and sheet size 23½ × 38 in. (59.7 × 96.5 cm)
Reference Mazur L-49

229
Tulip Pair, 1979–80
Medium monoprint with etching, aquatint, and monotype
Edition size variant edition of 10
Paper Arches
Plates/blocks 2 zinc plates
Inks green-black
Image size 23¾ × 35⅜ in. (60.3 × 89.9 cm)
Sheet size 31½ × 43½ in. (80.0 × 110.5 cm)
Reference Mazur L-58

230
Next Door, 1980
Medium monoprint with drypoint and monotype
Edition size 35
Paper white wove
Printed by the artist; letterpress by Copper Canyon Press, Port Townsend, Wash.
Published by Copper Canyon Press
Plates/blocks 1 magnesium plate
Inks black (drypoint) and violet (monotype)
Image size 9 × 8⅞ in. (22.9 × 22.6 cm)

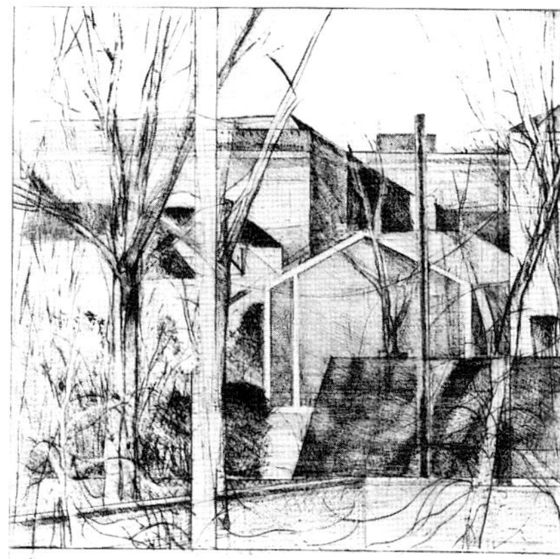

231

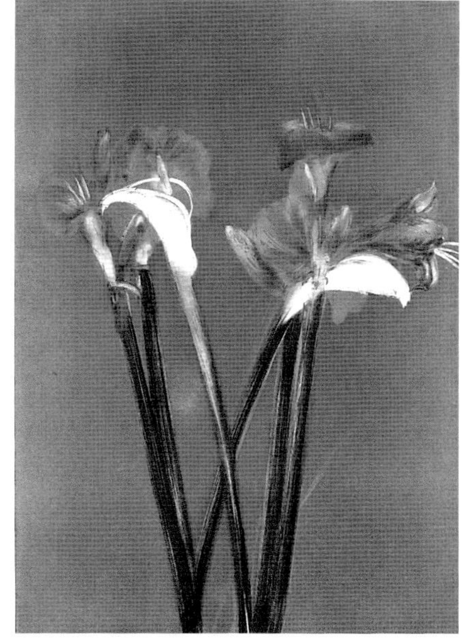

232

Sheet size 15 × 18¼ in. (38.1 × 46.3 cm)
Remarks part of a broadside with the poem "Next Door" by Gail Mazur printed by letterpress in black ink
Reference Mazur S-42

231
Carriage House, 1981
Medium drypoint with electric engraving tool
Edition size not editioned; 4–5 impressions printed
Paper white wove
Plates/blocks 1 aluminum plate
Inks black with *à la poupée* inking
Image size 17¾ × 16⅝ in. (45.1 × 42.2 cm)
Sheet size 31⅜ × 23½ in. (79.7 × 59.7 cm)
Remarks the view from the artist's Cambridge home, looking out over the backyard and the artist's carriage house studio; a preliminary to the *Carriage House* series of 1983–84

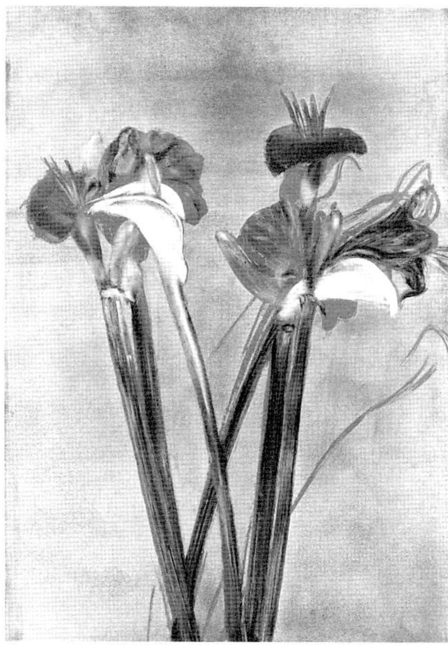

233

232
Amaryllis-Calla I, 1982
Medium monoprint with etching, aquatint, and monotype
Edition size variant edition of 20
Paper Arches
Printed by Robert Townsend and the artist at the artist's studio
Published by Pace Editions, New York
Plates/blocks 1 copper plate
Inks multiple colors
Image size 35½ × 24 in. (90.2 × 61.0 cm)
Sheet size 43 × 31½ in. (109.2 × 80.0 cm)
Remarks the artist first etched the copper plate, masking certain areas that would not etch in the acid and would remain smooth metal; after etching, the intaglio plate was inked in one color and wiped so that the smooth, unworked metal areas were exposed and clean; the artist then painted freely with multiple colors of ink in these areas, creating monotype images within the etched plate; the plate was then printed
Reference Mazur L-35

233
Amaryllis-Calla II, 1982
Medium monoprint with etching, aquatint, and monotype
Edition size variant edition of 20
Paper Arches
Printed by Robert Townsend and the artist at the artist's studio
Published by Pace Editions, New York
Plates/blocks 1 copper plate
Inks multiple colors
Image size 35½ × 24 in. (90.2 × 61.0 cm)
Sheet size 43⅜ × 31⅝ in. (110.2 × 80.3 cm)
Remarks see *Amaryllis-Calla I* (no. 232)
Reference Mazur L-36

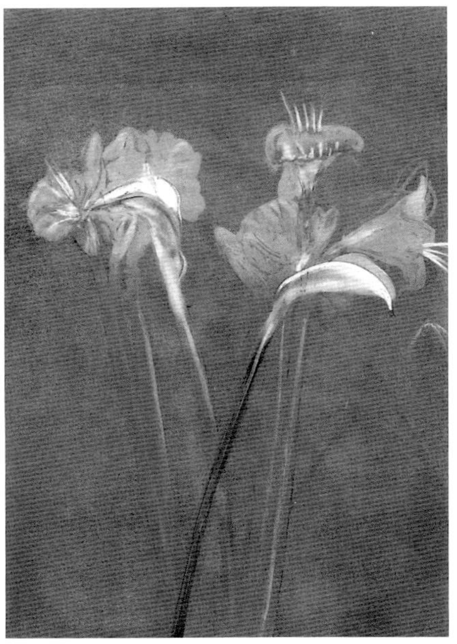

234

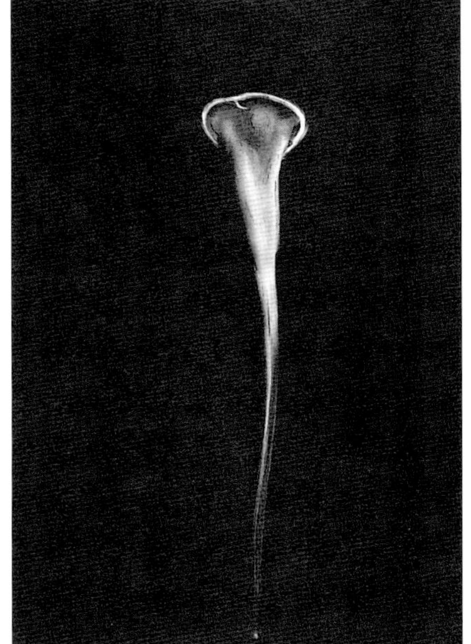
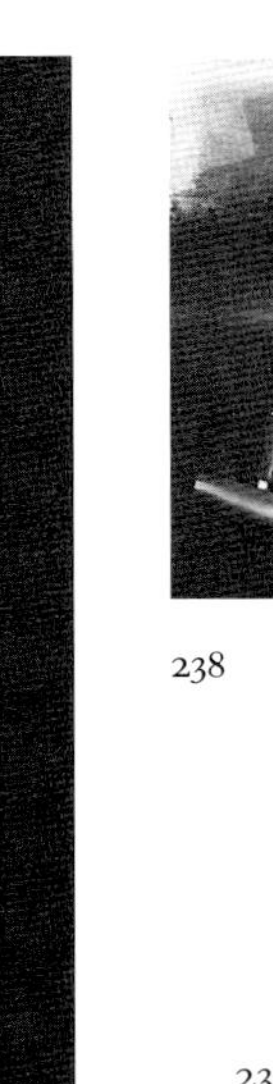

236

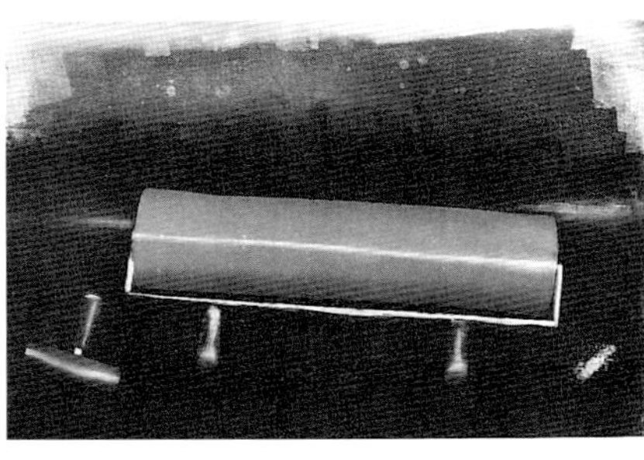

238

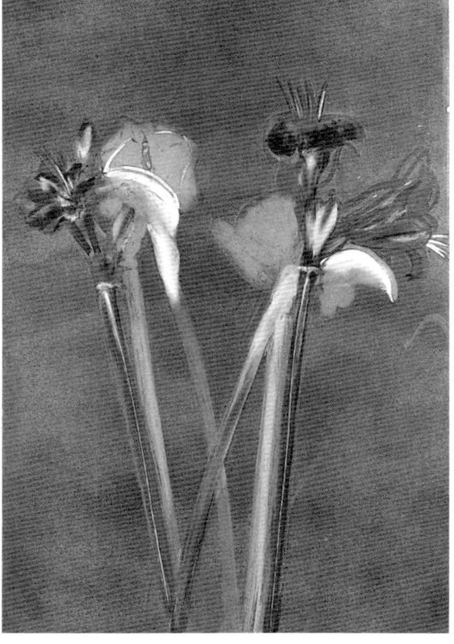

235

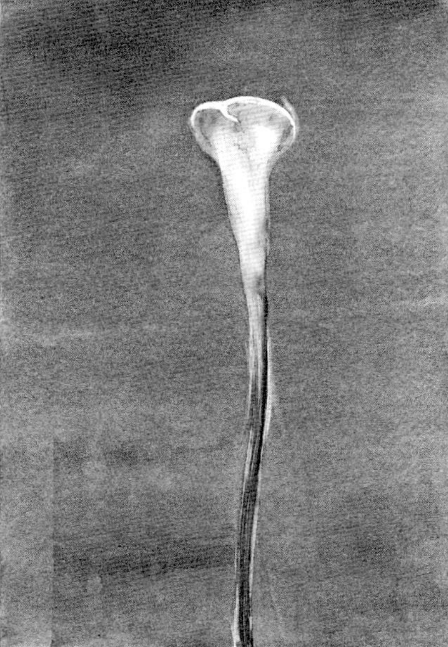

237

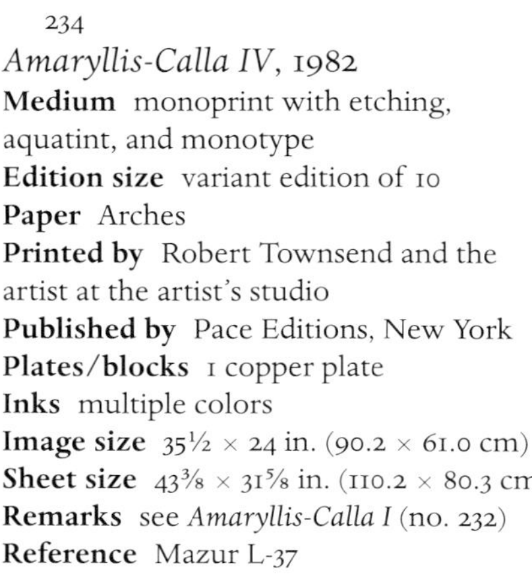

234
Amaryllis-Calla IV, 1982
Medium monoprint with etching, aquatint, and monotype
Edition size variant edition of 10
Paper Arches
Printed by Robert Townsend and the artist at the artist's studio
Published by Pace Editions, New York
Plates/blocks 1 copper plate
Inks multiple colors
Image size 35½ × 24 in. (90.2 × 61.0 cm)
Sheet size 43⅜ × 31⅝ in. (110.2 × 80.3 cm)
Remarks see *Amaryllis-Calla I* (no. 232)
Reference Mazur L-37

235
Amaryllis-Calla V, 1982
Medium monoprint with etching, aquatint, and monotype
Edition size variant edition of 10
Paper Arches
Printed by Robert Townsend and the artist at the artist's studio
Published by Pace Editions, New York
Plates/blocks 1 copper plate
Inks multiple colors
Image size 35½ × 24 in. (90.2 × 60.6 cm)
Sheet size 43⅞ × 31½ in. (111.5 × 80.0 cm)
Remarks see *Amaryllis-Calla I* (no. 232)
Reference Mazur L-38

236
Calla I, 1982
Medium monoprint with etching, aquatint, and monotype
Edition size variant edition of 25
Paper Arches
Printed by Robert Townsend and the artist at the artist's studio
Published by Pace Editions, New York
Plates/blocks 1 copper plate
Inks multiple colors
Image size 35½ × 23¾ in. (90.2 × 60.3 cm)
Sheet size 45⅛ × 31¾ in. (114.6 × 80.7 cm)
Remarks see *Amaryllis-Calla I* (no. 232)
Reference Mazur L-41

237
Calla II, 1982
Medium monoprint with etching, aquatint, and monotype
Edition size variant edition of 25
Paper Arches
Printed by Robert Townsend and the artist at the artist's studio
Published by Pace Editions, New York
Plates/blocks 1 copper plate
Inks multiple colors
Image size 35⅝ × 23¾ in. (90.5 × 60.3 cm)
Sheet size 43⅞ × 31½ in. (111.5 × 80.0 cm)
Remarks see *Amaryllis-Calla I* (no. 232)
Reference Mazur L-43

238
Red Roller, 1982
Medium monoprint with etching, aquatint, and monotype
Edition size variant edition of 20
Paper Arches
Printed by Robert Townsend and the artist at the artist's studio
Published by Pace Editions, New York
Plates/blocks 1 copper plate
Inks black with red and green monotyping
Image size 23¾ × 35⅜ in. (60.3 × 89.9 cm)
Sheet size 31¼ × 43¼ in. (79.4 × 109.9 cm)
Remarks see *Amaryllis-Calla I* (no. 232)
Reference Mazur L-44

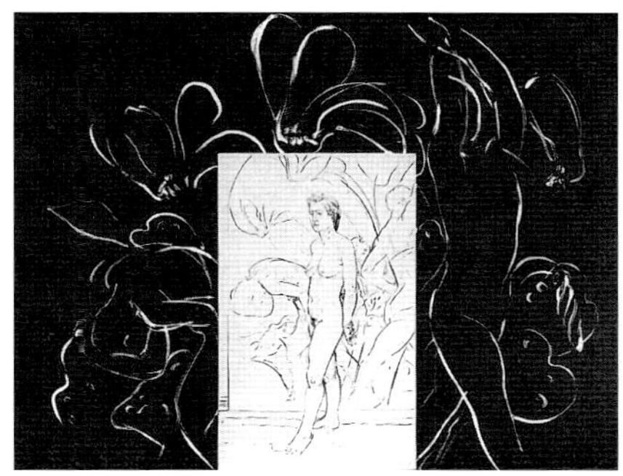

239

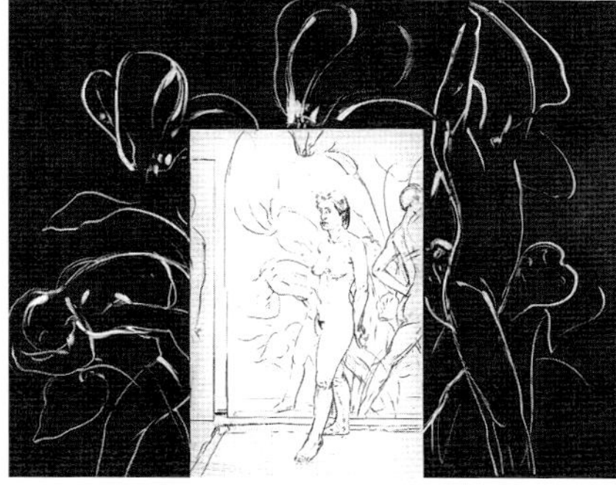

241

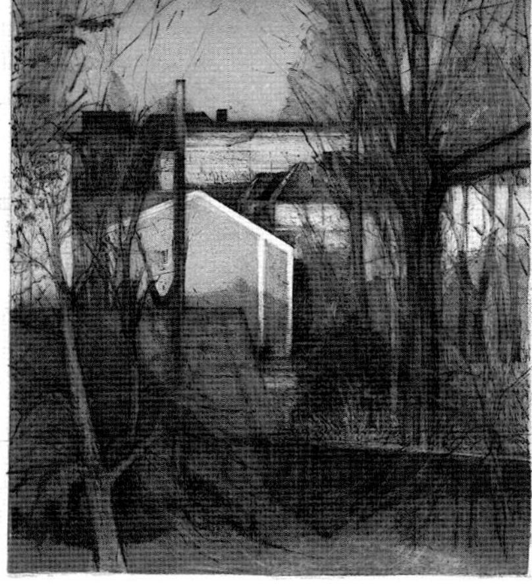

243

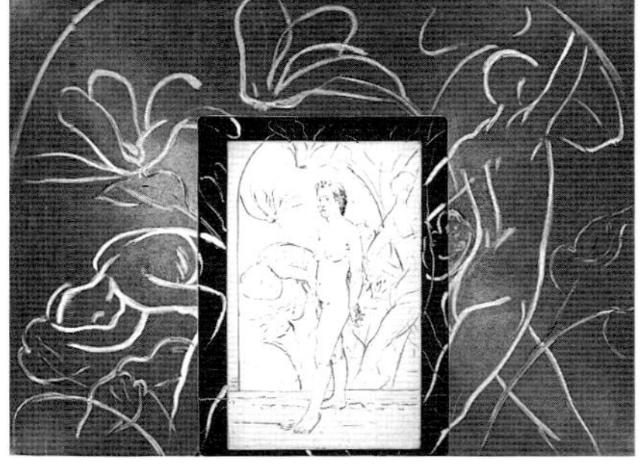

240

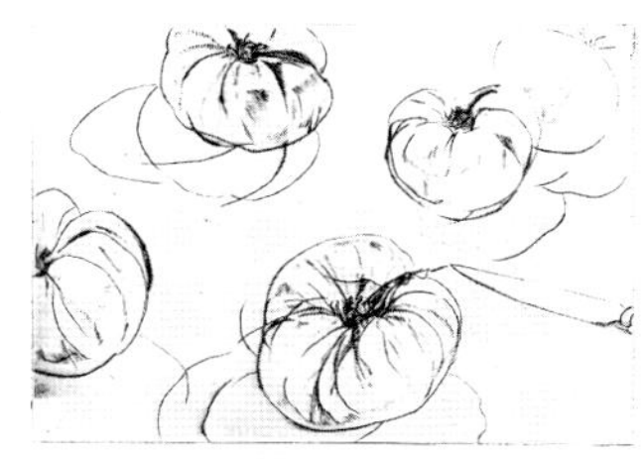

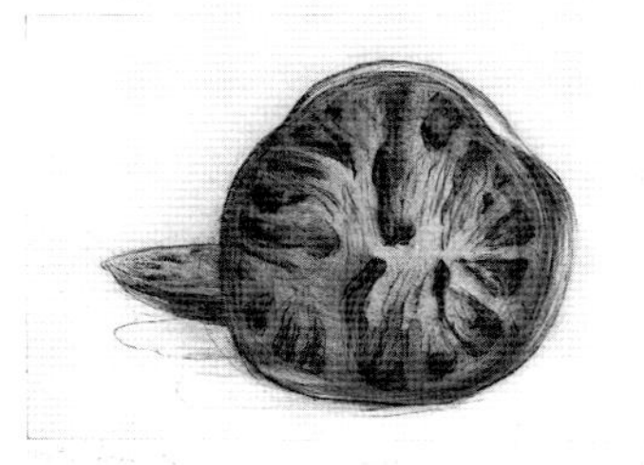

242

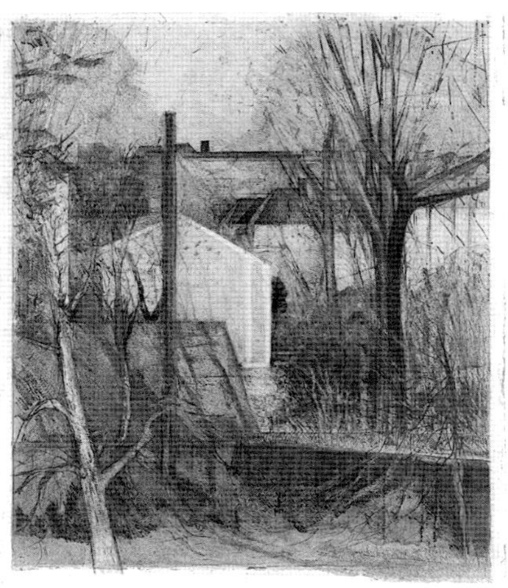

244

239
The Dancer or the Dance, 1983
Medium lithograph and drypoint
Edition size 25
Paper white wove
Printed by Judith Solodkin at Solo Press, Inc , New York, and Robert Townsend at R. E. Townsend Studio, Georgetown, Mass.
Plates/blocks 1 copper plate and 2 magnesium plates
Inks black
Image and sheet size 34¼ × 44⅜ in. (87.0 × 112.7 cm)
Reference Mazur L-45

240
The Dancer or the Dance (Variation 2), 1983
Medium monoprint with drypoint and monotype
Edition size variant edition of 6
Paper Arches roll
Plates/blocks 2 copper plates and 1 magnesium plate
Inks brown, sepia, black, and blue-black
Image and sheet size 34¼ × 44⅜ in. (87.0 × 112.7 cm)
Reference Mazur L-45a

241
The Dancer or the Dance, 1983
Medium monoprint with aquatint, drypoint, and monotype
Edition size not editioned; 2–5 variant impressions printed
Paper Rives BFK
Plates/blocks 1 magnesium plate and 1 aluminum plate
Inks black, blue, brown, and green
Image size 35⅝ × 47¾ in. (90.5 × 121.3 cm)
Sheet size 42½ × 53⅞ in. (108.0 × 136.9 cm)
Reference Mazur X-2

242
The Tomatoes (diptych), 1983
Medium monoprint with drypoint and monotype
Edition size 6
Paper Rives BFK
Plates/blocks 1 copper plate and 1 magnesium plate
Inks red and black
Image and sheet size 42⅜ × 30¼ in. (107.6 × 76.9 cm)
Reference Mazur L-59

243
Carriage House I (Late Winter), 1983
Medium etching and aquatint
Edition size 25
Paper Arches
Printed by Robert Townsend at R. E. Townsend Studio, Georgetown, Mass.
Plates/blocks 3 copper plates
Inks sienna, blue, and green
Image size 21⅞ × 17¾ in. (55.2 × 45.1 cm)
Sheet size 30½ × 26¼ in. (77.5 × 66.7 cm)
Reference Mazur L-50

244
Carriage House II (Spring), 1983–84
Medium etching and aquatint
Edition size 25
Paper Arches
Printed by Robert Townsend at R. E. Townsend Studio, Georgetown, Mass.
Plates/blocks 3 copper plates
Inks sienna, blue, and green
Image size 20⅞ × 17¾ in. (53.0 × 45.1 cm)
Sheet size 30¼ × 26¼ in. (76.9 × 66.7 cm)
Remarks an unusual process; using the same plates as for no. 243, each first printing was thrown away and three ghost plates were combined
Reference Mazur L-51

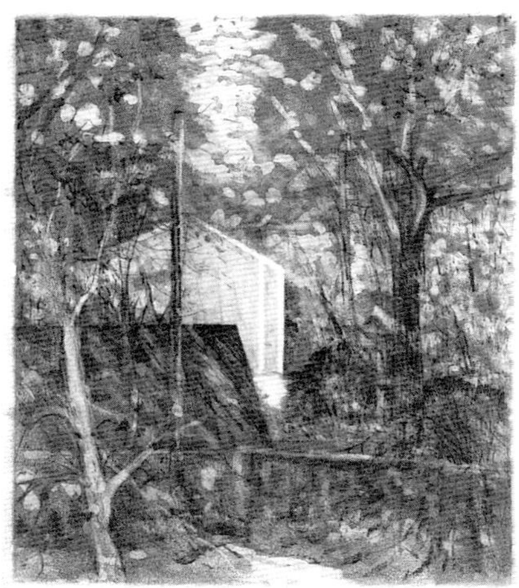

245

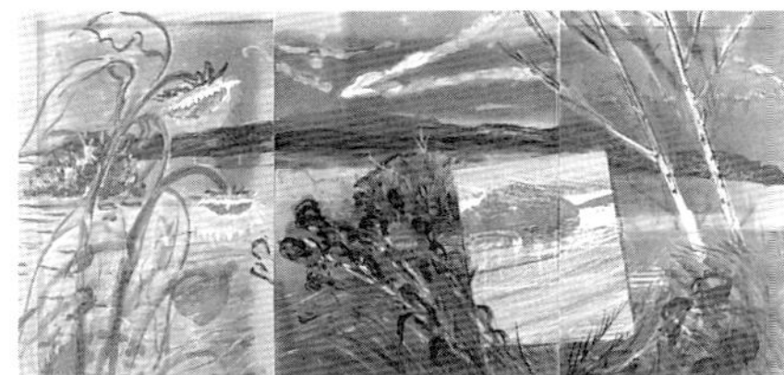

246

245
Carriage House III (Summer), 1984
Medium etching and aquatint
Edition size 25
Paper Arches
Printed by Robert Townsend at R. E. Townsend Studio, Georgetown, Mass.
Plates/blocks 3 copper plates
Inks Thalo blue, Thalo green, black, and transparent orange
Image size $20\frac{7}{8} \times 17\frac{3}{4}$ in. (53.0×45.1 cm)
Sheet size $30\frac{1}{4} \times 26\frac{1}{4}$ in. (76.9×66.7 cm)
Remarks uses the same plates, reworked, from *Carriage House I* and *Carriage House II* (nos. 243 and 244)
Reference Mazur L-51a

246
Wakeby Night (triptych), 1984
Medium lithograph, wood relief, and monotype with *chine collé*
Edition size 35 plus 8 artist's proofs
Paper Arches with Sekishu *chine collé*
Printed by Judith Solodkin, Toshiyasu Shinozaki, Arnold Samet, and Tim Regester at Solo Press, Inc., New York
Published by Solo Press, Inc., and Joe Fawbush Editions, New York
Plates/blocks 6 aluminum plates and 1 wood block
Inks light blue, green, white, blue, dark blue, red, orange, and blended color roller
Image and sheet size (left) $30\frac{1}{8} \times 20\frac{3}{8}$ in. (76.9×51.8 cm)
Image and sheet size (center) $30\frac{1}{8} \times 22\frac{3}{8}$ in. (76.6×56.8 cm)

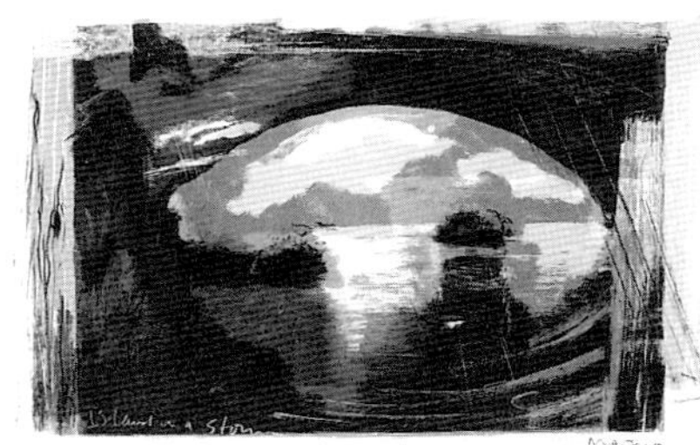

247

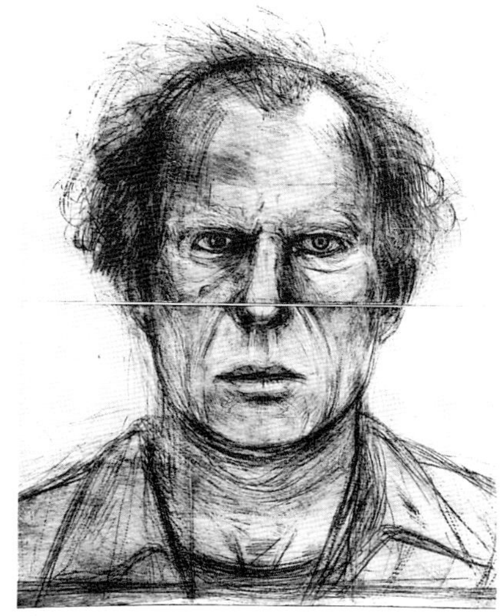

248

Image and sheet size (right) $30 \times 18\frac{1}{8}$ in. (76.2×46.1 cm)
Reference Mazur M-90

247
Island in a Storm, 1985
Medium screenprint
Edition size 100
Paper Arches 88
Printed by AM Editions, Boston
Plates/blocks 8 screens
Inks light blue, medium blue, dark aqua, gray, medium brown, dark brown, light brown, and light yellow-green
Image and sheet size $22\frac{5}{8} \times 30\frac{1}{4}$ in. (57.5×76.9 cm)
Remarks used for a benefit print and the poster for the traveling exhibition *Art for a Nuclear Weapons Freeze*
Reference Mazur M-88

248
Self-Portrait with Cut Plates, 1985
Medium drypoint monoprints using roulette and electric engraving tool
Edition size variant edition of 23
Paper Rives BFK gray
Plates/blocks 2 aluminum plates
Inks black

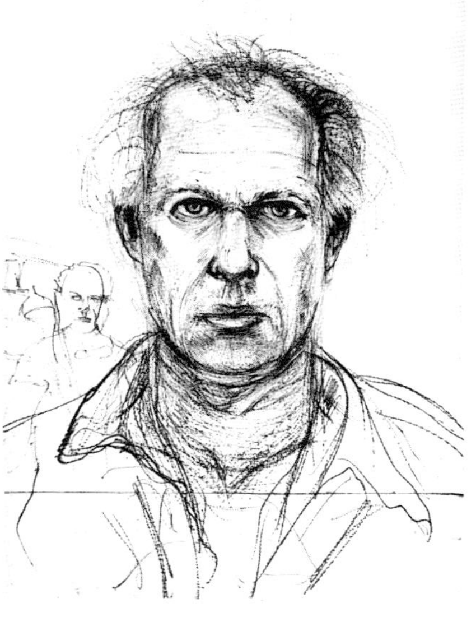

249

Image and sheet size $44\frac{3}{8} \times 30\frac{1}{8}$ in. (112.7×76.6 cm)
Reference Mazur L-57a

249
Self-Portrait Large Copper, 1985
Medium drypoint with electric engraving tool
Edition size not editioned; 2–3 proofs of each state printed
Paper Rives BFK
Plates/blocks 1 copper plate
Inks brown and black with *à la poupée* inking
Image and sheet size $40\frac{1}{8} \times 30\frac{1}{4}$ in. (112.1×76.9 cm)
Remarks the image was developed in five states
Reference Mazur L-57

250
Self-Portrait with Cut Plates, 1985
Medium drypoint monoprint using roulette and electric engraving tool
Edition size variant edition of 4
Paper Rives BFK
Plates/blocks 5 aluminum plates
Inks black and sepia
Image and sheet size $45\frac{1}{8} \times 34\frac{1}{2}$ in. (114.6×87.6 cm)
Reference Mazur L-57b

251
Wakeby Day (triptych), 1986
Medium lithograph, wood relief, and monotype with *chine collé*
Edition size 50 plus 14 artist's proofs
Paper Arches with Sekishu *chine collé*
Printed by Judith Solodkin, Toshiyasu Shinozaki, Dan Stack, David Belzyaki, and Brian Finley at Solo Press, Inc., New York
Published by Solo Press, Inc., and Joe Fawbush Editions, New York

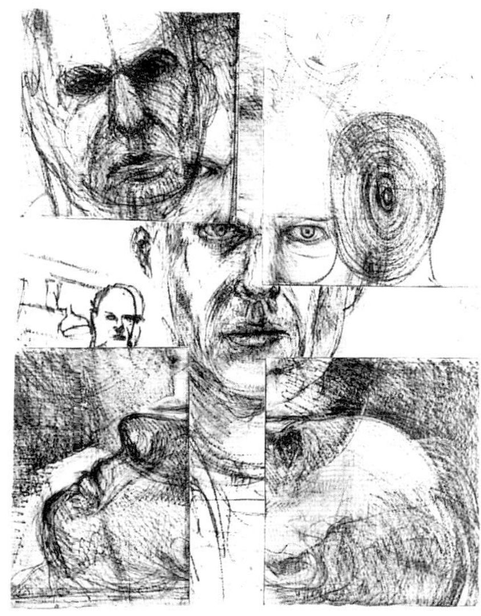

250

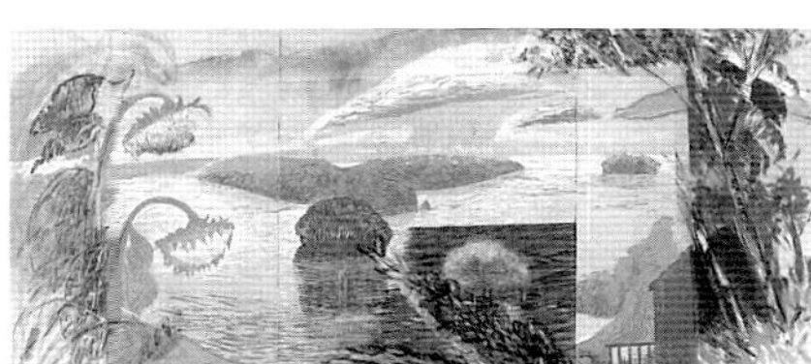

251

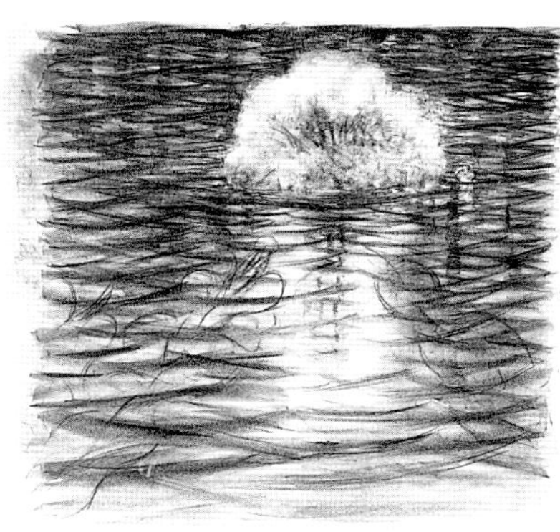

252

Plates/blocks 8 aluminum plates, 1 stone, and 4 wood blocks
Inks green, black, ultramarine, dark green, light yellow, light blue, medium blue, red, and dark blue
Image and sheet size (left) 30 × 20⅜ in. (76.2 × 51.8 cm)
Image and sheet size (center) 30 × 22¼ in. (76.2 × 56.5 cm)
Image and sheet size (right) 30⅜ × 18⅛ in. (77.2 × 46.1 cm)
Reference Mazur M-89

252
Wakeby Island, 1986
Medium lithograph
Edition size 20 plus 1 artist's proof
Paper German Etching
Printed by Toshiyasu Shinozaki under

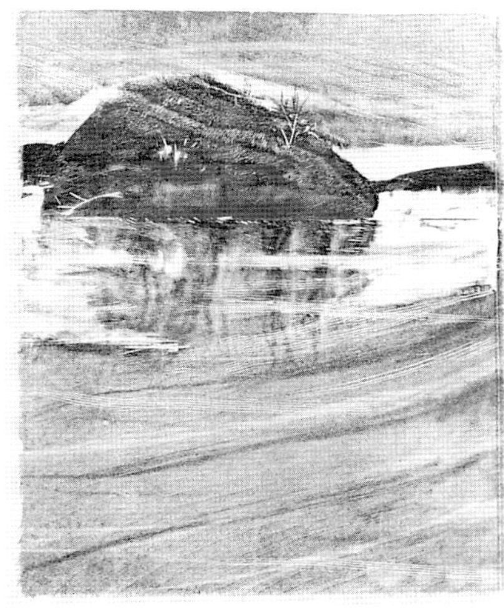

253

254

the supervision of Judith Solodkin at Solo Press, Inc., New York
Published by Solo Press, Inc., New York
Plates/blocks 1 stone
Inks black
Image and sheet size 27¼ × 22½ in. (69.2 × 57.2 cm)
Remarks related to the *Wakeby Day/ Wakeby Night* project; part of the edition was hand-colored by the artist
Reference Mazur M-86

253
Wakeby Island I, 1986
Medium wood relief with *chine collé*
Edition size 15
Paper Torinoko with Sekishu *chine collé*
Printed by Judith Solodkin and the artist at Solo Press, Inc., New York
Published by Solo Press, Inc., New York
Plates/blocks 2 wood blocks
Inks beige and blue
Image size 15 × 12 in. (38.1 × 30.5 cm)
Sheet size 25 × 20 in. (63.5 × 50.8 cm)
Remarks the same image as *Wakeby Island II* (no. 254) except for selective ink removal on the blue block by the artist

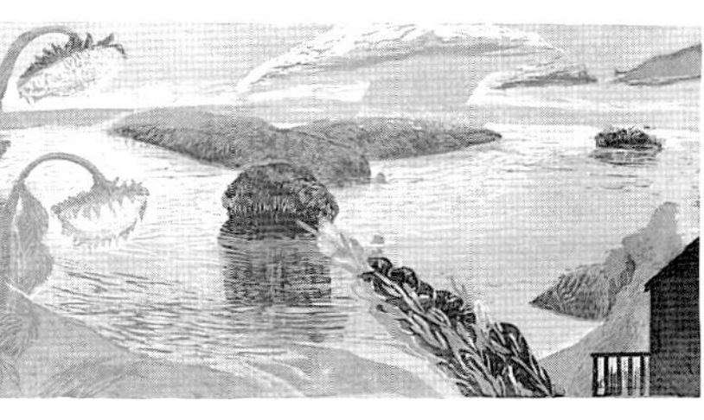

255

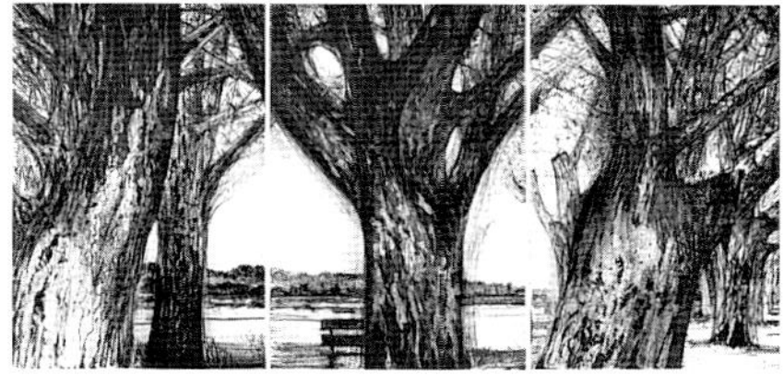

256

254
Wakeby Island II, 1986
Medium wood relief with *chine collé*
Edition size 15
Paper Torinoko with Sekishu *chine collé*
Printed by Judith Solodkin and the artist at Solo Press, Inc., New York
Published by Solo Press, Inc., New York
Plates/blocks 2 wood blocks
Inks beige and blue
Image size 15 × 12 in. (38.1 × 30.5 cm)
Sheet size 25 × 20 in. (63.5 × 50.8 cm)
Remarks the same image as *Wakeby Island I* (no. 253) except for selective ink removal on the blue block by the artist

255
Wakeby Rain, 1986
Medium wood relief
Edition size 10
Paper Arches buff with Sekishu white collage
Printed by Toshiyasu Shinozaki under the supervision of Judith Solodkin at Solo Press, Inc., New York
Published by Solo Press, Inc., New York
Plates/blocks 4 wood blocks
Inks light yellow, light blue, medium blue, red, dark blue, and green
Image size 24 × 44 in. (61.0 × 111.8 cm)
Sheet size 32 × 51 in. (81.3 × 129.5 cm)

256
Sycamores 1 (triptych), 1986
Medium etching
Edition size not editioned; 3 impressions printed
Paper Arches
Printed by Robert Townsend at R. E. Townsend Studio, Georgetown, Mass.
Plates/blocks 3 copper plates
Inks black
Image and sheet size 35½ × 71¼ in. (90.2 × 181.0 cm) overall
Reference Mazur X-4

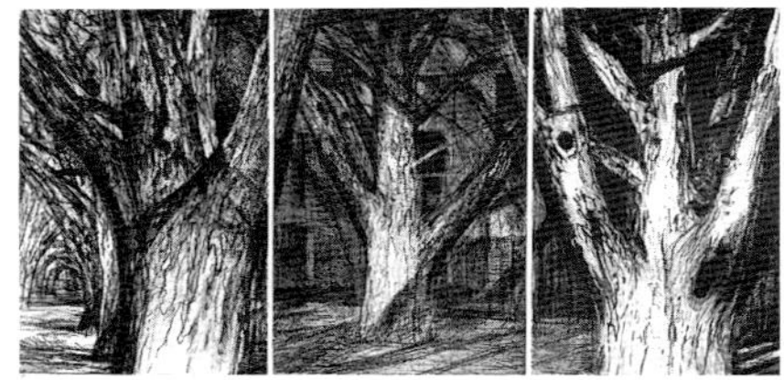

257

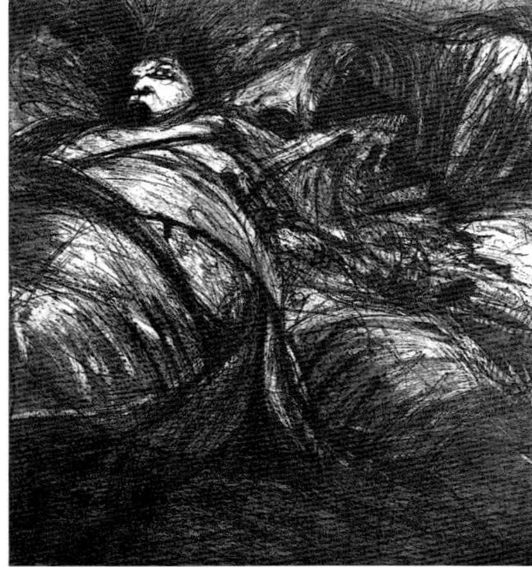

258

257
Sycamores 2 (triptych), 1986
Medium etching
Edition size not editioned; 3 impressions printed
Paper Arches
Printed by Robert Townsend at R. E. Townsend Studio, Georgetown, Mass.
Plates/blocks 3 copper plates
Inks black
Image and sheet size 35½ × 71¼ in. (90.2 × 181.0 cm) overall
Reference Mazur X-5

258
Nightmare (II), 1987
Medium etching and aquatint with electric engraving tool
Edition size not editioned; 3–4 impressions printed
Paper various papers
Printed by Robert Townsend at R. E. Townsend Studio, Georgetown, Mass.
Plates/blocks 1 copper plate
Inks black
Image size 26¾ × 23⅞ in. (68.0 × 60.6 cm)
Sheet size varies
Remarks the artist recreated the lost plate from the 1959 edition (no. 71) in a larger format
Reference Mazur L-52

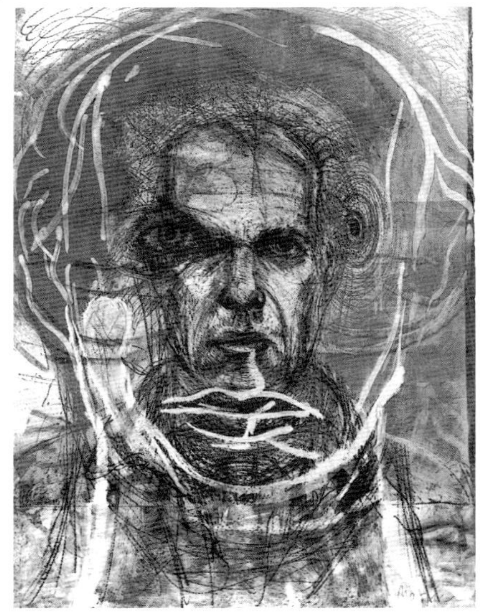

259

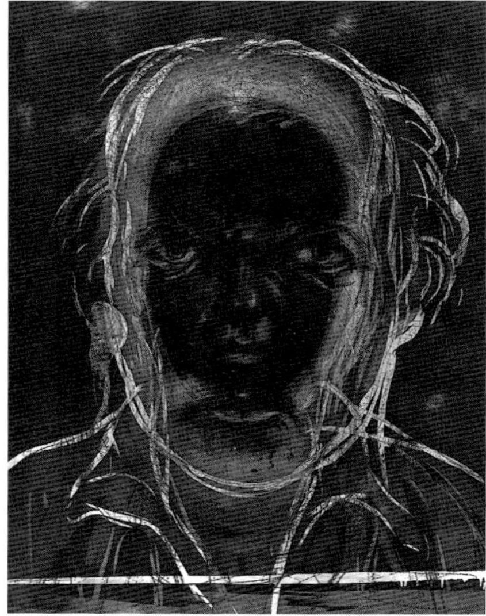

260

259
The Unknown Region (Self-Portrait), 1987
Medium monoprint with etching and monotype
Edition size variant edition of 10
Paper Rives BFK
Plates/blocks 1 copper plate
Inks black
Image and sheet size 47½ × 35 in. (120.7 × 88.9 cm)

260
The Unknown Region (Self-Portrait), 1987
Medium aquatint and drypoint
Edition size 10
Paper Rives BFK
Printed by Robert Townsend at R. E. Townsend Studio, Georgetown, Mass.; plate preparation by the artist

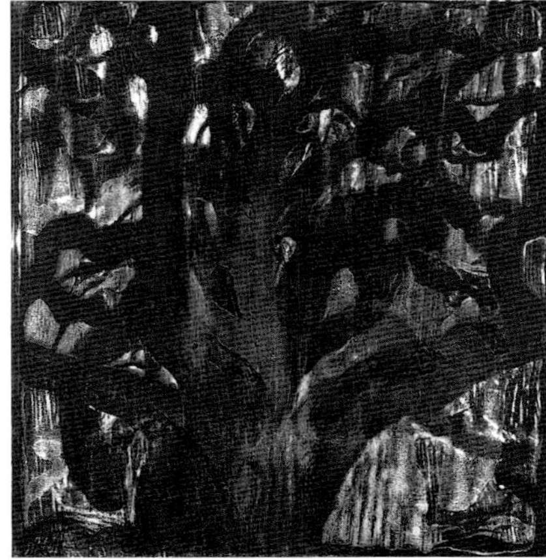

261

Plates/blocks 1 copper plate
Inks black
Image size 47⅞ × 35¾ in. (121.6 × 90.8 cm)
Sheet size 52½ × 39¾ in. (133.4 × 101.0 cm)
Reference Mazur X-1

261
Texas Tree, 1988
Medium monoprint with transfer wood relief and metal plate offset
Edition size variant edition of 6
Paper Arches
Plates/blocks 1 wood block and 1 magnesium plate
Inks black
Image size 25⅜ × 23¾ in. (64.5 × 60.3 cm)
Sheet size 35 × 31½ in. (88.9 × 80.0 cm)
Remarks the artist inked the wood block and ran it through the press with a metal plate that he then printed
Reference Mazur L-66

262
Mother's Boy '41 and '89 (diptych), 1989
Medium drypoint (left); drypoint with electric engraving tool (right)
Edition size 8
Paper white wove
Printed by Anne Clarke at the artist's studio
Plates/blocks 1 magnesium plate and 1 copper plate (each)
Inks black and brown with *à la poupée* inking
Image size (left) 15⅜ × 10⅞ in. (39.1 × 27.7 cm)
Image size (right) 23⅞ × 21⅝ in. (60.6 × 54.9 cm)
Sheet size (left) 31½ × 26⅞ in. (80.0 × 68.3 cm)
Sheet size (right) 31½ × 27¼ in. (80.0 × 69.2 cm)
Remarks image for left side taken from a childhood photograph
Reference Mazur L-78

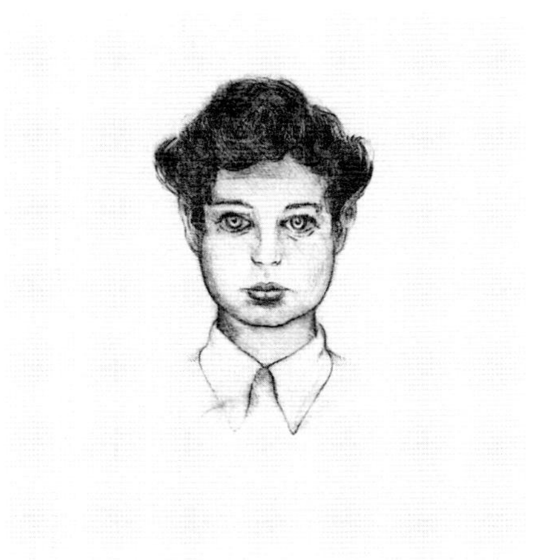

262 (left)

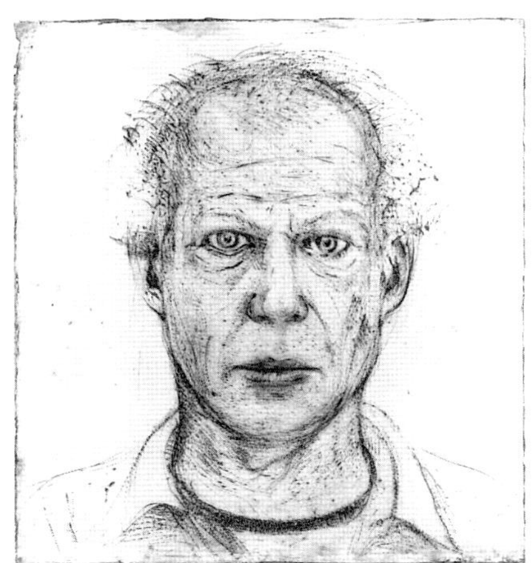

262 (right)

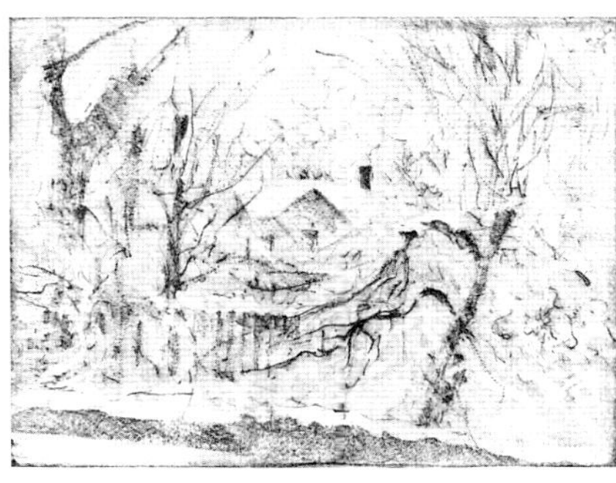

264

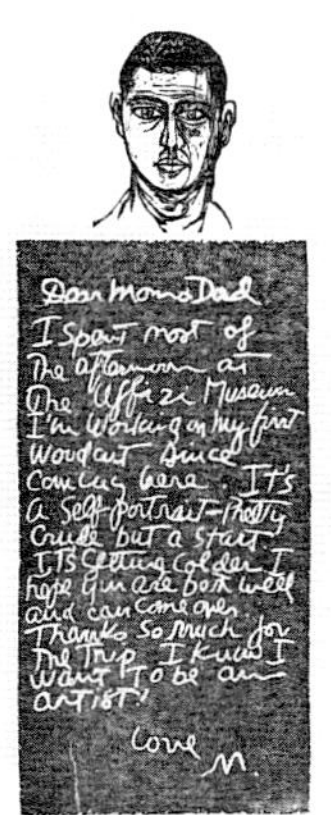

263 (left)

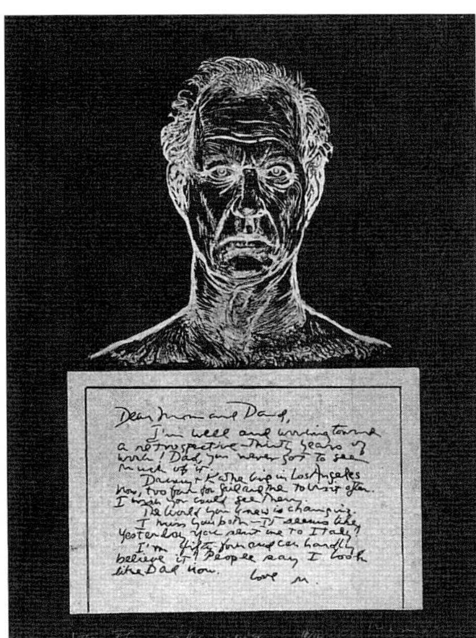

263 (right)

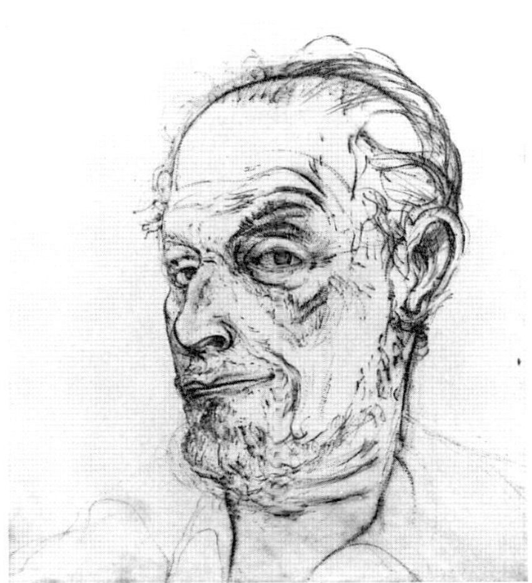

265

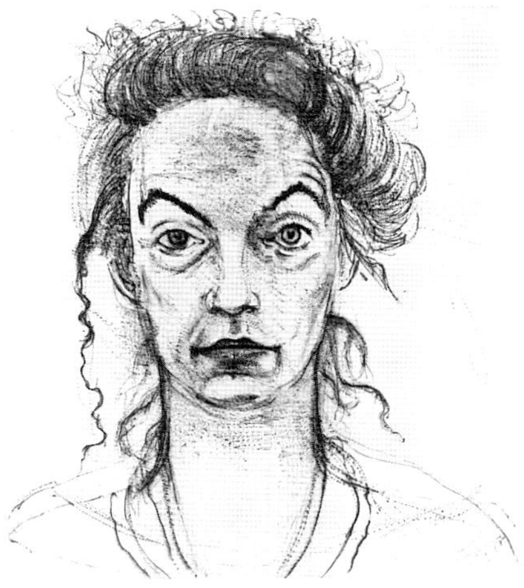

266

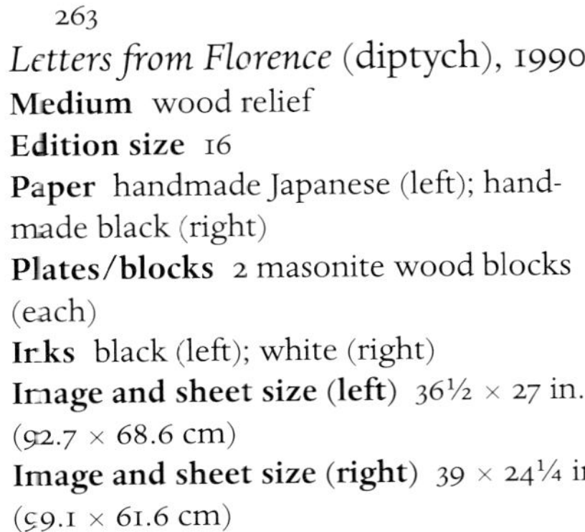

263

Letters from Florence (diptych), 1990
Medium wood relief
Edition size 16
Paper handmade Japanese (left); handmade black (right)
Plates/blocks 2 masonite wood blocks (each)
Inks black (left); white (right)
Image and sheet size (left) 36½ × 27 in. (92.7 × 68.6 cm)
Image and sheet size (right) 39 × 24¼ in. (99.1 × 61.6 cm)
Reference Mazur L-77

264

Yard — Winter, 1990
Medium etching
Edition size 10
Paper white wove
Plates/blocks 1 copper plate
Inks black
Image size 6⅛ × 8 in. (15.6 × 20.3 cm)
Sheet size 16 × 20 in. (40.7 × 50.8 cm)
Reference Mazur S-43

265

Portrait of Harold Tovish, 1990
Medium engraving with electric engraving tool
Edition size 10
Paper Rives tan
Plates/blocks 1 copper plate
Inks black
Image size 17⅝ × 15¾ in. (44.8 × 40.0 cm)
Sheet size 25¼ × 22⅜ in. (64.1 × 56.8 cm)
Reference Mazur M-91

266

Portrait of Anne Clarke, 1990
Medium engraving with electric engraving tool and hand coloring
Edition size 10
Paper white wove
Plates/blocks 1 copper plate
Inks brown-black
Image size 17¾ × 15⅝ in. (45.1 × 39.7 cm)
Sheet size 27¾ × 23½ in. (70.5 × 59.7 cm)
Reference Mazur M-92

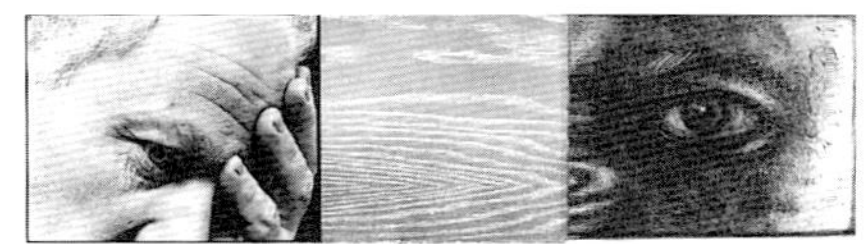

267

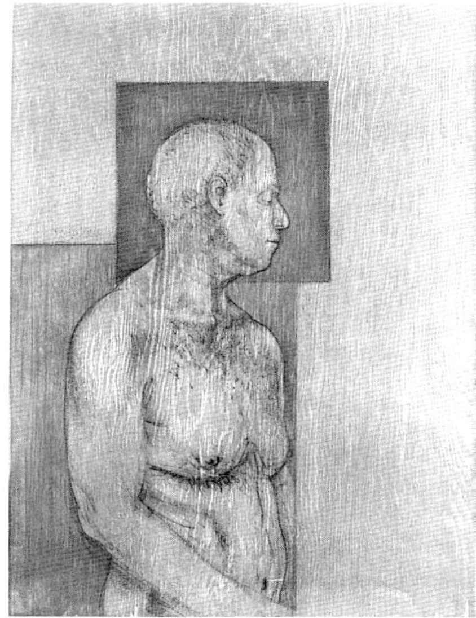

268

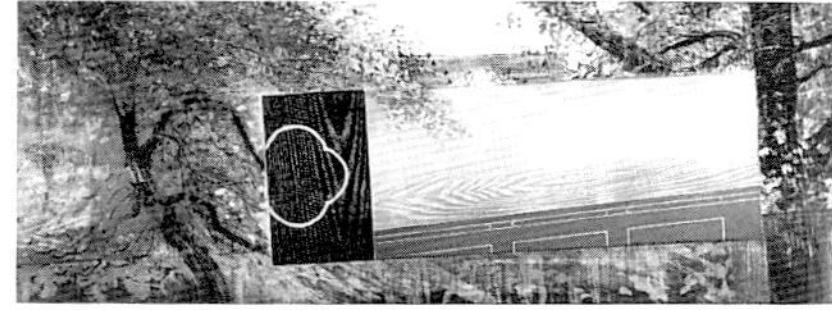

269

267
Portrait (collaboration with photographer Nicholas Nixon), 1990
Medium etching with wood relief, *chine collé,* and collaged photograph
Edition size 20
Paper Rives gray with handmade Japanese *chine collé*
Printed by Nicholas Nixon and the artist; collage by Anne Clarke
Plates/blocks 1 zinc plate and 1 wood block
Inks green and black
Image size 7¾ × 28 in. (19.7 × 71.2 cm)
Sheet size 20 × 40 in. (50.8 × 101.6 cm)
Reference Mazur L-61

268
Self-Portrait (Wood Grain), 1990
Medium etching and drypoint with electric engraving tool and wood relief

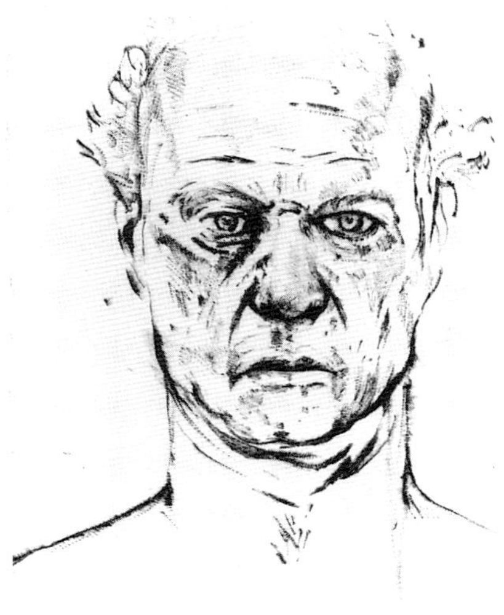

270

Edition size not editioned; 2–3 impressions printed
Paper Rives BFK
Plates/blocks 1 copper plate and 1 wood block
Inks sepia and ocher
Image size 19⅞ × 14½ in. (50.5 × 36.8 cm)
Sheet size 27⅝ × 21¼ in. (70.2 × 54.0 cm)
Reference Mazur M-93

269
Two Ideas about a Garden, 1990
Medium etching and aquatint with wood relief *chine collé*
Edition size 50
Paper Arches white with handmade Japanese *chine collé*
Printed by Robert Townsend at R. E. Townsend Studio, Georgetown, Mass.; inset printed by the artist
Published by Mary Ryan Gallery, New York
Plates/blocks 2 copper plates and 1 combination wood block
Inks multiple colors with *à la poupée* inking
Image size 21¾ × 57⅝ in. (55.2 × 146.4 cm)
Sheet size 27½ × 63 in. (69.9 × 160.0 cm)
Remarks two metal plates were printed in both relief and intaglio using multiple colors *à la poupée;* wood relief inset is of veneer plywoods and masonite pieced together and printed as one block
Reference Mazur X-3

270
Self-Portrait, 1991
Medium engraving with electric engraving tool
Edition size not editioned; 5 impressions of 1st state and 3 impressions of 2nd state printed

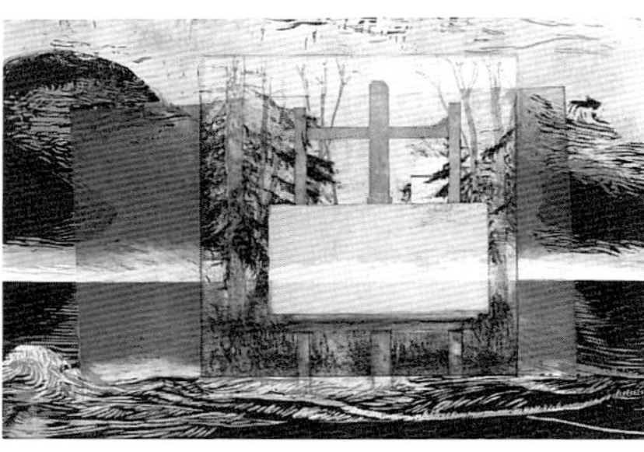

271

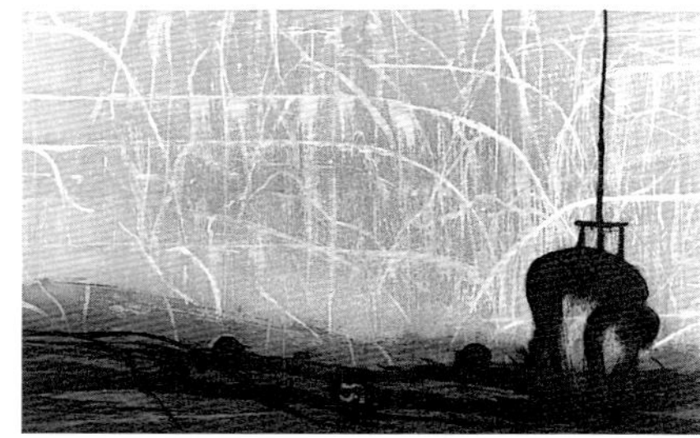

272

Paper Arches
Plates/blocks 1 copper plate
Inks black
Image size 15⅞ × 11⅞ in. (40.4 × 30.2 cm)
Sheet size 23 × 18⅛ in. (58.4 × 46.1 cm)
Reference Mazur M-118

271
Memory and Distance, 1992
Medium etching, aquatint, and wood relief
Edition size 50
Paper Arches white
Printed by Anne Clarke at the artist's studio
Published by Mary Ryan Gallery, New York
Plates/blocks 3 wood blocks and 3 copper plates
Inks aqua, blue, dark blue, green, brown, gray, and yellow
Image and sheet size 31⅝ × 47 in. (80.3 × 119.4 cm)
Reference Mazur L-63

272
Canto XXI (The Lawyers), from *The Inferno of Dante,* 1992
Medium etching and aquatint
Edition size not yet editioned; 6 impressions printed
Paper Rives BFK
Printed by Robert Townsend at R. E. Townsend Studio, Georgetown, Mass.; plate preparation by the artist
Plates/blocks 2 copper plates
Inks black and red

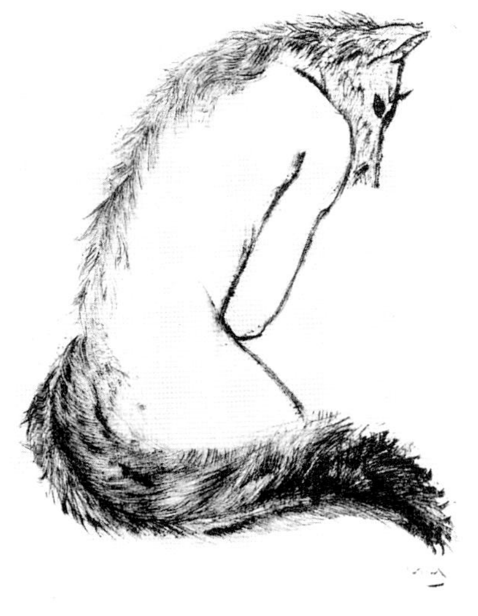

273

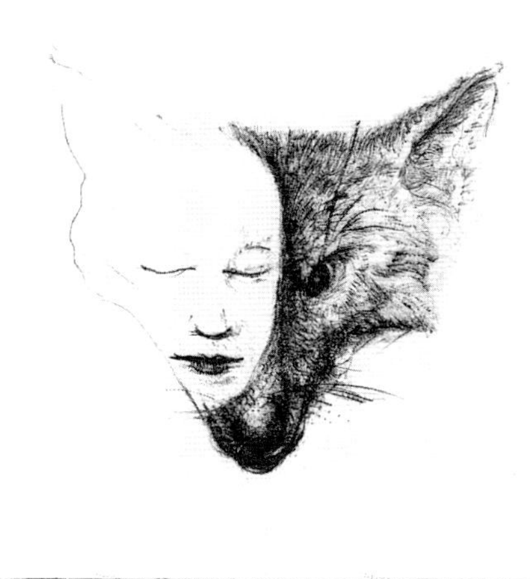

274

Image size 14 × 22¼ in. (35.6 × 56.5 cm)
Sheet size 22⅛ × 30⅝ in. (56.2 × 77.8 cm)
Remarks used on the dust jacket for Robert Pinsky, *The Inferno of Dante* (New York: Farrar, Straus and Giroux, 1994)
Reference Mazur M-117

273
Herna: A Story, by Melinda Marble (frontispiece), 1993
Medium drypoint
Edition size 50 (deluxe edition)
Paper Rives Heavyweight
Printed by Robert Townsend at R. E. Townsend Studio, Georgetown, Mass.; plate preparation by the artist
Published by The Bow and Arrow Press, Cambridge, Mass.

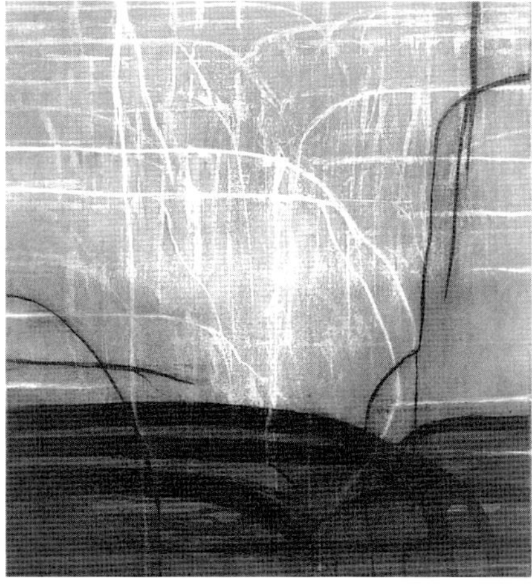

275

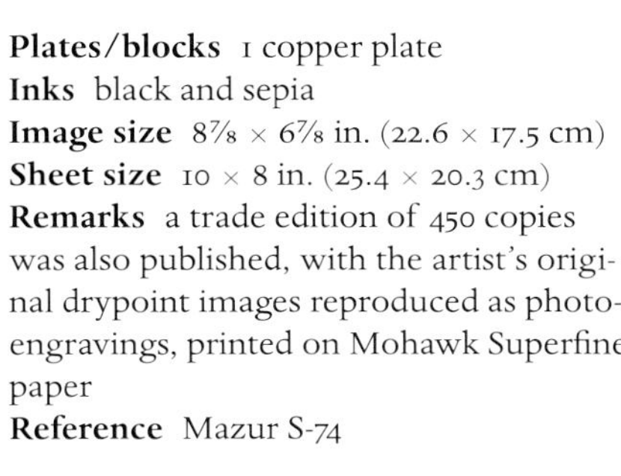

Plates/blocks 1 copper plate
Inks black and sepia
Image size 8⅞ × 6⅞ in. (22.6 × 17.5 cm)
Sheet size 10 × 8 in. (25.4 × 20.3 cm)
Remarks a trade edition of 450 copies was also published, with the artist's original drypoint images reproduced as photoengravings, printed on Mohawk Superfine paper
Reference Mazur S-74

274
Herna: A Story, by Melinda Marble (endpiece), 1993
Medium drypoint
Edition size 50 (deluxe edition)
Paper Rives Heavyweight
Printed by Robert Townsend at R. E. Townsend Studio, Georgetown, Mass.; plate preparation by the artist
Published by The Bow and Arrow Press, Cambridge, Mass.
Plates/blocks 1 copper plate
Inks black and sepia
Image size 8⅞ × 6⅞ in. (22.6 × 17.5 cm)
Sheet size 10 × 8 in. (25.4 × 20.3 cm)
Remarks a trade edition of 450 copies was also published, with the artist's original drypoint images reproduced as photoengravings, printed on Mohawk Superfine paper
Reference Mazur S-75

275
Inferno (CR), 1993–94
Medium etching
Edition size 15
Paper Arches
Plates/blocks 2 copper plates
Inks red and black
Image size 17¾ × 15⅜ in. (45.1 × 39.1 cm)
Sheet size 27¼ × 22¼ in. (69.2 × 56.5 cm)
Reference Mazur M-105

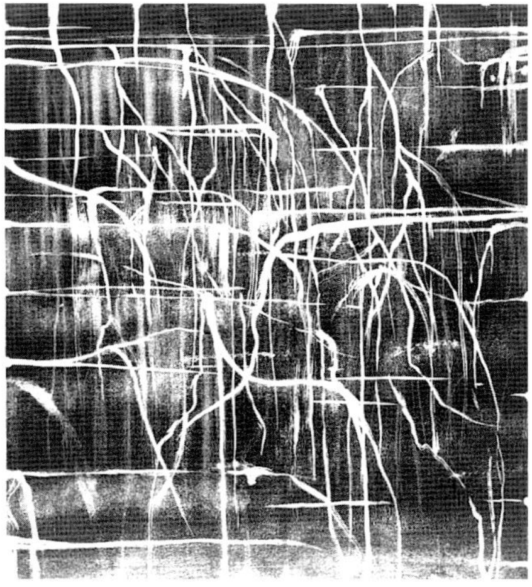

276

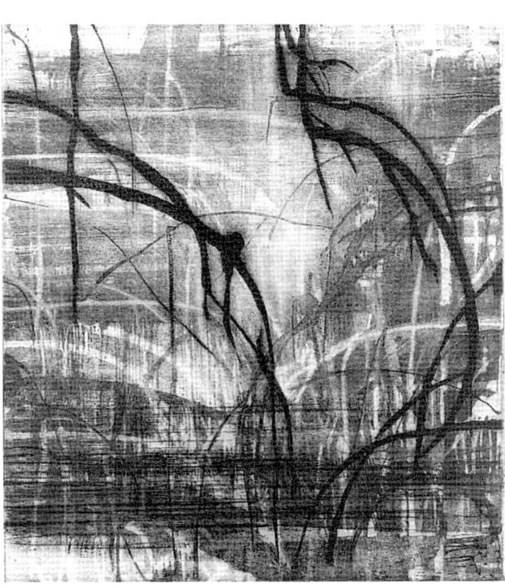

277

276
Ice Glen, 1993–94
Medium aquatint
Edition size 10
Paper Rives BFK white
Plates/blocks 1 copper plate
Inks black
Image size 17⅞ × 15½ in. (45.5 × 39.4 cm)
Sheet size 30 × 22½ in. (76.2 × 57.2 cm)
Reference Mazur M-104a

277
Black Branching, 1994
Medium etching and aquatint
Edition size 10
Paper Arches
Plates/blocks 1 copper plate
Inks black
Image size 19⅞ × 17 in. (50.5 × 43.2 cm)
Sheet size 27¾ × 23¾ in. (70.5 × 60.3 cm)
Reference Mazur M-106

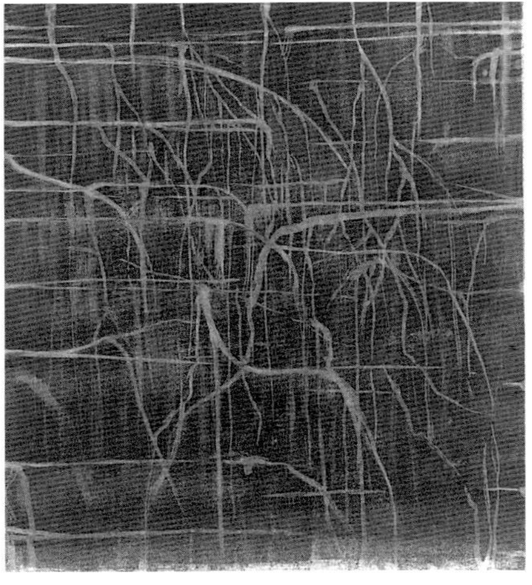

278

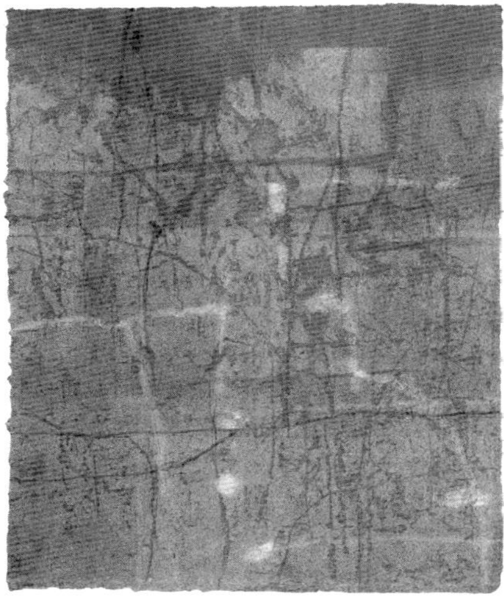

279

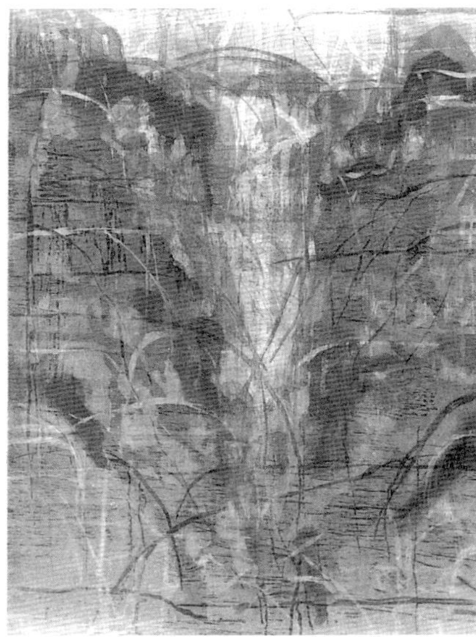

280

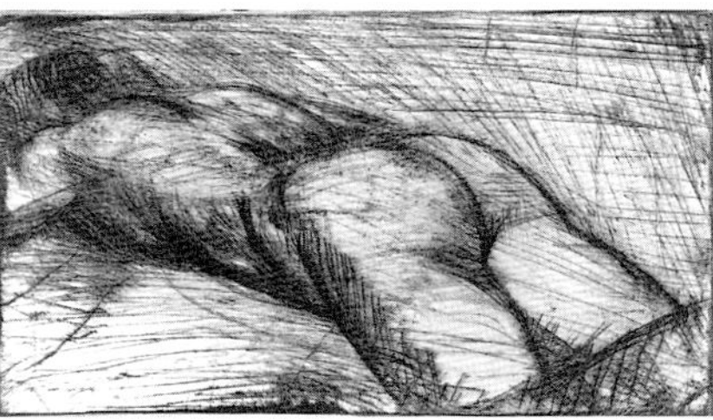

281

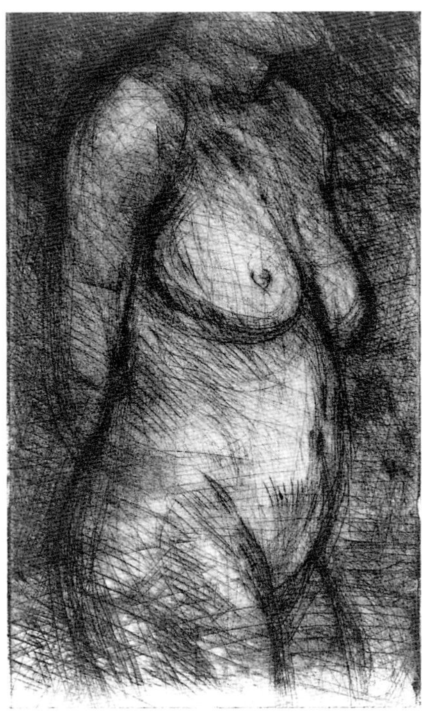

282

278
Fire Glen, 1994
Medium etching
Edition size 12
Paper Rives BFK
Plates/blocks 2 copper plates
Inks red and black
Image size 17⅞ × 15⅝ in. (45.5 × 39.7 cm)
Sheet size 30 × 22⅛ in. (76.2 × 56.2 cm)
Remarks the plates used for *Ice Glen* (no. 276) were reused for this image
Reference Mazur M-104

279
Provincetown, 1994
Medium monoprint with wood relief and *chine collé* over monotype with hand additions
Edition size variant edition of about 18
Paper Rives BFK with Kitikata *chine collé*
Published by New Provincetown Print Project, Provincetown, Mass., and the artist
Plates/blocks 1 aluminum plate and 1 wood collotype block
Inks white and multiple colors with *à la poupée* inking
Image size 20½ × 17 in. (52.1 × 43.2 cm)
Sheet size 28 × 22 in. (71.2 × 55.9 cm)
Remarks 12 impressions included in the annual New Provincetown Print Portfolio for 1994

280
Canyon, 1994
Medium etching, aquatint, and wood relief
Edition size 35
Paper Rives BFK
Printed by Robert Townsend at R. E. Townsend Studio, Georgetown, Mass.
Plates/blocks 2 copper plates and 1 wood block
Inks translucent warm green, Thalo green, burnt sienna with *à la poupée* inking, and white
Image size 30¾ × 22¼ in. (78.1 × 56.5 cm)
Sheet size 41⅞ × 29½ in. (106.4 × 75.0 cm)
Remarks the first plate was printed in translucent warm green and the second plate in Thalo green and burnt sienna inked *à la poupée;* the block was printed in white with selected areas wiped out before printing
Reference Mazur L-64

281
Harvard Evenings 1, 1994
Medium drypoint
Edition size 10
Paper Rives BFK
Plates/blocks 1 copper plate
Inks black
Image size 5⅛ × 8⅞ in. (13.0 × 22.6 cm)
Sheet size 14¾ × 19¾ in. (37.5 × 50.2 cm)
Reference Mazur S-64

282
Harvard Evenings 2, 1994
Medium drypoint
Edition size 10
Paper Rives BFK
Plates/blocks 1 copper plate
Inks black
Image size 9⅛ × 5⅛ in. (23.2 × 13.0 cm)
Sheet size 19¼ × 14¾ in. (48.9 × 37.5 cm)
Reference Mazur S-63

283
Harvard Evenings 3, 1994
Medium drypoint
Edition size 10
Paper Rives BFK
Plates/blocks 1 copper plate
Inks black
Image size 11¾ × 9 in. (29.9 × 22.9 cm)
Sheet size 19¾ × 14⅞ in. (50.2 × 37.8 cm)
Reference Mazur S-62

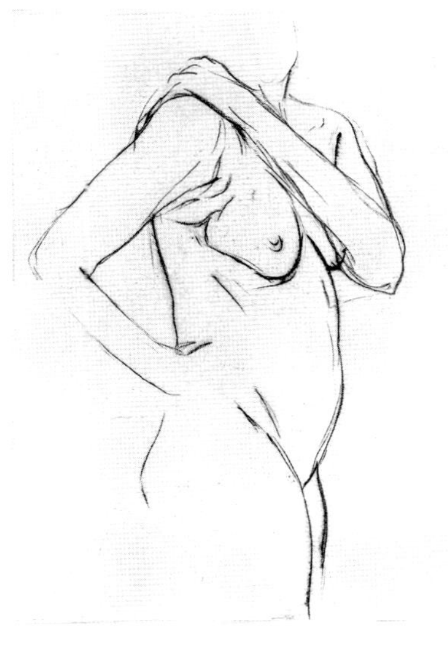
283

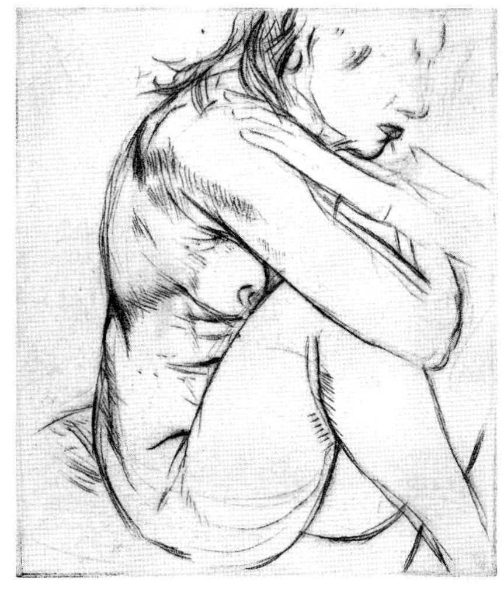
285

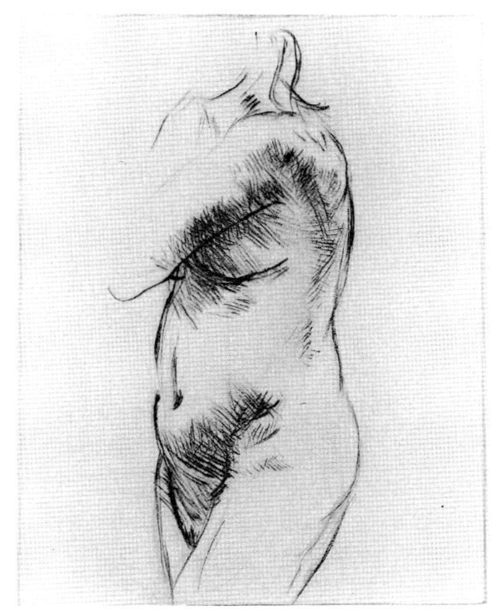
287

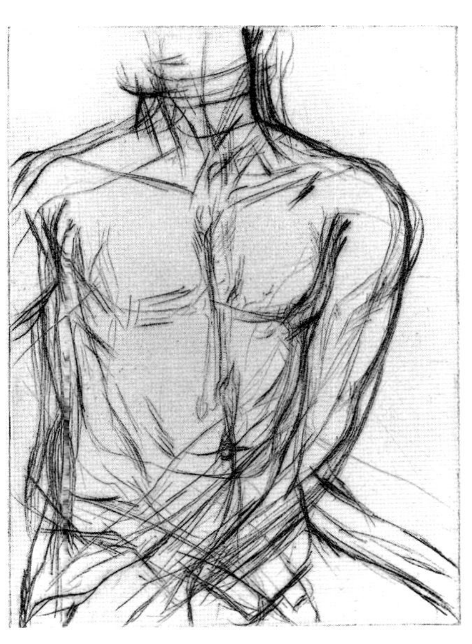
284

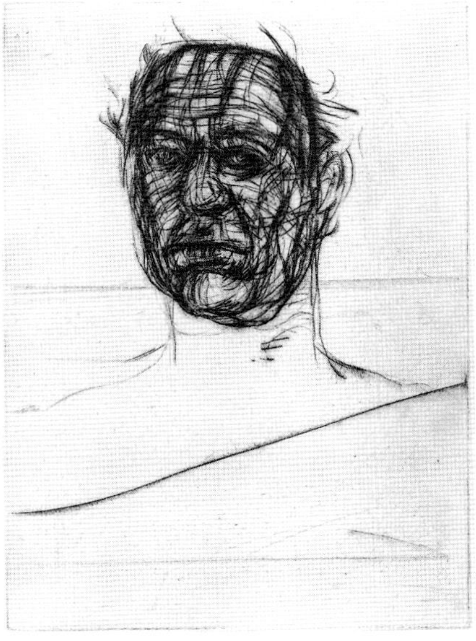
286

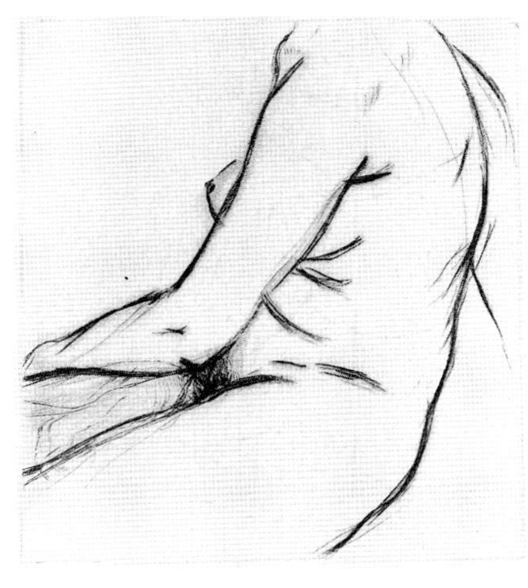
288

284
Harvard Evenings 4, 1994
Medium drypoint
Edition size 10
Paper Rives BFK
Plates/blocks 1 copper plate
Inks black
Image size 8⅜ × 6 in. (21.3 × 15.2 cm)
Sheet size 21 × 15 in. (53.4 × 38.1 cm)
Reference Mazur S-61

285
Harvard Evenings 5, 1994
Medium drypoint
Edition size 10
Paper Rives BFK
Plates/blocks 1 copper plate
Inks black
Image size 7⅜ × 6 in. (18.8 × 15.2 cm)
Sheet size 19¾ × 15 in. (50.2 × 38.1 cm)
Reference Mazur S-60

286
Harvard Evenings 6, 1994
Medium drypoint
Edition size 10
Paper Rives BFK
Plates/blocks 1 copper plate
Inks black
Image size 8⅜ × 5⅞ in. (21.3 × 15.0 cm)
Sheet size 19⅞ × 14⅞ in. (50.5 × 37.8 cm)
Reference Mazur S-59

287
Harvard Evenings 7, 1994
Medium drypoint
Edition size 10
Paper Rives BFK
Plates/blocks 1 copper plate
Inks black
Image size 7⅞ × 6 in. (20.0 × 15.2 cm)
Sheet size 21 × 15 in. (53.4 × 38.1 cm)
Reference Mazur S-58

288
Harvard Evenings 8, 1994
Medium drypoint
Edition size 10
Paper Rives BFK
Plates/blocks 1 copper plate
Inks black
Image size 6⅜ × 5¾ in. (16.2 × 14.6 cm)
Sheet size 21 × 15 in. (53.4 × 38.1 cm)
Reference Mazur S-57

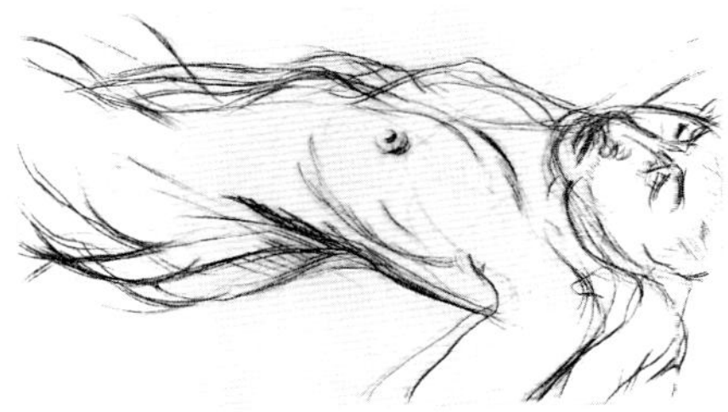
289

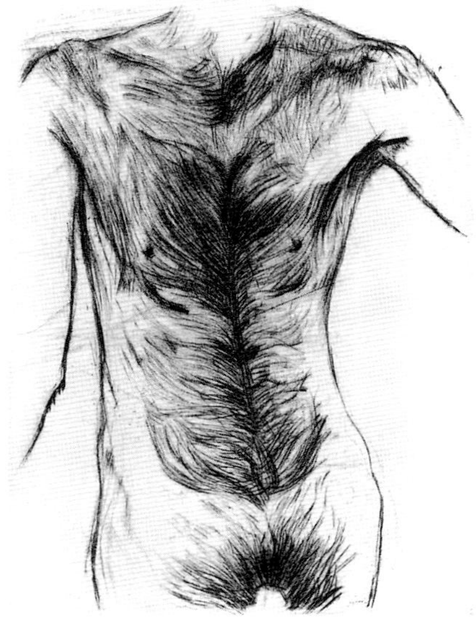
290

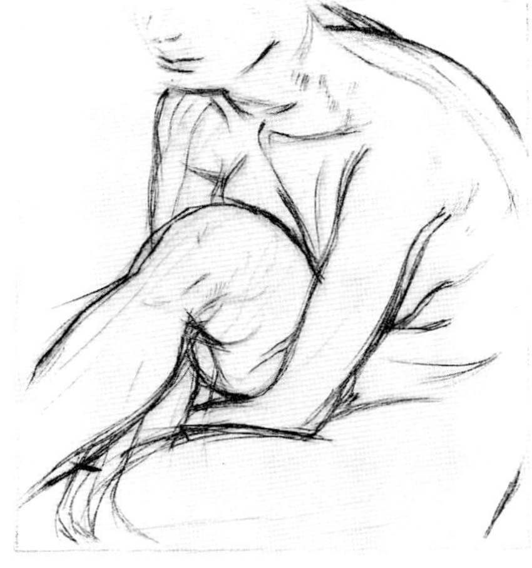
291

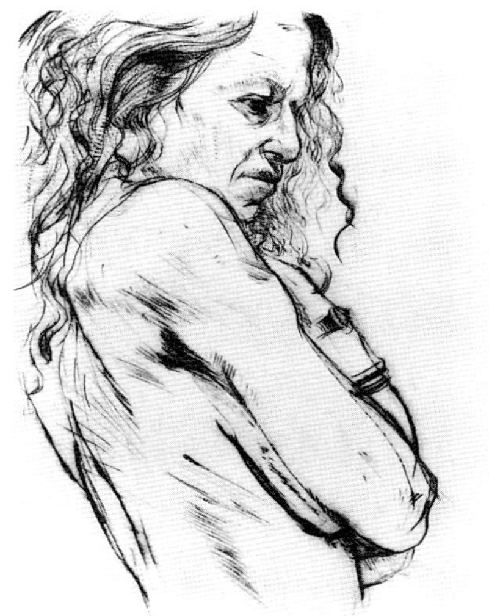
292

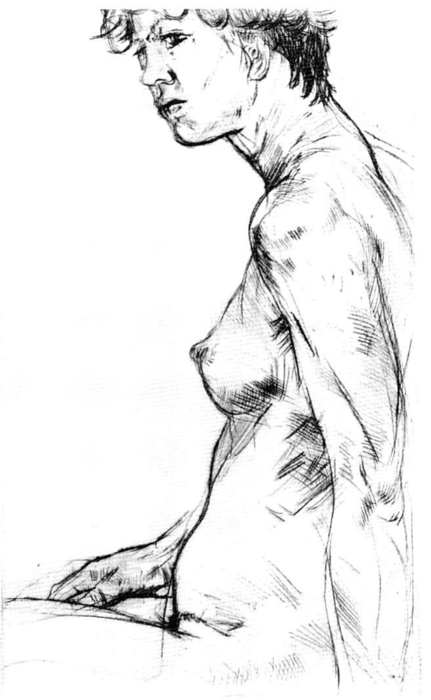
293

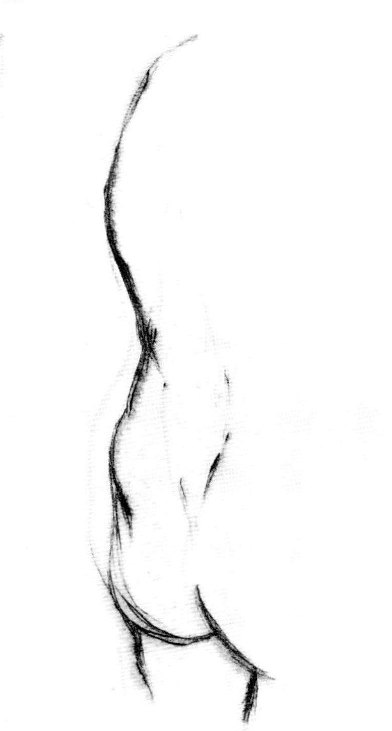
294

289
Harvard Evenings 9, 1994
Medium drypoint
Edition size 10
Paper Rives BFK
Plates/blocks 1 copper plate
Inks black
Image size 5⅛ × 7⅞ in. (13.0 × 17.5 cm)
Sheet size 15 × 21 in. (38.1 × 53.4 cm)
Reference Mazur S-56

290
Harvard Evenings 10, 1994
Medium drypoint
Edition size 10
Paper Rives BFK
Plates/blocks 1 copper plate
Inks black
Image size 8⅜ × 6 in. (21.3 × 15.2 cm)
Sheet size 21 × 15 in. (53.4 × 38.1 cm)
Reference Mazur S-55

291
Harvard Evenings 11, 1994
Medium drypoint
Edition size 10
Paper Rives BFK
Plates/blocks 1 copper plate
Inks black
Image size 6⅜ × 5¾ in. (16.2 × 14.6 cm)
Sheet size 21 × 15 in. (53.4 × 38.1 cm)
Reference Mazur S-54

292
Harvard Evenings 12, 1994
Medium drypoint
Edition size 10
Paper Rives BFK
Plates/blocks 1 copper plate
Inks black
Image size 7⅞ × 6¼ in. (20.0 × 15.9 cm)
Sheet size 21 × 15 in. (53.4 × 38.1 cm)
Reference Mazur S-53

293
Harvard Evenings 13, 1994
Medium drypoint
Edition size not editioned; 3–4 impressions printed
Paper Rives BFK
Plates/blocks 1 copper plate
Inks black
Image size 11⅞ × 6⅞ in. (30.2 × 17.5 cm)
Sheet size 19⅞ × 14¾ in. (50.5 × 37.5 cm)
Reference Mazur S-52

294
Harvard Evenings 15, 1995
Medium drypoint
Edition size not editioned; 3–4 impressions printed
Paper Rives BFK
Plates/blocks 1 copper plate
Inks black
Image size 6⅛ × 3⅜ in. (15.6 × 8.6 cm)
Sheet size 14¾ × 13 in. (37.5 × 33.0 cm)
Reference Mazur S-51

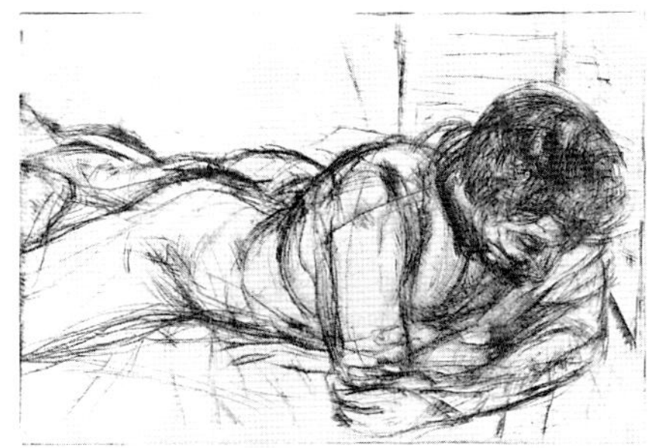

295

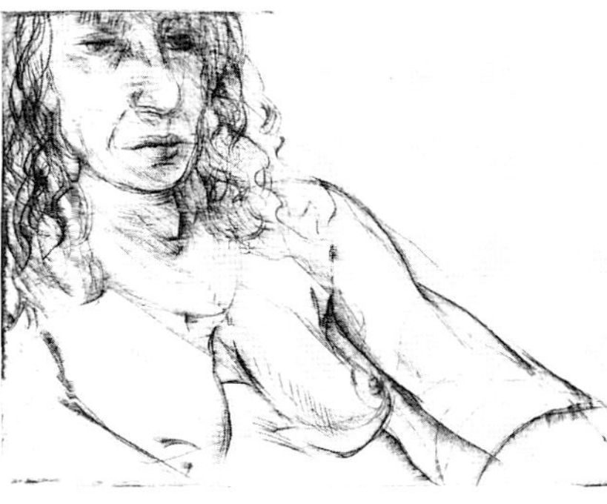

296

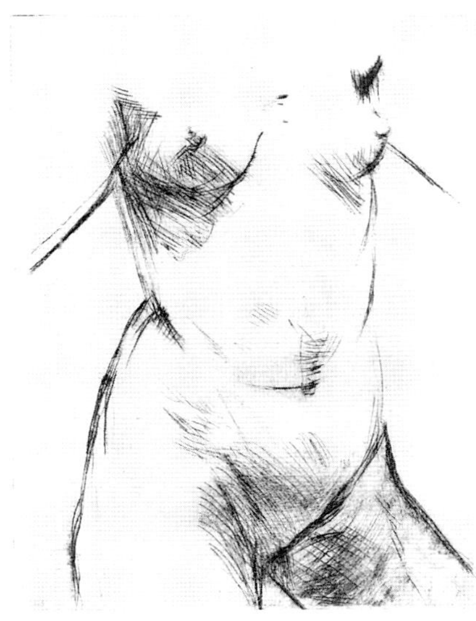

297

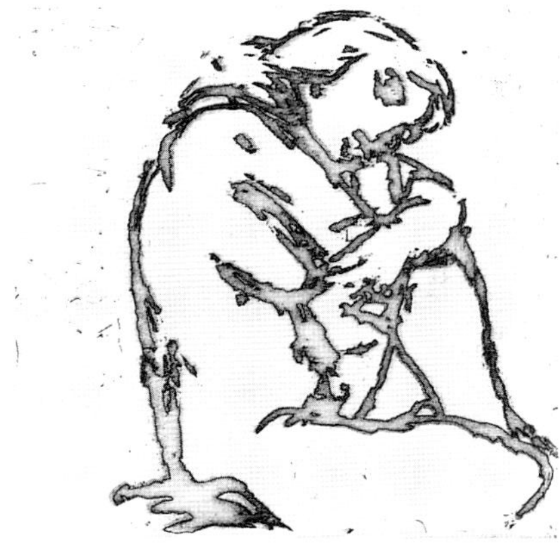

298

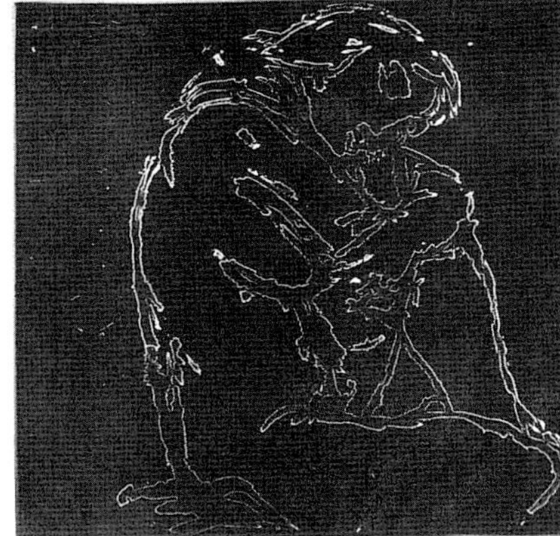

299

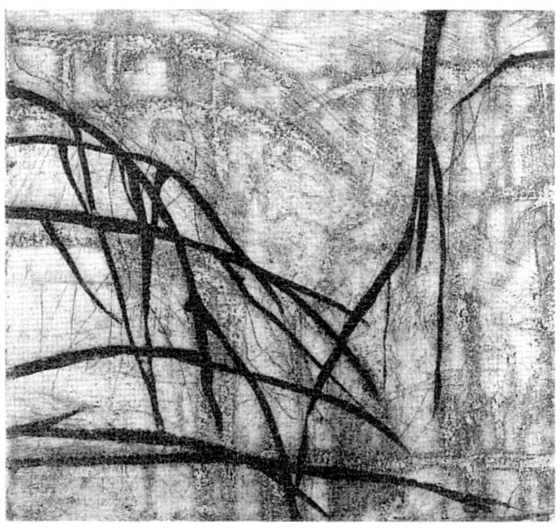

300

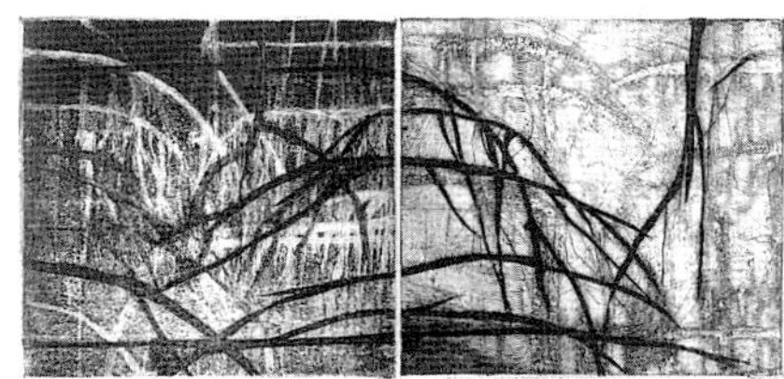

301

295
Harvard Evenings 16, 1995
Medium drypoint
Edition size not editioned; 2–3 impressions printed
Paper Arches
Plates/blocks 1 copper plate
Inks black
Image size 6⅛ × 8⅜ in. (15.6 × 21.3 cm)
Sheet size 13½ × 14⅝ in. (34.3 × 37.2 cm)
Reference Mazur S-50

296
Harvard Evenings 17, 1995
Medium drypoint
Edition size not editioned; 3–4 impressions printed
Paper white wove
Plates/blocks 1 copper plate
Inks black
Image size 6⅛ × 7¾ in. (15.6 × 19.7 cm)
Sheet size 15 × 15¾ in. (38.1 × 40.0 cm)
Reference Mazur S-49

297
Harvard Evenings 18, 1995
Medium drypoint
Edition size not editioned; 3–4 impressions printed
Paper Somerset gray
Plates/blocks 1 copper plate
Inks black
Image size 7⅞ × 6 in. (20.0 × 15.2 cm)
Sheet size 19¼ × 15 in. (48.9 × 38.1 cm)
Reference Mazur S-48

298
Harvard Evenings 19, 1995
Medium open-bite etching
Edition size not editioned; 6–8 impressions printed
Paper white wove
Plates/blocks 1 zinc plate
Inks black
Image size 7⅞ × 7⅞ in. (20.0 × 20.0 cm)
Sheet size 18⅛ × 14⅞ in. (46.1 × 37.8 cm)
Reference Mazur S-47

299
Harvard Evenings 20, 1995
Medium open-bite etching printed in relief
Edition size not editioned; 2–3 impressions printed
Paper white wove
Plates/blocks 1 zinc plate
Inks black
Image size 7⅞ × 7⅞ in. (20.0 × 20.0 cm)
Sheet size 15 × 12¼ in. (38.1 × 31.1 cm)
Remarks a cognate of *Harvard Evenings 19* (no. 298)
Reference Mazur S-46

300
Single Branching, 1995
Medium etching and aquatint
Edition size 50
Paper Rives BFK
Plates/blocks 1 copper plate
Inks blue-black
Image and sheet size 5¾ × 5½ in. (14.6 × 14.0 cm)
Remarks related to *Black Branching* (no. 277)
Reference Mazur S-65a

301
Double Branching (diptych), 1995
Medium etching and aquatint
Edition size 10
Paper Rives BFK
Plates/blocks 2 copper plates
Inks black
Image size 5½ × 5⅝ in. (14.0 × 14.3 cm) each
Sheet size 14¾ × 19¼ in. (37.5 × 48.9 cm)
Reference Mazur S-65b

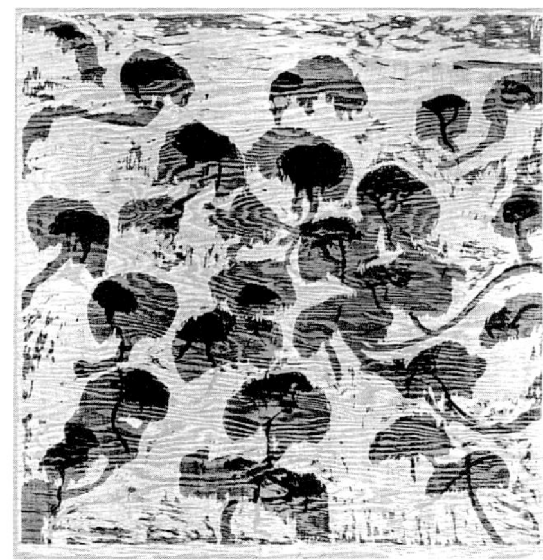
302

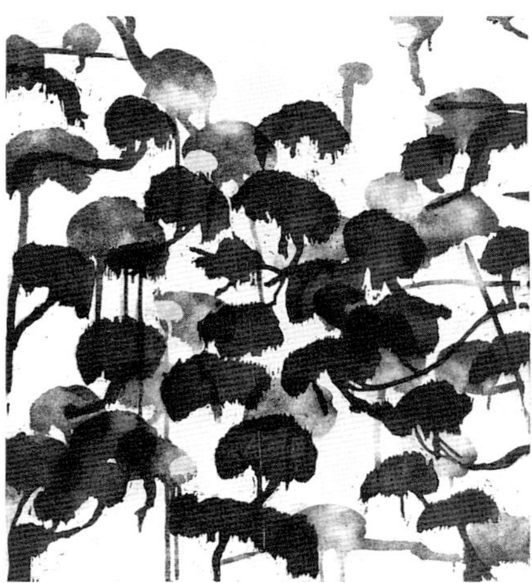
303

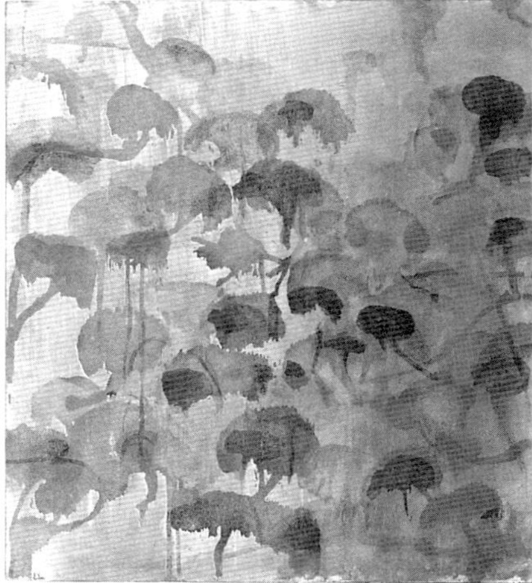
304

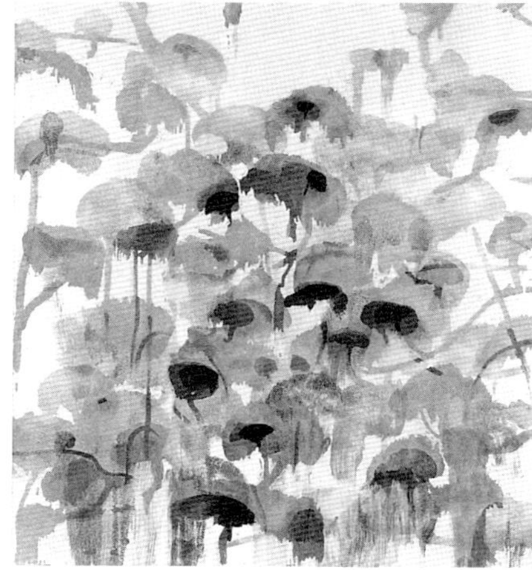
305

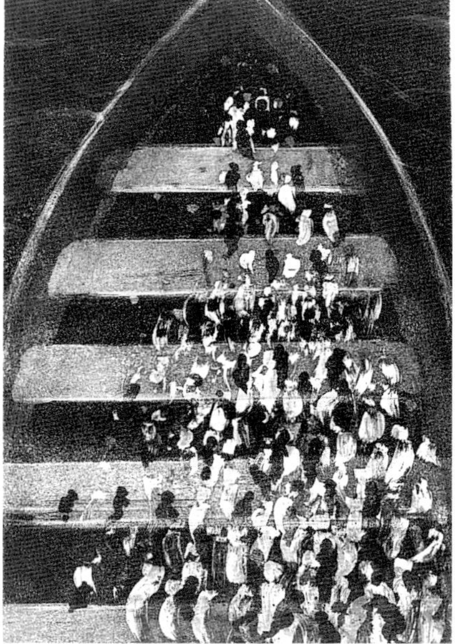
306

302
Mind Landscape (Cascade), 1995
Medium wood relief
Edition size 20
Paper gray laid
Printed by Anne Clarke at the artist's studio
Plates/blocks 2 wood blocks
Inks black and white
Image size 25¼ × 23¼ in. (64.1 × 59.1 cm)
Sheet size 28⅛ × 25⅛ in. (71.5 × 63.8 cm)
Reference Mazur L-70

303
Untitled (Cascade), 1996
Medium aquatint
Edition size 5
Paper Rives BFK
Plates/blocks 1 copper plate
Inks black
Image size 26 × 23 in. (66.1 × 58.4 cm)
Sheet size 34 × 28⅝ in. (86.4 × 72.7 cm)
Remarks the black wood block from *Mind Landscape (Cascade)* (no. 302) was reused for the preparation of this aquatint plate, using a Mylar transfer process
Reference Mazur L-67

304
Untitled (Cascade — Fall), 1996
Medium monoprint with aquatint and monotype
Edition size 12
Paper Rives BFK
Plates/blocks 2 copper plates and 1 Plexiglas plate
Inks brown, sepia, and multiple colors
Image size 26 × 23 in. (66.1 × 58.4 cm)
Sheet size 36⅜ × 30 in. (92.4 × 76.2 cm)
Remarks the aquatint plate from *Untitled (Cascade)* (no. 303) was reused for this image
Reference Mazur L-68

305
Untitled (Cascade), 1996
Medium monoprint with aquatint and monotype
Edition size 12
Paper Rives BFK
Plates/blocks 2 copper plates and 1 Plexiglas plate
Inks black, white, and multiple colors
Image size 26 × 23 in. (66.1 × 58.4 cm)
Sheet size 32 × 29⅞ in. (81.3 × 75.9 cm)
Remarks the two copper plates from *Untitled (Cascade — Fall)* (no. 304) were reused for this image
Reference Mazur L-69

306
Canto III (Charon's Boat), 1996
Medium etching and aquatint
Edition size not yet editioned; 2–3 impressions printed
Paper Rives BFK
Printed by Robert Townsend at R. E. Townsend Studio, Georgetown, Mass.; plate preparation by the artist
Plates/blocks 1 copper plate
Inks black
Image size 14¾ × 9⅞ in. (37.5 × 25.1 cm)
Sheet size 22 × 15 in. (55.9 × 38.1 cm)
Remarks two to three variant impressions with *chine collé* exist; the artist is creating a series of intaglio images based on his 1993 monotype series used to illustrate *The Inferno of Dante* (1994); the intaglio prints are intended to be published as a portfolio
Reference Mazur M-110

307
Canto IV (The Limbo of Antiquity), 1996
Medium etching and aquatint
Edition size not yet editioned; 2–3 impressions printed
Paper Rives BFK
Printed by Robert Townsend at R. E. Townsend Studio, Georgetown, Mass.; plate preparation by the artist
Plates/blocks 1 copper plate
Inks black
Image size 15¾ × 10¾ in. (40.0 × 27.3 cm)
Sheet size 22 × 15 in. (55.9 × 38.1 cm)
Remarks see Remarks for no. 306
Reference Mazur M-111

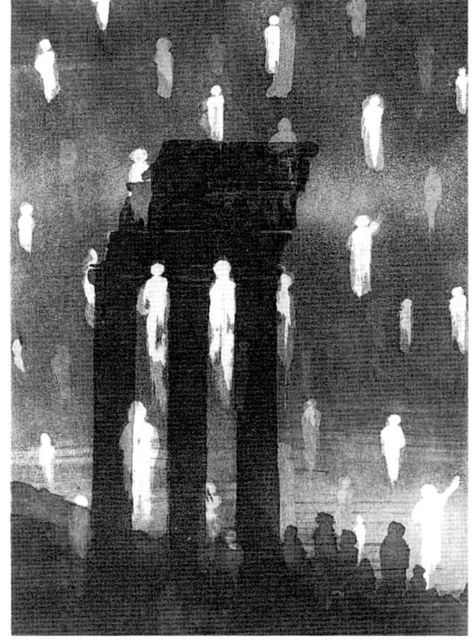

307

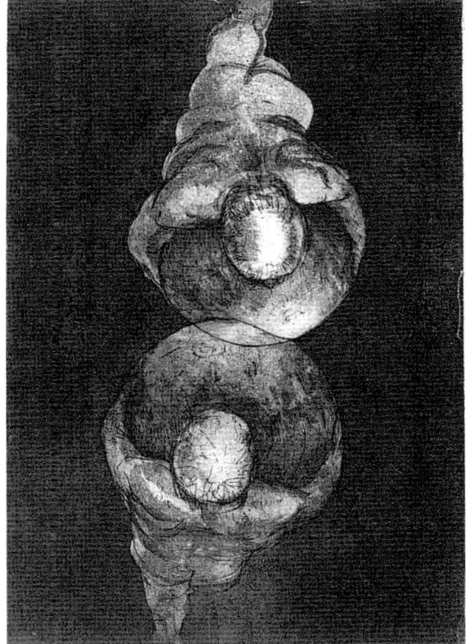

308

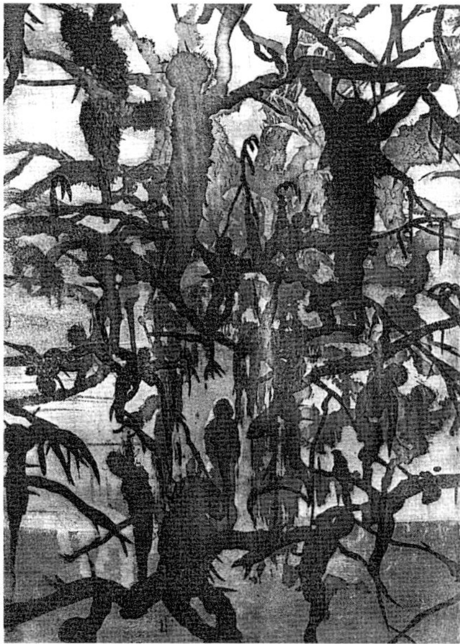

309

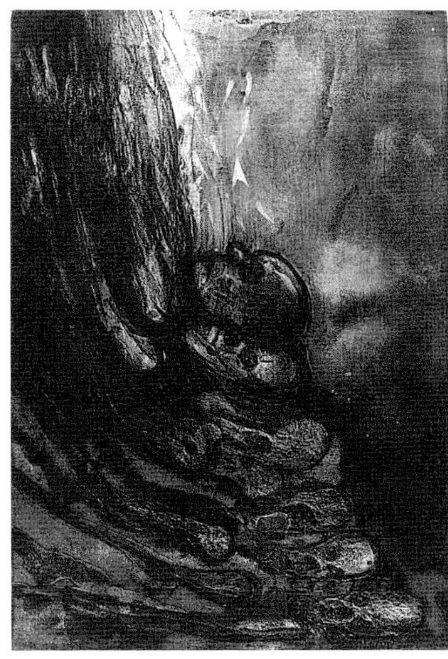

310

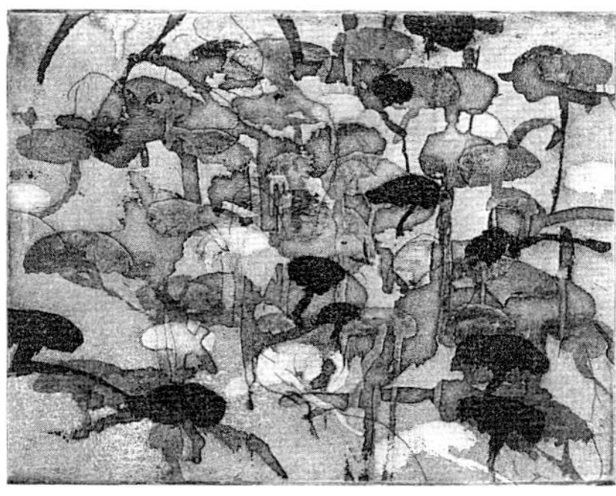

311

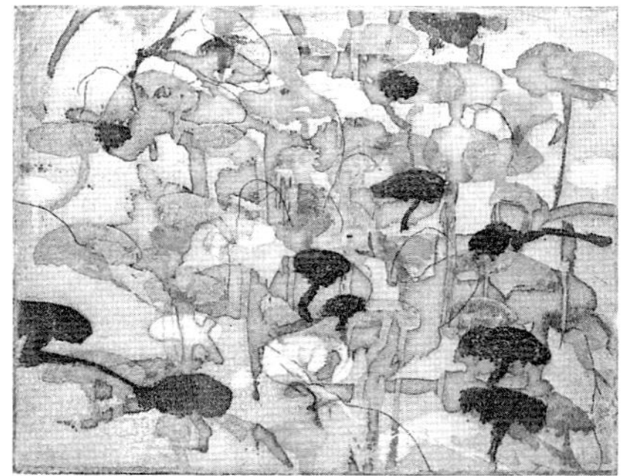

312

308
Canto VII (Spenders and Hoarders), 1996
Medium etching and aquatint
Edition size not yet editioned; 2–3 impressions printed
Paper Rives BFK
Printed by Robert Townsend at R. E. Townsend Studio, Georgetown, Mass.; plate preparation by the artist
Plates/blocks 1 copper plate
Inks black
Image size 14⅝ × 10 in. (37.2 × 25.4 cm)
Sheet size 22 × 15 in. (55.9 × 38.1 cm)
Remarks see Remarks for no. 306
Reference Mazur M-113

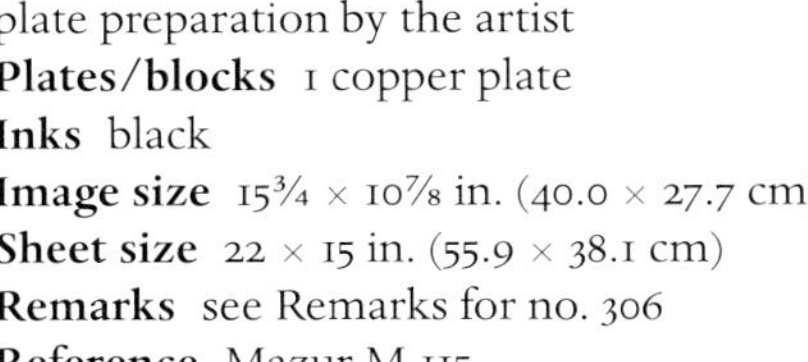

309
Canto XIII (Wood of the Suicides), 1996
Medium etching and aquatint
Edition size not yet editioned; 2–3 impressions printed
Paper Rives BFK
Printed by Robert Townsend at R. E. Townsend Studio, Georgetown, Mass.; plate preparation by the artist
Plates/blocks 1 copper plate
Inks black
Image size 15¾ × 10⅞ in. (40.0 × 27.7 cm)
Sheet size 22 × 15 in. (55.9 × 38.1 cm)
Remarks see Remarks for no. 306
Reference Mazur M-115

310
Canto XIX (The Simoniacs), 1996
Medium etching and aquatint
Edition size not yet editioned; 2–3 impressions printed
Paper Rives BFK
Printed by Robert Townsend at R. E. Townsend Studio, Georgetown, Mass.; plate preparation by the artist
Plates/blocks 1 copper plate
Inks black
Image size 14⅞ × 9¾ in. (37.8 × 24.8 cm)
Sheet size 22 × 15 in. (55.9 × 38.1 cm)
Remarks see Remarks for no. 306
Reference Mazur M-116

311
Mind Landscape, 1996
Medium etching and aquatint
Edition size 100
Paper Rives BFK
Plates/blocks 1 copper plate
Inks black
Image size 6 × 7½ in. (15.2 × 19.1 cm)
Sheet size 10¼ × 11⅝ in. (26.0 × 29.5 cm)
Reference Mazur S-66

312
Mind Landscape, 1996
Medium etching
Edition size not editioned; 3–5 variant impressions printed
Paper Rives BFK
Plates/blocks 1 copper plate and 1 Plexiglas plate

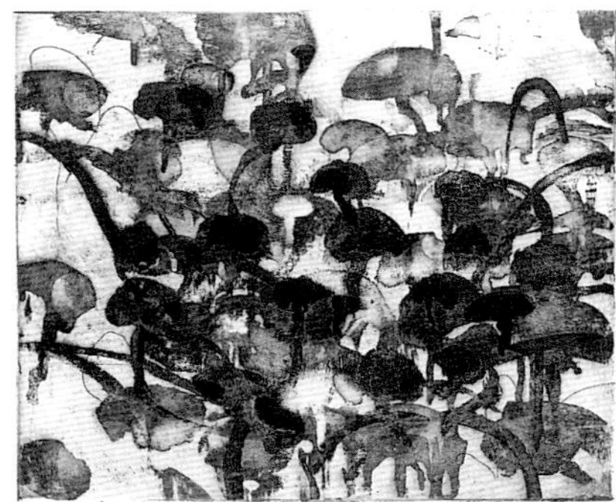

313

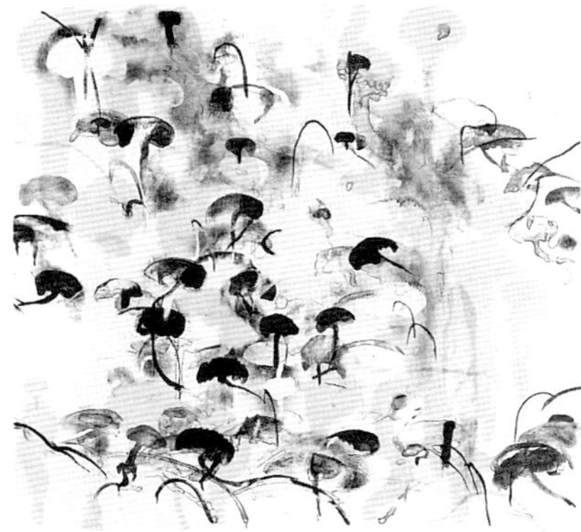

314

Inks brown; green, orange, and white with *à la poupée* inking
Image size 6 × 7½ in. (15.2 × 19.1 cm)
Sheet size 10¼ × 11⅝ in. (26.0 × 29.5 cm)
Remarks the plate from the black-and-white version (no. 311) was printed using brown ink, and a second color plate inked *à la poupée* in several colors was added
Reference Mazur S-66a

313
Mind Landscape III, 1996
Medium etching and aquatint
Edition size 3 plus numerous variant proofs
Paper Somerset
Plates/blocks 1 copper plate
Inks blue-black with white surface roll
Image size 11⅞ × 14⅛ in. (30.2 × 35.9 cm)
Sheet size 22⅛ × 22⅛ in. (56.2 × 56.2 cm)

314
Untitled, 1996
Medium lithograph
Edition size 40 plus 9 artist's proofs
Paper Somerset Velvet
Printed by Andrew Mockler assisted by Andrea Mockler and V. Stanejerle at Jungle Press Editions, Ltd., New York
Published by Jungle Press Editions, Ltd., and the artist
Plates/blocks 4 aluminum plates and 1 stone
Inks light gray, gray, light blue, yellow ocher, and black

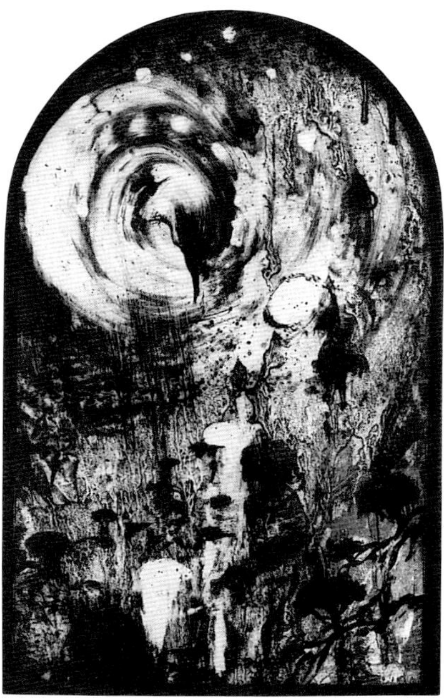

315

Image size 21¾ × 21¾ in. (55.2 × 55.2 cm)
Sheet size 26⅜ × 26¾ in. (67.0 × 68.0 cm)
Reference Mazur L-79

315
Genesis, 1996
Medium etching
Edition size 200 (book edition) with 26 lettered *hors commerce*
Paper handmade at Velké Losiny mill in the Czech Republic
Printed by Robert Townsend at R. E. Townsend Studio, Georgetown, Mass.; plate prepared by the artist
Plates/blocks 2 copper plates
Inks black and red-brown
Image size 11⅜ × 7⅛ in. (28.9 × 18.1 cm)
Sheet size 16¼ × 11⅜ in. (41.3 × 28.9 cm)
Remarks the frontispiece for the Arion Press publication *Genesis,* with a translation by Robert Alter and facing text in Hebrew from *Biblia Hebraica Stuttgartensia* (1967); a single sheet edition was also printed on Velké Losiny handmade paper in an edition of 25 with 5 artist's proofs
Reference Mazur S-76

316
After a Chinese Scroll, 1997
Medium wood relief and aquatint with *chine collé*
Edition size 50
Paper Somerset with Kitikata *chine collé*
Printed by Robert Townsend at R. E. Townsend Studio, Georgetown, Mass.; plate prepared by the artist
Plates/blocks 1 wood block and 3 copper plates
Inks Thalo green, burnt sienna, black, blue, and olive green
Image size 15⅜ × 17⅞ in. (39.1 × 45.5 cm)

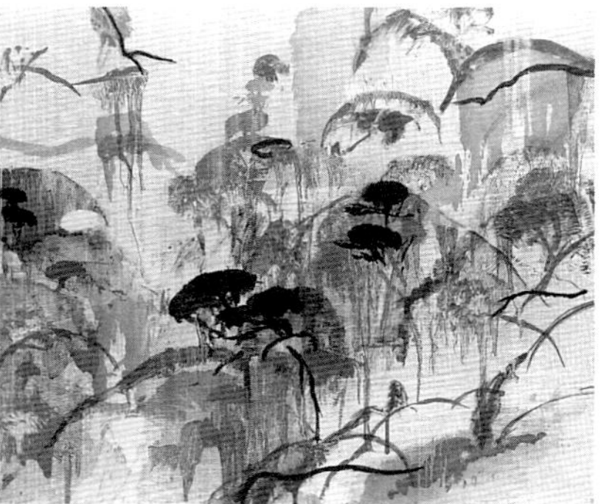

316

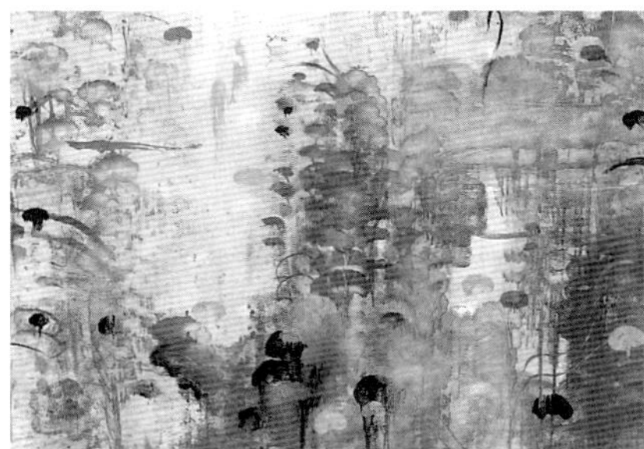

317

Sheet size 23 × 23⅞ in. (58.4 × 60.6 cm)
Remarks a benefit print in support of the exhibition *Branching: The Art of Michael Mazur,* Mead Art Museum, Amherst College, Mass., and DeCordova Museum and Sculpture Park, Lincoln, Mass., 1997–98
Reference Mazur M-107

317
Pond Edge, 1997
Medium etching and aquatint
Edition size 35 plus 3 artist's proofs, 2 printer's proofs, and 1 *bon à tirer*
Paper Rives BFK
Printed by Robert Townsend at R. E. Townsend Studio, Georgetown, Mass.; plate preparation by the artist
Plates/blocks 2 copper plates
Inks warm yellow, Thalo green, light blue, olive green, orange, purple, black-green, light gray, and white, with *à la poupée* inking
Image and sheet size 29¾ × 41¾ in. (75.6 × 106.1 cm)
Remarks the key plate was printed twice, first using Thalo green with warm yellow relief and then using the ghost of the first printing with selected inking and light blue relief; the second plate was inked *à la poupée* with multiple colors
Reference Mazur L-82

318
Storm Warning, 1997
Medium etching and aquatint
Edition size 35 plus 5 artist's proofs
Paper Copperplate buff

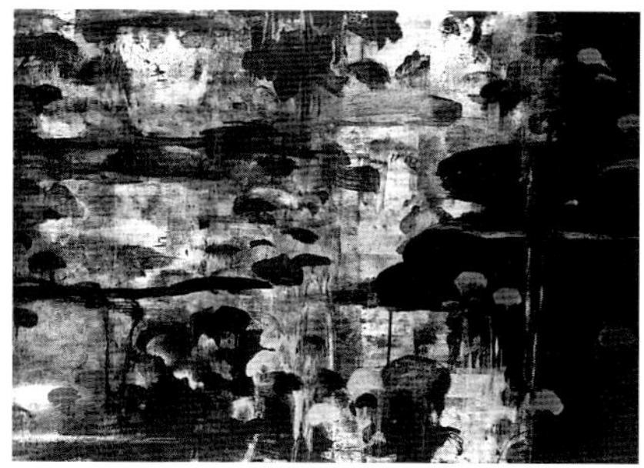

318

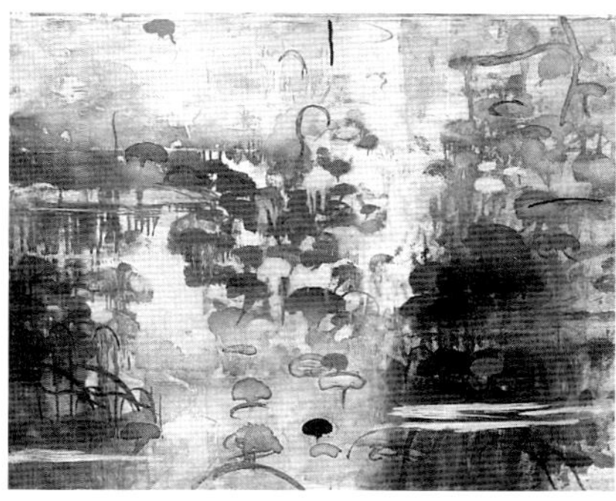

319

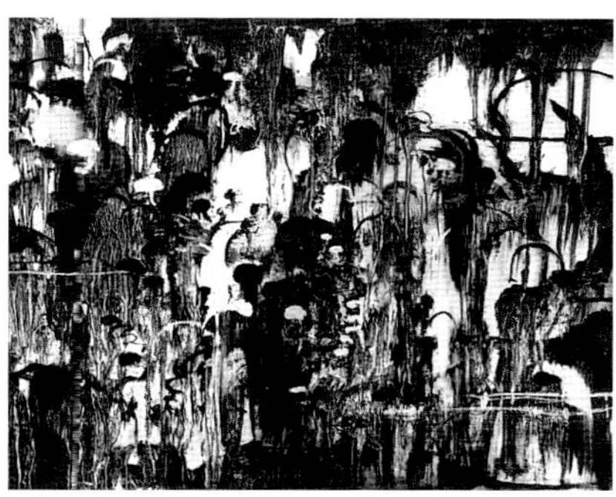

320

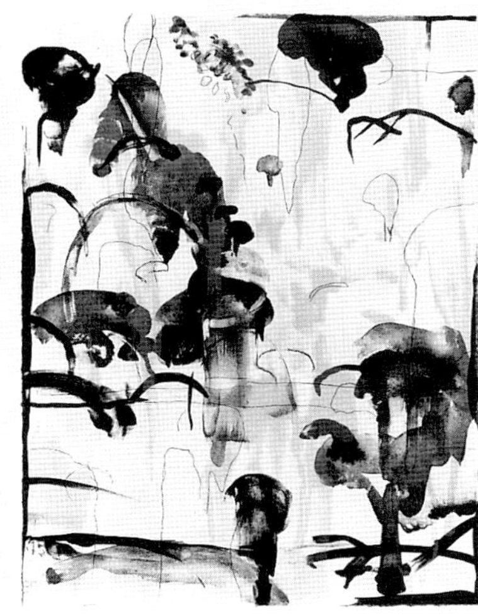

321

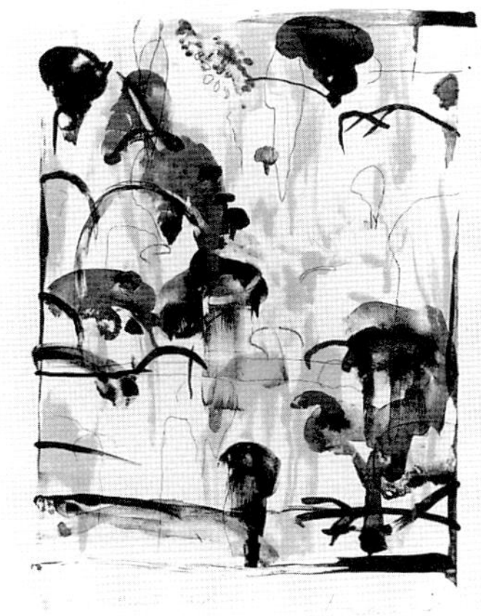

322

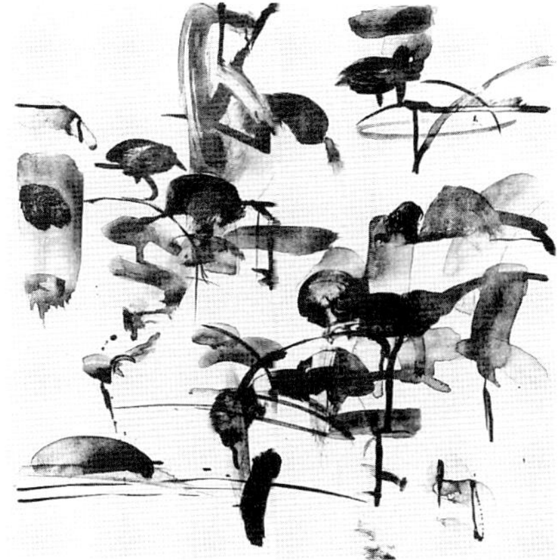

323

Printed by Robert Townsend at R. E. Townsend Studio, Georgetown, Mass.; plate preparation by the artist
Plates/blocks 3 copper plates
Inks black, transparent warm red, and white with bronze and gold pigment
Image and sheet size 31¼ × 42 in. (79.4 × 106.7 cm)
Remarks the first plate was printed in warm red relief and the second plate in black aquatint; the third plate was printed in white with gold and bronze dusting into the aquatint
Reference Mazur L-81

319
Pond Edge II, 1997–98
Medium etching and aquatint
Edition size 35 plus 5 artist's proofs
Paper Rives BFK
Printed by Robert Townsend at R. E. Townsend Studio, Georgetown, Mass.; plate preparation by the artist
Plates/blocks 4 copper plates
Inks warm yellow, blue, Thalo green, black-green, silver, purple, black, and orange, with *à la poupée* inking
Image and sheet size 32 × 39¾ in. (81.3 × 101.0 cm)
Remarks the first plate was printed in warm yellow and the second plate in blue; the key plate was then printed twice, first in Thalo green, then with black-green printed *à la poupée;* the fourth plate was printed with multiple colors
Reference Mazur L-82a

320
The Dragon's Rockery I, 1997–98
Medium etching and aquatint
Edition size 10 plus 5 artist's proofs
Paper Arches Heavyweight 190 lb. water-color paper
Plates/blocks 1 copper plate
Inks black
Image size 24 × 29⅞ in. (61.0 × 75.9 cm)
Sheet size 29½ × 36¾ in. (75.0 × 93.3 cm)
Reference Mazur L-83

321
Connection, from
The Art Connection Portfolio, 1998
Medium lithograph
Edition size 50 plus 14 artist's proofs, 1 printer's proof, 1 *bon à tirer,* 1 archive impression, and 2 *hors commerce* impressions
Paper Arches Cover white
Printed by Carolyn Muskat at Muskat Studios, Boston; portfolio boxes made at Portfolio Box, Inc., Providence, R.I.
Plates/blocks 1 stone and 2 aluminum plates
Inks black, gray, and blue-black
Image and sheet size 16 × 12 in. (40.7 × 30.5 cm)
Remarks published to benefit Art Connection, Inc., Boston
Reference Mazur S-77

322
Connection II (2nd State), 1998
Medium lithograph
Edition size 10 plus 2 artist's proofs, 1 *bon à tirer,* 1 printer's proof, and 1 archive impression
Paper Arches
Printed by Carolyn Muskat at Muskat Studios, Boston
Plates/blocks 3 aluminum plates
Inks black, gray, and blue-black
Image size 20½ × 12¼ in. (52.1 × 31.1 cm)
Sheet size 25⅛ × 19⅛ in. (63.8 × 48.6 cm)
Reference Mazur M-119

323
Thaw I, 1998
Medium lithograph
Edition size 40
Paper Somerset Satin
Printed by Andrew Mockler at Jungle Press Editions, Ltd , New York

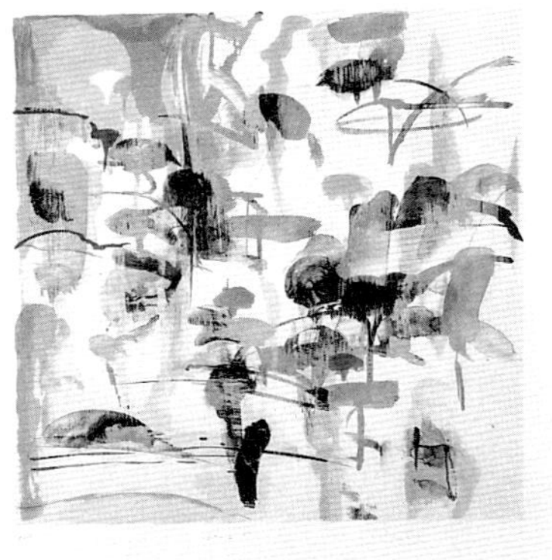

324

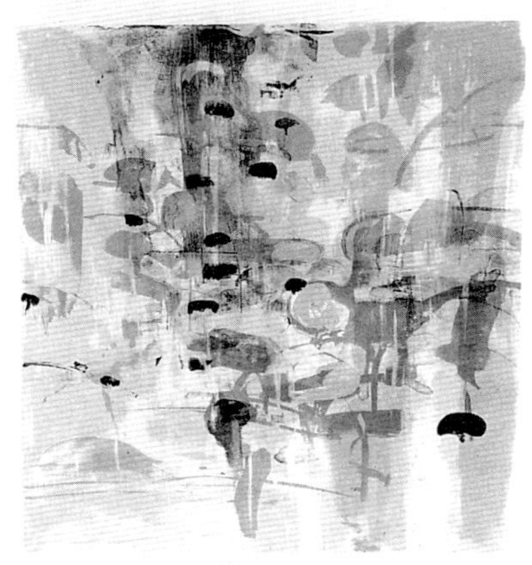

325

Published by Jungle Press Editions, Ltd., and the artist
Plates/blocks 2 aluminum plates
Inks transparent ocher and black
Image size 22½ × 21¾ in. (57.2 × 55.2 cm)
Sheet size 28½ × 26½ in. (72.4 × 67.3 cm)
Remarks black-and-white version; it is intended to take 12 impressions each from nos. 323, 324, and 325, and a final image yet to be created, to create a portfolio that will pair these images with Chinese poetry
Reference Mazur L-84

324
Thaw II, 1998
Medium lithograph
Edition size 40
Paper Somerset Satin
Printed by Andrew Mockler at Jungle Press Editions, Ltd., New York
Published by Jungle Press Editions, Ltd., and the artist
Plates/blocks 6 aluminum plates
Inks ocher, green blended roll, black, white, purple / sienna, and green / purple / yellow
Image size 22½ × 21¾ in. (57.2 × 55.2 cm)

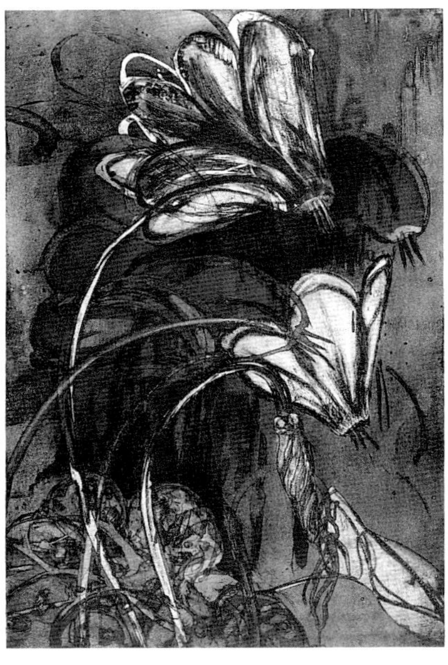

326

Sheet size 28½ × 26½ in. (72.4 × 67.3 cm)
Remarks see Remarks for no. 323

325
Summer Cascade, 1998
Medium lithograph
Edition size 40
Paper Somerset Satin
Printed by Andrew Mockler at Jungle Press Editions, Ltd., New York
Published by Jungle Press Editions, Ltd., and the artist
Plates/blocks 8 aluminum plates and 1 stone
Inks gray, green, purple, black (stone), gray, white, transparent yellow, white, and black
Image size 22½ × 21½ in. (57.2 × 54.6 cm)
Sheet size 28½ × 26½ in. (72.4 × 67.3 cm)
Remarks see Remarks for no. 323

326
Cyclamen, 1999
Medium etching and aquatint
Edition size 25 plus 7 artist's proofs
Paper Hahnemühle
Printed by Robert Townsend at R. E. Townsend Studio, Georgetown, Mass.; plate prepared by the artist
Plates/blocks 1 copper plate
Inks black
Image size 35¾ × 23¾ in. (90.8 × 60.3 cm)
Sheet size 42 × 31 in. (106.7 × 78.8 cm)
Remarks the plate for this print was first created by the artist in 1982 and a few proofs were printed; the plate was then extensively reworked by the artist for this edition in 1999
Reference Mazur L-86

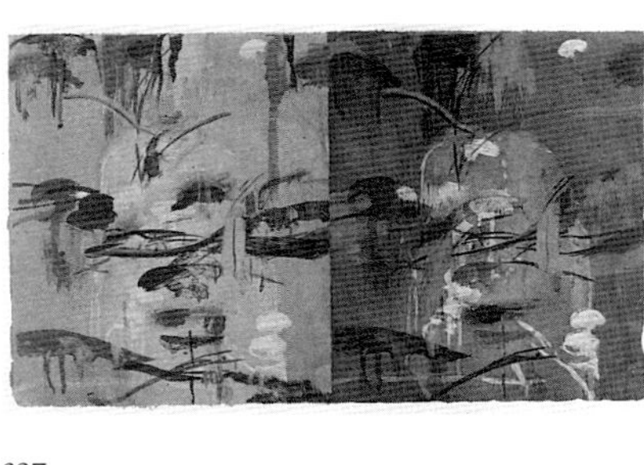

327

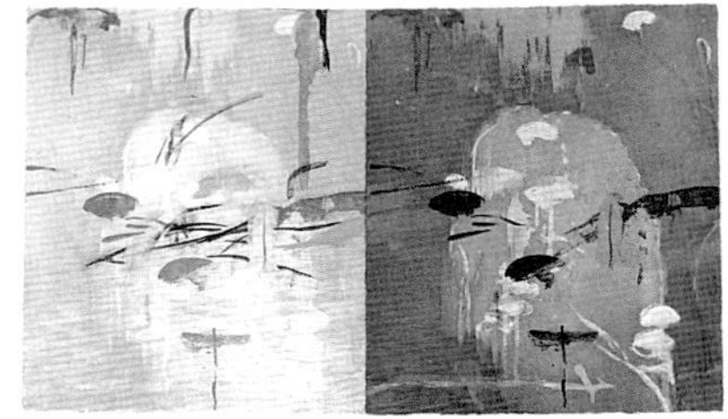

328

327
Mountain Dragonfly (diptych), 1999
Medium etching with *chine collé*
Edition size 25 plus 5 artist's proofs and 2 trial proofs
Paper Hahnemühle buff with Okawara *chine collé*
Printed by Robert Townsend at R. E. Townsend Studio, Georgetown, Mass.; plate prepared by the artist
Plates/blocks 1 wood block, 4 copper plates
Inks white, brown, green, orange, blue, and off-white
Image size 18 × 29¾ in. (45.8 × 75.6 cm)
Sheet size 31¼ × 42¼ in. (79.4 × 107.3 cm)
Reference Mazur L-85

328
Mountain Dragonfly II (diptych), 1999
Medium etching and wood relief with *chine collé*
Edition size 25 plus 5 artist's proofs
Paper Hahnemühle buff with Okawara *chine collé*
Printed by Robert Townsend at R. E. Townsend Studio, Georgetown, Mass.; plate prepared by the artist
Plates/blocks 5 copper plates
Inks gray-black, red-black, red, white, and blue-black
Image size 18 × 29¾ in. (45.8 × 75.6 cm)
Sheet size 31¼ × 42¼ in. (79.4 × 107.3 cm)
Reference Mazur L-85a

Glossary of Printmaking Terms

à la poupée French term for applying inks selectively to different areas of a printing plate; *à la poupée* inking enables the creation of a multicolor print using only one plate and one printing run.

aquatint an **intaglio** process developed to simulate the delicate tonalities found in watercolor washes. To create an aquatint ground, an uncoated printing plate is dusted with a resin powder that, when heated, fuses to the metal plate in small droplets. When the plate is submerged in an acid etching bath, a tightly spaced network of pits that will hold ink is created. When printed, there will be an overall gray tone, or various areas of the plate can be stopped out and etched to different depths to create darker or lighter tones across the plate.

artist's proof originally a test or trial proof of different states of a print. Today an artist's proof is one of a number of signed proofs, generally no more than one-tenth the size of the **edition,** made for the artist's own use in addition to the numbered edition. Printed to the same standards as the numbered edition, these proofs are often numbered using Roman numerals. While inherently of no lesser or greater value than the impressions in the numbered edition, artist's proofs can develop greater value if the artist later individualizes these works on paper with hand-drawn additions.

bite the corrosive effect of an acid on a metal intaglio plate.

bleed image a print in which the image extends beyond one or more of the edges of the paper, as opposed to a print that has blank margins on all sides.

blend roll a specialized inking technique in which a printing **matrix** is inked and printed with several strips of different colors at once. Also referred to as a rainbow roll. The colors are blended at the edges to produce a rainbow effect.

bon à tirer **(B.A.T.) impression** a French term meaning "good to pull." A final proof signed by the artist is used by a master printer as the technical and aesthetic standard and guide for printing the **edition.** This proof, which brings to completion the collaborative stage between artist and master printer, is also referred to as the right-to-print (R.T.P.) proof.

burin a steel engraving tool for cutting into wood or metal.

burnisher a smooth, curved steel tool used for polishing copper-plate surfaces, making corrections, or for producing light areas in **mezzotints** or for other **intaglio** techniques.

burr the ridge of displaced metal along an engraved or drypoint line. In **engraving,** the burr is generally removed with a scraper before inking. The burr in the **drypoint** process holds ink (in addition to the ink held in the incised line), and the effect of this dual line when printed is a characteristically soft and velvety line. The drypoint burr wears down quickly in printing, thus limiting the quantity of good impressions.

cancellation the destruction or defacing of the printing surface(s) after an **edition** has been printed. This is done to ensure that no additional impressions can be produced. A cancellation proof shows the actual scratching or gouging, or other defacement of the plate, stone, or block.

carborundum print a nonacid process for creating an **aquatint** texture by applying a mixture of carborundum grit and adhesive to a metal or plastic plate. When dry, the plate is inked and can be printed either in **relief** or **intaglio.**

chine collé French term for a method of adhering a thin sheet of paper of different color or texture to a larger sheet of paper at the same time the inked plate is being printed. Originally used for adding strength or color variation to the image, *chine collé* is now used in a variety of ways to create and vary texture, color, and ink absorption.

chop mark an embossed stamp, usually a design of the press that the printer, artist, or publisher places on the edge of the print. Also called a blind stamp.

cognate see **ghost impression.**

collagraph a collage of various materials attached to the surface of a plate or block, or the building up of a plate or block by any other means; the plate or block is then inked and printed either in **intaglio** or **relief.**

colored print a print with color applied freely by hand or by using a stencil after printing.

color print a print produced in color by using a separate plate for each color, by inking separate areas of the plate in colors (***à la poupée***), by printing through stencils, by using a blend roll, or by using inks of different viscosities.

color separation the process of preparing a separate printing plate for each color to be printed.

counterproof offset image from a wet print onto damp paper, made by putting the two sheets face to face and running them through an etching press.

deckle edges the rough, uncut edges on handmade paper. Originally considered an imperfection, the deckle edge became fashionable with the craft revival in the last decade of the nineteenth century and has become common in contemporary handmade paper.

drypoint the **intaglio** process of drawing directly on a metal plate with a steel needle, creating a furrow and a rough **burr** that each hold ink, giving a blurred, velvety quality to lines when printed. Because the burr wears down quickly when printed, only a limited number of good **impressions** are possible with this technique. Drypoint is often combined with other intaglio processes for added linear effects.

edition the number of printed **impressions** from one design that has been authorized by an artist for distribution; usually double numbered in sequence; for example, 25/50 (print number 25 out of a total number of 50 in the edition).

embossing in **intaglio** printing, the raised impression made by a metal or collage plate on dampened paper, creating a three-dimensional effect. Also called inkless intaglio or blind embossing (when the plate is printed without ink).

engraving an **intaglio** process in which a sharp tool such as a graver, **burin,** scraper, or electric engraving tool is used to cut lines into the metal plate. It differs from **drypoint** in that metal is actually dug out of the plate and any **burr** created is scraped away. Depending on the pressure and the angle at which the tool is used, and the skill of the engraver, the tool's cut can range from deep and broad to a finely tapered stroke.

etching the **intaglio** process in which a metal plate is bitten into by a corrosive acid (French, *eau-forte;* German, *radierung*). After covering a plate with an acid-resistant ground, the artist draws through the ground with various tools to expose the metal. The plate is immersed in an acid bath that **bites** (chemically dissolves) the exposed metal to create depressed lines or tonal areas that can be inked and printed. Etching techniques include **aquatint, hard ground, soft ground, spit bite,** and **sugar lift.**

ghost impression after a monotype has been printed, sometimes enough ink is left on the plate to print one or two lighter impressions that are mere "ghosts" of the original unique impression. An artist may choose to add ink or rework the image from one printing to the next to create a series of related images. Also referred to as **cognates.**

handmade paper a sheet of paper made individually by hand from a variety of cotton, linen, or other natural fibers, using a mold and deckle frame.

hard ground an acid-resistant etching ground that is heated to a liquid state and applied to a heated etching plate. The plate is cooled until the coating hardens and an image can be scratched through the ground and then etched and printed. It is a process often used in combination with other **intaglio** techniques.

***hors commerce* (H.C.) proof** a proof printed to the same standards as the edition that has been retained by the press, usually to be used for exhibition or demonstration and not to be sold. From the French, meaning "not for sale."

impression any image, whether a proof or signed print, that has been printed from a plate, block, stone, and/or screen.

intaglio from the Italian, "to incise," a generic term that describes all prints and printmaking techniques in which lines, tones, and textures are incised or etched into the surface of a printing plate.

laid paper a paper made on wire molds that give it a characteristic **watermark** of thin lines. In producing handmade papers, the **pulp** is usually drained on a wire screen composed of heavy, or "laid," wires and lighter, or "chain," wires in a gridded rectilinear pattern. These laid and chain patterns are evident on the paper's surface. See **wove paper.**

letterpress the relief process used for printing type and other material from raised-ink surfaces.

lift ground an etching ground applied over an image drawn on a plate with a water-soluble solution, often containing sugar. During the etching process, the drawn lines dissolve, lifting the ground and allowing the acid to **bite** into the design.

linocut sheet linoleum, usually mounted on a piece of wood for stability, is gouged or cut with tools to create an image. The block is then inked and printed as a relief image. Also known as a linoleum print.

lithography a planographic printing process based on the resistance of water to grease. An image is drawn on a limestone or aluminum plate with a crayon or a tusche, a greasy drawing medium that can be used in solid or liquid form. The stone or plate is then chemically treated to "fix" the image. To print, one printer sponges the prepared surface with water while the second printer rolls inks over the surface, allowing the ink to stick to the greasy image. A sheet of paper is then laid over the stone or plate and run through the printing press.

matrix literally, that which gives form or origin to a thing; a plate, block, stone, or screen that carries the image to be printed.

mezzotint an **intaglio** technique in which the entire surface of a metal plate is roughened by metal rockers with sharp teeth to hold ink and print a deep black; light areas in the design are produced by burnishing and scraping out the rough areas (French, *manière noire;* German, *schabblatt*).

mixed process a combination of more than one printmaking technique or unique process in a single print.

monoprint a unique print pulled at least partly from a printing **matrix** that has an image drawn, carved, or incised into it. Unlike a **monotype,** where the surface of the plate is unworked, a monoprint is made unique by the rearrangement of printing elements between the printing of impressions, by varying the ink color from one impression to the next, by the addition of handwork before or after printing, or by other means that result in a one-of-a-kind printed work on paper.

monotype a unique printed work of art on paper or fabric made by drawing or painting with printing inks, watercolors, paints, or other materials directly on an unworked printing plate such as glass, metal, Plexiglas, Mylar, etc., and then transferring the image to a sheet of paper either by rubbing or printing. Usually only a single print can be produced; the second or third weakened prints are called **ghost impressions.**

offset printing a method of printing that involves the transfer of an image by means of an intermediary, such as the rubber cylinder of an offset press; there is no reversal of the image because it passes from the plate to cylinder to paper.

open biting an etching process in which no ground is used. The image is painted using an acid-resistant solution, and the plate is immersed in an acid bath and deeply bitten. When the plate is inked, the ink holds only the sides of the recessed area, giving a hollow look to the printed image. See **bite.**

paper the most common support for prints. Paper can be handmade or machine manufactured. The traditional way of making paper is to beat cotton or linen rags, or other plant fibers, into a liquid **pulp.** Into this pulp the papermaker scoops a tray of crossed wires onto which a thin layer of fibers settle. The tray is then turned out (couched), and the paper is pressed and dried between felt blankets.

paper plate lithography a printing technique based on the commercial Multilith technology, which is a form of **offset printing** that utilizes plastic-impregnated paper plates instead of traditional stones or metal plates.

photogravure a photomechanical **intaglio** process, used widely at the turn of the century and enjoying renewed interest today. Continuous black-to-white tones can be achieved by means of photogravure.

planographic printed from a flat surface, such as a smooth lithographic stone.

plate mark an indentation on paper left by the edges of a metal intaglio plate as a result of the strong pressure of the printing press.

plate tone a film of ink left on an intaglio plate after wiping to produce tonal nuances; also known as selective wiping.

pochoir French for stencil; a method of hand coloring by applying ink through thin stencils of copper, brass, plastic, or paper.

press the pressure device through which an inked **matrix** and **paper** are run to transfer the image from a plate to the paper. Each of the main types of printing processes requires its own particular kind of press.

print an image produced on paper or other support by placing it in contact with an inked block, plate, or stone, or by pressing ink onto a sheet of paper through a stencil. Also known as an **impression.**

printer's proof identical in nature to an **artist's proof,** a proof made for the printer's own use. Printed to the same standards as the numbered edition, the printer's proof is often numbered using Roman numerals (for example, P.P.II).

progressive proofs a set of proofs showing the development of a multiple-plate print in progressive stages from the first color run to the finished print, with each stage superimposed over the last to show the building up of the final image.

proof any impression taken at any time, either to check the progress of the design, or a specifically designated impression of the finished image, such as an **artist's proof** or **printer's proof,** that is not part of the numbered **edition.**

pulp the basic ingredient of paper, consisting of cotton or vegetable fibers that have been chopped and beaten with water. Pulp can be made into sheets or molded, dyed, or used as a liquid painting medium.

reduction relief a **relief** printing technique in which one relief block (wood or linoleum, for example) is used for successive printings onto the sheet of paper. After each printing, the artist carves and cuts away on the block, creating the image out of gradual reductions in the printing block. Generally, the lightest tones are printed first, and the process may be repeated until virtually the entire block is cut away.

registration the correct alignment of separate plates, blocks, stones, or screens with respect to one another in printing an image with multiple matrices.

relief a printmaking method in which the raised and inked surface of a plate or block is printed, while areas or lines that have been gouged or cut into the block do not print. Examples include **wood engraving, wood relief, linocut,** relief etching, and relief **collagraph.**

roulette a small toothed wheel set in a handle, used to make dotted lines on a metal plate. These indentations hold ink along with any other etched or engraved intaglio lines or tones and when printed add variety and texture to the print.

screenprint a stencil process using a fabric or metal mesh stretched over a frame. Using a squeegee, ink is forced through openings in the mesh, which can be blocked out by a variety of methods to form all or part of an artist's image. During the 1930s, when the process was first used as a fine art medium, the term "serigraph" was coined to distinguish screenprints made by an artist from screenprints produced for commercial purposes. Today, however, the term "screenprint" is universally accepted. The term "silkscreen," initially used when screens were made of silk fabric, is no longer appropriate. Most screens today are made using synthetic fabrics, which are more durable and do not contain the imperfections inherent in silk.

serigraph see **screenprint.**

soft ground an etching ground mixed with wax or vaseline that does not dry to a hard finish. A thin sheet of paper is placed over the coated plate, and a drawing is made. When the paper is lifted off the plate, the soft ground is removed where the artist drew and a soft pencil-like line is revealed. The plate is then placed in an acid bath for etching. Textured objects such as fabric can also be pressed directly into the soft ground and lifted; the etching process then produces that texture on the plate.

spit bite the selective direct application of acid to an uncoated aquatint plate with a brush or dropper.

state/state proof a proof taken at a stage in the development of a print project. States are printed after significant changes have been made in the printing **matrix** and document the evolution of a print project. Sometimes a small edition is pulled for interesting, well-developed states.

steel-facing a process in which intaglio plates are coated, or electroplated, with a very thin layer of steel. This process greatly increases the life of an intaglio plate, although with some types of images there may be a slight decrease in the quality of the impression.

stencil the masking or stopping out material, such as paper, fabric, or plastic, that is cut or perforated to allow ink or paint to pass through and print on another surface.

sugar lift a water-soluble solution containing sugar, which is used to create an image on an etching plate. After the solution dries, the plate is coated with an acid-resistant ground and immersed in warm water so that the sugar solution dissolves, lifting the ground off the plate and exposing the original image painted with the sugar solution as bare metal. The exposed drawing can then be etched and printed (see also **lift ground**).

surface roll ink that is rolled on the surface of an intaglio plate and is thus printed in relief. If ink has already been applied to the incised or etched areas of the plate and then wiped, the plate will print in both **intaglio** and in **relief** when run through the press.

trace monotype sometimes called a printed drawing or a transfer drawing, made by rolling ink on a smooth plate or sheet of paper and then laying another piece of paper over it. The artist then draws an image on the top sheet, sometimes rubbing sections to create large tonal areas. When the paper is lifted off the base sheet or plate, a unique image is created. The artist's pencil or other marks remain on the back of the monotype.

trial proof any test impression taken from a block, plate, stone, stencil, or other printing **matrix** to test how that particular image, or part of an image, will print, or to experiment with ink colors, papers, etc.

unique impression usually a **monotype** or **monoprint,** any printed work on paper that is a one-of-a-kind image.

variant edition a recent term used to describe an edition of prints that employ the same printing **matrices** but that show variations in inking, in the use of different papers, in the arrangement of printing elements, etc. Variant editions, also referred to with the French term *éditions variés,* or as a series of monoprints, reflect in part the growing number of painters and sculptors making prints that expand the traditional notion of a uniform set of identical prints and present instead a closely related body of prints that can be viewed more accurately as a set of variations on a theme.

watermark a translucent image made within a sheet of paper by variations in **pulp** thickness. As a sheet of paper is being made, a logo or small image can be built up on the screen, which causes the pulp to be thinner, allowing more light to pass through and reveal the mark.

woodcut see **wood relief.**

wood engraving a **relief** printing process in which an image is drawn on the end grain of a block of wood, and areas that are not to be printed are cut away using gravers, gouges, chisels, and other sharp tools. As opposed to the often broad and bold effects of the **wood relief** print, which cuts along and utilizes the grain of the wood block, wood engraving can achieve fine, delicate line work and has the potential for great detail.

wood relief the most common **relief** printing process, often called woodcut, in which an image or design is cut with knives and chisels along the grain of a block of wood. The areas that are not to be printed are cut away, ink is rolled on the block, and the surface area that is in relief is printed. The lines of a wood relief print are generally broad due to the nature of cutting the wood along the grain and the physical pressure the block must bear in the printing process.

working proof a trial proof, taken at any time during the evolution of a print project, on which notations or corrections have been made by either the artist or the printer. These adjustments can include notes for color changes, indications of changes to be made in the plate, or any number of alterations that will be made and then proofed again.

wove paper handmade paper produced using a tightly woven brass wire mold that leaves no visible vertical and horizontal pattern (as in **laid paper**).

Selected Bibliography

Articles and Reviews

Canaday, John. "Art: For Sake of Expression, Not Esthetic Theory." *New York Times,* 5 March 1966, 23.

——. "Art: Michael Mazur Shifts Direction." *New York Times,* 27 November 1971, 21.

Corbett, William. "Michael Mazur's New Work." *Arts* 59 (January 1985): 114–15.

Divver, Barbara. "Michael Mazur." *Arts* 53 (May 1980): 2.

Edelman, Robert G. "Michael Mazur at Barbara Mathes." *Art in America* 73 (May 1985): 172.

Florescu, Michael. "Michael Mazur." *Arts* 52 (March 1978): 7.

Forman, Debbie. "Landscapes of the Mind." *Cape Cod Times,* 20 July 1996, C1, C4.

Glueck, Grace. "Michael Mazur." *New York Times,* 28 January 1977, C16.

——. "Michael Mazur." *New York Times,* 25 November 1983, C17.

Goodman, Jonathan. "Michael Mazur: Mary Ryan." *Art News* 93 (Summer 1994): 179.

Goodman, Linda. "Light out of Darkness: Michael Mazur's Infernal Monotypes." *California Printmaker* 1 (April 1995): 4–7.

Mazur, Michael. "The Foundation for a True 'Renaissance' in Printmaking." *Alumni Bulletin* (Rhode Island School of Design), June 1964, 16–19.

——. "The Monoprints of Naum Gabo." *Print Collector's Newsletter* 9 (November – December 1978): 148–51.

——. "A Work That Marries Painting and Poetry." *Boston Globe,* 3 October 1982, E12.

——. "The Case for Cassatt." *Print Collector's Newsletter* 20 (January – February 1990): 197–201.

——. "Looking at Art: The Mind Landscape of Hsieh Yu-yu." *Art News* 95 (November 1996): 84–85.

"Michael Mazur." *Artist's Proof* 10 (1970): 19–29.

Raynor, Vivien. "Mazur at the Rutgers Gallery." *New York Times,* 13 December 1981, 48.

Sandback, Amy Baker. "Not Fully Repeatable Information: Michael Mazur and Monotypes, An Interview." *Print Collector's Newsletter* 21 (November–December 1990): 180–81.

Silver, Joanne. "Mazur's Inferno." *Boston Herald,* 22 September 1995, S17.

Spring, Justin. "Reviews: Michael Mazur, Mary Ryan Gallery." *Artforum* 33 (September 1994): 107–8.

Stapen, Nancy. "Amid High Technology, Artists Seek the Elemental." *Boston Globe,* 27 December 1990, 65–66.

——. "A Mature Painter Branches Out." *Boston Globe,* 24 June 1993, 55.

——. "Michael Mazur: Interpreting Hell." *Art News* 94 (November 1995): 103.

Storr, Robert. "East Coast: Michael Mazur." *New Art Examiner* (Chicago) 8 (December 1980): 17.

Taylor, Robert. "Michael Mazur Monotypes a Breakthrough." *Boston Globe,* 20 March 1983, 49.

Temin, Christine. "Perspectives: Joel Beck Draws from a Lyrical Tradition." *Boston Globe,* 28 June 1984, 66.

Tuttman, Kathe. "Michael Mazur: Artist in Transition." *New Boston Review,* Winter 1975, 14–15.

Unger, Miles. "Massachusetts: Michael Mazur, Barbara Krakow Gallery." *New Art Examiner* (Chicago) 21 (September 1993): 35.

Waddington, Chris. "Saint Paul: Michael Mazur at Macalester College Galleries." *Art in America* 77 (February 1989): 170–71.

Walker, Barry. "The Single State." *Art News* 83 (March 1984): 60–65.

Weisberg, Ruth. "Michael Mazur: Affirming the Idyll." *Artweek* 13 (3 July 1982): 1.

Wilson, Douglas C. "Hours without Time: Michael Mazur Talks about Painting." *Amherst* 50 (Fall 1997): 10–18.

Books and Exhibition Publications

Arts Club of Chicago. *Michael Mazur.* Exh. cat. Chicago: Arts Club of Chicago, 1985.

Baudelaire, Charles. *Les Fleurs du Mal.* Translated by Richard Howard. Illustrated by Michael Mazur. Boston: David R. Godine, 1982.

Brockton Art Center. *Michael Mazur: Vision of a Draughtsman.* Exh. cat. Brockton, Mass.: Brockton Art Center–Fuller Memorial, 1976.

DeCordova Museum and Sculpture Park. *Expressionism in Boston, 1945–1985*. Exh. cat. Lincoln, Mass.: DeCordova Museum and Sculpture Park, 1986.

Dunham, Judith. *The Monumental Image: Prints by Jennifer Bartlett, Chuck Close, Michael Mazur, Susan Rothenberg, Donald Sultan, Terry Winters*. Exh. cat. Northridge, Calif.: California State University and Sonoma State University, 1987.

Finch College Museum of Art. *Two Aspects of Illusion: Paul Gedeohn/Michael Mazur*. Introduction by Elayne H. Varian. Exh. cat. New York: Finch College Museum of Art/Contemporary Wing, 1971.

Genesis. Translated by Robert Alter. Frontispiece by Michael Mazur. San Francisco: Arion Press, 1996.

Goldman, Judith. *American Prints: Process and Proofs*. Exh. cat. New York: Whitney Museum of American Art, 1981.

Goodyear, Frank, Jr. *Perspectives on Contemporary Realism: Works on Paper from the Collection of Jalane and Richard Davidson*. Exh. cat. Philadelphia: Pennsylania Academy of the Fine Arts, 1982.

Hayden Gallery. *The Narrative Impulse: Paintings, Drawings, and Monotypes: Robert Birmelin, Mary Frank, Michael Mazur, and Irving Petlin*. Cambridge: Hayden Gallery, Massachusetts Institute of Technology, 1979.

——. *Wakeby Day/Wakeby Night: Monumental Monotypes by Michael Mazur: A Documentation of the Commission for MIT*. Essays by Eugenia Parry Janis and Katy Kline. Exh. cat. Cambridge: Hayden Gallery, Massachusetts Institute of Technology, 1983.

Janus Gallery. *The Cyclamen Dance Series: An Exhibition of Paintings, Pastels, and Monotypes*. Exh. cat. Los Angeles: Janus Gallery, 1982.

Koslow, Francine Amy. *Henry David Thoreau as a Source for Artistic Inspiration*. Exh. cat. Lincoln, Mass.: DeCordova Museum and Sculpture Park, 1984.

Macalester College. *Michael Mazur: Paintings, Prints, Drawings, Monotypes, 1962–1988*. Exh. cat. St. Paul, Minn.: Macalester College, 1988.

Marble, Melinda. *Herna: A Story*. Illustrated by Michael Mazur. Cambridge, Mass.: Bow and Arrow Press, 1993.

Mary Ryan Gallery. *Michael Mazur: Color Prints*. Exh. cat. New York: Mary Ryan Gallery, 1990.

——. *Michael Mazur: Recent Paintings*. Essay by David Shapiro. Exh. brochure. New York: Mary Ryan Gallery, 1996.

Mazur, Michael. "Monotype: An Artist's View." In Sue Welsh Reed et al., *The Painterly Print: Monotypes from the Seventeenth to the Twentieth Century*. Exh. cat. New York: Metropolitan Museum of Art, 1980.

Mead Art Museum. *Branching: The Art of Michael Mazur*. Introduction by Robert Pinsky. Essays by Susan Danly and Rachel Rosenfield Lafo. Exh. cat. Amherst, Mass.: Mead Art Museum, 1997.

Mecklenburg, Virginia M. *Modern American Realism: The Sarah Roby Foundation Collection*. Exh. cat. Washington, D.C.: National Museum of American Art, 1987.

Moffett, Kenworth, and Clifford S. Ackley. *New England Works on Paper*. Exh. cat. Boston: Museum of Fine Arts, 1977.

Moser, Joann. *Singular Impressions: The Monotype in America*. Exh. cat. Washington, D.C.: Smithsonian Institution Press for the National Museum of American Art, 1997.

Picker Art Gallery. *Michael Mazur*. Introduction by Edward Bryant. Exh. cat. Hamilton, N.Y.: Picker Art Gallery, Colgate University, 1973.

Pinsky, Robert. *The Want Bone*. Hopewell, N.J.: Ecco Press, 1990.

——. *The Inferno of Dante: A New Verse Translation*. Bilingual edition. Illustrated by Michael Mazur. New York: Farrar, Straus and Giroux, 1994.

Rose Art Museum. *The Herbert W. Plimpton Collection of Realist Art: 18th Annual Patrons and Friends Exhibition*. Exh. cat. Waltham, Mass.: Rose Art Museum, Brandeis University, 1995.

Rutgers University Art Gallery. *Michael Mazur*. Exh. brochure. New Brunswick, N.J.: Rutgers University Art Gallery, 1981.

Tamarind Lithography Workshop, Inc., Catalogue Raisonné, 1960–1970. Albuquerque: University of New Mexico Art Museum, 1989.

Townsend Center for the Humanities. *Image and Text: A Dialogue with Robert Pinsky and Michael Mazur*. Berkeley: Townsend Center for the Humanities, University of California, 1994.

University of Iowa Museum of Art. *Monotypes by Michael Mazur for the Inferno*. Essay by Michael Mazur. Exh. cat. Iowa City: University of Iowa Museum of Art, 1994.

Walker, Barry. *Michael Mazur's Self-Portraits*. Exh. cat. New York: Joe Fawbush Editions, 1987.

Wellesley College Museum. *Wellesley Greenhouse: Janowitz, Kumler, Mazur*. Exh. brochure. Wellesley, Mass.: Wellesley College Museum, 1977.

Index

Page numbers in *italics* refer to illustrations.

Photograph Credits

Jack Abraham cat. nos. 3, 11, 12, 14–32, 35, 36, 38, 40–42, 46, 48, 49, 52, 53, 56, 60–63, 70–72, 78–80, 84, 85, 92–96, 108, 111, 115–17, 120, 127, 132–34, 136–44, 157–68, 173, 183, 212, 213, 221, 224, 231, 238, 239, 248, 250, 253–55, 259, 267, 269, 270, 272–74, 276, 280, 284, 287–92, 306–10, 313, 315, 321, 322; colorplates 1, 3–6, 9–13, 15–17, 25–27, 31–33, 37; figs. 8, 10, 11, 13, 15, 20–29, 37, 39, 41, 46–52
Courtesy The Art Institute of Chicago fig. 31
Courtesy the artist figs. 69, 71, 76–80; pp. 50 bottom, 143, 144 top left and bottom, 145 bottom left, 150 left, 152, 153 left, 154 top left and right
Brooklyn Museum of Art colorplate 18; figs. 3, 14
Elsa Dorfman p. 23
Brigitte Durr p. 150 right
eeva-inkeri fig. 75
Courtesy E.W.K., Bern fig. 35
Courtesy Experimental Workshop, Emeryville, Calif. colorplate 28
Michael Fischer and Gene Young, National Museum of American Art, Washington, D.C. colorplate 19
Greg Heins cat. nos. 1, 2, 4–10, 13, 37, 45, 51, 54, 55, 57–59, 64–66, 69, 77, 81, 87, 91, 97–100, 110, 118, 119, 128, 129, 147, 170, 174, 177, 180, 186, 189, 194, 196–98, 200–202, 208, 210, 211, 216, 218, 225, 227, 229, 230, 232–37, 242, 244–46, 251, 252, 258, 260–66, 268, 271, 275, 277, 278, 281–83, 285, 286, 293–305, 311, 312, 314, 316–18, 320, 323, 325, 326; colorplates 2, 8, 21, 30, 34, 38–41; figs. 2, 4–6, 17, 43, 44
Clemens Kalischer fig. 70; pp. 145 bottom right, 146 top
Courtesy List Center for Visual Arts, Massachusetts Institute of Technology colorplate 20
Courtesy The Metropolitan Museum of Art, New York fig. 40
Courtesy Museum of Fine Arts, Boston colorplates 22–24, 29, 36; figs. 32, 36, 38, 42
© The Museum of Modern Art, New York colorplate 14
Courtesy The New York Public Library fig. 12
Pinacoteca Tosio Martinengo, Brescia fig. 33
Courtesy Private Collection fig. 1
Nathan Rabin fig. 68
Carol Rankin fig. 72
Adam Reich, courtesy Mary Ryan Gallery cat. nos. 323, 324, 327, 328; colorplates 42, 43
Tom Rummler fig. 74
Mary Ryan Gallery cat. no. 319
Stephen K. Scher fig. 7
John D. Schiff figs. 45, 73
© Marc Teatum, courtesy DeCordova Museum, Lincoln, Mass. frontispiece; colorplate 35
University Art Museum, University of New Mexico, Albuquerque cat. nos. 181, 182, 187, 188, 190–93, 195, 199, 203, 206
David and Louise Webber cat. nos. 33, 34, 39, 43, 44, 47, 50, 67, 68, 73–76, 82, 83, 86, 88–90, 101–7, 109, 112–14, 121–26, 130, 131, 135, 145, 146, 148–56, 169, 171, 172, 175, 176, 178, 179, 184, 185, 204, 205, 207, 209, 214, 215, 217, 219, 220, 222, 223, 226, 228, 240, 241, 243, 247, 249, 256, 257; figs. 9, 16, 18, 19, 30
Louise Webber figs. 53–67